NICHOLAS BERDYAEV

Astride the Abyss

of

War and Revolutions:

Articles 1914-1922

Translated by Fr. S. Janos

frsj Publications

Astride the Abyss of War and Revolutions
Articles 1914-1922

Copyright © 2017 by translator Fr. Stephen Janos

ISBN: 978-0-9963992-7-2 *Hardcover*
ISBN: 978-0-9963992-8-9 *Paperback*

Library of Congress Control Number: 2017947245

No part of this book may be reproduced or transmitted in any form or by any means, graphic, electronic, or mechanical, including photo-copying, recording, taping, or by any information storage retrieval system, without the written permission of the copyright holder.

In the event of the eventual demise of the present copyright holder, in accord with United States copyright law, copyright of this work devolves to Andrew M. Janos, son/heir of Fr. Stephen Janos.

Printed in the United States of America

Printed on acid-free paper.

For information address:

frsj Publications
Fr. Stephen J. Janos
P.O. Box 210
Mohrsville, PA 19541

Contents

Forward i

1914

War and Rebirth 1
Russia and Poland 9
Futurism in the War 13
Modern Germany 19
Imperialism Sacral and Imperialism Bourgeois 29
On the Dormant Powers of Man 35

1915

The New Russia 41
Nietzsche and the Modern Germany 49
To the Feckless Devotees of Slavophilism 57
On the Givers and the Takers 65
Germany, Poland and Constantinople 71
On the Disputes Concerning German Philosophy 75
The Will to Victory 83
The Contemporary War and the Nation 87
The Sensation of Italy 91
War and the Crisis of Socialism 97
Concerning "Leftness" and "Rightness" 103
The Slavophilism of the Ruling Powers 109
Society and the Ruling Powers 121
On "Radicalism" 127
Self-Restraint 131
The Role of the Third Estate in Russia 133
On the Conditional Aspect of Vital Values 143
The Immediate Task at Hand 147

Spirit and Economics 153
Concerning the Spirit of Despondency 159
Are the Rightists Nationalists? 163
The Evil Will and Reason of History 167

1916

Concerning Inward and Outward Activeness 171
On the Prestige of Holding Power 177
On Justification of Love for the Fatherland 181
The Rightists and the Unity of Russia 187
Ideas and the Societal Movement 193
Power and Coercive Violence 199
Tolstoyan Non-Resistance and the War 205
The Religious Fate of Judaism 213
Positive and Negative Nationalism 223
Russia, England and Germany 229
The Social and the Bureaucratic Conservatism 237
Regarding a New Book on the Masons 243
On the Growth of Bourgeoisness in Russia 247
The State and Ownership during a Time of War 253
The Church Question in Russia 259
On Understanding the Souls of Various Peoples 267
The Awakening of the National Will 269
The New Religious Consciousness and History 273
On Citizenship 281
Concerning Power and Powerlessness 287
Barbarity and Decadence 293
An Account about Heavenly an Origin 299
On the Dispute between Pr. E. N. Trubetskoy and D. D. Muretov. 307

1917

The Strength of Russia 313
Reform of the Church 319
The Psychical Factours of the War 325
On Love for Russia 331

The Downfall of the Holy Russian Tsardom
Articles 1917-1922

Theocratic Illusions and Religious Creativity 335
The Psychology of a Survivable Moment 347
The Downfall of the Sacred Russian Realm 355
The Internationale and the Unity of Mankind 365
Concerning Political and Social Revolution 373
The Position of Russia in the World 381
Power and Responsibility 385
Russia and Western Europe 391
On Bourgeoisness and Socialism 399
Counter-Revolution 407
A Free People 413
In Defense of Socialism 419
The Mobilisation of Interests 427
Truth and Lie within Societal Life 433
The Triumph and Crash of Populism 441
The Populist and the Nationalist Consciousness 449
The Religious Foundations of Bolshevism 457
The German Influences and Slavism 465
The Free Church and the Sobor 473
Who is to Blame? 481
Patriotism and Politics 489
Concerning Freedom and Integrity of the Word 495
Democracy and Hierarchy 503
The Objective Groundings of the Societal Aspect 511
Concerning a True and a False Will of the People 519

Has There Been in Russia a Revolution?..527
The Tasks of a National Democracy..535
The Germanisation of Russia...541
The "Bourgeois" World and the "Socialistic" World......................549
Personal Good and Supra-Personal Values......................................557
Concerning Creative Historicism...565
Is Social a Revolution Possible?..571
The People and the Classes in the Russian Revolution 587
The Free Church...599
Class and Man..621
Spiritual and Material Work in the Russian Revolution..................629
The Power and Psychology of the Intelligentsia............................637
The Ruin of Russian Illusions..645
The Spiritual Foundations of the Russian People............................653
Russia and GreatRussia...667
The Recuperation of Russia..673
The End of the Renaissance..681
The "Living Church" and the Religious Rebirth of Russia.............715

Forward

Our present text, "*Astride the Abyss of War and Revolutions: Articles 1914-1922*", -- a sbornik or collection of articles written by the Russian religious philosopher N. A. Berdyaev, provides insights into his thought over this fatedly tragic period. As in any true tragedy in the classic purview, we sense with helpless a grim foreboding the catastrophic climax that will overwhelm all the bright hopes and views of the moment, moment after moment, over this protracted period. So also with our present series of articles, which serve as a sort of public Journal of Berdyaev's views and thoughts over a range of issues, which tenaciously continue to plague mankind into the present time.

Our present text is comprised of 98 articles, numerically -- nearly 20% of the total corpus of writings penned by Berdyaev. There are, of course, other Berdyaev writings from the period not included here nor in the two Russian texts from which translation was made, articles rather moreso subject-specific.

The primary Russian source, which in other places we have referred to as the *Padenie*, is a massive 2007 volume entitled "*Padenie svyaschennogo russkogo tsarstva: Publitsistika 1914-1922*".[1] The Russian *Padenie* title derives from an April 1917 Berdyaev article: "Downfall of the Sacred Russian Tsardom/Realm". We have chosen a different but still apt title for our English text, since emotions still run raw over the vicious murder of the Russian Royal Family and the brutality of the Civil War in the demonic madness of its aftermath. In Berdyaev's view, the Old Regime ended in a dark Khlystyite orgy in the person of Grigorii Rasputin, and after a brief interlude, continued on in the dark Khlystyite orgy of Lenin's

---

[1] "Падение священного русского царства: Публицистика 1914-1922", Москва, Асртель, 2007, 1179 с. (pages); compiled & edited by V. V. Sapov.

Our present book represents only a portion of the *Padenie* Russian text, which includes: Berdyaev's 1918 book "*The Fate of Russia*", the 1918 "*Crisis of Art*" booklet, extensive explanatory notes, the 1922 anthology "*Osvald Spengler and the Decline of Europe*" along with numerous contemporary commentaries.

Bolshevism, -- the former Black Hundredist mentality transformed into a Red Hundredist mentality, -- all one and the selfsame element.

We have included some several Berdyaev articles from this period, not included in the *Padenie* tome, from a second Russian source, entitled: "*Mutnye liki*" ("Murky Visages").[1]

Berdyaev's articles in our text have been annotated with the year of original publication, along with corresponding Klepinina № assigned within the 1978 "Berdiaev Bibliographie", and footnoted with the transliterated Russian title and bibliographic source info.

The plural in our title of "Revolution<u>s</u>" is deliberate, not a misprint. In 1917 Russia suffered two revolutions: the "February Revolution" of March 8th, following the tsar's abdication, which lead to the formation of the Provisional Government under Kerensky, and the "October Revolution" of November 7 1917, by which Lenin and the Bolsheviks seized power, effectively ending Russia's participation in WWI. This "Great War" continued to drag on for another year, ending only on November 11 in 1918, Armistice Day...

Our present text is timely in context of the Centennial historical commemoration of the "Great War" and its aftermath, reverberating in its tremours down to our own day, and perhaps with increasing intensity. Berdyaev's articles in our present text appeared in a small handful of literary journals and gazettes, to which he was a regular contributor, such as "Utro Rossii", "Birzhevye vedomosti", "Russkaya mysl'", "Russkaya svoboda", "Narodopravstvo" etc., as well as several pamphlets published during the period. The wide range of issues addressed by Berdyaev includes matters both merely of the moment, and those that remain eternal in significance. We leave it to the reader to engage the text itself, rather than to attempt limited a commentary on vast a scope. Proper scholarship has always considered primary source material to be of greater importance for study and attention, rather than mere partialised secondary or tertiary commentaries, limited in depth -- a matter of "appropinquity", proximity. Hence the importance of making available the hitherto untranslated material, such as these articles, to as it were complete the picture of Berdyaev's thoughts and mindset during this turbulent period, watching as though a catastrophe unfold in slow motion....

---

[1] "Мутные лики (Типы религиозной мысли в России), Москва, Канон+, 2004, 448 pages.

Astride the Abyss of War and Revolutions

As in any classical tragedy, we are gifted with a painful sense of hindsight, of what is doomed by fate to occur, its inevitability contributing to our own transfixed catharsis afar witnessing and sharing in it. In the murkiness of our own life and time we attempt to discern and peer through the beclouded dimness of events and augur what it portends; those gifted with such true foresight are considered seers, prophets, the perspicacious, but even their sight is dimly a fleeting glimpse. And well we remember the curse upon Cassandra. Christ, echoing Isaiah, was wont to say: "...яко видящи не видятъ, и слышаще не слышатъ, ни разумеютъ".[1]

Our present text serves likewise another purpose. Some readers quite likely may have already perused Berdyaev's intense book, "*The Philosophy of Inequality*", written in 1918 in the early days of the Bolshevik "turnabout", but published only abroad in 1923. To this work, our present text may be seen as a prolegomenon, a preliminary introduction of Berdyaev's preparatory thoughts and mindset which erupted forth into this later volatile tome.

And beyond this stands the spectral challenge of "*Osvald Spengler and the Decline of Europe*", and yet still untranslated works by Berdyaev and others, illumining the present via the past, in our ongoing efforts at the "eternalisation of memory", a grappling of the catharsis of tragedy amidst the religio-philosophic search for meaning...

27 June 2017

Fr. S. Janos

---

[1] "...in seeing they see not, and in hearing they hear not, nor do understand" (Mt. 13: 13).

War and Rebirth

(1914 - 182)[1]

In an era of great tribulations, when all the exertions of power have to be gathered and directed, to each people is proffered the challenge to realise itself and its position in the world not only materially, but also spiritually. And the war, which wherein act purely material weapons and which presupposes material might, both can and ought to be considered also as a spiritual phenomenon, and to be evaluated, as a fact of spiritual activity. Everything historical (wars, revolutions, the transmigration of peoples, etc.), presents itself to us as material an appearance and to quite many would seem explicable by external causes. But behind all the genuinely world historical occurrences there lie active hidden spiritual powers, and behind all the contingently external chain of events, behind the husk and covering aspect can be discerned the core, connected with the essence of life, with its fundamental dynamics. The great Carlyle so very well understood the spiritual meaning of war, its power of perishing and rebirth. His intuitive genius always penetrated into the spiritual activity, hidden beneathe the material trappings of history. The no less great Fichte in his speeches to the German people appealed for a spiritually in-depth attitude towards events, which might otherwise seem a meaningless clash of external forces. And now are needed suchlike speeches to the Russian people. The war -- is irrational, it has its murky source in the will of peoples, heedless to higher reason. And war has meaning, it punishes, it causes to perish and cleanse in fire, and provides rebirth for a spirit decrepit and weak. These contradictions are present to everything in life and that which is concrete. Only an abstract doctrinal mindset would refuse to know the contradictory and twofold aspects, rooted within all concrete life. And history is concrete life, uncontainable within the Procrustean bed of abstract doctrine, for it is complex and varied in reflecting the contradictions and dualities of spiritual activity. The abstract doctrinal attitude towards war is always deadly, -- in it is not the delicacy and

---

[1] VOINA I VOZROZHDENIE. Article originally published in the newspaper "Utro Rossii", aug. 1914, № 192.

plasticity of spiritual life, which should have to derive from the Gospel truth, that the "Sabbath" (abstract doctrine) is for man (concrete life), and not man for the Sabbath. A glaring example of suchlike an abstract doctrinaire approach consists in the Tolstoyan teaching concerning "non-resistance". This -- is a narrow straight-line denial of any plasticity of spirit, of all the vital flexibility and delicacy of nuance in reaction to the infinite complexity of existent being. This -- is a rationalistic denial of the truth of instinct, of the truth of passionate feelings of indignation, of honour, of fidelity to the point of death, of defending the weak against the strong. The doctrinaire "non-resistance", the doctrinaire cosmopolitanism, the abstract and lifeless love for the world and for man -- all these "Sabbaths" ought to give way in the face of the vital truth of love for one's native land, the instinctive impulse to defend it from the enemy, the sacred indignation against oppressors and the vicious. How many there are of the doctrinaire sort, proclaiming all kinds of abstract "Sabbaths", but now actually consumed by a true instinct of struggle for the honour and dignity of the native land, for its fate right down to the last drop of blood. Moral instinct is always closer to the truth, than is moral doctrine. But every great struggle transpires not only through flesh and blood, but also through spirit. The truth of the instinct has to be consolidated spiritually, not doctrinally analysed by the consciousness, but rather instead enlightened and strengthened by it.

If every war possesses some deeper meaning and deeper motive causes, than one would tend to think at outward a glance upon everything historical, when what is seen is merely the superficial chain of events wherein it would seem, that everything would have been altogether otherwise amidst an happier chance set of circumstances, then the present day war -- unprecedented in the history of world conflagrations -- is already totally inexplicable by any hapless and chance set of circumstances, by diplomatic failures, the evil will of individual persons, etc. The conflagration of the European world war was providentially inevitable. The fraudulent European world and no less the fraudulent European peace were doomed to lead into this fire. It was not the assassination of the Austrian emissary of the throne, not the brazen ultimatum, addressed by Austria to Serbia, not the mania of grandeur of the Emperor Wilhelm, which led to the European war, and it could not have been avoided, even if the surface events of history had been somewhat different. This unprecedented and terrible war was inscribed in the book of life from seemingly forever. Europe long ago already had become transformed into a fire-breathing Vulcan, veiled over by the superficial and fraudulent trappings of peacetime bourgeois life. The European world was something false, an illusionary world, behind which lay concealed a raging hostility and hatred, and foul greed. The peace had been preserved by militarism, which like a vampire, sucked up the blood of the peoples. The contradictions in historical life created a strange paradox: the European peace signified a realm of militarism, and only war could free it from its unbearable yoke.

Germany long since already had become the bearer of militarism and of a militaristic imperialism. It holds all the world in tension, and compels countries, themself having no sort of militaristic intents of conquest, to maintain enormous armies, to direct all their efforts towards defense against the threat of Pan-Germanism. The aggressive Pan-Germanism, thirsting for world domination, signifies a permanent realm of militarism, and this -- is a fist raised against all the world, a barbaric power, threatening the culture. If it were not for the German militarism, then all the cultured lands of Europe and the world gradually would have begun to disarm, and the idea of peace and peaceful international relations would have begun to win out. As soldiers intent upon war, and with their self-conceited militarism, are alone only Germany and Austria -- reflecting the anti-nature offshoot of Pan-Germanism. Pan-Germanism sets itself in opposition against all the world, since the Teutonic conceit does not permit, that Germany should consent with other states and peoples, to stand together with them in a single line. The current horrible days for the world have shown, that Germany has total disregard for the norms of international law and is not afraid to go it alone in the world. There has begun a sort of intoxication and heady madness with this brazen Pan-Germanism. It is totally apparent, that the German imperialism is the grip of schemes for world domination. Germany does not want to be one among many, albeit amongst the foremost, to be individual within an hierarchy of individuals. The ideologues of Germanism long since already have been saying, that world history has entered upon a period of the dominance of the German race, which is to replace the worn-out Latin race. The German culture is worldwide, as formerly was the Latin culture. The German ideologues desire the spiritual dominance of Germany, grounded upon militarism, and they consider power as higher than law. And both the one and the other sort have desired the Germanisation of Slavdom.

Nicholas Berdyaev

In opposition to the Germanic race stands the Slavic race, still culturally young, fresh, full of hopes for the future. The Slavic race has not yet bespoken to the world its say. With the Germanic race there is a worldwide historical antagonism towards the Slavic race. Pan-Germanism -- is an eternal threat for Slavdom, for its existence and future. With everything happening in the Balkans, among the lesser Slavic peoples, it would seem, while not having worldwide a significance, yet involving the whole world, has been dragged in the worldwide hostility of Germanism and Slavdom. This worldwide historical racial hostility has climaxed into a dispute between Germany and Russia, the great spokesman for the Slavic race and Slavic culture. Where worldwide powers and oppositions are in play, where across the expanse of the whole of history one spirit is in opposition to another spirit, therein are sufficiently quite foreordained by chance reasons, for a worldwide conflagration to ignite. And now there has struck the hour of the already long anticipated worldwide conflict of the Germanic and Slavic worlds. In this terrible struggle is presented an historical issue, the resolution of which we are consigned by the spirits, governing history. The question concerns not only the Russian state and the Germanic state and their international politics, but also goes deeper, whether the spirit of Russia or the spirit of Germany should prevail in the world. And herein is what consists the tragic aspect of this worldwide conflict. The Germanic race -- seeks to conquer and make war, and its militarism has reached monstrous proportions. The Germans have a need for the seizure of foreign lands. The Slavic race -- is not for conquest, and foreign to it is the pathos of an invading militarism, with its trait in spirit moreso that of defending and selfless sacrifice. Howsoever deficient the internal politics of Russia might be, its international politics has always been sacrificial and selfless. The spirit of a militaristic imperialism has always been foreign to the Russian people. If Germany -- be the worldwide bearer of the idea of militarism, then Russia -- is the bearer of the idea of peace. The victory of Germany would signify a victory of the militaristic spirit; the victory of Russia would be for a victory of peace. The current world war signifies a struggle for the world, for a liberation from the oppression of German imperialism. The outbreak of the world catastrophe, the likes of which are unprecedented within history, is inevitable, a bursting open of the festering ulcer of militarism and rapacious imperialism. The victory over Germany and Austria has to represent the bringing to a close of that whole period of modern history, marching beneathe the standard of a vampirish militarism. More than once already has fallen to the lot of Russia this selfless and sacrificial mission. Russia once formerly defended European culture from the onslaught of Tatarism, and covered with bones, it enfeebled itself in the name of this world task, by its sacrificial blood it saved Europe, which always has remained ungrateful to it. Russia indeed also saved Europe through the Napoleonic incursion, yet once again fulfilling its sacrificial mission. Russia indeed went to war for the liberation of the Slavs and crushed the might of Turkey, an oppressor of Christian peoples. A terrible and especial fate, with impressive a selectedness! And now a new sacrificial challenge faces Russia. Russia is called and chosen to guard not only Slavdom, but also all the cultural world from the Germanic peril, which has turned upon all peoples its barbaric visage. And now the war-mongering Pan-Germanism has become a threat not only for Russia, but for all the world culture. Beneathe the lofty cultural mask of Germanism is sensed the old German barbarian, nowise desiring to know the genuine cultural traditions and manners, prone to violence and knowing only his own capricious will. German militarism is set amidst an armed culturally technological German barbarism. The Prussian Junker, such as is aesthetically manifest in the personage of the Emperor Wilhelm -- is a barbarian, having donned merely the outward trappings of civilisation. This militaristic barbarism with its upturned moustache and puffed out chest, quite the utter blowhard, threatening total degeneracy and decay, has demanded that Russia together with other peoples should back down and yield. The task ahead is worldwide and sacrificial the same, as with the repulsion of Tatarism, the Napoleonic invasion, the Turkish brutalities. With the falling of this allowed duty to Russia is sensed the character of the Russian people, selflessly sacrificial, with a spirit free from temptations for power. Imperialism, nationalism, bureaucratism -- all these are traits, grafted onto the Russian people, and no small role here has been played by the German graft. The Germans have played a fatal role in our inner history, they have made hostile an incursion into the inner organism of the Russian people, they have undermined our civil life, have mechanised and bureaucratised it. External invasion by the Germans, threatening the honour of Russia, will perhaps free us from the inward Germanising and help create a civil life, more in accord with the spirit of the Russian people. This bureaucratic Germanising is worse than how the Tatar-Mongolism had crippled the life of the Russian people. The Germanism has befallen us from within, as a chastising for the sin of our inward Germanising, distorting our national visage. Germany has always supported the reactionary element within Russia. The moral task, facing Russia, is not easy: to manifest a great martial spirit, a military readiness, a military valour not in the name of aims of war conquests, but in the name of peace for all the world, the unification of all the Slavs, and in the name of defending and preserving justice. And it is not the first time that the Russian people is going to war not in the name of war, not for conquest, nor possessing at heart a militaristic pathos. The Russian people understands only such a war. It did not understand the Japanese war.

There exists an incontrovertible dialectic of history, transpiring through sacrifice. Evil reaches its own limit of developement, its extreme intensity and devours itself, explodes, gets burnt up. The moral preaching of peace, despite its undoubtable truth, will never defeat militarism, nor free the world from the dark will to war and violence, nor install the brotherhood of peoples. All the accomplishments of history are won through passionate oppositions. Peace can be won only through war, through the discharging of evil energy. A just war will defeat the militarism, in its discharge the evil passions and the evil will self-destruct and self-negate. War -- is a terrible evil, but not only evil, it is twofold, as is much in the world. In war will be forged the character of various peoples, will be strengthened a manliness of spirit, its trials and sacrifices putting a limit to the inevitability and mollification, the bourgeois smugness and calm, the personal and familial egoism. But the essential aspect to it all, is that the world war should demonstrate to various peoples the impossibility lodged within war. The technological perfectings for war lead to self-negation impeding the possibility of war quite moreso, than the preachings of peace. The world war cannot long continue: it manifests such a terrible devastation of cultural lands, such ruination, which the peoples cannot sustain. But the rapidity of the finish of the war depends totally upon victory over the Germans. Only the containing of Germany and Austria will lead to peace.

If the incursion of the German barbarism does not overly prolong the war, then the war should lead to a rebirth for Russia and the world. Peoples, demoralised by the thirst for bourgeois well-being, will once again manifest heroic a spirit, always dwelling concealed within human nature. A world and general approach for all peoples will prevail over the dominion of private interests, the personal and familial self-centredness. A war, in which there will be a defending of native land and truth, will impel feelings of honour and citizenship, a sense of the trans-personal right down to the last fellow. And finally, the terrible experience of the world war has to lead to a religious deepening of life, to a mysterious sense of meaning penetrating into it, to movement from the surface into the depths. An hundred years back, during the Fatherland War, the national consciousness of the Russian people was strengthened. And this consciousness was not nationalistically egoistic, was not for plunder, underlying the lie of imperialism. This was instead an awareness of a deed of rightful truth, done by the Russian people for Europe, for the world. The present war is a spiritual continuation of the Fatherland War. In it, the Russian people once again conceives itself singularly called for the world deed of rightful truth -- in repulsing the violent German militarism, and the pretensions of Pan-Germanism, the threat to all peoples. In a single fiery awareness will be burnt away the inner discord, lacerating Russia, the inner violence, poisoning its life. The character of the Russian people through trial and sacrifice, persevering in the name of truth, will ultimately mature for more free a life. Russia will cease to be the step-mother for those peoples, who in the hour of peril and misfortune have unanimously acknowledged it as their mother. Something bad and vile has gone stagnant within Russia, and in it already has begun the morbidity and rot. Peaceful developement has become impossible in Russia. Only a catastrophe could renew and revive the Russian character, and direct the Russian will to great deeds. Such a catastrophe indeed has burst over Russia, has faced all its sons with supra-human tasks, has compelled a forgetting of petty malicious settlings of accounts. In the life of various peoples occur periods, when there is needful a cleansing fire. The present war, in distinction from the Japanese war, will be a war of the people, of society, and not only of the state, not only of the government. In such wars the people and society tend to strengthen. Those moral strengths of character, which gather and strengthen a people and society in an era of war, in defense of fatherland, have to remain active, to be a new might even after the war, in peacetime life. These societal moral strengths cannot yet live in an atmosphere alternating between hatred and apathy, of violence and servile abeyance. The bringing down of the worldwide yoke of German militarism and imperialism, a yoke, unbearable for the German people itself, will expose before all the world the untruth and lie of all the militaristic and imperialistic pretensions. After this world war the lure of militarism and imperialism has to forever fail, its ideology become already impossible and the feelings supportive of it to nowise remain in the human soul. Because it will have become clear to every man upon earth, that the limitation and end result of all militaristic imperialism -- is death, and not life, destruction, and not flourishing, and its essence -- is a fiction, and not reality, and that this idea is an obsession. The bearer of this idea, totally obsessed, is now not the great genius Napoleon, but rather the diminutive and cocky Wilhelm. And the worldwide liberation from the oppressive fiction of militaristic imperialism will be on the order of a worldwide rebirth.

Russia and Poland

(1914 - 178xx)[1]

The [5 August] appeal of our Supreme Commander [of the Russian Armies, GreatPrince Nikolai Nikolaevich], filled with wise statesmanship, sets the basis for a just resolution of the Polish Question. It imposes a great responsibility upon Russia, since it has to be unselfishly fulfilled. In the age old historical hostility of the two Slavic peoples, Russia ought to be the first to extend the hand of brotherly reconciliation and brotherly assist, since the power is on its side to do so. Too often in Russia they have tended to forget, that the Polish are Slavs also. Our traditional Slavophilism has tended to discount the Polish, and by this they brought falsity into the Pan-Slav ideals. We have had greater love for the Germans, than for the Polish. We have not been afraid of the Germans, we have allowed them into our national organism, into the heights of the administration of the country. The Polish however represented an eternal danger. Aksakov placed the fear facing the Polish danger at the basis of his publicist efforts.

---

[1] ROSSIYA I POL'SHA. Article originally published in the newspaper "Birzhevye vedomosti", 10 oct. 1914, № 14424.

(*trans. note*) N.B.: Our year 2007 *Padenie* Russian text (from which mostly our Berdyaev articles are to be found) correctly notes (*page 1080*) that the 1978 Klepinina Berdiaev Bibliographie (*page 82*) erroneously considered this above title as identical in content with that of Chapter 18 in Berdyaev's 1918 book, "The Fate of Russia" (Kl. № 15,8), entitled "The Russian and the Polish Soul". Our 2007 Padenie Russian text is massive a work, and contains both the "Fate of Russia" (Kl. № 15) in entirety (pp. 15-206), and our present "Russia and Poland" article, which is the authentic (1914-Kl.№178).

However, back in year 2009 we contributed to the problem, by posting on berdyaev.com website "The Russian and the Polish Soul" article, coding it as (1914-178). Since then, it has been irreparably duplicated across the Internet in this format. Hence, in this circumstance, we have coded our present article as (1914-178xx) to distinguish the two variants. Thus be it noted! *Mea culpa!...*

This was adopted by the ruling authorities. The religious side of the question here played no little a role. The Polish Question is closely bound up with the Catholic Question. The Polish danger seemed both at the same time likewise a Catholic danger, and the Catholic danger -- the Polish danger. In this regard the Slavophils were no little to blame. They occupied at root a false position in regard to the Polish and in regard to Catholicism. Out of their harsh national self-assertion they did not want to admit, that in the separation of the Churches there was blame on both sides, that the Catholic Church is a Christian Church the same, as is the Orthodox, and that their differences are the result of human sin.

They did not desire a brotherly and Christian turning towards the Western Christian world and on this basis they set themself a bad position. They likewise did not want to openly recognise facing them and all the world, that Russia cannot sincerely and without hypocrisy decide the Slavic Question and the liberation of the Balkan Slavs, if it does not decide in truth and justice the largest question -- the Polish Question. The Polish Question -- is inward an ulcer for the Russian people, a great Slavic people. Only after Russia secures the re-uniting of unfortunate Poland, will it then conceive of itself as a great Slavic land, called to convey to the world a Slavic truth. The just resolution of the Polish Question coincides with wise statesmanship. The forceful Russification politics in Poland would merely exhaust Russia and not bring it any sort of benefit. Injustice in regard to the Polish would be not only a spiritual, but also material burden for Russia. An united Poland, the re-united brotherly ties with Russia, would serve as a bulwark against the dangers of Germanism, against the eternal threat of the Germanisation of the Slavs. The Polish in their blood do not love the Germans, they fear them. And these Slavic sentiments have not been rooted out from the Polish heart. This is expressed even now. Germanism has also been an eternal hindrance to the unification of Poland. And Germany most of all has been to blame for the division of Poland.

Now or never. For the Polish Question this hour of history -- is decisive. We encounter one only impediment upon our path, as punishment for our sins. The Polish have fared comparatively well-off in Austria -- they will not so readily renounce this fine living, and they would relate with mistrust towards an uncertain future. It would require an enormous and unselfish effort on the part of the Russian people, to persuade the Polish in Austria, that there better awaits them a better future in the event of detachment from Austria-Hungary and subsequently uniting to Russian

Poland. We would hope to believe, that there will not occur some blunder here, and that the appeal of the Supreme Commander will serve by way of a pledge on this. Our politics has to become Polishophile. This -- is the obverse side of the anti-German politics. The moral duty underlying our victory consists in this, that we are fighting not only for the Serbs, but also for the Polish, for all the Slavic world. We also have to ultimately get free from a wrongful hostility towards Catholicism and from degrading fears about a Catholic danger. Within the Russian people there are religious strengths and great religious possibilities, which even the Western nations acknowledge, and hence the weakening religious powers of the West should not present a source of fright. On the contrary, we are called to inspire new religious life into the decrepit Western world.

The noteworthy year 1914 opens up a new era of world history and a new era of Russian history. The Petrograd period of Russian history is at an end. In this great and auspicious year our national self-consciousness has to ultimately strengthen. A new Russia is being born. And all the old, the stagnant inner malice and strife, grant that it may be forgotten. Russia will ultimately enter into the life of Europe and the world as an independent and guiding spiritual force. All the peoples of the world will be compelled to finally recognise Russia, to look upon its unique visage, to hearken to its words. And ultimately there will dissipate the view on Russia, as a land Eastern and wild. The German Social Democrats even now still reckon it possible to divert their racial and spiritual hatred towards Russia under the excuse, that they are fighting against Russia, an eternal bulwark of reaction. The very possibility of such an attitude towards Russia has to vanish after this 1914 war. This war has already shown, that the Russians are less savage, than the Germans. In order to ultimately confirm the place of the Russian people in the world, there has to be within the national self-consciousness a departure and cleansing from the remnants of the chaotic aspect, veiled over by the German drill discipline mentality. It is for the ultimate realisation of this, of what Russia ought to be, whether it is called to be a Christian land, and the hour of history has struck, a second time not to be repeated. Vl. Solov'ev reckoned the national question in Russia not so much a question of existence, since this is already irreversibly decided by the enormous expanses of the Russian state, but rather as a question of *worthy* an existence. The worthy existence of a great people is connected with the awareness of its calling to defend truth in the world and for all the world to manifest a spirit, not in semblance of the grasping spirit of violence, of greed and gain for itself. If we desire everything only for ourself, we shall then be totally like the Germans, and there will be nothing uniquely Russian in us. But the justice of the world tasks of Russia have already been foreordained by the spiritual powers of history and have only to be followed through to the end.

Futurism in the War

(1914 - 179)[1]

Interests over the past season to a remarkable degree have revolved around the issue of futurism. A countless number of public lectures, published articles and private conversations have been devoted to the uproar over futurism. And as always happens, the significance of the trendy theme has gotten blown out of proportion. Anything too noisy and clamourous cannot be accounted prolonged an existence. When the world catastrophe erupted and people had facing them true questions of life and death, the theme of futurism proved of essential interest, along with much of the superficial and secondary. But in less raucous and frivolous, in deeper and inward a sense of the word, the problem of futurism continues to face us and manifests to the world with totally unexpected a side, passing over into the historical life of the masses. Futurism has assumed ugly a form regarding the war also, in the capacity of an obedient servant to an outmoded reactionary past. In the methods and the manners, in which the Germans conduct the war, there is very much of the futuristic, but the spirit, with which these futuristic methods and manners transpire, certainly, are profoundly passé. The ideals of the Prussian Junkerism are oriented backwards, and not forwards. Yet the German militarism is a recent phenomenon in modern history. This militarism is not only modernistic, but also futuristic. In vain does one search in it for traces of the old chivalry. In the recent militarism of the German Empire there has not remained even traces of the chivalrous spirit, a trait of the old Germans. This -- is a phenomenon of the XX Century, armed with all the methods and manners of modern technology and industry. The German militarism is a typical futuristic mechanisation and automatisation of the human masses and of human life. German militarism is a capitalistic militarism, inseparably interconnected with German industry.

German industrialism in recent times has stood at the head of world capitalism, and in it has been the strongest pulsating of capitalist

---

[1] FUTURIZM HA VOINE. Article originally published in the newspaper "Birzhevye vedomosti", 26 oct. 1914, № 14456.

initiative and capitalistic growth. It has out-distanced the English. But the industrial capitalism of Germany is very unique by virtue of its uniting with the Junker militarism. Upon the industrial capitalism of the German Empire lies militaristic an imprint, and upon the militarism -- a capitalistic imprint. And it could not be otherwise in a state, which looks to be a great power only through annexation and force, rather than upon the basis of greatness and strength of its essential position.

The free combination of militarism and industrial capitalism bestows upon German imperialism a futuristic tint. As much as Wilhelm would play at the role of Siegfried, in a simulation of ancient knighthood, it does not hide the fact, that the German Empire is not something holy, but rather instead a bourgeois industrial empire. And the power of the army of Wilhelm is first of all an industrial capitalistic power, a power of futuristic technology, and not of knightly a spirit, not of heroism, not of mass enthusiasm. And the auspicious future of a futuristic technology finds its expression in this, that it is ready to serve whatsoever spirit it pleases, not only the spirit of the future, but also the spirit of the past. The horrendous capitalistic enterprises of Krupp, readying futuristic ordinance, is certainly a manifestation of futurism in the military aspect. Automated masses of an army, transformed into total a mechanism, armed with modern technology and to a perfect degree disciplined, -- this is the futurism in war. Technology trumps the human spirit, outward fitness substitutes for inward value, destroys essential movement. The German army appears to the world as a technological wonder. Everything in it is armour-clad, everything is blindered, everything is automated, and automobilised. Its chain-tracked vehicles -- are futuristic horrors. Everything is set up in the German army with a cold lack of emotion. The army of the Germans is reminiscent of an H. G. Wells novel. "Siegfried" Wilhelm, wanting to play at his own version of a medieval emperor, not only wields as a weapon the futuristic technology and industrial automation, but he is also situated in the grip of this futurism and automation -- he is armed with fatal a power. Wilhelm in essence as an emperor -- is a parvenu, an upstart. Behind him there are no old traditions and customs, no sacred reminders. He is not heir to the Holy Roman Empire, as are the has-been Hapsburgs. His empire is purely industrial, bourgeois. And the pretension of the German Empire to world domination is not the same a sort as with the old pretension of the Holy Roman Empire, an empire worldwide and trans-national, ; this rather is the pretension of the German industrial capitalism to dominate the world. The military, the Junker character of the German army is merely a veil, a masquerade of sorts and it does not essentially changes matters, since the German militarism -- is completely industrial, capitalistic, technological a thing. Beyond that there remain only the words of Wilhelm, in imitation of what was sacred back in the Middle Ages.

The futuristic army of the Germans has already borne its own fruits. Part of the futuristic programme by its founder, Marinetti, is already being carried out by the German armies; they destroy the old culture, they devastate old cities, churches, works of art. The German newspapers write in justification of German barbarity, that there is nothing especially wrong in the destruction of the old architectural monuments, since Germany is called to create new and more beautiful ones. A totally futuristic mindset is something difficult to have been expected, namely from Germany. In Germany there was always less the aspect of futurism in literature and art. The cradle of futurism was in the Latin lands, seeking to get free of the weighty burden of their great past.

But in Germany was brewed futurism of different a sort, quite more effective and threatening, a vital futurism -- in its militarism and industry. This futurism imperceptibly has engulfed the human spirit, has transformed man into a means for a monstrous mechanism bereft of soul. The dualism of spirit and matter in Germany is stronger than was expected there. Since the historical, the massive embodiment of life there has become especially lacking in spirit, it has become subject to automation all more and more. The organic life, the elemental life in flesh and blood there is being transformed into an automatic "automobile-like" mechanism, subordinated to a mechanical discipline. In futurism there is a sort of true presentiment, that mankind is doomed to this, to go through the mechanisation and automatisation of fleshly organic life. Futurism is a tense and highly sensed acceptance of the inevitable results of the technological process... This is a technological process, in which the motion of time becomes all the more accelerated, wreaking havoc with the organic wholeness of life, with the organic bond of spirit and matter. This is a process of differentiation, of being torn and broken apart. In place of organic a connection, it substitutes instead mechanical a connection, the wholeness of spirit with instead the wholeness of the automaton. The current futuristic war rattles the organically sacred foundations of life. A most immediate result of this concussion of organic traditions, of cultural customs is in a partial barbarisation of mankind. This barbarisation in full measure has found expression in the Germans, possessing the most "advanced" and perfect armies, the most technologically armed. We are witnessing the remarkable phenomenon of barbarity upon the groundworks of the growth of a false civilisation. In the Germans there is their initial barbaric coarseness, inherent to their race, combined with a barbarity from the civilisation. The civilised barbarity is a spiritual barbarity. It is impossible to repulse and defeat this fatal process by any sort of guarding the organic wellsprings of life. It can be opposed only by freedom of spirit. And I believe, that in Slavdom, in Russia is that freedom of spirit, which can be brought to bear against the futuristic war with its automated monstrosities.

This alternate spirit ought also to find expression in the alternate spirit of our armies, in the predominating within them of factours spiritual over factours mechanical and automated. And this ought to be sensed also in an alternate attitude towards man, even though he be our enemy. The Slavs ought to appear to the world as more lofty a type, than the Germans, not because that they are technically backwards and less civilised and hold still to old sources, but because that in them is more lofty the spiritual potentials, oriented towards the future and not the past. The Slavs -- are a race of the future, and not the past, and in this race is impossible the barbarity deriving from a false civilisation. With us there is possible a fierceness out of wildness, but not a civilised fierceness, very pitiless and emotionally cold. We are called to create a new life, since the old is approaching its conclusion. Futurism technically is connected with the future, with what is to come. But in essentially negative a sense it is connected with the past and the present, it is inwardly chained fast by reaction to the past and the old, in it there is no inner freedom. The very word "futurism" is very imprecise and is applicable to various phenomena. Behind the term "futurism" lies concealed actually new searchings in poetry and painting and new, not yet manifest world-outlooks. The symptomatic significance of futurism is enormous. But in "futurism" as denoting a philosophy of the automaton, moving with increased a rapidity, there is nothing creative towards a fashioning of the new life -- its role is merely destructive. The militaristic futurism of the Germans in this war has made apparent, that the futuristic automatons and mechanisms serve not only the future, but also the past, not only progress, but also reaction. In the automatism and mechanistic consist no creative aims, connected with future a life. This -- is a future power, in which culture degenerates into barbarity, -- a very repulsive barbarity, more terrible, than the primitive and ancient barbarity of mankind. From the touch of this power perishes the beauty of nature and the beauty of art.

Modern Germany

(1914 - 183)[1]

It is useful to know one's enemy, to understand his character, to appraise his strength. And therefore the [1914] Russian language Sabashnikov edition of the H. Lichtenberger book, "Modern Germany",[2] could not have come out at more appropriate a time. Henri Lichtenberger [1864-1941] is already known to us by his books on Nietzsche and Wagner. This -- is a Frenchman impartial and even well-disposed towards German culture, who attempts to provide the synthetic characteristics of the average level of modern German culture, both the material and the spiritual. In general, his work has to be acknowledged as successful, and for us instructive. The world has been facing a perplexing question these days, as to why the Germans have proven such barbarians, wild devastators of culture, alien to all respect for truth, why they deny all moral decency in war. War is not a matter of brigandage, fraud and murder, war has its own morals, its own strict honour, its own sense of propriety, and not everything is permissible in war. Even a gang of thieves has its own code of honour, setting moral limits to its acts of violence, often to spare the weak. Even if one were to admit, that there is a dram of exaggeration, as is inevitable in such cases, to the accounts of German atrocities, then still they have been well established and witnessed to sufficiently, to exclude the Germans from the ranks of cultural Christian mankind. The consciousness of the Christian peoples cannot permit of any such unrestraint of power, it demands a restraint upon power by truth and it can tolerate only a rightful power, only with the power of rightful truth. What has happened with the German race, what strange moral sickness has struck it? It is possible not to love the Germans and difficult to find a love for them, but the Germans have always been esteemed, so much always has

---

[1] SOVREMEHHAYA GERMANIYA. Article originally published in the newspaper "Utro Rossii", oct. 1914, № 255.

[2] *trans. note*: "L'Allemagne moderne: son évolution", Flammarion, Paris 1907.

been said about German accuracy and integrity, so extensively read have been the German philosophers, and the erudite and the poets, and the higher culture studied in Germany.

Germany has provided so many geniuses, who belong to all the world. Often among us the very concept of culture has been considered identical with German culture, as the most contemporary form. What has happened? The great Germans now also remain great and will remain so forever, but as to the grandeur of German culture, but all the contemporary German spirit we instead have to deny and oppose to it a different spirit. The Russians are being forever cured of a servile attitude towards German culture. The book of Lichtenberger, which characterises the average and typical aspect in German culture, -- its fruits, destined for broad consumption, provides materials for a reply to this tormenting question: why have the Germans become savage, what has happened with the grand German culture in this hour of world history, so exceptional in its significance?

When one reads the objectively balanced book of Lichtenberger, it becomes clear, that the rapid developement of German might over the last several decades, -- from the time of the formation of the German Empire and the victory from the Franco-Prussian War -- it becomes clear that this was not developement in the German sense of the word, but rather a downfall, a disintegration, a spiritual degeneration of the German people. And this is clear in spite of the opinions of Lichtenberger himself. During this period of the imperialistic might of Germany and its militaristic dominance over Europe, invariably there has occurred a collapse of the German ideals of life, a lowering of the level of its spiritual culture, a dying out and forgetting of the great aspect, wrought by the German spirit in the past. This -- is a systematic victory of the German Junker and the German industrialist over the German thinker, the mystic and the poet. The finest people of Germany long since already are appalled at the lowering of the spiritual level of their people, bereft of a moral centre in the contemporary culture of Germany, and enslaved by a bourgeois militarism. The whole process of the developement of culture in modern Germany represents an uninterrupted cutting off and separation of the whole of life from the inner spiritual centre and the subsequent subordination to an external material centre -- the imperialistic might of the Fatherland, based upon militarism and crude force. Germany has known periods of a great spiritual upsurge, and suchlike was the religious movement spanning the

XIV, the XV and XVI Centuries, as well as its extraordinary creative upsurge of the late XVIII and early XIX Centuries. In these finer times, having created the spiritual prestige of Germany, the German people did not possess an imperialistic might and did not intimidate other peoples with monstrous armies. True, there are German ideologues who assert, that the great German mystics, philosophers, poets and musicians prophesied about the imposing might of the Teutonic Empire, and that this might is a reward for modern Germans in the spiritual efforts of the past. But in recent times, German might has brought forth quite bitter fruits and evoked in people a spirit of quite grievous disillusions. Modern German thinkers remember with regret about the past spiritual greatness of Germany and with anguish they look upon its current spiritual squalour. Modern Germany no longer still finds its Fichte in the threatening hour for "der Vaterland".

Lichtenberger sees the essential peculiarity of modern Germany to be in the will to power and might. The whole military, industrial, bureaucratic mechanism of modern Germany is an excellently organised will to power and might of the German people. The German in his past history did not know power and did not possess might. All the powers of his spirit went instead to thinking, to philosophy, science and literature, to the lofty dreams of individual creatively gifted people, to great ideas, cut off from the life of the people, the masses and society. In Germany there has always been an enormous inconsistency between its higher stratum of select people, those creating the culture, and the average level of Germans, a rift between the German philosophers and poets, and the German burgher, the mere Mike. The "land of philosophers and poets", as they love to call Germany, never was a land of developed citizenship, of a mass moral upsurge. The German burgher -- as a private man, can be free in his individual life, and yet he -- is a slave, a member of a mechanism within societal life. In him there is no sense of a citizen honour and citizen worth, traits of the Latin race, which even the modern Frenchman derives from ancient Rome. There is in him also none of the moral anguish over universal good and universal salvation, characterising the Slavic race, of that sympathy towards people's distress, which imposes a special imprint upon Russians, upon their thinking, upon their literature. The spiritual work of the Germans remains purely individual, oriented towards the culture of the individual soul, powerless to inspire their history, to overflow into their societal life. The average German is extremely uninspired, coarsely materialist even in outward appearance. The total disregard towards everything material among German thinkers reflects on the obverse side a triumph over the uninspired materiality of the German masses. In their higher spiritual stratum the Germans can be romantics and heralds of lofty ideas, but in their civil state and societal life, in their morals as a people overall they confess a cult of naked and crude power, nowise enlightened. The role of the German race within history is always negative, and the positive is but the creative work of separate individuals. When the Germans of the era of Bismarck, with the unification of Germany and the Franco-Prussian War, emerged finally on the path to power, they proved then to be bearers of crude force, showing the world an imperialistic fist. The German by nature is crude and morally limited, in him is no magnanimity nor sympathy, no surfeit of moral energy. He belongs to the Teutonic barbarian race, once flooding upon the Latin culture of Europe. In him is not the refinement nor the nervous energy of the French, nor the sympathy and world sorrowing of the Russians. The German by nature is unsociable, in him has remained a barbarian rather than cultural individualism of arbitrariness, and on his societal side he is oriented towards the world, as one prone to violence, a military Junker and bureaucrat. When the centre of gravity in their life for the Germans was transferred from the inner life of their "philosophers and poets" to instead the external life of their statecraft, this principle at present has gotten bound up with their barbarism. The greatest statesman of Germany, and actually of genius, Bismarck, has remained in history under the title, the "Chancellor of Blood and Iron".

The role of Germany reflects an historical paradox. The individuals of genius in the German race have given much to the world, have introduced great values into world culture. Their philosophers, mystics, the erudite, the musicians and poets belong to the world, and no sort of German atrocities can obscure the light, issuing from them. But the German state and its societal aspects, the German historical might has projected towards the world its barbaric and violent image, and hence its role is negative and anti-cultural. The growth of German might, always crude and ugly, has to have limits put to its violence. German might threatens not only Slavdom and the whole of world culture, it threatens also the spiritual culture of Germany. The religiosity of the Germans is such, that it cannot be strong, spiritually transforming their history and their societal mindset. Protestantism -- is a totally individualistic form of religiosity, which has something to give the individual soul, but too little to give to the life of the people. Protestant religiosity does not seek for the Kingdom of God upon earth, and unknowable to it is the Slavic searching for the City to Come. German Protestantism has broken off not only from the tradition of the Church, but also from the tradition of ancient culture, which organically has entered into the life of the Church. And not without basis do they assert, that Western culture is always a Latin culture, having assimilated the legacy of the ancient world. Culture always presupposes a tradition and an inherited legacy, it cannot be exclusively individualistic. Nietzsche -- moreso a Slav, than a German -- said, that in Germany there is no culture, that there exists only a French culture. And actually, in Germany there have been great creative individuals, people of solitary a contemplation, of thought, of dreams, who have introduced values into world culture, but a racial and supra-individual culture as a people the Germans do not have. They remain barbarians, and their barbarity has been uncovered to the horror of all the world at a decisive hour of history. However pitiful the condition of Russian culture, however much wildness we still have, nonetheless with the Russian people there is its own organic religious culture, inherited through the Church as connected with the Greek world. With us there is a Christian conscience of the people. And all the greatness of Kant and Hegel cannot help the German people attain to the heights of humannness, when its will to power and coercion have unleashed chaotic elements. A philosophy, always opposing itself to life, cannot morally help a people in life, in the larger scale historical life. German thinking has become detached from the moral centre. This sundering of the heights of German culture from the life of the people has not found expression in these days of an historical trial for the people's conscience. The Teutonic masses, pouring forth upon the world, have proven to be without a moral and religious compass, to be with barbaric instincts and violent intent, all which have developed in it over long decades the culture of a militaristic imperialism. Lutheranism all more and more is becoming rationalised and in decline. The Social Democrats, characteristic as a Germanic form of socialism, -- is the antipode to the militaristic Caesarism -- and is likewise indeed pervaded by a cult of power, by nothing spiritually enlightened. And it is powerless to save Germany from that moral and spiritual degeneracy, to which its cult of power and force is leading it, to the ideals of outward might and power. In the German socialist movement there are not those deeply human and magnanimous motifs of world citizenship, which in the socialist movement of France somewhat shine through all the falsehood of modern life.

Lichtenberger does not speak about this duality of German culture, does not shed light upon the contradictory aspect of its heights and its lowly baseness. His aim -- is to define the average resultant of the powers and currents, contending in modern Germany. He is objective, and without aversion describes, how economic materialism has taken hold with the enormous masses of the German people and how there has gotten worked out the system of German imperialism, in which industrial capital, thirsting for worldwide dominance, has organically aligned with an aggressive militarism. "Imperialistic Germany is not limited by the boundaries of empire, it encompasses the whole sphere of German interests, and in a measure extends to their farthest expanses, and develops in peaceful a way, in the measure of which is how the sphere of German activity grows, not only on German soil, but also beyond its boundaries".[1] Lichtenberger considers the imperialistic politics of the German government to be an expression of the will of the German people itself. "If the left parties tend little to sympathise with the government, which "unites world and imperialistic politics with the politics of Prussian Junkerism", then the masses of the people, evidently, do not share in their discontent. The voters at the time of the recent elections to the Reichstag came out in favour of a politics of national expansion, which the government incorporated into its programme, and came out on the side of the Emperor against the pessimists criticising the "new course". In view of this, it can be said, that the Emperor has continued quite successfully to find supportive tendencies existing in the land, and that the wellsprings of modern German imperialism are not only from the honour-loving dreams of the Monarch, but also from the highly-wrought intensity of the will to power of the people itself".[2] The present day war confirms the correctness of the opinion of Lichtenberger, that the German people in its masses sympathises not with the lofty ideas of its "philosophers and poets", but rather with the pillaging intents of an imperialism, in which the economic materialism of the industrialists is united in marriage with the militarism of the Prussian Junkers. Lichtenberger cites a series of German thinkers and erudite

---

[1] Vide Lichtenberger. "Modern Germany", p. 156.

[2] Ibid., p. 162-163.

figures, who bemoan the decay of all the ideals in Germany. The spiritual level of the politics in Germany has terribly fallen.[1] Werner Sombart considers it incomprehensible, by what manner a people with a great past "should have reached such a downturn of political life, as we have experienced at the end of the XIX Century... The great ideals, with which our grandfathers and fathers were still enthused over, have grown pale".[2] Lichtenberger characterises the societal political condition of modern Germany thus: "The place of political debates has not been occupied with discussions on material interests, in the parliament rather it is pervaded by opportunism, indifferent to whatever the principles as might be. The intellectuals, little disposed towards economic and political adventurism, gradually are being squeezed out of the parliament. The legislature and administration have passed over into the hands of the professionals, who deal with these difficult tasks, as experienced practitioners, with the greatest possible skill and the least possible exertion of efforts. Hence -- the decline in political life, which is noted and bemoaned by many modern German historians".[3] Since the time of the Franco-Prussian War, "national interests have stood higher than all other considerations. The powers have to uphold that which has created the power. In such manner, the cult of power gets still more deeply rooted within the German soul... The support of this exaltation of power, upon which rests the greatness of modern Germany, for it therefore appears a question of life or death. In such manner, the support and growth of the military might remains all the time as one of the foremost national aims of Germany".[4] In Germany has developed a nationalism, which rests upon power and force and it pursues a goal of world seizure, and not of world service. This -- is a classic land of a false nationalism, of a repulsive chauvinism, from which one mustneeds flee, as from a moral pestilence. The national self-conceit and national arrogance of the Germans -- is morally and aesthetically insufferable. "Upon the threshold of the new century the unified Germany more than formerly represents of itself a remarkably organised will to power, totally

---

[1] Lichtenberger. "Modern Germany", p. 183.

[2] Ibid., p. 184.

[3] Ibid., p. 139-140.

[4] Ibid.

disinclined to destruct".¹ The moral and cultural degeneration -- is the inevitable result of German nationalism and militarism. What has this modern nationalism in common with that consciousness of a great mission of the German spirit, which awakened with the great idealists of the early XIX Century, with the national expectations of the Romantic era? There is as little in common, as also little have our own modern nationalists and Black Hundredists with the Slavophils, with Dostoevsky or Vl. Solov'ev. In Germany is beginning a savagery of brute force and power, by nothing spiritually enlightened nor restrained. An idolatry of material power, having replaced the veneration of the power of God, leads always to savagery, to an unleashing of the beastly elements.

This spiritual degeneration of the German people has nothing in common with French Decadentism, with a debilitating refinement and complication of soul. The Germans "believe in rather coarsely rough an health of the race, in its growing might in the economic sphere, in its soldierly instincts, in the sense of discipline and solidarity".² "This somewhat ponderous and sluggish, but yet strong and healthy people reflects an exceptionally favourable soil for the growth of a capitalistic civilisation. The German -- is altogether unartistic, and not of the passionate nature striving after delights, as is the romantic... And here, in this lacking of elegance and lustre, but on the other hand by the strength and insistence of the people, there is developing a powerful will to mightiness, patient, methodical".³ *"The will for might is taking hold in the German soul in precedence over the aspiration for culture, imperceptibly relegating it to a secondary plane... Amongst the Germans grows a cult of power"*.⁴ In these words is a clue to our question. This degeneracy within crude power -- for the world is a most dangerous form of degeneracy. A people, which has entered upon this path, has to be outwardly rendered powerless, forcibly humbled, has to be deprived of imperial might as such. Having taken up the sword one perishes by the sword. Germany has lifted a sword against all the world. It aspires not still for the spreading of culture

---

[1] Lichtenberger. "Modern Germany", p. 147.

[2] Ibid., p. 386.

[3] Ibid., p. 402-403.

[4] (Italics mine. -- N. B.). Ibid., p. 404.

through all the world, it aspires after power for the sake of power. The cult of power, nationalism, making a god of the might of the Vaterland, has replaced the worship of God, has been turned into a pseudo-religion. The duality within Protestantism allows it to direct historical life along a course, which leads all farther and farther away from Christianity. The rationalism of the Germans has impeded direct religious experiences. The traditional German Idealism has not vanished ultimately, but it remains the religion of a select minority. "This religion of the metaphysicians, of the literary figures and artists, lacks sufficiently solid an hold... The German Idealism remains strong, which however enjoys esteem only within the higher cultural levels. It has not proven a strong influence upon practical life, does not attract to it the sympathetic interest of the broad masses".[1] And it is not the German Idealism, exalted and powerless, that now heads out into the world for the seizure of all and everything -- it has instead drowned without a trace into the enormous element of the barbaric Pan-Germanism, just as the cult of Goethe and many beautiful things have drowned. When the Germans unleashed a beastly reprisal upon the peaceful inhabitants of Kalisz [in Poland], the thought of German Idealism then became impossible, since the heart seems lacking at the core of the Germans. Truly: "Afront the mouth of the Dragon the cross and the sword -- are one". These words were spoken by Vl. Solov'ev concerning the danger of Pan-Mongolism. But now the danger of Pan-Germanism has proven *more terrible and more real than the danger of Pan-Mongolism.* There is being laid bare the lie of a culture, which has neither subordinated itself to the spiritual centre nor striven always for justice, but rather instead for earthly power. Germany is teaching us, what we ought not to become. God grant us not to follow upon the path of German culture, either outwardly or inwardly. We have our own particular paths of culture, more just, and our own greater potentials. The world war ought to free us from the false idea, that German culture is culture preeminently. To get free not only from German power, but also from the German spirit. The German spirit has its own destiny in the world, and certainly not that, to which German imperialistic might makes pretense. But this spirit for us, as Slavs, can only be foreign for us, an external norm, which hobbles our soul. Closer to us and less dangerous is the culture of the Latin peoples. This new Fatherland War frees us from foreign-land incursions both outwardly

---

[1] Lichtenberger. "Modern Germany", p. 277-278.

and inwardly and helps us to manifest pure a spirit. And does not indeed the full symbolic sense of the city name-change from St. Peterburg to rather the city of Petrograd signify *the onset of the end of the Peterburg period of Russian history*, in which a nationalism not Russian in spirit has held us, and in which a not-Russian bureaucratism has waged war against the Russian people itself?

Imperialism Sacral and Imperialism Bourgeois

(1914 -180)[1]

I.

The idea of empire -- is one of the ancient ideas of mankind. Within it is embodied the lofty idea about a trans-national, worldwide unity of mankind. According to this idea, there can be only one empire, and the one true empire -- is the Imperium Romanum. The Christian world inherited from the ancient world the idea of the Roman Empire and acknowledged it as sacred, as holy. The empire is not a national state, it is supra-national in its concept, and the coinciding for it with this or some other national state was merely a typical hedging of the pure idea in its empirical and historical aspects. And the Holy Roman Empire is something on the order of a Platonic idea. It held sway with the best minds of mankind and guided the will of the mightiest. The idea of a theocratic empire across all the expanse of Western European history tended to clash with the idea of a theocratic Papacy. And with both the one and the other there was sacral a pretension to world dominion and world unity. The Roman Empire played indeed an enormous role in fashioning the unity of mankind, in the consciousness of the very idea of the oneness of mankind. The Roman Empire provided the Christian Church a naturo-historical basis for the oneness of mankind and therefore it possesses the right to be termed holy. And the Holy Roman Empire continues with its ideal aspect, sundered off from a real geographic centre of existence right up through the XIX Century. As to the ideal existence of the Holy Roman Empire, while bereft already of any historically real basis, it would be difficult for mankind to renounce it, as a symbol of its world unity, without preventing European mankind from disintegrating into atoms. This great idea became empirically attached first to Germany, and then to Austria. The Holy

---

[1] IMPERIALIZM SVYASCHENNYI I IMPERIALIZM BURZHUAZNYI. Article originally published in the newspaper "Birzhevye vedomosti", 5 nov. 1914, № 14476.

Roman Empire was formally abolished in the year 1806, and its pitiful offspring remained the Austrian Empire of the Hapsburgs, the former Roman emperors. This was as a result of the great Napoleon, who dreamed about the founding of new a world empire, an empire of genius and the super-man. The XIX Century stands beneathe the standard of the ultimate formation of national states and the national self-consciousness of peoples. The unity of mankind becomes conceived of spiritually, an external appendage to the body of a world empire. The supra-human and genius-based pretensions of Napoleon to create a real world empire represent the final pretensions of a sacred imperialism in the West. The world empire of Napoleon was not a national state and Napoleon, victorious over the emperors of Austria and Russia, which had esteemed themself as heirs of the first Rome and of the Second Rome respectively, in their place himself claimed to be the sole heir of the Roman Empire. The collapse of Napoleon was a collapse of sacred imperialism in general -- in it the idea of a sacred world empire reached its ultimate limit and passed over into its opposite. After the Napoleonic wars there in turn began national liberation wars and movements. Imperialism did not however disappear during the XIX and XX Centuries, but rather assumes a completely new form, it degenerates from a sacred imperialism into a bourgeois imperialism and gets closely bound up with the national state. And in the XIX Century making pretension to being worldwide and sacred is international socialism, the Internationale.

II.

Bourgeois imperialism represents a degenerate form of the ancient idea of empire, its rebirth into a thirst for a material domination of a national state in the world and over the world. The imperialism of the XX Century is a struggle among nations for the great-power position in world affairs. This imperialism is no longer a striving towards a worldwide trans-national unity, towards a sacred universalism, -- it is merely a striving amongst nations to be great and hence the greatest power on land and sea. This struggle for political and economic dominance, for markets, for sea trade -- is a form of Darwinism in sociology. There remains nothing of the old Imperium Romanum, except for the profaning of its name. Bourgeois imperialism represents the selfish pretensions of national state particularism in place of universal a dominance, and its aims are attained through pillage and enslavement.

In the idea of the Roman Empire there was truly a sacred task, the sacred dream about an all-unity within the historical life of mankind. This sense of sacredness has not remained in the bourgeois imperialism, which has flourished into the capitalistic era. The present imperialistic situation -- derives from the free rivalry of capitalistic societies. One of the chief causes of the current world war -- is the rivalry of the bourgeois imperialism of Germany against the bourgeois imperialism of England, a struggle for dominance on the sea. England was the first as the model of purely a bourgeois imperialism, as was so brilliantly described by Chamberlain [Houston Stewart, 1855-1927]. This represents the imperialism of a capitalistic dominance by England upon the sea, an imperialism primarily of sea and colony, pushing its civilising mission, but totally free from any medieval sacred dream of a world empire. It is so characteristic to the spirit of modern times, that our times admit of the existence of several and many empires, which are in rivalry betwixt them. The modern period with its capitalistic economy has replaced the imperialistic medieval monism with instead an imperialistic multiplicity. In the old sacral sense there can only be but one empire, whereas many empires can be bourgeois. But even the bourgeois imperialism, behind which always must be taken into account the economic underpinnings, can be varied and variously considered. The English imperialism possesses obvious advantages over the German imperialism. England, by virtue of its position, is more given to be a great imperialistic power dominating the seas, than is Germany. The English imperialism is less vicious, more liberal, and it can be moderate. Germany as a great empire is less fortunate a land, than is England, and to it is apportioned unfortunate an allotted fate. The secret of the ugliness and insufferable aspect of German imperialism lies concealed in this, that with Germany it has lacked naturo-historical a basis to be foreordained to be a great empire, and that therefore its imperialist pretensions can only be realised by way of violence and plunder, by way of quite intolerable a wronging for the world. The German imperialism, in contrast to the English -- is conservative and in fatal a manner militaristic. The monstrous and insufferable militarism is an essential and engrained trait of the German imperialism, presenting a threat for all the world, and it exposes the weakness of vocation and non-essential aspect of Germany's aspirations as a great empire. This fact, that the unification of Germany was in realisation of a certain proper truth, has led to a counter-natural growth of militaristic imperialism; as such, it has been fatal for Germany and has led to its spiritual decline and moral degeneracy, as expressed in this war. The German people, to whom in the book of fates was deigned to be a people of "thinkers and poets", but not to create a great empire, has become gripped with the thirst for a bourgeois-imperialistic world domination. To drown this thirst was possible only through the developement of a contrary to nature militarism, arming all the world and holding all the world in the grip of extreme tension. This is not so with the rather more fortunate English imperialism. It is evident, that Germany is striving and attempting to be, quite other than it was predestined to be. The terrible current war, the responsibility for which falls on Germany, has to seem fully justified from the point of view of the imperialistic pretensions of Germany. And if the pretensions inevitably and as justified lead to such terrible acts of violence, then it means, that in these pretensions is rooted an untruth and lie. Germany, as a great and greatest empire predominant in the world, can continue its existence only by the ravaging of foreign lands and colonies, and only so by the permanent sustaining of militarism. To destroy the threat of German militarism is possible, only by destroying the imperialistic might of Germany. All the peoples of the world cannot indeed consent to this, that Germany should become the greatest empire, since the existence of this greatest empire is a threat for all the world, a threat of violence over all the world and of untruth in the world.

III.

Once upon a time formerly the Teutonic barbarians received from Rome the idea of empire. The ancient idea of a world empire and the Christian idea of the oneness of mankind fermented within the barbarian Germanic blood. It assumed very complex and confused an historical form, named the Holy Roman Empire, but sundered off from Rome. The Germans have always tended to confuse a world empire with their own local royal kingdom, and they stamped upon the empire the imprint of a national particularism. Thus it was in old Germany, living under the influence of the medieval idea of empire. After the Reformation, there ultimately appeared an organic disinclination with the Germans to the idea of an imperialistic universalism. The Germans in essence were desirous of a national German state and their own national German monarch, and for a long while they were lacking in a national German unity and national German might. The dignity of title passed over to the Hapsburgs and the idea of the Holy Roman Empire, completely free of any geographic centre and set boundary, by a strange irony of fate passed over to Austria. Fir the uniting and might of Germany there emerged Prussia, which least of all could be termed a centre of Germanism and a population of which was not purely German. These lands had formerly belonged to the Lithuanians and Slavs, and most everything remarkable in the history of the German spirit had not occurred in Prussia. If the Prussian kingdom itself can be termed a parvenu, a recent upstart, within the family of German states, then too the empire of the Hohenzollerns is likewise ultimately -- a parvenu. The finest of the Germans tend to protest against the hegemony of Prussia. The imperialism of the Hohenzollerns has in itself ultimately nothing of the sacred, no sort of connections with sacred traditions, it -- is thoroughly bourgeois, thoroughly national-particular, and not universal. The German empire is a profaning of the sacred idea of empire, its final degeneration into a bourgeois national state of the XIX and XX Centuries. In the spirit of the German empire is expressed the non-universal, the national particular nature of the Germans. The pretension of the German empire to world dominion is a pretension bourgeois, and not holy, a thirst for enslavement, and not world unification. The holy empire in its idea -- is not a state, not a monarchy, not a national unity, but rather an unity all-human, a worldwide power. The idea of empire -- is not monarchist, but instead of republican (in the ancient Roman sense) an origin, and the title of emperor -- is republican a title. Julius Caesar -- was the child of a republic that had become worldwide, and not the offspring of some sort of national monarchy. Monarchistic power is always of particularised, local, land-based an origin. Napoleon was also the last Western emperor in the worldwide, trans-national and supra-state ancient sense of the word. His empire was in the style of the ancient empire, and his imperial power was just as republican, as was the power of Julius Caesar. The modern German empire possesses no sort of the style of empire, in it there is no universal spirit. This is a falsely named empire -- actually a national monarchy, harshly German, with selfish plundering instincts. *Deutschland über alles* -- cannot be the slogan of an empire, for which most of all important should be the unity of the world and of mankind. The German national imperialism inevitably has to oppress and commit violence against both individual nations and individual humans, -- it desires, that Germany should be the all and the all should be Germany. The German empire -- is the eternal enemy of the liberation of various nationalities. Not in vain is it always situated in such a despicable union with Turkey. The modern imperialism inevitably possesses a tendency towards domination, it does not tolerate the individual existence of weaker peoples.

    The great and foreordained mission of Russia -- is to be the defender of the oppressed nationalities, the liberator of peoples. And within the world war this mission has to become totally apparent. Bourgeois imperialism with its selfish spirit is foreign to Russia and the Russian people. Everything of violence in Russia has been of foreign a source, not authentically Russian. Germany, Austria and Turkey -- are eternal enemies of freedom and of the independence of peoples, eternally violent against national individuality. After the great war the bourgeois imperialism will undergo a crisis to the death and the falsely appropriated names cast aside. The worldwide unity of mankind ultimately will be realised spiritually, outside of all material considerations. Russia will appear as the bearer of worldwide a spirit, of trans-national an universalism, which only likewise will represent an union amidst the existence of individual nationalities. In the sacred imperialism there was lodged the idea of worldwide brotherhood. But it has to ultimately be liberated from material a domination, has to provide a free life to human individuals. The trappings of a sacred imperialism have fallen, and in this is the great truth of the process of secularisation. The world spirit has departed the old forms, it is not contained in the historical bodies, it is freed of all materiality. Everything historico-corporeal is limited and particularised, and cannot pretend to be worldwide a power. This is a liberating truth that Russia has to convey to the world.

On the Dormant Powers of Man

(Concerning the Psychology of War)

(1914 - 184)[1]

The war evokes feelings so contradictory, that it is almost impossible to bring them into a mutual accord. The tortuous experience of the terrors of the war, the pall of death, suffering and destruction, which it bears with it into the world, is juxtaposed by the proud consciousness of the boundless powers of man, of the heroism of human nature, merely but veiled over by quite thick a layer of the peaceful life, but never dying away. Lethargic is man, and his enormous spiritual powers lay dormant. Great shocks are needed, catastrophes personal and worldwide, in order to rouse all the powers of man. In the bourgeois life of peacetime are active only an insignificant portion of human powers. Why in the life of individual creative persons there occur periods of an influx of creative energy, of an exceptional creative upsurge, -- remains a mystery of the individual, never completely to be solved. But in historical life, involving the masses, in a period of an upsurge of powers, of an heroic zeal, it tends to coincide with catastrophic impulses, with the setting of tasks, demanding sacrifice and selflessness. The nature of man is discerned only in the exceptionally responsible moments of life, when the powers of man can no longer still lay dormant. The war is a great trial for man, his powers and capacity for sacrifice. The war makes of man a beast and an hero, a barbarian and mighty, rousing instincts very base and very high. In this consists the ineradicable contradictions of war. It bears with it the danger of barbarisation and savagery and the hope for a rebirth into new life.

A great and inspirational war, presenting various peoples with great tasks, rouses into life and action the potential powers of man, powers immeasurable, but hidden and dormant. The current world war has brought

---

[1] O DREMLIUSCHIKH SILAKH CHELOVEKA (K psikhologii voiny). Article originally published in the newspaper "Utro Rossii", nov. 1914, № 272.

with it already not only the tragic account as yet unprecedented terrors of devastation and destruction, of savagery, the extent to which the cultured people of the XX Century have reached, but also the joyful account of heroism, which no one still expected of bourgeois peoples, seemingly concerned only about industrial prosperity, of human strength, of endurance and capacity for sacrifice, which they had become accustomed to think applied only to past ages. The war has shown, that bourgeoisness has not ultimately eradicated the heroic spirit, that the attachment to well-being has not ultimately extirpated the capacity for sacrifice and has not rendered man altogether soft. Whoever expected from industrial Belgium, ready to make the transition from a felicitous bourgeois prosperity over to a felicitous socialistic prosperity, a small neutral country, never having especially industrialised for war, -- who would have ever expected a spirit so sacrificial and heroic? Modern bourgeois life has seemed altogether incompatible with the heroic spirit. And here indeed the heroic spirit has manifested itself in the very core of bourgeois life. This happy account has reached across to us amidst all the terrors of the war. We are shaken both by the heroism of peaceful bourgeois Belgium and by the savagery of cultural Germany. There is reborn the hope, that bourgeoisness has not destroyed the core of the soul of Western man, but involved only its outer trappings. The spiritual power was there dormant, hidden beneathe a covering of bourgeoisness. The war -- present fine a test. It has uncovered both the heroism behind peaceful life, and the barbarity behind mechanical a civilisation.

It would be very important to concern oneself with the psychology of war, and the present war, certainly, will call forth a whole series of works in this direction. General Dragomirov has complained, that "we know nothing or almost nothing about those inner processes and phenomena, which occur in the soul of a man under the influence of danger".[1] The spiritual factours of war are too often ignored both by the military and by the non-military. Dragomirov himself is convinced, that "war, and war alone, evokes that terrible and conjoint exertion of all the spiritual sides of man, in particular the will, which evidences all the measure of his might and which is not called forth by any other kind of

---

[1] Vide: M. Dragomirov, "Sketches: Analysis of "War and Peace", the Russian Soldier, Napoleon the First, Joan of Arc", p. 3.

activity".¹ In these words there is of course an over-emphasis upon the military, the extremeness of an exclusively military point of view, but there is also a serious truth, upon which it is appropriate to turn one's attention. In Dragomirov there are interesting remarks on the psychology of the Russian soldier and on the effect of Napoleon upon the mindset of the masses in war. In contrast to the German directions in military science, Dragomirov bestows tremendous significance to the spiritual factours of war and does not grant the point, that the successes in the war have resulted exclusively from the technical and mechanical aspects. "If there have been entire eras, convinced, that masses of people should form entirely into linear and rectangular geometric figures, that for the army it is best that the soldier be close to an automaton, by which he is more ready for action, then this can be attributed to naught else, than to a total inattention to the spiritual activity of man, summoned to action in the masses, on the field of battle, under the influence of danger".² It is known, that the German army, possessing brilliant technology and amazing discipline, is quite given to mechanisation and automatisation. The Russian army is moreso inspired an affair, and its victory will be a victory of spirit over the mechanical, over mechanical a civilisation. But what is of interest to us is not so much the psychology of the masses during the time of battle, as rather the psychology of an entire people during the time of a great war. The enormous potential power of man is revealed not only in battle, on the field of combat, but also in a general upsurge of the people. War is a phenomenon more extensive and deeper, than what occurs in the acting armies, in the actual combats. Some now suggest to consider Russia as the rear-flank of the army and to subordinate the whole life of Russia to the interests of the army. In this point of view there is a dram of truth, but the reverse can also be said. It is possible to view the army, as the vanguard of Russia, to see in it only an important function of the spiritual war, which is being waged by all of Russia, all the Russian people. Such a view -- goes deeper, and it provides more extensive an understanding of war, which is a manifestation of the spirit, and not only of the clashing of armed masses.

In tranquil peacetime, when there thrives the thirst for well-being and comfort, people tend to lack endurance and they readily become weak.

---

¹ Vide: M. Dragomirov, Ibid., p. 4-5.

² Ibid., p. 3-4.

But in moments of danger, when he is pushed to an ultimate testing of his powers, a man proves capable of working miracles, his endurance has no limits, the intensity of powers can reach improbable extents. Average people are able to do battle 25 days at a stretch, not sleeping, not eating, overcoming the fear of death, to undergo such terrors, the mere thought of which in peacetime would chill the blood in the veins. Doctors speak about the striking ease and rapidity, with which the wounded recover. Gangrene may have set in, and with the slightest assist the organism is restored to life. People in ordinary times are afraid of a mere scratch and from the least illness are unable to recover. The powers of man lay dormant, in non-active a condition. But in a threatening hour all the powers of man awaken, and the power of life reaches utmost an intensity. Man is almost capable of exceeding the laws of nature. A true measure of the powers of man in the everyday, peaceful, tranquil times is inaccurate and deceptive. And base a thing it is in man, that he feigns to be weak and without endurance, when life does not demand an exertion of strength and endurance. Historical trials and catastrophes are needful to the masses of mankind: they provide an awakening, they test and punish. A great mystery of human life lies concealed in this, that for the full revealing of human powers there is necessary not only the good, but also the evil.

We face tormenting a question, -- after the war during peacetime will there be active those spiritual powers, which were awakened and revealed during the time of war? Certain now already fear, that after the exertion and upsurge evoked by the war, there will possibly ensue fatigue and exhaustion. In these apprehensions is expressed a great lack of trust in human nature. Only great tribulations, dangers and misfortunes tend to uplift human nature. When tranquility ensues, man withers. Human freedom has to have needful its stimulator. In such a pessimistic point of view on human nature there is, certainly, an element of truth, to which one ought not to close one's eyes. The freedom of man as such does not provide a guarantee, that he has no further wish to remain in the grip of necessity, lethargic and passive. And if as I believe, that after the world war it is necessary to await not a let-down, but rather a spiritual upsurge, this therefore is only what I do know: man awaits not a tranquil and peaceful life, but rather something other, a spiritual continuation of the world war, which pushes to the ultimate limit all the basic questions of human life. The current world war was preceeded by a profound spiritual crisis, a re-evaluation of all values. All the foundations of a world-feeling and a world-understanding , inherited from the XIX Century, have been shaken. That which transpired in the depths, in the substrate, will be brought out by the world war onto the surface, into the arena of history. What formerly involved separate individuals, at some intimate depth having experienced a re-evaluation of the meaning of life, has to become historical a matter. The world-historical catastrophe will prove a crisis of the old culture -- a crisis for international capitalism and for international socialism, for imperialism and militarism, a crisis of all the old fundamental aspects of life. After the war there will be demanded a still greater exertion of the spiritual powers of man, than during the time of war, but already otherwise, with a creative intensity, creating new life. It is because the old life will become impossible, and its inertial continuation would be deadly. The world war is leading many to an awareness of the instability of earthly life, to a presentiment of supra-human providential powers, which might direct and guide human life. In this awareness and presentiment there is a great truth, likewise for many of the modern people neither experiencing nor knowing, nor of deep an attitude towards life. But the world catastrophe is awakening also another awareness -- the awareness of the extraordinary powers of man himself, divine powers, potentially alive within man himself. Both types of consciousness express two sides of a singular truth about the revealing of God within man. This exceptional awareness of divine powers within man leads to an intense expectation of the appearance of great people, of leaders, of heroes in Carlyle's sense of the word, for whom it demands a culminating breaking point within world history, the shaking up of everything of the old and an engendering of the new. At present our gaze is directed towards the army, and we with reverential respect bow before the heroes of the war. But also at present we already have presentiment of the appearance of heroes, creating the new life, pointing out the way for Russia and the world. The tasks, presented by the world crisis, cannot be resolved by any sort of impersonal mechanical means, by any sort of average scope and considerations -- these tasks demand human genius, exceptionally gifted and chosen, of an as yet unprecedented creative upsurge of the human spirit. There is hence the determined and intense faith in this, that it will be a passionate summoning forth of leaders and creative persons, ready for what is to come.

The New Russia

(1915-188)¹

I.

When the war began, we experienced moments of happy a faith, that there had ensued an end of the old divisions, the hostility of party, platforms and doctrines, that there no longer would be "rightists" and "leftists", like two races, having no respect for each other as people, no "Slavophils" nor "Westernisers", no "typical sorts" and "intelligentsia". It seemed, that it is possible to have a sense of Russia, its sole visage, its whole organism. All the indeed doctrinising, as appended to life, had been a falling away from the being of Russia into a wont for abstract thought. The initial impressions from the war capsized all the doctrinalism. Granted, it was only in a single moment that we experienced the feeling of Russia outside the divisive categories. In a single moment became possible greater light, than we experienced in many a long year. In this lightning-quick awareness of the oneness of Russia was a truth, transcending all the platforms and all the doctrinal slogans. The united Russia -- is a free Russia, gathering its strength, aware of its dignity. [...] The Russians have been too accustomed to sense themself, as though in a conquered land, as not their own home. The German invasion has given the Russians joyful a feel, that they have their own home, their own native land. Suddenly it was felt, that it was possible to love the native land irregardless of "mindset", not to love it merely in the "rightist" manner nor in the "leftist" manner, but simply to love it. There came a flash of awareness, that love for Russia cannot have a "trend", it is initial and prior to all secondary distinctions, deeper than all the categorical determinations. In all lands there are parties and trends of idea, which are in conflict, but nowhere have the divisions gone so deeply, as in Russia. In Russia everything has been especially paradoxical and extreme. [...]

---

¹ NOVAYA ROSSIYA. Article originally published in the newspaper "Birzhevye vedomosti", 23 jan. 1915, № 14628.

trans. note: This article was heavily censored, as indicated by [...].

The "rightists" have tended to think, that the true Russia is the official Russia. And the "leftists" have tended to think the same, and upon this basis they considered Russia itself as something false or non-existing, whereas truly existing they admitted was whatever the trend or party. The "leftists" ceded to the "rightists" a monopoly on feelings for Russia, renounced the age-old right to have one's native land for oneself. Patriotism was considered identical with the attitude of the "rightists" towards the official Russia. Russia had eluded the "leftists", did not obtain for them. The "leftists" had proven very yielding: they surrendered Russia to the "rightists", and had left unto themselves merely their "trends". Russia -- became a matter of "they", not "we", and therefore all patriotism was disdainful. Russia -- this is the official government. And essentially it was not a matter of Russia and the Russian people, but rather only a matter of official government as against the matter of trends, of party and of class. The false and official nationalism appeals to life and gives rise to internationalism, an abstract cosmopolitanism. The consciousness of the "leftists" is situated in a slavery to the "rightists", tends to get defined and directed by the "rightists". The "leftists" experience everything only in the form of an emotional reaction against the "rightists", only in a negative opposition to everything "rightist", and not in essence, not freely. The "rightists" from their side are completely obsessed over the "leftists", the "leftist" danger, the need to restrict, oppress and divide. The "rightists" get transformed into maniacs over all the dangers. Their slogans are totally negative, destructive, and not constructive. The "rightist" reaction begets the "leftist" revolution, the "leftist" revolution again in turn begets the "rightist" reaction, etc. It is such an inescapable circle, a nightmare. Neither the "leftists", nor the "rightists" have been reflective of an authentic citizenship, a citizenship of the free sons of their native land. [...] Both the "rightists" and the "leftists" alike little believe in themself and they all think, that "they" the enemy, are stronger. Actually, it is because that genuine power obtains with a true feeling for Russia, in being one with Russia.

There has been something slave-like in the attitude of Russians towards the state, something immature, not manly. The most typical Russian rightists and the most intelligentsia-inclined Russian leftists always have thought, that the state -- is a "they", and not "we". The state is not a function in the life of the people, is not a construct of the people, reflective of its historical activity. The state is the utmost, standing over "us", for some it is good, for others bad, not "our" power, but rather a foreign power, "their" power. [...] The Russian state is perceived as something transcendent to the Russian people, something unapproachable from within for this feminine and stateless people. The Russian radical intelligentsia continues to sense the state as the legacy of the Varangians, but situates itself in constant an opposition to this legacy. Hence there occurs a constant confusing of the state with the government. But the government indeed is only a temporal and transitory function of the state. In the state aspect there are functions relative to the entire people. [...] And to such functions relative to the entire people belongs, for example, the army, which defends the fatherland and all the people. The army, just like the courts and m[uch] el[se], for a certain while might be the weapon of a given government, but the army in its idea is "our", and not "their" army, relative to all the entire people and the whole civil aspect, a Russian army. And this is vitally felt in a time of war. [...] With us it has been not only the "rightists", but the "leftists" also who have been lacking in a true correct-awareness, and therefore we have had so much fruitless opposition and so little struggle for legal rights in the English sense of this concept. Russian man is very passive. [...] He loves for everything to shift to the "middle", which he mangles. Our societal and political slogans are rooted in spiritual infirmities, in the feminineness and passivity of the Russian soul, in a certain incapacity to assert of itself power and strength. [...]

In the Russian character there is a certain metaphysical hysteria, which Dostoevsky so powerfully sensed and revealed. There is no tempering of character. Russia is torn between two opposing realms -- the realm of the "philistinists" and the realm of the "intelligentsia". If in the "philistinists" there is servility towards the state, then also in the "intelligentsia" there is an inverted servility. Genuinely free are neither the one, nor the other. The realm of the "philistinists" is proud, that it is the authentic Russia, that only it loves and knows Russia. The realm of the "intelligentsia" is proud, that only it loves and knows freedom and justice, it only fights for the interests of the people. And eternally opposed are these two realms, they lacerate Russia and hinder the birth of a free Russia, aware of itself and its vocation in the world. A true national self-consciousness has not been attained by either the "philistinists" nor by the "intelligentsia". The untruth of internationalism has been set in opposition against the untruth of a murky nationalism.

II.

Russia in its moving has to pass over into a sort of different scale of measurement. It ought to begin motion not along the flat plane towards right or left, but rather along the vertical of depth and height. The flat plane movement towards right or left does not lead to any sort of an egress, a way out. This movement remains caught up in a vicious circle, eternally repeating a cycle of two reactions, it essentially is situated always in the grip of emotional reaction, and cannot be creative. Everything creative within history has always been movement along the vertical, and not along the flat plane, has been a movement of depth and height. And only on the surface of history has it seemed, that a progressive movement occurs along the flat plane. This was a shifting about of the points of intersection of the horizontal with the vertical, a projection onto the horizontal of the movement from the depths. Only the vertical and deep motion regenerates the fabric of life, creates new life, and does not merely redistribute the old matter of life, covered over anew with superficial veils. Every motion vertically at depth is religious, its impulses derive from primordial a freedom, from the sensings of God by man. The religious nature of this motion can also remain undetected, subliminal. The true, the creative motion is movement from within outwards, from freedom, and not from necessity, from the freedom of the spirit, freedom-loving by character. [...] True movement [...] is filial creativity.

With sorrow it has to be admitted, that the ideology of our national consciousness, reinforced upon religious a basis, is situated in the grip of emotional reactions, impeding their movement at depth. They fatally move horizontally rightwards out of a reaction against everything of the "intelligentsia" and the "left". They judge about life not in essence, but with a constant gazing about both left and right. They therefore all remain within the same inescapable circle of mutual reactions of the "right" and the "left" camps. A cleansing from the dirt and an enlightened "legality" all remain upon the horizontal plane and do not improve the situation. Upon this path are sustained the old division and hostility, and have merely reinforced the former separation of Russia into two camps. With us has arisen a type of "concerned intelligentsia individual", just as formerly there has been the type of the "concerned nobleman". The concerned intelligentsia individual is very indicative of the crisis of the intelligentsia, but he is not a creative man, he is all still in reaction against his past. S. N. Bulgakov shows within him a sincere and pure movement along the horizontal plane "towards the right", from religious impulses. And this example teaches us, that upon the flat plane, where "right" and "left" feelings hold sway, where the "philistinists" and "intelligentsia" remain set in opposition, it becomes impossible to have an united Russia and it is impossible to pass over to the creativity of a new Russia.

And here is still yet another representative of the "religious consciousness" -- D. S. Merezhkovsky. He is moving along the flat horizontal "leftwards", all in an attempt to unite religion with intelligentsia radicalism and no less than Bulgakov he is situated within the grip of an emotional reaction, not going into depth along the vertical. Completely hopeless and ineffective are all the attempts to unite religion with something, to seek for religion a buttress in external historical powers, and in turn for the external historical forces to seek a sanction in religion. And it is totally irrelevant, whether this transpire from the societal "right" and the traditional, or from the societal "left" and the revolutionary. Since religion is the creative energy of the free spirit, it regenerates life from within, immanently. Everything of the flat horizontal, historically external in religion is merely a projection of the profoundly inward, of the hidden unseen. And this projection is not religious life itself, but merely what is seen. Religious movement "right" or "left", according to the criteria and categories of the external world, evokes a sort of sense of hopelessness. And thus is not engendered a creative and profound consciousness.

III.

Russia needs to free itself from the traditional platforms, from the contorted slogans, from the dead doctrines. Oh, if only it could happen for us as Russians, -- the awareness, that we should have to be not so much liberals, as rather freedom-lovers, not so much opportunists, as rather creators, not so much democrats, as rather seeing in each man the image and likeness of God and his higher dignity, not hysterical but rather volitional people, radicals not in the conditional, but rather the deep-rooted sense of the word, men moreso, and persons, rather than "leftists" or "rightists". And this means, that we, as Russians, ought first of all to become manly with a fully mature and self-restraining will, and to stand firm. In us, as Russians, there ought to show forth a creative spiritual fount, the impulse to new life, from within, from the will, from freedom. Without this, Russia is doomed to the result, that for it the masculine principle will be the Germans, who always have pushed themself forth as a suitor for the feminine Slavic race, both in the life of the state aspect, as well as in the spiritual life, in the formation of thought. To be inwardly freedom-loving, the freedom of the spirit, the energy of a personal worthiness and personal legitimacy -- these are necessary prerequisites for the creativity of a new Russia. Russia all still too much has lived in an impersonal collective, in the organism of natural an economy both in the spiritual and in the material. Its Christianity has been too much grounded in nature, too tied in with the natal existence. Russia has to go through a spiritual, a religious emancipation of the person, through a forging of what it is to be a person, of the personal spirit, to pass over to a collective not impersonal, not natural, but rather spiritual, constructively building. [...]

A free societal aspect can be created only by the free in spirit, only by those conscious of their own freedom. And our "leftists" and "rightists", our "intelligentsia" and "philistinists" cannot be termed people, free in spirit, creating from the depths of their will. A Russian societal renewal presupposes a Russian spiritual renewal, a renewal of the Russian creative will, a new spiritual rebirth of Russian man.[1] The "idea" of a new Russia has to stand higher than all the old doctrines, the platforms, the party and current trend divisions. And the repetition of the old words -- Slavophils, Westernisers, rightists, leftists -- has gotten to be tediously tormentive, an hindrance to new life. The power of inertia drags upon us with the old slogans, the old categories, the traditional divisions of "rightists" and "leftists". Thousand-pud weights hang on us and drag us downwards. The old sins still rule us. And our struggle for a free life always is poisoned, always is joyless, and too often fruitless by its hysterical emotional reaction.

The current world war provides an inducement for the rise of a new consciousness, a creative national consciousness. The war itself per se can create nothing, its nature is negative, it is moreso the end of the old, rather than the beginning of the new. But with us there is the will to believe, that a new historical period is beginning and that there awaits us

---

[1] It has been established, that the English consciousness of the rights of man, the English sense of freedom was begotten of a religious movement, from the religious Reformation.

something not foreseen by any sort of doctrines. the soldier, fighting for the honour and dignity of the native land, -- is not a slave; he has to feel, that Russia -- is he himself, and this valiant awareness is something he has to offer within Russia [...]

A movement at depth is always liberating, and it surmounts every slavery. The current world period stands beneathe the standard of a confusing of planes, from a shifting about of the points of intersection of these horizontal planes by the vertical and in-depth movements. The world war itself is but an horizontal flat-plane projection of those stormy motions, which transpire within, in the depths, in the substrate of life. And an egress and way out from this manifest chaos can be sought only in deep creative movements. The new Russia, not torn asunder by the old disputes, and [...] can be, by the creative action of the new man. And the new man -- is the child of a new religious rebirth.

Nietzsche and the Modern Germany

(1915-189)[1]

I.

Since the very start of the war we have had many an attempt made to discern the spiritual fathers of modern Germany and to explain the origins of its fierceness and brutality, its unrestrained and unenlightened will to might.[2] In these riddles of the mystery of modern Germany, each has begun to come up with his own account of where to lay the blame for those manifestations of spirit, which generally he has regarded as despicable and false. Pointed out as culprits in all the ugliness to begin with is Luther and Protestantism, and then Kant and critical philosophy, then Marx and economic materialism, then Nietzsche and the teaching about the superman. Others even reach back to the old German mysticism and already in Eckhardt they see the seed of that which will grow ultimately into the present-day world war. In Ern,[3] with his typical frenzied and blind and monolineal manner, he ties in Kant with Krupp, with the facile levity of doctrinaire a mindset, overlapping all the obstacles along the way. To Kant he draws a direct line from Eckhardt and Luther. Ern goes about this abstract pounding upon Germanism by means of the wonts and habits purely of German thinking, investing the matter with

---

[1] NITSSHE I SOVREMENNAYA GERMANIYA. Article originally published in the newspaper "Birzhevye vedomosti", 4 feb. 1915, № 14650.

[2] The best and most profound of everything written about Germany currently, -- is the article of D. Koigen [David, 1879-1933], "The Tragedy of Germanism", in "Severni zapiski" for December.

[3] Vide: "Russkaya mysl'" for December. Ern infers the rise of Krupp [the German military industrial firm] from the phenomenalism of Kant. But moreso extreme a nominalism is a trait of the English, and hence it is in England that Krupp ought to be.

concepts and ideas, and not with life in its multiplicity and individuality. It thus comes close to the plan of war constructed by General Pfuel in "War and Peace". But we have grown weary of the doctrinaire scene and should instead desire to turn pervasively into the individuality of actuality.

That tree of life, which can be termed Germany, grew and blossomed both in the individual and in the manifold. This tree has also borne some disfigured fruit. But the growth and blossoming forth of life never transpires in accord with the fulfilling of monolineal doctrines and their deductive conclusions. Only in abstract thought does it occur thus, that if Luther be a given, then by the power of incontrovertible deduction obtains also the modern German militarism. In life nothing like this happens thus, and it makes a mockery of it all. In life not only is German militarism not a legitimate offspring of Luther, but even Lutheranism itself is not his legitimate offspring. Since, truly it can be said, that Lutheranism is altogether incommensurate with such an immense phenomenon, as Luther, and altogether unanticipated as well. On the surface aspect of history it seems, that a great man, a creative individuality, begets a sort of massive historical phenomenon. But in the depths of life, in the authentic actuality, there is nothing the like. St. Francis did not create Franciscanism, nor Luther -- Lutheranism, nor Tolstoy -- Tolstoyanism, nor Nietzsche -- Nietzscheanism. And that what on the surface level of history is given the name of Christianity, was not created by Jesus Christ. There is full an incommensurability between the creative act of a great creator from that, which is begotten through the refractive distortion within the gravity of the world, within the gravity of history, within the gravity of the masses. Here is why it is so difficult to unriddle the secret of history, to view at the depths its creative motion. Here too is why it is necessary to have a great intuitive delicacy and great psychological pervasiveness in determining the spiritual sources of modern Germany, in explaining its baseness and fallenness.

II.

It pains one to see, how low-fallen at present is the proffering of a coarse, doctrinaire and superficial attitude towards the life of F. Nietzsche. It has revealed a very facile and shallow means of explaining away modern Germany and all its ugly aspects. Nietzsche preached the will to power, he taught about the superman, who has to stand beyond this side of good and evil and be fierce. Nietzsche extolled the spirit of war. But is he not the spiritual father of the German aggressive militarism? Has he not made fierce the hearts of Germans? Are not the Prussian Junkers the authentic Nietzscheans? Truly the fate of Nietzsche after death was still more tragic and unfortunate, than during life. At one point all sorts among the vulgar suddenly and conceitedly tended to conceive of themself as Zarathustras and supermen, and the memory of Nietzsche was defiled by its popularity amongst the herd element. The herd began to march as though single supermen, fancying, that to them all is permitted. The proud, heroic, austhere and severe spirit of Zarathustra was consigned to mockery. Enfeebled decadents, bereft of their higher "I" and indulging their lower "I", grabbed hold of Nietzsche and began to term themselves Nietzscheans. Clasping onto Nietzsche were also those, who had a will to plunder, to power and profit across the plains of the earth. At the present historical hour Nietzsche has appeared to be one of the guilty for the world war, for the German aggressive militarism and the German brutalities. And the connection of Krupp with Nietzsche seems more plausible, than the connection of Krupp with Kant. It is very easy to quote in light of such an opinion several citations from Zarathustra. "The benefit of war sanctifies every aim". "Love peace, as a means to new wars". Thus spake Zarathustra. And Zarathustra did not love the good and the just. "Be fierce", -- he taught. And furthermore he taught "to shove the falling". It has appeared all too tempting to see in the Germans, with their having discovered such a fierce will to power and so sanctifying by war every end, as the fulfillers of the commands of Zarathustra. And yet all the same I know of nothing more monstrous in its inner untruth, than to connect Nietzsche with the modern militaristic Germany. This means -- to read the alphabetic letters, without understanding the meaning of the words. They know Nietzsche only through certain fragmented aphorisms, turned round in reverse and filled with shoddy nuances, they read through and ponder on too little in him, and sense not his spirit and his fate. "Thus Spake Zarathustra" -- is a great symbolic book. In it -- "the profundity, this depth by day is scarcely evident". The words of Zarathustra need to be able to be unraveled. When Zarathustra says "war" -- this nowise means Krupp cannons. When he says "the will to power", -- this does not mean territorial seizures for the German empire. When he says "be fierce", -- this does not mean German atrocities in Kalisz [alt. Kalisch, Poland] and Louvain [Belgium]. About this it would be awkward even to speak -- this is so elementary, since even those who earlier held to the view that they profoundly understand Nietzsche, have not lowered themselves to such a street-bazaar understanding of him. But what can happen on the streets and the bazaars with the words of Zarathustra, who dwelt upon the lofty mountains? True indeed, Nietzsche is altogether unnecessary for Wilhelm, he can finely make war with his "old god", more compliant, than Zarathustra. With this "old god" much blood has already been spilt and many a brutality and atrocity has transpired amidst its conniving and approval.

Prussian Junkerism -- is the herd, the mob, hating Nietzsche, alien to him, and from which he fled to the heights. From Nietzsche nothing, decisively nothing is derivable for this mob; he nowise at all instructs state civil matters and politics, it is impossible to fashion any sort of politics from him, impossible to conduct any sort of war in the societal-historical, commonplace sense of the word. He is totally oriented towards the creative individuality, towards its path and its fate. Is it possible to base upon Nietzsche that societal and state discipline, of which modern Germany is so proud, to base the discipline of the masses upon the teachings of the solitary madman Nietzsche? Modern Germany is first of all a mechanisation of the masses, i.e. something absolutely polar, absolutely contrary to the spirit of Nietzsche. The mass organisation -- herein is the pathos of modern Germany, here is in what it has been successful at. In the old Germany there was many a creative individuality, something which has dried up in the modern Germany, and Nietzsche the romantic has rather something more in common with the old Germany, though it be in the cult of genius. But it is needful also to note, that Nietzsche did not love the Germans, he always stressed, that he was a Slav, Polish, he denied in Germany the existence of authentic culture and he loved French culture, as the sole one within Europe. He fled from Schopenhauer and Wagner to Montaigne and Stendhal. He aspired towards the sun, towards the south, he espoused a religion of the sun. Truly in the spirit of Nietzsche there was more of the Slav, than the German: in him there is something end-like, final, already flown beyond the bounds of culture, going beyond the religious limit, akin to our Dostoevsky. And how close Nietzsche was, by his pathos, to the Russian religious searchings!

III.

German militarism -- is an ultimate victory of the herd, the ultimate perishing of individuality, the triumph of that spirit, against which Zarathustra stood. German militarism -- is a path not from man to the superman, but from man down to the beastly herd, to pre-human a condition upon the basis of highly mechanical a civilisation. Was this indeed the path of Zarathustra? Zarathustra -- is the path of Man and the tragic fate of Man, of the human spirit in its ascent to the heights. This -- is a thankless and heroic path, in which man takes upon himself all the burden of suffering and all the difficulty of passage along as yet undisclosed mountain passes. In Zarathustra there is a spirit grasping towards the heights, there is a mountainous austerity, sacrificial in its unique asceticism. On this path there is no animal warmth, no cuddling back into the collective, the many comforts of the lowlands, of the flatlanders life. This path repels many, and it is possible religiously to reject it. But it is monstrous, unjust and simply unthinkable to make a comparison between Nietzsche and the modern German militarism with its ultimate dissolution of man into the herd. Nietzsche, who participated as an orderly during the Franco-Prussian War of 1871, with disgust speaks about the self-conceit, which occurred in the Germans after their victory. What would he say now? The self-conceited swinishness of the modern Germans would evoke loathing in him. Nietzsche, certainly, was not a pacifist, and indeed he need not be. Dostoevsky sang hymns to the spirit of war in quite more literal a sense, than did Nietzsche. The martial and triumphant pathos of Nietzsche is profoundest a manifestation of spirit, and not a preaching of Prussian militarism. He had no desire to beget super-junkers. "If ye cannot be zealous strivers of knowledge, then in extreme measure be its warriors". "Seek out your enemy, seek not his soldier to know -- but rather his thoughts!" "I call you not to labour, but to struggle. I call you not to peace, but to victories. Let your toil be struggle and your peace victorious!" "It is fine to be brave". Here is what Zarathustra spake. He taught about war, about struggle and the victory of the brave, as the path towards the supra-human condition, as the surmounting of the merely human condition. This -- is a forging of the will, a steeling of the spirit, an eternal symbolism of spiritual power and firmness. And may God grant us this power and firmness.

Why do they fail to remember about the attitude of Zarathustra towards the "new idol", the state? Those, who do remember, would scarcely tend to connect German imperialism with Nietzsche. "The state is called the coldest of all cold monsters. It coldly utters the lie, and the lie creeps forth from its mouth. An admixture of good and evil in all tongues: this sign I give you, as the sign of the state. Truly, this sign signifies the will to death". "There all, the good and the bad, imbibe the venom: the state -- there, where all the good and the bad lose themself; the state is there, where the slow suicide of all is called life". "Behold, how they scamper about, these nimble monkeys! They leapfrog about one after the other and therefore then wind up on the dirt and in the abyss. They all want to attain mastery of the heights: it is a folly of theirs, that they could be happy to sit upon these heights! Often the dirt sits upon them -- and often the same they sit upon the dirt". "Foul an odour issues from their idol, from this cold monster, and foul an odour issues from all these servants of the idol... break ye quick the windows and dart out into the pure air". "Stands free yet still the earth for great souls. Many yet still is the place for the solitaries and for those, who live double; there waft fragrant the quiet seas. Manifest still free is the free life for great souls". "There, where ends the state, begins first the man, who is not superfluous". Here thus was how Zarathustra spake concerning the new idol -- the state. But modern Germany worships this new idol. And truly foul is the odour that issues forth from German imperialism. And repulsive to Zarathustra is this idol. Zarathustra brands disdainful a stigma upon the will to power of the modern Germans, the will to power in worshipping the new idol. "The dirt sits upon their summits -- and often the same they sit upon the dirt". It is a different will to power that Zarathustra preached, a will to power there, where "free stands now the earth for great souls", "where waft fragrant the quiet seas". With disgust Zarathustra shunned the modern culture of the large cities and set off to the heights. Everything, that modern Germany loves -- the state, the industrial success, the mechanical civilisation, the leveling down, the organised masses, the disciplined masses, -- all this was hateful to Zarathustra. He loved individuality in its tragic fate, he loved creativity, he loved sacrifice, he loved all that, which is not in modern Germany. Where is the evident virtue of the modern Germans?

IV.

Nietzsche never indeed created Nietscheanism and is not to blame, that in the bazaars they speak concerning him. It is impossible to be a disciple and follower of Nietzsche, for Nietzsche -- was no pastor, no shepherd. He -- reflects great a fate, a complete in itself artistic manifestation. One who has sensed and experienced his fate, will have known his significance for the world and for the fate of mankind. But from his teachings it is impossible to make any sort of societal usage. Zarathustra cautioned his would-be disciples and followers, those, who assured him earlier, to be like him, i.e. to become Nietzscheans, -- he cautioned them that they did not know the fate of Nietzsche.

To transform into Nietzscheans the power-loving Prussian junkers and the rapacious German bourgeoise -- this is a final insult to the memory of Nietzsche, making a mockery of his suffering fate.

German imperialism and German militarism are just as incommensurate with the spiritual life of Nietzsche, the same as they are incommensurate with the spiritual life of Eckhardt. The tragedy of Germanism -- is namely in this incommensurability of the profoundly individual manifestations of the German spirit in contrast to the collective and massive manifestations of the German state and societal aspects. The German spirit has failed to inspire the German historical flesh. The German spirit has served the world only by its creative individualities, and not by its societal-historical fate. Germanism has never sought nor does seek a rightful truth, and in the period of its societal-state maturity has gone the path of the cult of power. In this the Germanic world is profoundly the opposite of the Slavic world, in which is lodged the seeking of a societal and universal right truth, of the City of God. And among the German Social Democrats the ideals of power have always predominated over the ideals of rightful truth. The moral pathos of the Germans has always been purely individualistic. And in Germany there is always a disconnect between the heights of its creative individualities, and the baseness of its philistine masses, formerly powerless, and now invested with power.

For us, as Russians, during these difficult days, I would wish there be a noble and free attitude towards everything valuable and universal in the German spirit and German spiritual culture. We, as Slavs -- are of a different spirit, we cannot and we ought not only not be slaves, but also not to be disciples of the Germans. We have our own tasks in the world. But it would not be good, will not be a fine thing, if a slave-like attitude towards German culture, which would bode ill for the Russians, instead gets replaced by a slave-like pogromme against German culture. A slaves revolt is just as vile, as is the cringing submission of slaves. We shall be free. A noble attitude towards the enemy uplifts: this -- is a virtue of the strong. And in German culture there is no phenomenon more transnational, more all-human in its significance, than the phenomenon of Nietzsche. And out of love for my native land I would wish, that within Russian people might be certain of the virtues of Zarathustra: a bestowing virtue, a creative exuberance, nobility, manliness, a solar quality, a proudly ascendant spirit. We have long and far gone down. It is time, it is time already to begin to ascend, to pass over from the life of the vast plains to the life of the heights. And in this ascending will be revealed to us an other, a mysterious visage of Christ, of Whom so passionately was sought the soul of the great blindman Nietzsche.

To the Feckless Devotees of Slavophilism

(1915 - 190)[1]

I.

Amidst all my literary activity I have never entered into personal polemics, have never replied to the numerous attacks on me, have not risen up in the literary mode even against the outright distortion of my thoughts. I have always on principle been antagonistic towards personal polemics, and never have I believed, that such could enable an explication of the truth or that it could be instructive for readers -- and I do not regard it needful to make an exception for V. Ern.[2] It is only the dispute of ideas that I consider to be worthy of a writer and thinker. There are possible still intimately-psychological discussions, but they presuppose a greater acuity, complexity and intuitive giftedness. I say only, that Ern is not at all well informed about my literary activity nor concerning my spiritual developement. But still my dispute with Ern and his ideational colleagues concerning Slavophilism and the Russian national consciousness may possess a very great significance -- it is a matter very relevant at the present hour of history. And I want to point out to Ern, how this dispute mustneeds run, so that it should be interesting and important not only for us and our household accounts. Regretably, the polemical article of Ern bears completely personal a character. Within it there was nothing said essentially about those thoughts, which I expressed in my article,

---

[1] EPIGONAM SLAVYANOPHIL'STVA. Article was originally published in newspaper "Birzhevye vedomosti", 18 feb. 1915, № 14678.

[2] Vide his 30 January article against me in "Birzhevye vedomosti". *trans. note*: our *Padenie* Russian text on page 1085 endnote notes that the Vladimir Ern [1881-1917] article in question was provocatively entitled, "Nalet val'kirii", ["Swooping of the Valkyries"], and which was included on pp. 926-932 of our present extensively enormous *Padenie* Russian edition, but which we do not include here.

"Concerning the 'Eternal Baba' in the Russian Soul".[1] There is no sort of a dispute on principle. Ern has refuted nothing in me. He has however used an old and tried method to undercut the person of his opponent, to destroy his credibility.

At the present time the wind blows such, that it is very easy to be a Slavophil and nationalist. Years ago I already wrote about our national self-consciousness and the highly important significance of Slavophilism within the history of our self-consciousness (I likewise wrote a book on Khomyakov[2]), and yet still I now experience that which Vl. Solov'ev experienced in the decade of the 80's, when he wrote his "National Question in Russia", -- for me it is unpleasant to float with the wind and I see a danger for Russia in such mere coasting along. Likewise also the beating up on Kant at the present moment seems to me too opportune and fragile. I am not an adherent of German philosophy and I long ago already laid bare its shortcomings,[3] but moreover a pogrom against German philosophy at present is rather too street-wise a matter. The judgement on Kant ought to be rendered apart from the street racket of bazaar passions.

As a Russian man, loving his native land, I am distraught over this, that in the Russian soul there is a "baba". A I desire for my native land and for its great future, that in it there should be a strong masculine spirit and that it should be freed from both inward and outward slavery. Even in revolt against Russia there can be moreso the Russian, than in the doctrinaire bowing before the Russia of Ern! Bakunin was moreso a

---

[1] Birzhevye vedomosti, 14-15 January. [1915; Kl. № 18; per the Klepinina Bibliographie this issue was "№ 14610-14612[?]"].

trans. note: Berdyaev incorporated this 1915 article, "Concerning the 'Eternal Baba' in the Russian Soul" into his 1918 book, "Sud'ba Rossii" ["The Fate of Russia"] as its 2nd entry.

[2] *trans. note*: book "Aleksei Stepanovich Khomyakov", Moscow, publisher Put', 1912, 256 pages, Kl. № 6.

[3] Back in 1904 I published in the "Questions of Philosophy and Psychology" journal an article concerning "The New Russian Idealism", in which I contrasted the ontologism of Russian philosophy in opposition to the transcendentalism of German philosophy.

[*trans. note*: the 1904 "New Russian Idealism" article was incorporated as Ch. 6 in 1907 book, "Sub specie aeternitatis" (Kl. № 3)].

Russian in spirit, than is Ern in his doctrinaire Slavophilism. The philosophic letter of Chaadaev, in which he said terrible things about Russia and denounced it, as no one ever had dared so to denounce it, was a Russian deed, a great act of Russian self-consciousness. It is inconceivable, why on the intellectual question about the need for Russia to have a spirit of manliness, why Ern should transfer it over onto a purely personal basis and transform it into a question concerning my own masculinity or effeminateness. Whether my nature be either masculine or not masculine, this has no direct bearing for my astute observation, that manliness is needful for the Russian people and that it will not grasp hold of manliness in its relationship to the state. When I wrote my article, "Concerning the 'Eternal Baba' in the Russian Soul", what interested me was the fate of Russia and Rozanov himself also interested me, as a reflection of certain features, which exist in Russia itself and which are a danger for Russia. What I considered fruitful and interesting was the dispute about Russia and its fate, about the masculine and feminine aspect within the Russian soul, and not about me and not about Ern. I did not make a personal comparison of Bulgakov, V. Ivanov[1] or Ern with Rozanov. I have to make individual distinctions and I well know, how little Ern resembles Rozanov. But I tend to think, as regards the societal and superficial Bulgakov, V. Ivanov and Ern fall together into the same current, into that selfsame gust of the wind, as obtains also with Rozanov. If they had the pluck to be totally open with their religio-societal and religio-state beliefs and expectations, then this would become clear. But they have no grasp of such boldness. Ern, perhaps, is personally also very masculine, though to me it seems not so, but his consciousness of Russia is not at all manly. Events sweep him along, and he bends with the elements and posits this as higher, than the person, than the person's will and activity. For him, the natural element within the national self-consciousness takes precedence over the humanly personal.

II.

It is totally inconceivable, why Ern accuses me of this, that I have said nothing essential concerning Orthodoxy, and he demands, that I

---

[1] It has to be said, that V. Ivanov, as a poet and a theoretician of art, stands higher than all this, and outside all these trends.

should frankly say, what it is that I have against Orthodoxy. Nothing in my article was said concerning Orthodoxy, except for indicating this, that Rozanov has nothing in common with Orthodoxy and is connected with it only by the lifestyle faults of Orthodox people. The theme of my article was altogether otherwise. Ern vainly thinks, that in provoking him, means to provoke Orthodoxy. Orthodoxy, as a great worldwide force, and the doctrine of Ern -- are matters, totally incommensurate. I sense that Ern is not so much Orthodox, as rather some sort of Protestant pietist, a Methodist or saved Baptist perchance. His religiosity -- is nowise Russian. Suchlike a serenity is unbecoming to our Russian heaven. In Ern there is neither a Russian humility, nor a Russian rebelliousness. Important is the spiritual type -- the man, his world-sense. And herein I tend to fear, that with Ern there is too little of the Orthodox and the Russian. There is nothing bad in this, but it is not necessary to prick the eyes of everyone with one's Orthodoxy and Slavophilism.

Ern quite inopportunely chose to speak about Orthodoxy, about which also there had been no discussion, instead of speaking about questions, concerning which actually, there was discussion in my article. It is these questions also that I should want to put to Ern, and also likewise to Bulgakov and V. Ivanov. The first question, touched upon in my article, is very important for the fate of Russia, and discussion of it is very much to be wished. This -- is the question over whether there ought to be or can there be a reinterpretation of Slavophilism? I posit suchlike a thesis: Slavophilism and Westernism alike ought to be surmounted within the creative process of the national self-consciousness. I decisively expressed this thesis in my book on Khomyakov.[1] The whole history of the Russian thought of the XIX Century was filled with the dispute between Slavophilism and Westernism, and through this dispute was born our national consciousness. But both Slavophilism and Westernism were still expressions of a national immaturity. In the Slavophil and the Westerniser ideologues there was a sort of provincialism, which ought to be surmounted. Vl. Solov'ev represents already an enormous step forward in comparison with the Slavophils and Westernisers. And I should want to continue his tradition on the national question. And from the past Chaadaev is no less dear to me, than is Kireevsky and Khomyakov. The significance of present day world events for the Russian consciousness

---

[1] Vide: "A. S. Khomyakov", publisher "Put'".

I perceive, first of all, as the end of the old Slavophilism and the old Westernism, and as the beginning of a new era. After the world war the opposition of East and West will lose its significance. Russia ultimately will enter into the inner circles of the life of Europe and will open for Europe its own great spiritual potentials. And those, who want to preserve and restore the old Slavophilism, in my opinion, would drag Russia backwards and downwards. All the basic theses of Slavophilism -- about the exclusive significance of Eastern Christianity in comparison with the Western, about the attitude towards Western culture, about the attitude of the people towards the state power, about the connection of the religious vocation of Russia with its lifestyle aggregate -- have to be radically reconsidered and replaced by a new national self-consciousness. Ern thinks evidently, that it is necessary to make a choice: either Slavophilism, or "A. Kizevetter", a third possibility there is not. I see in the articles of Ern, Bulgakov and V. Ivanov, a restoration of the ugly aspects in Slavophilism, not of that which is eternal, but rather the old within Slavophilism. And in this I see a great danger for Russia, against which it is needful to contend, similar to how Vl. Solov'ev in the 80's espied a great danger in the nationalistic degeneration of Slavophilism. Slavophilism can now be only ruinous, and the rot can poison with a compelling vileness. That which was valuable and non-ephemeral within Slavophilism, long since already has separated off from Slavophilism and lives an independent life. And at the current historical hour, when we await for the world a new life, the restoration of Slavophilism is spiritual a reaction, a reaction in the profoundest sense of the word. The consequences of this reaction permit directly of being known in practice. Let Ern and those like-minded with him express their thesis on the question of Slavophilism, concealing and hiding nothing. Let them express their hopes to the end. Needless are the liberal stipulations, which have remained, like an habit acquired in that society, in which they happen to live and with which they are resolved not to part with.

III.

With S. Bulgakov in his article, "Rodina" ["Native-Land"], printed at the beginning of the war in in the journal "Utro Rossii", there slipped by something which was more ultimate, more finalative. Then, evidently, he himself got scared of this. But it would be fine to be consistently open, on what was said there under only the aspect of lyrical musings. And here I approach another basic question, undertaken in my article, the question concerning the attitude of the Russian people towards the state. The national boldness and virility of the Russian people is likewise also its governmental maturity and virility, i.e. the ultimate awareness of this, that the Russian state is "our" state, the state of the Russian people, the expression of the power and authority of al the people. The state is not an object of worship and swooning over, and though it be distant and august, it is not some foreign power, which one mustneeds serve; it is rather a philosophy of the people's life, an immanent expression of the people's will. Rozanov preaches worship, almost a deification of the state authority, as a mystical fact and a mystical force. And in this there is something both characteristic and dangerous. This tendency exists also with Bulgakov, and in many of the expressers of a "Russian direction". And in this is to be detected not a manly attitude towards the state and authority, but rather instead the eternal Russian temptation of submissiveness and coming undone, the surrendering of oneself to a foreign will. And it is possible to express the problem philosophically: what is needful -- a transcendental religious sanctification of the state, or the immanent human growth? This first path I consider as false in a time demanding virility of the people, and for Russia it is dangerous. Along this path shuffles the "current" of Bulgakov, Ern, Fr. P. Florensky. They seek within the state a priesthood analogous to the priesthood in the Church, for them the state authority is of an angelic principle. To this decidedly must be contrast an understanding of the state power, as a principle human, with all the aspects of relativity within the natural historical process.

This second path is that of the secularisation of the state, detached from its transcendental sanctification in the name rather of its immanent reformation and transformation within the societal aspect, an inward sanctification of the human spirit and through its creative activity. Bulgakov dreams about a "theocracy of the white tsar". This is a path of religious servility, sustaining also a servility societal. And about this it is needful to speak and to argue. The transcendental sanctification of state power is a condition of infantilism and a source of slavery. Spiritual maturity makes instead a transition over to an immanently free sanctification of societal and state life from the depths of the spirit. The spiritual emancipation of the person in Russia has to rend the fetters and bonds, imposed upon the human spirit by a religious materialism, by the deifying of the objectively-corporeal, the materially-relative, regarded as something absolute. The whole relative and material historical life ought to be free, autonomous, ought to be directed religio-immanently, and not religio-transcendentally, ought to be spiritual, and not authoritarian. For the transcendental consciousness the state would remain that, which the "cavalry" was for Rozanov whilst standing on the pavement. For the immanent consciousness -- we ourself are the cavalry. Here is the problem, posited by me, and this is more important than the triffling concerns of Ern. Here is the serious issue of contention, the clash of differing spirits. Do Bulgakov, Ern, V. Ivanov desire that the Russian people act like a bride in attitude to the state authority, or do they desire, that the Russian people itself be manly, strong and powerful, in regard to their own land? Here is my question.

Within this also is connected the issue of how one ought to relate to Russia, to one's native-land? I think, that the attitude of Ern towards Russia is a matter of creating for oneself an idol and a fetish. Religiously it is impermissible to say, that the Russian soul is praeternally already betrothed to the Bridegroom Christ. The betrothal of the Russian land with Christ is something that still lies ahead, and this -- is a task, and not a fact, not a given. Holy Rus' -- is a religious ideal, and not an idol nor a fetish. Man -- is free and the soul is free and therefore the creative task faces him, as a matter of his activity.

If the fate of Russia were predetermined and there were for it no danger of downfall, then there would not be freedom, and facing the active will would be no sort of task and no sort of ideal. And thus do ideals get replaced by idols. An ontological affirmation of the praeternal betrothal of the soul of Russia with Christ is a source of spiritual reaction, passivity and slavery. Vl. Solov'ev asked of Russia, whether it wants to be of which sort the East, "the East of Xerxes or of Christ?" And this was truly a Christian query. The affirmation of Ern however -- is truly that of the Musselman. Amidst a veil of Platonism, the worshipping of Russia, as a fact and force, is the creation for oneself of an idol. This is a serious hindrance on the path of a manly awareness of the great tasks of Russia, the great ideals, to the realisation of which it is called, on the path of the creating of a new and better Russia. How different the contrast is this sense of love for the thirst after perfection and righteous-truth, lodged within the soul of Russia! Ern, Bulgakov, Ivanov, as also Rozanov, sense our native land exclusively as a mother, i.e. they want to love it unconditionally. But, in the beautiful expression of Hertsen, the native land is a child. And only love for the native land, as for a child, is a love responsible, a love manly and creative. Love for the maternal native land is of our source, natal, subconscious, not doctrinaire a matter, but love for the native land in the guise of a child is bound up with our masculine consciousness and with our creative activity. And I have one further question to put to our Slavophils. Can the apocalyptic vocation of Russia, connected with the final period of world history, can it be based upon its historical mannerisms of life, the churchly, the national and state-societal? Does not all the apocalyptic aspect and finality presuppose a catastrophic rift? In Russia does not the wandering, the itinerant, the spiritual hunger comprise the potentials of a great world vocation? I tend to think, that with the complacent lifestyle of the old Slavophilism we can no longer still have anything in common.

On the Givers and the Takers

(Regarding the Dispute on the National Question)

(1915 - 191)[1]

I.

The articles of P. B. Struve on the Ukrainian Question provide a basis to express some principal considerations on the setting forth of the national question in Russia. The initial point of view of Struve on the Ukrainian Question is accurate. And I think, that Ukrainophilism is merely a provincialism, which cannot and ought not to fracture the unity of the Russian culture in general. But Struve has entered upon false a path, having overstated to the extreme the significance of Ukrainophilism and having evoked the spectre of the Ukrainian danger. If there is something in particular dangerous for Russia, it is this -- the fabricating of various dangers. How many "a danger" has poisoned Russian life!

The Polish danger, the Jewish danger, the Finland danger, the Catholic danger, the sectarian danger, the revolutionary danger, etc. And may God preserve us from coming up moreover with an Ukrainian danger! Upon the spectral images of all these dangers the murkily dark forces of Russia have quite speculated. Being terrorised with dangers has held Russia in the grip of slavery. And thus moreover has been formed a degrading and shameful sense of self within a great and mighty state. The predominant Great Russian nationality within its own mighty state has sensed itself, as though all its subject and weaker nationalities are stronger than it and can harass it. And the dominant church has sensed itself weaker and less alluring, than the most insignificant of sects, than the heterodox confessions restricted within their rights. Such a lack of faith in one's own

---

[1] O DARYASCHIKH I OTNIMAIUSCHIKH (K sporu o natsionnal'nom voprose). Article was originally published in newspaper "Birzhevye vedomosti", 11 mar. 1915, № 14720.

nationality, in one's own state, in one's own church, in one's own truth -- is terrible, it saps at the root every creative impulse.

It is nowise possible, that the Russian should have always sensed himself weaker than the Jew and have feared the Jewish as a danger, or that the Orthodox should have sensed himself weaker than the Catholic, and have feared the Catholic as a danger. Such a terror in the face of dangers surrounding from all sides can only be an expression of childish immaturity. A mature people ought to sense itself otherwise: it has no need of an eternal nursemaid, will not put up with a nursemaid, it summons up its own inner might against everything foreign and hostile. A great and dominant people cannot go around crying about the dangers, issuing from the weaker and the subjected, often the oppressed. In the Russian people there ought, finally, to awaken a regal, a non-slave consciousness, and let it be accompanied by a manifestation of real virtues. Characteristic of the strong ought to be magnanimity, a greatness of soul, a capacity to assist the weaker. And the genuine strength of the Russian people is sensed not then, when it hems in and restricts out of fear in the face of dangers, but rather then, when it assists and gives from out of its own abundance. As the stronger, the Russian people should magnanimously liberate and assist the Polish and the Jewish. It bullies them however, like a weakling. And the Russian people conscious of its own strength could grant for the Ukrainians the having of their own provincial cultural particularities. The transforming of Ukrainian provincialism into an Ukrainian separatism was totally the effect of a false political hemming in and restriction, Russian as to the official slogan, but not Russian as to the Spirit.

A certain Polish person pessimistically sad of outlook said to me: "The Russians are accomplishing wonders, they are making friends of the Polish and Ukrainians over there in Galicia". For a Russian it is bitter to hear theses words. And we ought to make every effort, that such a sarcasm should become forever impossible. A genuinely Russian politics of our people ought not to be officially and contrivedly "Russian"; it will be Russian, if it becomes politically the truth. Let us seek the truth in the politics, and the rest will fall into place for us. Only atheism and non-faith do not want to admit, that the ideal politics -- is most real as to its results. It is very depressing, when the dominant nationality, possessing a powerful state, is mistrustfully minded, everywhere suspecting dangers and out of fear of finding itself restrained, instead does the restraining. It is needful to become cured of this.

II.

The sincerity and moral virility of P. B. Struve as a publicist merits great esteem. But, I tend to think, he makes hopeless efforts to inculcate the pathos of statecraft into the Russian soul. His nationalism -- is not national. This -- is not Russian, it is an international nationalism. In the abstract idea of statecraft, as an higher criterion for the resolving of all societal questions, there is nothing specifically Russian. This is an extreme Western idea, depersonalising for Russia, and likening it to Germany, England, and other European states.

Within the Russian soul live always the questions of Lev Tolstoy towards every state. The Russian soul senses more acutely than other souls, that "the state -- is the coldest of all monsters". The Russian soul never can reconcile itself to this, that all national and societal questions be decided from the perspective of a "state necessity". The state civil necessity ought to know its place, a subordinate place, it ought to yield in facing higher values. If we decide the Jewish Question, the Polish Question, the Ukrainian Question only from the perspective of a "state necessity", then we betray that which is most essential in our national soul -- that Russian and Christian awareness, that the human soul stands for more, than all the kingdoms and all the world. Struve at present is insufficiently attentive to the fundamental antinomy between the person and the state, which Christianity so acutely stresses. Only in the pre-Christian and pagan world was there possible a self-sufficing state aspect, restricted by nothing. A "state necessity" has no desire to know the human soul, it is without pity towards the human person. For a "state necessity" there exists only the overall, the mass, the quantitative and there does not exist the individual, the qualitative, the partial. "State necessity" with ease can run amuck over both the individuality personal and the individuality national, over everything humanly of value and divinely of value. The state itself is a certain value, but a value subordinate and increasing as such in the measure of surmounting the gravity of its "necessity".

Our consciousness cannot and ought not to be a docile reflection of the process of "state necessity", just as also with the process of economic necessity. A purely state ideology, in the final end, and in a fatal manner subordinates our moral values to "state necessity" and deprives us of spiritual freedom. Certainly, the Polish and Jewish questions can and ought to be considered from the state's point of view. But first of all, these are questions moral and religiously Christian, and within this qualification they do not depend on any sort of "necessity". For our Russian consciousness it is infinitely more important, that we should be good, rather than that it should be good for us. And better it should go bad for us, than that we should be bad. O certainly, on our side there has to be not only truth, but power also. An asserting of the powerlessness of truth is a lack of faith in it. But it is possible to believe in a righteously true power, a power sacrificial and giving, and not greedily selfish and plundering. Plundering and greedy taking represent still a powerlessness and poorness. Genuine power and richness represent profuseness. And the power of the politics of the Russian people can only be that of giving, of profuseness, magnanimous, ready for sacrifice. The bare "state necessity" and the state wisdom prompting it are so impoverished, so altogether weak! And I believe in the richness of Russia.

A great people cannot base its worldly aims upon the arithmetic of "state necessity". There is needful an higher mathematics of spirit. And if by the arithmetics of "state necessity" Russian nationalism proves to be a greedy and egoistic national self-assertion, the same as every other nationalism, then in the higher mathematics of spirit the Russian nationalism consists in a freedom from nationalism, in a supra-nationalism, in the people's sacrificial aspect and the giving from out of profuseness. To snatch and take away -- this is weakness, and not power. The sun shines its light and warmth, eternally it gives forth... To be powerful, means to be like unto the sun.

III.

The most terrible thing of all, is when "state necessity" transforms religion into a tool for it. A state utilitarian attitude towards religion always represents the utmost in cynical unbelief. An atheist tends to have more respect for religious life, than does a state religion. Forcible conversion to Orthodoxy for purposes of state and national interests is also a very genuine expression of atheism and materialism. To give of the light of Orthodoxy -- is a religious fact. But to forcibly make a conversion to Orthodoxy -- means not to give, but to snatch and take away, and this always is anti-religious a fact. The religious question in Galicia (the question concerning Uniatism) at present is so tightly intertwined with politics, so beset by state and national interests, that it is almost impossible to discern a grain of religion in it. Uniatism indeed is a matter entirely of politics, an utilitarian contrivance.

And may God grant us not to add to this unending politicising in religion still more with our own politicising. There is possible only one genuinely religious, Christian and Russian resolution of the religious question in Galicia -- a fearless assertion of freedom of conscience, of freedom of religious life.

And herein we ought to give, and not take away. Politicising in religion is a spiritual powerlessness, a non-belief in truth, a religious poverty. Spiritual richness, the religious power shines forth light, alluring and contagious. When "state necessity" begins to hold sway in religious life, spiritual death ensues. The religious life by its essence dwells in the sphere of freedom, and not in the sphere of necessity. I fear, that the state ideology of P. B. Struve, for all his liberalism on principle, in practice could lead to a state utilitarian point of view on the religious question. The mistakenness of the initial point of view can be verified thus. If Orthodoxy be regarded not so much as a religious value and sanctity, but rather a national value and state utilitarian matter of necessity, then the initial point of view was not religious. A purely religious point of view has nothing in common with utilitarian aims -- it instead posits freedom to the spiritual life.

I think, that the state ideology of Struve represents a state and civil maturing of Russia. In the person of Struve our societal aspect is rendered a civil affair and receives different a self-awareness.

This process, evidently, is inevitable the same, as is the growth of capitalism in the economic life of Russia. This -- represents an Europeanising of Russia. And the nationalism of Struve is purely Western and Westernising. But the social and the state civil Europeanising of Russia, assuming the form of a nationalistic and imperialistic consciousness, is situated in very complex correlatives with the unique and original spiritual life of Russia. I do not believe in the possibility of inculcating Western nationalism and imperialism into the Russian soul and I do not want this for Russia. The whole national uniqueness of Russia consists in this, that its national individuality excludes nationalism. Russia is most national, when it is least nationalistic. The triumph of a nationalistic and imperialistic ideology and its practices can deprive Russia of the most unique of its national features, its deep-rooted moral particulars, its spirit of searching and wandering. And I do not believe in the possibility of such a depersonalisation of Russia. The outward social Europeanisation of Russia is inevitable and is nothing to fear. The free spirit of Russia and the vocation connected with it cannot be chained down to material forms. The spirit of Russia will abide even amidst the total decomposition of the material trappings and garb of Russia. The deeply engrained defect of the Slavophils consisted in this, that they tied in the spirit together with the material trappings, and to an out-moded social lifestyle. But imperialism and nationalism are in profoundest a contradiction with the fundamentals of the Russian soul, with its eternal essence. The soul of Russia remains ever remote to the selfish thirst of seizing and taking away, and the ideal of a state's prosperity should never be its predominant interest. And Russia will ultimately be conscious of itself as powerful, when to the end it will be a giver, and not a taker.

Germany, Poland and Constantinople

(1915 -193)¹

In 1912, in a monograph on A. S. Khomyakov, I then wrote: "Khomyakov always gave preference to Germany over the Romance lands. I think, that in this he committed a great mistake in regard to the ideals of Russia and Slavdom. Germany -- is the bearer of the ideals of Pan-Germanism, which is deeply hostile to the ideals of Pan-Slavdom. Germany aspires to a world-historical effort of Germanising the Slavs, to engraft onto them its culture. *Germany -- is one of the historical dangers for Russia and Slavdom, similar in ways to Pan-Mongolism.* With the Romance lands for us there is nothing similar. Catholicism is organically closer to Orthodoxy, than is Protestantism, and the Romance peoples are organically closer to the Russians and the Slavs, than are the Germanic peoples. The worldwide Slavic-Orthodox politics ought to be a politics of drawing closer with the Catholic and Romance lands and peoples. We have already suffered enough from our historical ruling powers having become Germanised, Teutonicised, and in our religious life and spiritual culture there has crept in unnoticed a Protestant rationalism. Dostoevsky also shared the same basic mistake of Khomyakov and the Slavophils, wanting in an union with Protestant Germany to divide up the Catholic world. But Catholicism cannot be an inward danger for Russia. *The historical fright at Polonisation ought not to blind us; Poland has long since ceased to be a danger for Russia, and it already long since time to make our attitude towards Poland properly correspond to the spirit of the Russian people.* Germanism -- is quite moreso the real danger" ("A. S. Khomyakov", pp. 227-228). These words now bear repeating.

Germanophilism has skewered all our perspectives, it has been the chief hindrance to paths on the resolution of the question of the Near East and the Polish Question, which has been so unsettling of late. Even the Slavophils and Dostoevsky were infected by Germanophilism. In regard to

---

¹ GERMANIYA, POL'SHA I KONSTANTINOPOL'. Article was originally published in newspaper "Birzhevye vedomosti", 21 may 1915, № 14855.

Germany, Dostoevsky has proven to be an altogether poor prophet. He asserted, that Germany is fated ever to be in an union with Russia, and he was happy about this. He did not see, that Constantinople could become Russian only after the crushing of Germanism. But now already it has become perfectly clear, -- the connection of the fate of Constantinople and the fate of Poland with the fate of Germanism. It is quite clear, that the historical tasks of Russia can be realised only by a breaking off from Germanism, only in a victory over German might. The liberation of the Slavs, the liberation of Poland, having the [Dardanelle] Straits and Constantinople -- are such tasks, posited in the war with Germany and Austria. Victory over Germany and Austria would give positive a resolution of these goals. And an inward getting free from Germanism will, perhaps, be a very great achievement from this war. With this is connected a rebirth of Russia towards new a life. The bond with Germanism in all regards has chained down the creative powers of the Russian people.

To everyone is apparent the historical knot, tying in the woeful fate of Poland together with that of the relationship of Russia to Germany, with the successes of German might. Germany -- is the chief culprit in the partition of Poland. Germany has encouraged a Polonophobic politics in Russia, has aroused fear over the Polish danger. German might always has stood in the way of the unification and liberation of Poland. To our shame, it must be said, that not only Russian politics, but also Russian societal opinion in regard to the Polish has toed the German line. We never stood independent on this question, we consciously or unconsciously became subject to German influences. Even the Slavophils were servile dupes of Germanism.

And this has determined our spiritual and unjust attitude towards the Polish. We have oppressed the Polish not in the name of the interests of Russia, since Russia is not particularly interested in the oppression of Poland as such, but rather in the name of the interests of Germany. Our Slavophilism was essentially restricted by our Germanophilism. But all this selfsame historical knot in a terrible and unanticipated manner connects the fate of Poland with the fate of Constantinople. A formula, seemingly paradoxical at first glance, can be posited: when Russia holds Constantinople and completes its historical movement towards an egress onto the sea expanses through the Straits, Poland will be liberated.

In the XVII Century, the Prussian Frederick the Great deflected Russian Catherine the Great from the historical movement south, towards the Straits and Constantinople, by having offered the partitioning of Poland. Catherine succumbed to this temptation and instead of a prolonging of the war against Turkey, which so frightened Prussia, she consented to receive a part of Poland, having had a share in its partition. The partition of Poland arrested our movement towards Constantinople, we were diverted aside and took part in historical a sin. This temptation came from Germanism, which could not allow us towards Constantinople. That temptation to which Russia succumbed, was a sin both in relation to it itself, and in relation to Poland. And this sin has to be redeemed. We have been bound up with Germany in common a transgression. Russia now is moving towards Constantinople and aspires to complete its task of many centuries. With the Germans we have broken, we strive to overcome and defeat the Germanism. Nothing still can deflect us from our natural advancing south, to the seas. And the day of the occupying of Constantinople ought justly to be the day of the liberation of Poland, i.e. a motion, in everything the reverse to that, which occurred under Frederick and Catherine. There is symbolic a connection between the fate of Poland and the fate of Constantinople.

Germany has more than once deflected us from the historical advance towards Constantinople. Not so long ago it involved Russia in the Far East adventure [the 1904-1905 Russo-Japanese War] and by this provided distraction from the Near East. Our world politics were determined anew by the interests of Germany. And the results are too well known. For its non-intervention in the Russo-Japanese War, of which it was an instigator, Germany demanded a bribe by way of a terrible trade agreement for Russia. Germanophil politics has always been a great hindrance in the realisation of the historical tasks of Russia. But the Germanophilism has been not only to the diminishing of Russia as a great power, it has been likewise an inner poison, an hindrance to every inward movement, a foreign assault, intent on holding the Russian people in the grip of slavery. Germanism for us is no less a peril, than formerly was Tatarism. Germanophilism is an expression of the immaturity of the Russian people and serves as an eternal slogan of Russian reaction. And the war with Germany has in all regards a liberative meaning. It ought not only to liberate the Slavs, to liberate Poland, to free the advance of the Russian people towards the southern seas, but it ought also to free the Russian people from the inward grip of Germanism. It is difficult to say, whether these goals will be realised with an inevitable necessity. Within history there is always the unforeseen, there is an irrational freedom, not subject to any sort of necessity. But meaning is derived from such.

Germanism has always been a chief obstacle for the *world* role of Russia. Germanism has always been interested in keeping Russia in the condition of an isolated state, with provincial and particularistic an existence. Germanism has stood in the way between Russia and Europe, between Russia and the Near East. It has not permitted an exit point for Russia out onto the world expanse, has not allowed us to breathe the air of the world. Dismembered and enslaved Poland has stood as a wall between Russia and Europe. Germanism has solidified this wall every which way possible. Hapless Poland has stood as a symbol of our moral amputation from Europe. Every Russian advance towards Europe has stumbled upon the lacerated corpse of Poland. Germany and Austria have always intended, that Russia should remain Eastern, a state cut off from Europe and from the world, and have pushed us into Asia. The liberation of Poland has for Russia a symbolic significance. This -- is our own liberation from the grip of Germanism and the removal of a morally divisive wall between Russia and Europe. The world role of Russia only then will begin, when Russia finally has broken with Germanism. Then the Slavic race will stand as an independent power. It will go into history as a substitute for the German race. And its world role will be realised in an union with England and the peoples of the Latin race.

On the Disputes Concerning German Philosophy

(1915 - #185)[1]

The practical manifestation of Germanism in the current war has set in sharp relief the question concerning the spiritual sources of German culture. And since philosophy occupies a central place in German culture, this has ignited disputes concerning German philosophy. At the Moscow Religio-Philosophic Society there was a conflict that raged, and it concentrated around a thesis put forth by V. Ern, suggesting that the aggressive German militarism is an offspring begotten of German philosophic phenomenalism. For Ern, an extreme phenomenalism appears not only in the philosophy of Kant, but also in the philosophy of Fichte, Schelling and Hegel. The proponents of German philosophy very resolutely objected to this. In these disputes was sensed the typical tendency towards schematicism and simplification and an insufficient attention towards individuality of spiritual activity. What was most of all striking, was that the opponents of the philosophy of Kant discerned that his interpretation involved a servile dependence upon the Neo-Kantians. For them Kant -- is completely the same, as Cohen. But Kant is immeasurably far richer and more complex. It is inaccurate to characterise the philosophy of Kant, as phenomenalism. For Kant, the "Critique of Practical Reason" was no less essential, than the "Critique of Pure Reason", and inwardly it defines the latter. An authentic, consistent and extreme phenomenalist was Hume, and phenomenalism is characteristic for the English, rather than for the German philosophy. In German philosophy there has always been its own ontology and metaphysics. The German spirit -- is essentially metaphysical, and even the German gnosseology itself, towards which the philosophy of recent times all the moreso tends -- is metaphysics, insofar as not having denied this gnosseology itself. And the phenomenalism as such within German philosophy is but variant a viewing of the age-old German metaphysics. Characteristic and of essence

---

[1] K SPORAM O GERMANSKOI FILOSOFII. Article originally published in the Journal "Russkaya mysl'", mai. 1915, p. 115-121.

to German philosophy is *voluntarism*. Voluntarism however is unique an ontology. The volitional impulse has been conceived by the German spirit, as basic to being. voluntarism plays a definite role in the philosophy of Kant, in his teaching concerning the practical reason, concerning the autonomy of the person, concerning the realm of freedom. This selfsame voluntarism is there also in Fichte, in Schelling, in Schopenhauer, in Hartmann and Drews [Artur, 1865-1935], Wundt [Wilhelm, 1832-1920] and Paulsen [Friedrich, 1846-1908], Windelband [Wilhelm, 1848-1915] and Rickert [Heinrich, 1863-1936] and many others. Voluntarist motifs existed already back in the old German mysticism. Revealing the truths concerning voluntarism was a mission of German thought, which it fulfilled one-sidedly and in the extreme. The German spirit discerned the dark volitional wellspring of being, an irrational principle, the Ungrund. German philosophy variously, right up through Rickert and Lask [Emil, 1875-1915], tended to reveal the irrational, and in this it continued that aspect of German mysticism, of the revealing of an ungroundedness within the nature of the Divinity itself (Jacob Boehme). Gnosseological rationalism was merely the reverse side of a voluntaristic irrationalism. And modern German philosophy, all ever more picayune in scope, is powerless to emerge from the thicket of the fundamental contradiction of the irrational and the rational. But the setting itself, is not a resolution, and a setting forth of the problem of the irrational, -- is a merit of German thought. By this path immanently and to its finish has been lived out the tragedy of cognition.

Uninvestigable and eternally fleeing within our cognition, as the remnants of the irrational, the ungrounded, the dark, the killing off of all individual life within rational knowledge -- is the tragedy of cognition, which German thought has strongly revealed, but has been powerless to surmount. This -- is an inward splitting within cognition, a breaking apart of subject and object, an experiencing as it were of death within cognition. The mystics teach about a passing through a moment of spiritual death. This passage through a spiritual death is there also within the paths of the cognition of man. The primordially integral sacred knowledge has to be shattered. The breaking apart and differentiation are inevitable. It is impossible to remain in the primordial cognitive felicity and balance, to affirm the initially healthy identity of subject and object. The philosophy of

Kant is also a gnosseological expression of the immanent[1] tragedy of cognition, a passing through death within cognition, as a moment of developement. This I see as a fundamental meaning of Kantianism. And from the Kantian tragedy of cognition it is possible only to go forward, not backwards to the felicity of a pre-Kantian rationalism, a pre-Kantian correlation of the knowing subject with the known object. We do not see truth in the Kantian philosophy, for us Kant is unacceptable. But Descartes is still even less acceptable, than is Kant, but Thomas Aquinas and Aristotle are even still less acceptable, than is Descartes. There is an inevitable process of developement, transpiring in the fates of philosophy along the path from Thomas Aquinas through Descartes and Kant to our own time. This -- is the process of the secularisation of cognition, parallel to the process of the secularisation of all the spheres of culture. From knowledge is snatched away its transcendent sanction, which provided a guarantee to the philosophy of Thomas Aquinas and rendered it sacred. Knowledge enters upon an immanent, externally unguaranteed path. Thus is affirmed the autonomy of the knowing subject, which proves tragic for it. The knowing as it were has fallen away from the bosom core of being and started a prodigal wandering. But these tribulations of cognition have been necessary. The Slavophil philosophy did not want to deal with the tragedy of cognition. It wanted to remain amidst the primordial wholeness and to preserve for philosophy the transcendent religious sanction. It affirmed for itself a cognitive felicity, and in the splitting separate process it saw merely a falling away and sin. But the fall, the sin-fall, lies at the very wellsprings of free immanent cognition. In the cognition is a principle of differentiation. The philosophy of Kant was also an expression of the sin-fall within cognition, a falling away from the primordial integral wholeness. This does not render it true and does not impel us to follow after it, but it imparts the profound meaning of the philosophy of Kant within the worldly coursings of cognition. The philosophy of Kant has to be surmounted. There has to be found an exit from these thickets, into which German philosophic thought has fallen. But it is impossible to reassert thought as in the primordial integral wholeness, such as preceeded the tragedy of cognition. From the philosophy of Kant and from the

---

[1] I employ the terms "immanent" and "transcendent" in dynamic, and not static a sense. The philosophy of Kant statically -- is transcendent, but dynamically it is a passing through the immanent tragedy of cognition.

thickets of the irrational and the rational there has to be found an immanent egress. German voluntarism, having partial a truth lodged within it, of itself finds no way out. In it is lodged the seed of violence. German irrationalism always remains incommensurable with German rationalism. Only by having acknowledged the immanence of the cognitive being and the beingness underlying cognition itself, can philosophy emerge upon new paths.

It is proper therefore to avoid the simplified schemae concerning the German spirit and German philosophy. German culture is very complex, and within it are some several lines. The neo-Slavophils have already begun to work out certain tracings of German philosophy. They see in it both immanentism and phenomenalism, a denial of Sophia, a being torn off from the feminine principle, from the land, from nature -- here is what they regard as of essence to the German spirit and to German philosophy. Bulgakov, Ern and others are constantly talking about this. The old Slavophils discerned rationalism and a fragmentation of spirit within Western philosophy. The modern Slavophils purport more specific a sort of theses on *Germanic* philosophy. For them, the defect of immanentism is lodged already back within the old German mysticism. The whole history of the German spirit for them thus -- the mysticism, the Protestantism, the classical philosophic idealism and the modern philosophy -- is totally a falling-away from the Truth, from the Church, from the land, from nature. The great creative forces have been dissipated all in vain, gone to the serving of non-truth. It becomes almost horrible. In the neo-Slavophil theses on Germanism there is something correct, some certain features taken from German thought. And yet, despite this, there is a sort of great non-truth in the evaluation of the German spirit, the non-truth of a murderous, destructive and hostile schematicism. One would have to completely forget about Jacob Boehme, about Angelus Silesius, about Fr. Baader, about the Romantics, about Goethe, about Hoffmann and Novalis, in order to assert, that in the German spirit there has been no meeting up with Sophia. There have been great revelations concerning Sophia within German mysticism, and the teachings of Jacob Boehme on Sophia -- are at the highest summits in the conception of Sophia. And the great crazy Hoffmann's image of Sophia, eternally twofold, is so passionately compelling, as no one ever. And can it be said, that there was nothing of nature in Paracelsus, in Boehme, in Schelling? Germany is not only Protestant, but also a Catholic land. It is impossible to characterise the

German spirit by Kant alone, or even not Kant, but by neo-Kantianism. Neo-Kantianism -- is small a phenomenon, and there is no big deal to be made over it. Neo-Kantianism is something but derivative and of decline. The greatness of the German spirit and its mission in the world mustneeds be sought within German mysticism, a phenomenon all exceptional in its own right. The German great philosophy -- is an offspring of the mysticism, as are the great manifestations of German art. The German spirit is one-sided, it has its own limitations. And within the Slavic spirit lie concealed great riches. But in the German spirit have been its own authentic revelations. German immanentism -- is a phenomenon complex and deep. This -- is the fruition of a mystical maturity, a religious autonomy of man. And it mustneeds be stressed, that Kantianism namely least of all can be termed immanentism.[1] Kantian philosophy and Kantian religion -- are transcendent, and not immanent. This -- is an extreme assertion of the distance between man and God and of the activity of God. The quite impoverished enough religion of Kant was a traditional transcendent theism. The teaching about the thing-in-itself, about the unknowability of the noumenal, the rift between subject and object -- all this is transcendentism, and not immanentism. Immanentism is rooted within the depths of mysticism, transcendentism -- upon the surface level of positivism. It is impossible to see in Kant a type of purely immanent thought. In Kant namely was much of the transcendent.

There might possibly be established a connection of the modern German philosophy with the old mysticism. Thus, for example, in the "unconsciousness" of Hartmann is sensed the Ungrund of Boehme, of the Gottheit of Eckhardt, which is deeper than God. All the irrational and voluntaristic within German philosophy goes back to the old mysticism, revealing the dark wellsprings of being. Germanism is endlessly more complex and individual a matter, than it would seem to the fashioners of simplistic schemae, accusing it of a falling-away from the old truths. To know something is possible only through love. Hatred allows only the seeing of distorted visages. And it is impossible to honestly decide the question about German mysticism, about Protestantism, about German philosophy, about Luther and Boehme, about Kant and Hegel under the din of cannon, in the blaze of national and political passions, on the streets and public squares. Needful here is an intimate examination at depth. It is fully

---

[1] If it be taken in static a view.

permissible and fruitful to posit racial types of thinking. A culture is something profoundly national and through its national character it attains universally-human a quality. The German race tends to think uniquely and altogether quite differently, than the Latin or Slavic races tend to think. The Latin thought process -- is dogmatic or sceptical and always lucid, always pervaded by the rays of the Southern sun. The Germanic thought process -- is critical and bears upon it the seal of the metaphysical North; it attains light in the darkness, being immersed in the depths of the spirit. The Slavic thought process -- is essentially moral, practico-religious, it seeks truth, the saving of the world and of people, truth, inseparable from righteous-truth. The attainment of truth is possible through the racial thought process, always varied as to form and limitedly one-sided. To various peoples is fore-ordained to reveal various sides of truth. But every attainment of truth, essentially, is trans-national and trans-racial. It is impossible to evaluate and judge about truth from racial a perspective, its particulars and its action within history. The psychology of race is very interesting, but the psychology of race cannot be the arbiter of truth. There is a very great danger hidden in the positing of types of a racial thought process and racial culture. Truth can easily become a plaything of national-racial passions. All the attainments of German thought could thus be explained away as false, merely because they are German. And thus, the will for struggle and victory over a race can get turned round into an indifference towards truth and righteousness. For us still not so long ago German philosophy was reckoned as fine and true especially, because it -- was German.[1] Now they regard it as bad and false likewise, because it -- is German. Our Slavophilist philosophers tend to posit a type for German philosophy, for German religion, for German mysticism, which they consider already culpable and false, just because it -- is German. Against this one mustneeds resolutely object. It is impossible thus to subsume truth to a national principle. This is an altogether unallowable psychologism, which would lead to a total annulling of philosophy. And thus, for example, they try to assert, that German thought always is immanentism (in philosophy, religion, mysticism), and that every immanentism is assuredly a Germanism. immanentism is made to seem a sinful peculiarity

---

[1] Here I have in view not individual Russian thinkers, who early on had related negatively to German philosophy, but rather certain traits of the Russian character.

of the German race. By such a method the question about the veracity or non-veracity of immanentism, essentially unconnected with nationality and having arisen already back before there was a German culture, is relegated to a struggle of national racial passions. I think, that it is possible and proper to be at war against the German race, but it is impossible and improper to declare war against the attainments of truth within German thought. And it is indeed difficult to presuppose, that within German thought there are no attainments of truth. It cannot be a reprobate, a race accursed by God, in which everything should be sinful and false. And inaccurate also is this, that German thought always represents immanentism. I have already pointed out, that as regards Germanism the very characteristic philosophy of Kant -- is not immanentist. Within German thought there has been sufficiently enough also of transcendentism. And Lutheranism itself cannot be termed an immanent type of religiosity. But there remains still the question, in what measure immanentism is truth, and as in every truth, independent of race and nationality? It is impossible to brush aside the question about the truthfulness of immanentism by merely denouncing it as Germanism. the problem of immanentism, as with every problem, ought to be completely apart and free from the problem of race.

Our thinking ought not to be contrived and devised as something Russian, hollowly fleeing from everything German. This would be a great affront to freedom, the deficiency of a direct creative national strength. The Germans nowise ponder out such that they should be immanentists, phenomenalists and voluntarists; they freely did their pondering from the depths. And I think, that our Russian thought is essentially and profoundly distinct from the German. Facing it stand other tasks, a different spirit inspires it. Our attainments of truth and right are for mankind in general and for all the world the same, as with the German and Latin races. And we are the most national, most Russian, when we seek from our own depths the right and truth, rather than then, when we proclaim that only the Russian is the right and true, and the German -- the false and sinful. The authentic lie and sinfulness of Germanism -- is in the attempts to monopolise and nationalise truth and right, to declare the truth as German, and right -- as the expression of German power. This resides in Chamberlain, in Drews and the other ideologues of Germanism. Upon this basis develops a crazy self-conceit. Here the German voluntarism degenerates into a naked and nowise limited "I want". But God grant us not to resemble the Germans in this their national-volitional tendency. The Germans, having conceived of themself as solely chosen, the higher and pure race, endowed with the fullness of truth, are totally insufferable, in need of a shot from the cannons. Racial self-love and self-conceit are odious. the Germans spiritually have fallen into this, and they have to go through a moral and material humiliation. But we ought not to imitate them. And we shall be free in our appraisals of German philosophy, free from a servile narrowness and erudite stifling, and free from hatred and pogromme-like negation. such a positive or negative narrowness is always powerless. Power however obtains in a passionate striving for truth and a fearlessness in experiencing the tragedy of cognition, in accord with a perceptive lack of felicity.

The Will to Victory

(1915 -194)[1]

I.

A great nervousness and anxiety in our society can be noted on the issue of the war. The least setback leads to despondency and downcast a spirit. Many relate to the war, as merely chance residents, and not as citizens of their own fatherland. But the war has to be experienced, not externally, as something and someone other than us have it happen, but rather from within, as a matter happening with us ourself. We -- are citizens of our fatherland only then, when we realise, that it is "we" who wage the war, it is not "they", that it is "we" who want to overcome the enemy and have to gain the victory. Otherwise we are like mere slaves, when we become totally detached from the war and totally cast aside from ourself all responsibility, declaring it all on "them". Very superficial and shallow is the viewpoint, that the war is waged exclusively by armies and governments. Even wars unpopular with the people, in which is concerned only a particular portion of society, even these are waged not only by armies and governments. The great historical wars always involve the struggle of peoples. And this mustneeds especially be said about the present day world war. We are sharing in an historically greatest conflict of peoples, which it would be absurd to explain away as a mere clash of governments and their armies. Herein act the stirrings of thousand year old powers, deep energies, herein come into play the primordial elements of life. To stand outside and off from this worldwide struggle, to slough off from oneself all responsibility for it, to be critical of it all, as something for oneself external, detached -- is morally impossible. We are all within this raging element, we are all -- its participants and act in it. Against Germany,

---

[1] VOLYA K POBEDE. Article was originally published in newspaper "Birzhevye vedomosti", 3 jun. 1915, № 14881.

Austria and Turkey wars all of Russia, all the whole Russian people, all the whole Slavic race, all the totality of our powers.

It would likewise be superficial and shallow to view the war, as an event merely, being played out within the material world, a phenomenon of but a physical clash of the masses. The war is spiritual an event, a spiritual struggle, and first of all spiritual, and only then material. A mass unspirited cannot wage a struggle, it is powerless and crumbles into pieces, like sand.

And in war it is a force of spirit that dominates and directs, albeit evil, if not good. We live in the days of a great spiritual conflict, and not only a material clashing of the masses. And the war has to be experienced as a citizen of his native land and as a citizen of the whole world, as his own particular inward matter, as a spiritual event, demanding the entirety of his pent-up powers. In the worldwide struggle of peoples participates not only one, who is called up into the active army, but also every citizen, whose will is directed towards victory, whose awareness makes sense of the great conflict. The surrounding world is as it were magnetised by the will, from it flow currents, charges, positive or negative. From lucid an awareness sun-like rays fall upon the darkness.

In the historical struggle of peoples there act not only the individual will and the individual consciousness, but also the collective assemblage of the will and consciousness of peoples. And everyone, in whom the will weakens, who falls in spirit, who surrenders in awareness to darkness, debilitates his people, emits negative charges and in whatever substrate level demoralises the army, obstructing victory. Behind the sacrificial and heroic effort of the army ought to stand, from across all the people, a granite-like will to victory. And the matter of suchlike a collective will involves each of us. Many now are pushing it beyond the limits of their strength and human abilities, and each of us ought at least to be involved to the limit of their strength. And first off it ought to involve a struggling against the spirit of despondency, against a corrosive scepticism, against a sickly susceptibility. World events demand a self-discipline from each, the manifesting of personal character, of extraordinary endurance. And it is necessary to morally prepare oneself and all the people for the possibility of a prolonged struggle, for new sacrifices and new challenges.

In such a terrible worldwide conflict, the likes of which never yet seen by history, setbacks and disappointments are inevitable. But it would be shameful to fail in courage at every setback. And if within society there became widespread an outlook such, that the war is already become wearying and tiresome, and the will of each tends towards a quickest attainment of peace and well-being in private life, then this bears with it a deep demoralisation, an undermining of the will of the people.

II.

Only the will to victory, only the will of the whole people can expedite resolution of the great conflict and lead to victory. The will to victory by each, his spiritual participation in the historical matter at hand has an influence upon the whole totality of the life of the people, towards strengthening the army. A will completely isolated, bereft as though of any responsibility, cannot exist. Everyone, readily downcast and spreading despondency around oneself, bears both guilt and an historical answerability in this. The private and self-centered view on the world conflict is an indicator of social immaturity, and we ought to get free from that spiritual form of slavery, which hinders us from perceiving ourself as active creators of our own history. The true freedom of the Russian people will be spiritual a fruition of this liberative awareness of oneself as an active participant in the world historical events. No longer in the position of a slave is one, who has himself participated in such matters and by blood has sealed his involvement, who by his own will has emerged upon the arena of world history. The slave-like narrowness of a provincial existence has to cease. Every act of losing heart, of disdaining the historical will, of throwing it all off oneself to "them", tends to return us to the condition of a slave, and not a citizen. The war has to play an enormous role in the matter of the self-awareness of the Russian people and the attaining by it of moreso free a life. One is only free, who has taken upon himself responsibility. Society has taken upon itself suchlike a responsibility in the activity of the rural and urban [Zemgor] unions. And the war itself on the fields of battle is becoming all more and more a matter of the people.

The great conflict of peoples has gone too far. The die is cast -- there is no turning back. The war will continue until the crushing and humbling of Germanism, and it perhaps will be prolonged, contrary to the expectations, there at the start. The world conflict is assuming all the more grandiose a scale and will demand bloody sacrifices of enormous masses of mankind, such as no other war in the world.

Such sacrifices are possible only amidst an exceptionally intense and total will of the people for victory, and an awareness of its inevitability for the utmost worth of existence not only for one's native land, but for all the world. And such an unprecedented intensification of the human will and its suchlike sacrificial aspect presuppose a profound awareness of the aims of life, lodged beyond the limits of earthly individual well-being. This -- involves a religious tempering of the will.

An enthusiastic will to victory means a lofty upsurge of patriotism, which in ordinary times is little in evidence with us, but which always has appeared in the grandiose moments of our history. And it mustneeds especially be stressed, that for us now is necessary not only an upsurge of nationalism, which always we have in abundance, but rather an upsurge of patriotism. Nationalism bears within it a whole series of negative, antagonistic, exclusionary and pretensive emotions. Such feelings in parts of our society go too far, and they darken the image of our native land. Nationalism -- is a matter of the parties, and not of the people, it puts forth various craven interests ahead of a creative love for our native land. Patriotism -- is supra-party, of all the people, it involves a positive creative love for the native land. The great patriots among all the peoples burned innerly with pure a fire, they created new life for their people. The consolidation of a creative patriotism, rising above party interests, surmounting all the negative feelings and reaction, -- is a great task for the Russian consciousness and will. And in this war there has to appear for us a true patriotism. A gust of such patriotism was sensed in the speeches of the conference of manufacturers. And when the will to victory becomes a matter of all the people, when each gets involved, then also there will be victory. Setbacks on the path, however, always small in comparison with the total sweep of events, ought only still to reinforce the patriotic will to victory.

The Contemporary War and the Nation

(1915 -196)¹

I.

The present war differs deeply from former wars. Now there is an altogether different relationship of the warring armies to the entire life of the various peoples, than was so in previous times. Former wars were rather moreso a matter of professional armies, separated off from all the totality of a people's life and the people's forces. And it was then a clashing of comparatively smallish armies. A general in one army of the conflict tended to defeat the other, and this decided the outcome of the war. Wars were conducted not to the point of the total defeat of one people by another, not to the point of total exhaustion, the entire life of a people was not set at stake, and all the totality of its powers. It was not the qualitative aspects of the various peoples, but rather the qualitative aspects of the armies and their military commanders that had a decisive significance. The present day European war has shown, that ware are likewise becoming democratic, becoming societal and of all the people, just like everything else in life. At the basis of modern militarism lies an universal obligatory military conscription and the mobilisation of all the forces of a people. War now is not merely a battling of army detachments, separate and off from the total life of a people, and it does not involve merely decisive fights by generals. War has become the armed struggle across all the relationships of the various peoples, which mobilise all their forces. A tremendous significance obtains from the industrial productivity of a land, its technology, its science, its general spirit. To win involves the power of all the people, the might of all the country, the material, and so also the spiritual. Individual military successes cannot decide the outcome of the war, as they might not have been effective. The German successes in Galicia can grieve us, but they do little to decide the outcome of the overall

---

¹ SOVREMENNAYA VOINA I NATSIYA. Article was originally published in newspaper "Birzhevye vedomosti", 23 jun. 1915, № 14921.

conflict. And with confidence it is possible to say, that all the military brilliance of Germany and all the successes of its armies are tragically hopeless in the sense of a final result of the war. Individual victories of the Germans can be but Pyrrhic victories. The seeming success of the Germans conceals in itself a terrible self-destruction, a self-devouring. The present war has to lead to the full defeat of one people by the other, to an ultimate exhaustion. Victory will be decided not by specifically military qualities, which the Germans possess, and which are indisputably great. Those peoples will win, who have in their totality greater powers. And therefore there is no doubt, that the allies will win. This -- is a question merely of time and quantity of sacrifices. To ultimately defeat Russia, to push it to total exhaustion is absolutely impossible. The powers of Russia are inexhaustible. The tragic experience of Napoleon has shown, what it means to make an assault upon Russia. Russia, as a total organism, as a totality of the powers of the people, is unconquerable. And still less is it possible to defeat Russia along with France and England and Italy. The victory of Germany is arithmetically impossible. And it is impossible spiritually.

But the will to victory and a consciousness of the inevitability of victory nowise signifies, that a condition of self-delusion should obtain in thinking, that everything will go fine for us. Dispassion in the face of truth strengthens the will, while every sort of lie tends to debilitate. Alike ruinous to the cause of victory is a faint-hearted despondency over individual incidents of unsuccess, as is also a false self-delusion. The pathetic experience of an entire people having to mobilise all its powers and win presupposes not only embellishing the actuality, but also presupposes the inevitability of self-criticism.

II.

We at present are entering into a new period of a societal and patriotic upsurge by all the people, and this upsurge is connected with an awareness of our many failings and deficiencies. And thus it always happens. The upsurge issues from the awareness of a creative task, presupposing an enormous exertion of powers, without any slave-like bowing to the facts at hand. Within Russian society is apparent a creative patriotism, loving truth and shoving aside the illusions. The creative patriotism presupposes an absoluteness of will by all the people to carry on the struggle, the great struggle, to the end, to the full vanquishing of the enemy. This involves an ultimate awareness of the truth, that in the current war to win is possible only through all the people and victory will obtain only by the discovering and bringing into active a condition all the powers of the people. The war cannot remain still bureaucratic, a matter of professional armies, it has to be societal and of the people, national. But the time of partisan wars has past, and there cannot by this path be manifest a character as would involve all the people in the war. The first moral condition of such an organisation of the people's powers is a cessation of inward strife, the surmounting of the party aspect and of this eternal opposition of "us" and "them", in which both sides are guilty. The current war presupposes an enormous creative upsurge of the people, a totally exceptional exertion of the people's initiative and self-reliance. The potential powers of Russia are enormous, many times over exceeding the powers of Germany. But these powers are in dormant a condition, all tied up and disorganised. The upsurge and organisation of the people's energy for the aims of the war will have significance not only for the war itself, but also for all the future of Russia. The consequences of this organisation of societal energy will be innumerable within all the spheres of life. The mobilisation of our industrial productivity for the aims of defense will yield likewise an upsurge of industrial initiative for life in peacetime and will lead to an awareness by the industrial class of its political role. There will likewise get strengthened, under this threatening hour of history, the acquired habits of societal initiative, societal organisation and societal responsibility. And the most valuable thing is, that the gains for a new life will be gained not by a negative, but rather by positive a path, not by discord, but by unity, by a creative, and not destructive energy.

III.

The vitally essential thing, that we are experiencing at present, will heal us from the pestilence of the doctrinaire party aspect. Unneeded at present are the political intrigues, and they are very harmful. The unitive and constructive experience, the result of the war, should cast aside every attempt at political intrigue, whatever side it involves. In the current hour of history are needed people with positive, creative, national-historical instincts. There needs to be a trans-party, a national ministry, concerned with deeds, and not political intrigues. Our rightist camp tends to political intrigue no less, than does the left, and even moreso. [...][1] The uniting of the whole of Russian society and the people has to happen from both sides, to be by both, it presupposes a sacrificial ability from all the camps. The slogan "all for the war, for victory" presupposes a freedom of activity, a freedom of organisation for all the powers of the people. [...] And a land, in which the war be not a national matter, will thus not have an exertion of all the whole people's power, and it risks suffering defeat. Only a free and armed people can attain victory. And every patriotic upsurge of the people's energy is together with this also a self-liberation of the people. The matter involves, certainly, not the people in the social-class sense of the word, but about the people as a nation.

We are entering upon a completely new period and we stand now under the standard of a nationally patriotic progressive enthusiasm and dynamic. The lack of success and weakness of our liberation movement have had in it a non-national, cosmopolitan character... And the dark forces of inertia in the Russian people have found their justification, as a nationally patriotic reaction... But after the current national war, after the current awakening of the powers of the people, these dark and inertial forces cannot still make a show of their monopoly on patriotism and their exclusive national feeling. Patriotism and national feeling henceforth has to belong by right to a progressive societal energy. The dark forces of inertia henceforth will stand compromised under suspicion of Germanophilism. And those, who still not so long ago projected themselves as monopolists of patriotism, now least of all share in the patriotic enthusiasm -- and they impede the mobilisation of societal powers. These dark forces have not wanted, that the war should become national a matter, i.e. they did not desire victory. They stood in the way of an ultimate awareness, that the war could only be a matter for all the people, and they are therefore culpable in preferring their own selfish group interests over the interests of Russia. Germany will be defeated, if it is a matter involving all of Russia. And only a new Russia can conduct a victorious war. A great land, a great people -- is undefeatable.

---

[1] *trans. note*: our *Padenie* Russian text notes (p. 1091) that "the article was subject to censorship deletion", as reflected by the [...] in text.

The Sensation of Italy

(1915 - 198)¹

It is a great joy for us, a joy not only political, but also of soul and culture, that Italy is now with us.² For a few Russians, just like for the English, Italy was a visionary dream. Italy also for us was an image of beauty and of the joy of life. The misery of Russian life, the absence within it of a plasticity of beauty drives our fondness for Italy to the extreme. The journey to Italy for many -- is a genuine pilgrimage to the sacred things of beauty incarnate, to a divine joy. It is difficult to express then the stirrings of soul, of a sweetness almost to the point of sickness, which grips the soul at the mere mention of some of the Italian cities or Italian artists. Italy for us is not a geographic, nor a narrow political concept. Italy -- is an eternal element of the spirit, an eternal realm of human creativity. It is impossible to look upon Italy as merely just one land, like the other lands of Europe. The mere thought about the barbaric destruction of the cities of Italy and its monuments of art so chokes the heart, moreso than it would choke from the thought about the destruction of all the other cities and monuments of Europe. It is impossible to form one's attitude towards Italy with exclusively political, stately, and national points of view. Only the barbarian would not sense this. And it distresses many, that the Germans could render themself such barbarians. Though on the other hand, many

---

¹ CHUVSTVO ITALII. Article was originally published in newspaper "Birzhevye vedomosti", 2 jul. 1915, № 14940.

² *trans. note*: Italy remained neutral at the outbreak of war in 1914, although it had been a member of the *defensive* "Triple Alliance" with Germany and Austria, Italy declined to enter the war on grounds that Austria was the *aggressor* causing the outbreak of hostilities. Italy declared war on Austria-Hungary only on 23 May 1915 on the side of England, France and Russia -- hence this exuberant article of Berdyaev. Much of Italy's military action was against Austria on a number of battles on the "Isonzo Front", q.v.

indeed have sensed the this awful feeling about the destruction of the Italian cities by the Germans, the plundering of the works of art. These dangers are heartily espoused, but they have no real basis to them. It would never reach this point. A second wave of barbarism upon Rome would be an impossibility. But the love of Russia for Italy during these days intensifies.

Nowhere else does the Russian feel so fine, as in Italy. Only in Italy does he not sense the weight and oppression of the hostile philistine civilisation of Western Europe, he does not feel on him the smug contempt of people, better settled in and attached to their norm of life, -- a contempt, so poisoning the life for us in the other lands of Europe. In Italy a Russian can breathe freely. The Russian character both has an affinity and yet is deeply opposite the Italian character. In the Italian character there is not the effects of wanting to dislodge us, as Russians, which is there in the character of the Germans. But we love the Italians also then, in that there is no semblance with us, and that it gives us completion. We love in the Italians the gift of the experiencing of the joy of life, of which we as Russians, are almost lacking. We -- are weighed down, always sensing the burden of life and worldly vexation, and hence we love the levity of the Italians. We -- are a people of the North, and we love the closeness of the Italians to the sun. So burdensome has been our history and so difficult the character of our race, that we almost do not know the free play of the creative powers of man. And captivating for us in the Italian people is this abundance of free creative powers.

The Russian soul does not freely make bold to create beauty, and while it senses it as a sin, this creative abundance, it loves the creativity of beauty, the creative abundance of the sunny land of Italy. The Russian soul seeks the captivating completeness within the plasticity of Italian culture, which is so lacking for the culture of the Russian. We called to mind, how Gogol so loved Italy, how he yearned for it, how he bestowed it praise. And indeed Gogol himself very vexedly experienced life, always he sensed the burden of the weight of the world; the torments of moral conscience always stood amidst the paths of his creativity. In this, he was very Russian and as a Russian he loved Italy, as a completion, as a dream vision, as that, which in him himself there was not. The Russian anguish over Italy -- is a creative anguish, an anguish as regards the spontaneous abundance of powers, as regards the sunny happiness, as regards beauty as a value in itself. And Italy ought to be an eternal element for the Russian soul.

Astride the Abyss of War and Revolutions

With Italy we doctor the wounds of our soul, lacerated by the Russian sick conscience, by the eternal Russian responsibility for the fate of the world, for all and for everything. Not only from the despondency of Russian life, but also from its grandeur, from Gogol, from Dostoevsky and Tolstoy, from everything difficult and tormentive we strive in Italy to breathe with a free creative breath. The exclusive ethicalness of the Russian soul seeks its complement in the exclusive aestheticness of the Italian soul. Italy is endowed with a mysterious and magical power to regenerate the soul, to life the weight from the unhappiness of life. Such is the eternal, deathless and indestructible Italy.

Our love was always directed to the old and eternal Italy, and not upon the new and modern Italy. The residue of modern Rome, the Rome of the last decades, the memorials to Victor Emmanuel, the quarter of Ludovisi and others, atop the deeper layers of Rome of the ancient, of the medieval, the Rome of the renaissance and the Baroque, tends to shock and repel. And in this -- is the tragedy of the Italian nation: it disintegrated and as it were came to naught by its own too great and excellent past. But there is no nation that can live only by the past, only by memories -- for it wants to live a genuine life, to create. And if everything, which a nation creates in its modern life -- is insignificant and lacking beauty in comparison with that, which it created in the past, then this is very tragic. The eternal city of Rome as a modern city -- is only a second rate city, only a Paris of secondary a sort. The grandeur and eternity of Rome, gripping the spirit by the might of its very name, they now give to Rome as the capital of a modern bourgeois state. There is perhaps a need to be set free from the unsustainable grandeur of the past, to fling aside from oneself its legacy, in order to create a modern and new life, to build and expand the size of the city, to emulate the other great domains of Europe. Italians both as regards the traits of their race and the legacy of their history with difficulty adapt themselves to capitalistic production and to the bourgeois style of life. In this area they are entirely still unable to advance into the front ranks. And so it is perfectly understandable, that Futurism would be conceived of particularly in Italy, in the land of an old and a great Latin culture. Futurism is a spasmodic attempt to cast aside this enfeebled power of past greatness, to burn the past, in order freely to begin life anew, to create a completely new life and new beauty, which would be impossible to compare with either the early or the late Renaissance. In Futurism there is the boorishness of insignificant children descended from great fathers.

It mustneeds be understood as the fitful decline of the great Latin culture. In France there is likewise the decline of the Latin culture, the greatest ever known by Europe, and it begot decadence, itself manifesting an unique grandeur and beauty.

In Italy this was not or almost was not so. Futurism indeed is connected with the past, and yet it is a reaction against the past, and not a creativity of the future. Futurism as an ideology had to appear in Italy, but it has not borne there genuine fruits. These fruits can more readily be observed in the futuristic war, such as modern Germany conducts. Futurism points to this, how tragically acute is the problem of the Latin Renaissance. But its actual rebirth is difficult to expect from Futurism. In the great war Futurism is going up in flames, just like much else, and there awaken these powers of the Latin race, such as still remain genuine within it. The Italians mustneeds not destroy the memorials of their past grandeur, but the rather defend them from the Futurism of the Germans. And it is probable, that [the Futurist] Marinetti himself will defend them.

The beauty and grandeur of their own past stifles the modern Italians. And this is but an indicator of their weakness. But for us and for all the world, in Italy's past, in its great monuments and cemeteries -- is an eternal, inextinguishable source of creative energy, eternally engendering strength. I sensed this with an inexpressible intensity, when I gazed from the villa of Mattea on the Campania with the Baths of Caracalla, with the Appian Way, with the aqueducts and ancient graveyards. The beauty of Campania, the land of which is as it were not still alive, in which everything as it were is deathly-asleep, all the monuments of human creativity are transformed into aspects of nature undetached from the ancient Latin land -- all this is unique in the world and of supreme beauty. But how mysterious then, that the very deathly-slumber of Campania, casting over it the seeming pallour of death, that this be a font of creative life. In the deathly semblance is eternal life and an eternal summoning to life. The surroundings of Rome give a powerful sensation of the greatness of man and of his creativity. Not only the fruitful soil with its ripe for harvest grain is it that gives a feeling of life, but also the soil now fruitless from too great a creativity, planted only with graves, can provide an even stronger feeling of life and eternality and stimulus for creativity. In Campania, in the surroundings of Rome, the fruits of human creativity have acquired the character of the eternal grandeur of nature. But suchlike is the whole of Italy: in it human creativity and nature are inseparable. And all within it remains eternally for all the world. It -- is the natal land of the human creativity of Europe. And everything dead and expired within it is a font of life and rebirth of the soul. If Italy were to be threatened with the danger of destruction, the whole world ought to defend it, since its beauty shines forth for all the world.

In these days these has to be sensed quite strongly the true love of Russia for Italy, as an union in heart, the eternal aspect of Italy within us ourself. Great within us has been the effect of the Germanophilia. We both esteemed the Germans, and worshipped them, and were enthralled by them. But never has there been an intimate heartfelt relationship of the Russians with the Germans. And only by an union of national souls can there be any sort of state-body union.

War and the Crisis of Socialism

(1915 - 199)[1]

I.

The crisis of socialism -- is one of the apparent and indisputable results of the European war. The internationale, the doctrinaire, the Marxist socialism, evidently, has irreversibly ended. Long ago already it theoretically was subjected to serious criticism and surmounted, but now the elements of life are putting a finish to it. The teaching, that social classes and their interacting interests are basic and defining principles of the historical process, has proven to be an abstract doctrine, not holding up under the test of life. Has the "international proletariat" preserved its physiological character during the recent great events? Does it exist, as some real unity, as an independently active force? That abstraction, which in the teaching has borne the name "international proletariat", has been allotted almost the same universal traits, as Papism, and has proven powerless in the greatest historical happenings. In the raging elements of the world war the international proletariat has floundered, just as the Catholic Church as an international organisation has floundered. In such critical moments of history it is proving, as to what is genuinely active and vital, and what also is debris and mere doctrine, what has become moribund and has lost its power. The international proletariat and socialism has been powerless the same to halt the European war, as has the Pope and Catholicism. The power allegedly to come has been powerless the same, as has the withered power of the past. Racial instincts, national feelings, imperialistic interests are stronger than all these international principles, pretending to universality. A world war such as unseen within history has shown the absence within the life of mankind of international and universal moral instances, which should have the power, to which

---

[1] VOINA I KRIZIS SOTSIALIZMA. Article was originally published in newspaper "Birzhevye vedomosti", 7 jul. 1915, № 14950.

there could be appeal. There does not exist a materially expressive, organically embodied unity of mankind. There is no outward world empire, nor outward world church, no outward world socialism, nor solely-saving proletariat. The appearance of universality -- is false and illusory. The oneness of mankind is revealed only in spirit, and not in material life. In the outward and historically embodied life, mankind moves towards unity along the complex and painful paths of racial and national conflict.

II.

The war has vividly and graphically demonstrated, what theoretically long ago already has been clear. Social class is not a substance, -- it is essentially something secondary, and not primary, it -- is merely a transitory function of social life. Social class is not connected with the deep-set roots of human life, it is a product of the historical process, and is not its fundamental and defining principle. In contradistinction to the concept of class, the nation, just like also the person, is a substance, a deep-rooted principle in the life of mankind. Nation as such also dwells beneath the empirical surface of the historical process, wherein yet are no social classes, and by its roots it reaches down into the very depths of life. And class, as something secondary, is powerless to dissemble and subsume to itself the nation, which is something primary. Marxism conceived of the nation as nominalistic and thought of class as realistic. But the reverse is true. National instincts, in the final end, always win out over class instincts. The growth of class consciousness in the second half of the XIX Century, in the era of the rise and triumph of Marxist theories, had serious reasons for it and was a fatum, a fated aspect of capitalistic societies. This was an honest and as such a just reflection of the social falsehoods of our life. But the class theories, propped upon the newly arisen class instincts, were not creatively active, but the rather compelling passive in relation to the evil process within social life. This was a triumph of fatum, the fated aspect, and not of freedom. The social class consciousness and social class theories have tended to veil over the deeper planes of human life, have weakened deeper rooted human instincts, have overshadowed the more remote aims of human life. This has served by way of a punishment for mankind. The bourgeois objections against class socialism are likewise indeed a matter of class, and in the majority of cases these objections are hypocritical and hollow. Every class self-assertion -- and the foremost example of such a self-assertion has been that of the economically-ruling classes -- tends to merit a class rebuff and reaction. And the responsibility for it falls not upon class socialism.

But the manifestations of this discordance on the surface levels of social life cannot ultimately overshadow the deeper principles of life. These deeper vital principles have long ago already filtered through into the Social Democrat movement and have destroyed its doctrinal purity. Principles national, on the one hand, and individual -- on the other, have penetrated in to the Social Democrats and have put a limit to the autocracy of the proletariat, to its absoluteness. This crisis of the Social Democrats began already from the times of the rise of the Bernsteinist, or revisionist trend. And gradually the Social Democrats were transformed from a proletariat revolutionary religion into rather a business-like social reform party and made room for sanctities, not connected with the divinity of the proletariat. When the European war erupted, stripping away all the superficial veilings of life, it laid bare the elementary primal aspects of human life, and the German Social Democrats quite coolly began to engage in warfare against the Belgian and French Social Democrats. The unity of the international proletariat proved to be a fiction. By virtue of the power of life, national instincts and interests were affirmed as more primary than class instincts and interests. Customary phrases, that the French and other proletariat were closer to the German proletariat than were the German bourgeiose, proved to be moreso a lifeless doctrine. All felt not a class unity, but rather a national unity. Germany stands dearer to the German Social Democrats, than does the international proletariat, since Germany -- is a fact, and the international proletariat -- is a theory. It is not the bourgeois classes waging the war, as it ought to be in theory, but rather various peoples, each conscious of itself as a single organism. In the fire of war there tend to unravel all the secondary formations, but there remains and abides everything primary. It would be unjust to reproach the German Social Democrats for having proven to be Germans, that within them has awakened patriotism, when danger began to threaten their fatherland. But the moral bankruptcy of the German Social Democrats mustneeds be seen in this, that they have proven to be a tool of the aggressive German imperialism. The Social Democrats represent still too quantitatively large a force within Germany, in order for them not to bear responsibility before the world for the aggressively violent deeds of Germanism. And the world therefore morally deprives the German Social Democrats the right to henceforth pronounce ponderous phrases about the international proletariat, about justice, about the defense of interests of the oppressed classes, etc, etc. After the victorious Franco-Prussian War Nietzsche wrote about the Germans: "The attaining of might bears dear a price: might *brings stupidity*... The Germans -- they termed them once a people of thinkers, -- can they still now be thought such in general?"[1] Truly he himself thought otherwise, when he preached the will to power. And "made-stupid" are the German Social Democrats also. But the collapse of German might will bring them to their senses and reason.

III.

A power truly international and worldwide is the capitalistic trade economy. Capitalism breaks down every national self-containedness and draws the economic life of various peoples into the worldwide cycle. Within the capitalistic economy exists the contradiction: on the one hand, it forms the basis of modern national and imperialistic politics, and on the other hand -- it is a power international and uniting. Capitalism unites mankind through discord and the conflict of interests: the modern banks -- are horrendous international powers. The stock-exchange to a remarkable degree determines international relations. And it mustneeds be said, that the international aspect of socialism has been merely a reflection of the international aspect of capitalism. Socialism has always much defined itself by its enemy. The world war is subjecting the worldwide capitalist economy to the greatest of tests. Former large-scale wars occurred while still under an economy to a remarkable degree natural, rather more stable and sustainable, set upon a slow tempo of life. In the modern economy the tempo of life has accelerated, and the nature of this economy has not the traits for endurance and a long wait. The capitalistic trade economy -- is very large-scale, sensitive and nervous a thing, by its very nature inclined to crises and catastrophes. But such a catastrophe, as the current war, has not formerly happened within an experience. And there is much a basis to presuppose, that the world economy after the war will undergo great

---

[1] *trans. note*: per *Padenie* endnote p. 1093, the quotation is from Nietzsche's 1889 work, "Twilight of the Idols, or, How to Philosophize with a Hammer".

changes. In the worldwide conflagration there goes up in flames much of the illusory and fictitious, accompanying the capitalistic economy. Capitalism in truth has created many an illusion and fiction, many a false need and false satisfaction. Illusory and hollow is this insatiable thirst for profits, unknown to other eras. There will hold up and remain in the capitalistic economy only that, which has comprised its positive mission, the real growth of the productive powers of various peoples. In modern Germany the capitalism has reached an utmost intensity, and there under the strain it has to collapse. Germany has shown the world an unique combination of modernistic capitalism with modernistic militarism. The technology of German militarism is a monstrously fanciful chimera of its capitalism, as its self-destroying and self-devouring offspring. And the European war in a certain sense is a fated fatum of capitalistic societies with their unchecked and devouring interests, the war being a fatal and inevitable capitalistic explosion.

Marx was correct, in saying, that capitalism has its own inevitable dialectics and that within it is lodged the seed of catastrophe. But his rationalistic schema of the future has proven inaccurate. Within modern Germanism there is uniquely spliced together an aggressive militarism, an intense capitalism, and a Social Democratism which is bourgeois in spirit. The Junkerism, the bourgeoise and the city workers, so apparently all at odds in their interests, have united into the singular image of the modernistic and futuristic Germany, and a defeat of Germany will be the defeating of the most modern militaristic-capitalistic social-democratic society, technologically the most accomplished and most heartless of all hitherto former societies. The catastrophe of the European war signifies the beginning of the end of the two twins -- the international bourgeois capitalism and the international bourgeois socialism. We are present at the tragic end of the bourgeois ideals of life. The Social Democrats have been infected no less by these bourgeois ideals, than have the prevailing bourgeois classes. In the German imperialism, so fateful for world life, the crisis of bourgeoisness has attained final an acuteness, and in it much is coming to an end. The crisis of socialism is the crisis of bourgeoisness.

IV.

After the worldwide crisis of the war, new social forms have to appear. The instability and non-durability of the fundaments of the social structure are quite evident. But hopeless and ineffectual are all the attempts, all of them, to rationalise life and rationally predict the future. All the schemes and all the doctrines will get toppled over by life. What awaits us is unforeseeable and unexpected. After such a world catastrophe a new sort of human soul will be born and the life of mankind will enter into a great uncertainty. The old socialism was flesh from flesh and blood from blood of the bourgeois capitalistic society -- it was not the creativity of unknowable life. The creativity of life is always multi-faceted, never schematic. The war has shown us, that everything is infinitely more complex, than was thought, that always the unexpected lies in wait for us and that no sort of rational schemes have power over life. It is possible, certainly, to foresee the inevitability of the socialisation of economic life, the greater subsuming of the process of production to societal and civil organisation. It is impossible to relegate economic life, upon which depends the daily bread of mankind, to the caprice of fate, to the free and chaotic playing out of interests and insatiable human greed. It is very important, that the urgent needs of the war bring about a partial socialisation of the economy and a greater regulating of it by the state. In a regulation of the chaos, resulting from the world war, will be worked out new procedures in the organisation of human life. The inevitability of an organised regulation of the elements of nature and of human elements will become particularly apparent during this war. During the time of such a war, states become quite immersed in the question of daily bread for all the people, and societal forces become quite accustomed to organise for the satisfying of the daily demands of defense, so that after the war economic life can as of old go back to an unregulated and catastrophically chaotic a condition. The societal and state regulation of economic life, certainly, will not emerge in those forms, which doctrinal socialism predicates. The forms will be multi-faceted and unforeseen, just as the creativity of life is unforeseeable. [...] Human life tends simultaneously to develope on both the side of a greater individualisation, and on the side of a greater universalisation. The life of various peoples will tend to become both more national, and more worldwide. [...]

Facing the XX Century stand such grandiose creative tasks of the regulating of the powers of nature and the natural elements, as were unknown by the XIX Century with its limiting positivist worldview. Now however the XIX Century is ultimately done with, and we enter upon the unknown.

Concerning "Leftness" and "Rightness"

(Reply to D. Muretov)

(1915 - 200)¹

In my reply to D. Muretov,² which has raised very interesting a question, I begin by saying, that I am fully in accord in the desire expressed by him at the conclusion of the article. Like him, I think, that "never has there been a time, more demanding of discussion and deepening of quite the most general and theoretical differences of opinion". We live in a period of a profound crisis of consciousness, the re-evaluation of the fundamental values of life, and we are in need not only of an energy of will, directed towards victory over the enemy, but also an energy of thought, directed towards a national renewal. But the article of D. Muretov provides occasion for misunderstandings, which require clarification. I have called for the surmounting of the schism splitting Russian society into two hostile camps, and I have come out against all the political posturing. And I tend to place the blame -- within the political posturing of the "leftist" inclination. Long ago already, regarding the year 1905, I energetically wrote against the bad habit of our "leftist" intelligentsia to view the categories of "leftness" and "rightness" as identical with the moral categories of good and evil.³ The "right" -- as the villain, and the "left" -- as the decent man -- is a simplified philosophy of life, against which I have long and much already written. For me it is entirely beyond doubt, that the

---

[1] O "LEVOSTI" I "PRAVOSTI" (*otvet D. Muretovu*). Article was originally published in newspaper "Birzhevye vedomosti", 16 jul. 1915, № 14968.

[2] Vide in "Birzhevye vedomosti" (№ 14949) the Letter entitled "Necessary Thought on Party Reconciliation (an Independent Voice)", written by D. Muretov in connection with my article, "The Contemporary War and the Nation".

[3] Vide my book, "The Spiritual Crisis of the Intelligentsia", 1910.

rightist Marshall of the Nobility or the priest can morally stand infinitely higher, than the leftist advocate or literateur. This -- is a moral axiom, which ought to be admitted by our intelligentsia. This -- is moral, and not societal a problem, demanding a moral reform of consciousness. A moral extolling on the basis of "leftness" and radicalness is, certainly, an ugly phenomenon. But I refuse to admit that the very sincere struggle of the very venerable Marshal of the Nobility, on behalf of the privileges of the nobility, should be seen as standing on equal a plane with the struggle for freedom of the word. Because privileges of the nobility -- are an interest of "this world", but freedom of the word -- is a God-given value.

One mustneeds understand, that the Russian intelligentsia has divided the world into decent people and villains, into the saved and the perishing, into those representing the Kingdom of God and those representing the kingdom of the devil along the same emotional lines, on which this division is made by ortodoks-minded Catholics, Baptists and sundry other sectarians, and likewise also by rightist Orthodox Christians. This -- is a division on the basis of a religious, and not political order. It would be a mistake to think, that the Russian "leftist" intelligentsia is constituted and oriented politically and societally, -- it rather is constituted and oriented moreso religiously, although this religiosity, -- is distorted and attached to unsuitable objects. This was beautifully understood and revealed by Dostoevsky. The Russian intelligentsia has aspired not so much towards political and societal improvement, as rather to the salvation of mankind and the world, proffered in the form of social pipe-dreams and utopian phantasies. In this, our intelligentsia has been very Russian, and national. To implant into the Russian intelligentsia the instincts for state building and inculcate an awareness for real politics -- means to Europeanise our intelligentsia. A differentiation of values, the establishing of a complex hierarchy of values would be an Europeanising of the intelligentsia consciousness.

The Russian intelligentsia individual, as a certain ideal type, tends to jumble up the "good" into a righteous truth and justice, and in essence he does not admit of any sort of value, except the moral. How difficult it would be for him to have to admit the self-sufficing independent value of beauty. He is almost totally incapable of operating with any other sort of values, besides the moral, and he is always moralising over history, where the sociological ideas have always been a but smokescreen for his moralism. The Russian intelligentsia individual has contrived with so amoral and immoral a teaching, as Marxism, to purely accept and understand it materialistically. For him the "proletariat" -- are the fine, the good, the saved, but the "bourgeoise" -- are the evil, the villains, the perishing. Such an exclusive moralism strengthens sectarian a psychology. It is almost impossible to induce the traditional type Russian intelligentsia individual towards historical and societal thinking, to an admitting of the complexity and diversity of life, the clashing and mutual interacting of various values. And I think, that only such a catastrophe, as the world war, can change and broaden the awareness of the Russian intelligentsia individual. Certain changes of consciousness have begun, however, already back withe the unsuccessful events of 1905.

And to speak about myself. I do not think, that the "leftists" ought "to incline towards the right", nor the "rightists" -- "to incline towards the left". I think, that it is necessary to get beyond the stifling categories of "leftness" and "rightness", to cease evaluating life exclusively upon the flat and level plane of movement either "leftwards" or "rightwards", and rather instead to pass over to different a dimension, a dimension of depth and height. D. Muretov wants to make a "rightwards" revision to my point of view. Not noticing this himself, he wants to play it out moreso for the "right", to gain for it larger a place. Yet I think, that it is not necessary to play out anything whether for the "right" or for the "left", but rather it is needful to look at things essentially, from within, from their inner viewing of truth and rightfulness, neither glancing either "rightwards" nor "leftwards". I can be very mistaken in my evaluations, but on principle and to the measure of my abilities I attempt to do so. I do not desire to be moreso "towards the right" or "towards the left", since I desire different and deep a dimension of things, I want to move along the vertical, and not along the flat-horizontal. But such a point of view does not deprive me either of truth, or of the possibility to make an evaluation of what is transpiring upon the flat surface of Russian life, an evaluation of "rightwards" or "leftwards" in it. The appeal to unity, to the cessation of the evil discord and a getting free from political intrigue has to represent a new value within Russian life, and not represent a refusal of even very severe appraisals. Under the sacrificial aspect, I understand first of all a repudiating of interests, of greed, of exclusive self-affirmation, and not of one's own inner values and outlook. In the name of the great value of Russia -- the intelligentsia ought to repudiate their own exclusive self-assertion and immersion in their limited circles, whereas the bureaucracy and the nobility ought to a certain degree to repudiate their own selfish interests. I can be, perhaps very mistaken in my estimation of the role of "rightist" circles, which I might regard as neither patriotic nor national, and then happen to get disproved, but on the issue of such a sort of appraisal I sacrifice nothing and I recant nothing.

And yet it is inconceivable, why does D. Muretov regard my point of view as non-sacrificial? There does exist a "leftness", which can represent a national danger in onerous an hour for the land. About this one must speak and about this it is not difficult to speak. But there exists likewise a "rightist tendency", which represents a national danger and a betrayal of our native land, and to expose this -- is a patriotic duty. The slogan, "all for the war, all for Russia" demands an unmasking, the unmasking of also a "rightist tendency", debilitating the nation in the great conflict, subjecting the fatherland to danger. This unmasking needs doing not from a "leftist", but rather from a national point of view. But to speak about this is extremely more difficult. I assert, that in certain "rightist" circles there has existed a Germanophilism, debilitating for Russia, which has cast a pall over our national consciousness in facing the world catastrophe.[1] This has involved namely the matter of Slavism in the world under the direct influence of Germanism. These circles, which from national a point of view, have to be termed murky dark forces, have set certain state and social forms as higher than Russia and have been fond of such moreso than their native land: they have been devoted not to Russia, which is more profound and higher than transitory historical forms, and their intent rather is upon their hold on the state, the intent upon a social structure. And this devotion to certain state ideals above Russia is no more national, than is the devotion of the "leftists" to their own social ideals. With some of the "rightists" this has been entirely unselfish and intellectual a matter, but with others -- a selfish assertion of their own interests. But the national danger here is no less, than in the view on Russia exclusively from the perspective of the proletariat or of whatever other "leftist" social teaching.

I am in full agreement with D. Muretov, that the Russian intelligentsia has to, finally, admit of the independent value of nationality. But I little believe, that the true bearers of this value have been our

---

[1] Ivan Aksakov -- is altogether unsuitable an example. And least of all am I inclined to include him amongst the dark forces.

"rightist" circles or that the nationality value can be received by the intelligentsia from, for example, either the bureaucracy or the nobility. And likewise I little believe, that the "leftists" have always been bearers of a true value of freedom. Too much of the conditional lie has been piled on by both the one and the other. The national awareness in Russia is a creative task of thought and will, and the pathway to it lies outside the traditional "right" and "left". That which in me seems to D. Muretov to be a "political posturing", is merely my profound conviction, that in certain influential "rightist" circles there has long since already begun a process of moral dissolution. This -- is a question of fact, and not of principle, since there is fully possible a morally healthy "right". Among the "rightists" there are excellent, honourable and upright people, and among them are possible even saints and heroes. And on the other side, among the "leftists" are many bad people, selfish, insincere and corrupt, and I am not especially inclined to hold in morally high regard the average mass of our radical intelligentsia, the radicalism of which often becomes vile and trite. But in the best, the heroic part of the Russian intelligentsia, has been a valuable moral energy, without which Russia would be unimaginable, just as Russia likewise would be unimaginable without the repudiation of all nationality by L. Tolstoy. This all-fired thirst for truth upon the earth has been something deeply Russian and national: the value of souls stands higher than the value of the kingdoms of this world. And our rightist bureaucracy all too often has been non-national, German in spirit and even by blood, alien to the cherished expectations of the Russian people, and cut off from the soul of Russia. It is necessary, certainly, to get over the bad habit of viewing each government minister with mistrust merely because, that he -- is a government minister. But the bureaucracy ought to become more Russian and of the people in spirit, and not by the literal conditional letter of state slogans. In Russia, historical fate has rendered the question about a national awareness as impaired and tragic a thing. The error of D. Muretov, evidently, is in this, that he insufficiently individualises Russia and the Russian people, that he thinks about nationalism in Russia in too generally European a way, in insufficiently national a manner. He fails ultimately to understand my point of view, in that I desire a new creative national unity, and not merely a mechanical reconciling of old powers and outlooks. We are now entering upon a completely new period of a constructive national self-awareness and self-consciousness.

The Slavophilism of the Ruling Powers

(1915 -202)[1]

I.

The appointment of the Moscow Gubernia Marshall of the Nobility, A. D. Samarin, as OberProkurator of the Holy Synod -- is the most interesting and remarkable of all the appointments of recent times. In the person of A. D. Samarin, Slavophilism for the first time is receiving power and receives it within the churchly sphere, which always has stood at the centre of Slavophil interests. Slavophilism up to the present has been unauthorised, and the conservative character of its basic principles has not saved this current of thought from the eternal suspicions on the part of the ruling authorities. Many of the ideas of the Slavophils were irresponsible and in experience not accurate. We tend to remember, that the theological writings of A. S. Khomyakov were prohibited by the religious censor and appeared abroad in the French language. And Khomyakov was not only the greatest theologian of the Slavophil school, but he contributed also to an utmost degree, to the uplifting of the churchly awareness in the East, within Orthodoxy. And now it avails the OberProkurator Samarin to transfer over into life many of the ideas of Khomyakov, which seemed so dangerous to all the former OberProkurators. The uncle of the current

---

[1] SLAVYANOPHIL'STVO Y VLASTI. Article was originally published in newspaper "Birzhevye vedomosti", 3 aug. 1915, № 15003.

trans. note: our *Padenie* Russian source notes (p. 1093) correctly that the 1978 Klepinina Bibliographie was mistaken in considering this article as identical (pp. 31, 83) with the 15th Chapter of Berdyaev's book, "The Fate of Russia", entitled "Slavophilism and the Slavic Idea".

Padenie (p. 1093) *ed. note*: "A. D. Samarin was appointed as OberProkurator of the Holy Synod in July 1915, but through the opposition of G. Rasputin in September the same year he was removed". (*trans. note*: this present Berdyaev article appeared in the interim, 3 August 1915).

OberProkurator, Yu. Samarin, wrote: "Khomyakov himself represented an original, a phenomenon almost unprecedented among us *of fullest a freedom in religious awareness*".[1] This "fullest freedom in the religious consciousness" of Khomyakov was something that never could be understood, nor accepted by the official churchly circles, those situated in authority. "Fullest freedom": always indeed and to all seemed dangerous and treasonous. At the very same time as the Slavophils were asserting churchly life to be in "fullest freedom" and saw in freedom to be the very essence of the Church, the churchly authorities were asserting churchly life to be instead in fullest necessity and saw the very essence of the Church to be in coercion. The Slavophil and Khomyakov conception of the Church had many points coinciding with the genuine churchly life amongst the Russian people, but not in a single point did it intersect with the official churchly authorities.

The first point of intersection of the Slavophil Orthodoxy with the official Orthodoxy is now in the new OberProkurator of the Synod, -- A. D. Samarin.

The appointment of Mr. Samarin -- is very responsible a fact for the old Slavophilism, a great putting to the test of its suitability for life, its sacrificing of idea. A. D. Samarin -- is not simply some bureaucrat, who can foppishly adapt to whatever and be obligated to nothing. And perchance, never yet has a Russian minister come to power being so intense and devoted to his ideas. Samarin comes to power from a perspective most responsible to Slavophilism. Behind him stand very definite churchly ideals, those of his spiritual and by-blood fathers and forefathers. His very name already is terribly imposing. Upon him gaze familial portraits, and they connect him with familial traditions. How bound up or devoted to any sort of intellectual or familial traditions was Mr. Sabler? He indulged to the fullest in bureaucratic liberties, a license for endless connivance and officious fawning. But A. D. Samarin -- is no bureaucrat. His "legitimacy" -- is societal, and not some "legitimacy" based upon official rank. He aspires to be the bearer of the ideals of the people's conservatism. We are not accustomed to anything like this, that the intellectual and societal conservatism of the people should be in power.

---

[1] Vide: Yu. Samarin, "Preface to the 1st Edition of the Theological Collected Works of Khomyakov" (in Tome II of the "Collected Works of Khomyakov", or in the "Collected Works of Yu. Samarin, Tome VI).

The traditional bureaucratic "legitimacy" has never been of suchlike a conservatism. It was bereft of conservative ideas, the like of which evidently Mr. Samarin does have. A. D. Samarin -- is the first Synod OberProkurator deriving from the Moscow, rather than Petrograd Orthodoxy, i.e. in essence the first moreso Orthodox, moreso churchly, moreso nationally Russian an OberProkurator. In this -- is the significant meaning of his appointment. I do not know, how Mr. Samarin will be in his efforts, but as such he has to be on the basis of his position, his person, and his connections with the past. The Petrograd, the state-bureaucratic Orthodoxy has always indeed differed from the age old Moscow Orthodoxy, an Orthodoxy quite more closely tied in with the startsi-elders and the monasteries, with the people's sanctities and with the religious life of the Russian Land.

    A. D. Samarin, evidently, is strongly a Moscow Orthodox type of churchman. He can be a representative empowering the Moscow Orthodox circles, genuine believers and intellectuals, those circles, which not so very long ago were in sharp opposition to the Synod and the official churchly authorities on the question of the "Imyaslavtsi/Name-Praisers"[1] and on certain other major questions of churchly life. In these rightist Orthodox circles and enjoying the greatest reknown are a brother of the new OberProkurator, by the name of F. D. Samarin, and also M. A. Novoselov,

---

[1] *trans. note*: The Imyaslavtsi, apparently grew out of the Hesychiast practice of mystical repetition of the "Jesus Prayer" among the monks of Holy Mount Athos. In 1912-13 this practice was declared "heretical" by the official churchly authorities in Russia, and "477 monks were forcibly removed from Athos and dispersed among various monasteries in Russia" (*Padenie note № 2, p.1093*). Among the expression of outrage in public opinion at the brutal roughing up of old Russian monks by the Russian government, in August 1913 Berdyaev penned his fiery famous article, "Quenchers of the Spirit" ("Gasiteli Dukha" Kl. № 172, in the gazette "Russkaya molva", № 232), -- the publication of which caused Berdyaev to be officially charged with "blasphemy" which after a trial would have resulted in perpetual banishment to Siberia, except that WWI and the 1917 Revolutions intervened, with the Bolsheviks subsequently in 1922 banishing Berdyaev instead to the West. Another irony of fate...

V. A. Kushevnikov, P. B. Mansurov.[1] The intellectual conservatism and strong churchliness of these people has set them in opposition to the dubious Synod politics, which have ravaged churchly life and caused its demoralisation. A lack of success by A. D. Samarin in power would to a certain degree be also misfortunate for these Moscow Orthodox circles, an intellectual crisis for them. All Orthodox Russia looks to A. D. Samarin at present, all the genuinely churchly Russia, which has been repressed under the OberProkurator leadership, hemming in always the "fullest freedom" in churchly life, such as when the persecution against the "Imyaslavtsi" occurred. How will the Slavophil traditions of A. D. Samarin tie in with the sphere of churchly ideals?

II.

The Slavophils were in resolute an intellectual opposition to the bureaucratic Synod structure, although under the conditions of those times they could not fully express it. In the bureaucratisation of the churchly structure, which in their opinion began with Peter the Great, they saw an enormous evil. The Sobornost'/Communality[2] within the Church -- in this indeed was the pathos, the feeling of something unique, for the old and classical Slavophilism. They loved to set the conciliar-catholic spirit of the East in contrast to Western Catholicism. In the Sobornost' of the churchly people they saw a lofty sanctioning for a churchly lifestyle, and this

---

[1] The group publishes a religio-philosophic selection of books under the editorship of M. A. Novoselov and organises religious talks.

[2] *trans. note*: "Sobornost'" derives from the Slavonic word for "catholic" ["sobornyi"] in the liturgically used Nicene Creed: -- "I believe... in one, holy, catholic and apostolic Church" ["Veruiu... vo edinu svyatuiu *sobornuiu* i apostol'skuiu tserkov'"]. In contrast to the Romanist understanding of "catholicity" as "universality *of* the Church", an external mark, the Orthodox nuance of "sobornost'/catholicity" reflects rather an "universality or wholeness *within* the Church", an inner non-static dynamic Divine-human process, evidenced in the Epiklesis during the Liturgy, and similar invokings of the Holy Spirit and of Christ [Mt. 18: 20] at spiritual and churchly gatherings, and Sobors/Councils. Hence, Sobornost' at times is translated as "conciliarity", "catholicity", "communality" and suchlike...

conciliar-catholic Sobornost' they conceived of as non-juridical, not something external, but inward and free. In this sanctioning by the people of the Church Khomyakov considered to be a sign of veracity for a Council to be OEcumenical.

But in the Synodal arrangement from the Peterburg period of Russian history, the people of the Church ceased to play any sort of role whatsoever, and the idea of Sobornost' was completely distorted. The Synodal arrangement is non-conciliar not only from that inward point of view, upon which Khomyakov stood and which cannot be expressed juridically, but non-conciliar also from the external and canonical point of view. This arrangement was an expression of the servility of the Church to the state. The feeling of the Slavophils regarding the Church was beautifully expressed by Yu. Samarin in the following words: "*I admit, I yield, I submit* -- means consequently, *I do not believe*. The Church lays claim only to faith and anything less does not suffice; in other words, it accepts into its bosom only the *free*. Whosoever offers it a slave-like grudging acceptance, does not have faith in it, and that one is not truly in the Church nor of the Church". And still further on he says: "The Church is not a doctrine, nor a system nor an institution. *The Church* is a living organism, an organism of truth and of love, or more precisely, *truth and love as an organism*". But the official Synodal arrangement has asserted the Church as an "institution" and has demanded, that the Church "should be offered slave-like an acceptance, irregardless of any faith in it". Is it possible then to esteem one's churchly authorities as an adequate expression of the Church, as "a living organism of truth and love"? The Slavophils quite well understood, that their ideal conception of the Church nowise at all corresponded to the churchly actuality or to the churchly ordering of things in fact. Their harsh criticism of the Western Church with certain transpositions can be turned also on the Eastern Church. If it be regarded poor an affair, when the Church becomes in effect the state and is in everything comparable to it, then it is no less poor an affair, when the Church is subordinated to the state and becomes its tool, its foil. The conception of the Orthodox Church by Khomyakov, Samarin and the other Slavophils was an ideal construct, an expression of the OEcumenico-Universal Church of Christ as above all the historical embodiments, and this conception is to their great credit. The teaching of Khomyakov concerning the Church represents an utmost point of ecclesial consciousness in the East, but it is far remote from the churchly activity of the East.

I shall provide certain characteristic places in Khomyakov as reflect the characteristics of the churchly views of the Slavophils, very bold and free and inevitably clashing with churchly actuality and churchly authority. "The Church is not authority, just as God is not authority, just as Christ is not authority: since an authority is something external to us. Not authority, I say, but truth rather and at the same time within the life of the Christian, his inner life".[1] "Every act of believing, every meaningful act of faith is an act of freedom and indispensably issues forth from a preliminary free investigating".[2] The Church "knows brotherhood, but it does not know subjection".[3] "The oneness of the Church was free; more precisely, the unity was of freedom itself, structurally an expression of its inner accord. When this new oneness was sundered, churchly freedom had to be sacrificed for instead the attainment of an unity artificial and capricious, an external token or sign having to replace the spiritual sensing of truth".[4] "The clergy, in its *Christian* actuality, is indispensably a free clergy".[5] "Christianity is naught other, than freedom in Christ... I admit of the Church as moreso free, than do the Protestants... It is extremely wrong to think, that the Church demands compulsory unity or compulsory obedience; on the contrary, it abhors both the one and the other: wherefore *in deeds of faith compulsory unity is a lie, and compulsory obedience is death*".[6] "No sort of external token, no sort of external sign should restrict the freedom of the Christian conscience: the Lord Himself teaches us

---

[1] *Padenie note (p.1093)*: A. S. Khomyakov, "Collected Works", Moscow, 1900, Tom II, p. 54. (alternately, A. S. Khomyakov, "Works" in 2 volumes, Moscow, 1994, Tom 2, pp. 43-44. In following this latter source pagination will be indicated within ( ) brackets).

[2] *Padenie note (p.1093)*: Ibid, p. 43 (35).

[3] *Padenie note (p.1093)*: Ibid., p. 69 (55).

[4] *Padenie note (p.1093)*: Ibid., p. 72 (57).

[5] *Padenie note (p.1093)*: Ibid., p. 181 (141).

[6] *Padenie note (p.1093)*: Ibid., p. 192 (150).

this".¹ "The oneness (of the Church) is naught other, than the consent of the personally free".² "Neither hierarchical power, nor the significance of the clergy as a class can serve as a guarantee for truth; the knowledge of truth obtains only by mutual love".³

"It would have been better, if we had less of an official and political religion, and if the government could be persuaded that the Christian truth has no need of constant protection, and that excessive solicitude over it tends to impair, and not strengthen it".⁴ "In that the members of the Church are we ourself -- the bearers of its greatness and majesty, we -- the sole ones in all the wayward world the keepers of the truth of Christ. And keeping silent, when we are obligated to proclaim the word of God, we bring upon ourself judgement, as being craven and heedless slaves... Howsoever lofty a man might stand upon the societal ladder, be he even prince or ruler for us, if he be not of the Church, then in the area of faith he can only be as a learner for us, but hence not the equal for us".⁵ And thus Khomyakov proclaims not only the freedom of the people of the Church and of each member of the Church, but also the authority of the people of the Church in the matter of teaching. That Khomyakov was opposed to Caesaropapism, is evident from the following words: "We think, that in being free, the sovereign just like every man, can fall into error, and if, though may God grant it not to occur, if some like misfortune were to befall, despite the perpetual prayers of the sons of the Church, thereupon also this emperor should not lose any of his rights of obedience from his subjects on matters secular: but the Church should bear no sort of detriment in its majesty and in its plenitude: since never must it betray its true and its sole Head. In suchlike a presupposed instance the

---

[1] *Padenie note (p.1093)*: A. S. Khomyakov, "Collected Works", Tom II, p. 231 (181).

[2] *Padenie note (p.1093)*: Ibid., p. 235 (183).

[3] *Padenie note (p.1093)*: Ibid., p. 363 (279).

[4] *Padenie note (p.1093)*: Ibid., p. 364 (280).

[5] *Padenie note (p.1094)*: Ibid., p. 86 (68-69).

Christian thus astray would become lesser in its bosom -- and only so".[1] If a Slavophil were empowered and wanted seriously to carry out in life the churchly ideas of Khomyakov, then there would have to happen an enormous and radical turnabout. Khomyakov's ideas bear heavily upon his spirit of freedom. Khomyakov was a teacher of the Church for the Slavophil camp. Samarin was his student and follower, as were all the Slavophils of the time of its flourishing, they were inspired by Khomyakov's churchly ideals, unlike the later times of decline. But the inevitable course of life shows, that to be a Slavophil in 1915 signifies something altogether different, than to be a Slavophil in the year 1840.

The old Slavophilism at present is in a period of decline and decay. It is still possible as a closet and antiquarian interest, as a non-vital mindset of a not large number of people standing off afar from the prevailing currents of life. But it is almost impossible to empower. An active attentiveness to life demands a new creative religious energy or it will lead to a betrayal of the old, the good ideals. It is too late for Slavophilism to have come to power. And every delay in history gets fiercely punished. The children and grandchildren of Khomyakov and Samarin no longer still possess this freshness in the affirming of churchly freedom. Too strong in them is the fear of facing the disintegration of a fond lifestyle.

III.

The position of the new OberProkurator of the Synod is difficult, in that the Slavophil traditions obligate him to a diminishing of the OberProkurator authority, i.e. to a self-limitation and self-denial. And this always becomes very difficult for a man, standing in power. Yet what is needed is a directing of his power towards a lessening of the power of the OberProkurator upon the Church. This task demands enormous energy, will-power and self-assertion. It is necessary to overcome the terrible power of inertia in our churchly governance, to win out over the Synodal bureaucratic routine, to set on new rails all the colossal mechanism, so accustomed as it is to grovelling and toadyism. And for this within our episcopate there has to be, finally, awakened the feeling of churchly worthliness, that of being proud of the Church, which has nothing in

---

[1] *Padenie note (p.1094)*: A. S. Khomyakov, "Collected Works", Tom II, p. 37-38 (31).

common with human or personal pride. A. D. Samarin, if he be the Slavophil, has to make an attempt at the emancipation of churchly life, setting free the positive religious energy of the people of the Church. He has to apply all his efforts to this, -- the restoration of Sobornost' in churchly life. The Sobornost' of churchly life -- is a dogma of the Slavophils. But the Slavophils have yet another dogma -- freedom of conscience. Freedom of conscience for all the Slavophils was something sacred, they contrasted it against the obligatory within Catholicism.

We have seen, how the pathos for freedom pervaded the churchly ideas of Khomyakov. Khomyakov, and all the Slavophils together with him did not admit of obligation and coercion in matters of faith. A. D. Samarin has thus first of all and most of all has to be a defender of freedom of conscience, calling to mind the words of his uncle, that the Church "doth accept into its bosom only the *free*. Whoso offers it a slave-like grudging acceptance, is not in the Church nor of the Church".

But one should not overstate the role, which the OberProkurator of the Synod can play. His role -- is moreso negative, than positive, he is called not so much to do good, as rather not to do evil. The OberProkurator cannot be termed a churchly activist, he is only an intermediary between the Church and the state, he directs the affairs of the Church, insofar as they concern the state, and the affairs of the state, insofar as they concern the Church. But the OberProkurator is not a participant of the Holy Synod and churchly a power does not belong to him. Our OberProkurators often in fact have run the Church and had greater an influence, than the metropolitans and bishops, but this was only a factual expression of the correlation between the Church and the state, and nowise an expression of the principal position of the OberProkurator within the Church. But the OberProkurator of the Holy Synod, one such as who esteems the freedom and independence of the Church, at a minimum has to reduce the grip of the civil authorities over churchly life, the coercion in matters of faith. The persecution of sectarians has tended to be justified for us as necessary an activity by the state, and not the Church. The OberProkurator, as the intermediary between the Church and the state, can take a stand on this, that the Church is not interested in having privileged a position from the state for its faithful sons, and that the protective services of the state authority are degrading for the dignity of the Church. A church of persecutors cannot flourish. A church of the persecuted has always flourished more. A. D. Samarin, as a Slavophil and a conservative, certainly, cannot be a proponent for the separation of the Church from the state, he still believes in "the Christian state". But he can and he ought to preserve the sacredness of freedom of conscience, which for us has been proclaimed, but not fulfilled.

IV.

It is difficult to believe, that our churchly life can be revived by those measures, which usually among us would be regarded as of renewal and progressive: the convening of a local Sobor-Council, the restoration of the parish, the return to a conciliar structure, in accord with the canons, or a reconstituting of the Patriarchate. The outward reforms, which irreligious and non-churchly people often demand, can be wished for, but in themself as such they will not renew the churchly-religious life. Church life has stagnated not because, that for so long a time it was directed and run by Pobedonostsev, and that the living spirit within it was smothered by the bureaucratic structure, and that the Church had become subjugated to the state. The reverse is true: Pobedonostsev directed and ran churchly life, the Church was oppressed by the state, because the religious energy had weakened, because the living spirit within the Church had diminished. The Church in disarray is the result of a decline in religious life, a religious crisis within the Russian people. It is impossible to renew the parish by external measures. The factual absence of the parish is but an expression of the weakness of churchly life among the people. A genuine churchly renewal is possible and can occur only from within, inwardly, from a gaining of spirit. Sobornost' in the Church is a manifestation of spirit, and not an external, juridical expression of form. From the outside there can be attained only a negative emancipation, a liberation from lies and coercion. But the positive values of churchly life are not reached by such a path.

The grievous symptom of the decline of religious energy in our churchly life happens to be seen in this, that in this threatening and extraordinary hour of Russian and world history, the Church has proven to be so inactive. The churchly forces are not mobilising for the defense of the country, for the repelling of the enemy. Our monasteries have done shamefully little for the help of the wounded. Our clergy have least of all participated in the patriotic upsurge and exertion of all the forces of the nation.

One can say, that this is not the business of the Church to be bothered with. But we are mindful of the times of St. Sergei Radonezh and the role, which the Church then played in the saving of Russia. The Church has been one of the defining forces within Russian history. And now Russia anew is undergoing difficult days of responsibility. But in the Church is not felt historical an energy. The religious energy has as it were departed to different a place and in concealment it acts within all the great, the heroic, the sacrificial and spiritually precious, that now happens within life.

Slavophilism cannot still renew churchly life: it is too late. In late an hour of history has appeared a Slavophil OberProkurator. The old schema was already powerless over the infinite complexity of life. The ideals of pre-Petrine Rus' could be a beautiful dream of idealistically minded a clutch of literary landowners of the 1840's, set not upon actual deeds, and remote from the vital struggle. But it is impossible already to look upon A. D. Samarin as such an idealistic dreamer, remote from life. He has been very involved with life and in the affairs of "this world" in his capacity of Marshall of the Nobility and a visible representative of an united nobility. Within this thicket of life, in this struggle for the interests of an outmoded nobility, in the eternal resistance to the growth of new life there will have to have faded the ideals of Khomyakov and Yu. Samarin. The old gentry, though quite pure and intelligent, cannot still renew churchly life or any sort of life. The final beautiful and majestic gesture of the nobility can be only a gesture of historical self-denial and sacrifice. But not such has been the activity on behalf of the nobility by the new OberProkurator. In the quite energetic image of A. D. Samarin is sensed a final spark of a dying lifestyle. This -- is a final showing forth of old Russia, which has had to give way to the new Russia in all the spheres of life. A. D. Samarin, certainly, is better than Mr. Sabler, he is more churchly, more intellectual, and moreso societal a man. And he can prove more progressive in the life of the Church namely upon the strength of his conservativeness. But it would be mistaken to place any sort of special hopes on him. In religious life, just as with life in general, it is necessary most of all to rely upon oneself, upon the people of the Church, upon their religious energy. The Slavophils proceeded upon the assumption, that the entirety of the Russian people and society -- is Orthodox. And upon this conviction rested all their organic system. But now it is impossible still to sincerely construct one's civil state activity upon the principle, that all the whole Russian people is Orthodox and that the Russian state is truly Christian. And it is possible beforehand to say, that it will not be easy for the new, intellectually so overwhelmed OberProkurator to authoritatively establish an attitude towards the Church not as towards an "institution", but rather as to "a living organism of truth and love". Religious renewal is possible only upon the basis of a creative experience and creative ideas, which cannot be from a Slavophil of the old type.

Society and the Ruling Powers

(1915 - #203)[1]

There is no land, in which there has been such a sickly rift between society and the ruling powers, as there is with us. Our society always feels itself such, as though it had not created the historical ruling power and is not responsible for it. We are accustomed to regard ourselves as though in a conquered land, and the Russian state often has seemed to us as not our state. An eternally indignant opposition, which also is the only thing left us and which has fomented the incessant struggle of the ruling powers against society, has taught us to look upon the state aspect as something foreign, "theirs". "They" have regarded themself the bearers of the state national idea. Russian society is constraintly held in a condition of statelessness and there has remained to it nothing, except to construct stateless theories and on principle to cleave to a stateless opposition. A sense of civil responsibility is possible only for one, who is called to an active participation in civil life, who himself has to create new forms of life. But one who is cast off onto the sidelines and from the sidelines has ability to be indignant, tends readily to admit as immoral and vile any sort of participation in the state civil authority. And the Russian intelligentsia has not been given to even the thoughts, that there can ensue a moment, when it will be called to an active and positive participation in civil life, when the state will be "us", and not "them". The historically habitual alternative of a boycott on principle of everything civil has remained up to the present. The consciousness of an active citizenship among us is still weak. We are too accustomed to feel ourselves as slaves not at liberty and hence to revolt like slaves. Rarely possible among Russians is to be met the pride of a citizen in his fatherland. In the speeches of our extreme "leftists" is felt not so much the dignity of the citizen, conscious of his mature power, as rather the mutinous malice of the eternally downtrodden and oppressed. Russians too readily go into hysterics, in both their deeds and in their words are

---

[1] OBSCHESTVO I VLAST'. Article originally published in literary gazette "Birzhevye vedomosti", 10 August 1915, № 15017.

lacking the power of the citizen. Rare is the one who speaks among us, as one having power.

And it is very remarkable and joyful a thing, that in the historic session of the State Duma on 19 July Russia truly heard citizenship speeches, full of citizenship worth and citizenship indignation. This utmost worthiness of the citizens of their fatherland, responsible for its fate, was sensed not only in the speeches of the progressivist Ephremov and the Cadet Miliukov, but also in the speeches of the nationalist Count V. A. Bobrinsky and the Oktobrist Savich. Beautifully citizen-like was the speech of the peasant Evseev. The feel of citizenship was absent only in the speeches of Mr. Markov II and Mr. Chkheidze. The talk of the two extreme representatives from the opposite positions from that of the Russian societal effort was totally irresponsible. But the words of Count V. Bobrinsky and Mr. Savich, expressive of moderate-rightist circles of Russian society, spoke to the growth of a free citizenship, which would transpire in Russia under the effect of the war and patriotic concern. The same awareness of citizen worthiness and citizen responsibility was sensed also in the speeches of P. P. Ryabushinsky, uttered at the session of the industrialists and in the military-industrial committee; in them is sensed the growth of the political awareness of an entire class: into the arena enters our third estate and powerfully demands its sharing in the state civil life. A maturity of societal power is sensed also in the speeches of Prince G. E. L'vov. And behind all this stands a new power -- the army, the armed people.

These are all important symptoms of a change of attitude between society and the ruling power. *And this new correlation can be characterised not as the growth of the negative opposition of society, but as the growth of the positive authority of society, as the assuming unto itself of power in the state.* In political life everything is attained not by the pronouncing of abstract formulas, but by the obtaining of positive power and the consciousness of this power. And society assumes power for itself by this, in what it does positive for the war effort, for the defense of Russia, for victory, and by this, in that without the societal forces the state cannot conduct war, without the all-rural and all-urban unions, without the industrialists, without the State Duma, without the free press it is impossible to advance the defense of Russia upon heightened a sense of duty. It is a matter of objective historical and civil necessity, though also with delay, but it summons broad societal forces to the matter at hand, to a sharing in civil state life, to authority. And now the societal forces would win a free citizenship not by means of a negative opposition, not out of a struggle for power, but out of a patriotic upsurge and a patriotic concern, not so much a demand for rights, as rather a fulfilling of obligations. And now the indignation itself against the ruling powers -- is a patriotic indignation, a fulfilling of the awareness of national responsibility. What is established is not a parliamentary and formal-juridical responsibility along with ministers of state, which presupposes a deep-rooted change of the state structure and at the present time is hardly possible, but rather a moral and factually real responsibility for the country. And this would give a jolt to a ruling power, bereft of civil an awareness and responsibility towards its great country, a ruling power, unworthy of its great land. A totally irresponsible ruling power can no longer be tolerated. During these days of historical tribulations our society has to become involved in the civil aspect and take upon itself power for a positive national effort. Such a national matter should transpire in all spheres: the rural zemstvos, the cities, in industry, in the State Duma, in the press. we begin to feel, that the state -- is us, that we are responsible for it, that we share in its growth or decline.

Russians do not fully understand, that the state is a necessary function in the historical life of peoples, that it is created and works through the peoples themselves. However bad and rotten a given historical form of state might be, yet it is also compelled to carry on certain functions common to every people. For us, and for every society, for every people is necessary an army or court system, although the army or court system can be poorly organised, and we then also have to strive to improve them. The state always is called in its own way to contend against that chaotic element, such as would lead to the falling apart of the societal life of the people. But the state civil consciousness has always been weak not only for our society, but also for our ruling powers, which sooner instead would stand upon the basis of its patrimony and imagine, that through an inherited right it rules the Russian earth and people. Our "ruling" power has always been very capable of wreaking havoc and anarchy into the societal life of the people. After 17 October, when the State Duma was formed, the ruling powers failed to evidence the civil state awareness, that the State Duma is a state institution, an organic part of the state. The representatives of the ruling authorities continue to think, that the people's representation is but a sufferable societal opposition to the governing powers, themself the sole bearer and voice of the state. From the two opposite sides for us is merged the state with the government.

But indeed the legitimate power of the people's representatives is quite more deeply-rooted a principle of the state aspect, than is the executive power of the government, which is but one of the transitory functions of the state mechanism. The State Duma itself has to first of all consider itself an organic force of the Russian state aspect, an expresser of the unity of Russia, and not merely one arena for party struggles. The State Duma is society, with its contending forces, it itself is a force, it preserves the Russian civil state aspect and Russian national unity no less than the governing power, and rather moreso. With the government ministers, who have proven unfit in this verymost threatening hour for the Russian state, there has been no sort of civil awareness nor responsibility as regards the capacity of being bearers of the principles of the state aspect. They have been reactionary spokesmen against the fundamentals of the state aspect. The war has brought a casting aside of mere bureaucratic functions and a turning to realities. The civil and national phraseology of our rightist bureaucracy has proven illusory. And the war in the same a has brought a casting aside the fictions of all the abstract political declarations, with a turning to the concrete. We have ceased to believe in the phraseology of the rightist-bureaucratic, the leftist social democratic or the doctrinaire-liberal. We now believe only in concrete realities and in deeds, in inward power, finding expression in concrete outward actions.

The relationship between society and the ruling authority is entering upon a completely new phase. This new correlation first of all brings awareness of the unity of society and the army, which is an awareness all more and more. Russia has been led to ruination by those destructive circles, which the State Duma has acknowledged as worthy only to sit in the judgement dockets as transgressors. Russia will be saved and defended by all of society, by all the people. And that civil state position, which will in fact have been won by society, by a patriotic deed of saving the native land, cannot ever be taken away. This henceforth -- is greatest a reality and power, not an abstract fiction. The war has to cure us from the abstract formalism in politics -- it points to actual content, to the vitally factual. We have to leave off with the irresponsible boycott and the principle-entrenched opposition by people, standing as it were outside of Russia, outside the Russian state aspect, outside the national unity. We have to surmount the formal and on-principle opposition between society and the civil authority, have to conceive of ourself as a positive force, acting within the united Great Russia, as responsible citizens of their fatherland.

On "Radicalism"

(1915 -207)[1]

The newspaper "Den'" ["The Day"], having an opinion of itself as very radical and leftist, has systematically conducted a campaign against the State Duma. The first and historical session of 19 July was already very much not to the liking of "Den'". "Den'", evidently, has reckoned, that the chief enemy at present -- is the State Duma and the Cadets [Constitutional Democrats], dealing with party issues and not a single word is found of an awareness concerning the exceptional aspect of the historical moment, of pain for Russia, of sensitivity to what is happening, of responsibility for the fate of our native land. There is the spewing forth of the usual radical phrases, long since become ludicrous, and indicative of no signs of independent thought. The position of the "Den'" newspaper is the typical position of the Russian radicalism, and itself displays all the same faults. This radicalism is bereft of whatever the sort of independent ideas, and it -- alas! -- readily becomes trite. It is indeed possible to be a conservative in ideas, a liberal in ideas, a socialist or populist in ideas. But it is impossible to be simply a radical in ideas. Radicalism does not convey with it any sort of independent an idea. This is in essence intermediate a direction. For the traditional type of the radical, there is characteristic an incapacity for independent moral judgements: they live by reflecting aversions towards moral judgements. These traits of Russian radicalism render it a phenomenon morally feeble and bereft of significant idea, with the Russian radical median level morally lacking in character and soft-headed. There is a right to existence such as possessed by an energy liberal and an energy socialist, an energy conservative and an energy revolutionary, they all have their own place in the developement of Russia. But radicalism does not evidence any sort of independent energy. Certain segments of Russian society render themself as radical only from their incapacity to throw something together in idea, from the absence of having an independent place in the societal effort. And thus is created the most irresponsible of all

---

[1] O "RADIKALIZME". Article was originally published in newspaper "Birzhevye vedomosti", 7 sept. 1915, № 15073.

the societal positions. The socialist position is very real and independent in idea. One might not be sympathetic with the socialist doctrine and socialist tactics, but it is impossible to deny the significance of the socialist movement: without it there would be too much ignoring of the interests of the working class, about which it is needful to remember, though it be in an extreme and exclusive form. There is likewise a meaning also in the existence of populism, which calls to mind the interests of the peasantry. The bourgeois world has to have its delimitations. But radicalism does not convey any sort of obligatory societal function. The Socialist-Revolutionaries [SR's] all alike acknowledge radicals as representatives of the bourgeois world. Granted that radicals are quite ready to accuse the liberals of this, but they too -- are "bourgeois" the same, as are the liberals. And indeed the radicals morally lack confidence in themself. As is apparent. They themself think, that the Social Democrats and Socialist Revolutionaries are better. And in the liberal camp such become for us principled in their ideas as rightist liberals, for whom liberalism is an independent idea, more true and lofty, than any idea revolutionary or socialist. The leftist Cadets often become the same sort radicals.

In recent months the Russian liberal movement has shown great energy, true patriotism and a political sense of reason. This "ruling" State Duma, whilst certainly not manifest as genuinely representative of the people and in the past possessing no special merits, has been rendered into something more, than one might have expected from it. Justice demands one to admit, that the Duma has sensed the exceptional importance of the present moment and has become aware of the basic tasks of the moment. The creation of the progressive bloc -- is a fact of enormous importance, indicative of the maturity of our societal sense of reason. There occur moments in the life of peoples, when it is necessary to strive for maximal unity and unity upon the basis of minimum-programmes. Russia at present is undergoing such a moment. Disunity and discord in general are doubtful a good or value, and when the fatherland is in danger, every increase of disunity and discord -- is criminal. Neither the extreme rightists, nor the extreme leftists, want to realise this -- they continue to think, that it is necessary to dig deeper an abyss within the land, to destroy the national unity. The year 1905 created the impression, as though the Social Democrat "Bolsheviks" saw their basic task initially in the destroying of the Social Democrat "Mensheviks", then the Socialist Revolutionaries, and then the radicals, and then the liberals, and then already last in line, the reactionary government. And the first in line Social Democrat "Bolsheviks" themself had to be destroyed by the maximalists. And here this wild psychology has not fully run its course even in 1915, though history would have much to teach. Not only the revolutionaries, but also the radicals from "Den'" are ready to see their chief shooting target as the progressive bloc. [...] And I believe, that the workers and the peasants show greater a sense of reason, than do the doctrinaire intelligentsia sorts. There is an enormous significance at present in the leftward tilt in the rightist circles of our society, a growth in them of societal awareness under the influence of the war. This fact possesses a greater significance, than the endless repetition of radical phrases, -- it is indicative of a real change within Russian society. Eyes were opened within influential levels of Russian society. And this is very valuable, very actual. The formation of a progressive unity in the life of the people has historical a significance. And this is indeed basic a task, and not a sectarian-like deepening of the abyss. The unity of the nation ought always to be stressed, and in facing the threatening enemy this unity has to be stressed to utmost a degree. The task involves the salvation of Russia, both outward and inward, and in the name of this sacred task much can and has to be sacrificed. Are our radicals perchance not aware of this? Have they indeed learned nothing? It is time now to settle the party grudges against the Cadets! Let many failings be levelled against the Cadets, but at present it is not only the Cadets, at present even the progressive nationalists and Oktobrists are involved in the deed of the saving of our native land, at present all have been regenerated at this hour of history under the effect of the national danger, which threatens not only from the Germans, but also from murky forces within the land. Freedom of the press, and in part, freedom of the socialist press has exposed all the emptiness of content in Russian radicalism, all the hollowness of its phraseology. An authentic radicalism indeed signifies a *deep-rooted* attitude towards life, a change in the actual norms of life. And in our traditional radicalism there is nothing deep-rooted, nothing radical.

Self-Restraint

(1915 - 208)[1]

The outward and the inward tribulations, experienced these days by the Russian people, demand first of all and most of all -- self-restraint, a self-restraint exceptional and unprecedented, a self-discipline, self-control and calmness. To master the elemental forces, which readily lead to an explosion -- is a basic task at present. Howsoever great the trying of the patience of the Russian people, if it holds up under this trial, then it will ultimately assume its historical maturity and its readiness for the fulfilling of great and positive tasks. The spirit of the Russian people is under assault, and we cannot permit the thought, that it will be smashed and shattered by the heavy hammer of history. The immediate elemental feelings at present impel towards actions, which can prove irreparable. We cannot permit ourselves to go into hysterics, into a feckless chaos. We have to put Russia, its interests, its fate higher than one's own elemental feelings, one's own most noble emotions of indignation. In our attitude towards the tragic turn of events, the will and reason have to prevail over emotions, over the feelings, which can be very turbulent and stormy, but to which in yielding exclusively reflects always a passivity of spirit. The utmost activity of spirit -- is in self-restraint. Genuine spiritual self-restraint is inwardly a deed, the saving of the soul of the people from disintegration and chaos, by a turning inward, into the depths. When the grip of passionate emotions takes hold of me unchecked, my soul then is hurled towards the outward and scatters into the external. The emotional life has to be concentrated around the inner spiritual centre, independent of whatever external stimulus it be agitated by. And this is so not only in the

---

[1] SAMOOBLADANIE. Article was originally published in newspaper "Birzhevye vedomosti", 12 sept. 1915, № 15083.

trans. note: This article apparently refers to the depressing, and here deliberately unspoken, serious military setbacks in Summer 1915 on the Russian front against Austria-Hungary in Galicia. The brevity of this article and numerous [...] cuts would seem to suggest heavy censorship imposed by the background authorities.

life of the individual, but also in life societal. The soul of an entire people can be held subject in its emotional and passionate life, by its spiritual centre. And then it is well for the people. And -- the soul of a people can become dissipated through external events, can be hurled outwards and subject to the will of the wind. Every panic is suchlike a spilling off of the mass soul, a loss of the spiritual centre.

[...] But it is necessary to call for self-restraint, for a preservation and concentration of the people's energy, for an accumulation of inner strength.

Russian society has manifest a striking unanimity and has entered upon great sacrifices in the name of the salvation of Russia. The State Duma has been patriotic in the finest sense of the word. [...]

The initiative of the Russian people and society ought not to get bogged down through inner dissention. Granted the dark forces would rejoice at the loss of self-restraint and of division within Russia. [...] Our conscious aim has to be positive and creative, and not negative and petty. Every dissention within Russia brings joy to our enemy. News however about the self-restraint and unity of the Russian people would be a blow against the enemy. Self-restraint -- is a sign of maturity and virility, an indicator of spiritual freedom. We shall thus be free from the grip of negative and destructive feelings. We shall then safeguard the soul of our people from chaotic collapse. May God grant that self-restraint not be lost in the threatening hour of tribulation. We shall then not only individually, but also as a society live within itself rather than outside itself, to determine itself from within, and not be subject to determination from the outside. Dispassion in the face of danger and in the face of the terror of life -- is utmost a religious virtue. And it presupposes spiritual self-restraint.

The Role of the Third Estate in Russia

(1915 -211)[1]

I.

It has been pointed out many times long ago already, that the industrial bourgeoise does not play amongst us that liberating political role, such as it has played in the West, and that this is sad for the political developement of Russia. For us the bourgeoise has not been rendered into a politically conscious third estate. Our bourgeoise has been lacking in culture, afraid of power, has not broken yet with the old plundering aspects of trade, and has been shoved back by the advanced economic role of capitalistic foreigners in Russia. The estates in general have but weakly been developed in Russia and stifled by the bureaucracy. The source of our bourgeoise -- is the old Russian merchant trade. By way of inheritance it received no sort of feelings for citizenship nor any sort of political pretensions. The old habits, inherited from being merchant traders, has left our bourgeoise economically lacking in creativity, politically submissive and timid. The creative initiative has been too insignificant in the Russian bourgeoise. Only comparatively recently has it been emerging from its repressed condition and becoming a cultural factour. And it is very important to note, that the Russian bourgeoise has always been somewhat limited in scope of idea and rather on the outside of matters, never receiving any sort of ideological sanction. At first it was scorned by the nobility, and then it was scorned by the intelligentsia. This does not enable developement. And the Russian bourgeoise did not know a period of spiritual upsurge. It always tended to be defined, as serving its own personal and class covetous interests, and not the national interests of the people in general. It also sensed itself as such and therefore could not play any sort of creative role in the developement of Russia. This too was an

---

[1] ROL' TRET'EGO SOSLOVIYA V ROSSII. Article was originally published in newspaper "Birzhevye vedomosti", 18 oct. 1915, № 15136.

indicator of rather a low level of industrial developement. But of late there has emerged for us a third estate, and no one believes still, that it -- is of the people. In place of the nobility, as the vanguard estate of the past, it is not the bourgeoise that has emerged for us as a third estate, but rather an intelligentsia bereft of rank, and it has determined the course of developement in ideas. This is a phenomenon specifically Russia. We have nowise had a trend of bourgeois ideologies, nor bourgeois ideas.

And without an idea-based sanction, any sort of creative role is impossible. Class solidarity and the inclusion within it of a sense of worth is possible only upon the basis of idea. The bourgeoise in Russia has been scorned by an exclusive predominance of interests. In the eyes of the wide swathes of the Russian intelligentsia every bourgeois, and every manufacturer -- is a morally reprobate exploiter, for whom is denied any positive role. The soul of the Russian people has no desire, that Russia on European models should pass through a bourgeois period of developement. We are yet unable to believe that bourgeois ideals are common to mankind in general, nor are we captivated by the fruits of the bourgeois revolutions in the West. And it is very characteristic, how Marxism was transferred onto Russian soil. The Marxist schema admits of the creative role of an industrialist capitalism and the progressive role of the bourgeoise at a certain stage of developement. But in Russian Marxism nothing similar has occurred. In Russia, capitalism was still at an initial stage of its developement and the bourgeoise has not matured into its role. Yet the Russian Marxists have begun to assert, that the bourgeoise is already disintegrating and that the transition from capitalism to socialism is nigh close. This is what comes out of heads, rather than from life. In the head of the Marxists the bourgeoise has begun to disintegrate, at a time when in life it has only just begun to come together. The Social Democrats have wanted to take note of a class proletarian pathos in Russia, at a time when the bourgeoise has not yet entered into the arena of history and not yet said its say. In essence, the Russian Social Democrats remain a masked-over populism. From populism it has received a whole series of moral judgements, suspicious of industrial developement itself. The perspective of class interests has ultimately crowded out the perspective of national developement. This exclusive class perspective, tinted the same with the Russian-ascetic moral hue, has hindered the Russian Social Democrats from perceiving, that in accord with Marxist theory, in Russia there still has to be faced the issue of the bourgeoise playing a progressive political and economic role. The pure Marxism has not been accepted by the soul of the Russian intelligentsia, it is all still the same national soul, a soul, repelled by the bourgeois aspect, but lacking the ability to perceive, that the aversion towards the bourgeois is a phenomenon spiritual, and not materially of class.

But it is impossible to view the industrial developement of Russia as exclusively the class interest of industrialists. This industrial developement is likewise a national interest of the people in general, and it is needful also for the working class as well. Industrial developement at a certain stage cannot proceed without the captains of industry, without a vanguard class of industrials, though the necessity of this ought not to be rendered into rigid a schema. The industrial class can be a progressive cultural stratum, conscious of its nationally-common tasks and its obligation in dealing with the working class, rather than as a plundering class, for which exist only greedy class interests. Up til now the second type has been predominant for us. But there has ensued a time for a cultural and political upsurge in the industrial stratum, for an awareness by them of a nationally-common mission and for the limiting of rapacious appetites, without which no sort of national mission can be accomplished. The instincts of a national creative productivity ought to take precedence for the industrial class over the instincts for gain and unseemly enrichment. Then only will the class stand under the standard of a nationally-common historical aspect. In Russia's industrial class there ought to take form a cultural and moral energy, without which it cannot play any sort of positive role. Historical a role presupposes a consciousness of its mission and a capacity for self-limitation and sacrifice. The purpose of plunder itself cannot be historical a strength. If the will within the Russian industrial class be directed towards the oppression of the working class and towards a struggle against the incipient workers movement, then this will tend to win out over the will towards economic and political creativity, and this class thus will be transformed into a power reactionary and unable to meet its summons to historical an involvement. The exclusive class point of view of the Social Democrats is pushing the industrial class onto this path and dooming it to reaction.

But the class perspective ought to be subordinated to the national perspective, to the purposes of the land and the people as a whole, and from this point of view the industrialists also cannot be disdained, and they too have to be called forth to the issue of serving Russia. The third estate has its own issues against the working class, its own specific interests, which we can neither fathom nor have a feel for. But we can admit of a positive significance of the third estate for the industrial developement of Russia and for political liberation, irregardless of whatever the feelings specifically regarding its class interests. It is possible to understand and consider the role of the bourgeoise, whilst nowise becoming contaminated with bourgeoisness nor sympathising with bourgeoisness in spirit. It is possible to contend against the bourgeois spirit and yet all the same to acknowledge the role of the bourgeoise within the external historical plane, where all is relative and gradual. The struggle against bourgeoisness is moreso a spiritual fact, than a fact socio-political, and it presupposes a spiritual absoluteness, not directly transferrable into the relativeness of the historical world. From utmost a perspective the working class also is bourgeois, and socialism too is bourgeois, since bourgeoisness is a condition of spirit. The class perspective is a sociological abstraction, and it cannot define the concrete historical life of peoples, in which act complex forces. Thus, for example, the sociological abstraction of the nobility or the bourgeoise does not cover the extent of that complex Russian actuality, in which act the rural unions in general or the urban unions in general, but which rise above class issues for a national politics in general.

II.

The present historical moment in Russia is situated beneathe the standard of the coming of age of the third estate. The class point of view is very relative and it is impossible to make use of it too widely and unlimitedly. But one need not be a Marxist, in order to see the significance of the industrial bourgeoise within the ensuing historical hour. The war has acutely evidenced the importance of industrial developement for Russia, for its security and defense, amidst all the insufficiency, all the wretchedness of our industrialism.

The present day war -- is an industrial war, and it is profoundly different from previous wars, those connected with the traditions of knightly chivalry, with the nobility, with personal valour. Now there instead occurs a war of capitalist societies, the tone of which is set by Germany, and this war possesses nothing of the former noble military style. This -- is a bourgeois war, although it demands no less than before, and perhaps even moreso a sense of sacrifice and stolidity of spirit. The heroism of the army -- is extraordinary. And yet the present war is lacking in style compared with the Napoleonic wars. The bourgeois-industrial style of war has still not fully crystallised and it is most difficult to explain it to us as Russians, repelled by everything bourgeois. But to everyone is clear the twofold truth: victory is impossible without industrial developement and industrial developement is impossible without victory. The Russian industrial class has been aware of this, that it is bound up with the political position of the country. Our industrial backwardness has proven fatal for us. And our entire bureaucratic system has set hindrances for developement in every direction. This is all tangled up in a single knot. In order for the knot to untangle, the Moscow industrialists have to win out over the Petrograd bureaucrats. Those, who would seek to pit our Russian sense of holiness against the German industrial technology, tend to coarsely confuse totally different planes of reality, and this mix-up produces an impression almost blasphemous. Let those, who come up with these pretty theories, themself attempt to fight in the trenches unarmed, with their bare hands. The technology of armament is indeed one of the weapons of the spirit at a certain stage of its developement. And industrial developement is itself a manifestation of the human spirit, and the bourgeois spirit in being bound up with industrialism, is an enslaved spirit, correspondingly manifesting itself within the external. But spirit can grab itself a tool, whist not falling into the bourgeois captivity of the external. The necessity of industrial developement remains imperative for the acting of spirit in the external world, within the naturo-historical plane, at a certain step of worldwide developement.

    The spiritualistic denial of the necessity of material developement is a false dualism, of spirit in opposition to matter, and a false monism, in applying to the relative material world absolute spiritual criteria. Against this dualism mustneeds be opposed a true monism, for which the material actuality is but a manifestation and symbolisation of the spiritual actuality, and against that false monism -- mustneeds be opposed a true dualism, discerning and separating the inward-mystical from the outward-material planes. And then the necessity of industrial developement for Russia can be spiritually justified. Reactionary utopianism and romanticism would substitute the material weapons needed by us with already existing spiritual values. It is impossible to oppose the bourgeois spirit by means of an industrial backwardness -- it is necessary rather to oppose it with different a spirit, independent of whatever the economic factours. Economic backwardness and weakness is itself per se a deficiency, and not a surfeit of spirit. And one can only say on this, that industrial creativity should be inspired by different a spirit, and nowise, that there should not be industrial developement, or that it should remain in primitive a stage. In the Russian ascetic attitude towards the industrial enterprise there has been its own truth, but there has also been a totally false confusing of different planes.

The war has evidenced a threatening lack of a constructive industrial initiative on the part of the Russians, under the crush and pressure from the German initiatives. There is evidenced likewise a solid connection of industrial developement with the political self-initiative of society and the people, with the right of societally organising and active on its own. The industrialists are likely to play no small a role in victory. And this is directly connected with an awareness by them of their own societal and political significance. This growth of the third estate, as an independent societal and political force, is constantly to be felt in the speeches of P. P. Ryabushinsky, a very characteristic representative of the liberal industrial bourgeoise.

Our path runs along with this, though our goals be very different, and sooner or later our paths will diverge. We have to realise, that for the emergence of Russia from its impasse, a great significance is to be had with the growth of the economic and political power of the third estate, subsumed under the national idea. But Russia cannot and ought not simply to repeat the paths of Western Europe. There is no repetition in history, everything in it is individual. And the world war indeed is giving such a jolt to the basis of a capitalist economy, that after its unprecedented experience the economic life of peoples will enter upon the path of unforeseen socialisations. Hence also in the growth of industrial capitalism in Russia there will be introduced totally new features, limiting the chaotic aspect and avarice of private ownership.

III.

The war of 1812 took place under the standard of the nobility and was vividly tinted in noble an hue. The nobility itself was an advanced and cultured estate, to the utmost patriotic and active in the affair of saving the country from the incursion of the enemy. In the Fatherland War there was evident the nobility's noble style. "War and Peace" -- is foremost an epic of the nobility.

From the avant-garde officers of 1812 there emerged the Decembrists. The portraits of our ancestors, the heroes of 1812, bespeak the blossoming of the nobility. There is nothing similar in the 1915 war. A hundred years later Russia has changed to the point of being unrecognisable. The nobility all still continues to cling to power, but it is sinking away all more and more. It is withering of blossom, in it appear all the signs of declining a condition, and exiting from the historical scene. In the nobility, as a class, there is no longer the capacity for enthusiasm, for gratis a service to native land, for being caught up with ideas. The modern conjoint nobility bears upon itself the features of being creatively powerless, vexedly clinging to its own interest as a social group. In the guise of the nobility, as a class, there is no longer anything still pretty. The interests of the modern outmoded nobility are not identical with the interests of Russia. The national role of the nobility in common with that of the people has ended. The nobility, as an estate, does not play any sort of independent or remarkable role in this war, and it has not evidenced that patriotic upsurge, that other societal elements have tended to evidence.

True, individual nobles are doing very much for the war, but as persons, as individuals, in the capacity of landowners, as members of the State Duma, as writers, etc. But not as representatives of their estate. And this -- is a nobility, refusing the struggle for even the nobility's traditional estate interests. Prince G. E. L'vov works for Russia not as a member of the nobility, but as a landowner, with nothing specifically of the nobleman in his societal activity, although in his emotional composition are features of the old gentry nobility. The finer portion of our nobility has filtered off into the progressive non-estate societal effort, into landowners. The nobility, as a social unit, has not said its say in this threatening hour of Russian history. It has become incapable still for national service, and is capable only of reactionary intrigues. The traditional national phraseology of the nobility -- is that of old and empty words, rhetoric, which no one still believes. It is impossible to hear still yet living words from a formerly foremost and avant-garde estate.

The present day war is set moreso under the standard of the third estate, than that of the nobility, if one is inclined to speak regarding classes, and it is tinted in industrial a light. The industrial class is very active and patriotic in the current war, nationally and moreover progressively minded and desirous to provide service in the war and victory by the developing of Russia, rather than by an hindering of developement. The modern war demands not so much gentry qualities, as rather industrial qualities. I repeat, the modern war -- is not one of chivalry, but rather of industry. This can tend to sadden some, but this truth needs to be directly looked in the eyes, with no prettying over. The decline and withering of the nobility grieves me. With the demise of the nobility there perishes much of the old beauty and nobleness. Russian literature was created chiefly by the nobility. With the coming of the third estate as a replacement, much that is unpretty, coarse, ignoble, cynically grasping, and indeed quite imprudent, will pour forth in the first waves. And it seems to me, that the soul of Russia will never be captivated by the bourgeois ideals of life. Russia ought not to go the bourgeois path.

But there is a consolation in this, that what is fine and precious in the nobility's emotional tone -- the nobleman's sense of honour and noble magnanimity will become traits of humanity in general, will pass over into other social groups. The third estate is emerging upon the historical scene for Russia. It is necessary to admit and accept this, even if this be unpleasant for us. But to the third estate cannot be granted an unlimited dominance. It is impossible to cede Russia to the industrialists. Their dominance is dangerous. The self-serving interests of the industrialists class has to be held in check by the power of truth which is beyond class and which is national in common. We already well know, that the third estate -- is not the people. Russian liberalism ought not to be a bourgeois class matter -- behind it stands not only the class of the industrialists, but likewise that of Russian agriculture and the Russian intelligentsia. The agricultural land aspect -- represents a grain of seed in its own unique societal effort and unique governance. We can accept and admit the role of the third estate only in the measure of coinciding in its interests with the national interests. The industrial class ought to be merely one of the active forces, and ought to be held in check by the other forces. And the determining force always remains the unique soul of the Russian people, possessing its own special fate.

IV.

The industrialisation of Russia, its troublesome transition to an industrial capitalism signifies not only the emergence onto the historical arena of the industrialists, but likewise also the emergence of the workers.

The growing significance of the third estate has as its flip side the growing significance of the fourth estate. In the industrial developement of Russia it is not only the capitalist-industrialists that have significance, but likewise first of all and most of all do the workers themselves. The position of the working class has to be culturally and economically raised. The worker has to be granted the possibility to organise, to defend his own interests and to hold in check the interests of the capitalists. It would be absurd to speak about the role of the industrialists for Russia and for the war while forgetting about the role of the workers. The working class has to become national a force both as regards its own awareness, and as regards its evaluation, which the other segments of society have to allow for it. Within the working class there ought to grow an all-national awareness and thus to get beyond the class exclusive consciousness. The working class has to have a sense of its own oneness with Russia, with the whole. And this presupposes a deep-rooted change of attitude on the part of the ruling authority and the other classes of society. In the economic class struggle between workers and capitalists there ought not to occur a state monopoly for the capitalists.

  The state is obligated to defend the interests of labour and bring this into connection with a defense of the interests of the industrial developement of the country, of the industrial developement, rather than of the industrialists. The developement of industrial capitalism in Russia is inevitable, but the Russian industrial capitalism will not be a copy of the Western European sort. There will occur a parallel state and municipal socialisation of the economy. And the struggle of classes can be mitigated and subsumed to national values of the people in common. The exclusive dominance within the state of the interests of the industrial capitalists tends to push the working class onto the path of class struggle, disrupting the unity of the nation. And it would be hypocritical to blame the workers for this. Both the third estate, and the fourth estate play a positive historical role to the extent of subsuming their interests to the national interests of the people in general, to the extent of surmounting interests in the name of values. Besides classes and estates, besides social groups, there exists still and first of all Russia itself, as one entity, as a mystical reality, whereof exists the Russian people, the nation. Near and dear to us is Russia, the Russian people, and not these or some other classes, and it is for this that we seek to work. And from a beyond-class national perspective, we see that the third estate is coming to power in Russia, but this movement will find itself delimited within the ideal uniqueness of the Russian people and in the growing power and significance of the fourth estate, which has to find itself a defender in the beyond-class and beyond-estate state, in the national and social state, brought into conformity with the spirit of the Russian earth, and in organised a societal effort.

On the Conditional Aspect of Vital Values

(1915 -213)[1]

I.

All the perspectives on life are limited, all are oriented towards the relative and the conditional, and cannot make pretense to fullness and finality. Life can be oriented upon whatever the value -- upon the value of the state, the economy, morals, knowledge or art. All these orientations possess however a significance pragmatic, and not absolute. An exclusive orientation upon whatever the value creates as it were its own particular sort of activity. For someone whose basic point of view has been placed in the value of the state, the world facing him is different, than for one, whose basic point of view has been placed upon the moral or the aesthetic. A man sees activity involving this or some other matter, dependent upon whatever the value he has taken as basic to his orientation and upon which perspective he has become the more involved. A total activeness is something no one is able of, for a total activeness does not exist, since the activeness is not only a given, but likewise rather it is created. From whatever the point of view and whatever the value, taken as the basic criterion, it is possible to derive from the activity a certain inexhaustible quantity of justified facts. Each has for itself its own validity and the validity is entirely factual. For a pessimistic outlook on Russia suchlike a number of facts are offered, just like for optimistic an outlook. Amidst a certain orientation and amidst certain values, perceived as a derivative point of view, Russia can seem in view a speck of dust, unstirred in feeling by any sort of a singular soul, and for suchlike a representation, certainly, they offer no few number of facts by way of validation. But for one, with different an orientation on life and who beyond the initial aspects strives for deeper values, Russia remains a living organism, and the singular soul of Russia has not gone dead through the very frightful facts pointing towards disintegration and ruin. It is important to admit, that there exists a

---

[1] OB USLOVNOSTI ZHZNENNYKH OTSENOK. Article was originally published in newspaper "Birzhevye vedomosti", 12 nov. 1915, № 15206.

gradation of values, which can be adopted for orientation in the infinite and crushing complexity of life. Such an orientation defends a man from the total endlessness surrounding him on all sides, from the crush of its entanglement. But a man easily forgets the conditional and relative aspects of his orientation and falls into captivity to his particular point of view. Thus, one and the same thing helps him choose his way through the world actuality, and yet also hinders him. And it mustneeds be admitted, that in various eras various values tend to come to the fore.

II.

At the present historical hour in Russia, life essentially and necessarily has become oriented upon the value of nationality, since it has had to become rendered conscious and affirmed. All the energy of our spirit hence has to be directed upon a national self-determination and a national self-preservation. Such a directing of our spirit is prompted by a precipitous historical necessity, the verymost important tasks of the moment. We live in a period of intense work with the national problem. But false is that attitude towards life, which admits of the value of nationality as the sole and supreme one. There exist still higher values. P. B. Struve, for example, seeks to orientate life upon an assertion of the value of the state and the exclusiveness in his point of view creates not altogether accurate perspectives. The state is personified and made absolute, transformed into a being, totally independent of man and the people. The state represents a certain value, but not the highest, not the sole value, and it ought to be subordinated to other values. And thus, nationality already -- is a value deeper, than one's state. Germany conceived of its national unity earlier, than that of its state. The nation, the people stand beyond the state and preceed it. The nation -- is a substance. The state -- its function. The German people conceived of their national unity within the values of a spiritual culture. And only in the second half of the XIX and early XX Centuries did the German people begin exclusively to become oriented upon the might of the state. This exclusive orientation of the might of the state has led moreso to a moral and spiritual downfall of the German people, rather than to its upsurge and regeneration. History teaches us, that a fixed orientation upon the state is relative, just like every other orientation. In Russia at present the exceptional reliance upon the state aspect is but a struggle against anarchistic instincts within the Russian people. But in other eras and with other peoples the totality of life is perceived differently. In the XV Century at Florence the singular and highest values centred around art, painting, and upon it was oriented the whole of life. And in this was a great truth, and it created a great flourishing of culture, in one of the most creative eras of history.

III.

A conditional orientation upon whatever the chosen and fixated value is quite necessary, so that man should not get lost within the infinite complexity and entangling thicket of being. But it is always proper to remember, that such an orientation has merely a pragmatic significance, it is relative, and not absolute. A pragmatic simplification of reality can prove a source of slavery of the spirit. Spirit ought first of all to preserve its own inner freedom and be aware, that all orientations are posited by it itself. In actuality, however, spirit all to often becomes stifled by the orientation of whatever the value. Man is readily rendered a slave of that which for him represents urgent a need, a slave to the state as needful for him or the economic aspect as needful for him. Everyone knows this from personal experience. And now too this is well known to all from the collective experience of the war. The war pushes the necessity of new orientations and the acknowledging of new values. The war quite enriches our souls in something. But it is improper to fall into falsely sweet an optimism. The war is quite twofold in its results, and it bears with it for our spirit not only certain positive values. The tasks and interests of the war tend to narrow the awareness and evoke pragmatically necessary a limitedness. Upon this basis is possible also a quenching of the spirit, a weakening of the impulse to cultural creativity. The world war, having gotten too entangled, includes within it the danger of a partial barbarisation of Europe. Life has been cast down to elemental a level. We have at present an awareness of elementary questions of economic and civil arrangements. The orientation of life upon economics, the exclusive absorption with questions on supplying provisions, in the final end, can lead to emotional a grip of panic. If such a situation continues for prolonged a period, then this cannot but reinforce a weakening of cultural creativity. The elemental necessities too much supplant all the exuberance of spiritual life, all the subtle and complex surfeit. A condition of defense can evoke an enormous spiritual upsurge, but this condition is spiritually at element a level, narrowing the scope of life. A prolonged dwelling in a condition of extreme defense bears with it the danger of a narrowing of spiritual life and having it recede into the elementary, if there be not affirmed a certain freedom of the spirit, inwardly possible amidst every condition of the external world.

    Freedom of the spirit is the dearest thing of all, it has to stand behind everything. And even the exclusive assertion of the value of nationality or the state has to be born of freedom of the spirit. A pragmatic orientation upon whatever the value ought not to be transformed into a mania-like obsession. Let my spirit be a creator of the value of nationality, and not a slave to it. With the nationalists however, the assertion of the value of nationality becomes readily transformed into an obsession: they are in slavery to so exclusively affirmed a value of nationality and in its name they become quenchers of the spirit. No sort of orientation upon this or some other value can make pretense to being absolute, since absoluteness can only be in spirit, in its fullness. Everything imposed however upon spirit from without -- is conditional and relative. In the external world there cannot nor should there be idols. Every value is first of all spiritual life and its objectification on the outside ought not to be directed against the spiritual life, upon that begetting it. The value of nationality or of the state is likewise spiritual life. And every form of national or state idolatry is a sin against the spirit. Everything, being said here, presupposes a relationship towards life inwardly, and not on the outside. The human spirit discovers freedom, when he senses the whole of life as justified from its depths. The he cannot be a slave to the state aspect, but rather can only be its creator, since he cannot be the slave to anything in opposition to him inwardly.

    The point of view on life by the statists, the church folk, the nationalists, the socialists and many others too often becomes a slavery of spirit, a slave-like determinism to external idols, all-devouring idols. From this spiritual slavery let us be free. Let us asset, be it nationality, the state or the economy, or any value needful for us, let us assert such in an atmosphere of spiritual freedom, inwardly breathing freely. Only then will our national and state orientation on life in the present hour of history not quench nor impair the spiritual life. Then also it will not extinguish the higher values of religious contemplation, knowledge, artistic creativity. Even though we undergo grievous tribulations, in not lowering our spiritual level.

The Immediate Task at Hand

(1915 -214)[1]

I.

The non-acceptance of a deputation from the rural and urban union associations has brought to a close a certain period of the liberal societal movement. This movement was distinguished by a great restraint and unity, it was pervaded by a genuine patriotism and had worked out a fine plan. But this plan was not crowned with success. The reforming of the ruling authorities, upon which this movement reckoned, did not occur. The progressive bloc, which was a parliamentary expression of this movement, already at present does not possess the significance, which it had still not long ago. This -- was a formation of the historical moment, and hence it cannot possess stability and can always be replaced by another grouping. At present, we are experiencing an intermediate condition and no sort of new plan or new methods have yet been worked out. But our basic goal remains firm and resolute -- the defense of our native land, victory over the enemy. And here, from the point of view of this basic goal it is clear, that the societal elements, united within the progressive bloc, in the rural and urban associative unions, have underestimated the significance of the masses of the people, first of all the workers, in the defense of the country and in the societal movement. Without "the people" there cannot indeed happen any sort of historical movement, and if it not be drawn towards the national issue in a positive and conscious form, then it can but play an unconscious and negative role. Recently to be noted has been a certain movement among the workers, in connection with drawing them into the military-industrial committees. The workers are beginning to think over the historical events of an exceptional world importance and are attempting to emerge from the vise-jaws grip of doctrinal Social Democrat categories. And evidently, even the socialistic minded workers are pervaded with

---

[1] OCHEREDNAYA ZADACHA. Article was originally published in newspaper "Birzhevye vedomosti", 17 nov. 1915, № 15216.

national a feeling and want to defend their native land. The "defeatist" psychology -- is the psychology of slaves, who from their own lack of strength have no desire to win for themself their freedom and welfare, and hence dream of receiving such as a charity gift from the enemy of the native land. This -- is depraved a psychology, the self-feelings of the reprobate, for whom nothing gets determined from within, and everything -- is from the outside, and who negotiate with the native land and are ready to defend it only for a price.

To love Russia and be ready to defend it can only be unmercenary a thing, only but seeing in it one's own great value, and not because that it brings rewards and improved a position. And essentially important for the fate of Russia is a national education and societal organisation of the masses of the people. The education and organisation also has to be resolutely against demagoguery and agitation.

II.

Russia is experiencing an unprecedentedly tragic position: it has to decide its own fate whilst under a vise-jaws pressure, squeezed from two sides almost to choking. Never yet has there been conjoined such a terrible outward danger with such a terrible inward position. The danger of chaos and anarchy threatens Russia, if it should fail to gather the people's energy and fail to consolidate the people's awareness for an organised struggle against the ensuing darkness and collapse. To prevent anarchy ensuing in the life of the people there is needed an organising of the masses of the people who, in the opposite instance, could wind up in elementally chaotic a condition. The disorganisation of economic life, high prices, an insufficiency of provisional necessities might assume such forms, as to cause the threat of uprisings by the people. To avert this can only be through an organising of the people and the people's conscious participation within societal life. Not only as so-called "society", but also as "the people", there should be an appeal to a national defense of the land and for an active struggle against the disorganisation of economic life. Without organisation, self-disciple and self-initiative the people of Russia cannot escape the terrors. It can only be in an instance where the workers, the labouring population of Russia, itself participate in creating the inward and outward fate of Russia and share in the healing of its ulcerous ills, imposing upon itself the responsibility for Russia whilst getting beyond the condition of irresponsible opposition and the tendency towards anarchistic revolt. It is both dangerous and harmful to leave an enormous segment of the Russian people outside of all active participation in the fate of their native land.

It is essentially needful, for the fate of Russia, that both the workers and the peasants should be consciously patriotic and inspired towards service with the national idea. But this is possible only in an instance, where the workers and peasants sense themself as co-participants and creators of national life, actual sons, and not mere step-sons in their native land. The privileged segments of society have organised themself in mighty rural and urban unions and have imposed upon themself a great responsibility. But it is impossible to leave a large part of the people in irresponsible a position. Broader segments of the Russian people should be pulled into responsibility for their native land. Dwelling in an irresponsible and disenfranchised a position invites the threat of chaotic happenings and anarchistic outbursts. Those privileged segments of Russian society have to realise this, those who have already received the right to organise with the right take upon themself responsibility. The people has to find its own way towards organisation, its own methods of struggle against social chaos, the methods of providing form to matter in the life of the people. In the cooperatives there exist already the rudiments of such organisations. But the path for the people's energy has to be widened and its sharing in national life deepened. And what is most important, contact has to be made between our national liberal movement and the movement of the people.

But it is of essential importance, as to what sort of spirit will inspire the organisation of the people, the working class, which has to be called to a great national involvement, has to receive national an educating, which now hastily is given by historical events. The positive historical role, which the working class in Russia can play, is directly proportional to their awareness of the truism, that the whole stands higher than the parts, the nation higher than class, objective historical values higher than private and class instincts. And in essence they tend to call for this, in spite of their doctrines, including the most reasonable of the Social Democrats, as for example, G. V. Plekhanov. The Social Democrats, as alive Russian people, can prove themself as higher than their mere doctrines. A purely Social Democratic educating of the masses is very undesirable, since it tacks on the poison of class hatred, an exclusively materialistic view on life, and denies the value of national unity. But even a socialist workers movement is possible upon different a spiritual grounding, along with speaking about involving the workers in the matter of national defense. And it is certainly not for us to merely copy the German workers movement. A better form appears to be the English movement, which also is more business-like, practical, and of more spiritual and idealistic a mindset. An idealistic educating of the masses, involving them with spiritual values is both possible and desirable. An healthy state of soul in the Russian people is dependent upon this, whether spirit wins out over matter in the consciousness of the masses of the people, whether the religious attitude towards life -- wins out over atheistic an attitude. A disunitive materiality is always indeed an impairment. Health can be sought only in a co-unitive spirituality. When the industrialists, nowise wanting to curtail their interests in the name of their country, in turn then call the workers to patriotism and sacrifice, -- this is a manifestation shameful and of hypocrisy. There cannot and ought not to be a national unity gained at the expense of the workers. But a patriotic self-limitation is possible for the working class, just as it is possible for every Russian man. This presupposes a moral regeneration of the person, independent of his class position. It is not a matter of speaking about a falsified unity of workers and industrialists, but first of all about the consciousness of the workers own unity with Russia, with the national fate. The workers, certainly, are obliged to defend themself from exploitation from the industrialists. But this struggle can transpire within an awareness of the unity of Russia and in a subordination to the whole.

The fate of the societal effort is always dependent upon the quality of the societal cell, and this means, that behind the societal aspect always stands the person, his fitness, his quality. This spiritual selection of personal qualities bears into societal life a principle of the aristocratic-qualitative in opposition to everything merely of the quantitatively mechanical. And it is very important that this be realised, that this aristocratic-personal principle has nothing in common with the aristocratic class or estate. In the working class there is fully possible an awareness of the inevitability of such an aristocratism of personal qualities and its inclusion in connection with this truism for all the practical societal orientation. The prevailing dominance of the Marxist point of view of the mechanism of the quantitative adheres to the baneful illusion, that from poor and unfit elements it is possible to create a fine and vitally fit societal form. But to this false mechanism there has to be opposed a spiritual educating, always oriented upon the person.

III.

If in general a private propertied capitalist economy bears within it the eternal danger of economic anarchy, then this danger during wartime reaches extreme a degree. The peoples, caught up in the worldwide conflict, have to make enormous efforts, to avert disorganisation and chaos in their economic life. The war heightens to the verymost extreme the quite most elemental problems of human existence and in catastrophic a manner evokes the awareness, that supplying the people their daily bread depends upon the chaotic playing out of private interests, based upon interests of greed and plunder. The terrors of the war, facing a man with the prospect of personal perishing and death, ought to evoke unique a sense of brotherhood, a brotherhood in misfortune.

And I think, that the measures of socialisation, directed towards regulation of economic chaos and anarchy, ought to reflect a character national-civil and rural-municipal, rather than of class greed. A bare-faced struggle of classes and class interests, not held in check by any sort of higher idea, at present can only but increase the chaos and anarchy. And I want to believe, that the tragic experience of the war provides points of view towards the developing of Russia along directions national-social, in a spirit of social idealism. Without this spirit, Russia will become divided into parts. An authentic, a non-false, and not merely momentary unity is possible only upon grounds spiritual, and not material. And at the basis of social creativity, in the final end, lies spirit, and not matter, and the material is but an implement of spirit. Submersion into the element of materiality tears apart and disunites people, dissipates society into atoms. And it burdens man beneath the pressure of the exclusive prevalence of material interests. Here is why the Marxist conception of the unity of the proletariat upon the basis of material interests is totally extraneous and fictitious, it crumbles under the slightest puff. Without a moral, i.e. a spiritual unity, Marxism also cannot proceed. But Marxism allows for this moral-spiritual principle only as a sort of contraband and in a limited sphere. All the reasonable Social Democrats, evidently, have in mind this thought, that the working class ought to participate in the defense of the country, in that the national movement ought to be considered by the socialist movement. But it is very important, that this awareness be not merely a simple tactical calculation, that behind it there should stand the emotional perception of the self-worth of nationality and the moral unity of the nation in facing the world. And for this the working class has to be situated within a different psychical atmosphere, than that, in which it now stands and which can but further nurture the boycott and defeatist outlooks.

If the liberal, the so-called "bourgeois" elements of society ignore the masses of the people and contemptuously seek to shove them aside, then by so doing they will push Russia onto the path of anarchy. The masses of the Russian people in a most threatening hour of Russian history cannot be left remaining in formless and passive a condition. And our liberal societal movement in the name of Russia, in the name of patriotism is committed to a certain self-limitation and to unity with the people, which it would be criminal to refuse. The sharing of all the entire people in the matter of the salvation of Russia is important not only from the point of view of the interests of democracy, but first of all from the national point of view, from the perspective of the fate of Russia. The people, the nation is something broader and higher than democracy. The unification of the wide segments of Russian society and the Russian people is possible only upon the basis of a national feeling and national awareness amongst all the people. Abstract democratic and abstract socialistic principles are quite unsuitable for the accomplishing of the great historical tasks of the given moment and have to be spiritually surmounted. That power, which we have been wont to term "democracy", ought ultimately to play a large role in the fate of Russia. But this role cannot be realised upon the basis of democratic doctrinalism. There has to be an orientation towards the people upon a different spirit, which in the fundamentals of life has in view the concrete person and the concrete nation. The fate of Russia is the fate of a self-delimiting, self-disciplined and self-directing Russian people, inwardly determining its history. Russia from the outside can seem a mechanism, which is directed by a power foreign to us. Yet Russia from the inside -- is a living spirit, creative of life. And the conscious organisation of the masses of the people ought to be the organising of this living spirit, rather than that of a mechanism of interests.

Spirit and Economics

(1915 -215)[1]

I.

Interest and commotions this present Winter tend to centre round the issue of the food provisions question. We live under a crushing fear of a food provisions crisis. The provisions matter at present is of greater an interest, than the war. Firewood, sugar and flour are being talked about more, than shellings, attacks and wounds. With the provisions question is connected the problems at the rear, since the disorganisation of economic life and the outlooks, connected with it, tend to weaken the military might of the land. In the past year much has been said, written and argued about the meaning of the war. During this year has happened a lowering of the level of our interests. From thoughts about the meaning of what is occurring in life we have turned instead to thoughts about satisfying the elementary necessities of life. And upon this basis there is readily created a gloomy outlook. When it became known, that there was a shortage of military shells and that the danger from the oncoming enemy had become threatening, in society there appeared an emotional upsurge, and a societal effort began. But when it became known, that our economic life was becoming disordered and that we were threatened with all kinds of provisional crises, in society there appeared no upsurge, there began instead a gloominess and tendency towards panic. But every sort of societal impulse is possible only within an atmosphere of an emotional upsurge, it always takes its course within a psychical medium and presupposes an emotional energy. Depression cannot beget anything fine. In an atmosphere of emotional depression there cannot occur any sort of impetus. And we have now a beginning amongst us of suchlike a depression and against it is needed the waging of an heroic struggle. The outward and the inward fate of Russia, all its mightiness is dependent upon this, whether the emotional

---

[1] DUKH I EKONOMIKA. Article was originally published in newspaper "Birzhevye vedomosti", 27 nov. 1915, № 15235.

upsurge overcomes the emotional depression. The resolving of the fate of Russia in matters of the war and in matters of the internal order presupposes first of all a discipline of spirit. And it is here namely that there is the great problem.

The danger on the part of the Germans has evoked a feeling of national unity. In facing the enemy we have sensed ourself belonging to an unified Russia. Granted that this has been experienced only at occasional moments, but preciously and remarkably it has been experienced. The danger on the part of economic disorganisation and provisional needs evokes moreso an acute sense of disunited interests, of class antagonisms, than it does of national oneness. Class greed, the thirst for profit, speculation and corruption are rampant. There is the feeling, as never before, that in the national afflictions befalling us the poor and the rich are not comrades, not brothers in misfortune. An insufficiency of military shells provided a feeling of national brotherhood. An insufficiency of firewood, regretably, evokes non-brotherly a feeling, a disuniting condition among people. Hunger and cold are directly terrible only for the poor, whereas for the rich they are terrible only indirectly. [...] Economic disorganisation, the provisional needs during wartime should demand of the rich and well-off classes of the population an heightened moral level, the capacity for sacrifice and self-limitation in the name of the Rodina [Birth-Land], in the name of that patriotism, which is proclaimed in words.

One of the chieftains of German imperialism, Rohrbach [Paul, 1869-1956], writes: "The question concerning victory for us is a question of our moral national strengths, a question regarding this, how capable for sacrifice towards sustaining the labouring part of the people are those possessing classes, who are in a condition to spare from themself something even then, when the wages of the workers will all less and less satisfy its needs... Germany only then can lose this war, if its rich and its well-off citizens, in general all those, the revenues or wages of which are secure, if they happen to say: the sacrifices for the support of the unemployed, i.e. for the support of the Fatherland, has become for us too much a burden" ("The War and German Politics" [1914]). The problem as posited by Rohrbach exists also for Russia, though in less acute a form, since the war has not worsened, but instead improved the condition of the peasantry. But Rohrbach justly posits the fate of the war as dependent upon the moral and spiritual condition of society. We see however, that at present provisional needs weigh down upon our human spirit, like an heavy material mass. The consciousness becomes fixated upon economics and becomes burdensome, enslaving: the provisional crisis is experienced not as a national danger, but rather as a danger facing each person and class. An heightened experiencing of a danger uplifts a man. An heightened experiencing of personal and class danger spiritually lowers a man and readily leads to outlooks of a panicked terror. And to further aggravate the awareness over provisional needs could tend towards the criminal in this non-spiritual and demeaning direction.

II.

The danger on the part of the enemy has been experienced by us moreso, than as a provisions danger. But both towards economics, and towards the provisions issue there ought not to be exclusively an external, materialistic, slave-like dependent an attitude. Material concerns ought not to swallow up the human soul. The acute need of supplying provisions ought to be considered and resolved the best way possible by everyone involved in the management of economic means. But it is impossible to detach these questions off from the spiritual life, from culture and from the discipline of our people's and our own personal will. At a greater depth in meaning, economics also is a manifestation of spirit. Behind the processes of production, distribution and needs there stands the energy of the person, the selection of human qualities. It is only the character of discipline of the person and of the people that renders impossible emotional depression and the resulting on this basis of a consequent panic. And alongside with economic and political measures of struggle against economic disorganisation are needed measures moral and spiritual. It is needful here to create an atmosphere of an emotional uplift and emotional discipline, without which is possible only the onset of chaos and discord.

If beyond economic organisation there stands not an organisation of spiritual energy, then the whole of economic life is rendered but a chaotic material thing. We are living through a time, when there is readily possible a falling into slavery to one's own provisional needs. The concentrating upon provisional needs ought not itself to be accompanied by a spiritual dwelling upon it and independence from everything outward. Otherwise we are rendered slaves. In the vital connection of spirit and economics the preponderance ought to belong to spirit, and economics ought to be perceived only as a function imposed by spirit at a certain moment of its life. Economic life then also will be disciplined and organised. Sustaining the character of the person and the people preceeds every societal objectification. Only an orientation in the depths of one's own spirit makes of us free creators of a new societal effort. It is necessary with all one's powers to oppose all the demagoguery both from the right and from the left, every contrived uproar, every sowing of malice. Provisional needs cannot and ought not to be a cause for agitation -- of itself it serves no purpose. There are limits at present for a possible regulating of the economic needs, and these limits have to be perceived by the masses of the people itself. And for this, there is necessary a drawing of the masses of the people into an active participation in dealing with the struggle against economic disorganisation and provisional wants. Only a concentrated sharing in the societal effort can impose a sense of responsibility and avoid anarchistic tendencies. There is needed also a readiness to educate the individual person, as well as entire societal strata, for self-discipline, for sacrifice and for patience. [...] To spiritually undergo economic needs and crises -- means to undergo them freely. Contrived uproars over provisional needs with the aim of agitations is indeed always directed towards those, who do not sense themself as free citizens, not as sons but as slaves rather, mere step-sons. But a free citizenship and sonship is not only an external position within society, this -- is likewise also an inner spiritual condition, and an inner self-awareness. And from this it is necessary to take a start.

III.

Our basic ulcerous flaws -- are the flaws first of all in the character of the people: the weakness of the Russian will, the non-discipline, the weak capacity for organisation, a certain wont towards hysteria, a lack of self-restraint. Economic life however involves an objectified discipline of the will. Its qualities are dependent upon the qualities of the human material, concealed behind every societal aspect. Economic chaos is a chaos of the human spirit. To posit everything upon purely external conditions is a materialistic slavery or a demagogic contrivance. To render healthy our societal effort there mustneeds be restored the true relationship between spiritual life and economic life, i.e. to subordinate economic life to a tempering of spirit. Only then will the provisional needs, caused by the war, be experienced with a national worthiness. The national tribulation of the provisional crisis during wartime is totally a matter involving spiritual discipline, a moral capacity for self-limitation. The problem nowise consists in this, whether to choose an inner, a spiritual, a moral path of life, or a path external, material, political and economic. Such an opposition nowise exists, such a question cannot arise. An opposition between the spiritual-moral and the societal-political points of view is to an utmost degree superficial. Everything outward is rooted in the inward, everything material is but an expression of the spiritual. Spiritual energy inevitably becomes objectified and expressed on the outside, it creates the societal aspect. And no sort of societal aspect, no sort of economic aspect is possible without certain spiritual-moral presuppositions. Even purely class politics presupposes a certain discipline of spirit, a moral tempering, without which every class would be transformed into a speck of dust, of sand. It is impossible to expect, from purely external societal-economic changes, a rebirth of Russia, of Russian society and Russian man. Every change in the societal medium presupposes a spiritual stirring, a creative tension, changes in the motives of human activity. And the problem, facing us, consists not in this, whether to make a choice between an outer or an inner path, but rather in this, that societal activity be enlightened from within, inwardly inspired, whereby a people reborn creates a new societal aspect. Economics is a creation by the spirit. And a disintegrating economics is a manifestation of a disintegrating of spirit. The provisions crisis for us is likewise a crisis moral. We morally have to undergo the matter of provisional wants, and spiritually enlighten it. It is impossible to strongly enough emphasise, that only a religious experiencing of life is free. Every other, every other non-religious experiencing of life is slavery to natural and social matter and it cannot lead to renewal.

Concerning the Spirit of Despondency

(1915 - xxx)[1]

During Great Lent we pray the Prayer of St. Ephrem the Syrian,[2] -- that the Lord grant us not the spirit of despondency, of despair. In Christianity despair has always been considered a great sin. People that are non-believers, the positivists and materialists, often think, that despair is an objective condition, is connected with some unsightly activity, a scrupulous admitting of it without any prettying or idealisation. This -- is a self-deception and self-justification. A despondent apperception of life is

---

[1] O DUKHE UNYNIYA. Article originally published in weekly gazette "Birzhevye vedomosti", 28 nov. 1915, № 15237.

N.B. This is an article missed by the authoritative 1978 YMCA Press Tamara Klepinina Berdiaev Bibliographie.

[2] *trans. note* -- the Prayer of St. Ephrem the Syrian:

"O Lord and Master of my life! Grant not unto me the spirit of sloth,
of despondency, of lust for power, nor of vain chatter. (*Poklon*)
But bestow unto me, Thy servant, the spirit of chastity,
of humble sagacity, of patience and of love. (*Poklon*)
Yea, O Lord and King, grant me to perceive my own transgressions
and judge not my brother, for blessed art Thou unto ages of ages. Amen.
(*Poklon*)"

"Господи и Владыко живота моего, дух праздности,
уныния, любоначалия и празднословия не даждь ми. (*Поклон*)
Дух же целомудрия, смиренномудрия, терпения и любве
даруй ми, рабу Твоему. (*Поклон*)
Ей, Господи Царю, даруй ми зрети моя прегрешения
и не осуждати брата моего, яко благословен еси во веки веков. Аминь.
(*Поклон*)"

an indicator of a despondent spirit, of a lowered vitality, weakness and infirmity. One, to whom everything seems depressing, is himself depressed. And for one to whom everything in the world is a matter of despair, is he himself in despair, his soul is enveloped with darkness. Such is the truth, that the despondency of despair -- is within us, and not outside us, and that it -- is through our fault, as particularly discerned in perceptions and outlooks on the war. How infinitely varied are the impressions on the war! No two accounts come out the same. Each sees the war in his own way and tells about the war in his own way. And the most contrary accounts are simultaneously accurate. Accurate is much that is fine. Accurate is much that is bad. The war can be perceived, as a meaningless chaos, as purely an external series of frightful factours, in nothing enlightened. A man gets devastated by such a perception of the war and often in good conscience thinks, that his perception -- is the most objective and true. But this -- is a self-preoccupation of the weak and of those incapable of seeing the light. The ultimate truths are always discerned at the heightened, and not at the lessened perceptions, in the active perceptions, bearing meaning and light. For a spirit devastated in the mystery of life they become hidden -- they are discerned only in an upsurge of spirit. And I believe definitely, that only heroic natures know the genuine truth about the war. The war has to be perceived in creatively spiritual a manner. The perception itself of the war is a doing, an activeness of spirit. A perception of the war is a trial of strength of spirit. Every grey detail itself of the war says nothing about the war. For a manly, active, heroic spirit the war -- is otherwise, than it is for a weak, sickly, passive spirit. Even the dull routines of the war for other people can be experienced in an atmosphere of emotional uplift.

    I think, that the ideal attitude towards the war should be that of one, who is fearless in gazing into the eyes of actuality, who loves truth without embellishment or idealisation in dealing with the most murky facts, preserving boldness of spirit, the will to victory and faith in Russia. Not so long ago I heard an account about the war from an old acquaintance of mine, having come from the front for a few days in Moscow. In each word of this brave man, full of energy, was felt such an ideal and eager account towards the war. A former social democrat, disillusioned in the groundings of revolution, having experienced a religious crisis and having arrived at an apocalyptic religiosity, he formed heroic an outlook and is applying his technical knowledge to the military effort. Many accounts given by my acquaintance produced an impression of a picture right out of Dante's Inferno. He is nowise inclined to idealisations or embellishments. He well sees all the deficiencies, all our material and moral defects. Yet all the same his outlook is courageous, positive, believing, he sees a profound meaning in everything happening. The accounts from such a man tend to uplift, and not depress. A youth, who heard these accounts, exclaimed: "Now it would not be so frightful for me to go to war". And indeed, what was told had much in it that was frightful, much that was bad. But everything consisted in this, in what emotional atmosphere this was told. An inwardly enlightened approach towards the terrors of life leads to an uplift, to a surmounting of all the despondency. Only in too unenlightened a yielding of oneself to the terrors is there a plunging into the darkness. It is necessary to love the truth and to look directly at all the terrors of the war and all our defects. But despondency is something we ourself insert into the perception of life, and not something we receive from life. The despair is always our sin, our self-sufferance towards it. And insofar as despondency exists for us in the rear, it is to our disgrace. In the army, judging from all accounts, there is no despondency.

There is a faith in the Russian people and in Russia, which surmounts all the most distressing facts about Russia. This -- is a faith in the soul of Russia, in its great potentials, in its great destiny in the world. Such a faith has no need of self-deceptions and is not afraid of self-criticisms. The faith has to be fearless. Fear is always bound up with non-belief. Only one, who believes in himself, in his people, in his deed, is afraid of nothing. It is impossible to defeat the spirit of despondency by closing one's eyes to actuality. We need to exert a struggle against the servile spirit of despondency. The despondency -- is from within us, and a terrible culpability lays upon those, who exhale the magical vapours of despair and by this poison the atmosphere. It is as though up to each citizen in this regard to attend to himself to inspire within himself a sense of responsibility for his own emotional state. Totally irresponsible and apathetic emotional an outlook is unbecoming for Russia. What transpires within the soul of the individual man transpires also in the soul of the people. Each exhales from himself vapours either positive or negative, bright or dark. Emotional oppressedness, heightened pessimism, lack of faith and hopelessness tend to poison the soul of the people. Having despair in the atmosphere, is in the objective world a matter of having us ourself giving rise to the spirits of darkness. And then they come back to us anew. And we meet again with a spirit of despondency, attached to us in the objective actuality. This self-deception process has to be dispelled via a bright self-awareness. And we shall then perceive the despondency, merely as an objectification of our own particular weakness and incapacity. The war has to engender within us a new type of attitude towards life -- fearless, truth-loving and heroically enlightened. Grant it that no sort of darkness have the power to overshadow the light emitted from us. And that we shall again the yet oftener repeat the words of the Prayer of St. Ephrem the Syrian.

Are the Rightists Nationalists?

(1915 - 216)[1]

It is difficult to reconcile oneself with the thought, that there exist people, who learn nothing from the experience of life, from the grievous trials of life, who are capable of no sort of echoing historical life. And to such a breed of people, indisputably, belong our extreme rightists. The session of the rightists in this regard is very instructive. It is almost terrible to be a Russian man, when being served speeches, in which there sounds not a single human word -- not a living and honest word. In the given instance what interests me is not the political side of the matter, the possible backroom political intrigues, hidden behind the departures of rightist resigned officials etc., what interests me first of all is the moral and psychological side of the phenomenon. Our extreme rightists -- are an amazing moral-psychological phenomenon, deserving of some attention. This -- is a phenomenon of such an extraordinary mental, moral and in general emotional squalour, of such an aesthetic ugliness, as brings to mind a serious illness in the organism of the people, in spewing such filth. I long ago already have come to the opinion, that in Russia there is no genuine conservatism, and that this -- is a sick manifestation within Russian life. And indeed it mustneeds be admitted, that conservatism can be profoundly grounded in idea, sharp-minded and morally fine in form, and that in conservatism there can be its own aesthetic. We have had solitary, far off the beaten track of life, original thinkers, who could be termed conservative though perhaps but in their negative attitude towards what is considered progressive. But we have never had a conservatism, as a societal phenomenon, in a form morally and aesthetically presentable and mentally imposing. Our societal sense in the right is appalling by its moral and mental dullness. At its root -- is some sort of a Russian non-being, an inertia, an hysterical weakness. The loud shouting and raging of the rightists is not a sign of strength, it is a sign of weakness, an hysterical lack of strength. An incapacity towards learning from the life experience and an

---

[1] NATSIONAL'NY LI PRAVYE? Article was originally published in newspaper "Birzhevye vedomosti", 1 dec. 1915, № 15240.

incapacity for an healthy readjustment in life -- are characteristic peculiarities of the rightist circles.

We have had dished out to us the words, distributed at the session of the rightists in an hour of grievous historical tribulations for our native land. Yet in these words it is impossible to discern any signs of independent thought and moral will. This -- was an occasion with vicious outcries for general vengeance, which once were connected with some sort of ideas, but now already are connected with nothing. Is it possible to feel in the words of the rightists a faith in Russia, and its great vocation in the world? Have they made an attempt to think about the calling of Russia at this moment in the worldwide conflict, when the world fate of Russia is to be decided? It is all too clear, that for the rightists Russia does not exist as a single organism, as a mystical reality, foreordained to the accomplishing of whatever its deed in the world. The rightists are situated totally outside the process of a national self-consciousness. They are immersed in their own trivial doings and petty affairs, vile accountings, inner disputes and sniping. Within the considerations of the rightists there enter in no assertions of the oneness of Russia, the oneness of all the Russian people. The terrible war, the danger being experienced by our native land, has not changed their psychology, has impelled them to cede nothing, to sacrifice nothing. The progressive Russian societal effort has compromised and sacrificed much in the name of the oneness of Russia in facing the enemy, in the name of the national idea, in the name of victory. In the camp of the rightists nothing has happened, everything has remained the same old way. The spiteful will to discord and persecuting prevails as formerly. The rightists are gripped most of all by a malicious hatred towards the progressive bloc, towards the rural and urban associations, towards the intelligentsia and others. Russia and its fate is of very little interest to them. They have no strenuous will to victory, as a chief and basic task. For them the most important thing is the victory over an inner enemy, rather than the external enemy. The rightists have no sort of a world perspective, they possess no sort of positive aims.

When our fatherland is in peril, they remain completely immersed in their trivial spite and totally negative inner politics, i.e. they do the same thing that they usually reproach the leftists of. A conscious self-limitation in the inner political struggle in the name of the defense of our native land, in the name of national unity cannot be only the affair of the leftists -- it is in no less a degree a duty likewise for the rightists. But do they indeed fulfill this duty? The rightists go instead the reverse path -- for them the national duty and national idea do not exist. Totally foreign to the rightists is the awareness, that the national idea stands higher than the political idea, that the nation stands higher and goes deeper than all the transitory state-political forms. The verbal bombast of the rightists is all full of the same lies, the falsification of the people's opinion, the same vile negativity, to which we are quite accustomed. What is strikingly sick is the absence of historical responsibility, of an awareness of the noteworthy and important events happening in the world. I think, that the rightist camp is totally bereft of a national awareness, although not free of dark national instincts. The national-Russian phraseology of the rightists is completely conditional a lie. These people -- are not Russians first of all, as they might by feeling within themself the pulsing of life of the soul of the Russian people, rather they are first of all "rightists", i.e. people of certain interests, of certain political parties, of certain conditions, upon which they agree to serve Russia. Too great an over-estimation of certain state forms and a certain political course is already a sort of treason to the Russian national issue and as such is situated in an antagonism towards the spirit of the Russian people. The rightists esteem not Russia, but rather a certain political course desired by them and in the name of the triumph of this course they are ready to go against the interests of Russia. The rightists are totally immersed in an outward politicking, in the struggle of parties, and in this they are foreign to the Russian spirit, such as is directed inwards, acknowledging the value of the soul as more lofty, than the value of kingdoms. And from whence comes this malice, this hatred, this violence and destructiveness, so characteristic to the extreme rightists, purporting themselves as the true Russians? Can it be that this is characteristic of the Russian people, the good, the non-malicious, the humble such? It is difficult to believe, that in the depths of the life of the Russian people there is such an hamishness. The extreme rightists take their support not on what exists in the life of the Russian people, but rather upon what reflects non-being in the life of the people, the darkness, the passivity, the inertia, the lack of will and strength. Such manifestations exist only by the great sufferance of the Russian people.

In any case, everything tends to impel a conclusion, that our extreme rightist circles stand outside the process of national thought, outside the national moral sense of responsibility, -- whereof they do not participate in the formation of a national consciousness and national aims.

These circles first of all, and it is impossible to stress this strongly enough, -- are anti-national in spirit, in direction, in condition of awareness. They do not desire the oneness of Russia. They learn nothing and have regard for nothing. The power of these circles is a sham, not genuine, but insofar as the remnants of such power exist, they represent a national danger for Russia.

The Evil Will and Reason of History

(1915 - 217)[1]

There is prevalent these days that particular perception of life, which sees the source of everything happening to be in the ill will of people and groups of people. And on this qualification of the will of people, as both bad and evil, it also cannot but be accompanied by a moral imputing. For many, this represents an inevitable phenomenon of nature. Thus, for example, the causes of the war arise from the evil will of the German people. The failures of the war happen exclusively through the evil will of people, albeit holding the ruling power. The food crisis and scarcity they ascribe exclusively to the evil will of this or that class. Often it happens to be heard, that there are inner disorders in our land, because of the role played by dishonest people, that the ruling authorities are wrecking the level of society. And organised good however has not the wherewithal to oppose all these evil wills. And thus are begotten pessimism and despair. There are no sort of real human hopes for an escape from a terrible position. All begins to seem but a chaotic meaninglessness. The world's life -- seems but a game of evil human passions, greed and misery. Russia -- a speck of dust, in which it is impossible to find anything of value or meaning. For such an attitude towards life the characteristic thing is not this, that the war is perceived as evil. The important thing becomes rather this, that there is denied every connection of the war with the deepest groundings of life for modern mankind, there is repudiated the symbolic meaning of the war, pointing to something inward in the life of mankind. The war becomes viewed totally as the result of the vile and base will of the governing classes. And the war thus is rendered an external evil, signifying nothing inward within the life of mankind.

But there is possible a different attitude towards life. It is possible to see the profound meaning of the world war, its deep groundings, as incommensurate with the evil will of governments or ruling classes. It is possible to see in everything external a symbol of the inward. The war is

---

[1] ZLAYA VOLYA I RAZUM ISTORII. Article was originally published in newspaper "Birzhevye vedomosti", 16 dec. 1915, № 15273.

occurring not only in the trenches -- it has its start within us and continues on in us, and everything happening at present on the surface of the earth is war. And everything most evil and dark within human life possesses an inner significance and meaning, everything symbolises something. By means of suchlike a deeper and more believing an approach, it becomes possible also to look at the inner life of various lands. In them, it is not only the evil will and madness that are active, but also the objective reason of history, and in everything happening it is possible to see an objective meaning. And many historical attainments are inevitable, despite the madness and evil will of people and human groups, on the strength of an objective rational necessity. The most mad and most evil of human passions cannot reduce Russia into a soul-less speck of disintegrating matter. There is the soul of Russia and there is a force of reason within Russian history, in Russian historical fate. Only a believing, spiritually enlightened attitude can perceive this soul and this reason. Within history act not only the human, but also supra-human powers. And the triumph of the dark powers cannot be lasting and final.

If one tends to see everywhere the evil will of people and classes, and then explain everything by this, this tends to lead to hostility and discord and obscures from our view the inner meaning of life. The most striking thing is this, that our traditional radically positivistic worldview denies the moral meaning of life and does not admit the existence of a metaphysical evil, yet on the surface level of societal and historical life it is inclined to explain everything in terms of the evil will of societal groups and separate individuals, holding power. But indeed the source of evil in our life lies quite deeper, at deeper an inner plane.

The evil does not consist in this only, that societal classes are greedy. It is necessary to deepen our attitude towards life and towards everything happening at present with the world. The very triumph of evil itself within the world is not without meaning, and signifies something profound. Behind the external evil oppressing us lies concealed the meaning of historical happenings.

There exists for real and acts a force of reason within history, the meaning of history. Everything outward is but the manifestation of the inward, and a surface view sees not into the depths, sees only the surface. The reason within history and everything occurring eludes a view, which sees only the outer shell of life, and not its inner core. And much of the evil in the life of mankind is only the outer shell, the surface covering, giving an impression of an ultimate meaninglessness. But it is necessary to penetrate beyond the outer shell inwards, into the depths. And there then opens to us the meaning of the grievous tribulations sent us, the inner significance of these tribulations. And it is necessary to experience them with a faith in the triumph of worldwide a Meaning. It is needful to undergo the evil tribulations with an inner worthiness, i.e. a deepening, not permitting that life should cast us out onto the surface, where the meaning of everything tends to be concealed.

There are strong grounds for pessimism, and a certain bit of pessimism, perhaps, is even needful for us. An oversweet optimism on the contrary also has no justification. But pessimism for us can readily pass over into despondency, hopelessness and despair. Always there is found a sufficient quantity of facts for a justification for such a downcast feeling in life. But too often they tend to forget, that in history act powers greater, and in consequence of meaning more real, than vile governments, than the greed of bourgeois classes, than the intrigues of the rightists, etc. All this is merely the dressing of history, the castoff from the inner ailment of mankind. And beneathe the dressings, at a deeper level of life there occurs something remarkable and noteworthy, meaning is realised, it triumphs by the convoluted, tormented and often unperceived paths of reason within history. That which we outwardly perceive as Russia, is but its surface layer, from which are not exhausted the powers within Russia. Besides the powers, manifest and cast off into the external, there are in Russia enormous potentials, profound powers. The soul of Russia is hidden in the depths, in an underground stratum. And it is necessary to peer down into the depths of life, to recourse to the deep stirrings of life, to recourse to the spirit of history. Not only does this not snatch away responsibility from the human will, but rather imposes a responsibility still greater, and calls for a revealing of potential human powers and it augments human activity, since never does it permit a reaching of despondency and despair, the collapse of spiritual energy. And we therein become active creators of our life, when ultimately we sense, that with us and behind us is the reason within history, its inward spiritual potentials, i.e. powers, immeasurably greater, than all the surface evil of life.

Concerning Inward and Outward Activeness

(1916 - 219)[1]

I.

In the "Birzhevye vedomosti" daily paper was printed an interesting article by M. O. Gershenzon, "The Personal and the Societal Aspect" [1915, № 15283, 21 December]. In this article it touches upon very important a question, deserving of serious consideration. Not only is the manifestation of energy on the outside, in societal life, a matter of doing and activity, a form of action, but there is a form of action also with the directing of energy inwards, within the depths of the person. Superficial is the judgement of those, who are in denial of any activity in people, such as are not occupied with societal work or immersed in spiritual work within themself. This is an indubitable truth that we still need to acknowledge, since among our societal extremists superficial and inaccurate views all still tend to hold sway on this account. But M. O. Gershenzon has somewhat narrowed the setting of the question, and I should want to broaden it and continue discernment on this theme from other sides. He contrasts the personal doing in opposition to the societal doing, but it would be more correct to set the inner doing in opposition to the outer doing. That which M. O. Gershenzon conditionally terms the personal doing, in essence is an activity not only personal, but also general, societal, an activity relating to all peoples and to all the world. The personal activity in that sense, in which Gershenzon speaks about it, is not a matter solitary, cut off from the life of the world. We indeed speak not about psychological a process of reflection, not about an egoistic self-immersion, not about the fretting over one's ambition and self-love. We are speaking about an authentic inner spiritual doing, a profound as it were underground work, defining the character of peoples and their history. That, what transpires

---

[1] O VNYTRENNEM I VNESHNEM DELANII. Article was originally published in newspaper "Birzhevye vedomosti", 14 jan. 1916, № 15323.

within the depths of the person, transpires also in the nation and in mankind, and also within the world, leaving an imprint at all the stages of being. The inner ascetic feat of the saint in the wilderness is also a deed that is universal. Man -- is an entire microcosm, in him is comprised all the world. And the whole question consists merely in this, in that what transpires within the person has transpired not at the periphery level, but rather in the depths, at its core, i.e. that it be not only psychological, but also spiritual. I would prefer to term this wholistic process the spiritual life, and not only moral as such. M. O. Gershenzon, evidently, in quite extensive a sense employs the term moral, though from another angle, and hence the spiritual life gets too fixated upon moral reflection, upon the awareness of one's own personal imperfections. This then leads to a setting of the question, akin to L. Tolstoy's.

But indeed within the depths of the person, within its spirit there is a profusion of creative energy, engendering great values. When we turn to the personal activity, or as I prefer to say, to the inner activity, then we invoke not only a personal and moral accomplishing, but likewise an enrichment of life with new creative values, which are not there in the external societal doings. We admit of the existence of values more lofty, than the outward societal orderings of life. Purist societal activists, connecting their societal activity to a positivistic worldview, not only deny the moral forging of the person for societal activity itself, but they deny also the independent value of knowledge, of artistic creativity, of religious contemplation and experience. To suchlike a casting off of the human soul onto the surface level, into the externality, we resolutely have to set in contrast to this the inner spiritual activity, which also creates the culture of peoples. The spiritual inner life -- is not only personal, it is communalative, supra-personal, national a life in forming a culture. There is a spiritual inward life of an entire people, and the national visage of a people is determined first of all in accord with this inner spiritual life. But this life actualises itself, certainly, through a deepening of the person, its orientation inwards.

Without a forging of personal character, the forging of a people's character is also impossible. The inner activity is oriented to the very wellsprings of life, to the spiritual energies at the depths -- it regenerates the subject of all the creativity in the world. Societal energy itself is amassed unseen, within the life of the people, at a plane deeper, than that, which is visible with the outer societal activity, at the very core of every human person. That, what they term as societal activity, transpires upon an external plane of life, on the periphery, and it presupposes, that something has already transpired at greater depth. The state aspect of every people is a fruition of its spiritual life and upon it are imprinted its strong and weak sides.

II.

Truly, every life operates from the inner to the outer. Every movement along the flat plane of life, along the horizontal is already the result of movements transpiring along the vertical, within the depths of life. Energy is amassed there and manifests itself, it is projected outwards. It is absurd to think, that creative energy can be received from the outside, from the external medium, mechanically. Creative energy, in transforming life, always comes from within, from the spiritual depths of life. In the external world, abstracted off from the inner world, there can only be a moving about of the atoms of nature and of a social matter, in its mechanical redistribution. But nothing in this essentially changes, nothing fundamentally happens. What changes is only the coverings, the veiling clothing, but underneathe them it all remains the old, all the old at the depths of life. It is absurd to think, that from the old, the old human material it is possible to create a new society and a new life, that the external mechanical redistribution of the old and of the old souls can change and transform societal life. The authentically new society and its new life presupposes an inward activity, a creative regeneration of the spiritual foundations of life, the nourishing and rendering healthy the roots of life.

It is illogical to give increase to the deceptions and illusions of externality, which can be false and phantasmic. In that what they term the external, societal, political activity, much becomes phantasmic, non-real, superficial, and vapid, like soap bubbles. There is much futility within external activity, much bustle and noise, unconnected with the depths of life. Too often there happens a desire to forget about the meaning of life by escape into outward activity, to smother within oneself the bitter sense of the meaninglessness of life. Amidst quite futile external activity there is no time to think, to glance into the depths, to grasp the true purposes of life. Such an exclusive absorption with external matters, without any enlightening or pondering within, produces unhealthy an impression and cannot be admitted as proper. Those, who are consumed with external activity, -- either already have a necessary minimum of inner attainments and then their work is fruitful and genuine, or else they are caught up with phantasmic and illusory a thing, unreal in the profound sense of the word, not attaining its purpose. This superficiality, this non-radical reality transpires within many of the revolutionaries, and many of the turnabouts on the surface of life fail to penetrate down to the roots of life.

Everything external is only a symbol of the inner. But in the external world there can be false and deceptive signs. Slaves can wear the clothing of the free and feign being free. Those mutually hating each the other can give the appearance that they are one in unity. True inward freedom always finds itself an expression also in the external freedom, and a true inward unity of people leads to external unity. But there is an illusory and false freedom, an illusory and false unity. But this lie quickly unravels, and the outward, bereft of inner a basis, falls apart.

And thus it was with the French Revolution, wrought by too many of the old sort of souls, with their upbringing based upon despotism and slavery, and situated in the grip of violent instincts. They attempted to create a new society from out of the old and unregenerated human material. There occurred radical changes in the veils and trappings, but this did not correspond worthily radical shifts in the depths of life, within the inner, the spiritual life of people. This does not mean, certainly, that in the French Revolution there was nothing new for the life of mankind. The new there was, but a correspondence and harmony between the inner and the outer was sundered. This is evidenced in the results of the revolution, in its fatal disintegration and rebirth into a new despotism. There occur periods, when people tend to live too much upon the superficial and only the outward plane of life do they consider as real. In such periods there is formed a very superficial cult of affairs. When the sad results of such a prolonged period are laid bare, an appeal to the depths is necessitate, for the recovery and renewal of the very fundamentals of life, for inner activity. After too many externalities with the revolution, to which there have not corresponded sufficiently deep inward changes, there ensues a time for spiritual work, and it becomes necessary to ponder, and to penetrate down into the meaning of every activity. That, what they superficially term as the romantic reaction of the early XIX Century, was a time of creative spiritual work, a time of the amassing of new values.

The preparation in the Russian revolutionary tumult of 1905 was too superficial. The revolutionary ideologies of the Russian intelligentsia over the span of entire decades were pervaded by a faith in only the reality of the external plane of life and they denied the depths. There was formed an almost religious cult of external activity, of a superficial societal activism.

The fruits of such a path, in which had been sundered the obligatory relationship between the inner and the outer, between spirit and the flesh of the societal aspect, was expressed also in the character of the movement. When a soul is spilled out onto the surface and ceases to believe in the depths -- foul luck lies in wait for it and threatens its revival. It is necessary to go down deep, to ponder, to penetrate into the meaning of a vital deed, to know, in the name of what everything is happening. Even the Tolstoyan "non-doing" becomes useful at certain moments of life and should lead then to deeper a doing. Concentration is necessary, to gather together one's strewn about powers.

III.

M. O. Gershenzon takes note, that in Russian life there is a periodic shifting between the personal inner activity with the activity which is external and societal. Each shifting produces the impression of a reaction against the preceeding period. This -- is a sick phenomenon of Russian life. In the West, life tends to come together otherwise, and without such acute contradictions there. Gershenzon expresses the clever thought, that those among us who are given over to societal activism, are not tormented by inner moral contradictions, hence those in which there is an inner harmony. And in this is a dram of truth. A soul, not occupied with self-formation, tends to direct its energy outwards, into external activity. But the rub lies in this, that societal activity among us too often is the pursuit of people, who have not gone through inner activity, who are bereft of a moral balance and of spiritual depth, in whom the soul is not agitated with inner contradictions only because, that it has been cast forth onto the surface of life. The societal activism is created not from the spiritual depths, but from the surface level. The person tends to feel himself determinable in his energies by the external medium, while not determining the external medium. The materialistic theory of the medium, in the final end, acts towards a moral dissociation, it spiritually debilitates.

In their youth, Russians tend to get ardently devoted to societal activism. But when middle age ensues, they too often cool down, turn into the uncouth, whilst eternally lamenting and preserving only the radical phraseology, they sense themself devoured by the medium and love to speak about this. This also signifies, that societal activism is not created from within. The exclusive preponderance of the external activity over the inward snatches away moral responsibility from the person and lays it all upon the external surroundings. Societal activism proves uninspired, behind it stands no forging of the person. The impulses of youth we readily accept as a genuine inspiredness. But very soon is exposed the mistakenness of such a perception. The weakness of the spiritual energies of the person, the weakness in the character of people is expressed in the qualities of our societal activism. Can it be expected, that something essentially will change by way of mechanical changes in the external medium? Most of all needful for us is to co-unite every external societal activity with an activity that is inward, spiritual. There ought forever to be asserted the primacy of the inner act over the external. And indeed the external is merely an expression of the inward. And then ultimately it will become clear, that the personal act is an important, an urgent societal activity, without which the societal activism threatens rot and ruin. The sorrows from the war teach us this truth.

On the Prestige of Holding Power

(1916 - #221)[1]

I.

One of the paradoxes of Russian life can be formulated thus: our ruling power does not have prestige namely because, that being so obsessed with the idea of the prestige of power, it discredits itself namely because, that it is so afraid to harm itself. This almost maniac-like and choking idea of the prestige of power has very ancient sources. The religious sources of the idea have already become parched and withered, but the idea itself continues still to hold sway over souls. That which already has ceased to be organic, tends mechanically to choke. In suchlike the view, in whatever the idea of prestige at all still prevails in Russia, it presupposes an almost metaphysical opposition between the power and the people, the society, man. The power, according to this idea, is not of human a potential and the worthiness of power is not human a worthiness, but rather supra-human, of angelic or divine a worthiness, transmitted by the priesthood into life civil, societal, familial. All the old Russia, the settled-down portion, and not the nomadic Russia, rested upon the idea of the hierarchical prestige of power downwards and upwards, the prestige of ranks and not of the man, of position in society, and not the qualitative best. The prestige of power and position is not only a thrill and a delight for its bearer. This likewise -- is his vexing worry, his onerous duty. In the name of the prestige of power and position not infrequently they tend to sacrifice their human interests, their tranquility, their natural attachments. This -- is an eternal vigilance, of glancing round oneself, an intense dreading to harm prestige. In the name of this prestige good people commit atrocities, they suppress within themself human feelings, parents torment children, an authority torments subordinates, even though this be contrary to their nature. Every of itself reasonable concession represents shame,

---

[1] O PRESTIZHE VLASTI. Article originally published in weekly gazette "Birzhevye vedomosti", 18 jan. 1916, № 15330.

every emotional outburst has to be suppressed, when the discussion involves the position of the authority.

It is a mistake to think, that the aspiration to the prestige of power -- is always greedy an aspiration, it can be totally ungreedy and even sacrificial. When a man becomes obsessed with this idea, when it is inherited by him from a succession of generations and boils in his blood, it is difficult to refuse it, sometimes even more difficult, than life itself. Life is not dear and not needful, when the prestige of position falls, when there falls into disgrace an authority, a master, a father. People tend totally and entirely to live with fictions, and the fictions possess greater a power over their souls, than do immediate vital interests. The consciousness of the prestige of power, of position, of rank, had its roots in the old religious world-feeling. It passed also into Christianity from the pre-Christian consciousness, and the new and cleansed Christian consciousness can nowise accept this idea in its old form. But the old idea of the prestige of power, of rank and position, and not the worthiness of the man nor value supra-human, -- all still in Rus' tends to direct the police inspector in relation to his district, the governor in relation to his gubernia, the government minister in relation to all Russia, parents in relation to children, pedagogues in relation to students, land-owners and owners in relation to peasants and workers. The old Russia has not yet passed away, it lives on still within modern people.

The remnants from the dying off of the old days do not go away quite so easily. People all still remain martyrs to their sense of prestige, their hierarchical position in society, they -- are slaves to this obtrusive idea, they themself do not know freedom and to others they grant not freedom, they are unable to live thus as they might wish, creating in life that, to which their inner voice calls them. The opposite side to this in Russia is manifest in the anarchistic contempt towards all authority and its full negation. Western people have gotten free from the old idea of prestige and authoritative hierarchical position, but they are infected by the new idea of bourgeois prestige and bourgeois hierarchical position, in which likewise perishes the human person, its divine dignity of worthiness.

II.

The old idea of the prestige of power is false at its primal basis, or more accurately, it corresponds only to a certain age of mankind. It is inherited from times, when there was not yet an awareness of the dignity of the worth of the man, when the religious value of the person was not yet affirmed. But the power of authority ought to have worth, ought to inculcate esteem, ought to be endowed of the gift of holding power for real, and not merely formally. These necessary traits our powers of authority do not possess. The powers of authority, situated upon prestige, do not enjoy confidence of esteem, do not possess the gift of manifesting power, and are bereft of human worth. In order to possess prestige, it is not necessary to strive after it as towards a self-sufficing aim -- what instead is needful is to strive towards a creativity of values in societal life, towards a realisation of truth, towards service. With prestige occurs the same thing, as with glory. One who strives in whatever to come to glory, as a singular and self-sufficing goal, tends not to receive the glory. Fate dispatches glory only to one, who strives with all his being to create values in the area of his calling, i.e. to strive towards knowledge, towards the realisation of justice, towards the creation of beauty. To hold power does not mean the exerting of violence. The exerting of violence is always an ungiftedness, a lack of vocation for power. The gift for power -- is a great gift, an altogether special bestowal. And with us there are almost none thus bestown, to our great misfortune. A power of authority, residing merely upon prestige, is always ungifted and powerless. Puffing oneself up, pomposity, the love for the outward trappings of respect and bowing signifies always indeed the absence of real power, of inner might, of authenticity and accomplishment. Every genuine and real power is a power over souls, over the collective soul of the people. One who holds power only over bodies and is able to move about the atoms of matter of the outer world and purely so by external means, that one holds no true power and is already toppled. The ontological essence of power itself presupposes an inner connection with that over which one exercises the holding of power. When this connection is sundered, the holding of power is rendered dead.

The old prestige of power, based upon a supra-human hierarchical structure, upon an hierarchy of ranks, and not upon people, is already bereft of life. This -- is a left-over remnant. In suchlike an hierarchical order, atavistic instincts are already in operation. The old and decaying prestige of power clashes against our religious sensibility, and in it there is no faith. And that historical power, in which faith has been lost, is hence powerless, it can exert violent force, but it does not have power of authority. Now at present the dignity of worth and the strength of power can only be based upon human an hierarchism, upon the dignity of man, upon his qualities and values, upon his vocation. This means, that we can bow before a great man, but to bow before a great rank we cannot. Needful for us is a cult of greatness, needful is a selection of the high qualities of the person. In all the spheres of life and of exerting power over life there has to be for us an advancement of the persons most creative, gifted, energetic, with genuine a calling in their affairs. The human material in the matter of power ought downwards and upwards to be reborn, renewed, increased. This human material has sunk to too already low a level. The very idea of power, of every sort of power, has been compromised. The striving after the prestige of power has been to the impairment of power. And now at present a strong and respected power can only be that of the finest, a power based upon human qualitativeness, a power of genuinely a calling and selection, esteemed by the people, serving the trust of the people. Thus it ought to be in both state and society, downwards and upwards. The holding of power by the finest is not something readily attained and no sort of perfection is possible in this area. But in principle, power can be posited only upon oneness with the people and with mankind, not in opposition to the people and mankind. It has to be something immanent, an inner human potential. The counterpart to power, to every power, not the civil only, but also the societal, the familial, to lifestyle or to man, represents a slavery of man or childishness of man. The holding of power can only be as a value, affirmable by man from within and realised by his energy. It can be rendered sacred only immanently, and not transcendentally, not through a theocratic mindset, but only through an awareness of the Divine within man. The prestige of power represents a duty of power, its service, its human greatness and value, and not its conceited pretension. Every lower and unworthy sort of holding power -- that of the police inspector, governor, father, owner, government minister -- ought to be deprived of prestige.

On Justification of Love for the Fatherland

(1916 - 222)[1]

I.

There has appeared not all that long ago the Marxist anthology, "Self-Defense", characteristic and symptomatic of the evolution of Russian intelligentsia thought. Combined in it are those Russian Marxists, who want to defend the fatherland. In Marxist doctrine, which the authors of the collection still confess, there is no provision of a place for the fatherland, no admitting of the value of nationality. The teaching -- is totally international, cosmopolitan, and upon its basis arose the Internationale. Marxism has always asserted, that class unity runs deeper and more firmly than national unity, that the German proletariat is closer to the Russian proletariat, than are the Russian bourgeoise. The war has shattered this doctrine. The proletariat of all the lands are killing one another. International socialism has ended. The manner of activity of the German Social Democratic movement has no sorts of justification from the point of view of Marxist international socialism. National instincts have proven stronger than class doctrines. But it is not so easy a thing to repudiate doctrines, to transcend the customary boundaries of consciousness. And hence they begin here to adapt doctrine to the unruly aspects of life, and attempt to bring life into conformity to it. A sad impression is produced by the attempts of the Russian Marxists, loving their native land, in conforming their feelings with their doctrine. Simply to passionately love one's native land, as is typical of all love, and to straight-forwardly want to defend it, they do not decide as such. Love for one's native land and its defense demand special justifications. It then therefore needs to be pointed out, that for the issues of international socialism it is more useful in the

---

[1] OB OPRAVDANII LIUBVI K OTECHESTVU. Article was originally published in newspaper "Birzhevye vedomosti", 12 feb. 1916, № 15380.

current war to be defenders of native lands, than to be "neutralists" or "defeatists" (how terrible, and aesthetically reprehensible the word formations!), and that the victory of Russia should be to the advantage of the working class etc., etc. But indeed would there not be made a defense of native land, if this were not to the benefit of international socialism and for the working class? Is indeed love for native land permissible only in the measure of its usefulness for the proletariat? This is equally all the same sort of thing, as though the love between man and woman were permissible, only because it enables an heightening of mental formation or is useful for the physical developement of people. In the love for native land, just as in love for a woman, they do not want to see anything of value in itself.

The Russian intelligentsia person especially as it were needs to justify immediate vital values with world-encompassing doctrines. He cannot live and create life, unless this serves some world brotherhood, the international proletariat etc. with lofty aims. The direct creative instincts are weakened, sapped by endless moral reflection. A direct affirmation of nationality, as organic existence, seems suspicious, almost immoral. Such however has been the attitude towards art, towards philosophy and towards many other values. And here the authors of our anthology make an effort to show, that the defense of Russia will not destroy the Marxist piety, will not go against the moral testaments of the Russian intelligentsia. This absence of immediacy, this non-freedom of spirit, has to be unsettling for a cultural Western man, accustomed as he is to form from himself his values in life. There is an intimation of a certain emotional repression, the inability to freely think and feel, to affirm values as of value in themself. It is too much like with people, who are held in prisons and not given the ability to breathe free air. Only a certain V. Zasulich decides to say a bit about the "Love for Native Land". The others do not permit themself such lassitude. It is not permitted them to love their native land and voluntarily serve it. And those, who have not allowed the love for one's native land and the creating of new life in it, have poisoned the very wellsprings of love for native land, have rendered it suspect, a monopolised defense of nationality. I think, that these Marxists, now bent on finding justification in their love for their native land, are very typical Russian people and that they love Russia moreso, than the official nationalists, but their souls are distorted with a Russian fate and amiss with a false doctrinal consciousness.

It is necessary to welcome the wishes of the Marxists to defend the fatherland. But the entire scope of the spiritual crisis is not felt. This is merely a virtual adjustment, and not spiritual growth nor developement in idea. This -- is an evolution of Marxism from the doctrinising towards instead actual life, an acknowledgement of a greater complexity with problems posited by life. But this process of thought is elementary, it does not rise to the settings of creative goals. The level of consciousness remains the same old thing.

II.

The patriotic views of the Marxists fail to admit the independent value of nationality as a reality, something not to be abolished amidst the ultimate unification of mankind. Their position is purely negative: impermissible are any sort of annexations, the defense of oppressed nationalities is not to be undertaken. They tend to think in a manner abstract-sociologically, and not concrete-historically. The matter of nationality is however a concept concrete-historical, cultural, and not abstract-sociological, nor economic. The Marxists share in the traditional avenues of thought with the Russian intelligentsia, they are totally caught up in social ideas. Living historical bodies for them do not exist -- there exist only social categories. They perceive nothing concretely-synthetic, as an entirety, but rather they perceive everything abstractly-dissected, cut apart. Russia for them does not represent entire an organism, having its own fate and lot within the world. The reality of Russia is not granted, everything falls apart into contending social groups, their interests and class ideologies. The concept of nationality becomes atomised, disintegrated. At its depths nationality goes unperceived, and instead there is only dissonant social formations. The question concerning the mission of Russia in the world cannot even be posited amidst such a mindset. Loving is possible only for a living image, the visage of Russia, a concrete organic reality, and not an abstract sociological or economic category. And truly indeed, Russia is a concrete reality, a living existent, having its own biography. The "proletariat" of the Marxists however is an abstract sociological category. The concretely historical working class in Russia is not this idealised sociological "proletariat", this god-bearing class. And the concrete interests of the workers in Russia can in no way be abstracted away from the interests of Russia itself -- such an operation is possible only in abstraction. Suchlike a totality, as Russia, is undoubtedly more real, than such a functional part of this totality, as a class. There was a Russia, when there was no class, and there will be a Russia, when there will be no class. And it is totally impossible to set the fate of Russia as dependent upon the fate of some whatever class, and for example, to defend Russia only because this is advantageous to the working class and justified thus upon proletarian morals.

The question about nationality is nowise a question about fairness, just as it would not regard attitudes of fairness on the question concerning the individuality of man, the unrepeatable person. A moralistic attitude towards the mystery of the individual being is in general impossible and out of place, it would be a destroying of the individualness. Nationality however is an individualness, a lingual name. An affirmation of the individual nowise contradicts the asserting of the universal, and the national modality of life is not antagonistic to the common modality of life for mankind. The common oneness of humankind, without including in it the national individualities, would be an empty abstraction. The higher hierarchical level of being cannot obtain by an abolishing of the lower hierarchical levels. It is absurd to set mankind in opposition to nation, as the cosmopolitans tend to do.

Russia has to exist as an individual being, and to the end it has to reveal its potential and fulfill its mission not only from a national point of view, but also from the point of view of the universal, of all mankind. All the national individualities have to be manifest within history, and the path to the unity of mankind, to the brotherhood of peoples, lies through the national unities, living out their fate, and their national cultures. And this signifies the necessity of a national struggle within history. The authors of the Marxist anthology have already made a conclusion on this, that the path to international socialism lies through a national socialism and the path to the unification of mankind lies through a national citizenship. It is impossible to overleap the entire level of being, upon which transpires the histories of peoples. This is a great step forward in comparison with the sociological abstractions and utopias, it is oriented towards a concrete historical realism. It is fine a thing, that the Marxists also are conscious of the impossibility to realise the life of all the one entire mankind in a dull and formless emptiness. It is time already to liquidate the enlightenment rationalism of sociological teachings and utopias, and to swing one's gaze towards the irrational mystery of the individual within history. The secret of the individual within history, to which also nationality has to relate, is impossible to discover and assert by way of the old sociological-economic point of view. It is important for us to realise, that the defense of native land is demanded by the national feelings of Russian workers, and not by the interests of the workers.

III.

Accurate and not lacking in sharpness is the thought of A. Potresov and others, that the "defeatist" psychology of the Russian internationalists, considering themself bearers more purely of the worldwide socialistic idea than the Western socialists, is all however the selfsame Eastern and Asiatic psychology, which was there also within Slavophilism, and in Populism, and in the anarchism of Bakunin, all the selfsame faith of being a step ahead of the West. Suchlike a sort of maximalism ordinarily is a sign of backwardness. But it is impossible to set into a single line the populist and anarchist teachings together also in common with Slavophilism, which was quite deeper, more cultural, and which included within it elements that are non-transitory. The authors of the anthology well understand, that "defeatism" is a psychology of the slave, a non-belief in the possibility of conquering freedom by one's own efforts, by the energy of the people itself, the desire to receive freedom instead at the hands of the enemy. They want to admit of nationalness, just like Western people admit. But in their attitude towards the German Social Democrats there are great strains and contradictions. They happen to admit, that the German Social Democrats have tended to tow the line of German imperialism. The Social Democrats however lack an independent understanding of the goals of world politics and an independent attitude towards the clashing of cultures and races. The Social Democrat mindset is still all provincial and narrow. Lacking in its own higher culture and its own higher cultural consciousness, the socialist world has adapted itself to the "bourgeois" world. And there has begun a dislocation and differentiation between Social Democratic theories and practices. This dislocation is something the Russian Marxists do not want to admit of, and they thus attempt to revise their doctrine.

The authors of the Marxist anthology display greater a citizenship maturity, than do the defeatist-internationalists. And in them obtains a sad effort to justify their national feeling. But a national mindset, as is so needful for Russia, they have not. They all still lack the ability to ultimately turn their awareness away from the parts to instead the whole, to Russia, to its fate and its world tasks, to historical concreteness, and without doctrinal justifications to be themself creative Russian people. Russian internationalism was a matter of Russian immaturity, the utopianism of people, not yet called to the creativity of life. Russian progressive nationalism is perhaps an elementary schooling in citizenship, and at this school the Russian Marxists are beginning to study. But hence is impossible an higher creative national self-awareness, a self-awareness mature and not elementary. This is still remote a step for the Russian Marxists, as also it is for a significant portion of the more radical intelligentsia. When the war broke out, it caught too many unprepared. The traditional stock of ideas was nowise large and from it was impossible to draw upon ideas, such as prepared for orientation towards unprecedented world events. There thus began a process of an elementary justification of the war and nationality from the point of view of moral and social teachings, a liberation from old ideas, such as were unprepared for the values of modern world events. But with us there has to begin a creative upsurge of ideas, less elementary, capable of inspiring to great deeds. This process mustneeds be welcomed, and it is happening in the midst of the Marxists and as such is reflected in in the authors of the anthology. But to a reaching of creative national ideas, this medium has still not ascended. And needful for us are positive ideas, in the name of which we can worthily bear up under historical tribulations, which can inspire us within the world struggle, and the responsibility for which no one himself can cast aside. In the broad circles of Russian society there are not yet such creative ideas, there is still insufficiently an awareness of creative national tasks.

The Rightists and the Unity of Russia

(1916 - 223)[1]

I.

Ever since the war began, from all sides have been heard appeals for unity, for putting aside differences, for a cessation of the political struggle by parties in the name of the defense of country and victory over the enemy. These appeals have been distinguished by a newness and freshness within the progressive camp and have led to a the formation of a progressive bloc. Much was done by way of compromise, and the Cadets and nationalists reconciled. Even the representatives of the far left currents admitted the untimeliness of revolutionary efforts and the need for defense of the fatherland. Much was changed in the psychology of our liberal and radical circles, much was re-evaluated. People became focused exclusively upon events. The national instinct, the love for native land proved stronger than doctrines and interests. Attempts were made to stand up for the unity of Russia. What however has occurred in our rightist camp, has it learned anything after this year and an half of war? Nothing indeed has happened there, nothing has changed. The speeches of the right at the Duma witness to this. The war has produced no sort of an effect upon the rightists, it has evoked from their side no sort of sacrifices, no sort of any re-evaluations, no sort of intensification of thought. The rightists are so accustomed to abuse patriotic slogans in an inner struggle against the Russian people and its striving towards a new and free life, so that when a genuine patriotic upsurge was demanded in the fight against an active enemy of Russia, they proved incapable of such an upsurge, they were bereft of true patriotism. A lie run amuck. And the rightists have gotten so entangled in the manifestation of their patriotic feelings, that they have themself ceased to believe in the possibility of a patriotic upsurge. The rightists have always fancied, that they are the sole bearers and expressers of the unity of Russia,

---

[1] PRAVYE I EDINSTVO ROSSII. Article was originally published in newspaper "Birzhevye vedomosti", 24 feb. 1916, № 15402.

that only they are the ones contending against the strife of the parties and politicing, that their politics is a politics of all the Russian people, the solely national, the politics of all the people. The rightists have named themself the "Union of the Russian People" ["Soiuz Russkogo Naroda"], at the same time as others have called them the "Black Hundreds". And they regard every appeal for a cessation of political struggle, for oneness and for an awareness of the unity of Russia, as a joining up with their habitual point of view, as a repenting before them and as an approval of their orientation in life. You have to change, -- they say to the left, -- we however can remain as we were earlier, since we have always been patriots, nationalists and for the state, and always we have spoken about the common unity of Russia. What an hypocritical lie! No one has caused such discord, poisoned with such malice, wrought havoc on Russia, nor politicised matters so, as have our extreme rightists. This hypocritical lie needs ultimately to be exposed, the lie that the rightists as it were have renounced the political struggle in the name of the unity of Russia, that in them there has been a pathos for national unity. The rightists have subjoined everything to politics and to behind the scenes politicking, and nothing is regarded as of value in itself. They instigated political discord to the point of fury, they cursed and alienated and wanted as it were to exterminate a large portion of Russia, of Russian society and the people. They admit of Russia under the condition, that it be such as they would want, the old servile Russia, the Russia of state absolutism. But if Russia be not such as they demand, if it should want to be free and liberative, then the rightists would prefer to betray it to Germany. Their patriotism -- is mercenary a thing, and defending the country is something they want only under certain conditions and for plunder. Better the governance of the Germans, than the governance of the liberals. This -- is a special sort of "defeatist" psychology, a psychology of slaves. Better to let the enemy consolidate the old order of life, than for the Russian people itself to construct a new order of life. Such slogans more than once have been heard from the camp of the extreme rightists. The rightists love not Russia, but rather a certain order, a certain way of life, certain interests. A Russia united, the visage of such a Russia never do they catch sight of, nor love nor want to defend. The patriotism of the rightists -- is avaricious and conditional. Certainly, among the rightists there are exceptional people, sincerely loving their native land, but they do not stand out in that camp, they are not the ones conducting rightist politics. The sincere and convinced rightists stand on the sidelines of life and the tumult of the political struggle. The politicising rightist street is otherwise inspired, and idea-prone conservatives are wont to fail to recognise their ideas there.

II.

The rightists express not a maximum, but rather a minimum oneness of Russia, they are for the uniting of a minimum quantity of the Russian people, while a large portion of the people they want instead to expel and subject to persecution. And the prevailing of the rightists, the rightist running of things would be an act of violence against the Russian people. Such a manner of things is bound up with a past, no longer still possessing organic a life. The organic aspect, to which the rightists love to appeal, long ago already has ceased to exist, has disintegrated. And least of all prone to violence would be that ruling authority, which would unite a maximum quantity of the Russian people, maximally express the common oneness of Russia, the soul of Russia. Only such a ruling authority would be for the state, and not for party. A rightist party-based rule of authority cannot however be admitted as preferentially for the state. The rightists are incapable of self-limitation and self-denial; they represent a dooming of Russia with the poison of an evil discord, with denunciations and persecutions. Over all this time during the war they have nowise shown the capacity for change. In them is none of the suppleness of living organisms, there is only the immobility of the corpse. The rightist bureaucratic monstrosity and opportunistic wont for adaptability cannot be termed alive and stirring. The rightists do not believe in Russia nor in the Russian people, they do not see any sort of world mission for Russia, do not set before it any sort of creative goals. They never speak about the revealing of the potential spiritual powers of the Russian people, not a single word do they find in faith of its creative powers. Their programme is completely negative, prohibitive and coercive, all they stand for is "no", "no", "no". The scantiness and poverty of idea of the rightists is truly frightening and evokes pity. Anti-Semitism -- is their sole idea, with solid an attachment and transformed into maniac-like an obsession. They live exclusively off their hatred for the Jews and maintain in themself a bogey in life with an exaggeration of the Jewish danger. The rightists are always crying out about the powerlessness of the Russian people, about the dangers, threatening it on the part of the foreigners subject to the Russian people, about the incapacity of Russians to freely defend their own national features, and by this they have shown disdain for their own people, and demean its dignity.

If one were to judge about the Russian people according to our rightists, then there would have to be a denying of any future for the Russian people, as the result of very hopeless conclusions. It would be impossible even to desire a great future for such a paltry and powerless people, which eternally resorts to violence and is victorious over quite lesser nationalities within its own great state. The imperialistic idea is totally foreign for the rightists, it presupposes breadth and subtlety, worldwide dimensions. In the ideology of the rightists always there is lodged a greater faith in the devil, than in God, in the power of evil, than in the power of good. And for the most sincere of the rightists the goal can only be in this, by forceful measures not to ultimately permit the triumph of the devil, rather than by creative exertions to realise the Kingdom of God. Any sort of creative movement for them is seen as leading to the kingdom of the devil. The rightists are bereft of creative national instincts. They are out of touch with the revelations of Russian genius. The soul of Russia is foreign to them, with its great presentiments and expectations.

The rightists are totally engrossed in negative politics, the in behind the scenes sort of politicking. The sway of the rightists signifies a maximum of raging political struggle, a maximum of political discord, the rending apart of Russia. The rightist negative politics proves to be the very worst sort of politicking, and the rightist sort of non-partyism -- is a very fearsome partyism. When rightists tell a professor: "The university is for science, and in the university there ought not to be politics", then we quite well know, what this means, -- this means rightist politics at the university. The ideology of the rightists does not admit of anything of value in itself and the rightists are always ready to expel from the university the most learned, if he proves a leftist in political attitude. When the government forbids officials from belonging to some whatever party, then this signifies the demand, that officials should belong to the rightists. There is intolerable a lie in the assertion, that the position of rightist authority -- is non-party, apolitical and expressive of the unity of the Russian state. The rightist rule of authority -- and with us the rule of authority is always rightist -- is partyism to the maximum extent. The rule of authority therefore is also powerless for us, since it does not possess prestige, because that it is partyism, because that it -- is merely one side in the political fray. The rule of authority in Russia is insufficiently geared towards the state. The nature of statecraft is something objective, expressive of the mind of the societal life of peoples, and it ought to rise above party strife. The state cannot be for either the right, nor for the left. A strong rule of authority cannot be a mere matter of politicking, it rather is aware and expressive of historical necessity in the fate of the state. And a ruling authority is powerful only then, when it expresses the maximum unity of Russia. Neither rightist nor leftist authority can be strong, but only that ruling authority, which to the maximum expresses the oneness of Russia and tackles the historical tasks of Russia. A group or class rule of authority will always be powerless. We have become too much accustomed, that always the ruling authority speaks not about the visage of Russia, the Russian state and the Russian people, but rather the visage of mobs, of groups, of politicising parties. Within Russian statecraft are operative certain objective principles, without which national life is impossible, despite the rightist character of the ruling authority. But the dominance of the rightists in Russian statecraft and Russian existence presents a danger for the unity of Russia, an enormous hindrance in the matter of defending Russia. This dominance of the rightists extends only to the outward trappings of Russia, it does not reach down to the core of Russia, its inner core. But upon this surface level, where this dominance transpires, there occurs rotten a process. The old garb of Russia is in tatters. And soon these rotting clothes will crumble away, like dust. The healthy core of Russia will create itself new clothes, which will not fetter the powers of the Russian people in the realisation of its national calling. The slogan for the unity of Russia, the national slogan is now a slogan of liberation, the voice of a new Russia. Russia will be forged together as a nation, possessing wholistic a character and wholistic an awareness. And therefore only now are we making the transition to an authentic historical and manifest existence.

Ideas and the Societal Movement

(1916 -224)[1]

I.

What tends to strike one regarding our societal effort is its poverty with ideas, suchlike as would inspire and breathe some life into it. This insufficient lack of inspiration for our societal effort, the elementary level of the ideas, upon which it rests, readily hits one's eye. Yet we live in an unusual and exceptional time, and we have need for ideas that inspire. I am speaking not about the content of ideas from individual persons, but about from societal groups and currents. And here we meet with a phenomenon very interesting as regards the societal psychology. Be it the ideas of the extreme leftists or the extreme rightists, these ideas are at elementary a level, simplistic, creatively poor, but they are definitely explicit. The ideas of the far left and the far right tend formally to come together in this regard, that they convey the character of a catechism, which one pulls out of pocket for dealing with whatever an issue in life. The far left and the far right alike set out from a pre-defined worldview and faith-teaching. There is a Social Democrat catechism, with the morals of the revolutionary intelligentsia, possessing religious features. There is the catechism of the rightists -- "Orthodoxy, Autocracy, Nationality". And with both the one and the other there is an entire faith-teaching: for the politics of the one side Orthodoxy is religiously necessary, while for the politics of the other side in turn atheism is religiously necessary. Societal ideas both for the left and for the right do not convey the character of a workable programme, of a real politics -- in this is always an indicator in life of certain beliefs of absolute a character. These traditional rules of the leftist ideas are situated in congealed a condition, they have gone cold, in them is no creative growth, they no longer inspire as once before they inspired, but all the

---

[1] IDEI I OBSCHESTVENNOE DVIZHENIE. Article was originally published in newspaper "Birzhevye vedomosti", 9 mar. 1916, № 15430.

same both the far left and the far right should be able to say, in the name of whatever ideas and beliefs they are fighting. In the given instance it is not important to me, that the extreme rightists in fact in the majority cases are altogether lacking in ideas, and in what they believe. One judges principally concerning every phenomenon in consequence of its finest and most sincere representatives. There are suchlike sincere leftists and sincere rightists. However, all the moderate societal currents, the liberal and the radical, the Octobrists and Cadets and those, to the left of the Cadets, do not have their own definite faith and definite content of idea nor can they say, in the name of what final values they base their politics and wage their struggle. The individual representatives of these currents certainly have their definite aims, but the currents themself lack for inspiration in ideas. The real politics is conducted without inspiration, and readily passes over into mere politicking.

The traditional batch of liberal and radical ideas, to which our societal activists constantly resort, is no longer noticeably fresh and of sufficient power to truly excite, and in any case it is lacking against the demands of surviving a moment of responsibility. In the abstract religion of liberalism and democratism there are already few who believe that, and few who are able to become genuinely inspired. A whole series of would be practical liberal and democratic slogans tend to remain nowhere and without demand of a practical doing. But great historical deeds in the great moments of history presuppose a religious zeal. Our moderate progressive currents are more cultural than the far left and the far right currents and they possess greater a stock of specialised knowledge and greater a societal grounding of preparation. This cultural basis demands differentiation, the carrying out of a real politics in the specialised sphere, the separating of politics from ultimately mere beliefs. For the extreme leftists and the extreme rightists, for the sincere rightists, politics is a sacred deed. But for the moderate progressive currents politics is a secular matter, a practical matter in the arrangement of life. Extreme leftists have gone to the death for their politics, since politics for them has been their faith, their sanctities. Liberals however in the name of their politics tend not to go to such great sacrifices, since to go to such sacrifices is possible only in the name of one's absolute faith, rather than the name of the relative affairs of politics. The growth of the cultural aspect and cultural differentiation comes at the price of a weakening of fervour over an idea, a decline in the ardour of faith. Cultural people always tend somewhat to be sceptics, they see too well the relative aspect of everything that happens in political life. And these cultural progressive people, who believe in God, have lost the old tying in of politics with God and they remain disinclined to have it so anew. I speak about God here no in some sort of dogmatic sense, but in the sense of abiding sanctities. And in this sense it has to be said here with grief, that in our societal effort there is an aridness of idea and lack of creative uplift.

II.

The misfortune of Russia consists in this, that it historically has fallen so far behind in the carrying out of elementary and obligatory liberal initiatives. And sometimes it seems, that too much of late in our efforts is directed to the hour of political freedom, when already the pathos for it instead involves living it and not putting out the fire. The pathos over the liberal ideas has already happened once in the West, and for our times cannot recur. The fate of liberalism has cooled down too much in France and the other advanced lands of Europe. Over there, the dialectics of history has shown a defect with the liberal idea, the inevitable necessity of introducing into it some sort of different and positive content. Liberal political ideas in Russia have tended to burn out prior to their practical realisation in life, and such indeed were never strong among us, always getting mixed up with social ideas. Russian man is given to pathos and inspired not so much in the realisation of ideas and carrying them out in life, as rather their inner meaning for existence, in the craving for truth and the Kingdom of God upon the earth. Ideas too moderate and easily accomplished tend not to excite him. The aspects of ideas in thoughts, in outlooks and searchings, in baseless utopias, is something we have lived through far more extremely, than what Western Europe has gone through. We have experienced both a very extreme socialism, and a very extreme anarchism -- phenomena predominantly Russian -- and also very extreme an idea of theocratic a societal basis. And we have grown cool to too tardy a realisation of idea in practice. Russian man's radicalism and maximalism in ideas has tended to debilitate and exhaust him. And to him it has started to seem, that what is experienced by him in thought and outlook, is experienced already also in life itself. He becomes frozen into an idea, which while not yet having started happening in life, inwardly for him already is in a production stage. And thus, the Russian Marxists, despite the realism of their world model, have often jumbled up the process of life with that of the progress, happening in their heads. To them, for example, it has begun to seem, that the bourgeoise in Russia is disintegrating and generating decadent ideologies, since this is something that has happened in their Marxist heads, at a time when in life the bourgeoise have only just started getting it together and face yet a period of flourishing. Russian religious people often confuse remnants of the natural order, antecedent to cultural developement, with being of a supreme spiritual type, which can then be set in opposition to everything in the West. But the supreme spiritual type obtains not in the natural elements of Russian life, but rather in their soul. The deep Russian soul is essentially religious and in this is its grandeur. It is not satisfied by anything in the middle, by anything not sanctified. But it analyses poorly and easily confuses various planes.

The business ability and political ability of the Cadets, who quite well are able to separate and differentiate everything, might thus seem non-Russian, too European and not arousing of enthusiasm. And even the Cadets themself, evidently, are nowise too enthused in their activity, in them is not too much of pathos and fire. All admit the usefulness and urgency of the liberal-democratic slogans. Even the most moderate of these slogans, as formulated in the progressive bloc, tend for everyone to seem essential and important for Russia, for establishing the elementary conditions of its developement. But the liberal-democratic ideology is overall rather poor, insufficient, uninspiring. A programme can correspond to the demands of life, can be reasonable and overall well formed, and yet lack in spirit, yet lack in genuine inspiration. Politics ought not to rely on a catechism, and the awareness of this truth, certainly, is a matter of cultural conquest. But politics ought to rely upon spirit, ought to be inspired from within, otherwise it will be dead. A liberal-democratic catechism cannot and ought not to be. But it is a poor thing, if the liberal-democratic doings lack in spirit. Russian man readily confuses the aspects of having spirit and inspiration as something with a catechism and doctrine. This confusion can be the result of a cultural immaturity. But the true Russian man is sacredly pursuant in his thirst for having spirit, inspiredness, being fired up with an idea, and has dissatisfaction with lukewarm opportunistic politics. And always for us in this regard it turns out badly. For us in 1905 there was no genuine upsurge of idea or spirit and joyless was any motion. There was a raging of passions and opposition of interests. In this raging of passions and interests the spirit was quenched, and every single idea faded away.

Not only the liberal, but also the socialistic ideology withered up for us and evaporated beforehand, than beginning to happen in life. A great turnabout in the life of the people ought to stand under the standard of a single great idea, from which the souls are set aflame. There has not been for us such a singular idea. Too early have they begun to skin the hide from the not-dead bear, to settle class accounts, at too young an age have they lost faith in the value and reality of freedom. And this has debilitated us.

III.

Our societal movement has need of a spiritual deepening, of a turning towards primal sources of enthusiasm for ideas, of new creative ideas. We tend insufficiently to sense, that we live in an exceptional moment of world history, one demanding of exceptional powers and focus. That aggregate of ideas and spiritual energy, which sufficed in ordinary times, now appears paltry and insignificant. And I think, that in the experiencing by Russia of the historical moment amidst liberative political and social ideas, preserving its practical immutability, that it has to be combined with a national enthusiasm and upsurge, with goals, connected with the emergence of Russia into its full historical maturity, with its mission in the world. We need to get deeply into the meaning of the world war and of everything happening in the world, and not remain at the superficial aspects. Russians ought to be conscious of their own "idea", which provides justification of their existence in the world. Political and social liberation itself cannot still be based upon the old and abstract ideas of liberalism and socialism, already outmoded to a remarkable degree. Social creativity presupposes the spiritual renewal of the person and the nation, the organisation of the soul of the people and the upsurge of its inner culture.

At present there cannot yet be an authentic social and political enthusiasm that is spiritual-cultural and religious. The rights of the human person can be ardently affirmed only upon a spiritual-religious grounding. The abstract political basis cannot still inspire. Everything has gone dreary from an exclusively external dealing with existence and external understanding of life. Politics has become secularised, freed from authoritarian religious sanctions. But parallel to this, there has to be a growth of the inner inspiration of politics, its inner religiosity. Without this process of deepening, there will occur a lack of ardour and hollowness to all our societal effort. It is impossible to undergo and survive great tribulations without a spiritual concentration, without an enthusiasm of idea. Without such an ardour and enthusiasm we shall fall into a withering marasmus. It is necessary to invoke all the powers available to a creativity of idea, which can provide meaning for our societal life. Quench not the spirit with superficial and foolish politics! And with this appeal it is needful to recourse to our societal movement, to our parties, to those actively involved in our politics. The human soul is more precious than kingdoms! The consciousness of this -- is very Russian a thing in our national consciousness. This indeed religious truth is distortedly expressed also in Russian political maximalism. We have to fight on behalf of our spiritual values. We cannot automatically and mechanically repeat merely the path, provided by the peoples of Western Europe. We have much to learn from the West and first of all to learn the organisation of human activity and responsibility, and much for us will be the same as in the West, since it involves the matter of social and political forms, repeated with all peoples. But there ought anew and inspiredly be our social sense of building, and in it we ought to convey Russian religious values.

Power and Coercive Violence

(1916 - #225)[1]

I.

Particularly acute in our day arises the question concerning the nature of power and its relationship to coercive violence. The problem of power agitates Russian thought and nudges it along a new direction. With Russians here is no love for power, no cult of power, there is always a morally contemptuous attitude towards it. Power seems sooner diabolical, than Divine, and it readily gets confused and identified with coercive violence. The love for power, the religion of power we tend to imagine of the Germans and we see in this a lower spiritual type. But it cannot be said, that we have been altogether alien to coercive violence, that nowise possible is it to say this for all the austere Russian state aspect. We tend to be proud, that the ideology of power is foreign to us. The violence amongst us has to be examined as a fact, and not as an idea, as our sin, and not as our heresy. But it is time already for us to make better distinctions in the concepts of power and coercive force. This has great significance for our national consciousness and for our very national existence itself. And herein I tend to think, that for us it is inwardly needful to be fond of power, to cultivate and strengthen it in ourself, and only then will we not be bullied nor be bullies. Without a radical and spiritual transformation of our attitude towards power, in awareness and in action, we will remain in a condition of servility. Coercive violence in Russia has always been but the reverse side of powerlessness. Coercive violence anywhere and everywhere is the reverse side of powerlessness. Power however is a positive concept and value. Power -- is of God. God first of all is power. In every great man, genius or saint, is power. In every great deed in the world there is power. In a great value -- is power. In great creativity -- is power. In life itself is power. Powerlessness, an insufficiency of power is something very negative, bad a thing.

---

[1] SILA I NASILIE. Article originally published in literary gazette "Birzhevye vedomosti", 2 April 1916, № 15478.

It is time already to cease opposing power with Russian humility. This beloved opposition gets nowhere. A great and saintly humility is itself a spiritual power, a mastery over its lower elements. A bad and slave-like humility is however a matter of inability and dependence. Russian humility, recoiling from every aspect of power, frequently has become the fruit not of an inner spiritual power, but rather the woesome and dependent fate of Russian people, of the Russian people, of the inability to manifest its own inner might. The Russian people has not yet known an historically voluntary and world existence. Too much in it has been repressed and driven inward. Russian humility has often become an instrument of self-protection for the Russian people, its means of adapting to the grievous conditions of existence. The Russian creative power has not yet been summoned forth for historical activity, it has slumbered in the depths of Russian man. And in Russian man there has not been a consciousness of Divine power. Power to him has seemed a matter of coercive violence, since he is accustomed to acts of power external to him, over him and against him. Power tends to stand before the Russian in material a form, it seems materially crushing. Spiritual power however is not sensed as power, but the rather as humility, love, renunciation, as of an ineffable depth and not translatable into the language of the "world". But suchlike power tends to be that, which happens upon me, threatens me and violates me, and not that, what happens from me and transforms the world. And herein is the characteristic feeling of Russian man.

II.

No sort of a genuine power within human life can be merely an external and material power. Every power -- is inward, a spiritual power, might, drawn from Divine a wellspring. All the material powers of mankind, all the outward implements of his mightiness -- are the fruits of spiritual a power. And even though these implements can be directed towards evil, it does not diminish the essence of the matter. External material powers, nowise connected with inner spiritual powers, do not exist, this is only a deception from superficial a perceiving of life. Every authentic power, not merely seemingly so but for real, is an inward spiritual action upon that upon what the power itself manifests forth, is an inward and spiritual act of communion, of co-uniting and appropriating. Active powers in the human world cannot be by an external and mechanical impetus. One, who has power over me, has to establish an inner contact with my soul and spiritually act upon me, evoking from my depths a spiritual and free admitting of his power as not foreign to me. That which remains foreign to me, can with violence coerce me, but it does not have power over me. A power of governance, having lost contact with the souls, the spiritual community, is no longer a power of governance, it is already powerless. Whoso rules only the bodies and shifts around the atoms of matter, does not possess a true power of rule, his power of rule is illusory. Coercive violence is illusory a method.

Power by its essence is deeply contrary to coercive force. Coercive force is always powerless or in any case an indicator of insufficiency of power. Coercive force is a sign, that a given energy does not act sufficiently deep enough, skips a beat, does not penetrate at depth, does not inwardly act, does not set afire or take hold. An oppressive mechanical shoving in human life is of powerlessness, an incapacity. An authentic power and might sets free, grants freedom to all and everyone, it is a transition into the world of Divine energy, its taking root into the very core of things. Powerlessness always enslaves, is violence prone, and bestows beatings. Authentic power evokes a respect for itself, meets with acknowledgement, and in its supreme manifestations -- is a delight. Whoso possesses true power is one who rules over human souls or the soul of the entire people, and is never sensed as an oppressor. An oppressor however rules nothing. In every state there is coercion and force, but no state can rest entirely upon coercion and force. A state tends to fall apart and collapse, when the power of rule in it is violent force, and not true power. And thus, the coercive national politics with us has always been the result of he powerlessness of Russians in regard to the non-Russians.

A true power indeed amongst the Russians would lead to the freedom of the non-Russians, to a liberation of all the nationalities. Only someone, who has a sense of his own powerlessness in his own enormous state, would want a limitation in rights and restraints on others, and that they be under restraints enough, limited in rights and situated under minority status. This -- is shameful a powerlessness, unworthy of a great people. The exaggeration of dangers and fears reflects a break-down of the elementary national hygiene. The power and might of a true national politics is always creative, and not terror. The governing nationality of a great empire should be endowed with spiritual power, setting afire and taking hold, ought to captivate by its visage. And I believe in the spiritual might of the Russian visage. But in this might our rightist circles do not believe. The ruling prevalence ought always to belong to power, and not powerlessness. If the Jewish, and the Polish, and the Finns, and the Georgian/Gruzinians, the Armenians, the Tatars and other foreigners are spiritually stronger than the Russians, and the Russians can protect themself only by coercive force, to manifest their own national visage only by the repression of a foreign visage, then it becomes impossible to believe in the fate of the Russian people. Then the coercive force, which accompanies reactionary politics, the same as politics purely revolutionary, is always that of an insufficiency of power, the insufficiency of an inner contact, a spiritual persuasiveness and appeal, the absence of a national all-peoples inspiredness. Factually all the phenomena within the life of peoples and of mankind is complex, and in them there is an admixture of power and powerlessness.

III.

Material power is not itself per se an existent reality. Material power is begotten of a manifestation of spiritual power. The material technical aspect is a manifestation of the inner power of a nation. But insofar as a material manifestation of spiritual power resorts to coercive force, the spiritual power proves insufficient for mastering and co-uniting, for a mastery over existences, over the souls of people and things.

In the world there is evil coercive violence, insofar as Divine power fails to take root in the world, and does not take hold in the world down to its very depths. Power always proceeds from within and goes inward. Power -- is ontological, real in the deepest meaning of this word, it is contrary to all illusiveness and all non-being. An insufficiency of power is a diminuation of being. And insofar as the world cannot yield and be brought under the mastery of an inner spiritual power, it is illusory and of non-being. No other sort of power, except spiritual a power, can there be. Only God is powerful, the devil however is completely powerless, he only pretends to be powerful, and his mastery in the world -- is illusory a mastery. The powers of this world in an ontological sense can prove to be very weak. For the Russian people and for Russian man is needful a consciousness of the majesty of power, its spiritual and Divine aspect. And for us it is necessary to surmount the externalistic attitude towards power. For the purpose of the spiritual hygiene of the individual man and the entire people it is not good to sense oneself as weak, on all sides beset by dangers and dwelling upon one's weaknesses, such as humility, as a quality, almost unknown to other peoples. The ever eternal feeling of oneself as weak, as helpless and beset by dangers, tends to engender a mistrustful anxiety and, in the final end, leads to such phenomena, as with the Jewish pogrommes, -- this is an extreme example of a national powerlessness and inability. Power is not a given, received externally, power is drawn forth from the inner depths. Power can and ought to increase in oneself, and needful for this is a spiritual hygiene of the person and the nation. Out of a mistrustful anxiety, out of fear, out of an idealisation of weakness, power is lessened and falls for real. And power for real grows and rises forth out of an awareness of oneself as strong, out of a love for power, out of a fearlessness in the face of dangers.

It is needful to call forth from the depths a feeling of power and to strengthen the awareness of power as spiritually higher an existence. In the depths of each man and each people there is power, but in slumbering a condition and weighed down beneathe the external layers of life.

For foresight into the activity and discernment of power it is nowise indifferent thing, whether it be a consciousness of the majesty and spiritual value of power, or whether on the contrary, it be a consciousness of the sinfulness and untruth of all power. And needful therefore in Russia is a radical reform of consciousness in relation to power. Power -- is immanent to man and the people, and not transcendent. A transcendent consciousness involving power would hold the people in slavery. The cult of a spiritual power, as also of any power, would seem to many Russians to be a Germanic, and not Russian an idea. But this is a simplification of the problem and a self-deception. Within Germanism there is a specific cult of power, transitioning into a will to power over the world. But of itself the idea of power, as spiritual and Divine a potentiality, is worldwide, transnational and objective an idea. Only power conquers the inertia of the world. All ought to be powerful and uncover their power in the world. World conditions at present compellingly demand of Russians, that they be powerful in all regards, that they transfer into an active condition all their potential powers and ultimately be aware of the significance of power. The Russian people, as with any people, ought to realise, that they themself are the fashioner of their own fate, that from their own particular power depends their historical future, rather than from the powers, bursting forth over them. Neither the person of the individual man, nor the person of the entire people can presume unto themself power, they themself have to be powerful. Both the power of the person and the power of the nation have to be organised. Russian power has to be directed otherwise, than the Germanic power, it ought to be liberating, bestowing also goodness, but it ought also to be power, rather than powerlessness. Russians however have hitherto tended to think, that power is something Western European, a foreign land thing, and German a category predominantly. For Russian man very characteristic is the wont for non-resistance, passive refusal and withdrawal. But it is erroneous to set non-resistance as the opposite to violent force. If violent force reflects a powerlessness or insufficiency of power, then "non-resistance" is illusory a way out, a refusal of the cultivation of power, in overcoming world evil. It can be said, that the violent force in the war signifies an insufficiency of power, a powerless good, but the refusal from participation in the war, its boycott, nowise signifies a cultivation of power, indicative of positive might. This is only a powerless ignoring of the worldwide cycle of responsibility, of historical a cultivation of power, often fine for the sensitivities, but feckless for the awareness. And there is no other way out of it for the person and the nation, except a positive cultivation of spiritual power, creating for oneself also all the necessary material tools, along with the finding of oneself in the outer world. Christianity itself is a religion of power, and not of powerlessness, a struggle towards power and a matching up of spiritual strength. The perspective of power is a perspective of value, and not of utility. Power possesses sacrificial a nature, it bestows from its exuberance, and neither usurps nor plunders. Power -- is a supreme good. A powerless truth -- is ungodly. But a truth that is mighty is not a good and benefit of this world, it is but a path towards the transformation of this world. And all of life ought to be based upon a [true sort of][1] power.

---

[1] text of paper damaged, word restored as to contextual meaning.

Tolstoyan Non-Resistance and the War

(1916 -226)[1]

I.

In a Moscow military court not long ago there occurred a case dealing with the Tolstoyans. On the defendants' docket from all ends of Russia were gathered the most visible of the Tolstoyans. The government authorities at the time sought to portray these people to be basically people of a non-societal sort, denying all societal involvement and admitting only of individual perfecting, in contrast with people of the community. It was only the war that fully brought about the clash of the Tolstoyans with the state, and caused the state court system to regard them negatively in terms of society. They accused the Tolstoyans of spreading appeals, directed against the war and against the fulfilling of military duty. The Tolstoyans defended themselves at the trial, they pointed out the injustice of the charges levelled against them, and already by this, in contradiction to their own teaching, they took part in the life of the state. A non-resistant Tolstoyan was compelled to contradict himself at each step. He denies the state, he does not want to enter into any sort of compromises with it, and yet he is compelled to acknowledge the state, when he plants a potato and wants to keep it for himself, when he takes a railway train, lights a lamp, when he reads a book, when he breathes a breath in common with his people. Through each small trifle, through his quite inconspicuous acts in life, the Tolstoyan non-resistance person shares in the economy, in culture and the state, and such draw him into the world cycle, into the mutual cycle of responsibility. Everything finds its explanation in the cycle of civil and cultural life, and even the most elemental and simple basics for the life of the Tolstoyan presupposes an organic civil and societal mechanism. The Tolstoyans are incapable in practice to repudiate the state, they accept the

---

[1] TOLSTOVSKOE NEPROTIVLENIE I VOINA. Article was originally published in newspaper "Birzhevye vedomosti", 23 apr. 1916, № 15515.

civil aspect in small bits and snatches. They deny of its powers only the civil awareness, only the awareness of the necessity and value of the state. But the acceptance in practice and the repudiation in consciousness is a weakness of consciousness and also irresponsibility. The Tolstoyans do not want to take upon themself the responsibility for the state, always connected as it is with coercion, they want to work and render for themself the view, that they have no need of the safeguards and services of the state. This, certainly, is a self-deception, wrought by weakness of soul and feeble consciousness.

The Tolstoyans accept the state, totally in the externals. They tend to think, that the state is some sort of object to which they are situated, that it has arisen through a sort of blind chance and that it is the wellspring of all evils. But this evil object, named the state, is in their opinion illusory, and it is only blunderings of consciousness that compel one to admit of it and serve it. The Tolstoyans do not want to admit, that the state is not only an external, but also internal fact of life, that the state exists from within each of us, and each of us has shared in its creation. In the nature of the state resorting to force there is objectified our own nature, and the necessity underlying the state is connected with the evil living within us. Every act of our life in this relative world always presupposes the state, just as it presupposes an organised form of society, the economy, and culture. Nothing can be isolated and transformed into a disconnected object, with which the individual man has no sort of involvement. The outward attitude of the Tolstoyans towards the state is connected with their outward attitude towards evil. They regard evil first of all and exclusively as violent force, coercion, and the coercion they however understand as something primarily physical, material. From this there is begotten a logicalistic mindset, a petty and pedantic moralism in which, in the final end, the Sabbath is made to stand higher than man. The whole pathos of the Tolstoyan non-resistance consists in this, that they do not commit physical violence against man or beast, that they fulfill the law of the master of life, not to participate in war, not to participate in the court system, not to eat meat, not to drink wine, not to smoke and moreover many a *no*. But the nature of evil -- is ultimately inward and spiritual, and not external and material. And good mustneeds be understood inwardly and spiritually, seeing the supreme blossoming of good not in non-resistance, but rather in love, not in the negative, but in the positive. It is possible not to commit physical violence, and yet be a devil. And it is possible to commit physical violence, without which, it stands to reason, it would otherwise be impossible to live within the natural order, and yet therein be a saint. In the non-resistance of the Tolstoyans there is a tendency towards Buddhism. And their meekness -- is not a Christian, but rather Buddhist meekness. In it there is something non-human, hostile to life and existence. Moreover, this non-human, Buddhist meekness is sensed in the chief hero of the Tolstoyan proceedings -- Sergei Popov.

II.

In the whole atmosphere of the trial of the Tolstoyans was sensed a leniency and the impossibility of severe sentencing. These people do not evoke any sort of vexatious or evil feeling, and no one tends to think, that they can essentially change anything in the world, in the life of society and the state, nor cause harm in matters of the defense of our native land, nor weaken the strength of our resistance against the enemy. For every whatever sensitive man it is clear, that the Tolstoyan non-resistance -- is individual a phenomenon, rather than societal, and societal it never will become. Every attempt to transfer the Tolstoyan convictions into societal activity is already a suicidal contradiction and betrayal of the idea of non-resistance, and would represent an entry point into the world cycle of resistance. Tolstoyanism is an individual path, which no one and nothing can intrude upon. The Tolstoyan non-resistance is not for the saving of the world, but rather for the individual's soul. In the final end, the Tolstoyan is concerned only about himself, about his own purity and for him it is not a matter extending to others, to all the world. Proselytism is impossible in Tolstoyanism, in it there cannot be the fire of propheticism. And that, which L. Tolstoy himself wrote so much about in his teachings, oriented towards people, was in him a contradiction. The Tolstoyan path is an exiting from the world, and not a going into the world for its change and transformation. The Tolstoyans do not admit of any co-uniting paths between the world of non-resistance and the world of resistance. Light and darkness are sharply divided. Only the non-resisters dwell in the realm of light, in knowledge, in the law of God. The resisters however, and such are all the non-Tolstoyans, dwell in the realm of darkness, in non-knowledge, in the law of the "world". Each one for himself can discern the divine law and fulfill it. This makes being a Tolstoyan very easy for each man, since he nowise has any perception of the irrational mystery of evil. But the

Tolstoyans admit of no sort of a process, no sort of an advancing towards the Kingdom of God, towards the realm of light. For the Tolstoyans, in essence, there is no path with all its complexity, it is instead a sudden attainment of truth, from which for each man begins a new and true life. In order to become true, it suffices to recognise the truth. To recognise the truth however is very easy. This -- is pure rationalism, taken to the level of absurdity. And to such a man, as S. Popov, man is not of this world, all are called to be brothers, blest almost, to be termed a mad rationalist. A saint however knows, how difficult and complex everything is in the world, with its dark and irrational evil elements. S. Popov does not know this and does not want to know this, for him all the world is illusory and everything in the world can readily be subsumed under the law of reason. Is it all thus so simple and so easy for him, that he does not see the Cosmos, that the whole cosmic process for him is merely a misperception, an illusion of ignorance?

This S. Popov -- is characteristically a Russian seeker of righteous a life, withdrawing from the unrighteousness of the "world". He does not admit of a fatherland, nor state, nationality, the kingdom of Caesar, and he wants to live only by the law of God. But in his very own denial of Russia, just like with everything individual and particular in the world, he remains characteristically Russian a man, very national. He does not want to defend Russia with weapon in hand, but he in his own way expresses and keeps to characteristically Russian a visage, a Russian soul. And this evokes towards him different an attitude, than that, shown towards him by international types, of the doctrinaire cosmopolitanism, of the exasperated etc sort. L. Tolstoy denied nationalness, but he was its great expresser, he was national even in the very denial of it, and he likewise denied art and was one of the greatest of artists. Tolstoy's denial of war was a matter of national genius. It is quite impossible to balance the Tolstoyan denial of war and the defense of the fatherland with such societal devices of outlook, as "exasperation", which can be nationally dangerous. The state, in its nature as the "cold monster", always is oriented towards society, to the socially external, it knows nothing of the intimately individual, of the inner. To the representatives of the state it is difficult to make sense of such phenomena, as a refusal of military service on religious grounds, they make considerations only upon the external aspect, whereas the inner does not enter into their calculations. But the judges even, representing this coldly calculating principle, still remain people and can otherwise relate to the Tolstoyan appeals not to wage war, in contrast to dealing with ordinary law-breakers.

III.

The defective flaw of Tolstoyanism is first of all the defective flaw of a consciousness which is narrow-minded, abstractly moralistic and abstractly rationalistic. The Tolstoyans deny the sphere of the manifold and relative, in which transpires also the historical and world process, and straight off they apply the absolute to the relative natural order. This leads to the result, that they absolutise the relative, they acknowledge the divine as natural, of nature, of the people, simple, elementary. But this is an illusion of consciousness. The violence, which the Tolstoyan consciousness dreads like the devil, is in everything natural, of the people, in everything very simple and elemental an aspect. The whole cycle of the natural order of life is based upon violence, mutual devouring and destruction. It is a great delusion to think, that violence always derives from culture, and that an approach towards a natural order of life leads to non-resistance and the repudiation of violence. L. Tolstoy borrowed the view of Rousseau about the existence of a sort of blissful natural condition.

But if one go backwards from culture, back to a natural life, then the violence only but increases. In the life of wild peoples the violence -- is maximal. And the life of the peasant, which to the Tolstoyan seems so blissful in comparison with the life of cultured people, is full of acts of violence and untruth. To think, that in this natural world there are such places and such living conditions, which are completely free of violence and thus to get out beyond the bounds of worldly evil, is a self-deception and a self-comforting. The Tolstoyan attempt at simplification does not save one from the violence prone cycle of natural life. To be saved from the sharing in violence and ultimately to be freed is possible only with an egress from the natural order into absolute Divine life. The mistake of the moral judgement of the Tolstoyans lies in this, that they want to escape being responsible under the historical and world process, to remove responsibility from themself and thus remain singularly pure and righteous amidst those submerged in darkness, living with violence in the world. They want thus to isolate themself and safeguard their purity, whilst remaining in the body, as though the elementary physical life of the body is not already prone to violence and a participation in violence.

The Tolstoyan non-resisters do not want to change and transform the world, do not want to inspire it from within, nor to turn other people towards their truth, they seek rather to separate themself from the world, so as to emphasise their own purity, and refuse participation in the national and worldly fate. This consciousness however cannot be acknowledged as very lofty, for in it there is nothing of sacrifice, it is not oriented to the world's salvation.

Those confessing the religion of non-resistance cannot oppose with resistance anything, they cannot resistingly oppose even the evil of war, for they are concerned only with a negative withdrawing of themself from what transpires in the world. Tolstoyanism can never become a widespread societal movement. And it is namely on those principles, on the strength of which a civil court would have to acquit the Tolstoyans, that a moral and religious court could find cause to condemn them, for their non-resistance and non-action in the world, for their too great a concern over their own purity. The Tolstoyans occupy and have their own place in the spiritual life of the Russian people, and they -- are a phenomenon purely Russian, since non-resistance is so characteristic to the Russian people. But for the state, for the societal aspect, the Tolstoyan current is merely but elusive and inconsequential. In the matter of dealing with our national consciousness in an era of world war, Tolstoyanism cannot possibly prove an hindrance. Individual non-resisters, having withdrawn from the world, are necessary for the spiritual life of the people. The Tolstoyan doctrine however implodes and collapses from the least contact with life and thought. But the spirit of non-resistance, the spirit of a passive withdrawal is something we have to inwardly conquer within ourself, not through the courts, not through police measures, but through a spirit of creative activity. The Russian soul has been poisoned with an exclusively moral evaluation of life. This absolute and abstract grip of a sort of straight-line evaluation is there, where instead there ought to be an evaluation more complex, more flexible and sensitive towards the mysterious march of worldly life, for it debilitates and hinders us from freely creating a new life. Tolstoyanism is one of the doctrinal expressions of this spirit, this straight-line sort of moralism, permitting to be seen only one point in a directly straight line. This spirit, still even less justified, exists also in various social doctrines of the Russian intelligentsia. The living tragedy of the war makes a joke of all the doctrines, all the morals, aimed at more simple and elementary an actuality. In the doctrinaire and straight-line sort of moralism is revealed the seed of moral untruth, of an insufficient moral enlightening. And the supreme moral revelation remains that of the Gospel truth, whereby the one who saves his soul, is the one who suffers its perishing [Lk. 17: 33].[1]

---

[1] *trans note: (Grk.)* "Ὃς ἐὰν ζητήσῃ τὴν ψυχὴν αὐτοῦ περιποιήσασθαι, ἀπολέσει αὐτήν, καὶ ὃς ἂν ἀπολέσει, ζωογονήσει αὐτήν".
(Lat.) " Quicumque quæsierit animam suam salvam facere, perdet illam: et quicumque perdiderit illam, vivificabit eam".
(Slav.) "Иже аще взыщетъ душу свою спасти, погубитъ ю: и иже аще погубитъ ю, живитъ ю".
(literal Engl.) "Whoso however doth seek to save their soul, doth lose it: and whoso however doth suffer it to perish, doth vivify it".
n.b.: The word "psukhe/anima/dusha" above in English is "soul", not "life" as is found in some English Gospel translations; in respectively Grk./Lat./Slav. languages the word for "life" is rather "zoya/vita/zhizn"... This echoes the nuance of Christ's "Parable of the Grain of Wheat" -- that unless it first perish, it abideth alone, and bringeth forth not fruit in abundance [Jn. 12: 24].

The Religious Fate of Judaism

(1916 -228)¹

These days, like never before, quite many are agitated over the Jewish Question, having become disquieted by the fate of the Jews, which is becoming all more and more difficult. This question is posited upon a societal-political and moral perspective. Yet still only but few ponder however over the exceptional fate of the Jewish people and penetrate down to the mystical depths of the Jewish Question. And truly extraordinary is the historical fate of Judaism and it is inexplicable by positivist-scientific means. If within world history there is a sign given us concerning its religious significance, it is this -- the mysterious and tragic fate of Israel, the chosen people of God. The Jewish people -- is exceptionally a religious people, and its fate -- is exceptionally a religious fate, it can only be posited religiously. And how powerfully Vl. Solov'ev had a sense of this, when before his death he prayed in the ancient Hebrew language for the Jewish people! The Jewish Question -- is first of all a religious question, and only thereafter a question racial or political. And terrible sounds the quip: has Judaism introduced anything positive into the religious history of mankind? Judaism -- is the religious axis of the history of mankind, it is thoroughly positive or negative religiously. Judaism -- is the cradle, the earthly source of both the Old Testament and the New Testament. In Judaism and through Judaism has been accomplished a great religious turnabout of world history, which even for the non-believing in Christ has split the history of the world into two parts. And for those believing in Christ, the Jewish people remains forever the chosen people of God, to the very end of the world sealed with an exceptional fate. The Jewish people has had within the world an exceptionally religious vocation and destiny. The apportioned lot of this people has been a religious creativity. I think, that in all the other spheres of cultural creativity Judaism has not risen

---

¹ RELIGIOZNAYA SUD'BA EVREISTVA. Article was originally published in the monthly journal "Khristianskaya mysl'", 1916, № 4, p. 120-127.

above the average level of giftedness. It is characteristic, for example, that the musical giftedness has not begotten a creative musical genius. The aspect of originality to Jewish philosophy has always been religious. Suchlike was the philosophy of Philo [Judaeus]. Suchlike the occult philosophy of the Kabbala -- a very remarkable and powerful creation of Jewish thought, through which European mysticism received a Semitic engrafting. This engrafting of the Kabbala is strongly felt especially in the greatest of the mystics, Jacob Boehme. In the final analysis the philosophy of Spinoza bears religious a character. And as an example of Jewish chiliasm turned inside out, the reverse religiosity can be discerned also in the social philosophy of Marx. In its irreligious culture always there is sensed the creative powerlessness of the Jews, an average spirit. And this creative lack of power is manifest as the reverse side of the exceptional religious vocation of Judaism.

All our entire Christian Aryan culture has in itself a Semitic religious engrafting. In our spirit we are all not only Aryans, but also Semites. Those bearing Christianity and those realising Christianity within history may be Aryan a race, but it received its Christianity from the Semitic race. In Judaism -- is the salt of the religious life, the messianic idea. In the Aryan spirit itself per se there is a sort of flatness, a lack of saltiness, too great a spiritual smoothness. This is sensed within the religious consciousness of India, in the theosophic movement, in the strivings of German thought to create a purely Aryan religious philosophy, contrary to every Semitic engrafting. In the German mindset, which defines itself as Aryan predominantly, anti-Semitism leads to anti-Christianity. Both Chamberlain [Housten Stewart, 1855-1927] and Drews [Arthur, 1865-1935] are typical spokesmen of this spirit. In the anti-Semitic and anti-Christian religious philosophy of Drews there is this flatness and smoothness of the Aryan spirit, of the Aryan monism, not wanting to recognise any religious an antinomy.[1] A religious passionateness, religious contradictions, messianic expectations, an apocalyptic mindset, a prophetic spirit -- all this is received from Judaism. Apart from the Jewish religious spirit there would have been no awareness of the religious meaning of history and the religious fates of mankind. The Aryan consciousness, having its cradle in India, -- is external to history, abstractly spiritual,

---

[1] Vide the remarkable [1906] book of Drews, "Die Religion als Selbstbewusstsein Gottes" ["Religion as Self-Consciousness of God"].

dispassionately monistic. Every perspective on the end of world history, as movement towards an end, at the first was only given in the Semitic spirit, in Jewish religious creativity, with the Jewish prophets and Jewish apocalyptic thought. Only in Judaism is there this tension, awaiting and demanding the sense to life. The Aryan spirit itself per se would never have known a metaphysics of history. At the centre of the metaphysics of history lies the messianic idea. The messianic idea is an endless intertwining of the metaphysical and the historical, which for the Aryan spirit always remain separate.[1] Only the awaiting of the appearance of the Messiah, i.e. the implanting of the metaphysical at a certain point of the historical, as revealing the meaning of historical motion, grants the possibility to religiously sense history as accomplishment, as "progress", viewed as such in the vulgar terminology of the XIX Century. Neither in India, nor in Greece -- in cultures purely Aryan, though also very different in spirit, was there any consciousness of historical a motion seen as a progressive realisation of a certain meaning. The metaphysics was not possible there, and impossible also was propheticism. The meaning of history also is the Messiah, an unrepeatable point, at which in completion was given a metaphysical manifestation within the historical, of the eternal within time. Only within Judaism was there this messianic consciousness, this intense sense of an approaching egress, a salvation from all the evils and travails of existence, the chiliastic hope, that there would finally ensue the Kingdom of God. In the Aryan consciousness all is infinitely and inescapably to be repeated.

  Only in a people, living in an atmosphere of messianic expectations and prophetic presentiments, could Christ the Messiah appear, turning around the whole of world history. The question about the religious significance of Judaism is also a question about why only within the Jewish people that Christ would appear. The messianic, the prophetic, the apocalyptic consciousness is an exceptional matter of the religious creativity and the religious revelation of the Jewish people, of its endowment within the world's religious life, in the completion of history. Jewish messianism, always bearing the imprint of a national exclusiveness and self-affirmation, by miraculous and mysterious paths transformed itself into an universal messianism. The Jews awaited their own Hebrew Messiah, the Saviour of Israel to bring about His earthly kingdom and

---

[1] Vide Chamberlain, "The Aryan World-View", ed. "Musaget".

bliss, but instead they gave mankind the Saviour of the world, Whom they repudiated for not fulfilling and not justifying their national messianic expectations. Herein is hidden the mystery of the religious fate of Judaism. If the religious significance of the Jewish people be connected with this, that it gave Christ to the world, then its exceptionally tragic fate is connected with this, that it repudiated Him. After the national messianism of Judaism became transformed into the universal messianism of Christianity, the fate of the Jewish people changed abruptly, became tragic. No other such people has been gripped with a burning thirst for an earthly kingdom and earthly bliss, a chiliastic kingdom. And to this people especially has been hindered that, which all peoples of the world have, -- the possession of their own national state. The chosen people of God, the fate of which cannot compare to the fate of all the peoples of the earth, was dispersed amongst the other peoples and was persecuted and reviled. The Jewish people repudiated Christ Crucified, would not assent to the Golgotha sacrifice. It desired Christ the King, not His blood shed for the sins of the world, but rather with power to establish an earthly kingdom. And the fate of the people, in refusing Golgotha, was transformed into Golgotha. Particularly because the Jews had not accepted the mystery of Golgotha, the mystery of sacrifice, their fate became exceptionally sacrificial, and they came to be crucified by all peoples. The remarkable Catholic writer, Leon Bloy, in his book "Le salut par les juifs" ["The Saving of the Jews"], says that the Jews will accept Christ only in the instance, that He come down from the Cross, but Christ will come down from the Cross, when the Jews accept Him. The Jews genuinely, organically and metaphysically are unable to accept the sacrifice (cross) as the sole path to blessedness, to their kingdom. They desire the kingdom and blessedness without the cross and sacrifice, they awaited and await the Messiah as king and have repudiated the Messiah Crucified. The messianic consciousness of Judaism is twofold, and in this lies the knot of the religious fate of Judaism. The imprint of the sorrow of Israel is upon each Jew. The Jews are in want for a kingdom and bliss. Here in a certain way is how the Jewish Question presents itself to the Christian consciousness. What sort of vital deductions are hence possible?

The Jews have crucified Christ, and therefore we shall crucify them! This progromme cliché is heard from the mouths of anti-Semites, esteeming themself as Christian. And indeed, Judaism is a great test for the Christian world! The Jewish people -- is the chosen people of God. In its fate is a sensing of the inscrutable ways of God. I however think, that the Jewish Question is inwardly to be decided only by the acceptance of Christianity by all the Jewish people, -- not of that external Christianity, which provides advantages in this world, but of that inner Christianity, which the "world" cannot contain. This is a question of the inner fate of Judaism itself, its religious path. But there also exists, moreover, the Jewish Question as a Christian Question, as a Russian Question, and simply and finally as human a question. In a certain sense Christianity is inevitably a religious anti-Semitism, a surmounting of the Jewish spirit. After the appearance of Christ the religious role of Judaism became negative. The Judaism within Christianity itself, which is all still very strong in Catholicism and in Orthodoxy, is an hindering and Old Testament type of principle, the principle of a religious transcendence, in opposition to the immanentism of a new religious consciousness and creativity. We have ever had the Semitic religious engrafting, the messianic sort of Judaism, but now the Aryan spirit ought inwardly to free Christianity itself from the Semitic religious materialism and from the remnants of an Old Testament attitude towards God. The Jewish religious materialism and the Jewish chiliasm during the XIX Century took shape and was reborn into a very genuine materialism and positivism. But it was not only Judaism appearing as the bearer of a negative Semitic spirit. Such a religious aspect of Judaism is strong within the pervasive ortodoks[1] mindset and rightist Christian circles. And thus, for example, churchly nationalism is a manifestation of Judaism within Christianity. Religious exclusiveness and religious intolerance, a frenzy of religious zeal, a dividing of people into "our own" and "not our own" begets reviling and persecution, it is a manifestation of Judaic a spirit, in which already Judaism as a race is not to blame. Judaism and Semitism exist as spiritual manifestations, totally separate from the blood-kinship of Judaism.

---

[1] *trans. note*: In Russian are two words that in English are typically translated as "orthodox". "*ortodoks*" [*ортодокс*] is a generic term indicative of a negative and pejorative obdurate narrow-mindedness, which we leave uncapitalised for clarity, and hence by way of example, it is all to common to meet with an "*ortodoks atheist or Marxist*". The proper Russian word in contrast for religiously "Orthodox" as it relates to Orthodox Christianity is "*Pravoslavnyi*" [*Православный*] and which typically we capitalise in context, as in "*Russian Orthodox*".

Our extreme rightist churchfolk and nationalists are in a certain sense more Semitic and Judaic, than are the Jews by blood. The "Christian" world is nowise better than the Jewish world and is even quite worse, in that it regards itself as Christian and by this declares for itself the exclusive responsibility of light-bearing an awareness. The Jews are not obliged to regard Christians from a Christian perspective -- they rightly relate to them from Jewish a perspective. But Christians are obligated to relate to Jews in Christian a manner, and yet they tend to relate to Jews not even in Jewish a way, but rather in anti-Christian a way. The attitude of Christians towards the Jews is an immensely shameful disgrace of the Christian world, a shameful disgrace all still insufficiently apparent. Christians, who would crucify the Jews because that the Jews crucified Christ, actually themself again and anew crucify Christ. The Jews in crucifying Christ did not truly know what they were doing. Christians however do know what they are doing. Christians, in their heart having accepted Christ, i.e. the crucified Truth, never ever should be able to crucify anyone. Having accepted Christ and His mystery in this world always situates one in the camp of the crucified, and not the crucifiers. How can Christians approve of crucifying Truth? The fact that the Jews, in repudiating crucifixion, received as their apportioned lot a fate, which itself is crucifixion, -- is a mysterious matter between the Jewish people and God. But it is not for us, as Christians, to be executioners. And if the Christian world within history has been an executioner of the Jews, then this is only because it was pseudo-Christian, falsely named, fraudulent and hypocritical. The Jews in having repudiated crucifixion are crucified by all that selfsame "world", which in general loves to crucify. I cannot term myself a philo-Semite and I am not fond of the modernly Jewish type of culture. But for me anti-Semitism represents a fetid and shameful phenomenon, begotten of spiritual emptiness. What as such is anti-Semitism, and in what sense does it assert itself?

    The superficiality and shallowness of our anti-Semites is striking. Orthodox Christians consider it proper to shout, that the Jews -- are of lower a race. They do not think it necessary to ponder, over whether a racial anti-Semitism should even be possible for a Christian. Indeed within the Christian faith the Jewish people -- is the chosen people of God. And indeed Christ in His humanness was a Jew! And indeed to this selfsame "lower race" belonged also the Mother of God, and the Apostles, and the very first Christian martyrs. For the Christian consciousness there does not exist a rejected race, neither Greek, nor Jew. The ancient Jewish religious consciousness looked upon all peoples and races except the Jewish, as lower and reprobate. But this consciousness ultimately was surmounted by the New Testament revelation. The racial anti-Semitism of our rightist nationalists in consciousness is Jewish a remnant, and not Christian. A false Jewish chiliasm -- the thirst for an earthly national kingdom and earthly bliss, -- with the compulsion to repudiate Golgotha, has penetrated into the Christian world. The nationalists and imperialists, in worshipping nation and state as like a god, having subsumed everything to utilitarian ends, confess a Jewish sort of chiliasm and it is not for them to judge the Jews for having repudiated Christ. Anti-Semites at present by all their deeds and words repudiate and crucify Christ anew. Needful for them is not Christ and His truth, but rather earthly goods. And in the German anti-Semitism of Chamberlain there is an honest element: Chamberlain -- is not a Christian, not even an anti-Christian, he does not accept the Semitic religious legacy. This racial anti-Semitism we can entirely ascribe to the Germans, but from Germany also it has come to us and has begotten a Teutonic arrogance.

But if a racial anti-Semitism be consistently impossible within the Christian consciousness, having as it were reprehensible aspects for an idea, then still political anti-Semitism is something altogether more vile and shameful. Political anti-Semitism -- is a phenomenon downright bourgeois, the manifestation of a bourgeois fear, avarice and envy. At its basis lies first of all a fear of economic competition, a feeling of one's impotence in the struggle for life. It is shameful and demeaning for the mighty Russian people in its own mighty state to sense itself thus, that it should have to be oppressive to the weaker Jewish people. It is undignified for a great people to be petty, to exaggerate dangers, to bully the weak, lest these weaker become stronger than one happens to be. One might be led to think, that in an atmosphere of freedom and fairplay the Russian people always would prove to be the weaker, would always get beaten. But this already reflects such a lack of belief in the power of the Russian people, and as an attitude to be put up with, it is an outrage against even elementary a patriotic feeling. Our nationalism with the constant blot of anti-Semitism reflects a lack of confidence in the Russian people, an assertion of its powerlessness and worthlessness. And if I thus were not to believe in Russia and in the Russian people, then I would not have desired for such an insignificant people a great future nor would I have admitted for it any sort of mission in the world. But I believe, that the Russian people -- is a mighty people, that it has the ability to defeat the spirit hostile to it and that there awaits it a great future. A great and able people ought to be magnanimous, great-souled, and not oppress. And in the Russian people there is this magnanimity, this desire to liberate, and not oppress. The tendency to oppress is something grafted on from the outside. The existence of anti-Semitism in Russia -- is superficial a phenomenon, and not essential. It gets abused however for political ends.

The Jewish Question that we first of all have to decide, is likewise also our own inward Russian Question, as a question of our Russian, human and Christian attitude towards the Jews. And this question has to be resolved quite independently of whether the Jews themself be good or bad. Towards the Jews one must relate in human and Christian a manner, even if they were to be bad. This question is not about whether the Jews be good, but about whether we ourself be good. The oppressed condition of the Jews in Russia is morally demeaning first of all for us ourself. And in the Jewish Question what distresses me more than the fate of the Jews, is the fate of the Russians. The absence of elementary human rights, the rights of a free moving about the land of God, the threats of pogromme, the rendering of an entire people into scapegoats, the scorn for a people, hindering one to see the human person, -- all this is first of all shameful for us, as Russians. The human and liberative resolution of the Jewish Question is a matter of health for the Russian people, a cleansing of its conscience, a strengthening of its integrity. Only the religious flippancy of our bourgeois era allows for anti-Semitism, and has no desire to know of the religious fate of Judaism. The vulgar self-avaricious anti-Semitism does not even suspect, at what depths is possible a religious anti-Semitism and how a denial of the Jewish spirit at this depth evidences a reverse dynamic even within the anti-Semites themself. "Judaism" as a negative force and anti-Semitism -- are phenomena of the same order. The anti-Semites in a certain sense are spiritually "Jews". The Jewish almost always are extreme a type -- either very good or very bad. And yet I have rarely met among Aryan Christians such individually fine people, as I have among the Jewish. And if one quite openly might say so, if among the masses of the Jewish are readily to be found the unlikeable and unpleasant, then even still moreso unlikeable and unpleasant are the anti-Semites. The anti-Semites seem not to have a real life of their own. And hence their disgusting existence.

Astride the Abyss of War and Revolutions

The Russian national consciousness should desire the granting of human rights to the Jews. This is a matter of our own maturity, of our national dignity. No sort of merely utilitarian considerations ought here to obtain. And least of all appropriate here is the view, that improving the position of the Jews would lead to a victory of the Jewish type of culture over the Russian type of culture. Quite the contrary. We shall be Russians most of all, nationally unique, when we grant refuge to the chosen people of God, when we see in each Jew an human face; and we shall be least of all Russians, we shall lose our own national visage, when we torment and oppress. I do not believe, that the granting of equal rights to the Jews and their full freedom would lead to the assimilation of Judaism and its disappearance from the face of the earth, as independent an element. Judaism will always remain a tremendous and ineradicable original element. The religious fate of the Jews, as the chosen people of God, renders impossible its assimilation. To the very end of the ages will exist the Jewish people and its existence to the very end will be a reminder of the religious meaning of history. And the existence of the Jewish people predominantly in Russia imposes upon the Russian people a weighty responsibility. This -- is a testing of the Christian conscience of the Russian people and of its spiritual strength. Anti-Semitism and the repression of the Jews is just as fruitless, as would be a readiness to subordinate the Russian moral and cultural consciousness to the Jewish moral and cultural consciousness. The Jewish people has its own mission, distinct from the mission of the Russian people. But in the actual existence of the Jewish people in the bosom of the Russian people there is, perhaps, an indication of the exceptional religious meaning of Russian history. In the utopian aspect of Zionism there is its own bit of truth. Israel always had its own fate and will have its own end. In the Apostle Paul there are mysterious words [Rom. 11: 26] concerning this, that all Israel will be saved. These words ought to be by way of fore-warning to Christian anti-Semites. The slander against the Jewish people, by which dark forces seek to keep it in the grip of slavery and repression and therein to turn the Russian people against it, is so pitiful and vapid a thing in light of the religious context of the Jewish Question. In alienating Judaism from human society and expelling it from its own national organism, the Russian people would be depriving itself of something of value within its own particular fate, would be entering upon the path of bourgeois avarice and felicity. The Russian people ought to live however in a free struggling of spirit together with the

Jewish people, in a free human community and a free mutual effort of resistance.

Positive and Negative Nationalism

(1916 - 230)[1]

I.

Nationalism is very tricky [...] a concept. With us in Russia this term has moreso negative a nuance, and for us with nationalism are connected [...] associations -- of coercive constraints, restrictions [...] etc. We tend not to connect with nationalism a sense of the creativity, the constructiveness, the individuality of our people, our positive values. When they speak about "nationalism", no one calls to mind the great uniqueness of the Russian soul, of Russian genius, of the goings in search of the Unseen City in the life of the people, or of L. Tolstoy, or about Russian iconography, but everyone calls to mind [...] Russification politics, [...] odiose names, not worthy to be enumerated for Russian culture. Only in recent times, amidst the crush of the war, is there beginning to awaken a national awareness, and the mind of Russian man emerges beyond the vise-jaws grip both of the old constrictive nationalism and the likewise old abstract cosmopolitanism. Transitions occurring towards a creative national awareness are all still barely visible. On a deeper level of life the attitude towards nationality is changing. We can already make a distinction between the nationalisms -- the negative and the positive, the old and the new, the preservative and the creative, the hemming in arising from weakness, and the liberating derived from strength. Our Old Testament like nationalism, primarily negative in definition, always has been on the defensive concerning the worthiness of the Russian people, which issued from the firm conviction, that the Russian people is weak and worthless and mustneeds be treated like the ward under a guardian, leading it along with strings, guarding it both from itself and from other peoples, which are

---

[1] POLOZHITTEL'NYI I OTRITSATEL'NYI NATSIONALIZM. Article was originally published in newspaper "Birzhevye vedomosti", 16 mai. 1916, № 15561.

Padenie note: the numerous [...] are indicative of heavy censorship.

always viewed as stronger and more energetic. This protective and narrow nationalism has been in essence a lack of belief in the Russian people, it tended to believe moreso in the Jews, the Polish, the Finns, the Armenians and Gruzian-Georgians. All always seemed stronger than the Russians, more independent and more gifted in creative life, all seemed more capable to exert an influence on others, whereas Russians -- were capable only of yielding to the influence of authority.

Russian nationalism as it were never arrived at the thought, that Russians themself can have an effect, can influence by the strength of their spirit, can lead by themself. Everything Russian is presented as unattractive, and only everything foreign is presented as attractive. Russian man is presented as weak, sluggish, ungifted, subject to all sorts of influences and dangers. Only a police guard can provide Russian man an advantage. Here indeed is an amazing national sense of self and awareness! The nationalism is based upon the impotence of its people and upon an inadmissibility of its wellsprings of strength. This sort of nationalism also has had no desire, that the Russian people should direct their will to a discovery of strength. An admission for the wellsprings of strength can be found, since with God there is strength for all. But a certain tendency of will and of consciousness can hinder the access to a discovery of strength. And our official nationalism has always wanted to consolidate such a tendency of will and of consciousness within the Russian people, such as would not allow for the discovering of strength and a discerning of the energy of the people, which was as it were hypnotised with a perception of its impotence. This was self-hypnosis [...].

The programme of our negative nationalism usually has consisted of a whole series of "no", "no", "no", and this programme was primarily one of forbiddance. [...]

[...] and difficult it would be to wrest from the nationalism a creative word, its "yes", its affirmation of a positive calling of the Russian people. The nationalists have always been more interested with foreigners, with the Jewish or the Polish, rather than with the Russians. And always they were oriented primarily on the dangers. And very characteristic it is, that our nationalism to a remarkable degree is of a protective origin, it found its definition in the negative struggle in the South-Western and Western border regions. Such a negative self-defining nationalism, feeding off the demand to repress the Jewish, the Polish or the Ukrainians, cannot be conducive to a positive awareness of a national calling, of a positive expression of national might. Our negative nationalists always -- are of little faith, always they appeal to the weakness, and not to the strength of the Russian people. This negative nationalism is bereft of creative national instincts. It says nothing and does nothing without all these innumerable dangers exaggerated by it, the dangers of the Jews, the Poles, the Ukrainians, without the struggle against the danger, threatening from the awakening of self-initiative within the Russian people itself.

II.

[...] A great national politics first of all has to be creative, strong, gifted and of genius. It has to be of the people, resting upon the mysteried and intuitive discerning of the will of the people. [...]

Such a nationalism can contribute only to a period of national existence, when the strengths of the people are still in a potential and drowsy condition.

[...] The element of compulsion is inevitable in the state's existence and in the accomplishing of historical tasks in the modern age of mankind. But this element ought to play subordinate a role [...]

[...] Only creative deeds can be great and historically of significance.

The awareness of a national strength and creative vocation dispels the mistrustfulness and faint-heartedness, of the sort of outlooks, which our old nationalism is so infected with. Someone strong, having awakened his strength and conscious of his strength, does not act violently out of fear of getting beaten up. The nature of strength -- is exuberant, creatively bestowing, in it there is not the greed of hungry a want.

[...] But indeed for the Russian people the hour is already at hand with a possibility to discover its own positive strength, its spiritual charm, its creative possibility. Every pretense to power ought to be justified by a positive strength, has to be a manifestation of strength within historical life. When the pretenses to power are found to be manifestations of weakness, this produces repulsive an impression, this -- is anti-aesthetic a spectacle. Such a repulsive and anti-aesthetic a spectacle in a majority of instances is reflected in our negative nationalism. Both in personal life, just like in the life of the people, one can observe this repulsive anti-aesthetic aspect of violent impotence. But we believe, that in the Russian people there is a positive strength which can be revealed in images that are historically aesthetic. The historical period of the gathering together, the uniting and consolidating of the enormous Russian state, devouring so much of the powers of the Russian people, was but a preparatory period for the positive mission of the Russian people. This period has concluded. And now, if the Russian people has great a vocation for the future, it has to make the transition to a creative and positive nationalism, to show, for what sort of spiritual ends it was called forth into the world.

III.

The national programme ought first of all to be positive, a forging of values, in it there ought to be felt a mighty vital impulse, an impulse for a new and higher life, behind which ought to be sensed a throbbing of a creatively-elemental love for Russia. A programme of impotence, lack of trust and cravenness can be termed national only in some quite distorted sense of the word. We have to surmount that lack of belief and callowness, which leads to brutalities and the paralysis of creativity. Timid people out of timidness often act hesitantly. Weak people out of weakness are prone to acts of violence. People bereft of character from lacking such tend to become obstinant. The same transpires also in the life of various peoples. Behind our [...] official nationalism there is never a sense of genuine character, confident in itself of its manly strength. The lack of belief in oneself, in one's truth, in one's own strength has always been an illness, impairing our nationalism. [...] The national will and the national awareness can be inspired only by great creative ideas. A positive national consciousness tends to reveal its all-humannesss within the nationalness and under the form of nationalness, it -- is universal, and not provincial. Facing the Russian people stand great positive tasks, and not negative tasks. [...] A positive nationalism demands first of all a setting free of all the energies of the Russian people, [...] the self-initiative and self-discipline of the Russian people.

[...] A people in fetters cannot fulfill any sort of positive task. Creative tasks are connected with the emergence of Russia across the scope of world-historical life, with the word, which the Russian people will bespeak the world. The old negative nationalism, however, did not allow Russia onto the world expanse, it forcibly held it down in a shut-in condition, it sought to isolate it from the world, it feared the intrusion of the world into the life of the Russian people. And this was a disbelief, that the Russian people should bespeak its own word to the world. A positive, a creative nationalism has to first of all believe, that the Russian people will enter into world life and convey into it its values. Even more refined Western people tend to think, that in the spiritual life of the Russian people are concealed values, which are needful for the Western world. But in this, evidently, the Russian nationalists tend not to believe, all immersed as they are in the negative task of protection, restriction and prohibition.

Creative nationalism cannot be limited to tasks of building a national culture, whether spiritual or material, it inevitably oversteps its boundaries and becomes contiguous with a national messianism. Thus it was, for example, with Fichte in Germany, and thus it was with the Slavophils, and with Dostoevsky, with Vl. Solov'ev, all which cannot be termed nationalists in the strict sense of the word. But this is already another theme altogether, not here to be considered. A positive Russian nationalism cannot be merely a reflection and reproduction of the nationalism of the other European peoples, of the Germans, the French or the English. A positive Russian nationalism will be totally unique and upon it will be the imprint of the uniqueness, the oneness, the unrepeatability of the soul of the Russian people, of the soul of Russia. European chauvinism, having transformed nationalism into a religion -- and this is foreign to us, is non-Russian, all this is a German spirit upon a Russian soil. In a Russian creative nationalism there ought to be manifest and revealed to the world the Russian soul in its absoluteness, with its wont for wandering, with its seeking for the City of God, with its repugnance towards everything philistine and bourgeois, with its incapacity to reconcile itself with anything whatever relative. The awareness of the religious uniqueness of Russia leads to a creativity as yet unprecedented in life, and not to a negative preservation of the old propping up of life. The new, the creative Russian nationalism ought to be deeply distinct not only from the old, the preservative Russian nationalism, but also from the recent European nationalism, since it is called to express the age-old uniqueness of the Russian soul, its all-humanness, neither known nor understood by Western people. This Russian all-humanness is profoundly national, and not international a thing; it reveals itself in the national mode of life, and not in cosmopolitan a mode. The negative nationalism has its reverse side, a negative cosmopolitanism as its supplement. A creative nationalism is situated on the other side from such a nationalism and such a cosmopolitanism, and to it all the old ought to cede way, [...] currents of the Russian will and the Russian consciousness.

Russia, England and Germany

(1916 - 231)[1]

I.

Whatever might be the most immediate political results of the war, consideration from a cultural-historical point of view with worldwide a perspective is both possible and needful. I have more than once already written, about how the present day war presents critical tasks with the emergence of European culture beyond the bounds of Europe, that it bears with it a surmounting of European provincialism. In such already is the inevitable dialectic of the imperialist politics of the great powers. And suchlike is the meaning of the spiritual pull towards the East, which is to be noticed at the summits of Western culture. Russia, England and Germany are likewise those great powers, before which stand worldwide tasks of the setting of the world stage. The closed-in European culture has insufficiently recognised, that the enormous world expanses, of water and dry land, are still yet to play a role in world history and that the ancient races and ancient cultures are anew to be brought into the world cultural cycle. The war, into which have been drawn all the states and all the peoples of the world, and which involves even those, which are not direct participants in it, makes acute those problems, amidst unifying mankind in bloody discord, binding together West and East. The war presents a dilemma: either the world predominance of Russia and England, or the world predominance of Germany. Predominance in the given instance does not signify the domination and the annihilation of the independence of the other states and peoples. On the contrary perchance -- the world predominance of such enormous organisms, as Russia and England, can instead signify a guarantee of the freedom and independent existence of all the national organisms, including the very least. And in this hour of history mankind is faced with a task, such as never faced Alexander of Macedon,

---

[1] ROSSIYA, ANGLIYA I GERMANIYA. Article was originally published in newspaper "Birzhevye vedomosti", 21 mai. 1916, № 15571.

nor later faced Napoleon. This -- is the task of a worldwide uniting of West and East. Other personages act now within the drama of history. This task does not predominantly face France, as it did with the titanic dreams of Napoleon, who wanted to divide the world between France and Russia, to form two world empires, Western and Eastern. This task now first of all faces England and Russia, in opposition to that of Germany. This task assumes concrete a form in the so-called Eastern Question, which has always involved the danger of giving rise to a world conflagration. But the worldwide task will variously present itself, and will be variously decided, depending upon which side will prevail -- Russia and England, or Germany.

Germany is clearly striving towards world dominance and the formation of a new world empire. Germany wants as it were to Germanise all the world. The Germanisation of the Slavs -- is an old historical goal of the German race. The Germanisation of Turkey -- is a recent goal of German imperialism. Similar are the aspirations of German imperialism also in regard to China. But as to the aspect of uniting, Germany is incapable, it is capable only of enslaving. The instincts of the German race are those of conquest and of force. Such instincts are little suited to peaceful colonisation activity. It is not without basis that C. Sarolea says in his fine [1912] book, "The Anglo-German Problem", that the Germans are incapable of a colonising activity. Foreign to them are the adventurer and freedom-loving instincts of the English sea-farers. There is in the Germans too much of the ponderous, too much an attachment in their obedience to discipline within their own state, in them is no flexibility and capacity to be initiators of a new life in a new land. The German of genius, Bismarck, was neither an imperialist nor a coloniser in his ideas, he was merely a nationalist. Nationalism and imperialism are totally different ideologies and represent different strivings of the will. Imperialism tends generally to admit of diversity, tends towards being tolerant and flexible. The Germans in their outlook are moreso nationalists, than imperialists, but they push on with their nationalism across the expanses of the world. Germany does not admit of any sort of individual existence as of value in itself, does not tolerate any sort of national uniqueness. The military marching drill in a single line, the mechanical state discipline -- is in the blood of the Germans. And they everywhere evoke a reaction, they never become liberating. We, as Russians, know only too well through our own bitter experience, what the Germans bring with them for other peoples, when they intrude into their life. Germanism has sought to enslave Russia from within. But ultimately to enslave Russia is impossible -- for Russia is too great and mighty. This might however be done with Turkey, transforming Turkey into a German province. Likewise the intent to enslave the Balkan Slavs via Austria, the intent to enslave China, itself no easy task. There is too much that obliges us to think, that Germany is incapable of deciding the world historical problem of East and West, nor can it by becoming predominant effect the worldwide unity of mankind.

The position of Germany in many regards is tragic, for it -- is tragic in terms of its geographic position, in the course of its history, and in the instincts of the German race. The Germans themself are wont say, that they are late-comers in the appropriating of the worldly sphere. The German empire came to maturity at an hour of history, when the earthly sphere had already been appropriated. German imperialism is too intent upon catching up. And the Germans are consumed with envy at the more successful and felicitous English imperialism, as well as towards the enormous expanses that Russia has. The growth of the resettling of their people, the strong racial instincts, the consciousness of their cultural strength impel Germany to world expansion. The German people senses itself on all sides hemmed in, like in a mouse-hole. And it senses in itself an accumulation of strength, demanding greater a world role, than that, which has fallen to its lot by its geographic position and historical fate. The imperialistic spreading about of Germany cannot be a natural sort of spreading -- it can only be something forceful, by military force. Militarism -- is the ill fate of Germany, and German militarism -- is the ill fate of Europe. The tragedy of a surfeit of power, in encountering the resistance of historically surrounding powers, always leads to aggression and coercive militarism. The large-scale military armament -- is an expression of the historical lateness on the scene by Germany, its historical lack of having been passed over for a world imperialistic role, its offense at the world, for what the world has not granted it. In the German empire is the feel of a parvenu, an upstart. Germany has played a positive world role only in its spiritual culture, its mysticism, philosophy, music, literature. In its material and state culture it is now playing only a negative role.

II.

To England has been fore-ordained historically the fulfilling of a sort of special geographic mission. The English have always been attracted by the sea and the ocean, by the broad and distant world expanses. The island position of England has to a remarkable degree determined its fate. But of no lesser significance are the racial traits of the English, their unique temperament, their natural love for bold sailing, their yearning for the faraway, their freedom-loving sense for an enterprise. The English are imperialistically more gifted a people, happier and more successful at it. The imperialistic politics of England has been historically opportune. England made timely an entry into world affairs, into the appropriating of world expanses.

The English imperialism is not militarist a sort -- it is amicable, trade-mercantile and cultural. The imperialistic spreading about of England, as in everything in the world, involved struggle and has had no little of the dark sides. Colonial politics was advanced not out of higher motives. In the contacts of civilised Europeans with the native peoples and the old cultures of the East there is an element of coarseness and insensitivity. But this is not something especially English, rather -- it is a generally European evil. In European civilisation there is a limiting self-smugness, hindering it from understanding the soul of Asia. This finds expression in the attitude of the English towards India, an ancient cradle of Aryan culture. But the English culture stands to benefit and be enriched by the wisdom of the East, by inwardly having to reckon with the old religions. The soul of Asia has stilled, gone cold, gone inward, -- become static. The East has dropped out of world history. But the ancient races and cultures of the East have not yet said their final say, in them has remained a sort of as yet unquenched mystery. From deeper a contact of the West with the East might be awakened the Asiatic soul to begin a dynamic process in it. West and East would mutually enrich each other and perhaps realise a true universalism, which is lacking in the West. Christianity itself tends to become universalised in facing tasks of contact with the soul of the East.

But whatever the spiritual deficiencies of the English in carrying out their imperialistic politics, deficiencies typical for white Europeans, elated as they are with their positivistic civilisation, England in all regards has to be viewed as higher than Germany in the matter of spreading European culture across the surface of the earthly sphere, across the seas and oceans. There is a sense of historical chosenness in this, in that the English do not strive towards oppression, they provide freedom, and seek to form a worldwide federation. The colonies provide the sense of a free connection with England. The British empire is not the empire of an oppressive world domination. And the matter of an imperialistic expansion of the British empire is finished. England is imperialistically exhausted. It is such a colossal power, that it can no longer offer the pathos of the new imperialistic usurpers. At present, it is occupied with the setting in order of its world empire and defending it from German incursions. And in having enough to deal with this renders England non-aggressive, non-militarist. The same having enough to deal with applies also to Russia. The colossal dimensions of Russia, in possessing enormous expanses of land makes for it both irrelevant and unnecessary any sort of pathos for imperialist expansion. Russia has facing it its own task of defense and setting in order its own territories. England and Russia -- are the two greatest empires in the world, to them belongs a large portion of the world surface. And this is why they can be peaceable, not oppressive but liberative. With its historical bad-timing, the too late and hapless German imperialism was bound in a fatal manner to clash with England and Russia -- the holders of worldwide expanses. German imperialism began its growth at a late hour of history, and the violence, committed by it, had to exceed all the violence, committed by the imperialistic politics of other lands. The talented ideologue of English imperialism, Cramb [John Adam, 1862-1913], foresaw the fatal clash of England and Germany and he romantically fancied it thus for himself: "we can imagine for ourself the ancient and mighty divinity of the Teutonic tribes, dwelling neathe the clouds, tranquilly gazing upon the earth, at the clash of his beloved children, the English and the Germans, rushing into deadly battle; the divinity, smiling assent to the heroism of this battle, to the heroism of the children of Odin, the god of war!" Germany wants to snatch from England its mastery on the sea, but it lacking in the spirit of the free sea-farers.

The Germans can act in the world only with their ponderous weaponry. At a time, when the world has facing it the task of finishing off the historical period of imperialistic politics involved with a snatching of colonies and markets, with a transition instead to spiritual-cultural work, Germany has facing it the goal of initiating a new period of imperialistic politics, in its violent character exceeding all others in the world up til now. This position tends to isolate Germany and set it against the whole of Europe and all the world.

III.

Russia cannot remain alone. If it would not be allied with England, then in a fatal manner it would find itself in an alliance with Germany. But an alliance with Germany means slavery for it and a large obstacle to the paths of the realisation of its world role. Germany's interest however is in this, to leave Russia in a blocked-in condition, not allow it out into world life, to maintain within Russia a disorganising reaction, thereby weakening Russia's might. And indeed Germany by its nature does not tolerate alliances, it demands slavery and submission. Austria and Turkey -- are slaves to Germany. Alliance with England however signifies freedom for Russia and the possibility of fulfilling its world role. The world role has to be shared between Russia and England, the greatest dry-land and the greatest sea power, to which belongs a large part of the world. And even if this world task is not ultimately to be decided as a result of the present day war, then sooner or later it will be. Russia -- is the dry-land intermediary between West and East, and likewise England -- is the sea intermediary. Constantinople and the Eastern Question -- is that point, at which the problem of East and West is concentrated, where it all comes together or falls apart. Through the applying of its powers, at this point Germany wants to seize the world, to go East. And this impetus of Germany causes the uniting of strong bonds between Russia and England, annuls the eternal contempt of England in regards to Russia. The transforming of Turkey into a German colony bodes badly alike both for Russia and for England, and to oppose this our two great powers can do so only in a tight unity. The world domination by Germany in the East cannot be permitted. The alliance of Germany with Islam -- would be fatal for the world. This alliance would be a betrayal of the legacies of Christian Europe, and the non-Christian East would be rendered a weapon for German world domination. And no less European and worldwide a danger are the imperialist pretensions, connected with China. The movement of Germany to the East does not resolve the world historical problem of the drawing together of West and East, does not serve to the uniting of mankind across all the earthly orb. This goal cannot be fulfilled by a power, which in so late an hour of history and with imperialistic pretensions is entering upon an initial by-force occupation period of its expansion. And this task demands indeed a spiritual subtlety, which the German race is totally lacking. This task can be accomplished only by those powers, which are situated in the end stages of their imperialistic expansion and have no further need for encroachments, which is to say by those races, which include within themself a great spiritual universalism.

On the basis of the world challenges, presented by the war, there has to begin a political, economic and cultural drawing together of Russia and England. Only such an alliance can resolve both the great Eastern Question, and the broader question about the East and West in general. The England and Russian languages have to become dominant in the world of languages. But in this dominance there should be no sort of repression of other languages, of other national individualities, but rather the maintaining of their independent existence.

By this I have no desire to disparage the significance of the alliance with France, with which is to be sensed more intimate a bond. But in worldwide a significance, the alliance with England holds greater a relevance. The alliance with France is insufficient for resolving the tasks facing us. The inward and spiritual matter of Russia will be greater, than that of England, for in the potentiality of its powers Russia has comprised within it an incomparably great universalism. But in the externals Russia has need of England, not only politically, but also culturally. Nevertheless, Russia has to come into an awareness of its world role, which is quite still on the weak side for us. It is time for us to get beyond the limitations of Westerniser or Slavophil mentalities and to conceive of Russia as a great East-West, which as such sooner or later will be called to a world role of spiritual unifying, the acceptance into its spiritual universalism of the Asiatic soul, from of old making its way to God, and a repulsing of the dark and anti-Christian Asiatic danger. The Slavic race with Russia at the head would still be called to a great historical deed. But the fulfilling of this deed presupposes an inner strengthening of Russia, a setting free of all the energies lodged within it, the creative heightening of its activity, and a cessation of the old disputes of the Slavs amongst themself. In the matter of our strengthening and setting things free, the alliance with England can play a large and political role, directly opposite the role, always played for us by Germany. This alliance can enable us to get free from the inward poison of Germanism. The spread of the English language amongst us would be a symbol of worldly breadth and freedom. The German language however, itself per se very valuable and proffering the world great ideas, has become associated wit us as a sort of stifling and enslaving of our spiritual energy. For our strengthening and being free the drawing closer with England mustneeds be preached.

The Social and the Bureaucratic Conservatism

(1916 - 236)[1]

I.

In Russia, conservatism as an idea-based social current almost does not exist. Conservatism for us always has been something official, bureaucratic. An intellectual-social conservatism seemed inadmissible and has faced twofold an hindrance -- the hindrance of the reactionary powers, which had no need of its services, and the hindrance from the progressive social element, which feared it as something reactionary. From above such a conservatism seemed anti-state, while from below it seemed anti-societal. The ideological conservatism of the Slavophils did not have any sort of direct influence upon life. From the side of the official powers it however met with a most contemptuous and scornful attitude towards it. And then too on the side of the vanguard social movement the Slavophil conservative ideology has encountered the same contemptuous and scornful attitude towards it. As regards the state, active among us has only been Katkov alone, only in his person did the printed word find tremendous an influence with the state. But this transpired at dear a price, the price of denying all the ideas, of twisting words to utilitarian state interests. State interests and societal interests for us remained severed. Our ideology tended almost to be constructed upon a transcendental opposition between state-interests and societal-interests. Like lands at war. The state thrust was alienated not only from the societal thrust, but also from every vital idea, and it had no need for the service of ideas. The societal ideas of the Slavophils, concerning "Orthodoxy, Autocracy and Nationality" encountered quite suspicious an attitude towards it from the representatives of the official state. The official state mechanism as it were conceived of itself as the "actually existing", in contrast to every sort of "mere thinking", and had no

---

[1] OBSCHESTVENNYI I BIUROKRATICHESKII KONSERVATIZM. Article was originally published in newspaper "Birzhevye vedomosti", 9 aug. 1916, № 15729.

need of suchlike a thinking. Ideas were not regarded as serious a matter, rather only as an amusement or luxury, which barely could be allowed. The official state element did not seek out for itself grounds of support, of sustenance and salvation in ideas, which always reflect indeed the activity of society, but it instead rested itself upon its own factual self-complacent power. And in this was a certain self-deception, since the official state element only was both powerful and indestructible, and since that within society and in the people there was the "idea", supporting this and humbled in the face of it. In the final end, "ideas" tend to rule the world, and without them are powerless all the ministers and governors, all the bayonets and weapons. But few there are that are given to know this mysterious power of the idea, and least of all those, who come off as their outwardly obedient dupes.

For Russian bureaucratism -- a phenomenon unique in its kind -- it is nowise characteristic, that it should be conservative. Essential for it is this, that it permit of everything only from itself, as authorised from itself, that it sense itself a power transcendentally above both society and the people, that it not permit alongside it any other sort of a source of a societal-state life and developement. Bureaucratism of this sort can be every so often liberal, it is compelled to allow even reforms, but this liberalism -- is unfailingly bureaucratic, and these reforms -- are unfailingly bureaucratic. One of the paradoxes of the Russian state can be formulated thus: we would sooner allow for a bureaucratic liberalism, than for a societal conservatism. An idea-based societal conservatism represents a self-activity of society, it would try to express the will of the people, the faith of the people, the ideals of the people. And yet here is something the age-old Russian bureaucratism cannot allow. The forceful character of the reforms of Peter [the Great] prepared the way for such an attitude and such a sort of bureaucracy. It is firmly entrenched in the opposition between the "we" and the "they", between the ruling authority and the people, between the state and society. The "we" -- are altogether special, not of earthly an origin, this sort is not such as to arise from the bosom of the Russian soil. The concept is to an higher degree reminiscent of the nature of conquerors. The "we" can be conservative, the "we" can also be liberal, if "we" so desire and deem it necessary. The "they" however ought not to be conservative, their active conservatism would be a pretension as belonging to them, that which "we" have properly belonging to us. And it remains for "them" but to dwell in a condition of impotent and irresponsible opposition. The principal opposition, varying at times with the concrete forms of rule against the Russian state element, was also an inevitable ideological reaction of the "they" against the pretensions of the "we" to be the unlimited and sole expressers of the Russian governance. The bureaucratic "we" was always inclined to think, that "they", i.e. society and the people, -- are hostile an opposition, contemptible in its impotence and moreover evoking eternal dangers and suspicion.

The idea-based conservative "they" became vexed, for unacceptable to them was the bureaucratic-police point of view. Such a sort of the "they" can pretend to an active role in societal-state life up to the point of a "turnabout" which the oppositional "they" want and which the "we" will not permit. And insofar as the bureaucratic "we" have some sort of an ideology, in the majority of instances there is none, and is based on this, that the people have nothing to tell them and that it is the "we" handling state matters. But the societal conservatism presupposes, that the people is not altogether to be silent, that it has its own expressible opinion, its perchance conservative activity. The Slavophils were hostile to the bureaucracy and they felt, that the bureaucracy isolated the tsar off from the people. Societal conservatism is all however a form of societal self-rule by the people, though trending in a certain spirit.

II.

Not only is societal liberalism, but also the societal conservatism whether of the gentry self-rule, of the agrarian self-rule, of the city self-rule, of the merchant self-rule -- always it comes to naught afront the official, the bureaucratic conservatism. Every manner of societal self-initiative and activity is distressing, whether today a conservative direction, tomorrow perhaps a direction liberal or even revolutionary. When some whatever visible bureaucrat is rendered too popular in whatever societal circle, this is already undesirable and hazardous. Suchlike a popularity is already societal an activity, an indirect involvement of the societal element in the affairs of state. The officio-bureaucratic conservatism tends to be very jealous, it wants to share with no one, it is very mistrustful. A societal conservative, having not taken bureaucratic a path, even in the role of minister is seen as not his own man, a sort of stranger rather, he introduces into state governance strange societal twists, he seems a liberal, despite his own resolute conservative convictions. A merely compliant and not too much on principle liberalism of the bureaucratic type becomes more tolerable, than a principled and resolute societal conservatism. In the first type is an element of servility, which is not there in the second.

The bureaucratic realm -- is a shut-in realm, nothing from outside it is permissible, it regards itself absolute a realm, it does not believe in anything, not begotten of itself. The bureaucratic realm will not tolerate uniting with the rest of God's world, it begets all of itself and subordinates all to itself. The bureaucratic realm can set about to moderately and with facility reform the world, but the one thing it cannot consent to is that the world should reform itself, nor even that the world can take care of itself. Metaphysical bureaucratism cannot tolerate any sort of a self-sufficing, self-originating occurrence transpiring alongside it. This is a metaphysics totally transcendent; it is intolerant towards actions of immanent powers in the world, in society, in the people.

All these abstract thoughts are confirmed by the bureaucratic fate of such idea-based astute societal conservatives, as A. Samarin, Prince N. Scherbatov or A. Maumov. A. D. Samarin is more conservative than many a bureaucratic minister, he is definitely a rightist and was always a rightist in the capacity of a social activist. But his rightist aspect -- is a societal rightist aspect, his conservatism has pretense to be a populist conservatism, all his fabric -- is non-bureaucratic a fabric. And hence he is not to be tolerated within the bureaucratic realm. He introduced into this realm an element of independence, of an idea-based self-sufficiency, traits of the societal self-guidance, of stubbornness and dissent against servility. All this is alien to the bureaucratic realm and cannot be stomached by it. The societal conservative Pr. Scherbatov in his role as minister of Internal Affairs appeared a liberal, he spoke about a "faith in society", he allowed for societal self-initiative. But for the bureaucratic realm he seemed a man, corrupted by the habitual wonts of the societal element. Even the societal aspect, advanced by the conservative leaders of the nobility, is unacceptable for the bureaucratic realm. Convictions too firm, conservative ideas too definite, cannot come nigh this realm. Required there instead is a great compliance, flexibility, assent to a fully subordinate position. Societal conservatives in their role however as ministers come off moreso as "they", than "we".

But the secret of the bureaucracy -- is in this, not to allow the entry of the "they" into the "we", and ever to maintain this opposition. Indeed, behind the conservative societal aspect can be dragged in every other societal aspect. When the conservative is too societally-based, -- too independent in idea, -- he is already then very much the liberal, he breaches open a gap within the closed-in bureaucratic realm. Civil awareness in the Russian bureaucracy has been weak, particularly because it esteemed itself as the only civil affairs element. Every societal initiative is cast away from the state aspect and viewed as of the endured opposition. Not only the rural and city self-rule, but also the State Duma in the eyes of the bureaucracy are still all -- not an organic part of the Russian state, but rather of the societal opposition, which can be tolerated only up to a certain point. This however -- is totally anti-civil, indeed pre-civil a mindset. The state concept gets jumbled and identified with a given manner of governance. And indeed civil awareness has been weak both in the Russian bureaucracy, and in Russian society. The historical significance of the Russian bureaucracy can be defined as a preserving of the external aspects of the greatness of Russia, while neglecting the developing of its inner greatness.

III.

In the absence of whatever the remarkable idea-minded conservative segment, the role of having occur enlightened and doable reforms on behalf of our conservative elements, in all actuality, is fated to be played by moderately liberal segments, by the right wing of those elements, which are grouped in the rural and urban assemblies, in the military-production committee, and in the Duma progressive bloc. The exclusive dominance of the official bureaucratic conservatism not only cannot carry out the necessary civil reforms, it likewise cannot guard Russia overall. Idea-base and cultural conservatives exist among us in the capacity of a societal segment, endowed as such with a positive national-civil mindset, but rather especially in the capacity of separate personages. In our conservative masses the elements are of reactionary a mindset, they tend to be hostile to all culture and are bereft of a positive outlook, and in them is almost absent a feeling of responsibility toward our native land. Our "rightists" cannot play the role of conservative elements in the cultural, the enlightened sense of the word. The "rightists" tend to undermine the sense of the national unity, Russia. The cultural conservative elements can play the role of a link, a supporting connection for the times. Can our "rightists" be such a link? They indeed tend to undermine for the times our national existence, and they bestow catastrophic a character into our transition from the past to the future. The absence of a self-initiating and active societal element, a consciously national societal element, is dangerous for whatever the healthy civil and national developement.

The liberal-conservative elements of society can bolster the positive connection between past and future national life, whereas the reactionary-rightist elements can play a role only destructive and making for catastrophe. Healthy and positive national developement presupposes the existence of elements that are liberal-conservative and resolutely reform oriented, oriented creatively towards the future. The bureaucratic conservatism, semi-consciously propped up upon the destructively reactionary elements of society and the people, has no desire for a natural national developement and seeks to impede it every which way. Our state mechanism's casting aside of even elements that are societally-conservative will rupture the connection of the times and prepare for sad a future.

Bureaucratic conservatism inevitably gives preference to the extreme elements of society, incapable of taking upon themself responsibility for positive building. The bureaucratic realm has its own correlative as a revolutionary realm. This is very old a truth, which always is ignored by our rightists elements. The revolutionary aspect itself has twofold a nature. It can be a creative impulse towards new life, and it also can be purely destructive, anarchy-like for society. The bureaucratic realm gives prevalence to this second revolutionary type. The societal element, lacking in self-organisation, in self-initiative and self-discipline, always is doomed to anarchisation, in it ripen anarchic instincts, whether as "leftist" or "rightist", alike destructive. Only a positive societal creativity, organised and disciplined, will save matters from destructive catastrophes of anarchy. Societal conservatism tends also though to possess a certain one-sidedness, but nonetheless the connection with the life of the people and life itself gives impetus towards an awareness of the necessity of the growth of life, of a self-initiating society. Such is the conservatism of the English type. But the bureaucratic conservatism can lead to a closed-in type of existence, shielded away from vital influences, shutting off all the pressure valves, pushing back every energy of reform inwards, reducing it to a sickened intensity. Too often it plays the role of reverse-revolutionary. Our task -- is to give preference to creatively positive powers over powers that are negative, debilitating and destructive.

Regarding a New Book on the Masons

(1916 - 238)[1]

There has appeared a book by A. N. Pynin [Aleksandr Nikolaevich 1833-1904], -- "Russian Masonry. XVIII and First-Quarter XIX Centuries". In it are gathered old articles, revised by the modern specialist on Masonry, G. V. Vernadsky, and provided with his comments. I should want to say some few words about this book, but not from a specifically historical point of view. At the present time, interest on this theme has quite increased and the appearance of an informative work in this area is quite opportune. Within the cultural segment is to be noted an heightened interest towards secret societies, towards mysticism and occultism. However, works regarding the history of such sorts of spiritual trends are quite few. Mystical trends within the Russian society of the end-XVIII and early-XIX Centuries all still remain in the shadows, insufficiently known of and insufficiently known. And amidst this, we happen to be witnessing the rebirth of suchlike a trend. It suffices but to point to the growth of the theosophic movement. Regrettably, the perception of "Masonry" all still remains murky and is employed in too wide a sense. In recent times indeed in our Black Hundredist literature this term is used quite irresponsibly (vide the curious book by A. Selyaninov, "The Secret Power of Masonism"), and towards political ends. The whole mystical literature of the Alexandrine Era has gotten smeared for us as "Masonic literature", though in it is many a book having nowise a relationship to the history of

---

[1] PO POVODU NOVOI KNIGI O MASONSTVE. Article was originally published in newspaper "Birzhevye vedomosti", 16 sept. 1916, № 15805.

This present article was not included in the massive "*Padenie*" Russian text, from which most of the articles in our current English text are taken. Rather, the present article in Russian text was republished in the 2004 anthology of Berdyaev articles under cover title "*Mutnye liki*" ["Murky Visages"], taking its name from title of one of Berdyaev's articles contained therein: Moskva, 2004, Kanon+, this article p. 128-131.

Masonry in the particular sense of the word. And also in the book of Pynin, which provides much in the way of valuable accounts and material, the word "Masonism" gets employs in very broad a sense. The author speaks much be it about the history of mysticism, about occult teachings and orders, about J. Boehme and Saint-Martin [Louis Claude de, 1743-1803], and about alchemy and magic, and about Rosenkreuzerism [Rosicrucianism, the "Rose-Cross" order] and the Illuminati. Type-specific investigations involving the existence of differences between mysticism and occultism barely exist. And in the "enlightening" though insufficiently enlightened consciousness of Pynin, everything gets jumbled. The book was written in a very ponderous language, as is everything, that Pynin has written, and is not distinguished by thought either deep or broad. In it predominates the point of view of the rationalist Enlightenment, steadfastly denying any independent value in these spiritual phenomena, with which the author deals. And suchlike a sort of Enlightenment mindset tends not to stand at the summits of modern cultural inquiries.

  Towards mysticism, and towards the occult teachings and societies, there ought to be at present more penetrating an attitude, admitting of an independent significance behind this sphere of spiritual life. As regards his culture, as regards the character of his upbringing and the character of his era, and as regards his whole spiritual outlook, Pynin is completely unprepared to render judgements on such phenomena, as the Templars and Rosicrucians, or the teachings of Boehme and Saint-Martin, or the occult Masonism. To do so requires more refined and profound a spiritual culture, more empathic a spiritual outlook. Pynin provides purely an external history. He looks at Masonism from exclusively a societal perspective. Everything that goes beyond the bounds of positive science and the rationalist enlightenment mindset represents for him but charlatanism or obscurantism. But soon there will ensue a time and indeed has already come a time, when there will be termed as obscurantism this rationalist denial of the profoundest investigations of the human spirit. The Russian Masons of old in certain regards were wiser than our foremost enlighteners of the decades of the 60's and 70's. Pynin regards it all the time necessary to apologise for the hapless Novikov, in that this acknowledged activist of the Russian Enlightenment got caught up with mysticism, with the secrets of Rosicrucianism etc. Such a sort of making excuses for Novikov is not necessary, and this method itself of resorting to an excuse is not scientific, but rather the old, rationalist-enlightenment approach to questions. Pure science ought to be prepared to admit whatever is appropriately a phenomenon of spiritual life and to investigate it at depth, not itself inserting and introducing any sort of rational boundaries. A true science has to immerse itself in its object of study, intuitively to be alive within it, admitting as worthy of knowledge the mystery and the enigmas therein, whereas the old scientific theories and unscientific "enlightenment" currents would admit of nothing, except non-being. We already well know, that there is indeed possible a rationalist-enlightenment obscurantism, appearing under the guise of science.

The book of Pynin provides us very valuable materials, and imparts many an account. But this does not give it a basis to term this work a knowing of Masonry, a discerning of the meaning of this spiritual movement. For a genuine knowing of secret societies it is needful to be moreso an initiate into their secret mysteries, to make an approach towards these matters from within, and not externally. This is a truth quite indisputable in regard to the investigation of religions, wherein it is impossible to grasp the chiefest things, if one be merely negative to such and provide but external an explanation.

With the histories of Templarism, of Rosicrucianism, Martinism and the Illuminati, everything proves more complex and enigmatic, than is presented by Pynin in the shallowness of his enlightenment view. This is an area awaiting its own unbiased investigation. The profundities of gnostic-mystic contemplation stand totally beyond the grasp of Pynin's understanding, but he regards it possible to speak about them with contempt and pass judgement upon them. Chapters IX and X of his book are written without sufficient grounds, since the author is nowise a specialist of the history of mystical, gnostic and occult teachings. His constant complaints, that Masonry has not preserved the character which it had in England, where it had been connected with the rationalist enlightenment Deism, makes apparent his whole unpreparedness for orientations into the complexity of European Masonism. The sole thing that can be said for Pynin, is this scrutinising of Masonry in regard to the growth of our societal self-initiative. Russian Masonry was, certainly, a form of our societal activity and self-initiative, and it is subjected to investigation in this aspect. Its history is very instructive in this regard. And indeed at present our rightists love everywhere to uncover a "Masonic" intrigue. But within Masonry there was also an entirely other, a spiritual side, which has remained beyond Pynin's grasp. Masonism was a transplanted Westernism upon Russian soil the same, as was the French Enlightenment. In it there was little in the way of an independent national thought. The mystical "Masonic" movement has left almost no traces within the farthest subsequent Russian literature and Russian thought. But the mystical literature of that time in a peculiar way has filtered down into the spiritual life of the people, and at present finds a reading amidst the theosophists and God-seekers among the people. And in that J. Boehme via a Russian translation was cast into Russian life, is a remarkable fact of the spiritual culture. In terms of the materials of Pynin, just as in terms of many materials yet unpublished, the history of Russian Masonism has still to be written from the perspective of its inner attainment and thought process, as a moment of self-valued spiritual life. The history of the Russian spirit demands within all its spheres radical re-evaluations of the perspectives, proffered by the school of Pynin.

On the Growth of Bourgeoisness in Russia

(1916 - 239)[1]

I.

Russia of recent is becoming Europeanised. But this Europeanisation is of a sort, that leads to the saddest of thoughts. Our civil arrangement is still not all that Europeanised. With us there is no genuine European style of industrial initiative. Our industrial backwardness provides quite bitter an experience during a time of war. In too many regards within Russian life there is still tied in the insurmountable culture of Eastern elements. But of recent years in Russia is to be noticed a bourgeois process, which is an "Europeanisation" of Russia in the form of a borrowing of the most poisonous fruits of the European bourgeoise. During the time of war we have seen not only a national upsurge, a capacity for sacrifice and extraordinary endurance, but likewise also an orgy of plunder and dark speculation. The distributive necessity has led not to unity amidst all the people, but rather to discord and class hostility. They mull over an easy gain, they get rich off the war, grandiose financial speculations are made, shams by nature, and the power of money grows, which becomes all more and more fictive. The power of money, the cult of money is also the realm of the bourgeoise, an illusory realm. In this realm the genuine realities vanish and there is lost the capacity of appreciating their value. Life gets submerged into a fiction, all more and more enticing.

As for a genuine industrial sense of enterprise, a strong will to cultivating the Russian earth and its natural riches, there is not. In this regard we are first of all too inclined to place our hope on foreigners, now already not the Germans, but instead upon the English and the Americans. But we are quick to imitate the incidentals and moreover also the vilest wonts of the European bourgeoise, that which is least real in it, its scum as it were. We tend to assimilate for ourself not so much the habits of industrial

---

[1] O ROSTE BURZHUAZNOSTI V ROSSII. Article was originally published in newspaper "Birzhevye vedomosti", 20 sept. 1916, № 15813.

creativity, as rather the habits of money speculation, which are not only fruitless for the economic developement of the land, but also to high a degree harmful and dangerous. Speculators and swindlers abound, along with every sort of shady dealers, treading the fine line between civil and criminal law. The European bourgeois sector is morally inclined towards restraint during a time of war. The Europeanised Russian bourgeois sector is however morally dissolute. The instincts of personal-class greed seem stronger than instincts of national service. Russian literature, Russian journalism, Russian thought has been justly proud of its purity, its richness of idea, never has it gone off into serving some special interests, and it is impossible that it should be open to any sort of plunder and speculation. But all this can change and is already changing. We can become Europeans in the worst aspects, without having become Europeans in the best aspects. We have had very poor an experience with the process of the demise of the old organic order in Russian life, giving birth to a "bourgeoisness" bereft of any idea-based pathos or idea-based sanction. The bourgeoise in Russia has sensed itself limited in idea, and Russian people of the better sort have had little tolerance for it and granted it no progressive a place in life. And the bourgeoise have been scornful towards ideas.

When it became dominant, its dominance then became totally impudent and shameless. The Russian bourgeoise lacked any sort of mission in idea, any sort of national purpose, remaining all instead in the sphere of private interests and appetites. The Russian bourgeoise has not grown into a creative class and has not been transformed to a sufficient degree into a politically conscious "third estate". Within it are still too strong the plundering instincts of the old merchant world. The old populist intelligentsia is gradually dying out and vanishing. The intelligentsia of however the new type, with different a spiritual tempering of the person, is yet insufficiently strong and insufficiently numerous. And the spirit of bourgeoisness is beginning to infect Russia, though still at its surface level. But there is cause to worry, lest the poison spread inwards.

In regard to the soul of Russia and the Russian people, all our national ideologues have asserted, that this -- is the most non-bourgeois soul in the world, the least captivated by temptations of earthly wealth and earthly power. And in all these assertions was to be discerned a certain profound truth concerning Russia and the Russian people. Yet is it possible that this truth should relate only to the past and that it be inapplicable towards the future? Is it possible that the finest traits of the Russian people, upon which are based faith in its great mission in the world, were connected merely with the economic and cultural backwardness of Russia? In Slavophilism and in Populism, variously via their own unique view of Russia riveted tight to outmoded social forms, there was the danger of losing faith in Russia with the instance of the decay of old social forms and the arising of new ones. But for one, who believes in the existence of the soul of the people, as dwelling beyond all the changes from the historical process and its changes, such a person ought to find himself freed of these fears. Our people's soul is undergoing historical tribulations and temptations. Every historical tendency, every developement bears with it trials for the people's character. And yet here now we have a shallow, a superficial segment of the Russian people subject to the allure of quick and easy gain. The catastrophe of the war, rendering the whole of life so complicated and so confused, has made a muddle of everything. War is always twofold, it begets both heroism, and vileness also.

II.

That portion of the populace, which has profited during the time of war and from the war, cannot be something vitally alive. It quickly dissipates, cannot accept participating in the building up of a new life in Russia. This -- is but merely as it were the scum aspect of life, soap bubbles, which quickly burst. Insofar as the bourgeoise can still play a creative role in Russia in matters of economic and political developement, it will not be that part of the bourgeoise, which during the time of the war speculated and profited via murky means. After the end of the war there ought to survive and play a positive role only those powers, which during the time of war have contributed to matters of national defense, of national unity and national developement. Those powers, which during the time of war conducted themself shamefully and anti-nationally, which thought only of their own interests and appetites, ought essentially to be disdained and overshadowed in matters of national renewal. And this ought to be prompted by the direct national instincts of the people.

A people, which would allow the playing of a defining role and the holding of power by those elements, which vampire-like have profited on the war, on the great tribulations and sufferings of the people, cannot have great a future. This -- is a question of an healthy national biology, and not only of the people's ethics. Those murky aspects, which accompany the war

-- the dishonesty of merchants, greedy industrialists, the appetites of the landholders and sugar-producers, the monstrous speculation of the financial dealers -- all this will be given over to the severe judgement of history and the people, who will have survived and created their own historical destiny. The healthy instincts of a national self-preservation and historical reason likewise will itself cast aside these dark elements. The fact, that at the time of the war there was granted too great a power to the large landholders, the sugar-producers and dealers, will be looked upon as a sickness within our civil and economic organism, as an enslaving of the people. The interests of the property holders, already gained or still gainable, were set above the interests of the state. The economic chaos during wartime shows all the importance and necessity of civil and societal regulation of the economy. The anarchy brought about by private interests represents a national danger.

Russia mustneeds have national growth, industrial initiative and industrial creativity. And in this regard it has facing it likewise an "Europeanisation", just like in regard to its state structure, its political developement. Those, who are afraid of this, -- do not believe in Russia. The fear is the result of unbelief. The "bourgeois spirit", and in still indeed a most dissolute and baneful form, cannot hold sway in Russia, cannot take hold the Russian soul at its depths. All the great presentiments and prophecies are opposed to this. Russia with its own unique spirit has its own lot, its own vocation in the world. The compulsory, the "European" forms of social and political existence nowise signify the quenching and depersonalisation of the people's spirit. And within the people's spirit has to be revealed the possibility of creative developement. Spirit cannot be riveted fast to social a sort of matter and be in slave-like a dependence upon it. The dissolution of the old Russian patriarchal system, of the old ordering of the life of the people, based upon extensive a culture, gives rise to a whole series of monstrous and sickly aspects. The rapacious and criminal aspects of Russian "bourgeoisness" -- are but an ailment of growth. These aspects, accompanying our transition to a new order of life, such as might be based upon more intensive a culture, ultimately have to win out in further developement. This -- is a rotting away of the elements of old Russia, which as such lack in ability to creatively adapt to the demands of new life, and instead tend only to adapt to vampire-like a plundering. And it can be said, that although the "bourgeoisification" of Russia is something new, and is the fashioning of a new style, still however this is new only in the old and for the old. The authentically new powers of Russia have however to be mobilised and organised for the struggle against the orgy of dark impulses, assailing Russia and the Russian people. The grievous experience of the war has to lead to new beginnings in economic creativity and economic organisation, just as in the West, so also in Russia. Yet in our path of industrial developement we shall approach at different a timeframe, inspired by different a spirit, than that which occurred at the beginning periods of developement of European capitalism.

The State and Ownership during a Time of War

(1916 - 242)[1]

I.

Property owners are accustomed to regard themself as the chief supporting prop for the state. The dangers, threatening from a revolutionary socialism, have tended only to strengthen this view, though socialism in its potential involves an intensification of the state. But up til now private property has remained for the state an absolute and inviolable sanctity. This sacred as it were aspect in the XIX and XX Centuries has been acknowledged even by those, who admit of no sanctities. The statists and nationalists have usually conceived of themself as defenders of property ownership and have seen in it a strongly civil and national supporting prop. All those however, who have undermined the absolute principle of property ownership, are considered destroyers of the civil and national welfare. There has been worked out a conditional phraseology, connected with suchlike an understanding of the correlation between the state and property ownership. This phraseology flourishes even at present, though at the present time in history it has been transformed into a bald-faced lie. At the present time, the instincts of property ownership have clashed with instincts patriotic. The experience of the war forces quite much to be looked at anew, too much of the unanticipated, the unforeseen by any sort of theories or doctrines, has accompanied it. Even the reevaluation of this evident truth, that the immediate interests of the property owners are manifest as an assuredly civil and national supportive prop. In the moment of danger for the state, when heroic efforts and heroic measures are demanded, the interests of property ownership have proven unreliable and the bearers of these interests incapable of sacrifice.

---

[1] GOSUDARSTRVO I SOBSTVENNOST' VO VREMYA VOINY. Article was originally published in newspaper "Birzhevye vedomosti", 15 oct. 1916, № 15863.

Nicholas Berdyaev

The world war has brought with it unprecedented difficulties for economic organisms. Former large scale wars transpired amidst a natural economy, which was more balanced an affair, less dependent upon transport, on less worldwide a scope of interaction, less dependent on the power of money, and as such these wars were unable to provoke such acute crises in distribution, as with the present day war. The semi-capitalist economy is convulsively attempting to adapt to totally new and unanticipated worldwide conditions. And though it has proven more viable, than would have been imagined at the beginning of the war, the anarchy-like nature of this economy is all more and more to be felt. Daily bread for the warring peoples cannot be sufficiently guaranteed by an economy, in which there are no state or societal regulations. In many regards, the war in its elements tends to socialise the economy, to introduce into economic life a principle of collectivity and the limitation of individual initiative. The private interests of the landowners, of the industrialists and the merchants during wartime are clashing already now not with the interests of the peasants and workers, but rather with the interests of the state, with the interests of national defense and security. This -- is a completely new aspect, unknown during peacetime. The defense of the state amidst a worldwide struggle of peoples, the necessity of keeping people fed under quite exceptional conditions demands state limitation of the private interests of the large scale property owners. The objective needs of the state therein demand a series of measures in the direction of a partial socialising of the economy. Private property owners have been accustomed at the slightest cause to cry out about a socialist danger and appeal for state protection. But now their din of interests and wonts represents a danger to the state. Socialisation of the economy, called for by wartime demands, proceeds not by means of those paths, which were predicated on socialist doctrines, since life never develops in accord with doctrines. This vital process evokes alike a dissatisfaction both with the defenders of an inviolable private ownership and with the defenders of a class socialism. This social process, the result of the unprecedented catastrophe of the war, in all actuality, will be the end to both the old capitalism and the old socialism.

In Germany, where the state and national instincts for organising have been especially strong, enormous strides have already been taken in the direction of a socialising of the economy; the principles of a state socialism there are clearly winning out. The thesis point of private ownership serving as the chief prop for the state and nationality in Germany stands refuted by life, and even the most conservative of its defenders, assuming they are sincere patriots, are compelled to adopt a totally different point of view.

The objective nature of the state and national existence has itself compelled a socialising of the economy in moments of peril. This has nothing to do with class, this -- is a national process. The same process is occurring also in the other warring lands, but with less powerful state-organising instincts, than in Germany. And after the end of the war it seems scarcely likely that there will be a return to the previous forms of the economy, for new habits have too deeply taken hold in life.

II.

The greatest degree of the economic chaos with provision supplies in wartime can be seen with us in Russia, though our national wealth of resources is greater, than in other lands. The explanation for this is not that with us there is especially developed the principle of a private capitalistic economy, but rather, that Russia is an industrially backward land and that the authority of rule with us is cut off from the life of the people. Weakly developed in Russia is a civil-societal self-initiative, and anarchic principles can be discerned also within our state order of things. Measures are needed, winning out over the chaos and organising economic life, conformable to our greater backwardness. And yes there are always the half-measures, internally at variance and not leading to any sort of complete plan. We shall have to enter upon the path of a certain socialising of the economy, for this -- is of a state and natural necessity. But this can transpire all too late, under the threat of collapse. The purely class interests of the landowners, and in part also of the industrialists, penetrate all the way into the upper governmental spheres and render the state a tool of the property owners. And thus, the landowner class politics [...] is truly manifest as anti-state and anti-national; for this sort of politics the interests of the landowners stands higher than the interests of the state, higher than the national security during the period of this terrible war.

The provisions distribution process for us [...] is causing problems at the rear. It reflects a threat on the part of private interests, making for chaotic governance, in regard to the state interests, demanding national organisation. This -- should be problematic to the state, for betraying its objective nature, its calling to stand above all the private interests. If the state becomes an organ of class governance and of totally private wishes, then at a moment of national peril it would become a source of disorder in fomenting chaos. The nature of the state -- is objective, transcending this or that other wont of the governing authority, and certain objective forces are always active within it. But at certain moments there penetrates into the state governance an element of dissolution, it gets swamped with private, personal and class demands, and it comes to betray its objectively national calling and then there begin days of greater tribulations across the whole spectrum of national life. For us, this coincides with the terrors of an unprecedented war. At such moments the ruling authority ought to the utmost to be national, expressive of the will of the whole people. Our tragedy however consists in this, that the governing authority to an utmost degree digresses from this normal condition.

During the time of such a terrible war the interests of the state coincide with the interests of the consumers. The normal issue of providing food for the people is one of the essential aspects in the defense of the state. The war is leading to the exhaustion of various peoples. Entire states are being rendered into besieged fortresses. Satisfying the daily bread interests of consumers signifies order and health in our read-guard. The flaunting of the appetites of private property owners signifies however signifies a break-down at the rear and leads to the danger of a chaotic collapse. The immediate interests of the private property owners and private merchants, nowise limited, nor subject to any sort of overall national organisational plan, do not at present represent a supporting prop for the state. These unchecked interests now represent instead a danger for the state, a threat to our national health.

The state by its nature stands higher than property ownership, it is constructive towards property ownership, but it cannot be constructed upon property ownership. And when essential national interests and dangers demand it, the state not only can, but it must organise and set limits to the unchecked and unrestrained element amongst private property owners and private merchants. But only the state authority has the powers to get this done, in keeping with the public trust and genuinely expressing the needs of the people.

III.

A purely police understanding of the state, be it conservative or liberal, is long since outdated. Creative social tasks face the state. The principle of laissez-faire long since already has been consigned to the archives. During the time of the terrible experience of the world war least of all can the state be relegated to merely police functions, it is compelled rather to enter upon the path of the organisation and regulation of economic life. Measures for state and societal socialisation of the economy, which ought not to be confused with nor identified with a class socialism, are fully in accord with modern legal outlooks, such as long ago have surmounted the old doctrinaire liberalism. But amidst the currently constituted ruling authority, the measures for a state regulation of the economy would bear purely a political character and would dismantle the apparatus of a free market, but without replacing it by any other sort of organising apparatus. And the administrative arbitrariness would merely increase the economic chaos.

Amongst the left-wing socialist intelligentsia very widespread have been socialist utopias. But since our intelligentsia has never been called to creative historical work nor to the accomplishing of its ideas within actual life, its ideas therefore have been irresponsible and its confessed social teachings merely doctrinaire. With us there has been great boldness and radicalism in elaborating ideas together with an insufficient boldness with vital a start. We are afraid to take upon ourself responsibility, we fear to dirty ourself in the vital actual startings and we instead prefer to be left within an inactive and irresponsible purity. The Russian intelligentsia has become accustomed to think in a certain manner about the realisation of its social ideals. It is afraid of the state, and the radicalism of state measures evokes in it mistrust. Yet it mustneeds be said, that the path towards which the talking tends, is possible only amidst a tight connection of the state powers with the societal organisations, with the self-initiative of all the societal groups. It is essentially necessary for us to realise, that the Russian state is our own state, and not "their" state. Whereas there is our rightful mistrust towards this or some other governmental authority, our opposition however has passed over into a mistrust and opposition to the state itself, has led to a forgetting of the objective nature of the state, such as embodies our proper energy. The question concerning the organisation of the governmental power is impossible [...] to get confused with the objective nature itself of the state.

We have had difficult aims proposed, and because of them a struggle has blazed forth. But the difficult aims and of price-fixing itself in general represent a dangerous half-measure, which would lead to a disappearance of products. Firm aims would lead to the desired results only in connection with the application of requisitions, compulsory state purchases, etc. But the state authorities are afraid of these measures, in being pressured by the property owners, chiefly the landowners, and the societal front also is hesitant, in its mistrust of the ruling authorities. All the vexing crises of Russian life thus lead to the problem of the arrangement of the ruling authority, in utilising the trust of society, of the people, in its nature. Any other path for the ruling powers now appears as something anti-state, undermining the objective power of the state.

The property owners have to realise, that if they oppose the needed measures of socialisation, such as would bring order and organisation to our economic life, it would then threaten Russia with suchlike a chaos and suchlike an anarchy, that in the final end, would engulf them also.

Certain self-restraints and saving sacrifices are not only for the life of all the land, but also for those, who consent to self-restraint and entering into sacrifice. And it is the better to enter upon this path the earlier as possible, transcending a view on private property as some sort of fetish or idol. This demands a civil and national instinct of self-preservation, the elementary instinct of self-preservation. We, as Russians, have to fight within ourself against the anarchistic instincts, which are strong both on the right and on the left, both from above and from below. In the inevitable renewal and rebirth of our civil and societal life, the instincts for organising and legality have to win out over instincts chaotic and destructive. Anarchy in Russia is of our old life, and not of our new life. And the anarchistic dissipation under the instincts of property can now become feckless, in threatening the objective nature of the state.

The Church Question in Russia

(1916- #240)[1]

I.

The question concerning church reform has caught us in sort of an impasse. It seems impossible to find a mechanism, rendering it possible to move forward out from the point of inertia in matters of external churchly issues. They seem clueless, regarding as from what sides to approach church reforms. Too entangled have become the churchly and the civil, the heavenly and the earthly, the spiritual and the material. How is the breath of the Spirit to become embodied within the external, the material churchly transformations? And indeed, do we even have suchlike a breathing of the Spirit, which can be brought into church renewal? Has not everything gotten too ossified within churchly life, living by the laws of inertia, the lifeless mere imitator of the old life of the Spirit, rather than a living tradition, eternally creating life anew? There has been worked out an entire system Orthodoxy as exclusively a system of safe-guarding. But has not this safe-guarding gone too far, and reached the point of ossification?

That which seemed comparatively clear and simple a matter in 1904-1905 as regards the church renewal movement, has now been rendered verymost complex and elusive. It might seem quite strange at first glance, but the Europeanisation of the Russian civil and social order, initiated in 1905, has led within the sphere of churchly life to the formation and rise of clericalism as a class movement. Clericalism -- is Western European a phenomenon, and in Russia it never had genuine a growth. The Europeanisation of Russia ("Europeanisation" is but a conditional signification of an irreversible process of developement) gives rise to a whole series of differentiations and considerations. Various social groupings crystalise and isolate off, operating under the group and class consciousness. The "People" in the old Slavonic and populist sense of this

---

[1] TSERKOVNYI VOPROS V ROSSII. Article was originally published in the weekly "Birzhevye vedomosti", 28 sept. 1916, № 15829.

word is gradually vanishing, -- in its primordial, materio-organic wholeness is beginning a social and psychological differentiation. In the deeper, the metaphysical and spiritual signification concerning the "People", certainly, will remain and prevail forever, but its manner of life gradually is becoming free of its seemingly inseparable connections with an aspect social, with outmoded forms of economic and civil life. To the populists it has seemed, that the "People" is completely perishing, if finally there is to crumble away the age-old Russian foundations, such as flourished in pre-Petrine Rus', and that Russia is ultimately entering upon the path of "Europeanisation". But that which the populists and Slavophils were afraid, -- has become fact, a fact inevitable. The "People" in their old sense of the word has vanished. Already it has become impossible to speak about either the Orthodox Rus' of the Slavophils, or about the peasant Rus' of the populists, already upon these paths it is impossible to seek out the unique image of Russia. The course of Russian life has inflicted blow upon blow to all the Slavophil and populist conceptions in the sphere of churchly life. If populism and Slavophilism mustneeds be regarded as done with and passé in artistic life, and that too with state and lifestyle, then no less have they tended to crumble away, and no less reactionary-utopian are they in churchly life. The life of the Spirit, of the Spirit of Christ, cannot be but only attached to material forms, the connections with merely a certain stage of historical developement.

And we now have facing us the very complex problem of the relationship between the Kingdom of God (the Church) and the kingdom of Caesar (the state). New times demand also new decisions. And thus the resolution of this problem, which is based upon the idea of purely a Christian, or more precisely, of purely Orthodox a state, has been found to be sufficiently inconsistent and a great falsehood at its basis, a great hypocrisy in its fruits.

II.

All the external, the material historical whole of churchly life is by thousands of threads attached and tied in with the kingdom of Caesar, with all the civil, economic, legal and lifestyle structures of society. The Church is drawn into the cycle of social evolution, and in its external organisation it always has to be adaptable to changes in the kingdom of this world. When under Peter there occurred a revolutionary Europeanisation of the

Russian secular state, the Church then came to adapt to this process, and there began the Synodal period in the history of the Russian Church, in which very much was recast into German Lutheran settings, and the Church was put into quite servile a dependence upon the state. In the era of Pobedonostsev's control the Russian hierarchy groaned under the burden of the bureaucratic grip of the state over the Church. Many hierarchs dreamt about a restoration of the Patriarchate and a return to the pre-Petrine order. But here in the Russian kingdom of Caesar in 1905 there occurred a turnabout, which was, though neither decisive nor radical, still nonetheless a step towards the Europeanisation of our civil structure, -- there appeared the Constituent Assemblies, having to deal with all the issues of Russian life. Earlier on had begun the Europeanisation of Russian socio-economic life -- there started the growth of capitalist production, the village obschina-commune faded off, and the remnants of a patriarchal mode of life disintegrated. The life of the Church in its trappings does not possess that complete freedom and independence from the realm of Caesar, which would have given it the possibility to further survive, without having to take into account whatever should transpire in the life of the state. Everything became unstable in churchly life, there was an acute sense of churchly irregularities and a bitter dependency on the government, in which had been destroyed the old sense of harmony and the ensuing of inauspiciously transitory a period. The church organism lacked the wherewithal for self-administration. The Sobornost'/Communality of the Russian Church existed only as an idea, and not in life. A churchly people were nowhere to be found. There began a struggle of parties within churchly life: reform aspirations clashed with reactionary aspirations. A process of differentiation took hold also upon public churchly life. Outside this process remained only individual startsi/elders, devoting their life to mystical contemplations. The clergy came to sense itself as a social group within the Russian state, and in it awakened a class consciousness. In one part of the clergy this class consciousness assumed a form progressive, while yet in the other part -- a form reactionary. There became apparent a rather sharp difference between the strivings of the higher episcopate from that of the strivings of the average masses of the white clergy. The clergy began to take part in the political struggle, and the reactionary aspect itself of the clergy was rendered into a sort of Western European phenomenon, quite the opposite to the Slavophil and populist image of the clergy.

Clericalism is a matter of class party, actively acting within the realm of Caesar, pushing for earthly, too earthly aims. And in the midst of our upper hierarchs grows a spirit of reactionary clericalism. This -- involves their active reaction against changes in our state structure. The reactionary portion of the clergy is of a mindset very hostile to the Constituent Assemblies, and does not want to allow any sort of input from the State Duma into churchly affairs, nor any sort of Duma control over them. This seems to it a secularisation of the Church, a dependency of the Church upon secular measures, amidst which so many non-believers also have fallen away from the Church, and then too there are no little a number of people of different faith-confessions. From the outside one might tend to think, that in such a manner there is upheld the freedom and independence of the Church from the kingdom of this world. And every religious man ought to have a feel for such freedom and independence of the Church. Yet from purely a religious point of view it would be unpleasant to think, that the reforms of the Church could produce totally worldly people, not only foreign to the inner life of the Church, but consistently and entirely non-believers, atheists in toto. Clearly, it would seem, that the renewal of the Church can only be a matter of the spiritual powers of the Church itself. And as regards the spiritual powers of the Church it is necessary, certainly, not the churchly hierarchs alone, but rather all the people of the Church. A Sobornost' of the members of the State Duma, however, is not the Sobornost' of the people of the Church, in a religious regard it is something completely fortuitous. But in actuality, this problem is quite more complex. The government offices make pretense to have involvement with churchly matters only insofar as -- that they are civil matters and immersed in the worldly realm, which entirely have to be reformed and renewed. The inner life of the Church, the spiritual life is nowise affected by this.

III.

The apprehensions regarding government involvement on the part of the churchly hierarchy are hypocritical and but tend to mask a thirst for political restoration. Our churchly hierarchy long ago already surrendered not only its body, but also its soul to the realm of Caesar, it long ago already admitted of the defining role of the secular realm in the outward life of the churchly order of things.

Our whole Synodal arrangement is a total subordination to the state, is a denial of Sobornost' in the strict churchly sense of this word. Dependence upon the Uber-Prokurator and on the state power, that which lies concealed behind the Uber-Prokurator, is in no less a degree, a dependency upon the secular realm, no less a degree than in the dependency upon the State Duma. There is nowise a guarantee of genuinely Orthodox Uber-Prokurators, and among them have been people with clearly a sectarian, Khlysty-type tendency (Pr. Golitsyn) or Catholic a tendency (Graf Protasov), and others that in the depths of their soul were simply non-believers or merely indifferent. The Orthodox conception of the secular authority is either an accommodation to certain interests or a phantasy of ideologues. At present this conception is almost impossible to be sincerely held. Every state authority belongs to completely different an order, than does the Church of Christ, and these two realms are incompatible. But the abject servility of our episcopate in regard to the old state authority has reached to the extent of a negation of every churchly sense of dignity. I say moreover: the external churchly arrangement with its hierarchy has been and is to a remarkable degree a kingdom of this world. This -- is a phenomenon historical, and not a phenomenon of spirit. And it has to share in the fate of history, of historical evolution. Moreover, the external churchly setup in essence has always shared this fate. The churchly order of things tends also to have to adapt itself to a new arrangement, has to participate in the process of developement. Reactionary politics are no more spiritual, than is a progressive politics. The Church has to be inwardly prepared for its total detachment from the state, which is an indisputable tendency and aim of the developement of the relationship between the two realms -- the Kingdom of God and the kingdom of Caesar. This preparedness of the Church to be totally detached from every secular realm will also be a portent of its inner, invisible might. The secularisation of all civil, social and cultural life is not only inevitable, but also is good a process, behind which lies hidden a liberation of the spirit and of the life of the spirit from all manner of fetters, -- at congealed religious a depth. This -- is a demand of truth, a great cleansing of churchly life from hypocrisy, falsehood and violence. The old dependence upon the state was more enslaving for the free life of the Church, than this new, howsoever repulsive, yet in essence merely seeming dependence upon government authorities.

Nicholas Berdyaev

A progressive and liberating reform of the churchly arrangement will never be initiated by the upper churchly hierarchy. The local Sobor/Council, dominated by bishops, will but restore the Patriarchate and consolidate the clericalism, giving a certain predominance to churchly bureaucracy over the civil bureaucracy. A true and liberative process of churchly reform can only be initiated by the Church people, at the spiritual depths of which is amassed a creative religious energy. Only the voice of this gathered Church people, free from burden not only of the civil, but also churchly bureaucracy, would be authentic a voice of the Church. But the free expression of the will of the people of the Church presupposes a profound transformation in that realm of Caesar, in those strictly interwoven ties of state and Church, which led to the enslavement of the Church people, to its forced silence, which shackled down its free will. The local Sobor at present would be constituted and constructed on the basis of the old relationship of Church and state and of the old powers of a churchly bureaucracy, overlaying the civil bureaucracy. This -- is a vicious circle. The local Church Sobor would produce reform in the format of a class spirit, and not in the spirit of Christ, it would be spiritual only in the externals, but even moreso secular, than a Sobor/Council with laity. And finally and from Orthodox a point of view it mustneeds be admitted, that insofar as the churchly order is part of the civil order, being connected with it by thousands of threads, it has to be reformed together with the civil order and sever off much from it. The class dominance of the princes of the Church within the churchly order of things is a dominance civil, and not spiritual, and it ought to be replaced by the authority of the people of the Church, just as the class dominance of the bureaucracy, of the agrarian and large-scale manufacturers, in the final end, ought to be replaced by a self-governing people. All this has religious a meaning, but it is still not a religious rebirth. It is said, that the gates of Hell will not prevail against the Church of Christ. And this remains forever inalterable. But this selfsame Church of Christ is not in the externals of the churchliness of the princes of the Church, devoted to this world, it is not in this or some other churchly order of things. The sanctities of the Church -- are in the sacramental Body of Christ, of the Mystery of Christ, the saints, the Spirit of Christ, which "doth breathe, whence it will". A religious rebirth is possible only inwardly, from the depths, it cannot be created by any sort of external reforms, by way of whatever the Local Sobor/Council, the State Duma or other secular paths. The churchly disorders are the result of a decay in religious energy, of a creative religious energy. The decay of religious energy is however a symptom of the profound religious crisis within modern mankind. It is impossible to live vampire-like off the old, by those things that former generations accomplished, it is necessary to create a new religious life, as it was created in all the times of churchly upsurge, beginning with the Apostles. Only such a creative upsurge of religious energy within the Church people can resolve all the pressing questions of the relationship of Russian Orthodoxy to the Schism, to sectarianism, to Catholicism, to the developement of culture.

On Understanding the Souls of Various Peoples

(1916 - xxx)[1]

An intuitive understanding of the souls of various peoples would surmount the blind hostility, would help bring us closer to what is foreign and hostile. In the depths of understanding there is an utmost love. A mere dram only of love, engendered in our heart, can give intimate an understanding into the souls of the various peoples. This utmost love, bestowing strength, does not exclude strife and hostility. A selective love renders unequal our attitude towards people and the various peoples. Love towards a foreign people cannot be such, as in the love towards one's own people, and towards foreign peoples love becomes varied. I might particularly love the French and not love the Germans (independently of the war). This is totally irrational and demands no sort of justification. But in a certain higher sense I have to have an understanding of the German soul, and in this understanding there has to be a flickering of love towards every individuality created by God. This understanding and penetration into the soul does not weaken my will for the struggle and victory, it renders it evident and enlightens my own struggling. The pathos of strife and war is not a pathos of hatred and destruction. The strife and war ought nowise to be made dependent upon a lack of desire for understanding, via a denying of any sort of worth in the enemy, from out of a feeling of hatred. I can desire the defeat of the German people and its overall weakening, namely because, that I understand the soul of this people and can apprise its dangers as worthy of regard. Certain German virtues are for us most of all dangerous and for us most of all contrary. One suchlike German virtue is a boundless devotion to the state, well nigh idolatrous, a formalistic and heartless fulfilling of duty. The Germans wreak evil in the world out of a powerfully developed sense of duty, out of some sort of consciousness of fulfilling a moral categorical imperative. They wreak this evil as though morally and virtuously, out of a self-assertion and immeasurable devotion to the idol of nationality and the state. To understand this trait of the

---

[1] O PONIMANII NARODNYKH DUSH. Article was originally published in the Volgda gazette "Ekho", 11 nov. 1916, № 531.

German people -- means to be just towards it whilst intensifying one's will to victory over such a people. The struggle of a people cannot be based upon the grounds of elementarily conceived prerogatives. It would be inaccurate to regard the Germans, with their conducting so terrible and horrible a struggle against the world, -- as immoral beings, they in their own way -- are moral beings, but with harshly directed a moral pathos. In depth it might be possible to understand the motives of the present German struggle against the world, and not to regard the German will as exclusively malicious whilst opposing to this will our own unshakable will.

  I indeed desire, that the visage of the Russian people have its imprint upon world life, and not the visage of the German people. This act of will demands no justification, this is first of all -- an act of selective love and faith. This thirst to see imprinted the visage of my own people does not prompt me to any sort of a burning hatred against another people. An intense national feeling can blind one and beget a false nationalism. But it cannot contribute to the experiential knowledge of every national individuality. A breadth of understanding does not debilitate, it strengthens and enriches. Such a breadth of understanding -- is a necessary prerequisite to the existence of a great world empire. A national closed-in narrowness of soul is allowable only for lesser peoples, it is unseemly for Russia and for Russians. We as Russians have to emerge from the world struggle with sharpened and deepened an understanding of the souls of various peoples, with a gift for insight into souls quite foreign and hostile to us. This -- reflects a great strength and a great purpose. This strength of a breadth of understanding is needful for us both within Russia and beyond, it leads out into the expanse of world life. Russia can take pride, in that it has set upon its standard the liberation of all the small oppressed nationalities. It is needful for us to be atop these world tasks. And getting to this stature arises only through an understanding of the souls of various peoples.

The Awakening of the National Will

(1916 - 243)[1]

Quite recently there has begun to be felt a certain awakening of the national will. In the year past, Russian society stirred with a patriotic alarm and mobilised its powers in the name of the slogan for national defense. And now we are experiencing an analogous moment with but this diffference, that the patriotic sense of alarm has evoked the issue of a national danger, threatening us from within. We are in need now not of political actions, but rather national actions. The demands for change within the inner political scene result from patriotic motives and an acute awareness of national tasks. All the political demands of the State Duma have been subordinated to the national patriotic moment. Reaction presents a danger not from the point of view of these or those political parties and political aspirations, but from the point of view of the national and civil in general. The slogan of national unity and public safety has gotten passed on to the Russian societal activism, to the State Duma, to the rural and urban unions, the military-industrial committees, etc. This -- is an enormous, never witnessed historical turnabout. And in Russian history

---

[1] PROBYZHDENIE NATSIONAL'NOI VOLI. Article was originally published in newspaper "Birzhevye vedomosti", 13 nov. 1916, № 15921.

trans. note: The reader will feel puzzled by this volatile article, without some further explanation. Per the *Padenie* (pp. 1102-1103 note), on the 1 November 1916 session of the State Duma occurred a speech by P. N. Miliukov, followed by Shul'gin and Maklarov, spoke of rumours of treachery, of a "camarila/coterie" surrounding the empress/tsarina, specifically regarding the intrigues of G. Rasputin in governmental affairs, threatening dangers for Russia either through "stupidity or villainy". Reports of this speech were interdicted from the press by government censors, but spread nonetheless, causing great public outrage at the havoc wrought by Rasputin and the toadyism of those who fawned on him for power and position.

there have become forever impossible the national-civil justifications of the old reactionary politics. The patriotic slogans have broken away from the ruling authorities, in opposing themself to the societal activism.

All our political attainments are directly dependent upon the degree of our patriotic enthusiasm, upon the growth of a responsible national consciousness within Russian society and the people. And here we have to flat out say, that all is not going well for us. Our people's psyche has undergone a period of decline, a period of shameful weakness. We have not sufficiently gotten all our act together and our will has not always stood atop the tribulations sent down upon us. The events of the past recent days have as it were roused and in any case ought to rouse the societal psyche. A sense of responsibility has to awaken in every Russian citizen. Dark chaos is on the move against Russia and its waves threaten to engulf it. In such a terrible moment, reminiscent of the Time of Troubles era, each Russian man has to fight against the chaos in himself, to gain mastery over his own particular chaotic element by an act of will and consciousness, to fight against the anarchy in his own soul and in the soul of the people. Chaotic anarchy can have for us very contrary manifestations, either very revolutionary, or likewise very reactionary. Yet for the patriotically alert, behind which stands a strong national will, we ought not to go flying off into anarchistic and chaotic manifestations, but rather manifestations that are responsible, organised and constructive. It is not thoughtless revolts that will save Russia from ruin and lead it forth towards a new life, but rather citizen honour and citizen duty, organised patriotic actions, directed towards the guarding of Russia from danger outside and from derivative danger within, and to the freeing it from the darkness of disintegration. At the present hour of history all our liberation aspirations, all the struggle of the societal effort for the right to serve Russia, to guard it and save it from inward disaster, has been subsumed under the great patriotic alert, inwardly motivated by awareness of national tasks in common, threateningly demanding to be done. The struggle for rights now is a struggle for the fulfilling of national obligations and for service: politics has ceased for us to be a struggle of political parties and the struggle of various social forces for power, it has become an expression of an elementary national instinct.

We are experiencing at present a crisis of Russian statecraft. The crisis consists not in this, that some sort of anti-state currents have flooded out upon the Russian state and engaged it in struggle. Rather, this crisis first of all consists, in that a false foundation is laid bare, veiling over the actual workings of the state. Within the state aspect itself there has been a sort of anti-state engrafting. In the national body of Russia itself there has been something foreign, not engendered from the depths of national life, but introduced from the outside. We are therefore living in an era of profoundest regeneration of national and civil awareness. Everything has shifted from its customary spot. It has become impossible to think about anything regarding a regular routine. At the present hour to be a state supporter and nationalist -- means to deny certain groundings of civil and national existence, poisoning our civil and national life. Here is why the nationalist Count [Vitaly] Shul'gin, who in his consciousness has always been a rightist, at the present hour looks almost a revolutionary. The state national slogans at present sound so oppositional. This is also a deep-rooted peculiarity of the moment being experienced by us. This is a terrible knot, with which such difficulty and almost with despair they attempt to loosen, into which is tied up the prolonged historical fate of Russia. And in so onerous an historical hour for us there transpires likewise for us an accounting of all our past. In this setting, which is unknown to the peoples of the West, Russia is having to defend its worth before all the world. It is difficult however for the world to understand all the exceptional fate of Russia, all the contradictions of Russia, which seem absurd to the Western sense of reason.

The peoples of the West apply to Russia their usual evaluations. And yet nothing in Russia are they able to understand. Russia is so mysteriously contradictory, that the great baseness in it has also at the opposite pole its great quality. The Russian people at present has to make the greatest exertion of spirit, in order to show the world, that in Russia there is patriotism, there is a national consciousness, there is a dignity of citizenship. The Russians cannot permit, that they be reckoned slaves, dwelling in a pre-citizen type of condition. It is we ourself waging the war, and not behind us someone conducting it, who arbitrarily can compel us to wage it or compel us to stop with it. In us there has to awaken an aristocratic consciousness of citizenship, an aristocratic citizen attitude towards our native land. Patriotism -- is aristocratic a feeling, it is in those, who sense themself as lords, and not as slaves in their own native land. Patriotism is a great school for citizenship in dangerous an hour for our native land. We have to get through this school not only for the present hour and its urgent needs, but also for all our historical future. The maturity of Russia for world life and a world role will be directly proportional to its consciously manifest citizenship. This patriotism has to be manifest not only outwardly, but also inwardly, not only in relation to the external Germanism, but also in relation to the Germanism within, to the inward enemies of the Russian state, lodged at present on the right. All the correlations have shifted about for us to the point of becoming unrecognisable. The application of the old, the customary categories to these new correlations is totally impossible. We have to win out over the lethargy of thought, which hinders us from anew shedding light on and evaluating events. There has occurred a change of dress, a change of historical masks, and everything is twofold, everything is rendered dual and dual in meaning. There are needed enormous efforts of spirit, to make sense of all this, to separate light from the darkness and to choose for Russia the path of light.

The New Religious Consciousness and History

(1916 - 244)[1]

I.

The article by A. Meier [or Meyer, Aleksandr Aleksandrovich; 1875-1939] concerning my book, "The Meaning of Creativity" [Engl. title: "The Meaning of the Creative Act"], impels a reply.[2] It demands explanations on my part. I am fully in agreement with A. Meier on this, that the new religious consciousness can be based only upon a new aspect, a new fact within the religious life of mankind, and outside of this fact it would totally remain an abstract ideology. I also have a sense of basing myself upon suchlike a fact, upon a certain creative surge within human nature, within the structure of the spiritual experience of man, of mankind in general, of Man with a capital letter. But, as it always happens, this fact, stirring up within the mysterious depths, is not known by all, is not conscious a matter for all. For A. Meier it remains unnoticed, and therefore his discussion with me -- relates totally to the external. And his objections to me involve objects more visible and even on the side of being more perceptible.

The basic reproach, which A. Meier proffers me, is this, -- the reproach of having an "obdurate insensitivity" towards history. This is a

---

[1] NOVOE RELIGIOZNOE SOZNANIE I ISTORIYA. Article was originally published in the weekly "Birzhevye vedomosti", 18 nov. 1916, № 15931.

This present article was not included in the massive "*Padenie*" Russian text, from which most of the articles in our current English text are taken. Rather, the present article in Russian text was republished in the 2004 anthology of Berdyaev articles under cover title "*Mutnye liki*" ["Murky Visages"], taking its name from title of one of Berdyaev's articles contained therein: Moskva, 2004, Kanon+, this article p. 132-139.

[2] Vide "Birzhevye vedomosti" for 28 October.

reproach, which I not only cannot take seriously into account, but which I am quite compelled to retort in return to A. Meier and to those of like mind with him. There exist vital determinants of our sense of history, of our real relationship to it. The greatest testing for the genuineness of a sense of history and the vital determinant of a real attitude towards it is the world war -- an event historical to the extreme, in which all the threads of history converge. And while here in relation to the world-historical events of the present day war, some have had discernment of an acute sense of history, an acute consciousness of the historical hour, others however have but discerned an "obdurate insensitivity". A. Meier, evidently, is of like mind with and is a follower of D. S. Merezhkovsky, or in any case very close to the circle of his outlook and ideas. This is evident from the session of the Petrograd Religio-Philosophic Society, devoted to rendering an opinion on my book, and from all the comments of A. Meier. And herein I have decisively to say, that it is Merezhkovsky namely and his adherents that have displayed an "obdurate insensitivity" in relation to the world war. They tend to say nothing about one of the most shaking and most answerable moments of world history, they cannot deal with world history, since it moves not according to their schemes and outlines, their thought fails to produce new creative work over completely new and unforeseen historical events. Over the course of the war I have written sufficiently many an article (amidst others also in "Birzhevye vedomosti", wherein occurs my conversation with A. Meier) and, they tend to remark, that they have found in them a certain feel for history and historical events. More than once I happened to express the very thought, that the Russian intelligentsia always possessed a weakly developed feeling for history, and it had not the wherewithal for purely historical thought and historical appraisings. For concrete an history, which presents quite original a reality within the hierarchy of being and possesses values quite unique, Russians have been wont to substitute instead values abstractly-moral, abstractly-sociological and abstractly-religious. Within Russian ideologies the historical values always get replaced by sociological and moral categories. Our theocratic ideologies are anti-historical the same, as are our socialistic and anarchistic ideologies. The "sociologism" of the Russian intelligentsia, which so captivates Meier, and to which he would want to ascribe a religious character, always has been bound up with a weak sense of history and with almost a completely atrophied sense of historical responsibility. This is the traditional sociological mindset, behind which lies concealed an extreme moralism, with no love for history, it recoils from everything historical and shews an "obdurate insensitivity" towards such purely historical values, as nationality and the state, as concrete historical tasks within the life of peoples. But this is a very great mistake. "Sociologism" -- is anti-historical, hostile to the creatively-concrete, quite insensitive to the fate of peoples, to their tasks within the world. For "sociologism" such abstract categories, as classes, the international proletariat, are closer and more real, than are such historical concretenesses, such living realities, as nations. The philosophic working of thought long ago already has undercut the sociological world-view. And it has ultimately been swept away and cast beyond the pale by the worldwide conflict of peoples. What now remains of international socialism -- this by-product of "sociologism"? The "religious social aspect" of Merezhkovsky and his like-minded associates is anti-historical and utopianism the same, as is the old international utopianism of the Marxists, or the more recent syndicalism or anarchism of Bakunin etc. Social utopias upon religious a grounding always have manifest an insensitivity towards history and historical fate. All people confessing a social utopianism, either positivist, or upon a religious basis, tend to become castaways left behind by historical events and discarded beyond the pale of history. The coming unknown, to which we approach, belongs not to them, for they imbibe but the dregs of ideas from the XVIII and XIX Centuries.

The "religious societal aspect" of Merezhkovsky and Meier are detached off from cosmic life just the same, in wanting to isolate themself from cosmic energies, as is the sociological societal aspect of the positivists and materialists. This also is a by-product of utopianism, the ignoring of cosmic evil. The abstraction of the societal aspect off from cosmic life is a tendency also of the abstract "sociologism".[1] Those, who are entangled in this abstract sociologism, truly are doomed to an "obdurate insensitivity" towards this historical hour, in which world life has come upon. The cosmic world-sense is more receptive to history, than is the sociological world-view, since the historical process is concrete and an

---

[1] Vide my article, "The Cosmic and the Sociological World-Sense" [1916-Kl.#235] in "Birzhevye vedomosti".

trans. note: this above-mention article comprises Chapter 16 in Berdyaev's 1918 book, "The Fate of Russia" (Kl. № 15) and thus is not included in our present tome.

inalienable part of the cosmic process, and at present in the historical actuality is particularly to be felt the actings of cosmic energies. It is namely those, which have a feel for history and the current historical hour, who ought to sense all the significance of the transition from the sociological consciousness to a consciousness cosmic. The problem of the unification of East and West, of the emergence of culture beyond the boundaries of Europe, the movement beyond the oceans towards other continents, the ultimate formations of enormous imperialistic bodies and the liberation of small national bodies, all these -- are problems historical and cosmic. The very growth of technical mastery over all the powers of nature, is set within the cosmic problem and is contiguous with that of cosmic evil. Merezhkovsky and Meier who is like-minded with him stand entirely on the outside of these historical tasks and historical presentiments. They remain locked up in their own socio-religious utopias, they impotently attempt to substitute the absolute for the relative, confusing the various planes. A religious societal aspect, insofar as one can speak about it, is but an inalienable part of the cosmic societal aspect, a certain felicitous communing correspondence amidst all the cosmic hierarchy.

II.

A. Meier totally fails to understand my attitude towards history. With him, we seem to be speaking in different languages and, evidently, we belong to different planets. I have first of all striven to establish religiously and philosophically the distinctions between the sphere absolute and the sphere relative and to render impossible the absolutisation of the relative, which always has been a source of slavery. There has to be religiously admitted the right to existence of the relative, and a defending of the relative from its ultimate being swallowed up by the absolute. The absolutisation of the relative, the substitution of the absolute in place of the relative leads to a denigration of the absolute and a vanishing of the relative. Thus, the substitution of the religiously absolute in place of the historically relative denigrates and materialises the religiously absolute and devastates all the historically concrete within it. The relationship between the absolute and the relative is impossible to think of transcendentally, it can be thought of only immanently. The relative is a manifestation of the absolute, a certain periphery of it, and namely because the absolute cannot be encompassed or contained within the relative and the relative cannot be transformed into the absolute. The relative, the natural and the historical is but a manifestation within the absolute. Within the relative can only be discerned symbols of the absolute, glimpses from within. The whole of the natural and historical life is merely of the sphere of the relative as manifest appearance, and the absolute in this life can only be grasped symbolically. However, the absolutisation of everything natural and historical is slavery and a lie. History and all the historical ought to be admitted namely as of the sphere of the relative -- as having been manifest from the depths of the absolute and namely therefore not able to be the engulfing absolute nor a transcendentally-external subordinate for the absolute. History is merely that, what is imposed from the absolute, and is nowise, what is externally positioned for the absolute nor for it having to be from the outside subordinated or engulfed. The entire world process with all its relativity is but an inward-based manifestation within the absolute Divine life. Philosophically I can formulate its significance thus: my dualism (of the absolute and the relative, of the religious and the secular) is defined by my initial radical monism. The consciousness of Merezhkovsky and Meier ought to be formulated thus: their monism (subordination of the Divine absoluteness to the world of relativity, the religious societal aspect) is defined by their initial radical dualism. For a dualism (separation, differentiation, secularisation), which initiates from monism, existent within the depths of spirit, is a liberation. Monism however (the external sacralisation of life, a binding religious norm), which initiates from dualism, of a transcendental opposition between God and man, is an enslavement.

  Every utopianism, every maximalism, every theocratism, reactionary or revolutionary, ought to be toppled, as a false and externalised absolutisation of the relative. The absolute ought to shew and shine forth from within, from the depths, through the relative. History is of the realm of the relative and of multiplicity, and not of the absolute and the singular. The non-mediated direct and real connection of history with the absolute is realised only through the human spirit, through its depths, immersed in the life Divine. The absolute always -- is in spirit, and not in nature, and not in history. In the process of the secularisation of all the societal aspect and culture, in the removal of religious sanction be it from the state, from the family, from science and art, there is a liberating truth, possessing religious meaning and significance. All the spheres of life ought to be spiritified and inspired from within, from the depths and ought to be inwardly illumined religiously. The free, the secular societal aspect and the free, the secular knowledge can be inwardly religious, and in the final end ought to be religious. The absoluteness, the religiousness, the sacredness can be only within the human spirit, and not in an objectively object-based world and not within its products (the state, the societal aspect, culture, the sciences and art). This is the setting-free of the religious consciousness, which will effect a change from religious slavery and infancy. Such a religious reform is the greatest historical task of our times. The greatest historical task, facing Russia, I see first of all in a liberation from religious slavery, from the enslaving of spirit by natural and historical matter, and in a transition to spiritual freedom. In Russia, the person has not emerged yet from a condition of natural collectivism, has not surmounted yet the condition of the horde, which for us has been so idealised. Spirit has not yet gained mastery over the dark element of the Russian land, in which person always faces temptations towards dissolution. Russian "socialism" is merely a societal form of religious slavery, the unliberatedness of spirit and the spiritual "I" from the primitive organic collective. We have need most of all in a liberation from populism, and just as the social, so also the religious, in the awakening of the person-spiritual principle within mankind. This stands not in any sort of opposition to a spiritual sobornost', with churchliness, deepened to an extent cosmic.

The Kingdom of God cometh imperceptibly and unnoticed, unseen it is wrought from within, as a certain mysteried communing with spirit. The Church of Christ also always has been such a mysteried, concealed communing, such an union of reborn souls in Christ. The Church of Christ has been suchlike a concealed cosmic organism, a cosmic communing of all creatures. The Church of Christ has been manifest also within the naturo-historical plane, it had its own physical features. But this is of the sphere of the relative, possessing the same indeed rights to existence, as also all the historico-relative, and subject to the process of developement and change. The Kingdom of God is created neither by a path reactionary, nor by way of a revolutionary theocracy, it is not a matter of an outward societal aspect, it can imperceptibly and unseen dwell and abide. Imperceptibly doth come the Kingdom of God and imperceptibly it leads to this, that the texture of the Kingdom of God becomes the texture of all the world. But this does not free us from the obligation to create within a relative societal aspect, a completely free, and secular societal aspect, eternally incommensurate with the Kingdom of God, since nothing relative is incommensurate with the absolute. The monism of religious life needs to look inwards, and not on the outside, within spirit, and not in the naturo-historical plane. This leads however to a strengthening of a real sense of history with all its concreteness. The religious person, the religious people, the religious mankind can with a religious pathos work at a relative societal aspect and create values, outwardly not subordinated to a religious authority. Inwardly they make of it a religious deed. The societal aspect, just like everything of culture, cannot be something planned out and external-normatively religious, it can only be inwardly-religious, on the strength of the religious rebirth of the soul of the individual man, of the people and of all mankind. The new religious consciousness presupposes a shifting into the depths of human nature as an ontological reality, i.e. it presupposes the birth of the new man and his creative activity.

On Citizenship

(1916 - #245)[1]

I.

Facing the Russian people and society stands the urgent task of working out its type of citizenship, the strengthening of a consciousness as citizen and the feelings for citizenship. For Russia this is a vital question -- the surmounting of those of its traits, which forever have been acknowledged as Russian and which forever have been contrary to citizenship. The idealising of these traits, admitting them as of an higher condition in contrast to that of the citizen -- is most extreme a danger for Russia. The training towards citizenship proceeds with us very slowly, there have been enormous hindrances against it both in the composition of the Russian character, and in the composite of Russian history. Russian emotionality, extending over into elemental a level, the exceptional humility, manifest also at the summits of Russian spiritual life, the weak developement of a sense of honour, the passivity and weakness of an awareness of responsibility, the swallowing up of the personal principle by the organic collective -- all these are traits, not favourable to the working out of character, as a citizen. Anarchism, deeply lodged within the Russian character and seen both in the extreme left and in the extreme right, a distaste for the relative within historical and societal life and an eternal striving for the absolute and the maximal -- all this likewise is unfavourable for our citizenship developement. In Russia the idea of the citizen and citizenship tends to flounder and to sink whether it be upon ideas theocratic, in a sacred absolutism, or in social utopias, in an anarchistic and socialistic absolutism. But at neither of these polarities resides that consciousness of the person, of that revealing of the personal spirit, of the personal human principle, which solely alone is favourable to citizenship. It is time already to stop with the idealising of the quaint

---

[1] O GRAZHDANSTVE. Article originally published in weekly "Birzhevye vedomosti", 7 dec. 1916, № 15969.

remnants and survivals of the old Russian collectivism, which they love to proffer as whether be it the true "Sobornost'/Communality", or else the true "socialism" and which, in essence, is but a stage, antecedent to the developement of the person and citizenship. Russian populism in all its shades and hues has been unfavourable to citizenship. The Slavophil populism always repudiated citizenship, as comprising a lower Western European principle. And our radical populism has also repudiated it. Every manner of populism is a principle not only contrary to citizenship, but also a refusing of it. The citizen cannot bow down to the people as some sort of an empirical fact.

The citizen is first of all -- the person, a person, having taken upon himself responsibility for the fate of his native land and his people. The citizen imposes moreso possibly upon himself, and not upon the collective external to him, not upon the material medium and not chalking it off to the lifestyle of the people. The materialistic teaching about the mastery of the social medium is unfavourable the same for citizenship, as is the teaching about the determinism underlying the whole fate of the people and the person as exclusively by the powers of Providence. Russian man loves to impute it to powers, situated outside him, to fate, to "a stroke of luck", to a "white lie" allowing one to worm out, or to a social medium, to thrash it out, or to God, or to a collective from the people's lifestyle or a collective from a social group. The Slavophils and the populists, the Black-Hundredists and the anarchists, the extreme rightists and the extreme leftists, Bulgakov with his rightist religious societal aspect and Merezhkovsky with his leftist religious societal aspect -- are all alike hostile to the developement of citizenship in Russia. True citizenship presupposes a mastery by the person over the elemental aspect of the people, rather than being immersed in it, an existing from the condition of slavery under the people's collective, a liberation from the grip of the earth. In Russia there is a peculiar democratism upon moral a grounding, a peculiar populist morals, assuming quite contrary forms, which creates a spiritual atmosphere, unfavourable to the birth of citizenship. Citizenship in the profound sense of this word -- is aristocratic. Citizens -- are sons, and not slaves, free in their attitude towards their native land, and towards the state, and towards the life of the people. The feeling of enslavement and repression -- is the greatest hindrance to the consciousness of oneself as citizen. But it would be false to expect, that the citizen and citizenship will appear from changes in external conditions, from a new and more free life. On the contrary, it is from the growth of consciousness as citizen and feelings as citizen that one mustneeds expect changes in the external conditions, to await a new and more free life. Citizens will create a new Russia. There exists no sort of a social alchemy, which could create from the souls of slaves a free societal approach. Neither the acquiescence of slaves nor the revolt of slaves will lead to a realm of freedom. Citizenship ought to be an inner stirring within us, altering the course of our will and consciousness.

II.

The developement of citizenship in Russia represents something not only societal and political, but is also a spiritual turnabout, a liberation of the personal spirit from the grip of the natural and elemental. With the peoples of the West this already occurred long ago. But with each people this process occurs uniquely, since the spirit within each people is unique. Russian citizenship will be spiritually unique, as unique as it is in France, in England, in Germany. But it mustneeds be admitted, that in the Russian people, the land-working people primarily, such a spiritual turnabout has not at all yet occurred -- the person within the masses is still all too situated in natural and elemental a condition, in spilling about the emotionality of the Russian earth, and for us therefore there cannot at all occur an essential civil-political turnabout. The deficiency of citizenship, such as that created by the spiritual forging of the person, was very much felt by us in the year 1905. There was no genuine pathos of the citizen, nor were there citizen-persons. Impossible for a citizen is an attitude towards Russia, as towards something external and foreign, belonging not to "it" but rather to "them". The citizen takes ultimate responsibility upon himself for Russia and the Russian state. The citizen cannot set the partial higher than the whole, cannot forget about Russia and the Russian people in the name of whatever the class or group, in the name of whatever the trend of circle. With citizenship there is always a national perspective. It is only possible to be a citizen of one's fatherland, and not a citizen of circle or group. And here is why the great school of citizenship is the war. The war heightens the feeling of the oneness of Russia and begets an wholistic attitude towards it. The concepts of true patriotism and true citizenship are almost identical, and this is shown in the threatening hour of war. A conscious patriotism in relation to one's native land and one's state during an era of tribulation is also citizenship, the attitude of the citizen towards it. No citizen is one who sets conditions, upon which he consents to defend it in threatening an hour for it. The national-patriotic work of the State Duma, the rural and urban unions and other societal organisations during a time of war is also a citizenship training of the Russian societal effort, the consequences of which look to speak across the expanse of the historical future of Russia. The tribunes of the State Duma are accustomed to speak of the visage of Russia and in the name of Russia. Motives national tend to overshadow the struggle of party, and the deliverance of Russia from enslavement is rendered a slogan both of the national and of the people in general, and is not a mere party or group slogan of national security.

Our societal movement is not yet all impelled by the image of a great citizen. The pathos of class struggle -- is not the pathos of a citizen, in it there is no citizen-type attitude towards Russia. For the citizen, dearest of all is Russia and its fate. The pathos of all the social utopias upon a positivist or upon a religious grounding are likewise not the pathos of the citizen, for in them is no real attitude towards Russia. All this is very much to be felt at present. Our free citizenship is hammered and forged out not by the confession of abstract social and political doctrines, not by an abstract opposition, but by a concrete sense of service to native land in a patriotic concern for the fate of Russia. Our citizenship is created and consolidated by the awareness, that the fate of native land, the salvation of native land is dependent upon us, upon the Russian societal effort, having become a citizenship. In the nationalist Count Shul'gin [Vasilii Vasil'evich, 1878-1976], a man very much a former rightist, there is the sense of the citizen, and his conduct -- is a citizen's conduct. And in Count Purishkevich [Vladimir Mitrofanovich, 1870-1920] the war has brought out the features of a citizen. The growth here of citizen sentiments and citizen awareness on the right represents an undoubtable progress of the Russian societal effort. The same progress appears with this citizen trend among those Social Democrats, who stand upon the point of view of defending the native land, and of subordinating the class movement to the national movement. The defeatists of the left and the right are however a remnant of our pre-citizen and slave-like condition. A non-citizen sort of condition is manifest also within a neutralist attitude towards native land during a moment of an historical conflict amongst peoples.

III.

Needful first of all is to fervently desire for Russian society the aristocratism of a citizen's awareness and a citizen's conduct. Upon this path of citizenship will be manifest from among us guiding persons, citizen-patriots with clear an image. Russians need finally to get free from the false and harmfully evil idea, that citizenship is some sort of a lower condition and that in Russia there exists, as a given, a sort of higher condition. Upon this illusion have stood the Slavophils, and populists of all hues, and the Russian anarchists, and maximalists. all variously have idealised the pre-citizen condition of Russia. In Tolstoyanism, a characteristically Russian phenomenon, the negations of citizenship have reached quite extreme an expression. and this element of a Tolstoyan denial of citizenship is in quite much a characteristic of Russian people. About the salvation of their own soul, about their purity, about faithfulness to a teaching many Russians are more concerned, than about the fate of Russia. The traditional type of the everyday individual, on the one hand, and the intelligentsia individual -- on the other, for us ought finally to be replaced by the citizen type, a person, conscious of his rights and obligations, and bearing upon himself full responsibility. The citizen, capable of realising this, that in his programme he has to save Russia and bring it to a new life, is not one who washes his hands of the matter, remaining on the sidelines, and defending the purity of his abstract principles. Citizenship in Russia is a cure to the abstractness and absoluteness in politics. The absoluteness ought to be transformed over into the human spirit, into the forging of the person, whereas politics, whereas the civil-societal activity always -- relates to the concrete and relative. Russians are too accustomed to think of politics as a setting in order and saving of their souls, and politics has been as it were a particular matter of one's own soul. The attainment of definite results for Russia are not regarded as especially essential. There is likewise a non-citizen sort of attitude towards Russia and its fate, an insensitivity to history and historical tasks. Citizenship always strives towards the concrete tasks of the historical hour. The citizen is sensitive to the call of his native land. And of little interest to him are abstract utopias and abstract state principles. In Russia the citizen now -- is first of all a patriot, who with all his powers strives for the saving of Russia both from the outward enemy and from inner chaos and disintegration, for whom politics is a deed of national service, and the struggle for rights, for freedom, for responsible rule is also a struggle for the security of Russia, for its unity, for its historical future. The national slogans and the freedom slogans now coincide. In this mustneeds be seen the unique moments being experienced by us. And howsoever late for us is the developing of citizenship, it is comforting to think, that citizenship will provide strength for us in the difficult hour of the great struggle for Russia, for its security and its future, in the new troublesome era. This will endow our citizenship with special features, and it, perhaps, will be less torn by the conflict of political parties. Russia faces the vanquishing within it the inner anarchy, the inner chaos, which tends to occupy no small a place in the soul of the Russian people. Citizenship is a principle, the opposite to chaos and anarchy. In citizenship there is a will to organisation and harmonisation of national life. It is impossible not to see, that the condition of citizenship is very difficult for Russians given the traits of the Russian character. Russians readily fall away from the condition of citizenship either to one side or the other, the polar extremes, wherein either freezes up or dissipates every awareness and sense of citizenship. To hold back the Russian soul, so inclined as it is to fly off into the boundless elements, and restrain it instead for citizenship, is an enormous task for our national training. The developing of citizenship is first of all a matter of training and self-discipline, and not in an heightening of passions. And this training will be accomplished not only by persons, standing at the summits of national awareness, but also by historical events. Citizenship presupposes a stronger national consciousness and the will to lead to national action in common.

Concerning Power and Powerlessness

(1916 -246)[1]

The rightist organs in our press, as regards everything happening in Russia, are making an appeal for power. In the opinion of "Zemschina", only power gets attention. People since the very creation of the world have worshipped only power. It is power that creates every right, and everything else, not resting on power, is a joke, like a cute bubble. It mustneeds be admitted, that in these thoughts of "Zemschina" there is quite much that is true. Thus too thought Lassalle [Ferdinand, 1825-1864], when he gave his famous speech on a constitution. In a constitution he saw a correlation of powers. And indeed there is hardly anyone to take upon themself the thankless task and assert, that powerlessness can be fascinating a thing and that powerless one might worship the people. "Zemschina", perhaps, has already in too Germanic a manner expressed the thought about the primacy of power over rights. But in these very considerations on power and the desires for power there is formally much that is deserving of interest. Yet here is the only problem in it. The problem really and in essence is that in the affairs of our extreme rightists they tend to worship not power, but instead powerlessness; they want to compel the Russian people to acquiesce regarding powerlessness and they claim, that a total powerlessness is all still charming for the people. The question about power -- is a real, and not a formal question. It is impossible to esteem in power, that which I merely want to see as powerful. It needs looking, at what really is in power, and for the ideology of our rightists, this -- is a fateful question. That to which the rightists bow, in Russia is set in a situation of hopeless powerlessness and inability and it cannot be still anything charming. The power, once glorious and charming, is in collapse and decay. It holds on only by inertia. The past greatness will never, ever return to the old ruling authorities. And yes indeed, Russia has need of a strong ruling authority. And never yet has it been so necessary, as at the

---

[1] O SILE I BESSILII. Article was originally published in newspaper "Birzhevye vedomosti", 15 dec. 1916, № 15985.

present hour of great tribulations. But what sort of a ruling power can be acknowledged as powerful?

Moreover, in what is the power of a ruling authority? Demands for a powerful ruling authority can be heard from the reactionary camp. This is merely an expression of love for old words, long since weathered and having lost real content. And really, the slogan for a powerful ruling authority is now a progressive slogan. We have happened for us a process of downturns too entangled, the disorganisation and anarchisation of the ruling authority. This anarchy of the ruling authority, assuming ever more threatening dimensions, dismays the responsible progressive segment of the Russian societal effort. This segment demands a sense of organisation in the ruling authority, it desires power, and not powerlessness in the ruling authority, since the ultimate continuing to remain in disorganised powerlessness by the ruling authority threatens dangerous consequences for the fate of the state. A disorganised powerlessness is governing Russia and leading it to ruination. It has to give way to organised power.

From the very creation of the world the people have bowed only to power. "Zemschina" is accurate in saying this. But there is a reverse side also to this truth. From the very creation of the world what only was powerful in the state, was what the people admitted as such, what it loved and sanctioned in its consciousness. Power is something positive, and not negative. It would be absurd to confuse power with violence and coercion. The violent and the coercive in the final end are always powerless. True power otherwise has the ability to lead. Those principles, which are dear to "Zemschina" and "Russkoe Znamya", still have the ability to force and compel, but they can no longer still manifest power, cannot provide leadership for the people. In the consciousness of the people there has occurred a fracture, and the old power has lost its charm. Those times have irreversibly past. The old power has ceased to be an idea, it has ceased also to be power, and never can reaction make a true appeal to power, it can appeal only to violent force, which is what has still remained from the old power in the period of its decay. From the very creation of the world never has there been an enticing power, given as such to lead, whilst such has been merely a bare fact of moving around bits of matter. Every true power is, in the final end, a spiritual power, is a certain idea. But that sort of power, to which "Zemschina" appeals, has already ceased to be a spiritual power, it no longer expresses any sort of idea and is perhaps only thus a short-term moving about bits of matter. Such a short-term shifting about of bits of matter is for us very reminiscent of a shifting about of ministers. There is no sort of idea behind this shifting around, no sort of spiritual power is evidenced. The whole process of a quick sleigh of hand remains bereft of any sense. But a meaningless shifting around of atoms of matter, behind which are at play no sort of spiritual energies, cannot evince true power in the fate of peoples and states. For the extreme right there remains only to summon the powerless to violent force and compulsion. To call for the evidencing of power is possible only in the instance, if this power actually exists. But this power long ago already has become spiritually moribund and now at present act only the remnants of its disintegrating matter.

    This does not mean, certainly, that the power of the Russian state is faltering. This means only, that the state is experiencing a crisis. The objective nature of the state continues to act, and in an era of the collapse of the ruling authority, the state mechanism nonetheless is fulfilling certain necessary functions of national life. But the true might of the state is manifest not in this almost automatic activity of the state mechanism -- it presupposes the discovering of the creative will of the people, and here it is not the rightists, not "Zemschina", but rather instead that we who want this free discovering of the creative will of the people, which also only can manifest the might of the state. We desire the discerning of true power, its organisation, we want a strong ruling authority. Strong in power however can only be that ruling authority, which will be an expression of the creative will of the people. A ruling authority, suppressing every manifestation of the will of its own people, can be violently forceful, but it cannot be truly powerful. The organisation and forms undergo within history a complex evolution, in which there are catastrophic moments. But in the periods of its flourishing and power, a ruling authority always become so from the people as regards its character. The autocratic rule was also derived from the people at a certain stage of historical developement. But when whatever the form of rule loses its character as derived from the people, it is rendered weak, and ceases to hold allure. And the Russian people now at present at a most difficult hour of its historical existence is thirsting for a rule with allure, the allure of the historical might of Russia. It has yearned with longing for suchlike a ruling authority. But they reply to this longing, not with a revealing of power capable of allure, but rather with a powerless recourse to violence and compulsion. The Russian people sees only the collapse and decay of the ruling authority. And now the rightist organs want as it were to bestow an aura of power to this decay and disintegration.

But this is impossible, impossible ontologically, in accord with the very structure of being and its laws. Only a real power can be powerful. It is impossible to substitute shouts and ravings for this power. Everything has grown weary and tired from the powerlessness. There is not one people that can live without a certain aesthetique of state rule, without bringing it into correlation with the rhythm of the life of the people. The shattering of this rhythm for us is reaching monstrously anti-aesthetic forms. The allure of an historical ruling authority reflects also its aesthetique, and thus its accord with the rhythm of the life of the people. But the tendency of our historical ruling authority veering towards the side of the extreme rightists represents an ugly fracturing of the national rhythm, it is an hysterical cry and hysterical gesture, violently forceful, but powerless. Power always tends to express the national rhythm.

Power and a powerful ruling authority is created by the spiritual upsurge and spiritual might of the people. Without such a spiritual upsurge and spiritual might there cannot also be the material power. All the future of Russia and of the Russian state are both bound up with the organisation and consolidation of the spiritual energy of the Russian people, with the working out of its national character. A powerful ruling authority can only be as an expression of the will of the Russian people, and not of some "Union of the Russian People". In this historical misnomer it is time already to put a limit. The "Soiuz/Union of the Russian People" is not in any sense the Russian people, even the very stones sing out on this. The "Union of the Russian People" is not concerned about the fate of Russia and the Russian people, it is interested only in its own personal fate, what guides it are the instincts of self-preservation. It is connected not with Russia, but only with maintaining the control of certain principles in Russia. But the decoration of these principles cannot revive their significance. The Black Hundredist personages, who have appropriated the name, representing merely an ambiguous play on words, have no right to declare anything on behalf of the Russian people. Certain words have already lost their magic power. We have to call for a powerful and alluring ruling authority. This powerful and alluring ruling authority has to express the organised will of the Russian people, has to be a blossoming forth of its people. The might of the state is the organising power of the people. A realm of powerlessness -- is terrible a realm. The voice of "Zemschina" resounds from such a realm. But the hour is nigh close, when there will resound a different voice, from an authentic realm of power.

Barbarity and Decadence

(1916 -247)[1]

I.

The question about the mutual interrelationship of barbarity and decadence -- is one of the basic and most acute questions in the philosophy of culture. This question typically has involved refined and abstract thought and they dealt with it chiefly as regards currents in art. But now this question is beset with events of worldwide an impact. The decadent man suddenly has been rendered capable to display the power, which we have been wont to expect only from the barbarian man, with all the positive and the negative traits of barbarity. Herein truly is an enigma, which modern times has set before us. Human culture upon its summits has an inevitable tendency towards downward decline. Within culture itself on its own accord is not lodged the possibility of endless developement. It mustneeds ever eternally orient itself to the vital sources, lying within its depths. And in the history of culture, developement does not happen along a straight line, by way of a continuous and unswerving growth. Culture tends to develope in periods, it knows ascent and decline. Every type of culture passes through a primitive-organic period, followed by a period of its classic blossoming and a period of decay. Ancient culture, not only the greatest of cultures, but also an eternal source for every culture, displayed the greatest cultural ascent and the greatest cultural decline. It would not be a mistake to see in the decadence something exclusively negative and impotent. But decadence is likewise tremendously refined and complicated, in it there is its own beauty and its own light. In periods of decadence there are begotten great tasks, but not the powers for their realisation. Decadence is twofold, begetting knowledge, unknown entirely for the epoch. But every time, when there transpires a decline of culture, when its powers

---

[1] VARVARSTVO I UPADNICHESTVO. Article was originally published in newspaper "Birzhevye vedomosti", 25 dec. 1916, № 16006.

dessicate from too narrow and self-satisfied an existence, the salvation comes from an inundating flood of barbarity. There is a barbarity of flesh and blood, and there is a barbarity of spirit, unenlightened and not worn down by culture, which renews the decrepit culture, and provides it a new effluence of powers. The entirety of the ancient world with its great culture would have perished as though without a trace, if the new force of the barbarity both of flesh and blood and the barbarity of spirit, as represented by Christianity, had not entered into historical life. And thus, what they tend to term as the medieval barbarity, not only accomplished a disintegrating of the ancient culture, but also saved it for eternity.

And modern European culture cannot escape the fate of every culture. It fatally depletes itself and tends towards decline. Culture tears itself asunder from the wellsprings source of being, from the living roots. It is at its summit, in its art, its science, philosophy, statecraft, law, technology etc, and it begins to oppose itself to life, to being itself, and in it there ensues a depletion and decadence. Concrete being passes over into the abstract. Abstract being is however constantly evaporating. There is a shattering of the boundaries, separating reality from the phantasmic. The flesh has become word. The decadence of culture gives forth its final blossoms, beautiful and intricate. Thought and creativity become all the more cultivated and refined. The integral wholeness ultimately is lost, the old organicity becomes dismembered and stratified, and the division leads to an impaired condition. In the Latin race, which organically and directly is connected with antiquity and which created the European culture, there is particularly to be sensed the exhaustion and decline. The question concerning the possibility of a renaissance of the Latin race very vexingly has been put forth in recent decades of the past. This question troubles and distresses the finest minds of Latinism. They furthermore already say, that France is situated in a condition of decline, that the French nation has deteriorated, that a great exhaustion is to be sensed throughout all Latinism. This judgement has become commonplace. In contrast to the Latin race, the German race -- is barbarian. This insight is from its once descending upon Rome and upon the ancient world, bringing with it to that decrepit world another spirit and a fresh bloodline. The German race has no blood kinship with antiquity. In German culture there was a barbaric depth and characteristic purity, but also in it was not the refinement and elegance. In a certain sense Luther and Kant were barbarians, ignorant of traditions and legacies. In Germany the decadence was less to be felt, and there was not so acutely set the problem of the correlation of barbarity and decadence. But the forebodings of exhaustion have already been sensed in Germany, and it leads not to a refined and cultivated elegance, but rather to a decay connected with coarseness. The level of spiritual culture in Germany in the last decades has quite declined.

II.

It would seem, that within the whole of European culture there is no longer a great reserve of powers, that the whole of European mankind is too corrupted and spoiled by bourgeois culture, too much values comfort, and is already incapable of heroism, of sacrifice, of too great an effort. The decadent man, it would seem, is incapable of great deeds in history. And here within this decline of the modern European culture, a world war unprecedented in history has burst forth. And peoples that are exhausted, spoilt and in decay, are summoned to an unprecedented exertion of all their spiritual and material powers, summoned to sacrifice and effort. It would seem, that the things demanding continuation of the world war from peoples already into its third year, are beyond human abilities. At the beginning when all this started, no one ever believed, that such a war could last so protractedly long. But the war has spun out of control and taken possession of human powers, which draw forth from some sort of unfathomable well. And it has become clear, that the culture was not especially deep a stratum, that its refined trappings are too easily concealed, that the decline, the exhaustion and enfeeblement of the culture of mankind has not reached down to the very depths, that at an even deeper level there has remained still the barbarity and still yet fresh powers. But the barbarity at present comes not from the sidelines, rather it is from within, it underlies the trappings of culture. The world war is, certainly, a partial barbarisation of human culture, a present and serious danger amidst its character of spinning out of control. In any case, it has introduced into European culture a barbaric energy, wherein it rouses ancient instincts, it renders life all the more simple and elementary. The Germans first rediscovered their age-old barbarity and conjoined it with an high and forthwith futuristic technical culture. But other nations also, drawn into the world war, are rediscovering an extraordinary barbaric energy and strength. The decadence is surmounted. European man is refused his habits and comfort. The typical bourgeoise, fond of earthly blessings and delights, is resettled into the trenches and he assimilates himself to a severe life, one mere thought on which would terrify him in peacetime. When the war started, then almost everyone was of the mistaken opinion, that the war could go on for no more than half a year, that modern mankind possessed not the powers for more prolonged a war. But for the war no end is in sight, and human endurance has not yet been exhausted.

And herein this nation, which seemed the most decadent and degenerate, has rendered itself the most heroic. I speak about the French. The French have shown the greatest of heroism in the war, in them has awakened the valour of the old, the medieval and knight-chivalric France. The defense of Verdun will be acclaimed one of the most heroic pages in the war histories of the world. The willing and self-denying patriotism of the French is truly astonishing and instructive for all the whole world. Valour has not died out in these frail French, albeit degenerate and immersed in bourgeois contentment, in France where it threatened decline and decay. The tragedy of the war, putting France afront the threat of peril, spiritually has regenerated it. Facing the French is the question concerning the ultimate free existence of their France, -- "la belle France". In terms of the decadence, the war is perhaps a salvific barbarity, it brings into action certain hidden potentials in man. With it ends too great a period of refinement, and there begins a period of roughness. There are dangerous sides in this, threatening peril to certain values, but there is also a renewal of strength: man is so constituted, that he requires suffering. The tragedy of the war, the exerting of all the strength of man and leading him through the experience of suffering, surmounts the decadence of culture. This is clearest of all in France. It is not by chance that the Italian futurists, who ultimately are barbaric, have recognised the war as a means of the renewal of the decrepit race. In these barbaric-futuristic peals there was much of cynicism and quite little of a sense of tragedy. To consider the terror of the war as a means for curing and renewing of decrepit and decadent races -- is lunacy and immoral. The war can be acknowledged as the greatest of tragedies and a redemption. But one of the objective points of significance to it mustneeds be seen in this, that it conveys with it an end of cultural decadence and enfeeblement, that it opens up a new historical period, in which perhaps will be also darkness, but undoubtedly also will be a restoration of strength.

III.

The world war results from a condition of the narrowness of European culture, from its self-satisfied smugness, leading hence to decline. It ought rather to widen the horizons of culture and uncover new sources for it. No small role would be played in this by a tendency for the interaction and association of East and West, which the current war engenders. But the barbaric element of the war presents also tremendous dangers for the whole of human culture. Its prolonged activity is a throwback to the elementary and leads to coarseness. Yet before us stands the task of the preservation of a most complex and refined spiritual life, the synthesis of everything positive, of what is in the barbarity, with everything positive, of what was in the decadence, i.e. the synthesis of strength and value with complexity and refinement.

The raging elements of the war, sweeping away everything in its path, demands a tremendous spiritual energy, so that in this storm there can be salvaged the image of man, the image of the people and the image of mankind. Man directs his powers to the utmost, drawing on them not from the topmost level of culture, but from a far deeper source, from an unfathomable barbarity. Therein especially is so complex the task, standing afront man, and all the directing of human powers ought to be directed to the strengthening of the human image, which can be atomised in the whirlwind of the war. It therefore mustneeds be acknowledged, that the process taking place within mankind under the influence of the world war, is very complex, -- it has its own positive and its own negative sides, its own great possibilities and its own great perils. And therefore the mobilisation of human powers for the deeds of the war ought not to run parallel with the inner spiritual work of mankind.

The question about the correlation of barbarity and decadence thus enters into a completely new phase. The decadence of culture becomes evident from its refinement and complexity, an enlargement of differentiation, a withdrawing from the archaic organic integral wholeness, the growth of a sundering from the sources of life.

This decadence will be overcome. The exhaustion, which threatens the European nations after the quite long drawn out war, will not be a transcultural exhaustion. This will instead be of a biological exhaustion from the struggle, from the simplification of culture and its methods.

This already is entirely other a motif, different from the motif of decadence. The decadence will be overcome, but it threatens a coarseness and simplification of culture. Thus it was at the beginning of the process of the vanquishing of the ancient culture by the medieval barbarity. Mankind has coarsened, and culture has plunged into darkness. And only in the later medieval period was there formed a new type of culture, more complex than the medieval culture, but anew acknowledging in itself the ancient culture. That which they generally term the medieval darkness, can only be conditionally and superficially be termed darkness. Actually, in the epoch of the medieval darkness there was a very intense spiritual life and an accumulation of possibilities of the greatest sort. It is not baseless to say, that our own era is coming nigh to a new Middle Ages. Upon cultural mankind a darkness is descending, there is a night-fall, and in this darkness there is an extinguishing of the light of rationalism, the light from some several centuries. Into the life of European rationalistic mankind there enters an irrational principle, capsizing all the planes of too rationalistic a construct of earthly life. But the inward sun of human life cannot and ought not to be extinguished, it will shine in the darkness and lead to a new renaissance. If the worldwide catastrophe extinguishes the reflective and too externalised light of rationalist culture, then by this all the more acutely ought there to be posited the task of manifesting the inward and eternal light within man. We are at the boundary point of a new birth. Night leads to the rising of the sun. We ought ultimately to be aware, that at the present time mankind stands at a crossroads and is experiencing one of the greatest of its crises. Only such a radical awareness will lead to the search for new sources of light.

An Account about Heavenly an Origin

(1916 - #248)[1]

There has appeared a book under the unobtrusive title, "From the Manuscripts of A. N. Schmidt".[2] The name of A. N. Schmidt tends not to attract attention, it is nearly known to anyone. The book is prefaced by a short biography of Anna Nikolaevna Schmidt. In her life and in her appearance, apparently, there was nothing remarkable. She spent her whole life at Nizhnii Novgorod, was an unassuming contributor to the Nizhegorod newspapers, she provided reports on Zemstvo gatherings, wrote theatre reviews, and on almost everyone in meeting her, she produced the impression of a good woman, a bit eccentric, drab in the externals. They noticed nothing extraordinary, prophetic, nor visionary in Schmidt. In religio-philosophic circles they tended to say only, that with Schmidt there was some sort of a mysterious regard for Vl. Solov'ev and that their correspondence had been saved. And here now, eleven years after the death of Schmidt, her manuscripts are published with timid an introduction, pouring doubt into the character of the disclosures, formerly told the world, -- so extraordinary they are and so absorbing and bold. But the Spirit breathes, whence it will, and it can breathe also in an unassuming woman from Nizhnii Novgorod, earning her bread with newspaper articles. And the modest, unremarkable appearance of this woman renders her book all

---

[1] POVEST' O NEBESNOM RODE. Article was originally published in periodical "Russkaya mysl'", 1916, march, p. 5-9.

This present article was not included in the massive "*Padenie*" Russian text, from which most of the articles in our current English text are taken. Rather, the present article in Russian text was republished in the 2004 anthology of Berdyaev articles under cover title "*Mutnye liki*" ["Murky Visages"], taking its name from title of one of Berdyaev's articles contained therein: Moskva, 2004, Kanon+, this article p. 140-146.

[2] Iz rukopisei A. N. Schmidt. With letters to her of Vl. Solov'ev, p. XV+288. 1916.

the more remarkable. Without any exaggeration it can be said, that the book of Schmidt will come to be considered one of the most remarkable works of world mystical literature. This -- is the first mystical book in Russia in the strict sense of this word, a mystical book great in style, like to the creative works of Boehme, Swedenborg, Saint-Martin and other classic mystics. With time, Schmidt will be numbered amidst the classics of mystical literature. In Russia there is many a book of mystical bent, but no mystical books strictly in style. And amongst women-mystics Schmidt will occupy one of the foremost places alongside Angela de Folino, St. Theresa and Madame Guyon. But the type of mysticism of Schmidt is gnostic, cognitive, closer to Boehme and in this she is singular and totally unique amidst women-mystics. The mysticism of Schmidt is likewise uniquely Russian, concrete, apocalyptic. And all the more original, is that in this Russian, concrete, apocalyptic mysticism there is so much of an hypnotic appeal. Suchlike a work there has never yet been in the Russian art of writing.

Especially striking and attractive is this extraordinary concreteness of the mystical gnosis of Schmidt. Her mystical treatise, a "Third Testament", central within all the book, can be termed an account about an heavenly origin, about coelestial marital-unions and multiplications. For Schmidt, being becomes drained, emptying itself within marital-unions and multiplications. From some one point she discerns an initial heavenly conjugal type life within the bosom of the Holy Trinity, and thereafter tells about the history of marital-unions and multiplications in the world. At the basis of everything, which Schmidt discerns, lies a concrete mythologism. No sort of abstraction, no sort of philosophy does she have. There is described a mystical-vegetative process of the divine being, of the divine germination. The arising of the world is a matter of birth, and not of creativity. The description of the forming of matter as a congealing of radiant light-beams reminds one of the teaching about emanation. With Schmidt everything is a matter of birth, and the mystery of birth is always connected with the mystery of the conjugal union. The whole mysticism of Schmidt totally involves the natal and the sexual. The mystical insights of Schmidt -- are feminine, but very uniquely feminine. Her style of mystical writing is dry, objective, she is very systematic and schematic, in her is not sensed the feminine attractive allure. The apocalyptic feeling of the impending end of the world does not make her distressed nor unsettled. She -- is very calm, content, and satisfied. The dryness and calmness of the mystical book of Schmidt make it unique, dissimilar to the typical for Russia tormentive and tortuous disquiet amongst apocalyptic outlooks. Certain places in the "Third Testament" remind one of the old gnostic books, for example the Pistis Sophia, -- it likewise mythologically apprehends the mysteries of the world. There is an affinity in the basic truths, revealed in every mystical gnosis, -- the great mystics of all times tend each to echo the other. And this affinity speaks to the genuineness of mystical experience. Schmidt, evidently, did not know the works of the old great mystics, she was not all that well-read, she had not read even Vl. Solov'ev up to the final years of her life and she lived in an atmosphere, into which had penetrated not even a single ray of mystical knowledge. It was independently revealed to her much the same, as it was revealed also to Swedenborg, and to Boehme, and the old gnostics. But the light of a singular mystical knowing gets refracted into an individuality, into the psychological aspect of each mystic and often gets bedimmed. There is not only uniqueness, but also a dimness to the light within the individual soul of Schmidt. The mysteries of the Divine and the world life are perceived by her, as a feminine soul, sensing itself as the soul of the world. And already therefore she is unable to see and to know everything. The mystery concerning man is more fully discerned by the masculine nature, than by the feminine nature. And in the mystical gnosis of Schmidt there is an incompleteness and dimness of anthropology. Man, as a mystically autonomous principle, she tends not to see, wherein that man is formed from a conjoining of the angelic principle to a principle beastly. In the description of the Sin-Fall there is a dimness with Schmidt deriving from the feminine nature, from the feminine, and not the eternal-feminine. The root cause of people falling into sin she sees to be in the treachery of Eve, having united herself with beings of a lower nature and evoking the anger and jealousy of Adam.

    The mystical primal-perceptions of the eternal-feminine soul draws Schmidt towards a misguided concreteness in her attitude towards the Church and to Christ. The Church, to which she gives the new name Margarita, for her is a person, an entirely concrete being, the bride and spouse of Christ. The mysterious fate of Margarita is also the fate of a woman, having gone through downfall and profligacy and having become united with her Beloved. And this is an aspect very powerful, very original in Schmidt. In her final incarnation upon earth Margarita, the bride and spouse of Christ, is called Anna Nikolaevna Schmidt. Such an audacious awareness may tend to repulse and alarm many. But Schmidt is not the first to show such mystical experiences, they are frequent also amongst mystics and almost typical. At a certain depth is snatched away the opposition between the church, as the soul of the world, and the individual feminine soul, standing face to face with its Beloved. The deep, the mystically remarkable souls have a right to such boldness. And this does not at all signify, that there is being presented a superficial view from the sidelines. And howsoever terrible this may seem on the surface, it is not so in the depths, not in that mystical sphere, in which vanishes the antinomy of the one and the many. The coelestial, the divine history is likewise an history of the human spirit, and the mysterious love of Margarita for Christ can likewise be also the mysterious love of Schmidt for Vl. Solov'ev. This -- is on that other side of antinomy, safeguarded against suchlike confusions, just like from blasphemy. But mystics frequently have blasphemous a guise. Mystics perceive one and the selfsame divine truth, but each has their own form, their own symbolics, and each perceives with but a varied degree of fullness. Schmidt saw the divine truth in the form of a coelestial family, and heavenly race, and the Holy Spirit revealed itself to her, as the Daughter of God.[1] It is possible to accuse Schmidt of various heresies, but everything was posited by her in very Orthodox a delimited framework. Her mysticism -- is churchly and Biblical. She nowhere sees any sort of revelation, except in Judaism and in Christianity, neither in the ancient world, nor in India. Over all the book of Schmidt lies the imprint purely of Jewish religiosity and Biblical apocalypticism. There is little in it of an Aryan spirit. Most original and remarkable of all with Schmidt is the narrative about an heavenly birthing. Of genius is her teaching about the growth of spirits, about spirits odd and even. The mysticism of history with her is rather more weak. She tends to say too much of the commonplace, of the usual about Christian history, about the heresies, about the separation of churches. The feel for history tends always indeed be weaker in women, than in men. When the account of Schmidt gets around to the Apocalypse, to the end of the world, she again is rendered more remarkable and strong. A very powerful impression is produced by the constant hearkening for the destruction of this world. The world has to dematerialise. Christ has to ultimately destroy this world. The devil has wanted as though to uphold it

---

[1] N. F. Fedorov likewise taught about the Holy Spirit, as about the Daughter.

forever. The book of Schmidt is written about the Third Testament, but it would be difficult to say, in what the Third Testament consists. There is as it were no sort of a new revelation. There is a new perception of the mysteries of being, the mysteries of a mystical descent, of birth and multiplicity, there is the extraordinary consciousness of Schmidt herself, with a concreteness unprecedented in boldness, and there is an apocalyptic presentiment of the nearness of the end. The Third Testament is a revelation of the Spirit, as Daughter of God. It becomes through the Daughter of God -- Anna Nikolaevna Schmidt. But what now does the Third Testament convey with it, what does it signify in the fate of man? A third revelation can only be a revelation of man and concerning man, it will bear into the world an as yet unprecedented religious creativity. But in Schmidt there is not this exceptional self-consciousness of man, there is not an anthropologic revelation. She had presentiment of a new revelation thus, as only a feminine soul of genius could have presentiment of it. It was contemplated by her, as a revelation of femininity and about femininity, and not of man and concerning man.

There is something mysterious in the relations of A. N. Schmidt and Vl. Solov'ev. These relations were short-lived, they continued for all of three months, before the death of Solov'ev, but they were extraordinarily intense and remarkable. The letters of Vl. Solov'ev to Schmidt, supplementing the book, can produce disagreeable an impression. There is in them a peculiar dryness, a desire to hold himself remote, a timidity towards mystical risk. But this is quite understandable. It is not easy to undergo such an attraction towards oneself, as Schmidt had for Vl. Solov'ev, this is very tormentive and can repel. Vl. Solov'ev had to sense a dark rift with Schmidt, when she wanted to see in him the Beloved. But another thing even more essential also, it tends to cast light on Vl. Solov'ev himself. Vl. Solov'ev all his life sought encounters with the Eternal Feminine. He sought the charms in the Eternal Feminine, of a beauty unearthly. She allured him.

> Thine eyes emerald I behold,
> Radiant the visage set before me...

> All saw I, and all alone but twas, --
> One only image of feminine beauty...

> But by day thou forget or by midnight awakest, --

Nicholas Berdyaev

Here who... we be two, --
Straight in soul peer the gleaming eyes
The dark night and the day.

Not only once did the deceptive image of Femininity appear to Vl. Solov'ev and allure him. The attitude towards the Feminine was also the tragedy of his whole life. He did not know consummation and satisfaction. The image of Femininity was twofold for him, in this he was a man twofold in thought. And here close to the end of his life there appeared for him a very remarkable and genius-endowed image of Femininity -- A. N. Schmidt. And this image of Femininity proved not alluring, almost repulsive. In the image of Schmidt was nothing alluring. In Schmidt Vl. Solov'ev found a mystical gnosis, which he considered his own matter, not a feminine matter, and the allure he did not find. This is the final episode in the tragic attitudes of Vl. Solov'ev towards Femininity. Thus can be explained the reticence of the Solov'ev writing.

The anonymous editors[1] of the manuscripts of Schmidt approached publication with a great sense of peril. The preface was written timidly and

---

[1] *Translator note*: The editors of this 2004 anthology of Berdyaev articles, printed under the title "Mustnye Liki", suggest that the "anonymous authors" penning the so very timid preface to Schmidt's manuscripts are none other than Frs. S. Bulgakov and P. A. Florensky -- based on information contained in E. Gollerbakh's book, "K nezrimomu gradu. Religiozno-philosophskaya gruppa "Put'" (1910-1919) v poiskakh novoi russkoi identichnosti", Spb., 2000, c. 210-211.

Against the dark mid-WWI year of 1916, it is difficult to gauge Berdyaev's jestful tweaking of the extreme churchly timidity of these two noted but anonymous editors of Schmidt's manuscripts, as well as the perhaps extent of hyperbole employed by Berdyaev as regards the significance of Schmidt as a world-class gnostic mystic. Certainly her concept of the Holy Spirit as "Daughter of God" is peculiarly unique, to say the least. Perusing private correspondence, such as between Schmidt and Vl. Solov'ev, evokes a feeling of indecency peering into private lives. Thus, as a newspaper theatrical reviewer, Schmidt's identification of herself with being the personification of the Church, assuming the name of Margarita, and also of Vl. Solov'ev (finally finding a concrete personification of his visions of Sophia) as the Christ-figure, the to little effect. The author of the preface does not know, what to think of the mystical revelations of Schmidt, it awaits the decision of church. This author stands decidedly for a dividing of mystics into the graced and churchly, and the ungraced and natural. The mysticism of Schmidt he relegates to the type of ungraced and natural, and this type of mystic frightens him, evokes suspicion. He awaits a churchly sanction for indigenous free mystical revelations. It seems to me idle and unnecessary, these timid questions, as to whether or not follow through on publishing the manuscripts of Schmidt and tell the world about her revelations, and not whether she was an heretic, not whether it be a matter of seduction, with what was revealed to her. The source of mystical revelations is always singularly one, always in the Divine depths, and, it is always through the human that the revelation is made. Orthodox or heretical, harmful or useful, dangerous or non-dangerous -- all these are secondary questions of totally utilitarian human categories. The division itself of mystics into the graced and the ungraced -- is conditional and exoteric. Mystical works always are becoming but for few. The church on the outside has never sanctioned mystical revelations and has always been suspect of mystics. And this externalised church will simply ignore the revelations of Schmidt, it is not interested in such questions. But the voice of the inward church ought to sound forth within the preface-author himself for Schmidt. If there be possible a new revelation, then it will resound forth through Schmidt, through the preface-author for Schmidt, through everyone, in whom the Spirit intends to breathe, -- it does so freely. The greatest testimony, however, in favour of the genuineness of Schmidt I tend to see in this, that she hid within herself her revelation, she did not seek the glories of this world, she did not seek to form sects, did not seek after followers, she remained unassuming and unknown to the world. And this is great a thing in her. Her book is extraordinary and merits a pervasive reading.

Church's Beloved -- one might suggest represents but a bit of metaphorical flirtation and poetic license, more appropriate to private indulgence than public consumption. This is all speculative, of course, without having seen Schmidt's manuscript. But no wonder, then, that there were all these dark rumours circulating about Schmidt and Vl. Solov'ev in the years after their deaths!

On the Dispute between Prince E. N. Trubetskoy and D. D. Muretov

(1916 - 251)[1]

The particularly interesting dispute of Prince E. N. Trubetskoy and D. D. Muretov, regrettably, has been marred by polemical elements, which never enable a clear examination of the questions. The desire to get the better of one's opponent begets a petty nastiness, creates an altogether peculiar and fictitious life of an idea and overshadows onto a secondary plane the real and essential life of the idea. And a problem posited amidst a dispute quite often gets submerged into polemical elements, swirling and subject to their own law. Altogether unimportant, it seems to me, are the petty aspects in the polemics between Pr. Trubetskoy and D. Muretov. Very inconsequential it is, whether one of them succeeds in getting the other trapped in contradictions. In dealing with the noteworthy aspect of a posited problem, vexingly unnecessary would seem the polemical considerations, as to whom Pr. E. Trubetskoy posed his questions and raised objections, whether to D. D. Muretov or to P. B. Struve. The important and essential thing is merely in this, that there has occurred a clash of ideas and that in this clash has been posited an important problem. It always becomes uninteresting, when the clash of ideas gets explained away as a mutual misperception and misunderstanding. But it becomes very interesting, when the opposition of ideas and the points of view on life leads to a crystalline clarity. The intellectual dissonance existing between

---

[1] K SPORU MEZHDU KN. E. N. TRUBETSKIM I D. D. MURETOVYM. Article was originally published in periodical "Russkaya mysl', 1916, aug., p. 44-48.

This present article was not included in the massive "*Padenie*" Russian text, from which most of the articles in our current English text are taken. Rather, the present article in Russian text was republished in the 2004 anthology of Berdyaev articles under cover title "*Mutnye liki*" ["Murky Visages"], taking its name from title of one of Berdyaev's articles contained therein: Moskva, 2004, Kanon+, this article p. 224-230.

Pr. E. N. Trubetskoy and D. D. Muretov nowise devolves upon that one of them logically is more consistent, and the other logically less consistent. To think, that logical consistency can compel one to a betrayal of one's basic vital values, means to fall into rationalism, whilst forgetting its limits. It seems to me, that Pr. E. N. Trubetskoy in the method of his polemics is guilty of such a sort of rationalism. But neither is D. D. Muretov free from this, to bad effect too much relying upon formal-logical arguments and too much proclaiming hopes on them. In these mutual formal punches gets ignored the sharp gist of the problem. The sparring sides get insufficiently immersed in the object. In contrast, P. B. Struve has more acutely posited the problem. I on my part do not propose to indulge in polemics, I want rather only to highlight a principal aspect of the debate and to stress such sides of the ideational problem which, it seems to me, were not sufficiently emphasised.

In the dispute is raised to utmost a degree an important philosophic and ultimately religious problem: whether purely moral values are applicable to history, to the struggle of nations and states, and whether the values of individual life can be transferred to the historical life of peoples. P. B. Struve is correct, in saying, that Vl. Solov'ev set forth this problem and then fell into moralism and rationalism. And the perspective also of Pr. E. N. Trubetskoy is guilty of an extreme moralism. This is quite clearly evident, in that he regards the love between a man and a woman as a manifestation of the moral order and finds it possible to subordinate it to a moral value and a moral law. It is inconceivable, why Pr. E. Trubetskoy reacts with such indignation to the article of D. Muretov concerning a national eros, written with great moderation. I think, that D. D. Muretov is a thousand times correct, in recognising the nature of every sort of eros, of every erotic love, as standing outside of good and evil, beyond moral values, and subject to its own particular values, constituting a quite autonomous sphere of human life. This does not indicate, certainly, that for example in the relations of a man and woman and the eros connected with this, that there cannot also arise questions of the moral order, demanding moral values. But the moral values here can arise merely as questions of the relationship of the human being to one's fellow human being. The sphere of love itself per se remains however beyond the moral value, and to it in incommensurably greater a degree are applicable criteria moreso aesthetic, than moral. People in love to various degrees can commit immoral acts, for example, out of love for a woman a man might take bribes or resort to stealing. But love itself cannot be either moral, nor immoral, -- it is as a law unto itself and a value unto itself, it does not tolerate over it any sort of norms. Love always is divinely-free. It is possible moreover to say, that love is beautiful, but it would be improper to say, that love is moral. Pr. E. N. Trubetskoy, evidently, is too much the Kantian in moral philosophy, too much he tends to share in the absolute moralism of Kant and therefore he regards the formalised categorical imperative as applicable to everything, towards all the plenitude of life. One even gets the impression, that he introduces this absolute moralism into Christianity. Suchlike an absolute moralism does not exist in Christianity. Christianity is not a religion of law, but rather in essence a non-normative religion. Insofar as there is law within Christianity, it derives wholly from the Old Testament and serves merely as a support. The specifically New Testament revelation is a revelation of grace, of love and of freedom, and not of law and norms. The Gospel morality -- is a morality of love, and not a morality of law; within it would be impossible to discern traces of the categorical imperative, and in it there is not that sort of formal-moralistic pathos. In the Gospel, the Sabbath is made for man, and not man for the Sabbath [Mk. 2:27]. An absolute moralism ,the pathos for a moral law is there within Kant, within Tolstoy, but not in the Gospel, nor within Christian mysticism.

I think, that first of all there must be considered the problem of an absolute moralism, -- the pretensions to a formal universally-applicable and universally-binding moral law. In the dispute of Pr. E. N. Trubetskoy and D. D. Muretov, a formal moral absolutism has been presupposed as something already beyond doubt and inevitable. D. Muretov evidently shares in this view and therefore remains defenseless against the formal issues with Pr. E. Trubetskoy. Nowise does it follow, that it be possible to proffer a sign of equivalence between religious absolutism and a moral absolutism. The absolutism has to be in the religious sphere, since it partakes unto itself all the plenitude of values. Morality -- constitutes a great value within human life, but this is merely one of the values within the complex hierarchy of values, and hence it cannot make pretense to an absolute and universal significance, wherefore it ought to admit of the co-existence of other values, no less in their own significance, nor engage in tragic conflicts with them. The tragic aspects of human life have always seemed to me not in the form of a comparatively simple and elementary clash of the moral with the immoral, of good with evil, but rather in the form of more complex a clash of values of various gradations, alike making pretense to positive a significance, and alike oriented towards divine life. The human soul becomes the arena for the tragic clash of the value of the good against the value of beauty or the value of cognition. To this type belongs the living tragedy of Botticelli or Gogol. It is impossible to imagine for oneself the co-inhabiting and co-existence of values of various orders within the human soul and in the soul of mankind in too smoothly-monistic, too optimistic a manner. In the struggle of values there is an arbitrary freedom. Love for one's fatherland can take precedence over the love for one's personal moral perfecting. People quite often out of a burst of moral zeal, out of a devotion to absolute truth, tend to destroy a whole series of values and a wealth of being. There is possible even a demonic moralism. This inclination exists, for example, in Tolstoyanism. The tragedy of the Russian intelligentsia -- consists first of all in the conflict of variously-innate values, and not in a conflict of good and evil. Its will has been taken hold of exclusively by a value of the morally-societal, and alongside this it has no sympathy for the value of cognition, the value of beauty nor suchlike a value of historical life, as nationalness. In the earthly human life there is no pre-established harmony of values, and it is full rather of tragic conflicts altogether not of the moral order. An absolute harmony of values is to be perceived there only within the depths of the absolute Divine life. But it is also possible, that the tragic conflict exists as well in the Divine life aspect and that from this is begotten the entire world process with all its anguish. To Pr. E. N. Trubetskoy the tragic aspect in life represents first of all as though a conflict of the moral with the immoral, as a non-fulfillment of an absolute moral law. Scarcely would he admit, that an exclusive fulfilling of the moral law can also lead to a great tragedy, to a betrayal of certain utmost values. This is best of all illustrated for example by attitudes on war. The moral problem for every person is always very complex and very individual a problem, which ought to be decided not by a formal application of an absolute and universally-binding law, but rather by creative self-autonomous efforts. It is impossible to moralise on war, it is always terrible a matter, which tragically is taken up by us in the name of values chosen by us and beloved by us.

    I have pointed out already a number of times in my articles, written during wartime, that Russian thought is bereft of an organ for evaluations upon historical life.[1] We have always simplistically applied towards historical life values that are abstract, -- either abstractly-sociological, or abstractly-moralistic, or abstractly-religious. Specifically historical values are not recognised by our intelligentsia, and this is actually explicable, in that it has as yet lacked an awareness of vocation towards concrete historical life and towards a concrete historical creativity. Our theocratic religious constructs have likewise been extra-historical the same, as have our sociological constructs, and as also has been the Tolstoyan moral teaching. We have always moralised over history, and this moralising lies concealed there even in Russian Marxism, albeit under amoral a guise. The most consistent form of a moral absolutism, wherein all the wealth of being gets subordinated to a monolithic moral law, was there within the teachings of L. Tolstoy. And an elemental sort of Tolstoyanism, in essence, is to be found in all our currents. We have failed to recognise the historical actuality as an independent self-sufficing reality. Unique in their form historical values, incommensurate with the values of individual life, have been foreign to us, and have seemed as a "blunder" of Western history, begotten of so many evils. The war gets us facing a totally unique historical actuality and unique historical values. Our thought would thus tend to begin at independently and creatively working upon new questions, presented by life. And towards the infinitely complex historical tasks begotten by the process of life, we ought not to recourse to the too simplistic moral, sociological or religious doctrines, we ought rather to creatively tackle the completely new problems, not foreseen by the old teachings. Suchlike first of all is the problem of nationalness. I very highly esteem the significance of Vl. Solov'ev and I think, that his polemics against a "zoological nationalism" had great significance, but it is impossible doctrinally to apply his point of view to the completely new historical actuality. In Christianity there is nothing doctrinaire, neither morally, nor metaphysically. Christianity is the leavening of new life,

---

[1] I wrote about this in my article, "War and the Crisis of the Intelligentsia Consciousness" (in *Birzhevnye vedomosti* for July 1915 [Kl. № 201; № 15, 3], and also "Concerning Truth and Justice in the Struggle of Peoples" (*Utro Rossii* for April 1916) [*trans. note*: Klepinina identifies this latter article as Kl. № 15, 22 in Berdyaev's 1918 book, "The Fate of Russia", but fails to take note of it separately as from its initial "*Utro Rossii*" apr. 1916 source].

a seed, cast forth into the soul of people and into the soul of humankind, it is not an absolute norm set over outside of us. The absoluteness of Christian truth is the spirit of new life acting within us, and not an immutable law standing over us. And it is quite impossible to mechanically in a straight line manner to apply the Christian absolute aspect to what is naturally and historically relative. History is a manifestation of the absolute, but in the historical itself it is impossible to assert the absolute as a norm and law. Within history there never has been and there never will be an absolute morals, but hidden behind history there acts an absolute spirit, of itself revealing and creating a complex gradation of values. And one of these values -- is the uniquely original value of nationalness. If also there is a morality to the historical process, then this is a morality, incommensurate with individual morality. Historical a fate presupposes the tragic conflict between the absolutely-singular and the relatively-multiple. Demonic powers act within history, and they impel peoples to a living out of their historical fate to the bitter end. War cannot be Christian a matter, Christian only can be spirit and the realm of the spirit.

It seems to me, that P. Struve and D. Muretov are overly inclined to absolutise the value of the state, which is merely but one of the loftiest values. Absolutism of the state is less permissible, than is a moral absolutism. The value of the human soul stands higher than the value of kingdoms and worlds. Tactically on much I am in disagreement with P. Struve and D. Muretov in the sphere of national politics and in certain regards moreso in agreement with Pr. E. Trubetskoy. But I am moreso in agreement with them in the acknowledging of a complex hierarchy of values and in a denying of moralising over the historical process. The elemental impulse of a national instinct ought to become justified and become a source of creativity. The moralising over the struggle of peoples can become transformed into an immoral self-exaltation, and moreso lofty a moral awareness would have to admit, that within the historical clashing of peoples it never happens thus, that the good is entirely on the one side, and the evil -- on the other side. And this means, that the national struggle within history is not a struggle for moral justice, but is rather a struggle for the advancement of being, for the creativity of historical values.

The Strength of Russia

(1917 - #254)[1]

I.

It is said the Germans, only now during the time of war, have gotten a sense of the strength of Russia and admit that it is great a power. Prior to the war they tended to look down on Russia. This will sound paradoxical. The Germans all the while sense themself as victors, they have occupied our land. And yet it would seem, that not only the Germans, but all the peoples of the West in perplexity also will have to halt afront the enigma of Russia and admit the power of Russia forever by all the evidence. The peoples of the West, in accord with their total frame of mind, all their history of schooling on this, tend to define the power of a state , the strength of power of the national life according to its organised aspect, the order and self-initiating of a people, the revealing and developement of all the energy of a people. But Russia represents great difficulties for these traditional notions of European man concerning the strength of power. The Germans, the French, the English alike can only exist and keep organised, by an exertion of all their powers, by a disciplined intensiveness. The Russians -- are the sole people in the world, who can permit themself an extensiveness in everything. If the Germans had permitted themself for a short while that wont for the chaotic and disorganisation, which we admit as customary a basis of Russian life, they would have been defeated and perished.

Russia, only Russia alone can permit itself the luxury, which no other one people of Western Europe can permit itself. During the time of war these peoples have to intensely exert all their powers and bring the extent of organisation into utmost a degree. Only the Russian people can sit tight, neither pulling themself together nor intensely straining themself. And in truth it can be said, that the war has uncovered not only the sins, the

---

[1] SILA ROSSII. Article originally published in the literary gazette "Birzhevye vedomosti", 4 jan. 1917, № 16018.

ills and weakness of Russia, but also its enormous strength of power, incomprehensible to reason. This paradoxical fact has to alarm the peoples of Europe and in them evoke envy. Too much has been bestowed the Russian. The existence of Russia -- is paradoxical, and contradiction is its law.

II.

I myself, inwardly having the feeling of Russia and in myself sensing the Russian nature, am compelled to sense it as both perishing and undefeatable, as strong and weak, disintegrating and yet having a great future. This contradiction mustneeds be accepted and lived through to the end. It is alike a mistake and wrong to thus believe in Russia, that there is nothing poor and weak to be seen in it, as likewise thus not to believe in it, that there is nothing good nor strong to notice in it. Russia is undergoing terrible a time, which can only be compared with that of the Time of Troubles era. All its furthermost fate is being decided: whether Russia will emerge towards broad and free a life in the world and thus enter into a period of flourishing, or whether a decline has begun in it leaving it unable to have its say in the world. There ensues an hour, when the Russian people has to master its inner chaos, to gird up and discipline its spirit. Faith in the freedom of man and the freedom of the people in determining their fate impels us to admit, that the people can also perish, that the state can also disintegrate, if all the details be ignored. A blind measure of faith in the givenness of a thing is a denial of human freedom in the realisation of a task. To the Russian people much has been given, but there is still more awaiting it. A responsible awareness ought to make one see this. Forewarnings are given to the various peoples and they can ignore the details. Faith in Russia ought not to be irresponsible.

We cannot but sense the great power of Russia even in a period of its powerlessness and disorganisation: Russia is incommensurate with other peoples and lands. Russia -- is terribly rich both spiritually and materially, within it lie lodged vast potential powers, all still dormant. Germany has done everything, that it could, it has become overstrained in its exertion, it has nothing more to say, and nothing more that it can do. It has reached the edge and the limit. Russia however has manifest only an insignificant portion of its powers, it is not exhausted spiritually, has not overtaxed all its powers. On the one hand, Russia has been a wastrel and permits itself luxury. This -- reflects the extravagance of an extensive culture. On the other hand, Russia is stingy with the historical manifestation of its inner powers, it preserves them inwardly. In it there is no lavish throwing around of its powers upon an intensive culture. This contradiction is very characteristic for Russia. There is an inner force in Russia, which leads it out of its difficulties and saves it in all the difficult periods of its history. But Russian man does not love to exert himself beyond the necessary extreme. The inward strength of power in Russia is totally manifest only in the most extreme instances, under the powerful crush of undergoing an historical tragedy. Usually it remains in reserve. But always there is hope, that at the very edge of doom, in the most tragic moment, this hidden inner force of Russia will awaken and come into active a condition. And always upon this inner power there remains hope. But in the inner core of Russia is hidden an enormous power and inexplicable wealth, which is apparent to the peoples of Europe, cramped as they are and easily exhausted, everywhere stumbling up against boundaries both spiritual and material. The spirit of the Russian people courses its way in boundlessness and vastness, in the elemental. It has not yet gotten concentrated nor formed still for historical manifestation and action. In such a condition are situated also the material inward aspects of Russia, undeveloped for intensive a culture. This dwelling of the Russian spiritual and material powers in potential a condition engenders both the Russian extravagance and the Russian historical miserliness.

III.

Russia indeed can allow itself that, what no other people in the world can allow itself. But it would be immoral to take too much comfort in this. The has to start an ending to the irresponsible psychology of being rich, of being wastrels in the expenditure of one's riches and miserly in the expenditure of one's working energy. Russia is entering into very responsible a period of its historical existence. And it is summoned by history to a responsible organisation of its inexplicable powers. The active involvement of whatever a people into the arena of world history presupposes a transition from extensive into intensive a culture. Russia all still lives a provincially locked-in existence and its state economy has been still all too reminiscent of the economy of the provincial Russian landowner of the old type. Of suchlike a type has been not only the state economy of Russia, but also the economy of spirit. The Russian swaggering about has been irresponsible. The world war is leading Russia into the world cycle of events far more deeply, than all the preceeding world influences upon Russia. The psychology of a provincial landowner of the old type has become impossible already for Russia. Insufficiencies of a spiritual undergirding, of self-discipline, of an active, human energy have also led Russia to a rotten process in its outer trappings. The rotting clothes are falling off Russia, and it is subject to the danger of remaining naked.

But it is impossible to go bare amongst cultural peoples, for it is too fraught with immense dangers. We not only have to get clothed upon with new clothes, we have to don ourself in armour. Spirit has to master the Russian diffuseness of emotion. Spirit has to give form to the body of Russia and guide the life of this enormous body.

But our task cannot be merely negatively protective. Russia is facing an entirely new period of world historical existence. It has to either actively enter into this period, or ultimately fall out from world history and passively fade away into the East. This means also, that Russia stands at an historical crossroads and is experiencing a very responsible moment of historical choice. Russia either has to be a certain great East-West, the uniter of two historical worlds, uniting mankind into universal an unity, or it will be great, but not the greater East, disunitive to the unity of all mankind, bearing disunity into world life. The first, the great path, to which Russia is called, is possible only in the instance, that the Russian people and Russian man ceases to rely upon fate, upon chance, upon the "evil eye", upon "luck", upon non-human forces, and he rather oneself show a strength of power, to organise one's power. The fundamental question for Russia -- is the question of awakening the human self-initiating of the people.

Tiutchev said, that "in Russia one can only believe". But Russia is entering upon that period of historical existence, when it has to also admit the lack of belief in it. And this means, that the faith in the power of Russia has to pass over into a manifestation of the power of Russia. Russia as disclosed and currently manifest presents great difficulties for believing in it. There has to begin a disclosing and manifestation, supportive to this faith. Upon faith is based the initial stage in the life of a people, but the subsequent stage has to be based upon knowing. The peoples of Europe do not believe in Russia and it is impossible to demand this faith of them. But they also do not know Russia, and lack the wherewithal to know it. Russia has to render its power accessible to knowing by all the world. And for this, what lies concealed within the bosom of Russia has to be revealed, what is hidden has to become clear, what is potential has to pass over into active a condition. The hour ensues for ultimate a disclosing of the inner power of Russia.

Reform of the Church

(1917 - xxx)[1]

I.

A. V. Kartashev, in his talented and interesting brochure, "Reform, Reformation and the Manifestation of the Church", says: -- "The reform of the Russian Church, in the precise and technical sense of this word, is of especially vital and intense interest to people, that are either irreligious (upon societal-liberal motives), or else of that religious type, which perceives religion, as something, not subject to any sort of creative experience and is of interest merely from the point of view of the practical organisation of churchly life upon the best of principles... Genuine mystics in the church are little interested, with what is called church reform. Suchlike bearers of a churchly mysticism, as Theophan, bishop of Poltava, or of its theoretics, as the priest-professor P. A. Florensky, have no interest in these questions". One mustneeds grasp the meaning of this phenomenon as accurately noted by Kartashev. We live in an epoch of the rebirth of Orthodox religio-philosophic thought. This thought is profound and

---

[1] REFORMA TSERKVA. Article originally published in the newspaper "Utro Rossii", 14/27 jan. 1917, № 14.

This Berdyaev article was missed by Tamara Klepinina in her authoritative "Berdiaev Bibliographie", and hence lacks a Klepinina # in following her coding.

Likewise, this present article was not included in the massive "*Padenie*" Russian text, from which most of the articles in our current English text are taken. Rather, the present article in Russian text was republished in the 2004 anthology of Berdyaev articles under cover title "*Mutnye liki*" ["Murky Visages"], taking its name from title of one of Berdyaev's articles contained therein: Moskva, 2004, Kanon+, this article p. 277-281.

refined, and it will tend to blossom out later. Yet here is the remarkable thing, that in the loins of this Orthodox outlook, in its thinking so new in comparison with the old theologising, there are however no signs of a will to churchly reform, no sorts of an impetus towards the creation of the free church. In that circle of the Moscow Orthodox, which conditionally and not altogether precisely are called Neo-Slavophils, there is no pathos for church reform or a spiritual turnabout, which should be historically active. I speak about that religious current, which is represented by the priest P. Florensky, S. N. Bulgakov and others. Those reforms, towards which these currents tend, are quite anti-social and anti-historical in their tasks. The centre of gravity is transferred rather into a matter of the personal salvation of soul, into the deepening and refinement of a personal religious experience, lived through as a churchly experience, oriented towards the sacred tradition of the Church. It is pathetic to experience the all ever-continuing and endless conversion into churchly orthodoxy, the adoption of the churchly givenness with all the traditions, all the scope of which encompasses and extends across the spheres of civil and societal life. Apparent are the considerations of movement to the Church, and with this is bound up all the whole dynamic of religious thought, all the refined apologetics. But there are apparent no sort of signs of stirrings from the Church, from out of the Church, as a creative dynamic process, as growth of developement within the church itself, by way of fulfillment of promises and prophecies. They await and expect everything from the Church, but they desire to do nothing for the Church. It is as though they forget, that the life of the Church, as human an organism for the good, involves also our properly own creative religious life, and it is not only an obedience to tradition, but also a forming of tradition. A person, sensing himself as insufficiently deep within the Church, and in churchly life dwelling too much upon the experience of being a neophyte, a beginner, tends not to regard himself ready and worthy for creatively religious an involvement. And thus opens the perspective of that inculcation into the Church and process of perfecting within Orthodoxy, by which one never attains to an awareness of worthiness to be a religious creator and initiator. All our churchly disorder, in having assumed such pernicious forms, gets explained away as private sins and failings, not allowing even for the proper right to render a judgement over this disorder. Everything thus gets caught up in an inescapable going in circles and consolidates forever every given, every gloomiest actuality, that most evil coercive constraint.

S. Bulgakov and Father P. Florensky can hardly be delighted with the synodal churchly structure, they cannot but be vexed over the abasement and enslavement of the Church. But in all their spirit they tend only to strengthen the old and hinder every free impulse towards religious renewal. Their Christianity -- is not a religion of freedom, but rather a religion of necessity, a religion of humility. Their Orthodoxy does not but want to be a religion of the priesthood and it recoils from the prophetic. They are totally concerned with certain individual saints as alone trustworthy of sanctity. And they are profoundly correct, in that they await little from external churchly reforms, such as transpire within the political realm. But they are profoundly incorrect in this, that they are opposed to that prophetic breathing of the Spirit, which has to bring for us a religious renewal and a consummation of the promises, and which breathes, whence it will [Jn. 3:8]. The Church is situated in a great uncertainty and is experiencing both an inward and outward crisis, unprecedented in its seriousness. Through its historical trappings the Church has been immersed in worldly elements and is bound up with processes, transpiring within the state, in the realm of Caesar. And from that side there inevitably has to occur churchly reform, a civil-political reform of the churchly structure. The Church is unable to assume a role in the historical process of growth, and it has to be freed from its old connections with the state. But at its core the Church at an ineffable depth is immersed in Divine life. And it is necessary therein to seek out the sanctities of the Church, against which the gates of hell will not prevail. Within the depths of the spiritual life of the Church there has to occur a certain creative stirring, opening up something new, something incomprehensible yet from within, something quite other from the greater part of those active in churchly politics. But in our modernmost Orthodox thought there is no trend towards churchly reform, no trend towards a new revelation. It wallows its way in an atmosphere of psychical reaction against the year 1905 and bears but a restorational character.

II.

It is very instructive a matter to compare the Moscow Orthodox trend against that of the Kiev Orthodox trend, which is grouped around the journal, "Christian thought". The Kiev current, represented chiefly by the group of professors of the Kiev Theological Academy -- such as

V. Ekzemplyarsky, banished from the Academy for an article on L. Tolstoy, P. Kudryatsev, V. Zavitnevich and others -- are ever long since Orthodox. Those involved in this current are not caught up in getting converted into Orthodoxy, they dwell within it ever and initially. In the religious regard they are very conservative, very ortodoks, in them is no sort of a dynamics of religious thought, and unacceptable to them are suchlike Moscow novelties, as an aesthetic and erotic rapture over Sophia, threatening to transform it into a fourth hypostasis [of the Trinity] and swallow up the religion of Christ. These people are poor in thought in comparison with Father P. Florensky, in them is a greater simplicity, and the Orthodox manner of life for them is not an object of aesthetico-mystical a sort of delectation and taste. But it would seem, that in their total orthodoxness of Orthodoxy there is more heartfelt a directness, more immediate an awareness of Christ, more a sensing of oneself within the very bosom of the Orthodox Church and the Orthodox manner of life. They are somewhat leery of mysticism and in accord with tradition they safeguard churchly Christianity moreso in opposition to mysticism, rather than dabbling in it. This makes them religiously frozen in place, conservative, timid as regards new religious themes, insufficiently refined. But this also sets upon their Orthodoxy the seal of an especial integrity and unique pureness in its safeguarding. The safeguarding of Orthodoxy by Father P. Florensky -- is something murky, distrustful, not free of an aesthetic dallying, decadent. The safeguarding of Orthodoxy by V. Ekzemplyarsky is the guarding of a simple heartfelt faith of the Galilean fishermen, such as is revealed to infants and hidden from the wise. Father P. Florensky tends more to believe in the power of the Anti-Christ and with this faith concurs also his vital values. V. Ekzemplyarsky moreso believes in the power of Christ. And yet this Kievan thoroughly conservative Orthodoxy, nowise wanting to hear anything about a new revelation, still nonetheless with all its heart and all its will has been striving for the reform of the Church, for its deliverance from slavery, for the democratisation of the Church. In the social-churchly regard the representatives of this current -- are progressives and democrats, opponents of the domination over churchly life by the princes of the Church and against the compulsory tying in the Church with the state. In a certain sense they are more faithful to the legacy of Khomyakov, than are the Moscow Orthodox. They hold dear the Sobornost'-Communality of the people of the Church, and it is from within the Church that they want to reform it, to cleanse and renew it. They do not want a reformation, such as may be understood in the Lutheran sense, while they also do not seek for more profoundly spiritual a turnabout within Christianity, such as may be bound up with the possibility of a new revelation. But their outlook is of benefit towards that external reform of the Orthodox Church, which is inevitable from all points of view, even such as may not be specifically religious.

    Our whole churchly renewal movement, striving towards the reform of the Church upon conservatively religious a basis, clearly has to be aware of that enormous significance, which in this matter involves the perestroika-restructuring of our state civil structure, and the activity of the State Duma. The ties of dependence upon the State Duma are not great, and less a dependency upon the secular realm, than that, which exists in our synodal arrangement. The incontrovertible process of the secularisation of the state is likewise a process of the liberation of the Church and its significance yet in the final end is religious. However, so that within the state inwardly there should be realised religious ends and that an immanent religious energy should become active, it is necessary ultimately to repudiate "the Christian state", with which has grown up so many an intolerable lie and association of servility. Then only will there be freely decided the questions concerning the relationship of Orthodoxy inwardly towards Catholicism and inwardly also towards the Old Ritualists, the Old Believers, and sectarianism. A Church of domination can never spiritually become dominant, this -- is a law of spiritual life. Spiritual dominance demands freedom. This -- is an external aspect of churchly renewal, which has to be apparent to everyone, but from which are averted the eyes of the bearers of the modernmost Orthodox thought, caught up in the temptations of the old theocracy. The inward aspect however is bound up with the creative spiritual life, in which is enkindled a new revelation of man. But this already goes beyond the bounds of the theme concerning the relationship of Orthodox thought towards the reform of the Church. And it mustneeds be noted, that at present there tend very complexly to be interwoven for us motifs religio-restorative and motifs religio-reformative. The religiously new however can be created only by motifs that are religio-creative.

The Psychical Factours of the War

(1917 - 255)[1]

I.

It is difficult to predict, when the war will end, and indeed in vain even to try to predict. But for many a reason it can be said, that it is entering into its final phase, which may prove indefinitely lengthy. An unprecedented struggle between peoples is occurring, and in this struggle are engaged all the powers of the various peoples, all the aggregate of their energies spiritual and material. When they say, that the war will lead to exhaustion, then by this they mean to say, that ultimately the war will be decided not upon the fields of battle, not by these or those military actions, but rather by the accumulated aggregate of active powers. All these powers of varied peoples can be staked out on a map. Amidst such a setting of the problem of the war, the rear has no less a significance, than does the front. Moreover, one might say, that everything gets decided at the rear. This has become almost axiomatic. It is totally beyond doubt, that a termination of the war will be decided by factours psychical, and these factours will decide the beginning of the end. The war will finish, because on one of the warring sides will earlier be sensed the psychical impossibility to fight further on. And this psychical impossibility to further fight on will be determined not by a taking into account objective factours, as for example, a food provisions crisis or a purely military position, and not by way of a breakdown of purely spiritual conditions. War is not a matter of mathematics, although mathematics also serves as a basis of the military science and art. I am inclined to think, that the world war will end unexpectedly, and actually, quite otherwise than we would expect. Irrational moments will bring this about. In the final end, the psychology of the peoples will be the deciding factour in the war. There is beginning to be

---

[1] PSIKHICHESKIE FAKTORY VOINY. Article was originally published in newspaper "Birzhevye vedomosti", 19 jan. 1917, № 16048.

felt a sense of this all more and more. And it mustneeds be admitted, that all the peoples have shown greater a strength, than would have been presupposed. Sheer exhaustion has not so quickly set in, as was expected at the beginning of the war. The resiliency of human powers has proven very great, and the endurance of man seems to know no bounds. But the determining significance will belong to powers spiritual, and not material. In the current world war the material powers cannot be decisive, and indeed the very intensity of material powers is dependent upon the spiritual power and is fashioned by it. If within all wars an enormous significance obtains with the spirit of the army, then in the present war an enormous significance obtains with the spirit of all the people.

The Germans have excelled at studying the significance of the psychical factours. In the German proposal for peace negotiations there was a clever psychological calculation. They sought simultaneously to attain two aims by this: to lift the morale of the German people and to demoralise their opponent, to weaken him. And the Germans can thus say, that they were the first in wanting to stop all the horrid spilling of blood, which has so spun out of control, while the allies in contrast have insisted on pressing on with this horror. The impudence of Wilhelm has reached the point, that he has considered it possible to speak about the mania for war, gripping all peoples, with the exception of the German people. All this -- is a toying with psychology, and this is a calculated ploy to undermine the ability for psychical resistance. It is beyond doubt, that Germany is reaching the final limits of exhaustion. Psychically it still sustains and manifests a sufficiently significant power of spirit. The greater the material exhaustion of peoples as might be, then the greater the significance to discover psychical factours, needful to strengthen the resolve of spirit. The Germans are convinced, that in Russia matters stand not favourable in spirit. To demoralise the Russian people, to weaken its psychical resistance -- is a basic goal of the Germans. And to them this seems comparatively simple and easy, since they do not know and do not understand Russia. The resistance of Russia is immeasurably greater, than the Germans might judge it to be, in view of our disorder. In Russia act unnoticed psychical factours, not directly there under the eyes, by which it holds together. The resiliency of the Russian people, in all probability, exceeds the resiliency of all other peoples. And the Russian people can sustain itself without that intense exertion of powers, such as is unavoidable for the peoples of the West. In the patriotism per se of Russian man, which in the externals can seem suspect, there is an unique elemental quality, fully manifest only then, when ensues the decisive hour. Russians always tend to frustrate the calculations of enemies.

II.

But within Russian society however there is the need to expand a responsible awareness concerning the outcome of the war, that the deciding significance devolves upon the psychology of various peoples, the spirit of the peoples. The victor will be the one with the greatest steadfastness of spirit, the greatest firmness. The purely material outlook on powers runs unfavourable for us. But these material powers themself as such will not decide the war: the psychical collateral factours will decide it. Under their vexing burdens at the last minute it will be flung aside by the spirit of the peoples. That psychical condition, which one day will render totally impossible a further continuance of the war, is accumulating imperceptibly. This psychical condition is comprised of very vague and seemingly insignificant elements, and responsible for it is each man, irregardless of howsoever insignificant a place he might occupy. And here the people in the exertions of its collective spirit ought not to permit itself getting into that condition of a psychical debilitation, as would cravenly compel one to go to unworthy lengths to end the conflict earlier than is properly the time. This is a national moral imperative facing each individual person. Let the debilitating psychical condition set in earlier for our enemies, than for us. And this means, that needful is a spiritual effort as regards both oneself and all our societal psychical state of mind, there is needful a conformable positing of the idea. With individual people there is a subliminal subterfuge and they tend to imagine for themself all sorts of ideas by way of justification, when they are too fatigued, when they are too burdened, when fear grips their soul, when they become dispirited, -- justification for the quickest way out from a period of difficulty. Over this subliminal tendency towards subterfuge is needful a control of consciousness. In this regard we have to be strict towards ourself and those nearby. Our individual outlook has to put our national identity as utmost. Our national will, an enlightened awareness, has to set itself the task, the fulfilling of which is obligatory and under which we shall not consent to desist. The awareness itself of such a task can prove an active factour.

Nicholas Berdyaev

It would be criminal to desire a continuing of the war for the sheer sake of the war, and vile a thing it would be to go on forever with the horror of the war under the press of enflamed emotions. And this would be least of all characteristic for the Russians. To make war should be possible only in the instance, where the goals of the war are not connected with grasping appetites nor bloody instincts, but rather with certain utmost values. If the war is only a matter of evil, which in that case would imply stopping it as quickly as possible, then there vanishes any justification not only for continuing the war, but also for its start and any participation in it. Either the terrible aspect of the war, which is something no one can deny, can be justified by some utmost value and thus the bearing of its burden demands heroism and self-sacrifice, or this terror is purely a matter of sin and participation in it involves primordial an evil. This question has to be decided at the very beginning, and the resolution of this tormentive question is impossible to leave til a particular point of fatigue or of fright. The whole matter consists in this, in being conscious of the utmost values and to sustain in one's spirit these values as utmost. If there are no sort of values connected with this war, then there is impossible any sort of rendering a judgement on principle on the question, whether it is proper to continue the war or better to have a quick finish with it. Such an evaluation cannot be considered in context of a will selfish for expansion or seizure. But it is impossible to look at the war and its terror merely from the "private" point of view, from the point of view of the fate of individual people and the present generation. An exceptional soft-heartedness and sentimentality can sometimes ready for man a more fierce and harsh future, than the fierceness and harshness of war. If this is accurate with the personal life of people, then it is even more true in historical life. A premature peace with the Germans, a peace, not realising any sort of historical goals, and evoked by psychical weakness, can prove more fierce a matter, than the ferocity of following through with the war to the end, and fulfilling a necessary historical task. Unaware of this seem those, who are despondent over the gravity of the given moment and are incapable of historical foresight.

III.

It would be very terrible and very sad, if as a result of the war there should transpire, that so many sacrifices have been made and so much blood has been spilled in vain, if mankind were merely to return to things the way they were before, but with all the debilitating and exhausting flowing of blood, if not a single issue were resolved by it! This war has been one of a fatal necessity, it was lodged within the deepest composite of the peoples, within contradictions and unresolved goals. For the whole of European mankind a cleansing catharsis was necessary and with such a catharsis there could only be a catastrophe. But the war, without having resolved anything and prematurely ended, cannot be the catharsis. The tension will remain, it will only be driven inwards, and for the weakened peoples it will be still more difficult to bear. If in our experiencing of an historical catastrophe the basic goals remain unresolved, if the oppositions remain and the correlation of peoples remains basically the same, -- this will bode cruelest a misfortune for mankind. The purely spiritual and moral consequences of such a war, in any case, will be great. But the peoples are doomed to historical an existence, they have to live out their historical fate. And the undecidedness of the historical tasks will terribly burden the historical fate of peoples and all mankind, and hence the necessity of being aware of the fundamental historical goals, facing the various peoples, the deciding of which will lighten their burden. Such a basic and inevitable historical task is the resolution of the Near East Question, of this eternal cause of war, and deep-rooted changes in Turkey and Austria-Hungary, both which are instruments of German imperialism. Herein lies concealed a basic sort of opposition, in fatal a manner dragging matters into the worldwide clash. All the remaining tasks, undertaken by the war, are not so essential nor fundamental, nor so worldwide in their scope. And we have to clearly conceive of and posit the task, connected with resolving this Eastern Question and the radical altering of the position of Turkey and Austria-Hungary. Without this, the sting of the aggressive German imperialism will never be torn out and never will there be a lasting peace in the world. The Balkans as before will become troubled and again shatter the world balance of powers. It is impermissible from an higher point of view to propose a dividing and annihilating of Germany, but benevolence yet demands a knowing of its limits.

Nicholas Berdyaev

If the current war does not resolve these questions in a direction desired by us, then this will be a matter of the greatest misfortune not only for us and for our allies, but also for all mankind, and for our enemies. Our psychical disposition, upon which depends the end of the war, our spiritual fortitude and firmness have to be connected with an awareness of the tasks facing us, with historical a responsibility. When on the map is put not only our own historical fate, but also the fate of all peoples and all mankind, then it would be shameful to be influenced by whatever sort of private outlooks and considerations. We have to fortify our consciousness and our will and not succumb to temptations of psychic a weakness. Our state and civil psychical outlook has to be at the forefront of the historical task, allotted our generation. To live in such an "ultra-historical" time always becomes difficult, it weighs upon the private life of people, and in such a time there is savagery and cruelty. But also in the personal life of each man there occur moments very decisive, upon which depends all his future fate. In such moments people tend to gird themself up, exert all their powers, they forget about joys and comforts, and are capable of great sacrifices. Moreover, such moments happen also in the historical life of peoples. Many of the wishes, expressed in the note of President Wilson, are beautiful and with them it is possible to sympathise. Russia first expressed the desire for worldwide a settlement. But the path to the realisation of the highest human aims is very complex, and they involve sacrifice and suffering. And if we cleanse our consciousness from everything "private" and suchlike, then it become clear, that for us peace remains still impossible, just as it is impossible for all mankind. The path to it lies through victory. The catharsis has still not begun.

On Love for Russia

(1917 -#289)[1]

I.

The love for one's rodina, one's native land, -- is so immediate and elementary a feeling, that it would seem unnecessary to appeal to it, and necessary though merely to clarify and ponder it. But for us in Russia this -- is a total problem, altogether not so elementary a matter, and we even have disputes possible upon this theme. The question regarding the love for Russia, about the immediate instinct, the impelling to defense of native land and service to it, evokes a struggle of various currents and teachings. The present day war has revealed a vexing dichotomy within the national consciousness. Very characteristic for Russian man, is that for him it is indispensably necessary to find justification and a basis to his love for Russia, though the justifications be quite very contradictory. We have great difficulty to find that primal instinct and primal consciousness, by virtue of which each Russian would essentially want to devote all his powers to Russia, its security, its unity, its greatness. We as it were lack that assertiveness of a national will in its primordial proclivity, without which there cannot be any sort of a national consciousness, any sort of national purposes, worthy of world significance. The disputes over the national consciousness and the national question shew the impairedness of our national sense of self. It is quite abnormal a thing, that the attitude towards native land should be rendered an object of struggle involving political parties and state ideologies, that a national issue should assume so subordinate a position in relation to the state-political issue. What we have are "defeatists" of the right and "defeatists" of the left, a phenomenon that only with difficulty is conceivable to the Frenchman, the Englishman or the German. It is only with difficulty to be conceived that perversion of a national feeling, which permits of the defense of one's native land only

---

[1] O LIUBVI K ROSSII. Article originally published in "Velikaya voina v obrazakh n kartinakh", № 13, p. 180-182.

under certain conditions, only under conditions of subordinating nationality to a certain state or social principle and demanding a guarantee, that the defense of native land should directly lead to the triumph of the desired principles. How can there be possible the haggling in our relation to native land in the moment of peril! Some love not Russia, but rather an old state order of things, dear to their heart, others love not Russia, but rather a new social order desired by them; and yet others are close to the interests of the nobility or the bureaucracy, and yet others -- to the interests of the workers or peasants.

But still there is Russia as a certain wholeness and individualness, Russia as a living organism within the world, possessing its own essential fate. Russia is more profound a matter, and more enduring than this or that social group. It has its own living and individual soul, unlike any in the world. And herein this soul suffers and bleeds from the haggling over it, from an insufficiency of direct love for it in a difficult moment of its historical wanderings. In the strife of passions, in the struggle of interests and ideas, they too often tend to forget about Russia. For too many, Russia gets replaced by this or that private principle, involving some group, some party or abstract idea. Every great people has to have its unique own idea, which it conveys to the world, its vocation. It not only has to exist, but to exist pondering and worthily. This is indisputable the same, just as it is indisputable, that every individuality in the world has to ponder his existence, when it emerges beyond the elemental beastly condition. Each nationality, just like each individuality, possesses its own idea and it has to be resolved at the forefront of a national self-consciousness. his idea is its vocation, without which is impossible a worthy existence. And I believe, that Russia has its own great idea and great vocation. Each Russian is called to freely manifest this idea and fulfill this vocation. But there exists likewise the idea, that every nationality, just like every individuality, possesses an independent worth, that it has to exist, to reveal itself, to attain a maximum expression of its powers and flourishing. There exists not only the idea concerning nationality, but nationalness itself per se is an idea, is a self-value. Whereas non-love for the fatherland seeks to be justified by some whatever idea, the idea of love for the fatherland has to be admitted as great a value. Service to the idea, consisting of the vocation of our fatherland, is our duty to the fatherland, is a manifesting of its spiritual might to the world. And this means, that the love for Russia is a self-value, primordial, primal, that it demands no justification nor grounds.

II.

It is impossible to love Russia merely on the basis, that it has to be the bearer of some whatever Byzantine state principles, just as it is impossible to love it merely because, that it has o be the bearer of some whatever socialistic ideas. The love therein is directed not towards Russia as a living reality, but rather towards an abstract state principle or abstract social ideal. To love Russia needs to be just as capriciously willful a matter, as capriciously willful as one might love an individual image in the world, as one might love a chosen of heart. When the face of a chosen fellow or lady of heart is covered with a rash, true love is not deflected by this. It is impossible to love Russia only for its qualities and its attainments, impossible to love it on conditions or with haggling. The attainment itself of the utmost life for Russia, the heightening of its qualities is possible only, if we love it irregardless of these attainments and qualities.

Theocratic Illusions and Religious Creativity

(1917 - #258)[1]

I.

The paper of A. V. Kartashev, "Reform, Reformation and the Fulfilling of the Church", read at the Petrograd Religio-Philosophic Society and not long ago appearing as a separate brochure, is very interesting. In this brochure can be sensed the spoken version, expressed with great enthusiasm. Kartashev -- is excellent an orator. Particularly precious in Kartashev is his passionate push towards a new religious life. His theme -- is poignant and fiery. But the thought of Kartashev is unclear and confused, it is laced with contradictions, and is all the time twofold. Kartashev uniquely and with great a religious seriousness tends to posit the theme of Merezhkovsky. He is infected with all the poisons of Merezhkovsky, is fascinated with his setting of religious themes, and has an inclination towards his heresies. Yet Kartashev himself is nonetheless altogether different, he has different sources and a different religious nature. In him is sensed a man truly Orthodox and churchly both by flesh and blood, and by spirit. In him there is no sort of abstractness not literary affectation. He is not a convert from culture to Christianity. He is fond of the fleshly aspect of the Orthodox Church, its way of life, its unique aesthetics. The Church for him is moreso a matter in the blood, than in thought. And he is a master at providing a physiologically aesthetic feeling of Orthodox churchliness, he is proud of his forever belonging to the churchly flesh. But he has wanted as though to free himself from his too great an attachment to the old churchly flesh, he flees from the aesthetics of the Orthodox cultus, as might one from a temptation. A dividedness, a dualism in regard to the Orthodox Church tears at Kartashev -- within him there is no integral religious mindset, no integral impulse, he is not free,

---

[1] TEOKRATICHESKIE ILLUZII I RELIGIOZNOE TVORCHESTVO. Article was originally published in periodical "Russkaya mysl', 1917, march-april, p. 71-80.

filled with fears he flees from himself, he vacillates between temptations of the old churchliness, taken in its wholeness and organicity, and the temptations of the innovations and heresies of Merezhkovsky. All this tends to muddle the thought of Kartashev and leaves its impress upon the brochure of interest to us. His churchly theocratic conception is not organic, is not integrally whole, and within it become objectified the contradictions of his own spirit.

I begin my critique with the observation, that Kartashev has aspired towards the Universal Church, and all his pathos -- is in the expectation of a new universal Christianity, yet he however with all his religious experience, with all the positing of that religious thought, he dwells exclusively upon the Eastern, the Orthodox Church, both parochial and national. This is already evident from the fact, that he bestows such an enormous and central significance upon the theme concerning Orthodoxy and autocracy, a theme not universally Christian, but instead purely Russian, of interest merely for Russian Orthodoxy and the Russian state. Concerning Catholicism, Kartashev speaks externally, formally and only for propriety's sake. He desires "to sense the very heart of Orthodoxy, to overhear its golden dreams". And herewith he asserts, that "Orthodoxy, in its maximum and prime, esteems autocracy, the connection with the religious bearer of the power of the state, with the Anointed-Caesar; esteems it by virtue not only of moral a lifestyle conservatism, but also by virtue of necessity -- to religiously hold mastery over the world, by virtue of the theocratic tasks of the Church" (p. 15). Kartashev is ready to admit, that the instincts of the churchly Black-Hundredists run deeper and more vigourous, than the aspirations of church liberals. This is the method of deliberation, by which Kartashev in following upon Merezhkovsky wants to demonstrate the inevitability of a new revelation (and not reform and reformation). That, which Kartashev terms as "the fulfilling of the Church", is too exclusively bound up with the Russian Church, with Russia. Merezhkovsky even directly ties in this "fulfilling" with the Russian revolutionary intelligentsia, in which he sees the engendering of a new religious societal aspect. This -- is a Slavophil offshoot, a revolutionary variant of the Slavophil ideologies. Kartashev is not free from the illusions of a religious populism. But such a mindset and trend of the religious will is contrary to the spirit of universal a Christianity and its hopes. The assertion of a mystical aspect of autocracy, of its faith-confessional significance, though as a topic of contention and polemic, is already a deviation away from the paths of universal a Christianity. This assertion cannot be formally juxtaposed against the papal theocracy, which in any case assumes a character universal and essentially religious. Some tend even to see in papism the Anti-Christ principle. The Russian autocracy however is a phenomenon entirely local, nationally historical. It cannot be something mystical by virtue of its objectively historical position and role, but only by virtue of the psychology of people having accepted it with reverence. Kartashev, just like Merezhkovsky, also thus does not explain, why Orthodoxy is mystically connected with autocracy. For this it would be necessary to go at depth into religious psychology, which they fail to do. They reverently accept the idea, hostile to them, of a mystical aspect of autocracy, and against its wishes they seek to reinforce this venomous idea. They essentially fail to discern the lie underlying this idea, the prelest' delusive going astray, upon which it is grounded. They themself are situated in this delusively straying prelest'. And this occurs from a false identification of the Church with the theocracies, inherited by Christianity from Judaism and from pagan Rome. The Church for them is first of all a kingdom within the world and over the world. "The full and living Orthodoxy is theocratically indestructible in the same measure, in which it is truly churchly. It is because that theocracy and the Church -- are inseparable concepts. That which is not a theocratic church is not a church particularly" (p.15). Hence "the fulfilling of the Church" is something Kartashev thinks of in terms of a new theocracy, albeit of revolutionary democratic a type.

II.

Theocracies have been of significance at a certain stage of developement of mankind. They reflected the childish helplessness of man and assisted man with paternal a guidance. But the associating and identification of the Church of Christ with a theocracy, the interweaving of the Church with an earthly kingdom, is a source of enslaving illusions. And Kartashev is not free from these illusions; he is afraid of freeing the spirit, felt rather as numbing the spirit, as an impoverishment of the Church and denial of its universality. But this means, that he esteems the preserving of the religious immaturity of mankind, esteems within Christianity elements that are of the Old Testament and Judaist a mindset, upon which also theocracies tend to rest. The unfortunate aspect is only, that this experience cannot yet be something immediate and naive, rather it is contrived, in it always can be discerned a romantic utopianism. The prerequisite for theocracy has tended to be an objectified religious materialism, in which spirit remains still submerged within the bosom of organic matter. In this stage of developement of spirit God tends to be presented in the aspect of power and authority. The source of the power of authority is conceived of as totally transcendent to man. The absolute and inorganic power of authority upon earth is merely the image and likeness of the absolute and inorganic power of authority in heaven. Upon this path the principle of the power of authority becomes religiously objectified and materialised. The Kingdom of God gets presented as an outward material kingdom, an object objectively existing within the natural and historical order. The absolute becomes circumscribed within the relative, the relative becomes absolutised. The sources for the conceiving of the mystical aspect of autocracy mustneeds be sought out in the transcendent character of the religious consciousness. A religious slavery is always indeed tied in with an experiencing of the Divine in the transcendent aspect of opposition and distance. A profoundly inward experiencing of the Divine leads to freedom. But Kartashev, despite his religio-revolutionary aspirations, wants to remain in this transcendent and Old Testament sort of religiosity, he bestows mystical a significance to the customary churchliness, a customary organic wholeness, and while he is a populist, he remains essentially a churchly traditional conservative, though he is also an heretic and renegade. And thus in whatever the matter, he desires to have a theocratic, external, material, transcendent power of the Church and guidance of the Church. "We thirst for the positive enrichment of the scope of religious life. For us there is little of that theocratic scope it had, which obtained in the historical embodiment of the Church. We desire the expanding of the power of religion into all the newly discerned mainlands and islands of human creativity, we anticipate a new flourishing of its powers in its application to the new problems of the human spirit and of human society" (p. 26). We cannot fail to sense these aspirations and expectations of Kartashev. These are also our own aspirations and expectations. But why however does Kartashev not think of "the enrichment of the scope of religious life" otherwise, why in the form of an external theocracy, though it be a new, free and democratic theocracy? He wants nevertheless the "power of religion" over all the extent of culture and the societal aspect. And certainly, theocracy always would be a transcendent power of authority over all the "mainlands and islands of human creativity", for it would be impossible to apply this Old Testament terminology in different a sense. Kartashev creates for himself a tragically inescapable position, since he is himself impelled to say: "Everything immobile and non-creative of history is still under the power, as regards inertia, of the Church; but, alas, everything creatively alive, advanced, actively absorbing and fascinating, truly commanding, bearing upon itself the seal of youth and holding in itself the pledge of the future, cannot find room within the Church" (p. 31). True, Kartashev anticipates new revelations within the Church, which would encompass the entirety of world history, all human creativity, the whole of culture and the societal aspect. But indeed this new revelation would all however be transcendent in regards to human creativity itself, transcendent to culture itself and the societal aspect, to world history itself, would be *a power of authority* over it, i.e. a new theocracy. But there is indeed possible an altogether different path, the path of acknowledging the immanent religiosity of human creativity itself, the revelations of modern history, the revelations of human culture and of the societal aspect. Upon this path likewise is possible "the enriching of the scope of religious life", is possible the discernings for religious life of "new mainlands and islands", but amidst the total freeing from theocratic illusions and from expectations of a transcendent sanction and power of authority. The religious problem of human creativity is not a problem of power of authority and in no sense can it be connected with theocracy. And the religious problem of a free societal aspect can only be posited as an ultimate surmounting of every theocracy, as an immanently religious sanctifying of the societal. The question about the expansion or contraction of the scope of religious life for Kartashev gets too closely bound up with polemics against Protestantism, against which it justly arises. But this question ought to be transferred over to a different plane, in which Protestantism is not of interest.

III.

The inward and creative religious upheaval within Christianity ought first of all to capsize every theocracy, to get free of theocratic illusions and in the sphere of the secular societal aspect to affirm inwardly instead a religiously grounded anthropocracy, *an human self-directing*. One can accept the old Christian truth, that every power of authority is from

God, i.e. the power of authority also within democratic and social republics. In every principle of power there is a Divine energy, every true sort of power in the final end has Divine a source. But a transcendently-theocratic interpretation of this truth can be replaced by an interpretation immanently anthropocratic. The Divine energy acts within man and through man, and not merely within angelic a priesthood and through angelic a priesthood. The religious societal effort cannot be merely external a task, it cannot be constructed upon but external sanctions and sanctifyings, it can only be an inward sanctioning and sanctifying of human community in the Spirit. An immanent theocracy is anthropocratic, the self-directing of matured man, conscious in himself of the Divine image. All the theocracies have been by way of a training and guiding of the immature, a guardianship over them. And the task of fashioning a free and new theocracy is illusory a task, based upon confusions within the religious consciousness. The secularisation, which is happening in the modern history of mankind, as regards its inner meaning is nowise a contraction of the scope of religious life. Such -- would be very external a view. The meaning of the secularisation, snatching away all the transcendent religious norms and sanctions from the human societal effort and from culture, -- is religious; it is but the expression upon the surface level of the inward religious upheaval, a passage through a moment of religious dichotomy. But Kartashev, evidently, quite fails to understand and to accept the inevitability of the immanentisation of religion and the inevitability upon this path of a passage through dichotomy. In contradicting himself he has to admit, that "the historical process has not transpired without benefit of Christianity, though also the last century has occurred outside of union with the Church" (p. 40). On the outside the scope of the religious life has contracted, on the inside however has been readied its expansion. The human spirit was given freedom and it created an outwardly fenced enclosure of external churchliness.

Religion is not a *Privatsache*, not a private matter. To squeeze out religion into some sort of tiny dark corner is something that only unbelieving people want to do, those who are hostile to religion. This -- is elementary and beyond doubt apparent. But this nowise resolves the problem of Kartashev concerning the scope of the Church. The scope of the Church cannot be measured by any sort of external signs, it coincides with the scope of the Cosmos. Where are the criteria of churchliness for Kartashev himself? He spreads it out, imperceptibly he extends the scope of the Church to infinity and he is compelled to admit, that what has been transpiring outside the Church has been churchly a thing in the sense of a new revelation. The whole new revelation for him has happened outside the visible, the external Church. But thereupon vanishes the acuteness of his churchly sense of self. And unjustified is his contempt towards people, lacking in understanding of the Church, to which he includes the majority of modern people. It signifies, that there exists an hidden Church, immersed within the inexplicable depths of Divine life. The external church, embodied upon the material historical plane is a projection of the hidden Church. But this hidden Church is nowise a justification for individualism, since the sacramental spiritual life is churchly life. The hidden spiritual life, involving different planes is nowise merely a Privatsache, a private matter, it -- is universal, cosmic, and moreso universal, than the external churchliness. Kartashev simplistically makes use of arguments against Protestantism and against the teaching that "religion -- is Privatsache, a private matter". This is all rather more complex a thing and demands an in-depth gnosis. The churchly Christianity indeed in more strict and deep a sense of the word -- is non-mystical, it is grounded upon objectification and oppositions. Churchly Christianity always has warred against mystics. Mysticism always has been an experience of identity, of the immanence of the Divinity for man, it is always a concealed and aristocratic matter, and expresses primal revelations. Religion however, in its historical manifestation, is already not primal a revelation, but instead secondary. The nature of every historical religion -- is social, in it is always a looking about upon the human multitude, the acceptance of responsibility for the lower stages of life, an entering into mutual security. In this -- is the truth of historical religion. Religion -- is democratic. Religion implies a certain worldwide bond, it conveys the primal revelations of the hidden life of the spirit within this connection. This mustneeds be clearly perceived, in order to avoid falling victim to illusions arising from a confusion of various planes. There is in Kartashev too much of the Petrograd understanding of Orthodoxy, exclusively social, theocratic, in the aspect of realm. But indeed there is also a different Orthodoxy, there exist the startsi/elders, the wilderness dwelling, mental prayer, the wont for wandering, the communing of the people in the liturgical mysteries. The obliquely indirect mystical side of Orthodoxy mustneeds be sought in this, and not in a theocratic Orthodox kingdom. It is inaccurate and superficial to speak about the individualness of mysticism. Mysticism in the profound depths goes beyond the opposition of the one and the many. The problem of a social multiplicity exists only within secondary an objectification.

IV.

Kartashev is correct, in bestowing tremendous significance to the religious problem of cosmos. "In the modern sensing of the cosmos, in namely its religious perception, lies a central secret of all the modern fates of religion as regards its farthermost history" (p. 47). But the connection of the cosmic problem with the churchly consciousness is very complex. There has been within the churchly consciousness a tendency towards acosmism, towards an ignoring of cosmic mysteries. A religion of the fear of eternal perdition and of the salvation of the soul -- is an acosmic religion. On the other hand, the process of secularisation is nowise assuredly a denial of religious an attitude towards the cosmos. Kartashev herein is too oriented towards negative an accounting of Protestantism. The problem of the cosmos was acutely and profoundly posited in the era of the Renaissance, with its theosophy, nature-philosophy and mysticism. The extra-churchly consciousness as regards external indicators of a Giordano Bruno or Paracelsus were more cosmic, than was the Medieval churchly awareness. With J. Boehme, a Lutheran by faith-confession, there was a religious attitude towards the cosmos, and he never narrowed the scope of religious life, he never relegated religion into a Privatsache, into a private affair. And in the modern theosophic trends, possessing no direct connection with the Church, there is first of all an orientation towards the mysteries of cosmic life, in any case, moreso an orientation towards them, than for example, with Merezhkovsky, who is oriented sociologically, and not cosmically. There exists even an opposition of types of a cosmic and sociological world-perception. And what is altogether still inconceivable as such is this, how could Kartashev, so well informed in the history of religion, how could he fall for a crude factual error and admit, that a religious societal aspect is foreign to Judaism. He even makes mention of those, who aspire towards a secularisation of the societal aspect, thinkers of Judaist a type. The striving however towards a religious societal aspect, towards an historical ordering of mankind upon religious a basis he instead ascribes to Aryan religiosity. But indeed the directly opposite is true! A religious societal aspect is an especial doing of the Semitic spirit, the grandiose theocratic idea was indeed engendered upon the soil of Judaism. This is true to the extent, even in modern Judaism, that socialism assumes the character of an inverted religious societal effort. And with great a basis it can be stated, that the idea of a theocratic societal aspect is foreign to a purely Aryan type of religiosity. There is within the Aryan spirit a tendency towards pure monism, unfavourable for theocratic ideas. This is evident in the religion of India, nowise theocratic in its pathos, shunning any religious meaning of history, and also within the German religious consciousness, which is foreign to every eschatological perspective and every apocalyptic prophesying concerning the Kingdom of God. A very vivid example of such a type obtains with the ultra-Aryan religious philosophy of Drews.[1] The thesis of Kartashev, which suggests a misunderstanding, is toppled likewise by Chamberlain [H. S., 1855-1927], in his expressing of an Aryan Anti-Semitic outlook. In Judaism, theocracy is bound up with a transcendent awareness of God. The Aryan immanent God-awareness does not however admit of theocracy and allows only for the religious sanctification of the societal aspect from within.

    The negative attitude of Kartashev towards secularisation, which has been a freeing of the human spirit from its slavery to the natural, to organic matter, having received religious a sanction, leads to a negation of the religious meaning of all modern history. Here we hit upon a basic contradiction in the consciousness of Kartashev. He thirsts for new prophecies and revelations from the Church and from within the Church. He is almost scornful of those, who make bold to prophesy and reveal the new not from the Church, but rather from culture, from freedom, from the free spiritual life. In him speaks the instinct of the age-old Orthodox lifestyle, almost that of a churchly conservative. He desires only the *fulfilling* of the Church, which he basically sets in opposition to reform and reformation. But he is compelled however to admit, that prophesyings and new revelations are beginning within secular culture and the societal effort, that they come from humanism, from the free spiritual life. He even goes so far as to proclaim: "The whole social political process of modern times is an unconscious striving towards a new theocracy, is a complex constructing of its outer body" (p. 44). He falls into a religious absolutising of worldly relative processes, since he tends to think only theocratically. It thus results, that the whole creative process of modern history, creating a

---

[1] Vide his "Die Religion als Selbst-Bewusstsein Gottes".

free societal aspect and a free spiritual culture, is a fulfilling of the Church. This clearly contradicts the initial setting of the theme and is expressed too simplistically.

Between culture and religion there exists an irreconcilable contradiction and opposition. Religion creates life. Culture however creates values. Upon this basis is begotten the tragedy of creativity, the thirst to create new life, and not merely new "sciences and arts". Culture is not a revelation of man, but rather an embellishing of man.[1] Culture therefore has to be secular, it cannot but be external to the religious. Religion is but that creative energy, which lies concealed behind culture, merely its creative edifice, and not its realisation. And behind culture can be glimpsed the potential of a new religious revelation. But this never can be caught sight of in the light of a transcendent religious consciousness. Culture and the societal aspect can never be religious in the transcendent-theocratic sense of the word, they have to be free and human. But secular creativity can be immanently of the Church in whatever the concealed sense, outwardly inexpressible. This would be a revealing of the Divine aspect within human creativity itself, a justification of its self-worth, and not a forcible cramming of it into the Church, not an awaiting of sanction from the Church. It is necessary to cease being pre-occupied with trying to reconcile the Church and free culture, the Church and the free societal aspect. This -- is a theocratic illusion. We are facing a tragic sort of opposition, which needs to be followed out to its end. *The Church exists prior to those times, while it still yet is unfulfilled. The end of culture, its transition to a new religious life will be also an end-point of the Church in the external transcendent sense. This -- is a different dimension of being, an apocalypsis of all our worldly backdrop. The fulfillment of the Church is also a finishing completion of the Church, it is needful merely prior to the time, prior to the overcoming of the rift. The fulfilling of the Church in an external and transcendent sense never will occur.* Upon such a basis man would be consigned to a bad infinity of waiting. It is impossible to await still a new revelation from the outside, it will be conceived of by man himself and will be a mysterious upheaval within the Divine depths of man. This new revelation can only be as a revelation of man in response to God,

---

[1] Vide concerning this in my book, "The meaning of Creativity. Attempt at a Justification of Man" [Engl. title: "The Meaning of the Creative Act"].

and not the fulfilling of the Church in a theocracy, albeit one that is new. This new self-feeling and self-awareness would cease the strain, echoing forth in the words of Kartashev: "And people come to church to bewail their grief or in joy, to create however they go into the open fields, under the solar canopy of the heavens and there they breathe in a bracing whiff of prophetic eschatology. The wellspring of propheticism is not gone dry. It spreads forth and flows in a stormy torrent, beating upon the shores of the Church upon improvised a channel. The religious norm demands its return into a proper to it churchly channel. It is necessary for it to mingle with the encountered churchly languor concerning propheticism" (p. 56). This rift tends to exist in all, situated within the grip of theocratic illusions. But in the Divine depths of man particularly lies the depths of the concealed Church. And the revelation of man, and of his creativity does not abrogate any of the sanctities of the Church, it -- is about the other and from the other. In the mysteries of the Church -- is the movement from God to man. The new revelation -- is movement from man to God.

It would be very superficial to think, that this is Protestantism. Within Protestantism there has been nowise posited the religious problem concerning man, for within Protestantism there has been a tendency towards Monophysitism. And still too, it must be stressed, that only on the periphery does there exist the vulgar opposition between individualism and collectivism, within the depths it is already surmounted. Man -- Adam Kadmon -- is likewise the human multiplicity. It is needful to religiously admit the responsive revelation of man himself, his creative freedom and domain, i.e. there is need of God in man. This also is that mythos,[1] upon which is built the new revelation. But Kartashev wants from the old myth to build a new theocracy. And this is a chasing after phantoms. The path, for which I am speaking, preserves to a greater degree the connection with the unshakable sanctity of the Church, rather than the path advocated by Kartashev. Outwardly in Russia there is needed a reform of the Church, the freeing of the Church from forced connections with the state and the secularising of culture and the societal aspect, as an imperative of religious sincerity. Inwardly however there is needed movement in the depths, and not in a surface superficiality, a spiritual revolution, a revelation of man. The merit of Kartashev, is that he is so keen and fiery, though also insufficiently free, and he posits these themes, suggestive of these tasks.

---

[1] Myth as a religious reality.

The Psychology of a Survivable Moment

(1917 - 259)[1]

Still quite recently, yesterday, it would seem, some very wise Russian people had gathered and they held agonising conversations, on how to find a way out of the mess, into which Russia has fallen. And in a sort of inescapable gloom the wise people left it all up to chance and to fate. In only but few remained faith in the instinct of the Russian people, which always has managed to find a way to save in the difficult moments of historical life. And the Russian people in so doing has proven, that it is a great people and worthy of a great future. On the brink of destruction, in an inescapable position, under the threat of terrible an enemy with inspiration and genius it managed a most brief, bloodless and harmless of revolutions. Everything happened unforeseen, not by plan, not by calculation. The Great Russian Revolution did not resemble typical revolutions. This was a sort of impulse amongst all the people, an upheaval of the nation in general. Suchlike were its first days. The ultimately rotted top structure was gone, and no one was sorry about it. The unprecedented vileness of the old powers united everyone top to bottom. The Russian revolution -- was the most national, the most patriotic, the most deriving of the people from of all the revolutions, the least in matters of class as regards its character, not "bourgeois" and not "proletarian". That which occurred in Moscow on 1 March, when all the army went over onto the side of the people, produced the impression not of a revolution with its bloody struggle, but rather of happy an holiday celebration amongst the people. The instinct of the people had found a way out, just as it had found it during the Times of Troubles era, just as it had always found it, and had not allowed Russia to perish. A prolonged revolutionary struggle during the time of war would have been ruinous for Russia. And here with the speed of a lightning-flash, in enormous an unity there was swept away the old powers, which hindered Russia to live and spread forth a prolonged and oppressive nightmare, from

---

[1] PSIKHOLOGYA PEREZHIVAEMOGO MOMENTA. Article originally published in the weekly "Russkaya svoboda", apr. 1917, № 1, p. 6-12.

this ghastly enchanted realm the Russian people emerged into a bright realm of freedom. And the striking thing, is how ingloriously perished the old and formerly sacred realm -- it found not a single chivalrous defender, all the servants of the old order hastened to desert it, they all proved to be charlatans. In this regard the royalists of the French Revolution stood higher. Where indeed the sincere and true defenders of the old regime? Where the spiritual powers of reaction? The last of the autocrats, Nicholas II, has killed the sense of loyalty, has murdered the monarchistic idea and has torn it from the heart. In the elements of Rasputinism was drowned the remnants of loyal devotion to the old monarchy and dynasty. In these murky elements perished also the last remnants of a connection of autocracy with the Orthodox Church.

Striking also was the lack of discomfort and ease, with which the revolutionary turnabout transpired for the Church almost mechanically, the imperial chair was removed from the Synod, and there occurred some small changes in prayers for Divine Services. The clergy has proven completely loyal in regard to the new powers. There have not been any sort of signs of clergy resistance to the downfall of the thousand year sanctity on the part of the representatives of the clergy. No sort of clergy religious agitation has been sensed in clergy circles, no signs of activity or initiatives. Long ago already there evidently occurred a spiritual upheaval, and the external catastrophe merely confirmed it. Of the sacred status of the autocracy long ago already nothing remained, except the outward decoration. And indeed there never did exist a mystical connection of autocracy with Orthodoxy: the connection was but a matter of the national historical and of lifestyle.

If much was unforeseen in what has transpired, then one thing was foreseen -- the neutral role in the turnabout played by the army, and otherwise it could not be. By thousands of bloody threads the revolution was connected with the war, it obliged almost all to the war and reminded one of one's duty in regard to the war. This correlation of war and revolution is for us very contradictory and paradoxical. For a long time the war, evidencing the unfitness of the old regime, forestalled a revolutionary turnabout. Many, sincerely aspiring for a free life in Russia, out of patriotism became reconciled to finishing up the war with the old powers remaining in place. But the war also however terribly facilitated the revolutionary turnabout in Russia: it rendered it rapid and united. The war transformed the whole army into something of the people and therefore it facilitated its passing over to the side of the people. Now many elements, in the depths of their souls being conservative, have become reconciled with the new powers out of patriotism, and out of fear of harming the war effort by discord. The general staff, undoubtedly, has sanctioned the revolutionary turnabout out of patriotic motives, and for maintaining unity in the army. And this special connection of the revolution with the war cannot be sundered, it has to be continued. Patriotic indignation has enabled the overthrow of the old powers, the suspicion of treason and betrayal has morally finished off the old power; its incapacity to get atop the tasks of the defense of the country has rendered objectively impossible its further existence. This patriotic defensive motive of the Russian revolution obliges it to continue on with the war and intensify the free powers of the people for the war. In this is its justification of national a character. It is not the first time in history that powers, under the force of revolution, happened to wage war. The French Revolution had to wage war. And it mustneeds be said, that the question concerning the war at present is a most anxious and important question for a free Russia: it has to be at the forefront of patriotic tasks. The Russian people has to define its free-citizen attitudes towards the war, has to realise, that in its own hands sits the fate of Russia, its honour and its dignity. Failures in the war are dangerous to the very cause of freedom. The victory of Wilhelm could readily be transformed in Russia into a victory of counter-revolution. The dark powers could lift their head, and there could be attempts at a restoration. A defeated and humiliated Russia would be unable to be reborn into a new and free life -- it would be thrown backwards. The more lofty and civil consciousness of the workers has to lead to a remembering, that a real improvement of position of the working class stands dependent upon the worthy and independent existence of Great Russia. Advances are needed not only of the bourgeoisie, but also of the workers themself, of all the Russian people, of all its coming generations: on this depends the economic developement of Russia. The problem of the improvement of the position of labour in Russia is insoluble if unrelated to the problem of Great Russia and its place in world life. A non-national, abstract existence of the working class is impossible. Only a national democracy is possible. The international Social-Democratic mindsets are merely moments of delirium, after which is inevitable a sobering up and being thrown backwards. One should not underestimate the danger of counter-revolution and restoration -- in the case of revolutionary excesses. In France indeed it was only after 80 years following the great French Revolution that there was established a durable democratic republic. In a land, accustomed to a lengthy period of slavery, not immediately at once and not easily can there be established the people's self-discipline and free citizenship. Free citizens are not created in a single day. The task of nurturing democracy in Russia -- is very difficult and serious a task, and the greatest hindrance upon its path is that of demagoguery. If we have a fracturing of the unity of the all-national impulse, with the growth of discord, if in deciding the fortunes of the state there prevail principles of class struggle, if there be attempts to prolong the revolution in a social-class spirit, if among the masses there prevail the Social-Democrat "Bolsheviks" with their anarchist-revolt tactics, then counter-revolutionary attempts are inevitable and will have justification. It is unseemly to incite violence against a significant portion of the Russian people and society. It would present the danger to the liberal possessor classes to feel, that the new regime for them is more dangerous than the old regime. Thus grow thoughts of restoration. "Bourgeois" fear already begins to be sensed, and this unlofty outlook in certain circles poisons the joy of the resurrection of an entire people to new life. The impossibility at present of a "proletarian" revolution is realised by all the somewhat reasonable Social-Democrats.

The new powers, undoubtedly, face entering upon the path of bold reforms in the spirit of state socialism, upon the path of the socialisation and regulation of our economic life. This has to, certainly, lead to a clashing of the state itself with the diverse interests of the industrialists and land-owners, the workers and the peasants, to a limiting of these interests and desires. Another path at present is impossible for the state. There has to be revealed the broad possibility for the organisation of democracy and the defense of the interests of labour. But all this can happen under the standard of a national civil welfare and its inevitability cannot have anything in common with the striving of whatever class for control. The creative instinct ought always to win out over the "sharing" instinct.

We have lived through an ecstatic moment of uplift among all the people, which will remain forever in the memory of the people. More at depth a view would have to admit, that within the social fabric has occurred a turnabout not so profound and not so radical, as might seem. There has fallen away the rotting head, all has become stirred up and set in motion, But a profound regeneration of society cannot occur in a single instant. Russia comprises within itself some several historical eras: in the depths of Russia exists the inner core, which dwells still back in the

XIV Century. Much of the old will continue to act under a new outer covering. In revolutions, much involves merely a change of attire. Not all revolutionaries become new people. The revolutionaries of today can prove to be very old-fashioned people, full of despotic and cruel instincts. And to determine the real specific effect of all the active powers is not so easy, as would seem under superficial a glance.

The working class of the large cities always plays a large role in the days of revolutionary turnabouts. But still this does not signify, that its role corresponds to its real place in the social and state-organism of Russia. The formation of a soviet of workers deputies was an essential corrective to the absence of democratic organisations, of the labouring strata of the Russian people. But the Russian people itself is not some whatever class, it represents immeasurably more mysterious a power, and this power is not subject to quantitative a reckoning. No one themself in truth monopolises the voice of the Russian people. The greatest metaphysical, moral and aesthetic error of the extreme democratic ideologues mustneeds be sought in this, that these ideologues see the reality of societal life only in the quantitative aspects and not in the qualitative aspects. The innate and inseparable qualitative aspect eludes this type of democratic consciousness. Therefore the societal problem presents itself as a mechanics of quantities. But there exist qualities in societal life, not squarable with any sort of quantities and incomparable with quantities. Thus, for example, the quality of compositioning the organisational aspect and of responsible societal an effort. Our qualificatory Zemstvo and State Duma are based upon poor an election law. But this imperfect rural Zemstvo and the imperfect State Duma all have played a certain qualitative role within our societal and state-civil life, and without them the turnabout would not have happened, as it happened. The chief thing about the initial qualitative aspect mustneeds be seen in people, in the forging of the person, in the traits of the person, irrespective of class position, in the spiritual life of people, not attributable to any sort of material medium, in cultural traditions. Every creative cultural power has a right to a particular role in the societal building up of Russia and cannot be rendered totally and mechanically on a level with the powers of lower a cultural level. This would be in an utmost sense of the word, unjust. Inevitable and justified would be a qualitative selection of persons, of creative powers, of cultural levels. The truth of democracy can only consist in the establishing of conditions, favourable for a manifestation of qualities, for the selection of a true aristocracy.

The truth of social democratism demands, that a person should be defined and occupy a place in life according to his personal qualities and talents, and not in terms of a social-class and material position. But this truth collides immediately with the idea of a mechanical levelling. It is even possible to posit suchlike a paradox: if an ideal social democracy were possible upon the earth, then its truth would be in a manifestation of a qualitative inequality of people. One's belonging to the working class does not guarantee having any sort of qualities and does not give specific rights to social building, equally just as belonging to the industrial class. Democracy cannot be posited upon purely formal a basis. The empty form of democracy does not represent any utmost benefit. The centre of gravity has to lie in the content, and not in the form of democracy. And this presents us a close looking at the basic task -- the spiritual nurturing of democracy, creating higher a type of culture for all the people.

That which occurred during the first days of the revolution, was a manifestation of the spirit of all the people, in this equally participated both the chairman of the State Duma, Rodzyanko, in his past an Oktobrist, playing in 1905 more rightward a role, and consequently the workers, consequently the soldiers, -- this was a matter involving all Russia, its fate. In such an impulse among all the people, extending from top to bottom, there is a great spiritual value. And it would be vile to imagine, that this impulse was merely for the brief moment, that already has begun class and party hatred and malice, that the democracy should want to conceive of itself not as national, but rather of class. It would be ruinous to tie in the spiritual problem of the limiting of an all-classes empowered democracy by an asserting of whatever social interests, contrary to the interests of labour. It is possible to fight for very bold and radical social reforms and at the same time from purely a spiritual point of view oppose democratic absolutism, which is not so much political a form, as rather a false direction of spirit. We have become free from the grip of our despotism, and for this, merely to fall under the grip of another despotism,-- instead we want, ultimately, freedom! In contrast to the all-powerful democracy stands the lofty culture of the person, and not the greedy interests of the person and his social group.

For us, as Russian writers, one of the consequences of the turnabout happening in Russia has especial a significance. The revolution has to produce in Russia freedom of the word, a freedom to which Russian literature has so passionately aspired. But freedom of the word, just like every freedom, cannot be conceived of as merely formal and external. Freedom of the word is inwardly and spiritually something sacred. The word is an expressing of spiritual life, and its freedom is posited dependent upon spiritual life. Freedom of the word has to be spiritually won. The formal abolishment of censorship is not yet a winning of freedom of the word: this abolition merely opens the path for work on liberation of the word. Freedom of the word is not a profligacy and bacchanalia of the word. Freedom of the word, as also in general the freedom of man, presupposes ascetic an effort, self-restraint and self-discipline, a self-rectifying of the word. The word, though set free from slavery to external censorship, can begin to go to rot, and then its freedom becomes impossible, it can fall into slavery to quite vile elements. Already a boorish and unruly spirit has burst out in the daily press, and already making the rounds is talk so emotionally disagreeable and ugly, that this presents a peril for the soul of the people, having accounted itself so fine in the moment of turnabout. The triumph and dissipation of elements among the masses does not beget freedom. There is needed a spiritual enlightenment of these mass elements, the revealing in it of the principle of the person. For us is necessary a spiritual self-discipline, a struggle for qualities against the power of quantities. The spirit of freedom is always the spirit of the qualitative, and not the quantitative. And freedom of the word is a lofty quality of spirit.

I believe, that in the Russian people, in its emotional composition there is a special *qualitative* democratism, there is a great love for freedom and lesser a bourgeoisness, than in the soul of European peoples. But these higher traits of the Russian soul can become obscured and brought to ruin. Quench not the spirit, cherish the purity of the word! -- here is the summoning, with which we have to incessantly recourse to the Russian people and society. The world war in the final end has to shake up the foundations of the old societal arrangement. The whole world anticipates very radical social changes. But that which is created as a result of the world catastrophe, will not be socialism in the old sense of the word, it will be something unforeseen and unexpected. The spirit, which will enliven the new social order and new social forms, has to be already within us, has to proceed from our freedom. The Russian revolution cannot but have its say to all of Europe: it would stir up the peoples of Europe and get their stagnating blood circulating more rapidly. But God grant it not be an example that we give to the peoples of Europe, not to be an example of anarchy and elemental disintegration. The example should only be of a lofty upsurge of spirit, only a positive thirst for a free and loftier life. We have to be very strict towards ourself, to be very discerning in the occurrence, of what is from God, and what is from evil. We, as Russians, are less burdened by our past, than are Western people, and we can be more free in our creativity of a new life. This is to our great advantage. But in this is also hidden the danger of a rupture of the connectedness of the times, wherein can perish many values. Everything that was of value in the past should pass over into the future. But this transition can occur only through a fiery and cleansing catastrophe.

The Downfall of the Sacred Russian Realm

(1917 - 260)[1]

I.

Over the span of several days, with amazing an ease and lack of harm there has occurred greatest an event in Russian history and one of the greatest events in world history. Truly, in how this Russian revolution occurred, is something legendary. It all still seems, that it was from a dream of sleep from which we suddenly awakened. From an outward point of view what happened was a political turnabout, just like many in history. But from deeper a perspective what occurred was an event of exceptional importance and significance: there fell the thousand year sacred Russian tsardom, with which had been bound up great hopes and illusions, the last holy kingdom of the world. And this downfall of the sacred Russian tsardom in its significance can be compared with the downfall of Rome and Byzantium, though it occurred in quite different an historical setting and for different reasons -- the Russian state itself did not fall, it can moreso still flourish. After the downfall of the monarchical principle in Russia it inevitably will have to fall throughout all the world, since Russia was its final bulwark and its most mighty and intense expression. Henceforth in the world there will not yet be a kingdom, making pretense to sacred a significance, -- the various peoples are entering upon different a dimension of existence. There is ensuing an historical period of republics, a period of human self-governance as democracies. The Russian tsardom, insofar as it conceived itself sacred, made pretense to being the Third Rome. And this is the extent of pretension to every monarchy, aspiring to worldwide a significance. From the time of the XVI Century the Russian tsardom sensed itself as having accepted the succession from Byzantium. And

---

[1] PADENIE SVYASCHENNOGO RUSSKOGO TSARSTVA. Article originally published in the weekly "Russkaya svoboda", apr. 1917, № 2, p. 16-23.

certain sacred expectations, connected with this tsardom, derive from that time down through the XIX Century, through the Slavophils, through Dostoevsky, through the religious currents of the final period. The Russian tsardom with its anointing by God -- with an autocratic tsar at the head -- was as such a Christian, an Orthodox realm. It stood opposed to every secular and worldly state, in it the state flesh -- is a sacred flesh. This -- is not some mere human kingdom, this -- is a certain sort of imperial sanctity, God's leadership in the fate of earthly states. This idea on its strength pretended to be the equal to the idea of papal theocracy.

Such was the idea. But in what sort of correlation did it stand with the factual existence of the Russian realm, with its actuality? The Slavophils sensed a monstrous disproportion between the idea and the fact. They attempted to make a subtle distinction between autocracy (a Russian idea) and absolutism (a Western borrowing). But the arbitrary aspect and falseness of these constructs was too evident to overlook. Russia, in spite of all the Slavophil pretty-feeling ideologies, was a classical land of absolutism, of despotism, of bureaucratic rule -- in Russia namely moreso than elsewhere, power was severed off from the people, and the whole history of our state aspect was not the history of the people, it was rather an incessant exerting of violence against the people, and their slavery to foreign principles. At present it has become finally clear, what earlier had been clear to many, -- the Russian absolute monarchy was not of the people and it lacked firm support from the people. In the West, the state power always was moreso of the people, than in Russia. The idea of the Russian sacred tsardom, which undoubtedly was alive among the people, was merely a projection of the people's passivity and the people's despondency, an insufficient manifestation of the human principle in Russia. That power appeared sacred, which had not issued forth from the human will of the people, but which rather was over the people, high and unreachable. The slavery of the people was to something foreign to it, it was experienced as transcendent a power, as a sacred tsardom. In this there was much that was specifically Russian and Eastern. Forcibly imposed, the old world-historical idea of the Caesar, of tsardom, was rendered into a nationally Russian and Eastern element. The sacred Russian tsardom was first of all at its basis a peasant kingdom. For the peasant consciousness among the people the state unity could only be conceived of symbolically, only in connection with the person of the tsar, symbolising the state and national wholeness and preeminence. The peasant consciousness, hitherto having taken hold with many of the representatives of higher culture, understands tsardom but does not understand the state. Tsardom is symbolised by the tsar. In essence, every monarchy, even one constitutional and parliamentary, is not a pure form of the state, it is always hybrid and of transitional a condition, in it are many elements of the pre-state consciousness. The state presupposes a capacity for more abstract thinking and abstract an awareness, a greater freedom of spirit from the grip of material images.

II.

The sacred tsardom was affixed to materiality, in it the spirit was enslaved to matter, to outwardly external images and forms. It was less spiritual, than a secular state, in which have already occurred the separations whereby no sort of congestive matter is venerated as sacred. The sacred realm with the tsar, with its inevitable materialistic symbolism, signifies still the submersion of the spirit of the people within organic matter, the non-freedom of the human spirit. The sacred realm rested upon a religious materialism, upon an acknowledgement of matter as sacred, upon an apotheosis of the materially relative. A more free and more spiritual religious consciousness would lead to the undoing of a sacred kingdom, to a discernment between the spiritual and the material, the absolute and the relative, and would deliver from the need for materialised sacred tsardom. There would ensue a liberative awareness of the spectral aspect of the kingdom of God within the material plane of being. The sacred tsardom was a realm of symbols, in it the realities did not obtain. Matter was symbolically was rendered sacred and meant, stood for, symbolised the realm of Spirit. But the realm of Spirit itself was not immediately and directly revealed. Some one or another man (for example, the tsar) was not a realistic, but rather only symbolic, bearer of the spiritual principle, independent of his human nature. The sacred materiality (the kingdom upon earth in the flesh) never was manifest for real, it was only symbolised. This conditional symbolism of everything sacred within the historical embodiment is connected with materialism. The material cannot be realistically sacred, it can only be symbolically sacred. And this is determined, by that matter and materiality are never the final reality, and in essence always -- are signs, symbols of different a spiritual reality. And the material aspect of the sacred tsardom signifies only a certain stage in the developement of spirit, only a certain condition of spiritual actuality.

But at higher a stage of developement of spirit there is inevitable a transition to a realm of realities, free from the initial symbolism. Religious materialism, as in any materialism, is an unperceived and unconscious symbolism. A perceived symbolism is already a liberating principle. The source of slavery is however rooted in a mistaking of the symbolism for realism, mistaking the symbol for the real, in that emotional confusedness, which does not distinguish the spiritual realities from the material symbols. The material symbols are needed but for a period of time. A free spirituality leads to realism in state and societal life, it delivers from demands in the symbolic sanctification of material life. The symbol of the authority of power (the symbol of the tsar) ceases to be necessary, when the human spirit is risen to the point of a real assuming of the authority of power. All the theocracies in the history of the world have been but symbolic, the divine authority of power was realised only in symbols, only in the symbolic sign-tokens of man. Every symbolic sanctifying of a man as the bearer of theocratic power diverges away from the path of the realisation of human power, and moreover it renders the power of the symbolic person despotic and unbounded. Only a free human power of authority tends to free from the enslaving theocratic illusions. Within human a power of authority itself, the human self-governance, the Divine energy can be active for real, there can be present the unmediated spiritual reality. In theocracies however, in holy kingdoms, the Divine energy does not act for real, but is only symbolised, and the spiritual realities themself do not obtain, but are merely rendered as signs within material images. And the religious consciousness has to make the transition to paradoxical a truth: the Divine for real can only be within an anthropocracy, whereas theocracy is always but symbolically Divine. The sacrificial religious spirit ought to forego the comfort and delight, connected with a sacred kingdom, and fearlessly make the transition to the ultimate realities. Thus is consummated the mystery of the human "I".

III.

The Russian sacred tsardom rested upon a firm reinforcing of the Russian state by the Russian Church. The Russian Church provided sanctification for the Russian tsardom. The Russian tsardom was anointed and it gave its support to the Russian Church. The Russian state was an Orthodox Christian state. The Russian Church was the dominant and state church. The Russian tsar was anointed by the Russian Church for civil state matters. The immense turnabout, happening in Russian life, has struck a grievous blow to this reinforcing arrangement, and the enormous consequences of this blow will be recalled throughout all the utmost historical fate of Russia. There has ended the sacred Russian tsardom with its enslaving illusions, with its allures and its terrors, and we enter upon other a dimension of being, into a great unknown and uncertainty. And for those, who keep to our faith of the fathers, there is needed a great resoluteness of spirit and self-assurance, in order ultimately to get free of the old illusions, from the dear phantasms, and to plunge forth into the dark ocean of unknown being, in which nothing is guaranteed nor assured. The end of the sacred Russian tsardom has to evoke a great consternation of spirit for many of the religious Orthodox Russian people. The inevitable secularisation of our state and societal life has to be apperceived by them, as a principle of spiritual death, as a desolation of soul. Many dread the coming mechanisation and machinisation of life, the destruction of every sort of organic harmony. The sacred tsardom was an organic realm, in it was an organic beauty, an organic warmth and comfort, a cordiality, in which it was possible to shelter oneself from the terror of life. Replacing the sacred tsardom is a secular stateform, the coming democracy -- mechanical, soulless, cold, lacking in beauty, lacking in style. For people of higher a spiritual life, full of love for beauty, it is difficult to accept the mechanism, cold and soulless, even though perchance just, and this -- is a great sacrifice, a voluntary Golgotha. But only this resoluteness to proceed through the wilderness, past the barren rocks, leads to higher life, to the mountainous freedom. The mystical and irrational basis for the societal aspect has to be conceived of not in the tsar and not in the people, but in the "I", in the person.

    The romantic restorative mindset, clinging to the old sacred organicity, is unfree a spirit, a slave-like condition, begetting mistrust, fear and terror. The Russian Orthodox world has been accustomed to live under a guarding and protective Russian state, and now it senses itself helpless and cast off upon the vast ocean of world life. Everywhere is sensed danger and threats. It is impossible to press back into the folds of the feminine skirts of the old emotional realm. Severe times of freedom ensue, when nothing still is guaranteed or assured. To Orthodox people this freedom is disagreeable. It would be warmer in the realm of sacred necessity and sacred compulsion. Emergence from organicity into mechanism is either a loss of soul, or of a great freedom of spirit, upon which only some are capable. Yet nonetheless the Orthodox churchly people, accustomed to age old passivity and submissiveness, have stirred, they manifest signs of activity, and hastily they set about to organise the Church as free. A conservative now already has to be an adherent of the separation of church from state. It has all become very paradoxical and contradictory in the world. In the Orthodox Christian state, in the sacred tsardom, the Christian Church was enslaved and oppressed, and it could not manifest any signs of activity. Only in a non-Christian and secular state, in a democratic republic, can the Church finally feel itself fully free and can church people be active. It is possible to posit a paradoxical position: within a Christian state the Christian Church always becomes enslaved and oppressed, and only in a non-Christian state can it be free and active. This is adequately substantiated by the rebirth of Catholicism in France after its separation of church and state and after the persecution against the Church. Churchly people perchance in a way can ultimately be grateful for a revolution -- only with it obtains a cleansing of the churchly organism from all manner of filth. In revolution there is a cleansing threat for all the spheres of life, though also inevitably accompanied by the dissipation inherent with the lower instincts of the masses. True, in a secular state, in a democratic republic there can begin persecution of the Church and spiritual oppression against believing people. But the oppressions are not ultimately terrible for the Church and cannot bring Christians to naught, they renew it and prove their spirit true. It is terrible for the Church, when it itself does the persecuting, murdering for merely its sense of guarding and protecting. True Christians in a completely new historical era will once again appeal for this, so as not to sacrificially consent to be masters and lords in the earthly realm. And in this is a regenerative truth.

IV.

The end of the Russian sacred tsardom can lead only to a renewal of the Church. It will lose out in quantity, but win out in quality. Only the free sons of the Church will remain in it, no one still will be numbered amongst it by virtue of outward necessity, no one will belong to it out of greedy considerations. The churchly folk will pull together, and organise freely. And the churchly people will come to detect their own existence. The revolution, destroying the sacred tsardom and creating a secular realm, can be a great stimulus for the living spiritual powers of the Church, testing its vitality. I am speaking somewhat formally and as regards externals. If however one inwardly and essentially approach the Church Question in Russia, then it mustneeds be said, that we stand facing a great religious spiritual turnabout, that we are entering upon an era of a religious revolution. For the time being it is still vague, and it is impossible to gauge it by the measure, by which political and social revolutions are measured. But in the depths of spiritual life already the dynamite is piled up and a religious revolution will come. Only on the surface of religious life will all seem quite tranquil and inactive. But in another dimension of existence, in the higher qualitative levels of being will occur spiritual upheavals, and everything, that transpires quantitatively, on the external plane of being, is but a projection and muddled reflection of what happens therein. History in its finalative realities is created by the few, it is aristocratic, and every mass revolution with the transition to democratisation etc is but a reflection downwards, of what occurs above, the result of a sacrificial resoluteness of the select of the spirit to go to the heights, by new and unknown paths, sacrificially having broken with the past. The lofty spiritual resoluteness to go sacrificing the old organic harmony, the old bonding of spirit with organic matter, the old warm sentimentality, such as hinders the creative growth of life, assumes the form of a transition to mechanism and the machine. The mechanisation and machinisation is but a reflection on lower planes of a dichotomy of spirit, happening upon a summit-like plane, of a religious revolution in the depths. And there remains the task of creative spiritual work, of a religious renewal of mankind in its higher qualitative aspects, not coinciding with the social and political democratisation of society. The turnabout is happening simultaneously on several planes, and in all the planes there has to occur creative work.

V.

The sacred Russian tsardom long ago already had died, long ago already the spirit departed it, and it lived a phantasmal and pseudo sort of life. The end of this tsardom was scandalous: it ended with the reign of Grigorii Rasputin, in him it became totally altered and in him it came apart. The "mystic" darkness pervaded the final period of the old tsardom and the murky wine of the life of the Russian people intoxicated the supreme power at the hour of the end. The sacred Russian tsardom passed away amidst a dissolute Khlystyism. This realm fundamentally always was a peasant realm and it ended under the dominance of a dissolute peasant. In this fate lies concealed a profound symbolism. The Russian Church also in the final period of its existence within the Christian state was under the grip of Grigorii Rasputin. Our supreme clergy authorities have been Grigorians. The old Russian tsardom mirrored and expressed the age old peasant darkness, and it had to end its power amidst the peasant darkness, symbolised in the same form. And the last Russian autocrat was not Nicholas II, but rather Grigorii Rasputin. The imperial power was powerless to enlighten and transform the ancient darkness of the people, to free Russia from the murky wine's effect upon the lower aspects in the life of the people -- it itself became drunken with this murky wine and ended amidst a shameful orgy. And ultimately there was killed off and destroyed the sacred idea of the monarchy. Such a downfall of the monarchic idea is unknown by any other people.

The demise of the old tsardom ought therefore not frighten the Christian Church and Christians, since this kingdom never was Christian and holy in the deep and ontological sense of this word. The image of a "sacred kingdom" was merely a symbolic play on words, of a religiously immature mankind, reflective of its non-freedom, its dearth of spirituality, its submersion in matter. The idea of an "holy kingdom" in this world, in either the old conservative form, or in a new and religious form, -- is covetously greedy an idea, in it there is a pitiful desiring of this world, an attachment to this material plane, and not the true freedom of spirit and thirst for emergence of higher spiritual planes. And there is something pitiful and shameful in this spectacle, how some tremble with fear, sensing, how the kingdom of this world is passing out from underfoot and being snatched out of their hands, whilst others greedily in their hands grasp at the transitory passing earthly kingdom and in a delirium of greed increase their demand for holding power. The "bourgeois" fear of those, from whom the realm is departing, and the "democratic" greed of those, to whom it is passing, will stand alike together before the face of an higher truth, before the face of God. Christ said, that His kingdom is not of this world and He commanded not to love the world and that, which is of the world. Truly indeed the kingdom of Christ cannot be within this three-dimensional expanse, in this material plane, for it is incommensurate with this world.

Astride the Abyss of War and Revolutions

The kingdom of Christ can only be in an other dimension, in a different spiritual plane, in a different lofty world: to suchlike a kingdom belong those, who in their spirit are free from the lower spheres of being, from the slavery to matter and who grow inwardly upon the higher sphere of being, in the sphere of love and freedom. The kingdom of this world however always rests upon necessity and compulsion. The army of Christ in this world, in this kingdom can only be but a mysterious chivalric union, free from all avarice and thirst for power. This -- is the true aristocratic spirit, for which externally can be desired the triumph of democracy. But the growth of democracy can only be gradual. The secularisation of the state and of society, the killing at root of every sacred kingdom, is an act of liberation of the spirit from the enslaving projections of an other world into this three-dimensional expanse, an act of liberation, a great step upon the path of inward growth of a select portion of mankind upon the higher plane of being. A peaceful democratic societal effort, from more profound a perspective, can be understood, as a democratisation of life, as a dividing apart of spirit and organic flesh, such as the old sacred kingdom tended to reinforce. This is the same dematerialisation, as is involved in the growth of the machine, with its undoing of the old organic flesh, setting the spirit at liberty. Our free grasping of the truth ought not to be hampered by an aesthetic reaction against democracy, the secret thirst for a romantic restoration upon motives aesthetic. In this would be expressed a non-freedom and immaturity of our spirit. A great audacity and freedom of awareness would lead us to a different, and indeed paradoxical in the externals, truth: the old monarchy was democratic in its fundamentals, whereas a democratic republic -- is aristocratic. Monarchy expresses the submersion of the entire people within organic matter and the demand for a symbolic sanctifying of this material aspect in the life of the people. The old monarchy, for enormous masses of the people, was a strong excuse for comfort, warmth and the guarantee of stability. Behind it stood no tempering of the spirit nor ascent in spirit of a select portion of mankind. A democratic republic can however be spiritually conceived of as the consent of the select of mankind to pass through an ascetic wilderness, by nothing adorned, as a sacrificial consent to live amidst the bare crags, arid, without the warmth of images of outward beauty. This involves an heroic resoluteness to cast off upon the vast ocean of the spirit, to the ultimate freedom, without any illusions or consolations. This -- is the final austerity of the people of spirit, the austerity of freedom from any consoling and any embellishments, the austerity of sacrifice by the "gifting of beautiful intents". The free spirit ought forever to renounce the temptations of a kingdom, both old and new, of guarantees and security, of luxury and comforts of the flesh. This -- is a testimony of Zarathustra, this -- is a testimony also of Him with Whom the Grand Inquisitor of Dostoevsky spoke, this -- is a passing through of a voluntary Golgotha, without which is impossible the higher and lofty life. Holy Rus' has ended and ahead lies only the Rus' prophetic. And the downfall of the sacred Russian tsardom ought to be favourable not only for the builders of a new democratic realm, remote from anything of spirit, but also for people of spirit, for an unseen spiritual aristocracy, by nothing terrified, who go forth bravely to the new and unknown world, having broken with all the old comforts, as comprising enslaving illusions.

The Internationale and the Unity of Mankind

(1917 - 261)[1]

I.

The idea of the Internationale, long since already having fallen apart and having lost all its strength in life, over the past several days has anew been dragged out under God's light, and anew it grips the hearts and governs the masses. This can scarcely for long prevail, but it is very interesting to note, how and why so weather-beaten an idea can become active. The ideology of a socialistic internationalism was off-handedly readapted to the interests and currents of recent days. And as often happens, behind the slogan of internationalism can be hidden something quite other, than what it really ought to signify. The socialist movement in the West has long since already settled into a national channel, and therefore no sort of socialism exists, except a national socialism, be it the French, the German or the English. The idea of the Internationale was begotten in the revolutionary atmosphere of the green hopes of socialism, the first childish prattlings of socialism, and it corresponded to the childishly immature condition of the labour movement. This was an utopia, not corresponding to the spiritual stature of humanity, but eternally this utopia managed to revive in a certain revolutionary atmosphere. In the human soul there is a place for a quite heated social dreaminess, where the most foolish type dreams blaze up in a condition of social and spiritual immaturity. In the measure that the workers begin to sense themself citizens of their own fatherland and their own state, and as the labour movement becomes more matured, the socialism tends to become more national, more reform-minded and evolved, and the realism in it wins out

---

[1] INTERNATSIONAL I EDINSTVO CHELOVECHESTVA. Article originally published in the weekly "Russkaya svoboda", 12 mai. 1917, № 3, p. 9-14.
 IMKA Press "Berdiaev Collected Works" Tome 4 indicates date of article as "*22 apr. 1917*".

over the utopianism. Werner Sombart accurately termed revolutionary socialism a pre-historic phase of the social movement. And it mustneeds be said, that the German Social Democracy has been rendered more national and evolutionary reform-minded. It particularly most betrayed the idea of the Internationale, and when war broke out, the German Social Democrats were reborn as social-imperialists. This -- is not a reproach, but merely the stating of an indisputable fact. And it is necessary to deal with this fact, -- a dreamy denial of it can cost us too dearly. The idea of the Internationale has long since already become moribund and has continued to lead a pitiful existence in the Social Democrat ideology only but for the lack of its setting in order the whatever other ultimate ideas. The revisionism of the E. Bernstein type has in fact won out, it has won out even with such people, as G. V. Plekhanov, though he does not want to admit this. The idea of the Internationale, of an international socialistic realm, continues to fulfill the role of a grand idea, of an ultimate idea of those, who have failed to enter upon the path of spiritual deepening and rebirth, of those who have not broken away from a limiting positivism. The utopian dream about a socialistic kingdom of God upon earth is contrary to that healthy pessimism of the religious consciousness, for which the triumph of an utmost and final truth always is related to the other world.

Russian Social Democracy has however gotten theoretically entangled under the German influence and is situated in slavery to it, but it bears within it specifically Russian and completely Eastern features. Within it are very strong elements of a Russian-Eastern utopian populism and anarchistic agitation. And this is quite vividly reflected in the so-called "Bolsheviks", who nowise can be called Marxists and who in essence are typical Easterners. The Russian Bolshevism and maximalism is a product of the Asiatic soul, disdainful of the Western paths of cultural developement and cultural creativity. The fundamental Marxist truth, which the first Russian Marxists proclaimed in their struggles against the populists, was this truth, that Russia is still faced with having to pass through an era of capitalist industrial developement, that there faces us still the bourgeoise having a political and economic progressive role, that there cannot be a leaping off into a socialistic kingdom from in all regards the backwardness of the old Russian kingdom, -- all this was basically forgotten back still in the year 1905. Now however in the Russian Social Democracy there is being reborn the old populist utopianism, and the bourgeoise are being declared class counter-revolutionaries, and social revolution is reckoned possible in a land, having only arrived at the first stages of industrial developement and culturally backward, still not having arrived at the elementary schooling of a free citizenship. Russian revolutionary socialism readily passes over into a distorted Russian messianism, based upon a jumbling of different planes and different worlds. In the Russian revolutionary element there is eternally born the fervent dream about the kingdom of God upon earth, which will spill forth onto all the world from the flames, blazing within Russia. In this is to be sensed the age old Khlysty element, and within it drowns the consciousness of the person. With Bakunin there was the idea of Russian revolutionary messianism, the revolutionary light from the East. In its own way it competed against the conservative messianism of the Slavophils. The basis of this idea was in a bowing before the people and the common element in the people, and it passes over into an idolatry before the quantitative masses. This old idea blazes forth anew in the elements of the Russian revolution.

II.

The "Bolshevism" of Mr. Lenin is an extreme expression of this idea, and conceived of in an intoxicated condition. In Grigorii Rasputin the black Khlysty element found its expression. In Mr. Lenin and the circle surrounding him is vividly expressed the red Khlysty element. These extremes merge in a mutual hostility towards the principles of person and culture. In the Leninist Bolshevism, the idea of the brotherhood of mankind and a kingdom of truth upon earth, which will come into the world from the Russian revolution, finds its assertion in a delirious hatred and discord, in a consigning to period a large part of mankind, labelled as "bourgeois". Only the proletariat is acknowledged as human. In the "messianism" of the Bolsheviks and maximalists there gets combined the Russian dreaminess and sacrificial aspect together with a bloody delirium, a sheep-like spirit -- with a ravenous viciousness and hatred, and the sense of brotherhood -- with a thirst for disunity and discord. Thus is formed an element, in which evil assumes the guise of good, and good the guise of evil, in which everything is twofold, and in which the human person flounders. Behind the most beautiful and fine slogans can be hidden the most evil passions. The assertion of an extreme truth can become an obsession.

Nicholas Berdyaev

What actually is the idea of the Internationale, which at present is so captivating and bewitching? The idea of the Internationale is a sickly class distortion and mutilation of the grand idea of the unity of mankind and the brotherhood of peoples. The Internationale cannot be a brotherhood of peoples, it can only be an abolition of peoples, with the assertion of qualityless toiling human masses, in which drowns everything individual and concrete. The brotherhood of peoples in any case presupposes the existence of such peoples, it can only be a brotherhood of national individualities. The same is true in that the brotherhood of people presupposes the existence of human individuals and also their mutual love for one another. Nations -- are concrete realities, certainly existing, which have to be and which have to be for the purpose of enabling brotherly unity and sacrifice. If there had not coalesced a national lifestyle, if there were not a national visage, then there could not be any talk about a brotherhood of peoples, nor about the sacrifices and self-denial undergone by peoples. Russia first of all has to be, has to have its own visage and be mighty. There can only be talk about its relationships to other peoples and to mankind.

Between the national unity and the unity of mankind there cannot be on principle any sort of contradiction. It is meaningless to posit the dilemma: the nation or mankind, a national or an all-mankind consciousness. This dilemma is begotten of rationalistic humanism, which does not admit of steps in the hierarchy of concrete individualities. The unity of mankind, as a certain supreme hierarchical step, is realised through national unities, through the consolidation and developing of national individualities. The principles relating to all mankind are revealed in the national existence, through movement at depth and above. Nationality ought to be elevated to an all-human significance. Every culture at its heights is both national, and all-human. Goethe and Dostoevsky are in the same measure all-human, as they are national. This -- is an elementary axiom. An all-humanness cannot in any sense be a loss or abolition of nationality. One hierarchical step opens out onto another hierarchical step. Internationalism however seeks as though to attain the unity of mankind, of an all-humanness, through a turning aside, a detour movement, into a sort of desolation, having abolished the whole eternal hierarchical step of its genesis. Here is why it is proper to investigate the idea of the proletariat as a plundering of mankind, a snatching away from it of the qualities and values of a national lifestyle, of national individualities. This is the path into a desolate and unqualitative abstraction. No sort of utmost step of unity can be had in denying the preceeding steps, -- in it there has to be the reaching of higher developement and a realising of all the gradations of individuality. Into the all-humanity enter in all the nations, just as with all the human individuals. This is similar to how in God there neither perishes nor is abolished all the cosmos with all its steps, but rather therein receives its full and real existence. For the all-mankind, fro the brotherhood of peoples there are no other paths, than through nationality, through the small national unities and the larger imperialistic unities -- this is the sole concretely real path. The national individualities, formed and living out their fate within the bloody tragedy of history, have to be included not only into the all-humanness, but also into the Divine all-unity. The foundations and tasks whether as small national bodies, and so also with the large imperialistic bodies -- are cosmic. Internationalism however both anti-historical, and anti-cosmic.

III.

Russia comprises a certain concrete reality in the world, a certain individual existent, having its own fate, its own allotted portion, its own task. And concerning this elementary truth it is needful now to loudly shout. Russia can serve the all-humanity only through the assertion of its own unity and its own uniqueness, and not through its disintegration and depersonalisation. And if Russia ceased to be Russia, and the Russians ceased to be Russians, then Russia and the Russians would represent a loss for all-mankind, in failing to have their all-human say, and doing thus no great deed within history. Russian man can only through Russia imprint his all-human spirit. Without Russia, Russian people would be rendered into an unqualitative mass, nowise capable of enriching world life. Only an united, a great and strong Russia can say its idea to the world, only such a Russia can be giving and sacrificial, in exhausting its light. But if Russia begins its free existence with a self-abolishing, with a dismembering, with the loss of its image amidst the peoples of the world, then it will quench out the source of its possible light, and Russian people will be transformed into a scattered about dull and colourless mass. The weakening and fall of the Russian state will likewise be a weakening and fall of Russian spiritual culture. The Russian people would enter into a period of historical decline and prove relegated to a secondary significance. No one expects any longer great sayings and great deeds from the Spanish, all whose greatness lies in the past. No one expects anything further from the Persians. The national and state collapse would likewise bear with it the collapse of the creative person. For many among the Russian people, for the Russian intelligentsia and Russian workers it is no great sacrifice to renounce the fatherland, to give up Russia; they are readily prepared to do this, the international mindset is for them a natural condition and movement along a line of least resistance. But every sacrifice is valued only then, when it is movement along the line of most resistance. The source for sacrifice rests only in strength. For the Germans, the French and the English, the surmounting of nationalism happens in an atmosphere of strength, it is difficult and therefore a matter of sacrifice. The Russian absence of patriotism and the Russian internationalistic mindset can however be but weakness. Liebknecht and Lenin are psychological opposites. It is initially needful to exist and to exist in strength, only then is self-denial and sacrifice possible. This is true both for relatively an entire people and the relatively individual man. In Russia necessary first of all is a tempering of personal character and a tempering of the character of the people.

The idea of the Internationale, an idea which is abstract and empty, debilitates the Russian soul and undermines the strength of Russia. Within the Russian people there are great spiritual qualities, unknown to the Western peoples, there is an authentic all-humanness. But it has to be said straight out, that the ease, with which among us is adopted the internationalism whist spurning the nationality, is a manifestation of weakness of character. In the weakness of will, in the absence of a severe tempering of personal character lies concealed the greatest dangers for Russia. With the Russians it is the virtues, which are more dangerous than the vices, there is somewhat a debilitating moralism, there is something sheep-like. Weakness of character and sheep-like virtues -- are the fertile soil for every demagogue. For us, this is connected with an insufficiently expressed personal human principle, with a submersion into the collective. Always it has to be remembered, that in Russia there was no principle of chivalric knighthood. And this fact was fateful for our moral and societal developement. We too readily pass over from the old collectivism, from the old elementary condition, to a new collectivism, to a new elementary condition. And we avoid the discipline of the person, the culture of the person, the developing of the person. But the free new collective can only be forged out through a forging out of the person. The idea of the person in the XX Century cannot be something abstract, as it was formerly in the XVIII Century, it can only be something concrete. And it mustneeds be admitted, that the concrete person is forged out only through national disciple and in the nation. The person, the nation, humanity -- are realities. The Internationale however is an abstract and empty phantasy. It is just as empty a phantasy, as is also an international proletariat.

Even the proletariat within each land is a certain abstraction; concretely they exist only as groups of workers of various character, distinct in their interests and in their psychology. The idea of a proletariat is a pseudo-religious fiction of class struggle. At certain instants this fictitious idea can be gripping; but in it there is nothing genuinely real. Real politics, in the empirical and metaphysical sense of this word, can be grounded only upon ideas of the person and the nation, with which there has to be concurrence and to which there has to be subordinated all the group and class interests. Nation is a certain idea, going the distance, class however is an interest, untransformable into an idea. But the idea of the Internationale is also an attempt to transform class into universal an idea, all-engulfing and all-devouring. This anti-natural, pseudo-religious and anti-religious attempt dissociates all the hierarchy of realities, the reality whether of nation, of mankind, of the person. Everything drowns within the elemental intoxication with its ideas of an international proletariat, the real and the illusory get all jumbled up together. And now, facing the responsible consciousness and thought stands the task of separating the realities from the illusions and fictions. It is impossible to permit the confusing of a pure ecstasy and blazing of spirit with obsessiveness and an elementally-drunken dissipation. Alongside the political and social construction there ought likewise constantly for us to be a spiritual and cultural work and creativity. We have to spiritually fight for the person, for the nation, for mankind, against the disintegrative and elementally-chaotic currents. And this will be a true liberation from slavery.

Concerning Political and Social Revolution

(1917 -262)[1]

I.

In such a time, as ours, many words are employed uncritically and without a definite real content. Sloganeering words correspond to a certain mindset and therein find their strength, even though they perhaps be bereft of any strict meaning or content. Quite badly employed at present are the expressions, "political" and "social" revolution, and upon this contrast disparity tend to be oriented various points of view on the turn of events happening in Russia. Some very insistently declare, that in Russia has occurred a political revolution exclusively, while others demand however, that the political revolution should be continued also upon the social side and insofar as possible carry along further upon this path. For those, who uphold the second point of view, the revolution has only just begun, it is still ahead, it has arrived at only the first preparatory stage, beyond which has to be followed out the furthermost stages of the social-class revolutionary struggle. The Social Democrats have not been able to hold forth with a consistent point of view about social revolution and even with Mr. Lenin it has not been presented in altogether clear a view. The Social Democrats themself however very much love to say, that the Russian revolution -- is bourgeois, and not proletarian and not socialist, and as regards events happening they irresponsibly bandy about the words "bourgeois" and "bourgeoisness". And yet they insist, moreover, that this bourgeois revolution has been made by the working class, and that it ought to have the guiding hand in it. If under the expression "social revolution"

---

[1] O POLITICHESKOI I SOTSIAL'NNOI REVOLIUTSII. Article originally published in the weekly "Russkaya svoboda", 17 mai. 1917, № 4, p. 5-10.
 IMKA Press "Berdiaev Collected Works" Tome 4 indicates date of article as "*29 apr. 1917*".

there mustneeds be understood a socialist revolution, then it remains inconceivable, how in essence a bourgeois revolution can be transformed into a socialistic one by whatever the forceful and dictatorial measures, by a struggle for the political power of the working class, nowise corresponding to its social weight at the given historical moment. The expression "bourgeois revolution" in all regards is a very poor, and in terms of its moral motifs even, a very ugly expression, and simply it mustneeds be admitted, that the bourgeois revolution is a progressive step in the historical developement of peoples. Marx himself admitted the bourgeoise as an higher stage of a progressive and revolutionary role in history. The bourgeois revolution signifies essentially a national, an all the people revolution, a moment in the historical fate of the whole entire people, in its liberation and developement. The "bourgeois" revolution in Russia is not that of a class, but rather that of a supra-class revolution of all the people, realising tasks common to the nation and the state as a whole. And if at present in Russia there were to occur a "proletarian" revolution, then it would be exclusively a matter of class, anti-national and anti-state, and it would lead to a forceful dictatorship, behind which by an immutable law would follow some sort of Caesarism.

When a great historical turnabout occurs in the life of a people, then within it always there is a certain objective line, corresponding to historical tasks common to all the nation and all the state, a line truly creative, in which the whole people is pulled into by an instinct for developement and a secret voice in its own fate. A true politics involves also a perceptive insight of this national direction. And everything, that runs off into the sidelines, has to be acknowledged as non-creative, destructive and reactionary in the deepest sense of this word, as non-real, illusory. Much, presented as very revolutionary, is in reality reactionary. Ferdinand Lassalle considered reactionary both the Crusades and the extreme currents in the Reformation era; as progressive he admitted only the Lutheran Reformation, which was in our contemporary terms "bourgeois", but which accomplished a tremendous world historical deed. From this point of view he would have regarded as deeply reactionary the Russian Bolshevist and maximalist socialistic currents and would have deprived them of all historical significance. In the revolutionary maximalism there is always absent the creative historical instinct, and never is genius drawn to this side. And everyone endowed with the creative historical instinct, in grasping the destiny of peoples, has to admit all the maximalist socialistic currents in the present hour of the historical existence of Russia as but a reactionary disruption. This truth is brilliantly apparent, that by way of profound insight with what is happening for us, there proves to be no social movement nor any sort of socialistic idea. Socialism is in any case the idea of the regulation of the social entirety; it desires to bring everything into correlation with the social organism, it is opposed to economic anarchy. But that elemental mass movement, which we tend to term as social, is not inspired at present by the idea of the social entirety, by the idea of the regulation and organising of all our national economic life; in it there clearly predominate personal and group interests to the detriment of the whole, in it there is no self-limiting, in it there is too much greed and grasping. This anti-social character of the movement is a legacy of the old regime, of the old slavery, of the old absence of habits for a free societal outlook, of the free submission of the person to the whole. The temporary dominance of such currents can end only with such phantasms, as with John of Leiden's "kingdom of Zion" or the Paris Commune. But the forceful establishing of "the kingdom of God on earth" always reeks with blood, always there is malice and mutual destruction. In such a maximalism there is a profound religious and moral lie, not to mention its social and historical impossibility.

II.

The political revolution in Russia, so terribly belated, will certainly have its own social side, as happens in every great historical turnabout. Facing Russia are tasks very serious, with bold social reforms, particularly in the agrarian sphere. The political revolution in Russia nowise signifies the triumph of the old bourgeois liberalism, which long ago already fell apart in its ideas, unable to inspire anyone. And least of all does a so shrilly anti-socialistic type of liberalism resonate with the make-up of the Russian soul. Russia is entering upon the path of political freedom at a late hour of history, repulsed by the experience of Western European history, but light and free of any experience and binding traditions of its own. It enters upon this path within the exceptional setting of the world war, which is shaking the foundations of modern societies. And it is conceivable, that in Russia are possible further inevitably bold experiences of socialisation, quite outside of class or state, and dissimilar to any sort of doctrinal socialism. The coming days of history renders unforeseeable, and indeed delusional, the expectations of both the "bourgeois" and the "socialistic". The developement of capitalism in Russia cannot be similar to the classical English form in its developement. The struggle against the dark and evil sides of capitalistic developement with us has to begin at the initial stages of this process, and organised labour cannot prove reactive to its social structure. This has to be clearly recognised by the Russian thinking class and with this consciousness it has to prepare itself a creative role in the rebirth of Russia. The idea of a "social revolution" is essentially not a creative idea, and it presupposes the inevitability of a social cataclysm, namely because that no sort of a creative social process has occurred as regards the evil, rather there has occurred only but a fatal and irreversible growth of social evil. Classical Marxism also has gotten itself entangled under the influence of the English type of the initial phase of the developement of capitalism, which has provided a clear view of the evil sides of this process. But all social creativity runs counter to social revolution.

We need to be mindful of that ultimately apparent truth, a truth both scientific and philosophic, that a social revolution in a strict sense of the word in general is impossible, it never has been and never will be. In this sphere the word "revolution" can be employed only allegorically, only in a very broad sense. Thus, for example, we tend to say, that in the XIX Century the great technical discoveries were great revolutions, transforming the whole of human life. But essentially it has to be said, that there has become possible only a social evolution with a more or less speeded up tempo, there became possible only social reforms more or less bold and radical. The change in the social fabric of societies is always a prolonged molecular process; it depends, on the one hand, upon the condition of productive powers, upon economic creativity, upon manufacturing and agriculture, and yet on the other hand -- upon unseen changes in the human psyche. The creative attitude of man towards nature and the creative attitude of man towards man, this is an economic creativity and a moral creativity, it changes the social fabric. It is impossible to change anything in social life with conspiracies, revolts, uprisings and dictators, all this is but scum. Forced experiments, productive of a semblance of order, only throws everything away backwards in social developement. For Marx the socialistic revolution, the Zusammenbruch implosion of capitalistic society, presupposes a prolonged process of developement of capitalist industry, -- and to it leads not the dictatorially violent actions of the proletariat, but rather the objective dialectics of capitalistic developement, the objective economic collapse of the capitalist economy, via a concentration of ownership, overproduction and crises. Marxism does not allow for such a socialism, as would lower the productivity of labour. Socialism can only then replace capitalism, when it can prove itself as more productive. But Marxism has facing it its own extreme uncritical and confused points of view on objective evolution, made fatally irreversible, with its perspective as class-subjective, and overvaluing the significance of the revolutionary activity of the proletariat. And the critique of Marxism has come from two sides.

III.

The Marxist Zusammenbruchstheorie Implosion-Theory and the Verelendungstheorie Pauperisation-Theory have proven inconsistent from all perspectives. These theories are not only scientifically inaccurate and completely out-moded, but with them is connected a false moral mindset. The developement of capitalism has proceeded along other, more complex paths, with mitigating contradictions, by debilitating evil, by increases in the significance of the working class and its condition of well-being within the capitalist society itself. And therefore the Social Democrats have to resort to a fatal process of "bourgeoisation". And indeed its ideals have always been bourgeois. The spiritual bourgeoisness of socialism, its slavery to social matter, its negation of values, its inability to undertake the delimited end of human well-being to reach ends more remote and lofty, is quite beyond doubt and apparent all more and more. And least of all is it able to seek an antidote against this bourgeoisness in its idea of a social revolution, which is begotten by a slavery of spirit. The Marxist concept of Zusammenbruchstheorie was constructed via an Hegelian dialectical schema. But in this theory there was nonetheless a greater appreciation for the fact of social evolution, than there is with Mr. Lenin and the greater part of the Russian Social Democrats, who essentially but combine the old Russian populism with the old Russian wont for rebellion.

The world war has put exceptional demands on the economic life of peoples and tends to set in motion an irreversible process of state regulation and socialisation. But the war-socialism, this socialism of woeful need, beyond class and state, does not provide any sort of vital grounds for the rebirth of the idea of a social revolution. Upon this bitter path are cast aside premises, which would have significance for the furthering of the social process, but hardly can it be possible after the war to turn backwards, to the quite unregulated economic life of the capitalist societies. But this will be only a new phase of social evolution, which will not lead to any sort of "socialism" in the doctrinal sense. Socialism, as constructed in the socialistic doctrines, always will be either premature, or too late. When the time for socialism does ensue, it will then have proven itself already unnecessary and out-moded, since already there will be new a life, dissimilar to that, pre-suggested in the socialistic visionary dreams, which are bound up with the negative connections of the bourgeois capitalistic order. In the socialistic idea there is almost nothing creative.

Many of us, as Russian critical Marxists of the second half of the decade of the 1890's, experienced deeply the collapse of the idea of a socialist-inspired Zusammenbruch, the idea of a social revolution. The intellectual work done since then has not left standing a stone upon a stone of the old social utopias; it not only scientifically, but also religiously has surmounted them. The social problem was broken up and set in connection with the cosmic problem. For people of spiritual experience and involved thought, it has become clear, that it is impossible to have a perfect organisation of the human societal aspect upon the surface of the earth, isolated from the world totality, from all the Divine world-order. Between the human societal aspect and cosmic life there exists a mysterious endosmos and exosmos. And what so quickly arose among us and the so quickly victorious childishly-immature, muddled idea of a social revolution is but an indicator of the backwardness and shallow culture of the broad masses, not only of the people, but also of the intelligentsia, of the intellectual apotheosis by those circles, with which such great arrogance term themself democratic. For everyone, given to precision in word usage, it ought to be clear, that not only with us at present there is not occurring a social revolution, but a social revolution in general never will occur within the confines of this material world. But one can readily admit that behind any social revolution there is a social disorganisation and social chaos, the uprising of part against the whole. This anti-social movement can seem to both its protagonists and its antagonists to be revolutionary in the socialistic sense of this word. And yet anyone in his right faculties would have to admit, that the grasping struggle for power on the part of individual persons, groups and classes, has nothing in common with the natural social process and social tasks. In a single day the ruling powers might fall and be replaced by another, and this indeed after a prolonged preparatory process. But in the social fabric in a single day there can occur nothing, besides psychological and economic molecular processes and formulas of social reform, prepared in correlation with this molecular process. And for the classes, hostilely disposed towards socialism, it would be proper for them to get free of the degrading fear about a social revolution. This fear conveys a poison into our national life. The governing economic classes ought to move towards a self-limitation and sacrifices in the name of the social rebirth of the Russian people. But trusting upon a revolutionary social cataclysm, which is conceived of as a leap across from the realm of necessity into the realm of freedom, is but merely a muddled and unconscious experiencing of the eschatological presentiments of the end of this material world. Prior to those mysteried times and seasons there can only be a social evolution, only social reforms, regulating the whole, but always leaving an irrational remnant in social life, but never prior to the end surmounting the evil, rooted within cosmic life and in the dark energies pouring forth from its bosom. Facing Russia stand tasks of a social process of building, and not social revolution. A social revolution for us at present however can only be but a social deconstruction, only an anarchisation of the economy of the people, a worsening of the material position of the workers and peasants. And in facing these infinitely difficult and complex tasks, which fate has set before Russia, any rosy optimism would be out of place and even immoral. The powers of evil in this world are stronger, than the powers of good, but they can appear under the most enticing convictions and the loftiest of slogans. And Russian democracy has facing it first of all to get itself through the severe school of self-limitation, self-criticism and self-discipline. There awaits us not a social paradise, but rather grievous tribulations in life. And it is necessary to have a tempering of spirit, in order to withstand these tribulations. All the social tasks -- are also likewise spiritual tasks. Every people is called to bear the consequences of its history and to be spiritually answerable for its history. Our history has however been exceptionally grievous and difficult. And foolishly mad are those, who in place of calling for the awareness of a severe responsibility, instead enflame the instincts of greed and malice, and who lullaby the masses with sweet dreams about an unseen social bliss, to be shown to the world by our unhappy and woefully suffering native land.

The Position of Russia in the World

(1917-263)[1]

There are those, who turn their gaze upon Russia, as comprising a certain sort of reality, upon its national unity, and the question concerning its position in the world, amongst other peoples, tends to alarm and disturb them. For people of a firm national awareness and patriotic mindset the questions of international politics always hold great significance, they cannot in this regard remain unconcerned. The honour and dignity of Russia, its position in world life, its historical vocation and the strength for its fulfilling -- all these questions are very real, very complex and responsible. And to these questions, always the people of an international socialistic mindset have tended to be indifferent. To them this has all seemed very simple. Simple indeed seems always that reality, of which one has no grasp. For resolving the problems of international politics, our socialistic minded intelligentsia are totally unprepared, and even less so prepared for this are the masses of the workers. Within this current the thought has never been worked out nor has the heart beaten stronger, over the might or weakness of Russia as a whole, bearing a singular visage before the world, whether it will uphold its dignity or collapse. With us there has been too little by way of thinking, in the extended circles, about the world-historical vocation of Russia and the Russian people, about its existence upon the world stage, about the say it should bespeak to the world, and the spirit, that it should imprint upon world life. The world entirety, the world stage has always seemed to our socialistic and revolutionary consciousness exclusively but for the triumph of internationalism, as a cosmopolitan directing of every national idea and even of national existence itself. The whole complex cycle of problems, connected with the ordering of the surface of the earthly orb, with the struggle of nationalities and imperialisms, with the smallish and the larger historical bodies, not only are dealt with simplistically, but even are

---

[1] POLOZHENIE ROSSII V MIRE. Article was originally published in the weekly Journal "Russkaya svoboda", 1917, № 5, May, p. 8-11.

completely ignored. These problems have an aspect unique in themself, they are not conjunctive with social problems nor resolvable by any sort of purely social movements, by any sort of modifications in the correlation of classes. There exists the world historical Eastern Question, bequeathed to our generation via the history of prior centuries. No sort of triumph of democracy, no sort of social turnabout can decide the Eastern Question, in which are concentrated a whole series of concrete historical questions -- concerning the relationship of Europe to Asia and Africa, concerning the fate of Turkey and the Balkan peoples, concerning the world historical gateways, which lead from East to West and from West to East. The world war is but an acutely tragic moment in the worldwide problem of East and West.

In the present historical hour Russia can fall victim to a profound ignorance in regard to these world questions and to the ignorance of the simplistic illusions begotten thereof. The Russian people for too long has been held in slavery and has endured this slave-like existence, narrowing it down horizontally, holding it in the grip of a dark ignorance. The old powers, having decayed and fluttered downwards, were powerless to resolve the world problems, which have faced Russia; all the time it balanced on the very edge of treason and betrayal of the fatherland. And it failed to provide the Russian people the possibility to become enlightened, to get prepared for the deciding of the fate of Russia, and assume responsibility. This slavery was rooted in the emotional passivity of the Russian people. And at present this selfsame passivity and selfsame irresponsibility can be sensed in the revolutionary maximalist passions now set free. To entrust responsibility for the resolution of all the acute and agonising questions, raised by the world war, to entrust it to the international proletariat, to the socialist Internationale -- means to abdicate from oneself all responsibility and to live in dreams and illusions, in which there is not a dram of reality. But this wont for an irresponsible dreaminess can lead to quite fierce a squaring of accounts, the awakening from the dreamland can prove quite frightening. It would be folly to entrust the deciding of concrete historical tasks to a power, which does not exist and which derives from dreams. Serbia, Belgium and Poland cannot rely on a resolution of their fate by depending upon a non-existent Internationale. This would mean in fact for these lacerated and divided lands that their fate would be decided by the German proletariat, which meanwhile displays no sort of an inclination towards internationalism. At present in Russia internationalism in practice signifies a defending of Germany and German socialism, signifies an outlook moreso imperialistically and nationally against France and England, against French and English socialism. What this meanwhile would establish is not a worldwide brotherhood of the proletariat, but merely a brotherhood of the Russian and German proletariat. Would this not be horrid a thing, would this not too closely resemble the brotherly feelings of the representatives of the old regime towards the German government, their mistrust and hostility towards France and England? The fate of Russia would be relegated over to the force of fictions and phantasms, and they would want to defend it by a power, which does not exist and which evidences no sort of signs of reality, except for the dreamland of the Russian Social Democrats. The real powers of genuine history however continue to act and they act against Russia, readying its degradation and humiliation. If even it be granted, that after the war the Internationale will prevail, then still it is impossible to presuppose, that it will prevail prior to the finish of the war, during wartime. Let Germany show for real its internationalism! Meanwhile however it occupies our territory, it has carved up several lands, and it all still senses itself a conqueror. From the Russian dreamland, from the fantasies and utopias France also can get carved up, and then the eternal shame will fall upon Russia.

There exist international relationships, international tasks and international obligations, as an unavoidable reality. This reality compels one to admit it and to awaken from dreamy thoughts. In Russia a social republic cannot be established, isolated from the world in its international outlook. The green sort of Russian kids from the intelligentsia and the people by short shrift would get cured from the irresponsible dreamings and get compelled to an awareness of realities. This would deliver a terrible blow to Russia as a great power, would plunge the Russian people into degradation and misery, but for a long time would cure them from dreams about the Internationale. Russian internationalism, which now is so in fashion for us, will not unite us with the peoples of Europe, but will ultimately instead disunite us from them. We would anew risk remaining the solitary East, and upon us just like formerly the peoples of the West would look, as upon Asiatics, unprepared for entry into the cultural life of Europe. Internationalism will not unite us with Germany, but it will disunite us from France and England. The attitude towards Russia was one of contempt under the old regime, incapable of upholding our prestige.

It can prove even more contemptuous after the turnabout that has happened. If among the entire people there is no will to upholding the honour, the dignity, the greatness and power of its own native land, then no sort of government, no sort of a bunch of people of loftier an awareness can accomplish anything. But the will of the Russian people is an uncertain factour, the people has not said its say. And I believe, that it will be otherwise, than from the words of those, who would usurp the will of the people and regard themself the voice of the people, whilst being a minority. There occurs at present the selfsame violation of the will of the Russian people, as was also under the old regime. The will of the entire people is a certain qualitative matter, not merely quantitative, and the true will of the people has to be reckoned as regards all the history of the people, from its remote past and remote future, and not alone merely from the interests and instincts of the present day. The will of an historical people cannot be clearly expressed in a climax of passions, in a struggle of greed, in the uprising of a part against the great whole, departing its roots for an eternity. In such moments individual persons can better conceive of the aims of all the people, the idea of all the people, than can the masses. But these individual persons have to have the support of the masses of the people. It is impossible to force a free people to love its native land, to defend it, to think about the remote reasons for its existence upon the earth. The people itself has to freely conceive of this and assert its will towards higher aims. But it would be improper to hide the fact, that the position of Russia facing the world now is truly tragic and frightful, it can be brought low spiritually and ravaged materially. And by way of answering for it will be only the appeals of social dreams and fantasies. It is impossible to permit the aloneness of Russia in the world. It has to have allies in Europe and such allies can only be England and France. It has to be faithful to the allies and pursue common goals. Only then will it for real, and not merely in dreams, enter into all humankind, into the world culture, onto the world expanse. The dreamy internationalism would however squeeze us back into Asia and isolate us. It would doom us to a solitary ignominy. Let this not be so, let the Russian people rise up against this, and save Russia as they did during the Time of Troubles and in the Fatherland War! Let there awaken in us the spirit of a free and knightly-noble citizenship!

Power and Responsibility

(1917 - #264)[1]

Prior to the revolutionary turnabout we had a prolonged crisis of power. The old powers had ceased to be national and statelike, had assumed an hostile attitude towards all the nation, and was overthrown into non-existence on an impulse by all the nation. The entire people's revolution has had to put forward a provisional government, to express a maximum of national and state unity, and to lead in line with the historical tasks, corresponding to the level of the societal developement of Russia. Power itself possesses objective a nature, it cannot be totally subjective and capricious, a matter of party and class. When it happens thus, the power of authority degenerates and falls. The old Christian wisdom taught, that all power is from God [Rom.13,1]. It would be inaccurate to interpret this truth merely in the context, that an autocratic monarchy or some other defined form of state power is something mystical and divine. This truth mustneeds rather be understood thus, that every power of authority by its nature is mystical and divine, if it fulfills its objectively destined purpose, if it is expressive of the civil and national nature in general, if it transforms chaos into ordered cosmos, sets limits to the triumphing of an evil will, and organises the people's life. In this context, the power of authority in democratic republics is mystical and divine the same, as is also every other power, congruent with its destined purpose. In the nature of the power of authority and in the attitude, which it evokes towards itself, there is a sort of mystery, which cannot be rationally grasped. The power of authority can degenerate into an evil principle, into a self-assertion merely, and then it betrays its divine wellsprings and its destined purpose, then it ceases to be of service. Such an evil degeneration of the power of authority long, for quite long occurred under the old regime. And it mustneeds straight out be said, that the power of authority of the provisional government, so unstable and transitory, is moreso divine, moreso in accord with the eternal nature

---

[1] VLAST' I OTVETSTVENNOST'. Article was originally published in the weekly Journal "Russkaya svoboda", 1917, № 6, May, p. 3-6.

of power, than was the power of authority of Nicholas II, set upon so ancient a grounding, than was the power of his temporary governments. The power of authority by its nature and its destined purpose is not a right, is not a privilege, is not a matter of interests. Power is a duty of obligation, a burden and service. In the self-satisfying and self-asserting struggle for power there is always a great untruth. It is because anyone taking upon himself the burden of power first of all imposes upon himself a great responsibility. One having taken upon himself the burden of power cannot still look upon all from partial a perspective, from the perspective of a group, class, party, from the perspective of opposing some private power against the whole. Unperceivable on the part of the life of the great whole, he enters into the mysterious life of the whole people and the whole state, he enters therein not only at some given moment of its existence, but into its historical continuance, into the connection of the times. In having assumed upon oneself the burden of power, it obligates one to think about the enormous whole, to organise it, and not permit the falling apart of the whole, or an ultimate uprising of a part against this whole. To this mystery of the whole, of the whole people and the whole state, is united only one who bears upon himself the responsibility. Power is inseparable from responsibility, an irresponsible power has to fall, it has to be overthrown. The old hence fell, because it was unable to bear the responsibility for the fate of Russia, because it irresponsibly helped ruin Russia, shoved it towards the abyss.

Our provisional government can be criticised from various points of view, but it is indisputable, that in it is an highly developed sense of responsibility, it has taken upon itself the responsibility for the great whole, for Russia namely, in very difficult moment of Russian history and it is prepared to bear this responsibility to the end. The provisional government has expressed a line of action objectively-national and objectively for the state, a line of action for the great whole. It has concerned itself with the fate of Russia, with the accomplishing of daily historical tasks. The provisional government, under the impetus of the Russian revolution, possesses original features, distinct from those of other temporary provisional governments of other revolutions. In it there is not the self-serving lust for power, not the self-assertion, nothing of the dictator. Moreso rather it consolidates upon too great an humanness and gentleness, almost akin to a Tolstoyan non-resistance. It -- is sacrificial, completely unselfish and it bears the power of authority, as a burden and obligation. It desires nothing to grab for itself. It is responsible for the whole, it is immersed under weighty considerations for the administering of Russia, for its defense, and the averting of anarchy. In this "bourgeois" government, as regards the irresponsible street terminology, there is something characteristically Russian, a Russian dislike for holding power, a readiness to resign power, if this be necessary for Russia. The provisional government holds power not out o a sense of a right and greed for it, but from a sense of duty and responsibility. At the present historical moment the power in Russia is a cross, and with reluctance is the resolve to take it upon oneself.

It has impossible a position. Those Social Democrats, which are hostile to the provisional government, organise demonstrations against it and want to overthrow it, they struggle for power, as though it were their right and privilege, but they are afraid of holding power and lack the resolve to take upon themself the responsibility, connected with power. And it mustneeds be said, that this hesitancy and fear of taking upon themself the responsibility for power is not only the effect of cowardice and lack of resolve, it has deeper real roots. Power in the hands of the socialists, with their class proletarian perspective, cannot be responsible. This power in its administration would not have the perspective of the enormous whole entirety, bearing the name Russia, it could not in essence be national and of state in general. Upon everything it would be impelled to look only from a perspective of private interests. Dealing with the mystery of power, certainly, there would have to be a change somewhat in the nature of those, who now stand upon purely a class point of view without any concern about the whole. But this is something they also are afraid of, something they do not want to do. One, who enters into governance, becomes fatally involved in the state aspect and looks with a statewide perspective upon that, which he previously regarded from private a perspective. And the Social Democrats are afraid of being rendered as the object of an irresponsible opposition, fighting for private interests, they are afraid to dirty their socialistic purity, their red socialist attire. To administer Russia in that hour of its existence, when an extraordinary revolution is combined with an extraordinary war, when the ruling power has been left such a terrible legacy from the old powers, is not only difficult, but also horrendous. The Social Democrats wanted to hide behind the sweetness of an irresponsible and pure confession of their abstract teachings. But every power in the world is a sacrificing of purity in the name of responsibility for the fate of peoples and states. And it mustneeds be said, that in certain regards the "Mensheviks" are worse than the "Bolsheviks", since they want it both ways and yet are afraid. It is immoral to want power and not want the responsibility. This is a denial of the great mystery of the whole, the mystery of the national and state being, a denial for which history will fiercely punish.

It is not only now that the working class in Russia cannot rule, but also never can any sort of class, rule. The nature of power -- transcends class. Class dominance would subvert power. A socialist, having entered into governance, would the same defend the citizen rights of the bourgeiose, as would also every other minister, he would have to concern himself over provisioning all classes of the population, the security and defense of the Russian state, the organisation of police, the courts, securing the rights of citizens, whatever the class they might belong to. Every power has to be powerful -- a powerless power is meaningless, and no one needs it. An example of a powerless power was manifest in the final period of the old regime. And a power has to be especially powerful in the era of such a crisis, as Russia is experiencing at present. But a powerful power has to have credibility and possess support among the people. It has to feel, that it expresses the middle line of the will of the entire people, which only can bring Russia out of the crisis. A power is responsible, when upon it they have imposed responsibility for the administration of the country, when they allow it freedom of action and do not hinder it at each step. The mania of mistrust, which at present has infected the Russian people, subverts not only the power, it subverts Russia, it is killing the soul of the people. This irresponsible preaching of mistrust everywhere, this hunting for "bourgeoisness" is the greatest evil of our day. The principle of democracy is perceived for us first of all as a mistrust and suspiciousness towards every manifestation of a personal principle. And this is the legacy of the old Russia, having undergone the old slavery. The preaching of mistrust by soldiers towards officers and generals subverts the army and puts Russia in defenseless a position. The preaching of mistrust towards the "bourgeoise" and the "bourgeois" government breaks up Russia into parts, seeking to abolish every remembrance about the unity of the people. And this -- is a slave's preaching. It seems further, that after the revolutionary turnabout the mistrust has become greater, than under the old regime. The first days of Russian freedom have become poisoned. The preaching of mistrust repudiates man in Russia, repudiates the dignity of the person, it repudiates the Russian people. And for the salvation of Russia and Russian man there has to ensue a moral sobering up and renewal of health, an austere awareness of moral responsibility. The moral and religious ascetic aspect has to put a limit to the irresponsible and dissolute orgies of social fantasies.

Russia and Western Europe[1]

(1917 - 265)[2]

I.

The world war has to facilitate a genuine closeness of Russia and Europe. We live at a moment of deeper a convergence of Eastern and Western mankind, than during the time of the Napoleonic wars. Russia ultimately will be pulled into the cycle of world life and will organically enter into Europe, as inseparable a part of it. There will end the period of the isolated and confined existence of Russia, as some sort of an East, set opposite the West. There is the aligning of Russia with Western Europe and its unprecedented alliance with France and England, and its unprecedented struggle with Germany and Austria-Hungary. The existence of Russia is rendered worldwide, is brought into conformity with its position in the world. The very demands of the world conflict already compel Russia to be on a level with European materiel and psychological armament. Russia had previously seemed a threat to Europe, in it they saw a strange and mysterious power, but Europe failed to perceive the Russia within itself. Western Europe shared its civilisation with Russia, but did not want and did not conceive of receiving anything from it, except raw materials. They viewed the Russian state, as a state half Asiatic. The existence of an unique Russian culture was something that Western Europe did not take seriously. They were unable to understand the soul of Russia in the West. And our neighbour Germany, which especially had pretended to civilise Russia, least of all wanted to admit of the existence of an independent Russian culture. The German self-confidence would not permit the thought, that the Germans could receive something spiritually

---

[1] This article was written prior to the turnabout happening in Russia, but its theme -- is eternal, and it is not so out of date, with what has happened.

[2] ROSSIYA I ZAPADNAYA EVROPA. Article was originally published in periodical "Russkaya mysl', 1917, mai.-jun., p. 76-81.

from Russia. They viewed Russia exclusively as an object for exploitation. But Russia itself also was insufficiently aware, that it could give something to Western Europe; in it predominated either a studying and dreamy attitude towards the West, or a repulsion from it and isolation in an Eastern self-smugness. Our Westernising consciousness reckoned it necessary only but to learn from the West, to adapt to the Western culture, and it viewed the Russian people as a people, going through an elementary grade school. In this was a grain of truth, though also not creative. The Slavophil consciousness tended however to isolate Russia from Western Europe, set itself opposed to it and assumed an Eastern insularity of Russia as a self-suffering higher type. And in the ideologies of the Russian radical Populists there was no sensing of the worldwide expanse, always there was a provincial isolatedness. The broad circles of the leftist Russian intelligentsia stood not upon the heights of European culture, in them rather predominated Eastern features.

Neither in the Westernism, nor in the Slavophilism, did Russia acquire worldwide a significance. East and West remained divided and opposites. For some, Russia was exclusively the East, albeit Christian also, and they had no desire to involve themself in a mutual responsibility for the fate of European culture; for others, Russia had to be made exclusively Western, and they would not take upon themself responsibility for the uniqueness of Russia. But Russia in fact by virtue of its position in the world and its purpose in the world is a great East-West, it stands at the centre of two worlds, two world historical torrents. Through all its history, through all its peculiarities it belongs both to Europe and to Asia, both to the West and to the East, it unites in itself two opposing principles. Russia is called to communicate to European culture a completely new principle and by this to broaden and deepen it. In this combination of two historical worlds -- is a source of the wealth and the complexity of the Russian soul and all the contradictions of the Russian nature. The entirety of Russian culture -- and it indisputably does exist, though also in insufficiently developed as yet a form -- is a culture of East-West, combining in itself two principles. But in this is a source of the greatest difficulties, standing upon the path of creating Russian culture. To create in pure and abstract a form of Western culture in Russia is impossible, but it is likewise impossible to let Russia stay in exclusively an Eastern culture or Eastern unculturedness. In a Western European sense, Russia can readily seem unsuccessful. Russia -- is quite a very difficult land, and insufficiently understanding this difficulty are not only foreigners, but even Russians themself. With Western peoples there is a great smoothness of spirit, less contradictory. In Russia, in the Russian soul always there occurs a conflict of two opposing elements -- the Eastern and the Western. But also within the Eastern element itself there occurs a division between the more extreme and non-Christian East and the less extreme and Christian East. In the depths of the soul of the Russian people lives not only a Christian and Slavic East, but also the Mongol East, entering within Russia during the time of the Tatar/Mongol Yoke.

II.

Russia has to also remain as an East, if it does not want ultimately to forfeit its uniqueness and originality; yet however it has to conquer in itself the extreme and exclusive east, eternally pulling at it inwardly, into the dark element, if it desires ultimately not to lose worldwide a significance and fall away from world culture. And thus, it was not in vain that Vl. Solov'ev posed his question to Russia:

> Which East wouldst thou be,
> The East of Xerxes or of Christ?

And it mustneeds be said, that in Russian Christianity itself, in the Russian rendering of Orthodoxy there are elements of the extreme East, and they drag at Russia inwardly, they hinder its ascent, do not permit it an active role in the world historical process. The extreme West in Russia, however, has always been either as an elementary level of learning, or of an international blandness. For us, the extreme West is merely the reverse side of the extreme East, and not of positive a creativity. German ideologies view Germany as central to Europe and they regard Germany as the bearer of the centrally European idea. With great a basis, it is also possible to see in Russia the centre of East and West and to regard Russia as the bearer of the East-West idea. And this idea is essentially more universal, than the German idea. Russia has to be consciously the great East-West, the unifier of two worlds. It is called to create a special type of culture, the synthesis of opposite principles, and the basics of such a type of culture are already apparent. The mission of Russia -- is for a leading of human culture towards an unity, its ultimate universalisation, bringing it out beyond the bounds of an isolated and self-sufficing Europe. The extreme East for Europe is something alien, neither understood nor receptive: Europe can accomplish nothing with it. Only through Russia can East and West come close to each other. It is not by chance, not in vain, that Russia rules a significant portion of Asia. And there is a sort of historical meaning in this, that to Russia has fallen the lot to transform in itself the Eastern element, to enlighten and humanise it. If Russia be the East also, then the East -- is rendered human and not inhuman, and is called to manifest of its bosom the image of man.

Such a conceiving of the position of Russia and its tasks has to lead to a surmounting of both Slavophilism, and Westernism. The conflict over East and West in Russian thought and life has to be rendered into loftier and more creative a type of thought and life. We have to overcome twofold a fear -- the fear to remain the East and a fear to turn towards the West. Russia -- is an European state, and it has to be in all regards armed with Western technology, which cannot be nationally derived. But all the various peoples tend to enter into the family of European states and cultures with their own unique and original image. Russia however has to convey still more trenchantly unique and original an image. The West also is a certain unity in multiplicity, and not a formless and ugly unity. Vl. Solov'ev already attempted to emerge beyond the opposition between Slavophilism and Westernism, but he too much involved this task with the reuniting of churches, and he was perhaps too inclined towards Catholicism. The centre of gravity to this question lies not in formal distinctions and affinities of the churches, but in different types of spiritual experience and different types of culture. Dostoevsky attempted to reveal the Russian universality and the significance of Russia for the West, and likewise also of the West for Russia. But in him likewise there was a deep attraction towards the Eastern element, which they then put to quite bad use. The asserting of Russia as an East-West centre has always presented great difficulties, and very easy are ruptures on one or the other side. But all the future of Russia and all its role in world life are dependent, upon whether it manages to overcome within itself the extreme East and the temptation to become immersed in purely the Eastern element[1] and

---

[1] In the elemental aspects of the developement of the Russian revolution are expressed features of the extreme East, in an hostility towards culture and evolution.

together with this also not to get transformed into the extreme West, forfeiting its originality. The faith, that Russia can bespeak a new word to the world and in it can be revealed something unknown, both to the extreme West and the extreme East, is based only upon the meeting together and interaction within the soul of Russia and within its historical body by two worlds, two world historical principles and cultural types. For the spirit of a people, in which has occurred this meeting and this mutual interaction, much has to be revealed, in it there has to be the knowledge of the one and the knowledge of its opposite. This means, that Russia would infinitely esteem Western Europe, the "land of holy wonders", but that it can better and more acutely than Western Europe be itself aware of the limitation and one-sidedness of Western European culture, in sensing the inevitability of its crisis. The Russian spirit always sees the limits and endpoints, does not remain in the middle as does the Western European spirit, and this is a sign, that Russia represents also a different world, is not contained within a single world. But this certainly does not mean, that Russia ought not to learn from the older European culture nor become Europeanised in the outward forms of its life.

III.

This Russian complexity, this richness of the spirit, this knowledge of opposites and polarities is revealed within the greatest Russian genius, the world genius -- Dostoevsky. The spirit of Dostoevsky and his creativity cannot have been begotten either purely by the West, or purely by the East. In the East, there is no suchlike acute a setting of the problem of human fate, such revelations of human nature, such a sense of the person, as with Dostoevsky; in the West in contrast there are no suchlike dangerous polarities, suchlike extreme and radical a spirit, such a striving towards the end and finality, such an incapacity of remaining content with everything average, with everything in order. Dostoevsky expresses the contradiction and richness of the Russian spirit, its ascent and fall, its difficulties upon the paths of the ordering of life, of the creating of culture. Dostoevsky in particular says, that Russia can open up to Western Europe much that is new, and unknown to it. But the hopes, connected with Russia, always have their reverse side and pitfalls, attending it. The Russian spirit truly -- is very insecure a spirit. How secure, how smooth and lacking in contradiction is the German spirit, the German monism! This -- is one aspect in comparison with the Russian spirit. "Wilhelm Meister" [Goethe] and the "Brothers Karamazov" -- herein is the difference between the German spirit and the Russian spirit! It has been easier for the Germans to create their culture not only in the outward conditions, but also in the inward ordering of their spirit. The contradictions in the Russian people tend to go at depth and hinder a manifesting of itself in the outward construct of the societal aspect and culture. The impression might even obtain, that the Russian people wants to let all its spiritual energy remain in the depths and inward, not wanting to manifest it in outward actions, in the making of history. And much in Dostoevsky has to be surmounted, as Russian a temptation. In many regards the effect of Dostoevsky was harmful. But he will forever remain a greatest expresser of the Russian spirit and a prophet of the worldwide significance of Russia. The attitude of Dostoevsky towards Europe was more complex and different, than with the old Slavophils and their modern continuers. For the expression of his attitude towards Western Europe he found such fiery wordings, as pure Westernisers never could. We might call to mind, what Versilov said in "The Adolescent" [alt. "Raw Youth"]. Dostoevsky, who not without basis can be reckoned a Slavophil, of the soil, an Easterner, managed however to express both the Russian anguish concerning Europe and the Russian reverential attitude towards its values and sanctities. Russians can more deeply appreciate the Western sanctities, than can the West itself.

The world war sets before the Russian consciousness the question concerning the worldwide vocation of Russia, about what Russia can give Western Europe, and not merely to receive from it. Russia faces a closer conjoint life with Western Europe. The vocation however of each people is determined by what it can give, and not only by what it is compelled to take. And herein clearly it has to be realised, that a pure Westernism within Russia can give nothing to the West, since it is only an affective studying, only a borrowing from the West. For Western Europe there is no interest in the Western side of Russian culture, no interest in its own reflected image. One can hardly be interested, for example, in English positivism upon Russian a soil, the Russian refraction of Mills or Spenser. And hardly can the Germans take interest in their own Neo-Kantian philosophy upon Russian a soil. And hardly can Western people find interest in Russian Marxism. But people in the West take great interest in Tolstoy and Dostoevsky, in Russian original literature, the embryonic concepts of independent Russian philosophy in Vl. Solov'ev and others, the unique religiosity of the Russian people, the special composite of the Russian soul, dissimilar to the Western, reflected also in the whole visage of the Russian intelligentsia. In Dostoevsky and in Tolstoy, Western people have long already become versed and have hearkened to their voice, within them they have sensed a light from the East. Russian literature is a factual thing, conveying Russian culture to worldwide a significance. Even the Germans are compelled to admit this, though they love to put forth the view, that the Russians -- are a lower race. In all that comprises the Russian spiritual composite there is much that is unrepeatably original, of interest and instructive for Western Europe, of that which aligns the authentic image of Russia and Western Europe. And hence each land enters organically into European culture, under pretension of being worldwide, -- not then when it merely borrows and moves along in elementary school, but rather when it begins to give of its own, to enrich the world with a new type of culture. The Russian people, rather later than others, is entering into the family of European peoples, but it has to give no less than others, since for European culture it will open up a whole new world, with riches as yet undiscovered. This awareness imposes upon the Russian people a great responsibility. The image of official Russia has long obscured the image of the true Russia. The Russian people has to ultimately surmount within itself the darkness of the extreme East, to emerge from a condition of isolation, and has to cease fearing the Europeanisation of the external forms of life; it has to turn its face towards Western Europe, not in order to become depersonalised and bland, but rather to manifest to the world its own visage and to convey to the world its truth and beauty, that up til now is so distorted and darkened.

On Bourgeoisness and Socialism

(1917 - #266)[1]

I.

Many a word, now enjoying wide currency on the streets, bears a character of magical effect; many a formula, now wending its way, assumes a sacral guise and is accepted by the masses not only without criticism, but also without understanding. And to such magical-incantational words belongs the word "bourgeoise" and "bourgeoisness". This word at present has a grip upon the masses, the masses find themselves enslaved to this word, the meaning of which cannot be adequately comprehended. The word falls into a dark obscurity, not prepared to encompass complex meanings, and it does not enlighten the darkness, but instead only increases it. The incantation arouses some sort of dark instincts, corresponds to some sort of interests, but no sort of clear concepts and ideas can be connected with it. What is the understanding of "bourgeoise" at the present day? Under "bourgeoise" is understood not simply the industrial class, not simply the capitalists, not the "third estate". With us at present the category of "bourgeoise" is employed in immeasurably more broad a sense. All of Russia, all of mankind is divided into two irreconcilable worlds, two realms -- a realm of evil, of darkness, the devil -- the bourgeois realm, and a realm godly, good, of light -- the socialistic realm. In its own way in this psychology there is a re-experiencing of the old, the age-old religious division and opposition, but in a distorted form. The Social Democrats, having poisoned the working masses with a destructive hatred for the "bourgeoise" and "bourgeoisness", make use of these words in a social-class, materialistic sense, and upon their own social-class point of view they bestow an almost religious stamp.

---

[1] O BURZHUAZNOSTI I SOTSIALIZME. Published originally in the weekly "Russkaya svoboda", 13 June 1917, № 8, p. 3-8, Petrograd-Moscow.

This positivist-materialist, social-class sense of the world cannot ultimately hold up. And the socialists, the materialists are compelled to admit, that "bourgeoisness" reflects a certain psychological disposition. A certain frame of values regarding life, not so much a condition of social matter, as rather an attitude of the human spirit towards it. A "bourgeois" disposition and a "bourgeois" set of values can be in a man, not belonging to the bourgeois class, no wise possessing property, and on the contrary, someone bourgeois as regards his class position can also be without such a "bourgeoisness". It is quite indisputable, that "bourgeoisness" is a condition of the human spirit, and not the social-class position of a man, -- it defines itself by a relationship of spirit to material life, by a spirit unfree and powerless to overcome the force of matter, rather than by material life itself.

  The great strugglers against the bourgeois spirit within the XIX Century were Nietzsche and Ibsen, who were not socialists, they did not have any sort of relationship to the proletariat and at present, surely, they would be consigned to the realm of the "bourgeoise", since at present the street wisdom consigns to the "bourgeoise" all the people of spirit. And perhaps the most vivid expression of the anti-bourgeois spirit in Russian literature was that of the reactionary, K. Leont'ev, -- all his life's work was a struggle against the impending grey-dull realm of Philistinism. His spirit was less "bourgeois", than the spirit of all the "Bolsheviks" and "Mensheviks", aspiring to the dull happiness of their earthly paradise. In France there is the remarkable writer Leon Bloy, unique as a Catholic, a reactionary's reactionary, having nothing in common with socialism, and he rose up with an unprecedented radicalism against the primary foundations of bourgeoisness, against the bourgeois spirit reigning in the world, against the bourgeois wisdom. As a Christian, he revealed the metaphysical and spiritual grounds of bourgeoisness and he grasped the mystery of the bourgeois, as in opposition to the mystery of Golgotha. The "bourgeois" always prefers the visible over the invisible, always prefers this world -- over the other world. Nietzsche would have said, that the "bourgeois" always loves more what is "closer at hand", than the "remote". The spirit of bourgeoisness is opposed to the mountain-heights spirit of Zarathustra. Ibsen would have said, that to the bourgeois spirit is opposed the spirit of that man, who stands the path of life alone. To the bourgeois, spirit is profoundly and essentially opposed -- not to the socialist and proletariat spirit, but rather to the aristocratic spirit. The bourgeois realm is a realm of the quantitative. To it stands opposed the realm of the qualitative. The bourgeois spirit builds everything on the basis of welfare, felicity and satisfaction. The spirit such as is the polar opposite to it tends to build on the basis of values, it has to gravitate towards the great spiritual far-off. The bourgeois spirit therefore does not love and indeed is afraid of sacrifice, whereas the anti-bourgeois spirit at its basis is sacrificial, even when it asserts power. The bourgeoisness was not created by socialism, it was created by the old, the decrepit world. But socialism accepts the legacy of bourgeoisness, it desires to increase and develop it and carry this spirit on to an universal triumph. Socialism is but a passive reflexion upon the bourgeois world, it has been wholly defined by it and received all its values from it. In it there is no creative freedom.

II.

The ideal of the ultimate arranging of this world and of an ultimate satisfaction and happiness in this world, killing off the thirst for an other world, is also a bourgeois ideal, is also within the bounds of bourgeoisness, an all-encompassing and just distribution of bourgeoisness over all the earth. The bourgeois spirit -- is first of all an anti-religious spirit. Bourgeoisness is an anti-religious satisfaction with this world, the desire to assert in it an eternal principle and to fasten down the human spirit to this kingdom, in preferring the world -- over God. And the very idea of the Kingdom of God upon earth, in this three-dimensional material world is a bourgeois distortion of a true religious expectation. In the old Jewish chiliasm there was a bourgeoisness, which has passed over into the new with its socialistic transformation. The bourgeois senses himself exclusively a citizen of this isolated world and of this surface of the earth, foreign to him is heavenly citizenship, the citizenship of other worlds. For the bourgeois, heaven is always exclusively contrived for the interests of the earth, and the other world -- for the interests of this world. Suchlike is the religiosity of the bourgeois. And truly the anti-bourgeois is that one, who puts the holding of values as higher than well-being, puts the inward higher than the outward, sacrifice higher than satisfaction, quality higher than quantity, the remote higher than the near at hand, the other world higher than this world, the person higher than the impersonal masses, and who loves God more than the world and one's own self. This means also the clash of two polarly opposite world principles. The bourgeois is a destroyer of the eternal in the name of the temporal, a slave of time and matter. The duping of the world, the duping of men and the human mob is also a basic trait. But the inward freedom of spirit, the victory over the power of temporality and materiality is also a victory over "bourgeoisness". Christ condemned wealth, as being a slavery of spirit, as being chained down to this limited world. The meaning of this condemnation is not social, but rather spiritual, oriented towards the inner man, and it least of all can be used to justify envy and hatred for the rich. This envy and hatred is a bourgeois stirring of the human heart and reveals all that selfsame slavery of the human spirit.

And it mustneeds resolutely be stated, that within socialism there is nothing opposing the spirit of bourgeoisness, there is in it no sort of antidote against the ultimate reign of bourgeoisness in the world. A worker can be no less the typical bourgeois, than the industrialist or merchant, his economically oppressed position does not guarantee him any sort of spiritual qualities, and often it even deprives him of nobility of character. Bourgeoisness is not dependent upon belonging to a particular class, though whole classes can be caught up in a spirit of bourgeoisness. In essence, every class psychology -- is bourgeois, and the bourgeoisness is conquered only then, when man gets above the class psychology in the name of higher values, in the name of truth. The workers and the peasants, in their purely class psychology, in their interests, can be spiritually bourgeois just the same, as the industrialists, the merchants and the landowners, and this is nowise affected, in that the interests of the former be more just, than the interests of the latter. For a class socialism, making pretense to the creativity of a new culture, it is fatal that all the higher values, the values of spiritual culture, the values of "science and art" should have been created by the bourgeoise, in the social class sense. The working class has not created any sort of values, has not discovered the rudiments of creativity of a new culture, of a new spiritual type of man. It borrows everything from the bourgeoise, it feeds off it spiritually and fatally becomes "bourgeois" in the measure of its growth of being cultured, its consciousness, its sharing in the blessings of civilisation. For the fifty years of its most heroic existence, the socialist proletariat -- this "messiah-class" -- has created nothing. In the sphere of religious awareness, the socialist proletariat has appropriated for itself the old bourgeois atheism and the old bourgeois materialistic philosophy, in the moral sphere -- the old bourgeois utilitarian morality, in the sphere of artistic life it has inherited the bourgeois alienation from beauty, the bourgeois dislike for symbolism and the bourgeois love for realism. The level of proletarian culture has not been lifted higher than the quite old, banal and as regards a more cultural segment -- the long since decrepit "enlightenmentism". The intellectual wretchedness of the socialist movement is striking. Is this how Christianity entered into the declining world of antiquity with its good news about new life? Where is it possible to find the signs of an original proletarian creativity? It is not the impulses of creativity, but rather the biding of interests that guides class psychology. The value itself of socialism was created by the bourgeoise, by the bourgeois cultural segment, to which belonged also the first utopian-socialists, and Marx, and Lassalle, and Engels, and the Russian ideologues of the Social Democrats, and of the Social Revolutionaries. For the proletariat, socialism is an interpretation of their interests and immediate instincts. And only for the ideologues from the bourgeois cultural segment has it been an idea, a value. How the interests and greedy instincts of some particular class can be transformed into an idea and value for separate figures who have emerged from other classes, -- this is a most interesting problem of the psychology and ideology of socialism.

III.

Socialism also is an ideal ultimately bourgeois, of a bourgeoisness as such equitable and universally spread about, the ideal of a forever attachment like serfs to this world in a bourgeois well-being. It would be foolish to expect from socialism a victory over the modern "bourgeois" culture -- it would only carry it on further to its end. The bourgeoisness mustneeds be sought not in the outward forms of socialism, but in its inward spirit. This spirit regards quantity higher than quality, well-being higher than value, the impersonal masses higher than the person, satisfaction higher than sacrifice, the world higher than God, -- this spirit is fastened down to this world, it is caught up in necessity, and not in freedom. Socialism through the present time has not come out with any sort of values, besides the values of material security, satisfaction and satiety. Spiritually it lives by values, created by the "bourgeois" world, its creativity, its sciences and arts, its discoveries. The promises to manifest forms of creativity purely proletarian, purely socialistic, have not been fulfilled, and the socialist movement draws away all farther and farther from the fulfillment of these promises. The socialistic spirit stands with an hostile attitude towards every sort of creative personal originality, in which only can there be sought an antidote against "bourgeoisness". Socialism represents spiritually a leveling, it leads all to a median dull-grey level, it gains a certain raising of the level of equality at the dear price of the disappearance of all the heights. Listen to the talk of the Social Democrats, read their newspapers, their brochures, their books. They all say one and the same thing, they write all the same language, they repeat the same words, they relive the same dull-grey thoughts. Nowhere is there apparent the person, personal thought, personal creativity. It is almost to the extent of being vexatious. There descends a grey foggy mist and promises a grey paradise, a paradise of non-being. The ideal of socialism -- is not creative, but rather expansive, not lofty, but equitable, and flat. The "bourgeois" world -- is indeed half-fast and sinful a world, in it are no enduring values. Socialism desires as it were to affirm an ultimate "bourgeoisness", a sacred "bourgeoisness", an equitable, a correct, an wholistic "bourgeoisness". The religion of socialism falls for the temptation of the loaves of bread, spurned by Christ in the wilderness. Socialism makes bread into a religion and for bread it betrays the spiritual freedom of man. Dostoevsky reveals this in his legend about the Grand Inquisitor. And Vl. Solov'ev also reveals this in his story about the Anti-Christ. Christ spurned the temptation of bread and taught to pray instead for daily bread.

I think, that the spirit of the materialistic class socialism, particularly in its Social Democratic form, is a deeply bourgeois spirit, a deeply anti-Christian spirit. But I say this not as an enemy of socialism. I think, that in socialism there is its own great truth and its own great question. But I think likewise, that the blame for the spiritual lie and untruth of socialism rests not upon it, but upon those social segments, which first entered upon the path of bourgeoisness, the path of the enslavement of spirit by materiality and class assertion. Socialism has but a reflective nature, it only continues on with the process, and does not start it, it lacks for initiative spiritually, and is only completive. The truth such as it is in socialism can only be realised in a different spirit, in a different spiritual atmosphere, in other than a materialistic consciousness, and without the class hatred, without pretension to the forceful establishing of the Kingdom of God upon earth, through some revolutionary cataclysm, but rather with a preserving of inward spiritual freedom. In the thralldom to its own passions, under the deceit of the interests and instincts of the masses there cannot be created a kingdom of freedom. The spirit of class hatred and malice leads to a denial of the image of God in man, it breaks down the idea of mankind and leaves it situated in an irreconcilable contradiction of the hopes of socialism itself. Social greed is an human sin, but social greed, established as an utmost sanctity, is already the spirit of the Anti-Christ. Everything is twofold within socialism and within democracy, -- the truth gets jumbled together with lie, the light with darkness, Christ with the Anti-Christ. World life is entering into a period, when there is no longer a crystal clear clarity, there are no easily recognised boundaries, separating the realm of light from the realm of darkness. The human spirit has set facing it the greatest of trials and temptations. Temptations of the greatest evil can appear under the guise of the good. And there is needed a vigilance of spirit and a sobriety of spirit, in order to unriddle the twofold nature of socialism, which moves along in the world with a newly promised realm. And incapable of discernment are those, who remain in a condition of primitive drunkenness and spiritual slavery.

Into the still dark masses of the Russian people have been thrown -- the seeds of hatred towards the "bourgeoise" and "bourgeoisness". The meaning of these hateful words remains misunderstood for the masses. And the way in which the masses assimilate these conjurative words about the "bourgeoise" and "bourgeoisness", tends to arouse something dangerous not only for the fate of Russia, the Russian state, the Russian people's economy, but -- a thousand times more importantly -- for the fate of the very soul of the Russian people, a soul feminine, dejected and frail, not having gone the way of the severe school of self-discipline and self-direction. The preaching of hatred towards the "bourgeoise" and "bourgeoisness" also makes the Russian people "bourgeois", distorts its Christian visage. For awhile we have still a quiet, a sort of benevolent anarchy, so characteristic for the Russian tribe. But there can come about something more vexing. And then the responsibility will fall not upon the people, but upon those segments of the Intelligentsia, which in having no wont for perceiving the deep meaning of words, tend to throw them around irresponsibly, and superficially. Thus within the Russian soul is killed what is holy, giving way to the rule of special interests. But the Intelligentsia itself ought to be preaching, that the basic division within the world and mankind remains not some temporal division into a realm "socialistic" and a realm "bourgeois", but rather a division into realms of truth and of lie, of good and evil, a Kingdom of God and that of the devil, of Christ and that of the Anti-Christ. In the spiritual sense of the word, only Christianity stands forever against "bourgeoisness". In it, the inner man gains victory over the outer man.

Counter-Revolution

(1917 - 271)[1]

I.

The word "Counter-Revolution" at present is being abused in ugly a manner. The manner, in which at present this word is employed in the leftist socialistic press, at street meetings, in private disputes, is impossible to term otherwise, than as moral blackmail. This -- is an easy method of shutting the mouth of one's opponent and depriving him of speech. Counter-revolutionary is termed every opinion, which is found displeasing, which does not fall under this or some other social doctrine. Too individual a thought at present already will certainly be regarded as counter-revolutionary. Only the regurgitated trite thoughts, only the group thoughts can be admitted as revolutionary. They assail as counter-revolutionary every guarantee of freedom and rights, every consolidating the conquering revolution into a new order of law. With the epithet of counter-revolution they try to compromise a dissident or hostile opinion and thereby evoke an attitude of suspicion towards it. This -- is a direct violence against the human person, against its thoughts and conscience, a denial of the elementary respect for the human person. The abuse of the word "counter-revolution" has poisoned Russia with mistrust, suspicion and hostility. The popular masses, who readily believe the first encountered demagogue or provocateur, have already been precipitated into a sickly mistrust and wicked suspiciousness. From this mass sickness is no easy cure. The moral blackmail has already borne its fruit, it has almost practically abolished the freedom of speech, has deprived speech of its own value. The hapless Russian people even after their liberation have begun to hide their thoughts, they sense the difficulty of free expression, they cannot breathe with the air of freedom. The atmosphere is beginning to be reminiscent of

---

[1] KONTRREVOLIUTSIYA. Article originally published in the weekly "Russkaya svoboda", 28 jun. 1917, № 10-11, p. 3-7.

that, which there was before the revolution, in the days of the orgy of reaction. And this oppression is created not by those, who would want to make counter-revolution, but by those, who brand as counter-revolutionary every free and independent word. The Russian revolution here already for several months is concerned with an inquest into a non-existent counter-revolution and is obsessed with a mania over espionage. Since the counter-revolutionary object was not evident, they then gradually had to invent and create it. The counter-revolutionary "bourgeoise" is, undoubtedly, the creation of a sick and frenzied imagination.

  The abuse of the epithet "counter-revolution" is growing at a dizzying tempo. The sphere of "counter-revolution" is ever expanding and the stigma of "counter-revolutionary" seizes upon newer and newer victims. The revolution in its fatal dialectic tends to consume its fathers and children. The revolutionary element knows no gratitude, it never rewards for merits. History and historians will take upon themself this latter mission. In the first days of the Russian revolution they decried as counter-revolutionary the supposedly hidden forces of the old regime and from them they anticipated threats in the matter of freedom. But soon there came to be dubbed as counter-revolutionary forces the People's Freedom Party, and then all the Russian liberals, and the State Duma, and the Rural and City Unions. There was shaped a counter-revolutionary "bourgeoise", in which they included wide circles of the intelligentsia. The head of the counter-revolution was considered to be P. N. Miliukov. There has been no halt to this process. We are entering into a period, when in counter-revolutionary designs will likely come under suspicion the Menshevik wing of the Social Democrats, and the Socialist Revolutionaries. From among the socialists, the first to fall victim of this moral blackmail was G. V. Plekhanov. Thus it became apparent over the course of three post-revolutionary months, that a major part of Russia was counter-revolutionary in its concealed or clear outlooks and intents. Pitiful was the result. P. N. Miliukov -- head of the counter-revolutionary bourgeiose. G. V. Plekhanov -- gone over to the bourgeoise. The socialist-ministers, Kerensky and the Menshevik I. G. Tsereteli, -- have schemed to go to the bourgeoise and already they have taken up with counter-revolutionary designs. What is to become of Russian freedom? The solely bright and truly revolutionary element remains the Bolsheviks, who also want to arrange a new revolution against the major portion of Russia, against the *bol'shinstvo*-majority, deemed "bourgeois" and "counter-revolutionary".

These luminous and pure bearers of the revolutionary and socialistic spirit do not halt in facing the conspiracies against their own comrades the Social Democrats, they also with them find counter-revolutionaries. The Russian revolution and Russian freedom are being lacerated. The sphere of pure revolutionism gets all narrowed down and in the final end becomes identified with a small heap, calculating on the demagogic fanning of passions among the dark masses. As long as the Bolsheviks sense themself the total expressers of the revolution, all are then suspect of bourgeois counter-revolutionism, and they alone stand above suspicion. They indisputably are not corrupted by the bourgeoise. True, certain of them are suspected of having been subverted by Germany, but in this there is nothing counter-revolutionary or bourgeois. In this process of "developement" of the revolution there is no end.

II.

The process of the inquest into counter-revolution, the spreading of its sphere and the concurrent narrowing down of the sphere of the revolution tends to move right along. There will be found also such, who will expose counter-revolution amongst the Bolsheviks. For the time being the Bolsheviks still are at one with the anarchists, but soon the anarchists will note within Bolshevism the indisputable signs of a bourgeois counter-revolutionality. For the true anarchist, every socialist -- is bourgeois, and the anarchist in this regard is correct. The ideals of socialism -- are suspiciously bourgeois ideals. The bourgeois nature of every socialism sooner or later cannot go unsaid, and it is strongly there also in Bolshevism. The Bolsheviks desire an all-encompassing, communistic bourgeoisness. In comparison with them, the anarchists would be wont to sense themself the outcasts of society, eternal losers, the expressers of the inner outlook and interests of a fifth estate. But the final act of this tragicomedy will ensue then, when within the anarchists themself will be seen a split and part will be written off to counter-revolution, while the other part will remain the singular, the ultimate and final bearers of revolutionality. In the midst of the anarchists themself will be found such, who in their outlook will be greater maximalists, than others. Part of the anarchists would undoubtedly detect the signs of counter-revolutionality and call forth a suspicious attitude towards the other side. By that time, part of the Bolsheviks would have been dispatched to the other world, and the part remaining among the living, would constitute quite seemingly rightward a current. All of Russia is becoming transformed into being seen as counter-revolutionary and bourgeois. And this will be the fruition of long inquests into counter-revolution and a moral blackmail, connected with this kind of preoccupation. Facing us is a bad infinity of fragmentation, exposing counter-revolution amidst a perfective selection of revolutionality. The revolutionary element devours itself, the revolutionary suspiciousness makes for a powerful self-destructiveness. This as it were law is apparent to us from the course of the French Revolution. The revolution destroys its hero Danton, having exposed him as a counter-revolutionary, and then in turn it destroyed Robespierre as well.

Who will stand to the left of the anarchists against all the rest of the world, seen as counter-revolutionary? From whom will be constituted this final remnant, in which will be concentrated and incarnated the "revolutionary" spirit? There can be no doubt. These elements are already to be noticed and are already active, these -- are the former or future criminal transgressors, the convicts, the misfits of society, former Black Hundredists and pogromists, provocateurs and traitors, elements already totally free from every "bourgeoisness". The dialectic finishes up, and the revolution at its end point will pass over into its opposite, will return from whence it started. At the furthest extremity of the left they prove to be the same, what they had been at the furthest extremity of the right. We shall but return to a purest Black Hundredism, to a purest demonic darkness, to a purest reaction. The genuine counter-revolution would seem to be in the extreme left wing against all of Russia, which nowise would be counter-revolutionary. The extreme, the maximalistic wing of the Russian revolution will be compelled to rely upon those selfsame elements, upon which relied also the extreme maximalist wing of the Russian reaction. We come facing the genuine counter-revolution, against which a very moderate liberalism presents itself as a saviour and liberator. The Russian rightist maximalism and the Russian leftist maximalism -- are of the same nature, the same element, alike denying every norm and law, alike anti-cultural and anti-state, alike not admitting of rights and freedom, alike it swallows up every face into a faceless abyss. The danger of counter-revolution actually does exist, and this is also that danger, threatening from the Bolsheviks and anarchists, from the dark instincts of the masses, towards which is directed the Bolshevik and anarchist demagoguery. The Bolsheviks not only can evoke reaction, as a movement directed against them; and no rather, it is the Bolsheviks themself per se that are reactionary, demonically-dark people, vomited forth from the chaotic pits of the past world. Reaction indeed against the Bolsheviks and maximalists is a liberation of man, and not some sort of counter-revolution. The Bolsheviks, the anarchists, the maximalists -- this is a remnant of a very gloomy, very servile past, and these -- are the enemies of the creativity of a new and free life.

III.

In order to get an orientation on the raging elements of the revolution and to derive an appraisal, there is needful a freedom of spirit, a freedom from the obsessiveness of that element, and it is necessary to draw upon one's own criteria and evaluation from a greater depth, from a Divine and not worldly source. The worship of an earthly goddess, named Revolution, is a slavery of spirit and idolatry. Such a goddess does not exist. It is possible only to worship and serve the One Lord God, the living and existing God. Every other god is an idol and the one worshipping it -- is a slave of the world. If revolution were to be acknowledged as some sort of being, with a personification of it, then it would be necessary to acknowledge it as a sinful earthly being, begotten by the sinful past of mankind. This being would be full of all the weaknesses of mankind, of all the ugly human passions. It is impossible to draw one's evaluation from the element itself of the revolution, it is needful rather to draw one's evaluations from the higher Divine source, such as exists within one, and impose them upon the revolution. And then it will become clear, what revolution is -- a being twofold, truth mixed up together with falsehood. On the face of the being, named Revolution, there is an ambiguously twisted smile, and with each day it becomes all more and more ambiguous. The Russian revolution -- is providential, in it there is a cleansing threat and a cleansing fire, in it burns up the old falsehood. But in this same element there is formed a new lie and much of the old appears in but a new form. Freedom -- is a Divine value, an utmost goal, the visionary dream of many generations of the finest Russian people. The revolution however per se is not a god by nature, by its essence, and it -- is but an inevitability. The revolution and freedom are not at all identical. Revolution sets free the fettered powers, but too often it manifests itself as the greatest violator against freedom and as a destruction of freedom. The powers are liberative, but not transfigurative, and they get directed against freedom, they do not love freedom, do not permit of breathing the air of freedom. Eternally twofold is the nature of revolution in relation to freedom. Why is this so? This happens because every true freedom possesses a spiritual basis, whereas revolution drags the masses onto the surface of life and permits only of a freedom torn away from its spiritual roots. An era of revolution per se is not an era of depth, is not an era of creativity. Revolution provides an enormous experience for the people, but this experience becomes deeply and creatively reworked later, after the restoration of health. But the Russian people needs a spiritual sobriety in regard to the stormy experience, it is in need of an asceticism of soul. There is the need to surmount every fear and terror, enslaving the soul, and it is likewise needful to surmount every rosy optimism, every social daydream, every deceit in the masses of the people, every idealisation of the dark element and its connivance at power during the present day. This -- is a demand for a propriety of character. It is necessary to protest with all one's strength against the sham connected with the word "counter-revolution". This is a blackmail that enslaves thought and speech, and deprives us of freedom. We have to struggle for freedom of thought and speech: this is both a very minimal and a very maximal demand of the revolution, a demand of spirit and not of flesh. The shouts about "counter-revolution" have to be exposed as to their true nature, as to their moral deficiency. It is impossible to allow this enslaving of thought, which is now being done. Time will show, where the genuine counter-revolution is, in the ontological sense of this word. It -- is there, where they would brand as counter-revolutionary every free thought, every free speech and free creativity. Against suchlike a "revolution" there ought to be made a "counter-revolution", i.e. a true revolution ought to be made against a false and pseudo-revolution. We live within the magical power of words and gestures, which enslave the Russian people, which make it obsessed. A true liberation, a liberation of the spirit of the Russian people and its body from hysterical convulsions and distortions lies still ahead.

A Free People

(1917 - 267)[1]

I.

The Russian people has emerged from constrained a condition, from a long period of historical servitude, and is making the transition to free a life, to power of the people and rule by the people. Great was the long-endurance of the Russian people and it prompted foreigners to think, that the Russian people -- is a slave at soul. And here now the Russian people has had to show all the world, that it truly is a free people. After the great turnabout that happened, Russian man himself has to govern himself. The source of the ruling power, upholding the social order and defeating all anarchy, is already within him himself, and not outside him, nor over him. And by this a free man is also distinct from the slave, in that he is capable of managing for himself, whereas the slave is capable only of submission or rebellious revolt. Rebellious revolt is merely the obverse side of slavery. A free man can make a revolution, but he cannot make a rebellious revolt, since a free man imposes upon himself responsibility for the fate of his state and his fatherland. And only those, who remain slaves at soul, can relate to their state and their fatherland, as to something foreign, attached to them, hostile. A people is worthy of maturity of citizenship, when it begins to govern itself. Freedom is also first of all the capacity for self-governance. To govern others, to direct an entire land can only involve those, who have learned to govern themself, their thoughts and feelings, their own particular aspects. Only those can establish order in the land, who have established order within themself, who have brought order by their own will and have directed it towards higher ends. But the end, in the name of which Russian man ought to learn to direct himself and govern others, cannot be the matter of the greedy interests of individual people or classes. Such a proper end can only be for the good of the whole, for the

---

[1] SVOBODNYI NAROD. Article originally published in the weekly "Narodopravstvo", 30 jun. 1917, № 1.

welfare of Russia, for the good of all the people, the ascent of the people towards higher a life in truth and right. Freedom does not signify arbitrary caprice, does not mean, that each can do, whatever comes into his head, -- freedom presupposes respect for every human person, the acknowledging of the person's inalienable rights, a cautious attitude towards the proper and the improper for the human soul. Those who have anarchy within, anarchy in thoughts, in the will and feelings, who have nothing but anarchy, are unable to constructively build within the land, the state, the life of all the people. And then the part rises up against the whole, each then strives after his own private, personal and group interests, without regard for the interests of Russia, for the welfare of all the Russian people. Freedom is impossible without discipline, without self-restraint and self-control, without subsuming oneself to that truth, which also renders man free. In the Gospel is said: "Know ye the truth, and the truth will make you free". And an entire people is made free only then, when it knows the truth and serves it.

The loss of all discipline among the people, of the capacity for self-direction and self-restraint, for subsuming itself to higher ends, transforms a people into an herd of wild beasts and returns it to the slavery of primordial times. Failure to govern oneself, to show restraint in one's interests and to subsume them to the whole is a sign of slave-like a condition and would lead to a disintegration of Russia, transforming it into a strewn heap of sand. Each hauls off for himself what he needs, and from this depredation, the people as a great totality ceases to exist. One who is free does not coerce anyone, does not extort anything from anyone, towards all he respects freedom, taking account of their rights. One prone to coercion, is still already a slave. The people can accomplish their aims, and realise all their powers only within a state; undefended by their own state, a people falls into slavery to other peoples. But a state cannot be a scattering of sand, it has to be crystalline, having strong features and edges. The forming, the guarding and developing of the state demands from the people a tempered character of firmness of national will. A lack of character in the people would subject the existence of their state to danger and threaten the people with slavery. The Russian people is entering into a new period of its historical existence, making the transition to a form of state, a democracy. A democracy however is grounded upon a self-governing people, upon the high qualities of a people's character. A people, which evidences a slave-like spirit, which does not want to direct itself and is instead given to acts of violence, such a people is not capable of democracy, lacks the maturity for it. Montesquieu already had taught, that democracy is based upon *valour*, upon love for the common task. If this valour does not exist in the soul of a people, if there is no love for the common effort, then democracy degenerates into despotism. And the Russian people now have an examination on the subject of democracy to pass, history is putting its "valour" to the test, its matureness for citizenship.

II.

What is the Russian people, what is the people as such? The people is not some whatever class, some whatever social group, is not the peasantry or the working class. Into the people enter all the Russian people, all classes and groups. The people is a great totality, a thousand years existing in history, and in it are conjoined the remote historical past with the remote historical future. It is impossible to arbitrarily term the people as present-day history would want me to, and posit a definition of the people as dependent upon the class struggle of the present day, upon the correlation of social classes, which exist in the present. The people goes deeper, than that which happens today, deeper than all the transitory classes with their opposing interests. And to discern the visage of the Russian people and the fate of this people within history, it is necessary to gaze at not the peasant and the landowner, not the worker and the industrialist, not the merchant and the intelligentsia, but to the Russian man concealed within them, to his soul, which is deeper than all these outward social trappings. This soul of Russian man, the soul of the entire Russian people, has found its expression in the Russian great literature of Pushkin and Gogol, of Tolstoy and Dostoevsky. And no one Russian man, irregardless of whatever class he might occupy, can be excluded from the people. The nobility, the bourgeoise and the intelligentsia alike belong to the Russian people, comprise alike an inseparable part of it, as does the peasant, and the worker. There exists the Russian people, Russia exists, and not merely the classes of workers or industrialists, peasants or landowners. Interests exist for all of Russia, for all the Russian state, the interests of the great totality, and not merely the interests of individual classes and individual people. And it is needful moreover to remember, that the very existence and welfare of each Russian man and each class depends upon the existence and well-being of all of Russia, upon its strength and greatness. Russia is the mother, nourishing its sons. The Russian workers and peasants can lead only national an existence at the maternal bosom. If there were to be abolished the Russian state with Russian industrial production weakened, then there would be abolished and weakened all Russians, all classes, all the peasantry and workers. No one Russian citizen can posit his existence as outside of Russia -- he can exist only in it and through it. Only the slave is capable of easily renouncing his native land and betraying it.

The Russian people -- is a single great people, and not a mechanical amalgam of disconnected parts, each pursuing only their own interests. The Russian people is endowed with its own visage in the world, dissimilar to any other people, it has its own history, its own great past and great future, it has tasks, allotted to it. And the Russian people has to remain itself, as an entirety, to defend its place in the world, its purpose in the world. With every healthy, life-capable and free people this feeling runs stronger, than class interests, than class contention. This great feeling of a national unity and national vocation is there in the French, the English, the Germans. If it were altogether to disappear with the Russians, Russia would cease to exist and the Russian people would dissipate, like dust. In Russia there is occurring at present a painful and tortious transition over to a new national consciousness and a new free patriotism. The old has died, and the new is not yet born. The revolution was made by all the Russian people, as a great totality, and not by this or that class, it was made out of a sense of self-preservation and from the impulse towards a new and free life. And the transition over to democracy is a transition to the self-directing of the entire people, irregardless of belonging to this or some other class. Democracy is a political matureness of citizenship of the entire people. It is impossible to posit democracy as in opposition to the bourgeoise, as now some among us do out of churlishness. Democracy signifies the supreme power of all the people, and into it enters each Russian citizen, the rights of whom have to be safeguarded on equal a level with the rights of all the rest of the citizens. Democracy cannot be understood as the domination of the working class or the peasantry. A dictatorship of the proletariat would be an act of violence by a minority against the majority, and it is in essence hostile to democracy, it is anti-democratic, and would infringe on the sovereignty of the people, involving a conspiracy against it. A free people cannot tolerate a dictatorship of whatever the class.

III.

The transition of an entire people, so long having dwelt in slavery, the transition over to a democratic form of governance presents first of all the task of educating the people, the growth of awareness, of enlightenment and culture among the masses of the people, of a spiritual rebirth of those, the human souls, of which the people is comprised. If the people in its masses consists of the souls of slaves, full of slave-like inclinations towards violence, lacking in respect for human dignity and for freedom and the rights of the person, then it is still unready and incapable for democracy and there will threaten it the inevitable arising of despotism, a return of some whatever form of Caesarism. Acts of violence, perpetrated by an immature revolutionary democracy, always prepares the way for tyranny. The violent will suffer violence, this -- is a law of nature. And here is why the task of educating and enlightening the masses of the Russian people is a fundamental task, in positing the transformation of Russia into a democratic state. Democracy can only be a special sort of the culture of the human spirit or it will be worse a thing from slavery, from despotism. Only those who are free, governing their own souls are capable of creating a free democratic state.

A people only then is worthy of being termed a free people and a people of mature citizenship, when it becomes conscious of its own national unity and totality as within its own state, outwardly to face other peoples and states. When a people disintegrates into parts inwardly and does not want to defend its totality and its dignity outwardly, it returns to slave-like a condition, it is not ready for freedom. Here is why the attitude towards the unity of state power in Russia and to the war is a testing of the maturity of the Russian people as regards a new and free life. The Russian people in the current threatening and responsible hour of its history has to be aware of its moral, civil and cultural unity, of its inviolable entirety amidst those fractional parts, classes, regions and peoples, comprising mankind. The social struggling of classes has to become subordinate to this awareness of totality and unity. The people has to more quickly determine its free citizen attitude towards the unity of the state and towards the war. Time will not endure. Each day the elemental spreading of anarchy and disintegration drags Russia towards the abyss and readies it for slavery. A slavery to foreigners and a slavery to one's own dark powers, lurks there alike from the extreme right and from the extreme left sides. Between the "Black Hundredists" and the "Bolsheviks" there is no essential difference: in them exist one and the same element of violence and enslavement, one and the same violating of the dignity and rights of the human person. A dictatorship of the Bolsheviks can rest only upon those same dark elements, which arranged the Jewish pogroms and wrought pillaging and expropriations. This is one and the selfsame black-red, Eastern Asiatic murky darkness, a remnant of the savagery and barbarity of the Russian people.

It would be a shame to think, that the Russian people managed to have a great and unified state, only while it lived under slavery and compulsion, and instead passed over into anarchy and disintegration, when it became free. And it would be even more shameful to think, that the Russian people managed to have a valiant army fulfilling its duty to its native land, only while it was forced to do so, like a slave. If it proved, that for the Russian people the possibilities are either a slave's submissiveness and coercion under the whip or a slave's revolt and anarchy, then this people will have been doomed to perish. Then the people will disintegrate and be rendered into disorderly hordes, which anew will lead to the summoning of Varangians. It will involve a return to the very beginnings of Russian history, and anew Great Russia will have to form. Too many at present preach this going backwards and with ease they dismiss all the adversities of Russian history, all the sacrifices, made by the people for the building of a single, great and powerful Russia. But I believe, that the Russian people, having already experienced a troubled period, is now also experiencing temptations and pitfalls, but will make the transition to an higher and free life. However, it is needful openly to say and to shout, that those, who at present agitate the people onto a path of anarchy and disintegration, are thereby agitating it onto the path of slavery and humiliation, and that they are murdering the soul of the people. Every people lives within history and accomplishes great deeds by the power and totality of its spirit. When the spirit of a people becomes corrupt and exhausted, the people exit the historical scene, move off onto a secondary plane and fade away. But the Russian people still has facing it a great role within history, and it only just now is entering into world life, and I believe, it will not perish.

In Defense of Socialism

(1917- 268)[1]

I.

Is socialism triumphing in Russia? On the surface level -- yes. Everywhere in the masses of the people is evidenced the victory for the socialistic slogans. The world has not yet seen such an outburst of socialism. It might appear, that from an absolute and dynastic monarchy Russia in a mere instant has become transformed into a socialistic republic. The peasantry, which in its darkness supported tsarism and rendered it "of the people", now goes with the slogans "land and liberty", and the army, which was accustomed to obediently shoot at the people, now demands full autonomy not only for each individual part, but also for each individual soldier. Fellows of the dubious sort, the petty sort, civil servants, all those, who by their political indifference and baseness supported the old order, now sympathise with the extreme socialist parties. Yesterday's Black Hundredists are become today's Bolsheviks. The People's Freedom Party is considered the most rightward and the most "bourgeois", since no one has the audacity to form a party farther to the right. There is the impression, that all Russia, still altogether not long since submissive to slavery and groaning under the oppression of despotism, has suddenly become extremely leftist, revolutionary, socialist. It would seem, that no powers can withstand the precipitous rush of Russia to the realm of socialism. Yet nonetheless it beggars belief, that socialism is triumphing in Russia, that this triumph goes deep and that this socialism itself -- is authentic. The very psyche of the masses of the people, and indeed, their manner of thinking, their moral character has changed very little. Socialism not only has not become ascendant in the soul of the people, it has barely touched the soul. Soldiers, peasants, workers, the intermediate democratic segments among the enormous masses do not at all understand, what

---

[1] V ZASCHITU SOTSIALIZME. Article originally published in the weekly "Narodopravstvo", 3 jul. 1917, № 3, p. 8-10.

socialism actually is. The peasants know, that they have lived poorly and that they need land. The workers know, that they have been repressed and that they need a shortening of the working day, an increase in workers pay etc, and elementary benefits. But such an "intelligentsia" and seemingly "educated" indeed contrived idea, like socialism, is totally foreign to the peasants and quite little as yet conceivable by the average working masses. The word socialism gets aligned however with daily, elementary, very proximate needs of the labouring masses, and therefore at present they live under its spell. Socialism is instinctively accepted and is understood as a private and personal satisfying of needs and demands of each working man from among the people. There prevails not a public rights approach, but rather a private rights perception of socialism. The very idea of socialism is not only not triumphing, but it is nowise even on the ascendant, it -- is too complex, it presupposes a great awareness and it demands sacrifices by the parts in the name of the whole. The soldier, the peasant, the worker all think, that socialism will bring immediate good to him himself, will now alleviate his bitter need. And the demagogues, desiring to sway the masses to their side, unscrupulously exploit this murky attraction to socialism. And thus obtains a fictitious triumph of socialism, behind which can be hidden its intellectual downsides. Socialism at present is merely a Russia means for making political and lifestyle revolution.

For the choices of the Moscow Duma there was put forth seven party lists. And right off it was sensed, that two numbers were as good as lost and would stand no sort of success. These -- were the party of populist socialists and the Social Democrat group "Edinstvo" ["Unity"]. Both the one, and the other were declared not to be socialists. The Soviet of Workers and Soldiers Deputies called for a vote on № 3, 4 and 5, i.e. for the Socialist Revolutionaries, for the union of Social Democrats with the Mensheviks at the head, and for the Social Democrat Bolsheviks, whereas № 2 and 6 were acknowledged as not meriting support. This is very characteristic a phenomenon. The defeat of № 2 and 6 is, in essence, a defeat of the traditional socialism of the Russian intelligentsia, a defeat in aspects of the revolution and a destroying of aspects of the revolution from the recognised intellectual leaders of our revolutionary intelligentsia -- N. K. Mihailovsky and G. V. Plekhanov. These are populist socialists -- to the utmost pure and intellectual socialists of the populist stamp, aligned with "Russian Riches", an organ of Russian populism, i.e. owing its lineage of ascent to N. K. Mihailovsky and "Fatherland Notes". They are more purely expressive of Russian populist socialism, than are the Social Revolutionaries. The Social Revolutionaries, though also at present having become imbued with a civil-state aspect having in their midst such people, as A. F. Kerensky, tend all to be too much demagogues, and their socialism is oriented towards the unenlightened instincts of the masses; they themself little believe in any near or real realisation of those slogans, with which they seek to captivate the masses, as for example, with the slogan for the uncompensated confiscation of all the private property landownings. The Social Democrat groups of Edinstvo are also authentic Social Democrats in the European sense of the word, aligned with the father and leader of the Russian Social Democratic movement, G. V. Plekhanov. They express in more pure a form the socialism of the Marxist outlook, than do the Mensheviks, not even to mention the Bolsheviks, who ultimately have forgotten the basics of Marxism. Not only the Bolsheviks, but even the Mensheviks -- are demagogues, seeking to take advantage of the instincts of the masses, and on the same basis have proclaimed the slogan of a social revolution, in which they themself do not believe, and which in contemporary Russian conditions in accord with their teachings is impossible. At present, however, the Mensheviks tend to insufficiently distinguish themself from the Bolsheviks, their tactics are ambiguous and they are weakened by a lack of moral courage.

II.

The representatives of List № 5, i.e. the Bolsheviks, nowise can be considered socialists, the ought to be cast out from the midst of the socialists. And the fact, that the Soviet of Workers and Soldiers Deputies has appealed to vote for this list equally with № 3 and 4, has no sort of inner justification. But as to the representatives also of Lists № 3 and 4, it is impossible at present to term as socialist in essence, as preserving and expressing socialistic ideas. The rub is in this, that up til now after four revolutionary months both the Social Revolutionaries, and the Social Democrats, have been little interested in developing the awareness and enlightenment of the masses of the people, of the peasants and workers, and they have done almost nothing for a positive socio-economic organisation of the masses. Thus, for example, our workers unions are left in the background, for them almost nothing is done and this threatens a sad lot for the working class. The essence of an healthy socialism -- is in the developement of the awareness and organising ability of the workers. This -- is a task positive, constructive, formative of a new social fabric, and not something negative and destructive. But the Russian socialists up til now have been too interested in a political manipulation of the masses, aimed at the instincts of the masses for a forging of revolution, i.e. rendering the people's darkness into a weapon for them. They have developed and organised for revolution only after it occurred, instead of developing and organising social life. For the Bolsheviks there is nothing else, they are totally like the Black Hundredists and need also to manipulate the pogrom instincts of the masses, they fear the enlightening of the masses, just like the powers of the old regime feared it. But even the Mensheviks and the Social Revolutionaries also have not been fully free from certain aspects of Bolshevism and only now do they begin to get free from it. They have not been expressive of that basic socialistic concept, that every attainment in the social sphere is dependent upon the level of social developement and upon the social organising ability of the working class. Their tactics have consisted in this, that as much as possible they promise the masses more, than corresponds with their level of awareness and organising ability. They have striven too much to take advantage of the masses with flattery and by this means they seek to gain power, to attain an easy victory. The bitter fruits of these tactics have been reaped in Bolshevism, and they have alarmed all the sundry responsible and honest Russian socialists. Bolshevism has provided a graphic object-lesson on Russian revolutionary socialism and has roused a statist mentality among the Social Revolutionaries and the Social Democrat Mensheviks. Only a lack of boldness and follow through have led to their choosing in preference the List № 5 over Lists № 2 and 6 on the city ballots.

There is mention of the fact, that a Moscow servant woman decided to vote for List № 4, and when they asked her, why she did not vote for List № 2, they then received the reply: № 2 -- these are socialists, and we know, who the socialists are, and we do not want them. Here is an example of the level of awareness of the voting masses. And there remains the impression, that the level of awareness of the masses is of little interest to Russian socialists, not only № 5, but also № 4 and 3. List № 4 is geared towards the servant woman with the appeal, to wit, that this party is especially concerned over the interests of city servants and will express their needs. And saying this are the pure ideologues of the proletariat, in addition to the large and petite bouergeoise, all except for the large industry workers, and yet they pin all their hopes upon the especial socialistic psyche of these workers! List № 3 has promised the servant both land and liberty, and has suggested to the cooks and chambermaids the thought, that the land will be received as the result of municipal elections. There is nothing also to say about List № 5. For it, actually, there voted all the Black Hundredists, the pogromists, a person with criminal a past or future and those masses of soldiers -- big children, who can be swayed by whatever the agitator-demagogue. The Bolsheviks already have nothing in common ultimately with the intellectual socialism, and they are totally without interest in the level of awareness and organising ability of the working class. These -- are most purely the destructive. But regrettably, also the Social Revolutionaries, and the Menshevik Social Democrats up til now have been too idle and indifferent as to what they present of themself to the masses, to which they turn, with the mental and moral condition are in. Here is why the now dominant parties to a remarkable degree represent a fiction and evoke mistrust. Genuine parties with a real programme we do not yet have. The party slogans -- are totally conditional, unintelligible by those at whom they are directed, and are not taken seriously, by those who proclaim them. Thus for example, what sort of a real significance does the slogan, "All the Land to the Working People", possess in municipal elections, where everything is involved in the affairs of the well-being of the city administration? The city Duma is not called for deciding the question of land for the peasants, and to it does not belong the right of such legislative functions. And those chiefly the city masses of servants, who are tempted by the slogan of "land and liberty", have been led astray without being aware of it.

III.

A true socialism has altogether failed for us to penetrate into the awareness of the masses. Many fear, that Russia will enter into a period of too intensive a sway of socialism. This -- is a groundless fear. Already there has begun a reaction against socialism, at a point in time when for us a genuine socialistic movement has not as yet existed. Somewhat greater a scope of socialist awareness would have been more useful for us. After four post-revolutionary months almost nothing has been done for the developing of a socialist consciousness and socialist creativity among the masses. The masses of workers, of soldiers and peasants are altogether unfamiliar with the elementary aspects of socialism and are not pervaded by a socialist psychology. The socialistic consciousness has dimmed also among the masses of the intelligentsia. It is improper to confuse revolutionism with socialism -- one could the sooner say, that they are incompatible. Social creativity presupposes an emergence beyond the negative and underground psychology of revolutionism. But with us there is a basis to fear, that with the finish of the sway of purely revolutionary a psychology there will be an end to socialism also, on the basis of negative feelings. It would be incorrect to say, that the ideas of Mikhailovsky and Plekhanov will win out and advance. One could sooner say, that these ideas will drown in a triumphing of demagoguery. Plekhanov also will remain a genuine socialist of the Social democrat stamp, but he will be ignored and cast aside. Back in 1905, at the height of an epidemic of revolutionary maximalism, he spoke and wrote, like a genuine socialist. To a genuine socialist, the enlightening of the masses cannot be something foreign, he cannot be insensitive to the developement of the industrial powers of the land, and he is first of all concerned with the qualitative raising of the level of organisation and consciousness of the masses. And here one has to admit, that socialism among us is suffering a defeat. What seems its triumph, is totally on the outside and superficial. This can be explained by the cultural backwardness of Russia. Our psyche is being rendered not socialistic, but all the more private and greedily egoistic. After the revolutionary turnabout, when the country is in the process of preparing for the Constituent Assembly on the basis of an universal, direct, equal and secret electoral right, revolutionary socialism is totally absurd and meaningless. Revolutionary socialism at present in Russia can only be a compelling reminder about the old slavery and oppression, carried over into the new and free Russia by the old underground psychology. At present is needed a positive social constructiveness, creative work. There do not exist those restraints upon a social developing of powers, against which making a revolution would be necessary, for all the paths are now open. Socialism can be only creative, positive, based upon the growth of awareness, upon the organisational and cultural level of the working masses, upon the subsuming of the partial to the whole. But of such a socialism we have quite little, almost none at all. The total exclusion of Lists № 6 and 2 shows, that more consistent a socialism at present will have no success and is unnecessary. The socialism seems merely a totally conditional slogan of the revolutionary maximalism. But the socialistic movement itself among us is in total disarray, since there is no positive social organisation of the masses, no creative social enrichments.

I am no worshipper of Plekhanov, and his ideas to me are foreign. But at present he evokes towards himself great respect and reknown. He could have been the most popular and acclaimed man in Russia, he was for many years the leader of the Russian Social Democrat movement. But for this, he would have to have in him at least a tiny smidgen of the demagogue, and enter upon the path of deceit and manipulation of the instincts of the masses. But he at present has preferred to say what he considers right, what he sees for the salvation of Russia, for Russian freedom and for the working class itself, and thus he is cast aside as superfluous. At present a "scientific socialism" is not needed, nor is an "idealistic socialism" needed. Socialism has become abased and disbarred. Class hatred and greed are what is necessary. Plekhanov appeals for the defense of the fatherland, and this demands sacrifices and hence cannot be acceptable with those, who veil over their customary abstemption under the guise of internationalism. But this will not last for long. The people will soon sober up and demand real spiritual and material a nourishing. It will have need of those, who will tell it the truth and will enlighten it. The question of socialism is not a question of politics and the struggle for power, this -- is a question of the social organising of constructive labour, a question of social culture. The Social Democrats and the Social Revolutionaries up til now have been concerned with the organising of the working masses for the political struggle to gain power and the growth of the revolution, and therefore they have been disinclined for positive social tasks. The "growth of the revolution" -- against whom directed is unknown, and it is time to make the transition to social creativity.

The Mobilisation of Interests

(1917 - 272)[1]

I.

The revolutionary turnabout has evoked in Russia a mobilisation of interests, which all more and more is growing and threatens to turn into a genuine orgy. The great turnabout nowise occurred under the standard of these or those special interests, in it there was nothing of class or greed. But that which they term as the "continuing of the revolution" and which essentially is its disintegration, is posited exclusively under the standard of special interests and greed. In the modern "continuance of the revolution" it is impossible already to discern any idealistic motifs. If the revolution itself in its first days was a manifestation of the unity of Russia and within it was active the spirit of self-salvation and self-liberation of the entire people, then with the ultimate course of the revolution is a manifestation of division in Russia, its breaking up into parts, with part contending against part. It started with this, that the whole people, the whole nation rose up against the old powers. This revolt was wrought in the name of an united Russia, in the name of the free self-determination of the entire people. But in its ultimate course, in the revealing of its vile element, the revolution has been transformed into an entire series of partialised uprisings, the uprising of one part against another, of one interest against another interest. There cannot be a transition to a creative and constructive effort without the strength of a national cohesion and state rescuing. All more and more the moral unity of the people is falling apart and hence subjects to danger the very existence of an unified and great state, which is impossible without a minimum amount of such moral unity. In our times without hypocrisy it is impossible to deny the very fact of the existence of opposed class interests and the inevitability of class struggle in a sinful mankind. A naive and sentimental idealism, ignoring this severe fact, hiding from reality, is to be

---

[1] MOBILIZATSIYA INTERESOV. Article originally published in the weekly "Russkaya svoboda", 17 jul. 1917, № 12-13, p. 3-7.

met with all more and more rarely, and now would be inopportune, and in this justly can be glimpsed both its limitation, and its desire to evade responsibility. But the struggle of elementary interests has to be subsumed to higher and uninterruptible realities, to the realities of the whole, the realities of the nation, the realities of the state, to the ontological reality of truth and the good, which in the final end cannot compel one to sympathise only for the tragic fate of people, of groups and peoples. When a people has gone too far in its betrayal of the realities of truth and the good, then these realities turn against that people and inflict upon it the fate of a series of grievous trials and misfortunes. The raging struggle between private interests sooner or later has to meet up with not a sentimental idealism, which is not terrible for it and evokes merely a smirk, but rather with realities more severe, than any private interest, with the realities of an higher degree of being, in the final end with the reality of God Himself, from whom there is nowhere to flee.

And insofar as the ideologies of the private and class interests do not want to take into account the higher realities, they -- are naive and short-sighted; their adherents are afflicted with blindness and they live with self-deceptions and illusions, and their realism -- is illusory and superficial, and facing them is a grievous and painful collision with a realism that is genuine, of deeper an actuality. The severe trudging on of history has still not ended, the masses of mankind have still not escaped the need to live under the law, and the mission of the state has not yet been fulfilled to accomplish its purpose. The primitive chaos yet stirs within the depths of human nature and has not yet been transformed into cosmos, and when this chaos emerges from beneathe the grip of norm-based law, mankind is thrown backwards. The realm of a graced freedom is a realm beyond-law, beyond-state, and not contra-law, not contra-state; it is not a return to the pre-state and chaotic existence. To abolish every law for human society is possible to an higher Divine freedom, but not anarchy, which always merely hinders the completion of the law. The objective reality of the state will deal a grievous blow to those, who deny it in the name of private interests, in the name of conditions, standing lower, and not higher than the nature of the state, and this incontrovertible, as a fact. In the nature truly of the state, independent of the forms of governance, is a moment mystical, and as regards the inner structure of the world, the possibility does not obtain that immature people can abolish it and administer ultimately at their own caprice, in the name of their chaotic instincts. In the finest

Russian people there has always been a profound striving for the realm of grace, the realm of freedom, for the Kingdom of God. But terrible and ruinous is a confusing of this higher kingdom with the lower chaotic realms, into Russian people so easily slide into. The chaotic element easily takes hold of Russian people in the masses, as something standing lower, and not higher than the state, and it bewitches them. The person, set afront the dissolute element, fails among us to possess spiritual tempering and grounding, it is captivated by the "mystical" element and drowns within it.

II.

It is a victory still, when individual people and social groups pursue their own private and selfish interests and are yet conscious of this as their sin and weakness or as something rather impersonal and neutral. But the genuine woe begins then, when the dominance of classes and private interests are advanced to the rank of truth, right and good, when the mobilisation of interests is conceived as an higher form of justice, as the source of all moral values. From religious life it is well known, that the devil is not so terrible when seen in his diabolical visage, but is the more terrible, when he appears under the deceptive guise of some saint or angel, when he is charming under the guise of something good. And the Anti-Christ likewise has to captivate people through their confusing of him with Christ, in that his image be twofold, including a seemingly Christ-like visage. In democracy and socialism there is likewise a twofold image. The material interests of individual people and entire groups possess a relative right to existence in this sinful world, they possess a relative right to existence in the struggle for these interests and for the improvement of their material position. But to see in the struggle for material interests some highest truth and ultimate aim, to render absolute so relative and subordinate a thing -- this already is terrible a lie and great temptation. But this exactly at present is occurring in Russia. In the mobilisation of interests is seen some sort of a realisation of the kingdom of God. The devil has appeared under the captivating guise of justice and good. The Russian people is being corrupted by a very ugly lie, by the lie of its selfish interests, to which are ascribed all the attributes of an higher truth and justice. In the social hatred, to which the mobilisation of interests leads, they want to see the pledge of a speedy realisation, as yet unseen in the world, of a righteous societal aspect. The mobilisation of interests provides ultimate a triumph to a very unscrupulous and unabashed demagoguery.

Many events of recent years and recent weeks suggest serious dangers for the soul of the Russian people, for its moral health. Two significant historical events have happened -- the war and the revolution. And here at first the war began the mobilisation of interests, and then the revolution mobilised anew the interests. Both in the war, and in the revolution there were many that wanted to get rich. The thirst for increased profits and wages overspread too wide a circle. There occurred a mobilisation of interests, but there did not occur a mobilisation of responsibility, a mobilisation of patriotic feelings, the mobilisation of higher ideas of moral and religious an order, the mobilisation of all the powers of truth within Rus'. Russians readily give in to dreams, to illusions and self-deceptions, they readily become captivated with the possibility of a quick realisation upon earth of an ultimate kingdom of justice and a social paradise, but there fails to take hold upon them the more austhere virtues, the more valiant and responsible virtues. Constructive work fails to entice Russian people, they all blame it on the catastrophic leap from the realm of necessity into the realm of freedom. The Russians are corrupted by autonomy, morally distorted by too lengthy a period of slavery, for too long accustomed to lay all the blame on others, upon the rulers and those in power, with the baleful shadow of the past obscuring our present and future. In contrast to the lies now holding sway it has to be straight out said, that in the Russian people there is a fateful lack of integrity, and this lack is connected with the long existence under slavery. The lack of integrity and the total absence of feelings of responsibility and duty readily get excused among us by the social ideologies, which spew poisonous lies to the masses of the people. The mobilisation of interests evokes a complimentary movement of lies. The intelligentsia betray their purpose of being an independent and free organ of higher awareness and of higher a culture of spirit. With us is to be discerned a fatal lack of moral courage, an incapacity to oppose the dissolute elements, to condemn that which now prevails. Russians tend so readily to come under the spell of every element, and in the ambiguous forms of the dissolute element they but poorly distinguish light from darkness, truth from life. Among us there is no great love for truth, for a sense of right within societal life, for honesty irregardless. And the Russian people is in need at present of the sort of the

Old Testament prophets, who would accuse them out of love for them in the name of faith in its higher purpose.

III.

A totally unrestricted and totally unsubordinated mobilisation of interests can lead to the moral downfall of the Russian people, to the atomisation of the Russian state, to the disintegration of Russian society. The state and society will break up into splintered parts, reversing a thousand year process. All want to grab for themself the most that is possible, to rip off anything not firmly nailed down, to take advantage of the passing revolutionary condition for their own selfish ends -- be it of class, of nationality, profession, group, district, and individual people. There is occurring an unabashed exploitation of the revolution, vampire-like in regard to it. Such a mobilisation of interests is anti-social as regards its nature, in it perishes not only the person, but also society, in it disintegrate even classes as a whole, since classes also demand a certain self-restraint, of sacrifice by the part in the name of the whole. From all sides are heard outcries for unity in the name exclusively of their own interests, for an awareness and assertion of their own interests, to a leading forth of their own awareness and their ideologies into compliance with their own interests. Even the representatives of spiritual labour and spiritual creativity call for an awareness of their own interests, for uniting and organisation in the name of the struggle for these interests. Thus with the higher intelligentsia of the land, with its higher cultural stratum, they want to deprive it of its genuine vocation to be an organ of national awareness in objective a spirit rather than expressing a subjective interest. The infection has taken hold with all ever newer circles and threatens to destroy in Russia every unselfish movement, every objective idea, every truth. Soon sucking infants will unite in the name of their interests and put forth their demands. School children already in the second grade have been called to a meeting for an awareness of their interests and for an uniting on the basis of these interests. In this orgy there tends to fall apart the soul of the people and the soul of a man. And the salvation from this can only be in the arising of a strong re-centring movement, re-centring of both the soul of the individual man, and the soul of the whole people.

But meanwhile there are not heard calls for a mobilisation of unselfishness, for a mobilisation of ideas, a mobilisation of conscience and reason. The mobilisation of interests in the era of a great revolution and terrible war signifies a poverty of idea and lack of inspiration. And indeed no sort of great ideas tend to guide our revolutionary movement, it is relegated to the whim of the wisp. All the time is sensed a belching forth of the old Russian nihilism. The appeals, apparently, for such lofty things, as peace and the brotherhood of peoples, are likewise indeed not matters idealistic, they are based rather upon the mobilisation of interests, the mobilisation of interests of weariness, the interests of a calm and content life, the interests of a speedy parceling out of land and wealth, upon the fear of everything, that would demand heroism and self-sacrifice. The demand for a speedy peace based however upon the poorly comprehended international interests of the workers. The demand of a speedy realisation of socialism totally oriented towards selfish interests and the manipulations of demagogues upon these interests. There is no one demanding a spiritual upsurge and spiritual rebirth. But I want to believe, that the mobilisation of interests -- is temporary and not deep. And if it proves deeper, wider and prolonged, then for the Russian people will ensue a spiritual death. A great people during the most answerable days of its history cannot exist without a great idea, without a spiritual shining forth, it risks dying from spiritual starvation. Such an idea cannot be that of any sort of special interests, even the most just interests of the workers. And if the Russian revolution has to be prolonged, then not on behalf of a socialistic revolution, which at present is impossible and in which the socialists themself do not believe, but rather on behalf of a spiritual revolution, of a spiritual renewal of the Russian people, a freeing of it from that infectious illness, which at present lacerates it. The salvation can only be sought in the depths, and not on the superficial surface. And the day of salvation will come, perhaps, after quite grievous and terrible tribulations. On this day an unifying love will win out in the soul of the people, will win out over the divisive hatred.

Truth and Lie within Societal Life

(1917 - #269)[1]

I.

During the final years before the Revolution we were smothered with lies. The provocation was made at the instigation of the Russian statecraft of the Old Regime. The atmosphere was thick with betrayal. Azefovism, Rasputinism, Sukhomlinovism -- all this poisoned the life of the people and rotted the Russian state. In the final months before the turnabout, the muddled air became intolerable, it was impossible to breathe, and everything became ambiguous. The image of the old powers became twofold. The Old Regime a long time already had lived by the lie. It continued to exist through inertia, and the passivity of the people sustained it. The moral disintegration had reached unprecedented dimensions. Amongst those active for the old power in the final period of its existence it was difficult to encounter people with a clear human image, such people comprised the exception and they did not long last. In the hours of the finish of the Russian tsarism, it was surrounded by the likes of Grigorii Rasputin, the Sukhomlinovi, the Shtiurmeri, the Protopovi, the Voeikovi, the Manusevichi-Manuilovi and suchlike, duplicitous and nebulous figures. The old Russian monarchy drowned in its muck, in its lies, in its wont for betrayal and provocations. It not so much was overthrown, as rather that it disintegrated and collapsed. The Russian Revolution was not so much the result of an accumulation of creative powers, of creative impulses towards new life, as rather the result of an accumulation of negative conditions, of processes of rot in the old life. This facilitated the triumph of the Revolution in its initial days and gave it a strong push in its ultimate course. The destructive powers seized the upper hand over the creative powers. The sickness seemed too far-gone, its consequences passed over into the new Russia, and they remain active, like an inner poison. The Revolution in its accomplishments of an elementary

---

[1] PRAVDA I LOZH' V OBSCHESTVENNOI ZHIZNI. Article originally published in the weekly Journal "Narodopravstvo", № 4, p. 7-9.

political freedom has come too late, and namely because in it there prevails a social maximalism, which always is the result of the unpreparedness of the masses, beset by darkness. The storm has abated, it was irreversible and was sent down by Providence. But the atmosphere has not cleared. For us it is no easier to breathe after the revolutionary storm, the air has not become clear and lucid, the muck remains, and as before there prevail ambiguous and duplicitous figures, though also in new guises, the lie as before reigns in our societal life, the wont for betrayal and provocation has not been removed, although Sukhomlinov and Shtiurmer sit in prison. The old people, entangled in lies and having lost their moral centre, appear in new attire and veil themselves behind new words. As before there are no people for truth, there is no acknowledgement of the self-sufficiency and absolute value of truth, something which cannot be sacrificed away for any sort of utilitarian and greedy aims, parties, classes or persons.

There are mouths, spouting hatred and contempt for Nicholas II, that formerly spoke about "the God-given monarch", about fidelity and service to the tsar. Much of this, that never was sacred, was transformed into a conditional lie, and the words had lost their real content. All the frightful part was in this, that long ago already the "God" aspect being honoured was not God, but rather "Caesar", and this transgressing of a basic commandment, this fashioning for oneself idols of every sort upon the earth, this idolatry has poisoned the life of the Russian people. But here the old idol of autocracy has been cast down and trampled in the dirt. Just as always happens, the crowd, shortly before worshipping it, now tramples it underfoot. But after the casting down of the old idols, have we become free of all idolatry, from everywhere honouring as God the Kingdom of Caesar? No, we have not become free of such. There have arisen new idols, which have been set up higher than the truth of God. The idol-worship, which always is a betrayal of the Living God, has remained, it has but assumed new forms. There has begun a new fashioning of idols, there has appeared many a new idol and earthly little-gods, -- "Revolution", "Socialism", "Democracy", "Internationalism", "Proletariat" etc. All these idols and little-gods belong the same to the kingdom of "Caesar", just as did the old idol of the tsar's autocracy, and upon them are bestown godly honours. The realm of Caesar in a Christian, Gospel sense of the word is not some sort of perpetual autocracy, monarchy, connected unfailingly with tsar or emperor, it is broader and more varied, and to it also can belong a democratic realm. Around the worship of new idols in the Kingdom of

Caesar there has already well accumulated many a lie and murkiness. The new idolatry, just like the old, screens out the sunlight of truth. Never does the idol-worship proceed along gratis for the moral nature of man and the people, it morally cripples and maims by way of the lie. Man, in worshipping something on earth in place of God, already ceases distinguishing truth from falsehood, he is rendered obsessed, he -- becomes a slave of temporal relative things, in the name of which everything becomes permissible.

II.

Revolution is but a moment within the life of a people, a temporary function, a passing and transitory condition, through which it can pass over to an higher and free life, but always sickly and onerous, evoked by the piling up of the old evil. When some whatever the man lances a festering boil, then it would be terrible to acknowledge this as something most luminous and divine in the man, and to substitute replacing the man himself with this moment in the developement of the process of sickness within him. But with us namely this is the process occurring in relation to the Revolution, which is but the opening up of a festering boil on the body of Russia. The transforming of the Revolution itself into a god and bestowing upon it the honouring of a god is a repulsive idol-worship, a forgetting of the true God. This is no better, than to worship Caesar as an idol, it is of the same nature. Russia previously replaced dynasties, which led it to make sacrifices; now Russia has it replaced by the revolution, which likewise will cause it to make sacrifices. If the "God-given monarchy" is transformed into a repulsive and ugly lie, than in suchlike a lie it can be transformed into a "God-given revolution", if it does not become subject to an higher truth. Truth however stands higher than all the changes into the Kingdom of Caesar, in it [i.e. truth] there is nothing ambiguous, wavering and variable, it is lodged by God Himself within the human heart, and its discernment is a foremost task and most accurate path to a new and free life. Idolatry always precipitates down into the realm of lies and enslaves one. And we are already situated in a quite terrible slavery of lies. An innumerable quantity of lies has poisoned the awareness of the people, the heart of the simple people in the dark, those little ones, and dimmed their minds. Formerly, before the Revolution the people were poisoned by one lie, now they are poisoned by another lie. Demagoguery is a lie, elevated into a principle, into a guiding principle of life. The demagogue considers every lie appropriate to the attaining of his goals, for enticing the masses. All the revolutionary-socialistic phraseology of our day is being transformed all more and more into a conditional lie, similar to the lie from that phraseology, upon which rested the Old Regime. Those, who hide themselves behind the veils of lofty words about the sanctity of the Fatherland, the state and the Church, too often in fact have betrayed the Fatherland, undermined the state and surrendered the Church into the grip of the dark powers. And thus do many of those deal with the Divine value of freedom, veiling themselves under the new revolutionary phraseology. The real significance and the real weight of words is lost, since behind these words stand the human souls of scoundrels.

"Dark and irresponsible influences" the same thus begin to govern the revolution, just as they had governed the old ruling powers. Betrayal, provocation and cruel greed thus veil themselves the same behind loud slogans of "Internationalism", "Revolutionary Socialism" etc., just as earlier they had been veiled behind loud slogans of "Monarchism", "True-Russian Patriotism" etc. Bolshevism has too much in common with Rasputinism and the Black Hundreds. The Reds and the Blacks in the colours of the masses has ultimately gotten all jumbled together. Even prior to the Revolution one tended to hear from respected Social-Democrats, that in the midst of Bolshevism it was difficult to distinguish the revolutionaries from the provocateurs and traitors. The moral principle itself in revolutionary maximalism is such, that it makes difficult any distinctions, since everything is declared permissible for revolutionary aims and truth is not considered essential. There coalesces an underground atmosphere, an apprehensive fear of light. In this atmosphere Azeph flourished. This atmosphere was always muddled with the security forces, with the departments of the police, with murky underground Court influences. This underground and ambiguous atmosphere did not disappear after the turnabout, it passed over into the new and free Russia, where thee ought not to be such a place for underground intrigues. The conveyers of this atmosphere were primarily Bolsheviks. The disclosures, which were made after 4 July about the German espionage, about the treason and betrayal among those, who called themselves internationalists and the solely true Bolshevik-Socialists, tend to have too much in common with what was revealed about Myasoedov and Sukhomlinov, and with what fell out surrounding the name Shtiurmer and the German party at Court. It reeked in spirit. We have not gotten free nor cleansed, we are all still in slavery to the dark powers, we are all still languishing in the underground. The Revolution has undergone a moral corruption, its idealistic elements have been squeezed out and fallen into slavery to dark ambiguous elements. The nihilism from the right and the nihilism from the left -- are of the selfsame nature.

III.

In the name of "Revolution" now is permitted the same sort of lie, as earlier was permitted in the name of "Monarchy". The prestige of the idol is set higher than the truth, the simple and in its simplicity Divine truth. The Revolution has not freed us from the false guarding of the prestige of the prevailing powers, it demands the guarding of its own prestige foremost of all. And this provides the push onto the path of falsehood. The new, the free life will begin in Russia only then, when in the name of truth, set uppermost, there is the consent to sacrifice every prestige, every conditional lie, -- of the Revolution, just as with the Monarchy. Let reign the prestige of truth itself, which with all its powers ought to be revealed in the heart of the people, and let vanish every falsehood, all the conditional phraseology! It is time already to loudly declare, that the lie with its principle has poisoned the Russian freedom and plunged us into slavery. The Socialist parties with their maximalist bent have from their very start permitted the lie for the guarding of their own prestige, the prestige of the Revolution, since they worshipped not God but an idol. Many a lie and untruth has begun to hold sway in Russian life. All these demagogic cries about the "bourgeoise", "bourgeoisness" and "bourgeois", to which also have been enumerated all thinking and educated Russia, all these inquests into "bourgeois countre-revolution" from the very start have been an ugly lie. Beyond pushing off from the coasts and sailing the sea, the bourgeoise of the Russian peasant-kingdom do not in any genuine and precise sense of the word play any role amongst us. Such still faces a progressive developement. The real danger, countre-revolution, threatens exclusively from the side of the Bolsheviks and anarchists. Reasonable and respectable Socialists finally begin to perceive this, but they do not want to loudly talk about this out of fear of causing a loss of prestige for revolutionary socialism. There was an ugly lie in the assertion, that the war was being waged exclusively in the name of the grasping interests of an international bourgeoise, led by P. N. Miliukov. And this then, when it involved the matter of the elementary defense of the Fatherland and its honour. There was an ugly lie in the veiling over of desertion and quite greedy egoism with loud words about internationalism and the brotherhood of peoples. All this lie undermined the army and prepared for us an unheard of scandal of treason and flight from the field of conflict. An ugly lie -- was in the assertion, that the human mass as it were could exist and fulfill its duty without state, churchly or cultural discipline. The masses, having returned to the natural state, are transformed into disorderly mobs and in the final end into beastly hordes. It is an ugly lie to term as socialism the greedy and grasping interests of the elemental masses, not subject to any sort of a common and higher truth. An ugly lie is in the view, that the Petrograd events of 4 July have no direct connection with the Bolsheviks, and that the responsibility for this rests upon the emergence of some sort of countre-revolutionary elements and even upon the withdrawal of the Cadet ministers. It is an ugly lie that cries out, that the People's Freedom Party -- is bourgeois, that it defends the interests of the capitalists, and that in it is lodged the seeds of countre-revolution. Honestly and as regards the actual reality, this party can as it were be accused of a certain academism, an over-reliance upon external constitutional forms, a clumsiness in attracting to itself the broader masses, in evoking any passionate responses from them, and in insufficient strength and will. This -- is the party of a legislative idealism, the least greedy of our parties, clean of any demagoguery, but suffering with party bureaucratism. In its composition, the Cadet Party is the party of the utmost Intelligentsia of the land, of professors and Zemstvo members, while any "bourgeois" elements in the precise sense of the word play in it but an insignificant role. It is an ugly lie to confess the principles of democracy, to demand a Constituent Assembly, while deciding everything prior to the Constituent assembly and without out. The revolutionary Socialistic Democracy prior to the Constituent Assembly, i.e. without the will of the sovereign people, is deciding the form of governance, the agrarian question, regional autonomy and suchlike basic questions. But the truth consists in this, that for revolutionary socialism altogether unneeded are the principles of democracy and unneeded is the Constituent Assembly, since it represents a danger for any purely class party, because it subordinates every class to the will of the nation. And it is the Cadets namely that appear at present to be the most consistent democrats. There is the falsehood too in proclaiming maximal social slogans, the actual and real achievement of which there is no belief in, and which are proclaimed only for attracting the masses. There is an ugly lie in bowing down to the mass elements of the Revolution, to seek in it itself the criteria of truth and right and to term as countre-revolutionary every attempt to subordinate this mass element to criteria of truth and right, such as is independent of the capriciousness of the human masses. It is a lie -- to proclaim freedom and at every step to impede it. An heap of lies forms the murkiness in the revolutionary atmosphere. Only the truth, independent of rapid shifts by days and hours, and not dependent upon the inconstant instincts of the masses, can set us free. Politics has been poisoned by falsehood, with some -- for craven ends, and with others -- for ends more lofty, but still bereft of a moral basis. All this leads to an awareness of the eternal truth, that the rebirth of a people cannot be exclusively external and material-social, that it has to be first of all an inward changing of the soul of a people, a victory within it of truth over the lie, of God over mere idols, with a spiritual restoration of the health of the human person. The voice of truth and a basic moral instinct compel one to admit, that in the present threatening hour what matters is the saving of our native-land, the saving of Russia, and not the Revolution, and that the governance of a national salvation can only be of such a government, in which are included representatives of all the groups, and all the parties, and not the party of a single class, which cannot hold the trust of the nation. The politics of a governance of national salvation can only be a politics of all the nation in common.

The Triumph and Crash of Populism

(1917 -273)[1]

I.

One can view the Russian revolution and its developement as a triumph of populism. Our revolution is not rich with original ideas, but if there is some sort of ideology inspiring it, then certainly it would be the vintage ideology of Russian populism. This is not immediately apparent, since deceptively it can seem as variously derived from the German doctrine, very widespread amongst us. But a more perceptive look would catch sight of the totally Russian and Eastern element behind the socialism triumphing among us, tongue-tied as it were, lacking the ability to adequately express itself. The whole Western world has to be amazed, that the most backward, the most reactionary Russian realm, the age old bulwark of monarchism, should suddenly with the quickness of a lightning flash be transformed into a most extreme democratic realm, almost to the point of a socialistic realm. In revolutionary Russia there is occurring an unprecedented outpouring of socialism and there is nowhere that the socialistic slogans have not triumphed. On the outside, Russia over the course of several weeks has outstripped the most advanced European lands. Russians are proud, that they -- are the most advanced people in the world, the most democratic people, that the example of the bourgeois European peoples holds no weight with them, that they are the ones instead teaching the West and sooner than the West they are realising the ideals of socialism. The radical and democratic People's Freedom Party has proven with us to be on the extreme right, almost reactionary to the extent of "bourgeois", and hence not safe in our days to set out under its flag. It is a phenomenon -- quite totally Eastern, and hence for the West difficult to understand. The Social Democrats -- were extreme Westerners, having

---

[1] TORZHESTVO I KRUSHENIE NARODNICHESTVA. Article originally published in the weekly "Russkaya svoboda", 31 jul. 1917, № 14-15, p. 3-7.

borrowed from the West their teaching, always denying any originality for Russia, and suddenly they are transformed into a peculiar type of Slavophils, confessing a sort of Russian socialistic messianism, believing in light from the East, which would spread its rays into the bourgeois darkness of the West. The Western teaching about evolution, about steps of developement, about the significance of the developement of industry and culture for all the social accomplishments was forgotten. With the Russian Social Democrats nothing has remained of Marxism, besides the faith in the exclusive mission of an all powerful proletariat. Quite wide circles have proven in the grips of the faith of the exclusive democratic and socialistic messianism of the Russian people, in its calling to be the first to realise a social paradise. And this in a land industrially and culturally very backward, where the masses of the people in a significant portion are illiterate, bereft of an elementary enlightenment, having no sort of nurturing nor preparation as citizens. But the Russians believe in a social miracle and they do not want to know about the laws, under which other peoples live. In the Russian revolutionary element blazes a faith, that the Heavenly Jerusalem suddenly is come down upon the Russian land. In this is expressed the age old Russian faith in a miraculous leap, by which is to be attained social righteousness and social bliss without the historical toil and prolonged efforts. And this is an expression of the age old Russian passivity, the Russian dislike for the responsible involvement in history, of the Russian femininity, of the old customary habit of Russian man, for whom someone has to do everything.

  The ideology of the Russian revolution, insofar as it can be discovered behind the orgy of special interests and dark instincts, is based upon a faith in the people, in its truth and wisdom, in an idealisation of the people, as the common people, as the toiling class, as workers and peasants, and not as a complete whole, not as a mystical organism. And the ideology of our revolution is pervaded by a deep mistrust towards culture, towards creative construction, towards personal initiative and personal responsibility, towards the significance of the qualitative in societal life. The suspicious and hostile attitude of the masses finds its sanctions in the revolutionary mindset. In the revolt of the quantitative against the qualitative is seen a democratic truth. This is all characteristic of the age old Russian populism, of the populist psychology and populist ideas, formerly mere daydreams, but now acted out and applied to life. There is occurring a populist experiment of enormous proportions. Populism does not believe in the culture of the person and has no desire to adapt it to itself, it believes only in the people's collectives. This -- is a peculiar sort of pseudo-Sobornost', a pseudo-churchliness, a substitute for the Church as the sole true collective. Can it be said, that this Russian people's collective is an utmost step of existence, can it be believed, that it will outstrip Europe, with its constrictive norms of bourgeois culture? In this, apparently, have believed not only our socialist-populists, but also our Social Democrats, and in this also various Russian writers and thinkers want to believe, in their inclination to go with the prevailing currents. And this is a very great Russian temptation, a temptation of a social miracle, a Russian self-deception and illusion, a dreamy nonsense, which faces an harsh awakening.

II.

The Russian revolutionary populism is bound up with the past, and not with the future, the populist illusions -- are offspring of the old, and not of the new Russia. The Russian socialism now spilling forth and raging is not the creativity of new life, -- in it there is felt the age old lack of will in the Russian people, the Russian irresponsibility, the insufficient disclosure in Russia of the personal principle, of personal creativity, of the forever submersion in the primordial collectivism, a collectivism deriving from the natural condition. At the basis of Russian socialism lies the Russian extensive economy and the Russian extensive frame of character. And therefore the pathos of Russian socialism is on the order of a pathos of division and distribution, never the pathos of creation and the constructive. The transition to socialism among us is not thought of, as a transition to an intensive culture. Not only with the socialist-populists, but also with the Social Democrats, the intensification of culture is completely set aside to the secondary plane and lacks inspiration. The cause of social misfortunes and Russian woes is too exclusively wont to be sought in the wicked will of people, in the bourgeois and possessing classes, and never is it sought in the low level of the culture, in the weak degree of the mastery of the elemental forces of nature. The Russian Social Democrats always had a very poor grip on that side of Marxism, which lays down at the basis of social progress the developing of industrial productive powers, but they very well got a grip on the other side, with the preaching of class hatred. For Russian socialism, the agrarian question was always a question of a redistribution of the land, and not a question about the raising of the culture of the village economy. The Russian revolutionaries and socialists consider themself as not "bourgeois", in that they had weak instincts about production, and were exclusively caught up in the social morals of distribution. To tie in the growth of the people's well-being with the growth of the productivity of labour and with the intensification of culture with us always has been regarded as "bourgeois". The social problem has transformed itself for us into the problem of an investigation of these "villains" and "rogues", these "bourgeois types", from whom all the evil happens. The exclusive moralism leads to morally ugly results and it paralyses the sense of personal responsibility. The objective and constructive side of the social problem completely vanishes. Socialism then conceives of itself not as tasks of the regulation of elemental natural forces, not as an harmonisation of the whole, but rather as class hatred and divisiveness.

The extensive and widespread nature of Russian socialism suggests the thought, that in Russian socialism quite much has to be disregarded on account of the remnants of the primordial condition of the primitive democracy, of that village communism, from which started the developement of peoples. Russia always was and has remained a vast peasant realm, a land of ploughmen, a land of an extended economy and an extended culture, with undeveloped backward classes and conditions, with an insufficiently differentiated sense of person, with a non-expression of activeness and self-initiative. Although Russia long since already has entered upon the path of capitalist industrialism, it has not been rendered a "bourgeois" land, it has not passed over as yet to a more intensive form of economy and to a more differentiated social structure. The alarmist shouts of recent days about the "bourgeoise" and "bourgeoisness" are a jumble of demagoguery and ignorance. The role of the "bourgeoise" in Russia is all still completely insufficient, it still does not exist among us in the genuine and European sense of the word. This is perhaps to be explained, in that only of late have we won political freedom. Everything comes down to this enormous grey mass of the peasantry, bound up with the land and with dreams about redistribution of the land. Russian tsardom was by its nature a peasant-democratism. It was supported by the same peasantry, which at present on the outside is tempted by socialism, though also not for long. Neither the gentry, nor the bourgeoise have played an underlying role among us, and in Russia therefore there has not developed a societal and political self-initiative. The uppermost cultural segment among us always was very slender, it did not go deep, and was easy to destroy. The hostility towards the "educated" on the part of the Black Hundredists and the Bolsheviks has one and the same source and one and the same nature, this -- is the hostility of an extensivist mental frame of reference, thirsting for division, an hostility towards all creative intensiveness. The peasant realm earlier on expected everything from the tsar, and now it is prepared to expect everything from the fictitious being, named socialism, but the psychology remains the same, passive and anti-cultural. And the whole future of Russia depends on the raising of culture within the peasantry, a culture both spiritual and material.

III.

The Russian leftist intelligentsia in its broad masses has always situated itself in slavery to the peasant realm, and it bowed as before an idol to "the people". And now occurs the payback for this. Those, who comprise now to the utmost an orderly and corrective party of populist socialists, -- are typical of the populist intelligentsia. But they are already being boycotted, and the socialists refuse to acknowledge them. Revolutionary populism in its fruits is devouring itself. Populism at present is triumphant, it has become the dominant religion. But in this triumph there is also at the same time the crash of populism, its end, its death of idea. The experience from life has proven, that there are no sort of grounds to believe in the empirical people, in the quantitative masses, that its worship is but idolatry and leads to the extinguishing of spirit, to a betrayal of the living God. The people should believe in God and should serve Him; it is impossible to believe in the people and it is impossible to serve it. Worship is proper only for qualities, never for quantities. The people has to be lifted to an higher spiritual and overall culture, in the people there has to be revealed the human person, its qualities, its responsible creativity. The experience of the Russian revolution confirms the truth of "Vekhi". Those intelligentsia, who so fiercely assailed "Vekhi", now by bitter experience are quick to know and acknowledge this truth. In the enormous mass of the people, the peasants and workers, has been revealed not an utmost truth, but rather still dark instincts. The pressure of the dark peasant realm threatens the Russian state and Russian culture with a qualitative lowering, with the disintegration of attained values, and the responsibility for this not upon the people itself, which strives towards the light and is blameless for having so long been in the grip of darkness, and now suddenly, has had set before it impossible tasks. The responsibility falls first of all upon the revolutionary intelligentsia, with its idolatry towards the people, an intelligentsia which cannot be a source of light. And least of all right are those, who want to give this populism a religious hue.

Christianity calls for belief not in the quantitative masses, but in the Divine image within man, which can become obscured and plunge into darkness, and which mustneeds be revealed through the arduous path of religious effort and spiritual culture. Only by the surmounting of the initial darkness and beastly image in man will be revealed the image of God. And this is always a matter of quality, and not of quantity. Christianity does not abolish the Old Testament commandments as regards the sinful and still dark and slave-like external nature of mankind. The higher truths of the law, the truths of the state and culture with their norms -- is not a matter of caprice and anarchy, nor is it the return to a primordial and natural condition, but rather a graced freedom, an ascent to a condition which is supra-natural. It is a pernicious mistake to connect Russian populism with Russian Christianity, -- since it is the sooner bound up with the age old Russian paganism, with the enslaving of the Christian revelation of the person by the Russian element of the earth. The Russian socialism and collectivism, which to many seem so original and which evoke a distorted chauvinistic feeling, is essentially a remnant of primitive naturalism, of a primitive communism, in it there is the sense of an as yet incomplete liberation from the state of the horde. The arising of a cultural and progressive socialism lies still ahead for us. Meanwhile for us there is the triumph of a reactionary socialism, bound up with just as chauvinistic a self-conceit, as there was with our Black Hundredists, as there was with our old nationalism. And meanwhile the originality of Russian socialism is expressed first of all in this, that it lowers the productivity of labour, i.e. it throws everything backwards. The whole task of Russia is in this, that within it should be revealed the qualitatively higher and more free life of the person and that every new collectivism should proceed through the cleansing fire of personal rebirth and uplift. The originality of Russia cannot consist in that it should forever remain in the condition of a natural primitive collectivism. Russia has to proceed through a personal culture and discover within it its originality and uniqueness. The populism henceforth can still inspire no one, it has become transformed from a pretty dream into a grievous reality, and it is experiencing the last of its days. After sobering up, there has to begin the severe tempering of the person, a passing over to responsible creative work. The worship should be to the One Living God, and not to earthly idols. It should be understood, that the people needs enlightenment, and not the fawning before it. And the new Russia ahead will be born only after the surmounting of the old populism, after the inner victory over the old slave-like psychology.

The Populist and the Nationalist Consciousness

(1917 - 274)[1]

I.

It is now very timely to consider that age old Russian trend and frame of mind, which bears the name of "Populism". At the present hour of Russian history there is occurring a sharp clash of the "populist" consciousness with the "national" consciousness, and the first of these two types is clearly winning out. In the populism there is something very Russian, very national even in its denial of nationality, and it has assumed the most varied forms, from the most religious and mystical down to the most materialistic, from the most rightist down to the most leftist. The extremities for us always merge, our black and our red elements -- are one and the same element. The predominance of the emotional side of human nature, of the life of the feelings over the volitional and thinking side, the denial of law and norms -- are alike characteristic both for our rightist, and for our leftist populism. The Slavophils were populists and so have been the Socialist Revolutionaries, the Tolstoyans and the intelligentsia revolutionaries, who in the decade of the 1870's went to the people, Dostoevsky was a populist and Mikhailovsky was a populist. And the Russian Social Democrats, which began their existence with a struggle against populism, in essence psychologically and morally have remained populists even at present, during the time of the revolution, they remain under the grip of all the populist illusions. "Bolshevism" is, certainly, a revolutionary, anarchistically-rebellious populism. Populism always had a special fascination for the soul of the Russian intelligentsia, and even the greatest Russian geniuses, like Tolstoy and Dostoevsky, could not free themselves from it. A rare exception was in Vl. Solov'ev, who was not a

---

[1] NARODNICHESKOE I NATSIONAL'NOE SOZNANIE. Article was originally published in periodical "Russkaya mysl', 1917, bk. VII-VIII, p. 90-97.

populist. In Russian societal thought over the last decades, a most resolute antagonist against populism has always been P. B. Struve, and in this aspect perhaps it is necessary to search out the reasons for the hostile attitude towards him in certain circles of the intelligentsia. Many consider populism to be that original word, which Russia will say to the world. For some this word -- is Slavophil, for others -- its is Tolstoyan, and for a third group -- it is revolutionary socialistic, but only in a special Russian sense, while for a fourth group it is in a Russian and idealistic sense an anarchistic word. In Russian populism always there is sensed the element of the East, deeply contrary to the Western idea of culture, to Western societal norms. The Russian revolutionaries, the Russian socialists and anarchists, howsoever fanatically they may have confessed Western teachings, always though in their nature were Easterners, and not Westerners. Russian populism -- is anarchistic and feminine, in it there is no masculine mastery of the element, as a formative principle.

The reasons for the rise of Russian populism and its long dominance over the intelligentsia consciousness usually are sought for in the deep and prolonged rift between the upper cultural stratum and those lower down in the life of the people. In the most conscientious part of the cultural stratum there awoke the desire to serve the people and to receive from it truth that is direct and integrally whole, of life, in accord with the rhythm of nature. This became focused into the unique moral framework of the Russian soul, in its wont for sympathy, in its anguish for universal salvation. In the Russian nature there is an eternal tendency towards repentance, and the working of conscience always predominates in it over the working of honour, over the sense of worthiness, such as primarily derives from the Western knight-chivalry. On the outside and historically, the Russian populist mindset was determined first of all by this, that Russia -- is a rustic land, a peasant land, that it for too long was a land of a natural economy, that in it everything still remained under the force of a primieval patriarchal democracy, from which the people had started with its developement, that in it everything still had a primitive tight connection of spirit with the organic matter. Democratism in Russia too often can be attributed to the remnants of the old, and not the birth of the new. Among us, the personal principle never was strongly expressed, and the person tended to sense himself dwelling within a primitive collectivism. Classes as such were little developed and little active, and they tended to form no genuine cultural traditions. Russia thus came to present itself as an obscure peasant kingdom with an autocratic tsar at the head. Our ideology of autocracy itself was essentially populist. Our faith was strong that Russia should forever remain a natural and organic peasants kingdom, which would reveal of itself some higher truth. Our cultural stratum however was very thin, it sensed itself lost in the mysterious immensity of the peasant realm and out of a sense of self-preservation it sought its support in this kingdom, it idealised the element of the people, it attempted to listen in on the people's understanding of truth. The populist feelings and the populist mindset extinguished the creative impulses, they morally poisoned the very wellsprings of the creativity of spiritual culture, since in creativity they saw an avoidance of the fulfilling of duty to the people or a betrayal of the people's truth.

II.

The populism of our intelligentsia's cultural segment was determined not only by the Russian sense of sympathy for the downtrodden and humiliated, not only by a conscientiousness, but also by an insufficiency of spiritual manlihood and spiritual freedom, by the weak developement of a personal sense of worth and independence, by a need to find support outside oneself, a lack of responsibility, to let to others the activity of spirit in the seeking out and determining of truth. Populism in Russia always was a sort of pseudo-Sobornost', a pseudo-churchliness. The Christian Church itself, universal in its nature, received in Russia a sharply populist imprint. The Church defined itself as a Russian peasants church primarily, in it the feminine element of the people prevailed out over the masculine Logos. It fell under the power of the state, since within the people's church the Russian anarchistic principles were stronger than any organising principles, the principles of a true self-administration. The upper religious hierarchy despotically governed the Church, as an officialdom, with a bureaucracy set up by the state power, but never was it a self-governing Church [since the Petrine reforms], never did it play a guiding spiritual role. The Russian populism, if it be taken at depth, was the reverse side of the enslavement of the people, the absence of self-administration in the life of the people, its eternal dependence upon some foreign ruling authority. The servility of spirit was expressed in the populist mindset. For this consciousness, the source of right and truth is revealed not by the Logos, not by the reason and conscience, not by the

Divine within man and within the Church, but by the people empirically, understood as the common folk, as the physically toiling, close to the earth and to nature. Not qualitatively was it necessary to seek out the source of truth, but rather in the quantitative, within the people's majority. Some religiously, and others materialistically sought for truth in the people's wisdom, within the dull grey masses they hoped to discern the truth. The demand for a submersion into the elemental collective -- is characteristically a Russian demand. Through the weakness of consciousness, it is experienced as a demand of religious Sobornost'. With us, the populism passed over into a worship of the people, a bowing down to the empirically given. The people was assumed by us as an empirically given, i.e. as quantity, and not as quality. In this sinned not only the populist-materialists, but also the populist-mystics. With the populists of the second type there was the temptation to see in the people, as a given, the true church. Upon this path, the Church lost sight of its universal quality and fell under the sway of the quantitative empirical given.

Particularly from the churchly and religious point of view, populism has to be acknowledged as a greatest of lies and a substitution: it infringes upon the universal qualitativeness of the Church, and replaces it by a limiting empirical givenness of the people. In this is a danger of the extreme nationalisation of the Church, a transference in identifying it as the people. But it is necessary to finally and irrevocably set down, that the collectivism of the people is not the churchly Sobornost'-communality, and it is as distinct from it, as heaven is from earth. The religious populism turns us away from Christianity back to paganism, to the pagan elementalness and the pagan nationalism. And it is impossible not to see a great truth of Catholicism in this, that it is radically opposed to such a sort of populism, and is incompatible with it. Populism is contrary to spiritual freedom, as revealed within Christianity, and to the utmost self-consciousness of person. The self-consciousness of the person coincides with the universal qualitativeness of the Church, but it incompatible with the idolising of the delimited quantitative aspect of the empirical people. In Eastern Orthodoxy always there has been a great defenselessness against the pretensions of a religious populism. Eastern Orthodoxy has not been able to withstand the danger of its being engulfed by the people's element, just as it has not been able to withstand the danger of being swallowed up by the state. And this fateful fact of our churchly history can be explained only by this, that Eastern Orthodoxy has not properly manifest itself as the

Universal Church, that in it has been a certain deviation from the universal Christianity on the side of particularism and provincialism. The populism is always a provincialism, and it is deeply contrary to universalism.

III.

Truth for the populist consciousness always is within the feelings, never within the reason. Culture thus only obscures the truth, concealed within the people. Culture is grounded upon the non-truth and evil of the inequality of the people. That qualitative stratum, which creates the spiritual culture, stands guilty before the people. Spiritual work for the populist mindset is not of equal value with physical work, it is something lower, and needing to be repented of. Truth always -- is in the simple, and not in the complex. Truth -- is in the totality, and the loss of the totality, a characteristic of the cultural segment, always is a lie. The simple peasant knows more, than the philosopher. For some, within the common people there is the truth, connected with nature, an organic and integral mysticism; for others -- it is the truth, connected with the material conditions of its life, and not benefiting off the physical toil of others. Populism denies a division of labour, it seeks to transfer the division of labour into each human person and to completely abolish it in society, to make all persons equal and alike, making society all the same and simple, bereft of every differentiation, a dull grey. In this attitude as characteristic populists are L. Tolstoy and N. Mikhailovsky, who despite their seeming individualism, have to be admitted as enemies of any individual elevation. For populism, the problem of distribution always overshadows the problem of production, in the spiritual sphere, just as in the material sphere. The upper, the creatively cultural level, building up spiritual values, always for the populist mindset is an apostacy, a loss of the sources of truth. With the simple toiling people there is much suffering, upon the exposing of which one mustneeds direct all one's strength, and there is truth, which of necessity is to be learned from it. Populism however always turns away from history and historical tasks.

For the populist mindset the people is not a complete whole, which would include all the classes, all the groups, all the human persons, and it is not an assemblage of persons, a being, a thousand years living its unique life, in which the past and the future are organically connected and which is not subsumed under any sociological definitions; for this mindset, however, the people is only a part, a social class of the physically toiling, peasants and workers, but most of all and first of all the peasants, while all others are considered to have fallen away from the people, to be apostates from the life of the people. From this social-class perception of the people even those populists are not free, who stand upon a religious soil. The religious populism of the Slavophils always understood by the word people the common-people, true to the old Russian principles and commands, and it quite bound itself up with the material conditions of life, with the peasant obschina-commune, with the natural economy, with a patriarchal democracy. But this is materialism, a chaining down of spirit to organic matter, and this is a naturalism, oriented backwards, towards the remnants of primitive life. In Slavophilism, though, there was also an underlying and different understanding of the people, free of social-class determinations, free of the fetters of the material conditions of life. The Russian people thus is first of all a certain metaphysical unity, a certain mystical organism, the subject of the thousand years of Russian history, indefinable by any sort of social-class structures, nowise bound up in its depths with material conditions. And the Russian people finds its most perfect expression, as a mystical whole, in the Russian geniuses, in Pushkin, with Dostoevsky or Tolstoy, who belonged to the cultural level, and not to the common-people. The people per se is purely a spiritual category. Each Russian man ought to say to himself: I myself am the people, in my own depths, for being of the people is something revealed internally, not externally, and I sense myself as the people and of the people, when I am not at the superficial level but rather at the depths, wherein are stripped off all the class and social trappings, and it is from this depth that sounds the voice of the people. And those, who are situated at the greatest depth and who surmount the surface trappings, these also are a true expression of the people, of the soul of the people. Between the peasant and the gentleman, between the simple worker and the man of utmost culture at this depth there disappears every opposition, they commune in the spirit, in the spirit of the people. I know this through my own experience of interaction with the sectarians. The populist consciousness only but increases the abyss between the "people" and the "intelligentsia", between the "people" and "culture", it fails to discern the spiritual depths in the life of the people, in which vanishes all the differences, connected with the social trappings.

IV.

The populist understanding of the people has long since already been subjected to a sociological analysis. The people in a sociological sense simply does not exist, it breaks down into classes, sub-classes, groups with manifold interests, with manifold psychological outlooks. And the peasantry does not represent any sort of unity in a purely social regard, it is already quite differentiated. Marxism has struck an irreparable blow to the old populist consciousness with its faith in an organic wholeness of the people, bound up with the remnants of a primitive patriarchal democracy in Russia. The people cannot be conceived of materialistically. The people exists authentically only in the metaphysical sense of the word, and this people is deeper than only its social aspects. The people is a mystical organism, which was there a thousand years back, and it dwells in the eternal. In the modern French people with its bourgeois culture we discern the features of the medieval French people with its old-fashioned valour, so vividly flaming up during the time of war, with its old knight-chivalrant culture. And in the modern Russian people we discern features of the people from the Time of Troubles and even from the appanage period, -- of a people, in which good and humility get mixed up with tendencies towards anarchy and discord. There exists one unrepeatably individual visage of the people, which can be distorted, but it cannot be abolished. This people, not subsumable to any sort of sociological definition and analysis, is a nation, and it is recognised as such within a national, rather than populist consciousness. Those expressing and bearing a national mindset have to be of an higher intelligentsia of the entire land, a spiritual aristocracy, comprised of persons of loftier a qualitative level. The populist mindset in the final end has been a bowing before the quantitative, before the simple masses; it relies on faith in the immanent truth of the mass collective, the truth of a subconscious simplicity. Populism is the refusal of all the complex worldly tasks, a refusal of emerging beyond the bounds of the visible horizon, it seek to facilitate matters through simplification. The higher national consciousness has to preserve the created values and to create the new values of the people, as a great historical end; it connects the remote past with the far off future. The value of a Russian great state, won by the Russian people over the course of its long and tortuous history, is conceivable only for a national consciousness and inconceivable for the populist consciousness, which has always had an anarchistic tendency.

Nicholas Berdyaev

The populist mindset regards it fully possible to renounce the significance of the whole of Russian history and to go back to its beginnings, in order to redo all the history anew, but without the untruth of the state and the untruth of the culture. At the bottom of the populist mindset always there lies the feeling, in spurning the state and culture, that they are gotten at too great a price. But if one actually does believe in a subconscious truth of the people, then inevitably it has to be admitted, that the people subconsciously has consented to pay the precious price for the state and culture and has not held back on its sacrifices of a thousand years. Only an extreme rationalism could see in this a violation of the people, an exploitation of the people. The national mindset understands however the place of Russia in the world and its great vocation, there exists for it first of all the whole, and not the parts, it is not indifferent to the greatness and power of Russia. The populist consciousness -- is first of all provincial and narrow and in these features it is a philistine consciousness.

The old reactionary Russian nationalism is finished. A new and creative national mindset is needed, free as it were of the poisoned memories and associations of the past. Facing the national consciousness stands first of all a great creative task, as an obligation, not a given, of which we have had enough and which is but idolatry. The national consciousness has to be free of all chauvinism, from all boastings and conceit. The populism in its deepest sense is no less reactionary, than the old nationalism; it is chained to the past, it hinders the setting free of the spirit. At present this old yet newly revived populism is tearing apart the unity of the Russian revolution, it is destroying the very idea of a single nation and impedes the passage over to the creativity of a new life. Populism gives sanction to that hostility to culture, to education, to people of spirit, which at the present day can transform it into a great national misfortune, no less, than famine, pestilence and invasion of foreigners. It is hostile to everything productive and it thirsts to divide. The new creative national consciousness is being born amongst us amidst torments and tribulations, through discord and division. Only a minority conceives at present of the unity of Russia, the unity of the Russian people, only a minority is oriented to the values of the entire whole. But a minority can be more correct than the majority and it can spiritually win out. Only a spiritual, religious regeneration of Russian democracy can lead it to the awareness of the great, the supra-class values of all the people, can turn it away from special interests to instead truth and right.

The Religious Foundations of Bolshevism

(*From the Religious Psychology of the Russian People*)

(1917-#275)[1]

I.

Such a setting of theme might evoke astonishment. What relationship has Bolshevism to religion? The Bolsheviks, just like the overwhelming majority of the Social Democrats, -- are materialists, positivists, atheists, foreign to them is every religious interest, and they mock at any religious setting of themes. Everyone tends to say, that Bolshevism is a phenomenon totally non-religious and anti-religious. All this is indeed so, if we stay at the surface and regard as conclusive those word formulas, in which people tend to cloak their consciousness. But I think, that the Bolsheviks themself, as so often transpires, know not the final truth about themself, do not perceive, of what sort of spirit they are. To recognise about them a final truth, to recognise, of what sort of spirit they are, is possible only for people of a religious consciousness, endowed with a religious criterion of distinction. And here, I am wont to say, that Russian Bolshevism -- is the manifestation of a religious order, in it are active certain ultimately religious energies, if by religious energy be understood not only that, oriented towards God. A religious substitute, an inverted religion, a pseudo-religion -- is indeed likewise the manifestation of a religious order, in it there is its own absoluteness, its own final end, its own all-encompassing aspect, its own pseudo and phantasmic plenitude. Bolshevism is not merely politics, not simply a social struggle, it is not a partialised and differentiated sphere of human activity. Bolshevism is a state of spirit and a phenomenon of spirit, an entire world-sense and world-outlook. Bolshevism has pretentions to seize upon the whole of man,

---

[1] RELIGIOZNYE OSNOVY BOL'SHEVIZMA. Article originally published in the weekly Journal "Russkaya svoboda", Petrograd-Moskva, 8 aug. 1917, № 16/17.

all his powers, it seeks to give answer to all the questions of man, upon all the human torments. Bolshevism seeks to be not merely some-thing, not merely a part, not some separate sphere of life, but rather the all, and all-encompassing. As a fanatic faith-confession, it does not tolerate anything alongside it, does not want to have anything separate from it, it wants to be the all and in all. Bolshevism indeed is socialism, having reached a religious disposition and a religious exclusiveness. In this it is akin to the French revolutionary syndicalism. In all its formal signs Bolshevism displays religious pretentions, and it is necessary to define, of what sort is this religion, of what sort is the spirit that it conveys with it into the world.

Revolutionary Social Democracy has become subject to a process of fading intensity, of becoming bourgeois, of differentiation, it gradually is becoming transformed into a practical social politics of the evolutionary-reform type. The pathos of revolutionary socialism imperceptibly has become weather-beaten. The European Social Democrats have become cultural people, they have acknowledged such "bourgeois" values, as nationality and the state, and their teleological world-concept has become transformed into a partialised matter. Only within the consciousness of the Russian Bolsheviks does the revolutionary socialism remain a religion, with which by fire and sword they want to thrust upon the world. This is something upon the order of a new Islam, in which they want to merit themself paradise by the killing of unbelievers. The Bolsheviks, just like all religious fanatics, divide all the world and all mankind into two realms -- the realm of God, the realm of the socialistic proletariat, in opposition to the realm of the devil, the bourgeois realm. But all the while I shall be speaking about the sincere, the believing Bolsheviks, since in this medium there are also many dark elements, provocateurs, spies, the corrupt, and moral idiots.

The religious basis of Bolshevism for the time being is very unclear and for many unnoticed. But a Christian, believing in the Christ having come and awaiting the Christ to come, has to assume the audacity to declare, what sort of spirit it is that enters the world with the fanatical revolutionary socialism of the Bolsheviks. The Russian great writers -- Dostoevsky in the "Legend about the Grand Inquisitor", and Vl. Solov'ev in his "Tale about the Anti-Christ" -- help us to solve the riddle of this spirit. Russian religious thought has done much for exposing the ultimate religious foundations of socialism, for making apparent its twofold nature, it has done this moreso, than has Western thought. Within Russian religious thought there has always been an apocalyptic disposition and striving. And therefore it has succeeded in making clear, that this is the spirit, of one who is to appear at the end times and who will tempt with his semblance to Christ, who will act in the name of the happiness and well-being of people, in the name of a million happy infants, not knowing sin. This spirit desires to leave people happy, having deprived them of spiritual freedom. For the renouncing of their spiritual birthright, the renouncing of the image of God in man and his Divine destiny, the Grand Inquisitor promises happiness, bliss, world-unity and tranquility. "He sets about to the merit of himself and his, that the final thing is that they shall have vanquished freedom, and rendered things thus, that they have made people happy". "Yes, we shall force them to work, but in their hours free of toil we shall arrange their life, as child's play, with childish songs, with choruses and dancing. Oh, we shall absolve them also their sins, for they are weak and without strength". "And all will be happy, all the millions of beings". "If it were to be in that light, then certainly already it is not for such, as they are". And the hero of the "Legend about the Anti-Christ" -- is a great philanthropist, he likewise wants to make people happy, he ultimately resolves the social question and installs a social paradise, but all this at a terrible price.

II.

Dostoevsky and Solov'ev prophetically and with genius revealed this twofold image of suchlike future alluring millions of infants. When one ponders what at present is occurring, one tends to remember then the truth of the words of the Legend of the Grand Inquisitor: "Nothing ever for man and human society has been more unbearable than freedom". Both the "Legend of the Grand Inquisitor" and the "Tale about the Anti-Christ" posit the problem concerning the Anti-Christian connection with the problem of socialism. And truly within socialism, as a worldwide phenomenon on a massive scale, there is something twofold and divided -- within it truth is mixed together with lie, Christ with the Anti-Christ, a principle liberating together with a principle enslaving. Socialism -- is a very complicated phenomenon, complicated both in idea, and complicated in life. And it is impossible simply to be a friend of socialism or its enemy. The alluring temptation of the Anti-Christ is grounded upon this, that the ultimate evil manifests itself under the guise of seeming good, that this ultimate evil is impossible to distinguish on the surface, that the evil power acts in the name of the well-being of mankind, in the name of lofty, just, beautiful aims, in the name of equality and brotherhood, in the name of universal happiness and felicity. Upon this basis rests all the whole seductive dialectics of the spirit of the Anti-Christ, as revealed by Dostoevsky. This spirit accepts all those temptations, spurned by Christ in the wilderness. This spirit conducts the Inquisitor's acts of violence in the name of the well-being and happiness of people, in the name of justice and equality. Socialism, as a religion, is first of all also the acceptance of the first temptation in the wilderness, the temptation of the loaves of bread. "And see Thou these stones in this barren and scorched wilderness? Turn them into bread, and Thou wilt win over mankind, like an herd, grateful and obedient, though also eternally trembling, lest Thou hold back Thine hand and cease Thine bread for them". And the obedient herd is won over by those, who would tempt it with the turning of stones into bread. Bolshevism follows in the footsteps of the Grand Inquisitor. In the name of happiness and equality this spirit would destroy everything uplifting, everything of quality, everything of value, all freedom, all individuality. This spirit preaches a worldwide equality of bliss in non-being. This spirit hates being, as qualitative, as uplifting, all in the name of equality and blissful tranquility it would destroy and subject it to non-being. Hateful to this spirit is that ontological aristocratism, which sets at the basis of every religion and most of all -- Christianity, an aristocratism of spiritual freedom and spiritual birthright, of the Divine descent of man. This spirit of Hamism affirms instead a lower descent of man's origin. People for it -- are not sons of God, but rather sons of the world. From a verymost low matter and material darkness it seeks to arouse revolt and rebellion in the name of a leveling down and equating being with non-being, in the name of submerging all the qualities of being into a qualityless non-being. This -- is a mystical Communism.

This spirit accepts not only the first temptation with the loaves of bread, but also the two other temptations, and upon them it desires to create a kingdom of this world. This spirit consents to worship the kingdom of this world and plunges into the abyss. The worldwide revolutionary socialism of the Bolsheviks wants to transform stones into bread, to plunge headlong into the revolutionary abyss in the hope of a revolutionary miracle and to found a forever kingdom of this world, replacing the kingdom of God. This religion of socialism is opposite in everything to the religion of Christ, which teaches, that not by bread alone doth a man live, but also by the word of God, it teaches to worship the Lord God alone, and not the kingdom of this world, it repudiates the temptation for a miracle, in the name of freedom. The religion of socialism wants to destroy everything qualitative of being, everything uplifting, and to drown it in non-being. It spurns freedom, the freedom of the sons of God, and it accepts the necessity and coercion of the sons of this world, of the children of lower matter. The temptation of a world social cataclysm, "of a leap from the realm of necessity into the realm of freedom", is also the allure with the temptation to plunge into the abyss, the temptation for a social miracle. The social revolution, having taken on a mystical hue, is also the third temptation, spurned by Christ in the name of the spiritual freedom of man. To this temptation has to be opposed a social sobriety, as a demand for ascetic religious discipline. Socialism, as a problem of social politics and social ethics, as social reformism, as a real bettering of the lot of the toiling, providing daily bread, is religiously neutral and can comprise an inalienable part of the Christian attitude towards life. In socialism there is its own great truth. But this true socialism issues forth from the freedom of the human spirit and does not permit of the enslaving of the human spirit at the price of bread and the dark abyss, the promises of a miraculous bliss in an earthly kingdom. Socialism however, in its dreaming about the creation of a worldwide kingdom by mechanical revolutionary miracles, is a temptation of the Anti-Christ, it denies the freedom of the spirit and deprives man of his filial relationship of sonship to God.

III.

Russians by their feminine nature readily fall subject to the allures of twofold images, to the temptations of evil, masked under the guise of good. Imposters and pretenders are so characteristic in Russian history. Within it have often appeared twofold images, the nature of which are indeterminate, not as a person, but as a mask. In our mystical sects amongst the people there have been no little of such masks, twofold images, pseudo-Christs and pseudo-Mothers of God. In the Russian people there is a very peculiar element, the Klysty element, submerged within the depths of the pagan roots of the life of the people. Russian Klystyism in the final end is bound up with an incorrect and impaired interrelationship of the masculine and feminine principles in the soul and the character of the Russian people. Within the mystical depths of the Russian people there has not occurred as it were a marital consummation, a true union of the masculine and feminine principles within the people's character. The soul of the people remains feminine, separated from the masculine principle, eternally awaiting a bridegroom and eternally not accepting any as her destined one. Upon this basis has developed a metaphysical hysteria in the character of the Russian people. Dostoevsky discerned it. Upon this basis blossoms forth every sort of obsession. The obsession with Bolshevism is a new form of the age-old Russian Klystyism. This Klystyism can alike be both black, and red, the Klysty-like hero can alike be either Grigorii Rasputin, or Lenin. And all this would be thus a manifestation of the passivity, and not the activity of the Russian soul, its sickly ugly and hysterical femininity. The Bolsheviks, certainly, are under the domination of a sort of spirit unrecognised by them, they are passive to the core and they mislead otherwise only by their revolutionary shouting on the outside. A masculine and active spirit would never be dominant in such elements.

With the more masculine peoples of the West, having received a Catholic or Protestant upbringing, there is a sharper sketching out of the boundaries, moreso a separating apart good from evil, God from the devil, than in the Russian indistinctness. The Catholic world has been tempted by the devil, as evil, but this is a distinctness of form, a crystalised world perceptive of its boundaries, and is not so readily tempted by the Anti-Christ -- by evil, having assumed the guise of good. Satanism, the demonic aspect has always been a specialty of the Catholic and Romance world; the Anti-Christ however is a specialty of the Orthodox Slavic world, with its indistinctness and unlimitedness. The devil is not a temptation for the Russian soul, but the Anti-Christ can quite readily be a temptation for it. The devil presupposes distinctness, the Anti-Christ however is grounded in confusion and substitution. This -- is a very interesting contrast in religious psychology. The satanic sects are impossible in the Russian Orthodox East, but very possible there is a confusion of pseudo-Christs with the true Christ, and in the Russian mystical sects this is always occurring. The piously pure cult of the Virgin Mary readily gets jumbled together with Astartism, and the Mother of God gets identified with a pagan goddess of the earth.

The West has everything set within its place, has in place all its religion, its culture, all its activity, its manly history, its chivalrous past, its free submission to law and norms. This makes the West little sensitive to the mystical impulses of the spirit of the Anti-Christ. The feel of the Anti-Christ is a religious specialty of Russia. It was there always in the religious life of the people and also at the heights, in Russian literature, in Dostoevsky and Solov'ev, and in the modern religious searchings. Within the Russian nature there is no sharp separation of good and evil. Russians tend to be captivated by evil, under the guise of good, whereas that selfsame evil, in not assuming the guise of good, rarely tends to captivate them. Here is why for Russians the dread thing is not the devil, but rather the Anti-Christ -- an ultimate and approaching manifestation of evil. And with Russians particularly strong has taken hold the religion of revolutionary socialism, of a magical socialism, the religion of Bolshevism, captivating with its equality, justice and world triumph of an ultimate social truth and social paradise. Western socialism -- is a matter of laws; the Russian socialism however -- is lawless. Bolshevism is a Russian, a national phenomenon, and this -- is our national ailment, which also in the past has always existed in Russian history, but in different forms. Germany is making use of this sickness of the Russian spirit, turning it into its own obedient tool. The manly German spirit is committing violence over the feminine Russian soul, abusing its sick passivity and hysteria. Germanism has presumptions to be the bridegroom in marriage to the Russian earth. To conquer this Russian sickness is impossible merely by rational, state, political methods of doctoring. To conquer it is possible only religiously, only by opposing against the false semblance of the Good with rather the authentic power of the Good -- of Christ. In this world the kingdom of the Anti-Christ can occur only as the result of the non-success of the matter of Christ in the world, -- it proposes to unite by violence this world, which is not being united in the love and freedom of Christ. If the principle of the Anti-Christ triumphs, then the blame will fall upon the Christian world, upon Christian mankind, upon its spiritual bourgeoisness. Christians do not show even an hundredth part of the energy, that the Bolsheviks show. In truth, the energy of the latter -- is misleading, is illusory, it is only an obsession. But a most important matter is the uniting of all the powers of the Christian world against the coming evil, since the struggle with it has to be conducted not only on the external, the political and social plane, but also in the inward, the spiritual and religious plane.

The German Influences and Slavism

(1917 - #277)[1]

I.

The struggles among parties and classes, with their political and social passions, is causing many to forget, that the Russian revolution is transpiring under the atmosphere of a terrible war, and that all the party groupings with their loud slogans are taking place under the pressure of the war. The parties with their programmes and tactics cannot at present appear in their pure form, they are all dissimilar to how they were in peacetime, in the calm conditions of political activity and the social reformation of society. At the present tragic moment of Russian history, all the parties are determined first of all by their attitude towards the war and towards international politics. In Russia at present there exist really only two parties -- the party of the patriots, wanting to save their native land, not having lost the healthy sense of the nation and the state, aware of their responsibility of all the future of Russia, and conversely the party of the non-patriots, denying the independent value of nationality, indifferent towards their native land, to its honour and worth, betraying it either from a fanatical adherence to abstract utopias and false internationalistic ideas, or from a craven mercenary greed. The division into "bourgeois" and "socialistic" parties possesses at present only a literal significance, and this -- is conditional a phraseology. Plekhanov's "Unity" socialistic group has been termed "bourgeois" exclusively for its patriotic stance. And the Black Hundredist elements, hiding themselves under the mask of Bolshevism, are wont to be termed "socialistic" for their anti-patriotic stance. This is not at all a matter of socialism, essentially. The serious discussion about socialism is historically here inopportune and misplaced. I would not, on my life, now endorse socialism for the Russian people and the Russian

---

[1] GERMANSKIE VLIYANIYA I SLAVYANSTVO. Article was originally published in weekly Journal "Narodopravstvo", 9 August 1917, № 6, p. 2-4.

state. It is possible to acknowledge a certain truth to socialism, but in the given historical hour I would be for every party and every class, that is patriotically and nationally disposed, that would want to save our native land from ruin. Only such parties and such classes can be considered truly progressive. The anti-patriotic, anti-national, anti-state socialism is deeply reactionary, and for it there should be no place in a future free Russia. The Russian revolutionary socialism has with us morally failed and disgraced itself, since it has proven itself non-patriotic, it is not for the nation and the state, at a moment of a greatest danger for our native land, and upon it hinges a wicked overshadowing of the German influence. Russian internationalism reflects a seamy side of German imperialism. This -- is objectively so, irregardless of the subjective mindset of individual internationalists, who might be sincerely attracted to this idea. The patriotic activity of Kerensky most recently is not typical to our revolutionary socialism. More typical is Mr. Chernov or the Menshevik internationalist Martov, not to mention the Bolsheviks. It constantly has to be remembered, that to a remarkable degree our parties represent fictions, party labels -- conditional signs. Behind these signs is hidden the real struggle, signifying quite other than what is expressed in words.

Internationalism on Russian soil is Germanism, Russian pacifism is a German debilitating of the Russian national will. What have the internationalistic and pacifistic ideas on Russian soil led to? They have shaken the unity of the Russian state, they have killed within the people our sense of national bonding-together, they have demoralised and disintegrated the Russian army, they have undermined all the Allies confidence in us, they have brought Russia to humiliation and disgrace. The fruits of internationalism are bitter for Russia, but very sweet for Germany. The German influences ought not invariably to be considered to be behind all the corruption, the spying and betraying of the Russians. With us no few have proven to be traitors, betraying their fatherland and proclaiming pro-German slogans, they were there in the old order and they are here in the new. But this is not the essential thing. The important thing is this, that too many Russians are situated under the German influence, inwardly poisoned by its venom, in the grip of devils, set loose by the Germans against Russia, and they have lost their national semblance. The Russian people has weakened not only materially in its struggle with Germany, it has weakened first of all spiritually, it has not conceived is own idea in the world conflict, it has not gathered its spiritual powers for the enduring of those sacrifices and tribulations, necessitated by this conflict. In the terrible moments, bearing upon the fate of the people, when the war has been combined with revolution, the Russian people is lacking for its own *word*, it speaks in a foreign tongue, it pronounces foreign words -- "internationalism", "socialism" etc, distorting the European sense of these words, spitting them out in a stumbling tongue. The Russian people both could and ought to have its own word in this historical hour, when there is raging the terrible struggle of the Slavic world and the Germanic world. But the passivity and femininity of the Russian people, its wont for foreign influences hinders it from conceiving its own idea and speaking out its own word. It was needful for Germany, that in the hour of struggle the class passion should win out over the national passion, and these two passions -- are basic to the life of various peoples.

II.

The German spirit, manly and forceful, tended to enslave the Russian soul earlier on, than when it set out to enslave the body of Russia. And it has acted via various paths. The international temptation with the Social Democrats has been one of the paths of the Germanisation and enslavement of the soul of Russia, of the depersonalisation of the Russian intelligentsia. But for Germany itself this international Social Democracy has remained something national, and it has been one of the expressions of the Germanic idea. For all those, to whom such an assertion may seem unjustified, I advise to read through a remarkable indeed book by K. Marx, "Revolution and Counter-Revolution in Germany". This book tends to be little known or understood. Such a strong and sharp mind, what a brilliant talent in a publicist! How could this original and sharp mind beget all those drab grey Marxists, impossible to distinguish one from the other? But then too, Tolstoy did beget the Tolstoyans! Marx speaks the strong and powerful language of German imperialism, in him are no traces of humanitarian internationalism and pacifism. He eloquently conceives of the racial calling of the Germans to civilise the Slavic East, and in the Germanisation of the Slavs he sees a progressive revolutionary process and even almost the classic formulas of German imperialism. The German race -- is the higher; the Slavic race -- is the lower. The higher race has the right to conquer, to colonise and civilise a lower race. The self-determination of lower nationalities is reactionary a matter. How far removed Marx is, from the declarations of his disciples on the theme of "without annexation or indemnities" and "the free self-determination of peoples". Marx argues that "from the time of Charlemagne the Germans have gradually directed persistent efforts at conquest, the colonisation or, in extreme measure, the civilising of the European East". ("Revolution and Counter-Revolution in Germany", p.79). Concerning the liberation efforts by the Polish he said: "It would however be disputable still, whether it be proper that whole districts, settled primarily by Germans, and large completely German cities should be ceded to a people, having nothing to show of an ability to emerge from feudal a condition" (p.80). Concerning the Czech liberation efforts he says: "Bohemia in future should exist only in the capacity of a component part of Germany, even though part of its inhabitants have continued over the course of several centuries to speak not in the German tongue" (p.82). Here is how Marx characterises efforts towards unification and liberation by the Slavs: "There was conceived in the work offices of certain Slavic dilettantes of historical science that laughable anti-historical movement, which schemed at naught else than the subjection of the civilised West to the barbaric East; the subjection of the city to the village; of trade, industry, science -- to the primitive agriculture of the Slavic outposts. But behind this laughable theory has stood a dreadful fact -- there has stood the Russian empire, in each movement of which appears pretensions to regard Europe as an appanage of the Slavic race, and in particular there is the singularly strange component part of this race -- the Russians; this is an empire, which with its two capitals -- Peterburg and Moscow -- all which has not found its centre of gravity, for as long as Tsargrad [Constantinople], in which each Russian peasant sees as the true genuine metropolis of his religion and his nation, for as long as Tsargrad fails to be rendered the active residence of the Russian emperor" (p.83-84). As we see, Marx did not tie in the Russian gravitation towards Tsargrad with the interests of a capitalistic bourgeoise, he was not merely banging his head with the routine spiel from all the common spots, he saw here first of all a gravitation of the Russian peasantry with its religious and national world-outlook. In Marx there as serious hatred towards the Slavs and towards Russia, he was a Turkophile, he was a German down to the marrow of his bones in questions of international politics. The same also was old Liebknecht, an hater of Russia, always preferring the Turk over the Slavs. As regards the [1848-51] war with the Danes over Schleswig and Holstein, Marx says: "These are districts, undoubtedly German by nationality, language and inclination, needful for Germany both for the guarding and developement of its maritime movement and trade" (p.86). This is all very expressed in the spirit of German imperialism. And here is a very characteristic spot: "Thus have the Slavs ended... the German attempts to conquer for themself an independent national existence. The shattered remnants of numerous nations, where the nationality and political manner of life has long since faded and which therefore already over the course of a thousand years they have been compelled to live under, makes proper their conquest by a stronger nation... all these past their prime nationalities -- the Bohemians, the Croats, the Dalmatians etc, have attempted to utilise the common period of unrest in the year 1848 for a restoration of the political status quo, as it existed 800 years after the Birth of Christ. The history of the elapsed thousand years ought to have shown them, that such a step backward is impossible; that if the whole area to the East from the Elbe and the Zaale, never settled by a coherent family of Slavic peoples having affinity amongst them, as has happened with the German, this fact then but indicates an historical tendency together with this physical and intellectual ability, for the German nation to subjugate its old Eastern neighbours, to swallow up and assimilate them; it indicates that *this assimilating tendency of the Germans always has served and still serves as one of the mightiest means of spreading Western European civilisation to the East of the European continent*" (italics mine -- N. B.) (p.116-117). "How can they (the PanSlavists) expect, that history will march a thousand years backwards on account of certain withered peasant communes, while on every stretch of land inhabited by them they are surrounded on all sides by Germans" (p.117).

III.

Who could imagine, that these forceful words were written by the father of Social Democracy, rather than by some German imperialist, that they were written by the prophet of internationalism, rather than by one of the German national idea? The modern German Social Democrats, reborn into social imperialists, as they ironically term themself, tend to follow along on the course set by their teacher Marx. Marx was sufficiently intelligent, talented and original, as to understand in his finer moments the significance or race, to recognise its connection with the world imperialism of that state and people, the culture of which he was raised and educated in.

Nicholas Berdyaev

Marx himself was never so doctrinaire as are his disciples and followers. Although Jewish by blood, he to sufficient a degree sensed himself a German and with the eyes of a German he looked at world events. And this does him honour. But we however, fools that we be, we think, that Marx was an internationalist on humanist grounds, that he wished for the brotherhood of peoples, that he commanded no making of "annexation" and presupposed free self-determination for all peoples. People are very naive, all these Russian chaps, dreaming about the brotherhood of peoples, about the free self-determination of nationalities, about internationalism and deriving the basis for the idea from the German Social Democrats! Actually, all these Russian stupidities are taken seriously by not one German, even though he be a Social Democrat. Marx approved of all the "annexations", made by the chosen German race, and he did not allow for the free self-determination of the lower Slavic race. Marx would have approved of the "annexation" of all of Russia, as a spreading of the German civilisation into the barbaric East. Marx knew, that history is an harsh struggle of powers, and not some humanist sentimentality. With the German there can be the idea of internationalism, but this will be the internationalism obtaining after the fulfilling by the German race of its civilising mission, after the Germanisation of the Slavic East and the subordination to Germany of all the Near East. For the attaining of this worldwide and all-human end the German never would allow himself to grow teary and slacken over any sentimentalities, from any abstract high-minded ideas. This he would leave to the Russians. International Social Democracy -- is totally German in spirit. It is also one of the German influences, hindering the Russian people from realising, that in the world is occurring a great worldwide historical struggle between Slavism and Germanism, of two hostile forces within history, and that the Slavic race will either emerge from this struggle victorious, repulsing the pretensions of Germanism and fulfill its own mission within history, or it ill be brought down and hacked apart. In the revolutionary element at present has been extinguished the Russian and Slavic consciousness. And in the quenching of this awareness, behind which stands an healthy racial instinct, the propaganda of German Social Democratic ideas has played no small part. Socialism can be national, but in Russia socialism has been made into a weapon of powers, hostile to our race, it impedes Russia from the fulfilling of its Slavic calling.

The Russian and Slavic feeling and consciousness with all its powers has to be awakened. We need a mobilisation of the national spirit. And recollection about the German self-consciousness of Marx is very useful in this regard. Against the German mindset of Marx concerning a world vocation of civilising by the German race in the East, we have to oppose our own Russian mindset concerning the mission of Slavism, which still has not had its own say in the world. We believe, that a strong Russia will provide a greater freedom to the world and to all the peoples of the world, than would a strong Germany, and that in the Slavic spirit there is greater an universality, than in the coercive German spirit. Howsoever great might be the significance of the Russian Revolution in Russian history, yet the world struggle of peoples is an event still greater in its significance, than is the Revolution. The Revolution has erupted because of the war, and it can be thought of only in connection with the war. The Germans have got their own idea in the worldwide struggle. Is there an idea with us? The Russians have shown such vulnerability, that they have fallen under the spell of a German idea. But our final word has still not be said.

The Free Church and the Sobor

(1917-#278)[1]

I.

The Russian people has always sensed itself a Christian people. Many Russian thinkers and artists have been inclined even to regard it as a Christian people preeminently. The Slavophils thought, that the Russian people lives by the Orthodox faith, which is the sole true faith, having within it the fullness of truth. Of Russia Tyutchev sang:

> Bent neathe the crush of cross,
> Throughout all thee, O native land,
> Hath traversed in humble guise
> The King of Heaven, giving blessing.

Dostoevsky preached, that the Russian people -- is a God-bearing people. The finest of Russian people believed, that in the hidden depths of the Russian people lay concealed the possibility of higher religious revelations. But here now has burst forth the Revolution and led to tempestuous stirrings within the immense sea of the people's life. The people, silent a thousand years, has wanted, finally, to speak out, and here, in hearkening to the multi-voiced people amidst the raging elements of the Revolution, it has to be admitted, that the Name of Christ is not to be heard within this din. It is not in the Name of Christ that the Revolution has been made, and it is not Christian love that directs its course. All the attempts to transform our national Revolution into a social one have been movements aspiring to the point of wrath with a thirst for equality, conceived of mechanically and materialistically, and least of all is there to be sensed any spirit of Christian brotherhood. The Revolution has uncovered a spiritual apostasy within the Russian people. And this apostasy is the result of too

---

[1] SVOBODNAYA TSERKOV I SOBOR. Article originally published in the weekly Journal "Narodopravstvo", aug. 1917, № 7.

ingrained a servility, of too far-gone a process of disintegration within the old order, of too long a paralysis of the Russian Church and the moral withering of churchly authority. The sanctities in the people's soul for a long time have been corroded both from the right, and from the left, and this has prepared the way for that cynical attitude towards the sanctities, now being discerned in all its ugliness. Revolutions are good, in that they show the true position, they cast down every conditional and hypocritical lie. The significance of the Revolution will be great in abolishing the old lie and rot.

The Revolution has struck the Church a blow and destroyed the old connection between church and state. Externally within church structures everything has been set into flux. The Russian Church has to set about restructuring from the top on down. But in the elemental spreading growth of the Revolution, the church movement has proven totally at a loss. The voice of the Church is not heard in the roar of the Revolution. During the days of great danger for Russia, the Orthodox Church is not playing that role, which it played in former times, when St. Sergei of Radonezh saved our native land and guided it spiritually. There are grounds to fear, that just like prior to the turnabout, when the Church was brought low before the autocratic state, it will again be brought low before the new democratic state. But during these days, when Russia and indeed all the world is living through unprecedented catastrophes, when everything in the world has become shaken and unsteady, Christians cannot but want, that there should be heard the voice of the Free Church of Christ. The free Church is first of all the Church, independent of the ruling authority of the state and from every element of this world. It of itself per se draws upon the source of its own revelations, it receives its freedom in Christ as its Head. The Church cannot receive its freedom by the Revolution nor by the changes, occurring within the state, the freedom of the Church cannot derive merely from a democratic structure. And if in the old connection of church and state there was transgressed the commandment of Christ as regards the relationship between "the things of God" and "the things of Caesar", then this was an inner pitfall for churchly people, for churchly mankind, its temptation and enslavement to "this world". The Church, however, in its inner sanctity, against which the gates of Hell cannot prevail, cannot be enslaved. It itself is the wellspring of graced freedom, it limits the all-encompassing power of the state, before which the pagan world bowed and scraped, and it guards the infinite nature and infinite rights of the human soul. Only

Christianity acknowledges the infinitude of the human spirit and its incommensurability with whatever the kingdoms of this world. But the Church is God-manly an organism, and the human will of the churchly people can be tempted with all manner of temptations, it can fall and become enslaved. The people of the Russian Church, situated under the spiritual lead of Byzantium, has passed through great temptings, it has rendered "God's due" -- to "Caesar". The autocephaly of the Russian Church has signified its being headed by the tsar. And upon this path, the Church's people in Russia has lost its independent significance in the life of its Church. The freedom principle remained at the forefront of such ideologies of Orthodoxy, as the Slavophils, but it was absent in the actual reality of the Church. Both the Church's people and the Church's hierarchy became accustomed to an abased passivity, and all activity was lodged within the organs of the state. And our present-day task for the life of the Church mustneeds be seen in this, that the Church's people itself and the Church's hierarchy now are summoned to activeness and self-initiative in everything (amidst other things also in the matter of religious nurture and education). It has become impossible still to count on the expectation, that the matter of Christianity upon earth will be handled for Orthodox Christians by someone else, by some protecting and guarding ruling power.

II.

The outwards structure of the Russian Church, which has been the largest and strongest part of the Eastern Orthodox Church, was upheld by its connection with the power of the tsar. The collapse and downfall of "the sacred Russian tsardom" signifies a new period in the history of the Eastern Church. The Byzantine idea is finished. The Church's people has freed itself from one of the temptations, that of slavery to "Caesar", and to it is given the freedom of choosing its ultimate path. There is nothing that still upholds the outward unity of the Eastern Church. And this represents an enormous trial for the spiritual powers of the Church's people. The Eastern Church henceforth can be upheld only by its inner unity, only by the rebirth of churchly power and strength. And therefore particularly, there has to be awakened the churchly will for the restoration of the universal unity of the Church. The collapse of the Russian autocracy removes an impediment in the movement for the re-uniting of the Churches. But this movement is needed first of all is not some external union, but rather as an inner orientation of the two halves of Christian mankind each to the other with love, nowise denying the unique experience of each of the halves. Only the One Universal-OEcumenical Church can be fully free, not chained down to states and nations, not dependent upon the ruling powers of national states. Every division in the Church is already a partial loss of freedom. The autocephaly of the Russian Church was also a source of its unfreedom. The temptation of Papocaesarism in the Western Catholic Church was suchlike the same a source of division and suchlike the same a source of slavery, as was the temptation of Caesaropapism in the East. But it would be a mistake to think, that Protestantism was a movement towards the freedom of the Church. The Lutheran Reformation in its consequences was a subordination of the Church to the territorial principle and was a surrendering of it into the hands of the ruling princes. Every detour towards Protestantism represents a division in the Church, its splintering and the loss of its freedom. The Russian synodal structure was an insertion of Protestant principles into the Orthodox Church, borrowed from Germany, and it represented a means of control over the Church. The finest of Orthodox people have felt only but contempt for the synodal structure, they regarded it as non-canonical and have instead sought out the spiritual authority of the Orthodox Church in the starchestvo, in the heeding of spiritual elders. The Church administration was bound up with the old state ruling authority and is sharing in its fate. The Holy Synod in the final period of its existence became subject to the same disintegration, as was in the bureaucracy, in it there was the same rottenness, that there was in the state authority. The princes of the Church found themselves enslaved to Grigorii Rasputin. He determined to a remarkable degree that composition of the Holy Synod, such as the revolutionary Provisional Government was to encounter. Facing the first revolutionary Uber-Prokurator was the task of undoing the old relationship of church and state, to remove the fetters from the Church, to free the Church structure from that which was bound up with the old ruling powers. From this point of view certain forceful measures of the Uber-Prokurator in regard to the old composition of the Holy Synod and the upper churchly hierarchy can be justified, though in future the Uber-Prokurator ought not to play any sort of churchly role, and instead be transformed into a minister of religious confessions. In the first revolutionary moments, the defense of the freedom and dignity of the Church and churchly authority was indefensible given the composition of the Holy Synod, the selection of which was nowise churchly, and which completely tied in the Church with the collapsing state powers. The first revolutionary period of churchly life proved to be tinted in the bureaucratic light of the new style, and this was an inevitable consequence of old sins. The body of the Church has already long since fallen sick, long since already has been in disarray, and the Revolution but merely uncovered the true situation with this, and cast off the hypocritical falsehood. The clerical class view is not wont to defend the freedom of the Church, it itself has been in captivity to the realm of Caesar and tends to aspire after earthly advantages. And it ought not to be forgotten, that the Russian Church has lived through a prolonged period of decay and suppression of spirit. The people of the Church have become silent and inactive. Much of their religious energy has become filtered off into the sects and was redirected into a struggle against the Church and the fullness innate to it. The soul of the people was in consternation and was shocked over the moral wantonness amongst the ranks of the Church hierarchy, and over the spiritual degeneration of the "official" Church. Such a religious condition for the people sets immense spiritual difficulties upon the path to churchly renewal. But one has to expect, that the great tribulations and upheavals in life will lead the Russian people to a religious self-intensification.

III.

The hopes for the renewal of our Church have for a long time already been bound up with the convening of a local Church Sobor, a national Church Council. The conciliar Sobor principle has to be restored to the Orthodox Church. The old ruling powers were afraid of having a Sobor, and its convening became possible only after the turnabout. The Church has to restructure itself upon elective and democratic principles. And henceforth there ought to be tolerated nothing, which should impede it inwardly. But it would be a mistake to conceive of the restoration of the conciliar principle and the democratisation of the churchly structure beyond purposes of churchly creativity and churchly rebirth. One of the temptations, waiting to ambush our Church life -- is the mixing up of religion with politics. The politicising of the Church either from right or left is alike pernicious. Transition over to a political or social democracy is not a religious sort of movement, and for the rebirth of the Church it as such per se can do nothing. An authentic Church renewal can only come from within, from the depths, from the breath of a new spirit. A creative religious stirring will begin only then, when the people goes down into its depths, within itself, and ceases to live in the externals. Then an autonomous and original religious and churchly stirring will bring into politics and the societal aspect an higher truth, not otherwise found therein. In the revolutionary movement at present God is forgotten about, and from such a movement it would be foolish to await a religious rebirth. Man has been cast out onto the surface level of things, the superficial. It is impossible to expect too much even from a local Sobor. It would be scarcely possible to have in the Church Sobor a greater quantity of religious energy, than that, which exists in the people of the Church. However sad, but it must be admitted, that the Church Sobor has not been proceeded by any sort of churchly stirrings from below, there has been no sort of pent-up creative spiritual energy in the people. The specially convened Sobor was called for by the external necessity to restructure the Russian Church and avert the possibility of its being torn apart. The Sobor will have to define the relationship of the Church to the state, and to decide a whole series of questions relating to the Church's existence. *The Sobor has to first of all strengthen the position of the Church amidst the raging of the elements, which is sweeping everything along in its stormy path, it has to position the Church into a setting independent of the changing and fickle elements of revolution and reaction, i.e. to manifest the Free Church, subject only to its proper Head, Christ, and not fall into enslavement further under any changes in the affairs of the state.*

But dangers and temptations lie in wait from various sides. On the one side there is possible a tendency towards a reformation of the Lutheran type. On another side, there is possible the arising of a clerical political current, which would lead to a class struggle within the Church and throughout the Church. Both the one and the other danger deviate off from the path of the Church, -- as Free, One and Universal. And in both the one and the other tendency there would be a false inter-linking with politics and the state. Throughout all the dangers there has to be maintained and preserved the inner hierarchism of the Church, which also is a true freedom and independence from the world. Only a Church free and preserving its hierarchical succession can prove a spiritual fortress, in which it can defend against both inward and outward temptations. Sectarian tendencies always become a fruitless waste of religious energy. And it is impossible not to desire with all one's soul, that the religious energy of sectarianism should be returned to the Church. The true path of the Free Church lies far off alike from both the inert and pharisaeical conservatism, which impedes every creative religious stirring, and from the destructive revolutionism, directed against the inward hierarchical harmony of the Church.

The free Church of the new Russian state ought to act as an inward spiritual power and to aspire to make the state more Christian inwardly, and not from the outside. A compulsory Christian state is an hypocritical lie. But the admitting of this negative truth does not signify a refusal from the right and obligation of a Christian people to impose a Christian imprint upon their state. Insofar as the Russian people remains a Christian people, it cannot but want, that the Church should occupy in its state an especial place, not consigning it to fragmentary aspects of society. The churchly freedom within Christianity is combined with religious freedom. But religious freedom, freedom of conscience for the Christian is not a formal and empty freedom, it is a truth of the Christian religion itself as the religion of freedom. Only irreligious people hostile to Christianity would assert, that religion is a partial matter for the individual man. No, religion is universal a matter, in it is the fullness of everything. The complete separation of the Church from the state, as doctrinaire liberals and socialists tend to demand, is undesirable and impossible. In France it assumed the form of a persecution against the Church. In principle there ought to be a separation of "the things of God" from the "things of Caesar", and "God's" ought to be completely free from any encroachments from "Caesar's". But "the things of God" are active in "Caesar's", from within, through churchly people, in which there ought to be an integral wholeness of spirit. The true Church is a combining of freedom with oneness. The Russian local Sobor is but a moment in the universal churchly stirrings, which ought to begin to unite in the world all the powers of Christianity for the struggle against the anti-Christian powers, which are on the increase in the world.

Who is to Blame?

(1917 - #276)[1]

I.

One can consider it already apparent, that if the Russian Revolution has also been something good, insofar as during its first days it freed Russia from the nightmare of the collapsing autocratic power, then subsequently all the "developement" and "deepening" of the Revolution has marched off along a false path and has not produced any sort of good fruits for Russia and the Russian people. Fatal mistakes were made, the consequences of which many of us had foreseen and predicted. It was a repeat on a larger scale of 1905, and can anticipate a largescale reaction. In the Russian Revolution there has very quickly begun a process of disintegration and decay. It moral visage becomes all more and more repulsive. The Revolution was inspired not by any sort of creative and original ideas. There tend to predominate long ago discarded and decayed socialistic ideas. These moribund ideas have lost any moral hue and have been stoked by the unrestraint and fury of greedy interests and passions. These ideas have led Russia to disgrace and humiliation, and have plunged it into chaos. In the revolutionary socialistic circles there has begun a sobering up after the wildness and an awareness of mistakes, there has begun a learning of elementary truths by way of lessons plain to see. But this obvious lesson is had too dearly, and coming generations will call us to account for the too great efforts at learning by the Russian revolutionary intelligentsia in elementary school. We leave our descendants a twisted and ravaged legacy. We have received Russia from the old powers in a frightful form, sick and lacerated, and we have led it into a still worse condition. There occurred after the turnaround not a return to health, but rather the developing of a sickness, a progressive worsening of the position of Russia. It is not a new life that is being revealed and flourishing, but rather the old life, coming apart and rotting. If the consciousness of duty has

---

[1] KTO VINOVAT?. Article originally published in the weekly Journal "Russkaya svoboda", aug. 1917, No. 18/19, p. 3-9.

always been weak in Russia, at present in Russia it ultimately has vanished. Where though to seek the culprit? Why so ugly that the Revolution is proceeding, why does the destruction within it take precedence over building, why does it conceal within it the seeds of a perhaps inevitable ugly reaction?

Revolutions never have happened all quite fine, in them always have been a falling away from reason, always they are connected with a piling up of evil from the old sins, always the negative aspect in them has been stronger than the constructive. But in the Russian Revolution there is much particularly its own, its own Russian ills and temptations, there is a requital for its own Russian sins. The cause of all the woes and all the sins of the Russian Revolution mustneeds be sought deeper, than is usually sought. These causes are not only in the false tactics, adopted by the socialist parties, not only in the Bolsheviks, not only in the economic backwardness and in the terrible pressure upon the Russian Revolution exerted by Germany. These causes are first of all in a false direction of spirit, in false ideas, by which over the course of many decades lived the Russian revolutionary intelligentsia, and by which they poisoned the masses of the people. The Russian Revolution has seemed to be an attempt at a consistent application to life of the Russian nihilism, atheism and materialism, an enormous experiment, based upon the negation of all absolute spiritual principles in personal and societal life. From a philosophic point of view, the Russian Revolution is a pure psychologism, limited by nothing and subordinated to nothing, the uprising of an arbitrary caprice of the human masses against every ontologism. In "Vekhi" ("Signposts") long before the present revolution there was shown the danger, threatening from the left, there was revealed the lie set at the basis of the revolutionary movement and the intelligentsia revolutionary world-view. Now the truth of "Vekhi" is being verified by living experience, and confirmed. And this truth has to be admitted now even by those, who made a fierce attack upon "Vekhi". The Russia revolutionary intelligentsia, who are reaping the fruits of their activity within the course and the character of the Russian Revolution, and who themselves were cast beyond the pale by the dark masses of the people, for too long have lived by a false faith, a faith in idols, and not in the living God, and its soul was distorted by this falsehood and this idolatry, it was corrupted and lost its connection with the spiritual truths of life. The centre of gravity in life was transformed from the inner to the outer. The intelligentsia venom poisoned also the soul of the people, it corroded away from it the living God. The Bolsheviks -- are the ultimate Russian nihilists, in them the nihilism of the intelligentsia is united with the nihilism of the people. The sources of all our misfortunes mustneeds be sought in the uniting of the nihilistic ideas of the intelligentsia with the darkness of the people. The revolutionary turnabout was itself a national deed, it was made by the Russian people, as a great goal, it was not the deed alone of the revolutionary intelligentsia or of the working class, it was not preceded by an intensification of the revolutionary-socialistic activity. But the Russian national revolution was misappropriated for themselves by the revolutionary intelligentsia circles and by the masses, which marched under their demagogic slogans. And this coincided with a religious crisis of the people.

II.

In the Russian Revolution there is the gathering of the harvest of an old and stale Russian nihilism. Within it is sensed the breathing of this old, not new spirit. The Revolution was inspired by nihilistic ideas, it is directed first of all at the destruction of the hierarchy of values, the hierarchy of qualities, upon which is based the Divine world-order. The revolutionary-nihilistic hostility towards every hierarchism is of a spiritual nature first of all, rather than political or economic, and it reflects the psychology of the masses and their moral disposition. At the core of this psychology lies a feeling of envy towards everything that is higher, that is endowed with already established qualities. But never yet has creativity issued forth from this source. The nihilistic disposition and ideas amongst the masses yields strange results. Russian revolutionary socialism as regards its spiritual grounds is violence-prone, materialistic and atheistic, and this negative pathos conveys it into a sort of pseudo-religion. Russian revolutionary socialism is obsessed by a thirst for equality in what can never thus be. This temptation of an absolute equality leads to the extermination of all qualities and values, of all upsurges and ascents, in it -- is the spirit of non-being. Being was conceived in inequality, in an heightening of qualities, in individual distinctions. In it the star from star is distinguished in glory. The "extinguishing of all qualitative distinctions" and of all the uplifting would be a return to the primordial non-being, wherewith is a complete equality, a total confusion. The uprising of the primordial chaotic non-being occurs periodically within history, whole societal movements can be reflective of its light. It would be a mistake, certainly, to identify all socialism and every socialistic movement with the spirit of non-being. There is possible a socialism of a completely different spirit. But atheistic socialism, in fancying itself a new religion, is certainly a religion of non-being. They have believed in the earthly total-bliss, the fabricated earthly paradise, because they have ceased to believe that there could be anything higher. When the religious hopes have dimmed and the spiritual life has weakened, there remains but to grasp at an earthly paradise, to utilise an instant of this meaningless life. The thirst for a difference holds sway.

Russian nihilism, which was a broad trend at the end of the decade of the 60's, by bearing this name repudiates not only in words and not only in thoughts all the indisputable and absolute sanctities and values, it repudiates them and the spirit of everything associated with them, by the exertion of its will, it repudiates them in deed and in life itself. Nihilism not only has ceased to think about the other and divine world, it has ceased to be in communion with it. Not by chance has the Name of Christ been forgotten in our revolutionary movement and in our Revolution. It is not there within the souls, within the basic directing of spirit for choosing out a path. Words and names -- are not chance accidental and conditional signs, as the nominalists think, they -- are real energies of spiritual life. Upon this is based the significance of prayer. Least of all should I want to suggest, that the Russian revolutionary-nihilists -- are wicked and bad people; among them always have been no little number of fine people, sincere, self-denying and ungreedy in their enthusiasm. But these people are under the grip of a false negative spirit, the nature of which they themself do not understand, and these people not rarely are situated in a condition of obsession. They are cast off onto the surface, torn off from the spiritual core of life, rotating within the outer orbits of life. In Russian nihilism and Russian nihilistic socialism there is no freedom of spirit, there is not the spiritual health needful for creativity, there is no sort of inner discipline, of subordinating man to sanctities standing higher than him. The revolutionary intelligentsia consciousness has repudiated all the objective spiritual principles, all the supra-human values, and it has subordinated human life to the caprice of the human passions, the interests and strivings for well-being and pleasure. Triumphant only are the utilitarian values. Everything is made subject to the good of individual people and to a mechanical quantity of people. The inward, the spiritual core of the human person is denied. Good and evil are acknowledged as relative and are evaluated as dependant upon societal usefulness. The moral decay of the Russian revolutionary intelligentsia and of the Revolution itself was quite facilitated by the traditional identification of the moral and the good with the "left", and the immoral and the evil with the "right". Those therefore, who sensed themselves as "leftists", have acknowledged for themself that everything is permissible. The religious feeling of guilt was replaced by the social feeling of victimisation, and this bestowed upon the soul an ignoble visage. The consciousness of obligations was replaced by endless demands and pretensions. The materialistic theory of the social medium ultimately paralysed the awareness of personal responsibility. They did not and they do not assign any significance to the personal tempering of will and discipline of character. According to this world-view and world-sense, the person sets forth his demands and pretensions, independent of his qualities and services. Irresponsible pretentiousness, having paralysed the awareness of obligations, is a moral ulcer, polluting Russian societal life. The noble and eternal feelings of respect and reverence have ultimately been cast out from the revolutionary-nihilistic type. The nihilism of our revolutionary consciousness is the offspring of an old and long slavery. A large portion of the guilt for this falls upon the guiding and governing classes, upon the moral decay at the top. Within these classes the heart long since already is deadened towards the sanctities, and they hypocritically used the sanctities for their own greedy ends.

III.

Both at the top and at the bottom they have ceased to see the objective and spiritual principles in the state and in nationality, which instead they have subordinated to the arbitrary and subjective aims of social well-being. Some have fashioned themself an idol out of the autocratic state and tsarism and have worshipped it as God, while others -- have done so from the people and the proletariat, and similarly worship it. The revolutionary nihilism, derivative of the reactionary nihilism, has tended to worship quantity over quality. All the spiritual realities and spiritual values are subjected to atomisation and fracturing. The church, the fatherland, the state, culture -- all long since already have been subjected to decay and behind everything they have tended to see but naked interests. Marxism they would accept in Russia, as a theoretical justification of nihilism, as a cynical denial of spiritual life as a value and reality in itself. The Russian intelligentsia of the nihilistic sort are quite happy to learn from the German booklets, that there does not exist any sort of independent spiritual life and that all the values in it -- are mere ideological veilings for vested interests, only reflections of economic activity. The state presents itself as an organisation of class domination, nationality -- as the creation of bourgeois interests, the good and truth -- as the reflection of economic attitudes. Marxism has found its reception amongst us first of all as a cynical nihilism, directed to the destruction of ontological realities. The cynical nihilism long ago already had been a vital practice of the right, among the dominant strata of the old regime, which resulted in a total moral collapse. Long since already there also triumphed the nihilism of the left and it found its justification within Marxism. The oppressions, the sufferings and hardships have morally given a noble aura to the Russian revolutionaries and have veiled over the spiritual consequences of the nihilism. But when the revolutionary nihilism itself began to govern and hold power, there became apparent its moral ignobility, its spiritual emptiness. Russian nihilism has combined with a sort of a peculiar moralism: all the spiritual realities are denied in the name of the morality of equality, in the name of the well-being of the people. Over a series of decades there was denied amongst the people the value of the fatherland, the value of nationality, and every national feeling was killed as being immoral. The politics of the old powers ultimately did attain an healthy national instinct. What however would it be amazing, is if the Revolution were to prove anti-patriotic and anti-national?

    These nihilistic dispositions and thoughts flourished in the spiritual atmosphere of the underground, created by the acts of violence of the old, the decaying powers. The bureaucratic nihilism and the intelligentsia nihilism -- are twins. The free creative spirit and free creative ideas lacked in strength at the top and lacked in enticement at the bottom, the left and the right were not governed by spirit, did not have a living faith in God and in the spiritual meaning of life. Russia long since already had fallen grievously sick in spirit, sending it into obsessive convulsions, in it the devils made merry, first the reactionary ones, then the revolutionary, first the Black and then the Red ones. Russian maximalism, hurling us from one extreme to the other, is a sickness of spirit, a metaphysical hysteria, an inward slavery. In the soul of the Russian people long since already there began the crisis of faith, the soul of the people was in agitation and found itself at the crossroads. And at such moments the soul is rendered defenseless against the many temptations. The old with its spiritual discipline was dying out in the soul of the people, while the new proved however to be a nihilistic negation. Thus was wrought out within the people that ugly aspect of soul, which yesterday led to the pogrom against the Jews and the leftist intelligentsia, and which today can lead to a pogrom against the "bourgeoise" and all of cultural society, as being too rightist. Over all reigns one and the same thirst for dividing things up, the envious glance at the spiritual and material riches of one's neighbour. And this is accompanied by a total creative impotence, an incapacity for building up and a distaste for it.

    Needful for the Russian people is an healthy and strong national feeling, but such there has not been and there is not. And there is not that national enthusiasm, which is necessary for the salvation of the native-land. We are being paid back for the old sins, we are gnawed at by the inherited ills. We need an inner cleansing and a spiritual turnabout, the ultimate expulsion within ourselves of all nihilism. Without a change in the human fabric, constituting society, it is impossible to reckon upon a more perfect societal life. From feeble human souls it is impossible to make a fine society, this would be but an outward shifting about of atoms. From this point of view no sort of external revolutions can change anything substantially. There is needed a spiritual tempering of the person, its inward rebirth, the elevating of its qualities. The human person cannot expect everything from a new society, it ought first of all as possible to give more to it. Regretably, in Russian cultural society, the liberal and enlightened, there is not that strength of spirit and that heated faith, which might save Russia from the demonic ragings. Purely liberal ideas -- are warm-cold ideas, in them there is no fire. And it is necessary in truth to say: if the Russian revolutionary circles have confessed nihilism, then the Russian liberal circles have confessed a quite superficial enlightenmentism and a superficial positivism, which alike corrupt the spiritual life and impair the faith in spiritual realities. Russian liberalism in its inability to take wing was rendered nationally minded only during the time of war, and the Revolution has consolidated it in this frame of mind. But in it the national idea is lacking of deep roots, and for Russian liberals the patriotism in the masses is a question of political tactics. They are patriots through power. The spiritual national movement with us lies still ahead, it will take form after the surviving and making sense of the tragic experience of the war and the Revolution. It has to lead to an original societal creativity. It will not resemble the old nationalism. But it will also not resemble the traditional humanistic liberalism. Not only the old revolutionism, but also the old liberalism has to accept upon itself part of the blame for what is happening at present in Russia. The Russian Revolution is a chastisement by God for the obvious or secret nihilism at all the levels, of all the classes and all the currents, from the extreme rightists to the extreme leftists. The creative national movement and rebirth presupposes a spiritual crisis, a turning towards the deep, the Divine sources of life.

Patriotism and Politics

(1917 - #279)[1]

I.

We, as Russians, are all too accustomed to say, that our native land is on the brink of ruin. We have been talking about this for so long, and our words are of such little effect, and their practical consequences so unremarkable, that soon there will be no one left to believe in the sincerity of our words. All the words have lost their allotted gravity and ceased to be effective. There occurs only a quick shuffling of ministers, who spasmodically try to form a strong national government, but this reconfiguration of the atoms produces the impression of a sickly impotence, and nothing essential is changed by it. This phenomenon, fully analogous to a "ministerial leap-frogging", happened too in the final period of the existence of the old regime. The basic thrust of the societal will remains the same. To get out from the condition of this tragic impotence we need an inner psychical push, a different spiritual atmosphere to the ruling authority, more free, more loving of rights, inspired not by the greedy, by class and the all too human ideas, but by objective national and state ideas, such as are not dependent upon human caprice. Many admit, that at this terrible and tragic moment of Russian history, that Russia can be saved only by a patriotic upsurge, only by an exceptional exertion of national spirit. But we lack this impulse, there are only appeals for it and words about it. All the patriotic and statesmanlike words of the government, pronounced by the Moscow state assembly meetings, have thus remained merely words, without passing over into action. All this terminology, new for the Russian revolutionary intelligentsia, signifies but that our infant statesmen are passing through grade-school and are learning by rote to pronounce the words: fatherland, nation, state. Essentially it would seem, that the power at this difficult moment should have belonged to those, who long since already had learned these words and whose

---

[1] PATRIOTIZM I POLITIKA. Article originally published in the weekly Journal "Narodopravstvo", sept. 1917, № 10, p. 2-4.

psychology more closely relates to the saving of the state and its setting in order.

But in this exceptional time they want to save Russia by political combinations, essentially changing nothing, repudiating nothing, sacrificing nothing and risking nothing. These past several months already have realised such an inertia of the revolutionary authorities, which it took the span of a century to form under the old ruling authorities. The psychology of governance of the revolutionary democracy is too reminiscent of the psychology of the governance of Nicholas II. Compromises are made exclusively under the influence of fear and danger, and not from inner awareness of national duty. Our revolutionary politics is infected with falsehood, it is quickly going to rot and decay. The lie was set in place into the foundation itself of the ruling powers of the revolutionary democracy -- no sort of an utmost and objective truth binding for all the people was set within this foundation. Everything was justified by the interests of social classes, of separate groups and of separate personages. But every ruling power, which is directed exclusively by the interests of social classes, inevitably has to fall apart. At the basis of a strong national authority inheres always something, standing higher than all the special interests. A ruling power by its nature cannot be either bourgeois, or proletarian, and it is conducted neither by class interests, nor the special interests of people, but rather by the interests of the state and the nation, as a grand whole. There is nothing easier, than to go astray in politics via the path of falsehood. The means for the political struggle imperceptibly gets substituted for the ends of life, and in the raging of political passions it is difficult to preserve alive the soul. This soul is being murdered by the dominance of interests and by the greedy struggle for power. Those, who value the health of the people's soul, have to admit, that in patriotism there is something more primary and more connected with the spiritual basics of life, than mere politics. In the national feeling there is something more intimate and more profound, than a state mindset. And the political motives essentially have to be subordinated to the patriotic motives. One who is fighting for his native land, is fighting not for his own interests and not for foreign interests, but for a value, standing higher than any well-being of people. Every great struggle can be justified only as a struggle for one's own truth and for God. And politics, lacking in this political core, will always be a lie and subject to rot. Now more than ever it can be said, that it is not a time for politics, estranged from the spiritual basics of life and merely shifting for itself and its vacillating and ambiguous elements. It is the matter involving the fate of a great people, and not only concerning its outward political and social fate, but also its inner fate, the soul of the people, which can become undone in the name of illusory benefits.

II.

The great significance of the Moscow conclave of societal activists, gathered on 8-10 August, must be seen in this, that it was convened exclusively upon a patriotic impulse and it pursued the aims of national unity. This was not sufficiently appreciated by our press, not only the "socialistic", which is dead to national motives, but also not the "bourgeois". The Moscow conclave did not represent any sort of political combination, it was not a matter of class unity, it aspired to create a national bloc, into which there could enter representatives of all the classes and social groups, insofar as they were patriotically disposed towards the state. It cannot be denied, that within such an unity there could enter in the reasonably disposed and the conscientious peasantry, such that its popular basis could be very broad. Such a national bloc, or patriotic union, having united various parties and groups, could prove a formation stable and lasting. In it a truly national power would find its support. And it mustneeds be said, that this current in the Russian societal effort, which coalesced at the Moscow conclave, was disposed patriotically and nationally, at it there were expressed thoughts concerning the saving of our native land, rather than of that ambiguous creature, which we tend to call "revolution" and which all more and more is immersed in falsehood and moral rot. And if it were possible to criticise the Moscow conclave on something, it would be on this, that its national character was not strongly enough expressed, that there was too much, in the contemporary terminology, of the "nation in common", and not of the nationally-Russian. There are three basic passions, which can be awakened in a people and which can become impulses in its historical fate, -- the social class passion, the national passion and the religious passion. Unscrupulous demagogues have already employed the most base of these passions -- that of social class. It has poisoned Russia, it has killed the feel for truth in the masses of the Russian people, it has formed in their souls a nihilistic apostasy. And only the awakening of passions national and religious can save the Russian people from total disintegration and decay. Concerning the religious passion this is not the place at present to speak, it is too immense a question, whereas the national passion cannot be that of the "nation in general" for political tactics, it is an arousing of a fiery element in the people.

In Russia at present there have formed three tendencies: the one wants unconditionally, without haggling and without further considerations to save our native land, in which it sees an eternal value, and it demands discipline in the army for ends patriotic and national; the second however wants conditionally to save the native land, and in its calculations it tends to say that the native land should be subordinated to the "revolution" and "democracy", and it demands exclusively a "revolutionary" discipline; whereas the third would unconditionally betray their native land and demand its destruction in the name of worldwide revolution. To characterise these three tendencies, as "bourgeois", "moderate-socialistic" and "extreme-socialistic" is both a conditional lie and nonsense. It is time to cease bestowing significance to a black-balling terminology, even though it fancy itself as of the intelligentsia. Only people, obsessed with false ideas or completely ignorant and limited, can see something "bourgeois" in the unconditional defense of one's native land and in a national perspective, whilst terming as socialism either a conditional defense of one's native land or else its outright betrayal. That which among us over the course of half a year they have tended to call a "socialistic" moment, represents an intolerable lie and fraud and is a smokescreen for the very lowest instincts of the masses and the shameless demagogic indulgence of them. About socialism at present in Russia it is impossible to speak, it does not at all exist, there is only a dragging in the dirt of the socialistic idea. Russian revolutionary socialism is a phenomenon completely reactionary, it is but the legacy of the processes of the disintegration of the old Russia. With us there is no sort of an healthy and creative democratic movement. Democracy is understood among us so distortedly, that it brings to mind some sort of a lampoon and caricature. The demonic obsession with the idea of equality is not democracy, since a true democracy is a search for ways of selection of the best, the establishing of a true inequality, and it is possible to imagine, that the mission of the Russian revolution -- is an exposing of the falsehood, lying at the basis of the democratic principle, with its lack of desire to subordinate itself to an higher truth. The tangle of lies in democracy and the tangle of lies in socialism is a phenomenon morally ugly. And we most of all have need of a moral restoration of health to the nation, its spiritual renewal, an awakening of faith in the truth of God. The Russian people cannot worthily wage war, since it has lost faith in the sanctities, such as surpass every earthly blessing. War in the name of one's own special interests, in the name of "land and freedom" cannot be justified. The terror of the war cannot be faced in the name of rational and utilitarian considerations. This tragic terror can only be faced by those, who believe in the ends of life and the sanctities, put higher than the givenness of empirical life with its limited interests. But faith in the Divine meaning of life has weakened in the Russian people, it has lost its strength in the most terrible moment of the struggle.

III.

The tragic events, connected with the name of General Kornilov, are a telling indication that we continue to live in an atmosphere murky and ambiguous. In the way recent events have played out, there is the feel of demonic linkages of lies and intrigues. There is occasion to think, that the dark powers are in collusion against Russia and allow it no escape out of its tragic position. The powers now dominant in the Russian state are just as intolerant of truth and light, just as intolerant of them, as were the powers governing in the old order. The old powers lived exclusively by fear of revolution, and the new powers live just as exclusively by fear of counter-revolution. Both the one and the other condition are alike non-creative, alike degrading, both alike doomed with falsehood and fear of the light. This -- is the path of a morbid mistrustfulness, imperceptibly passing over into a wicked vindictiveness, and crowned with provocations. This -- is of the bleak realm of the underground mindset, from which our miserable land seems unable to escape. Even after the turnabout, which was to set us free, we continue to be choked with murky lies. Freedom of thought, freedom of speech are trampled upon for us. It is too clearly apparent for honourable people, that in the accusations against General Kornilov there was piled up a monstrous falsehood, deceit and intrigue. And all Russia ought first of all to demand explanations of the truth and for what is right, which cannot be sacrificed for anything in the world. It is impossible to tolerate, that a seal of compulsory silence should again be imposed upon our mouths. And if a disturbing lie is governing our lives, then it ought to be exposed and shouted about at all the crossroads. The revolutionary power can as little free itself from Bolshevism, as the pre-revolutionary power could free itself from the Black Hundreds, and therefore it cannot be national and patriotic. That which our revolutionary insipidness terms a "developing and deepening of revolution", is a sip of the poison of Bolshevism, which in but a more diluted form is present also in the Social Democrat Mensheviks and the Social Revolutionaries. The Bolshevik disease-germ has had an excellent culturing in the blood of the Russian revolutionary intelligentsia, and this -- is but a new form of its age old social maximalism, which is but the flip side of its age old religious nihilism. The radical freeing from Bolshevism presupposes a spiritual turnabout. And until there is this desired spiritual turnabout, the ruling powers in the hands of the Russian intelligentsia never will be patriotic and national.

It is possible quite variously to view for the given moment the fateful clash between General Kornilov and the Provisional Government, but to deny the heroic patriotism of Gen. Kornilov and his supreme fidelity to our country is but malice of will or from greedy considerations. This has to be admitted from out of an instinct for what is right, irregardless of belonging to this or that party. Politics with its passions and calculations, its struggle of interests and struggle for power, ought not to obscure the vitally direct truth. Every lie has to be cast down, and for this occurring there have to unite all those that are honest and upright, all that are conscientious in loving the light. The rising up against falsehood is a sacred right and a sacred duty of man. The whole of politics and all the social interests and the social arrangements -- are nothing in comparison with the eternal light of truth, with the spiritual life of man. In a direct patriotic impulse there is an immediate vital truth, which there cannot be in politics. In Russia there has to begin an organic patriotic stirring and a demand for truth in politics. An atheistic politics cannot be other than a lie, it sacrifices what is right and true in the name of the well-being of people, whilst transforming this well-being into an idol. But higher than people's avaricious well-being has to be posited the truth of spiritual life, without which there is not man, there is not in him the image of God, and there is not the people with a great historical destiny.

Concerning Freedom and Integrity of the Word

(1917 - #281)[1]

I.

When they speak with pathos about the freedoms won by the Revolution[2], then first of all they ought to have in view those rights of man, which cannot be taken away in the name of whatever the earthly blessings. But it is about these sacred and inalienable rights of man among us that they least of all think and least of all care about. Pathos for the freedom of man does not exist within the elements of the Russian Revolution. There is a strong basis to think, that Russians do not love freedom and do not value freedom. Our so-called "Revolutionary Democracy" is obsessed with a passion for equality, such as the world has never seen, but under freedom it however understands the right of violence against neighbours in the name of its interests, and arbitrariness in the overall leveling. In the name of equality it is ready among us to destroy whatever freedom pleases it. And the moral source of the denial of rights, such as guarantee freedom, mustneeds be sought in the weak awareness of the sense of duty and in an undeveloped sense of personal dignity. The rights of man presuppose first of all a sense of duty in a man. Without an awareness of the duty to preserve the sacred right of one's neighbour, it is impossible to speak

---

[1] O SVOBODE I DOSTOINSTVE SLOVA. Article originally published in the weekly Journal "Narodopravstvo", oct. 1917, № 11, p. 5-7.

[2] [*translator note*, n.b.: this is the 27 Feb.(Old Style)/12 Mar. 1917 Russian "*February Revolution*" which formed the Provisional Government under A. F. Kerensky, which was supplanted by the 15 Oct./ 7 Nov. 1917 Russian "October Revolution" under the Communist Bolsheviks and V. I. Lenin. Berdyaev's present article here was published on 7 October 1917, late in the life of the Kerensky revolutionary democratic Provisional Government, and reflects the increasing chaos that led to its collapse.]

seriously about any sort of rights, for all rights will be squashed. The Russian revolutionary consciousness however initially denies the sense of duty in man, it stands exclusively upon the pretensions of man. And one, in whom the pretensions and demands are stronger than the sense of duty and obligation, morally loses his rights, morally buries his freedom. In the Russian revolutionary democratic emotional outlook there has completely faded the sense of guilt, such as is characteristic of the children of God, and it has been replaced by a sense of endless pretensions, as is characteristic to the children of this world. Any awareness of duties has faded in that element, which now is dominant in Russia, and therefore outrages are committed incessantly against the rights of man. In the guarantee of the rights of man most important -- is not the pretensions of one, who possesses a right, but rather the sense of duty in one, who ought to respect these rights and not infringe upon them.

Russian revolutionary democracy sees as its most valuable conquests the universal electoral right, as in the Constituent Assembly, in the developing of the class struggle, in the democratisation and socialisation of society, but it fails to see them in the rights of man, in the free rights of man. And indeed this is no surprise. The spiritual understanding of freedom is totally foreign to the revolutionary democracy, and it is prepared to betray freedom, such as is bound up with the birthright of man, for a motley pottage of interests. And the Russian Revolution has given us no sort of the real and substantial rights and freedoms of man. We have no *habeus corpus*. On the contrary, in the measure that the Revolution has "developed" and "deepened", all the moreso there has triumphed the outrage against every human right and every human freedom. And first of all it has proven a stifling of the most sacred of the rights of man, the most sacred of freedoms -- the freedom of the word, the freedom of speech. We are experiencing a period of the most terrible servility of word and slavery of thought. In our nightmarish days, few are those who are resolved freely and independently to think, freely and independently to express their thought in words. Our press is in sore straits; it is in a condition of restraint, and tends to support the conditional lie, connected with the ruling powers. Formerly it tended much to speak about "his majesty the lord emperor", now in no less quantity it tends to speak the conditional lie about its majesty the revolutionary democracy. And no one makes bold to say, that the king has on no clothes (as in the saying of Anderson). On the streets and squares few are those who are resolved loudly to express their thoughts and feelings, everyone is afraid to turn upon them the heads the comrades in the neighbourhood. The Russian people have begun to speak in whispers the same, as during the worst times of the Old Regime. And it is necessary straight out and loudly to say, that the freedom of thought and the freedom of speech at present is in greater peril, than it was in the Old Regime. Back then for speaking freely they threw you in prison and exiled you to Siberia, now they might tear you to pieces and murder you. Back then, under the old oppression, free speech did work and it radically criticised the governing powers, morally it made a protest against the oppression and for a whole century it morally undermined the prestige of the powers, which had deprived people of rights and freedoms. Societal opinion went against the fundamental principles of the old tyranny and it always expressed this, though in a roundabout language. Now societal opinion has been rendered less free. Few are those who might resolve to rise up against the fundamental principles of the modern oppression and expose the moral ugliness of the present-day tyranny. The tyranny of the mob is more terrible, than the tyranny of the one or of several. Russian thought is situated in a grievous state of captivity. Societal opinion has become paralysed, it has lost its moral centre. There is no sounding forth freely and independently, rising above the struggle of interests, above the raging elements, there does not sound forth such a voice of the national conscience, of the national sense of reason, of thought-word (logos).

II.

Many among us tend to criticise the tactics of revolutionary democracy, they appeal for unity and coalitions, but morally they capitulate before that element, which breeds tyranny, which forcibly abuses thought and speech. Too much already everything is blamed on the Bolsheviks, who have become a common target, at a time when the evil is not only in them and it not only they that are destroying freedom in Russia. The evil has spread widely and its sources run deep. Our intelligentsia has confessed the world-concept of the slave, it has denied the very sources of freedom -- the spiritual nature of man, of man's sonship to God. The people for too long already have lived in slavery and darkness. And the most sacred rights of man, justified by his boundless spiritual nature, have been surrendered over into the grip of the quantitative human masses, the harrowing crowd. And if the fate of the freedom of the word is being entrusted to utilitarian interests and calculations, then in recent days the right to have this word is admitted only insofar as it is of service to the revolutionary democracy, but they abuse and refuse the right to words, which serve other ends, more lofty and deeper ends, upon this shaky ground that it is only words, playing up to the interests and instincts of the masses, that should receive unlimited freedom. All other words however, resounding from a greater depth, are subject to suspicion and violence. An hideous sense of blackmail connected with accusations of counter-revolution leads to a tyrannical mob justice against free thought and speech, the inviolable freedom of the person. It is necessary finally and forcefully to declare, that a true freedom of the word in Russia presupposes the possibility to have a say by everyone, even by those, that are proponents of monarchy. If the freedom of the word be given exclusively to the proponents of the democratic republic, then it will not be greater, but less so, than under the Old Regime, -- then it would be unlimited freedom for words, but merely only by the former opposition current. And in a free Russia they want to limit the freedom of the word to only but one current! And indeed it is presupposed, that the Constituent Assembly, i.e. the sovereign people, will decide, whether in Russia there will be a republican or monarchical order, and that consequently segments having the most varied opinions can freely prepare for it. But monarchical convictions none of us dare freely express, this would be not without danger, the freedom and rights of such people could not be guaranteed. And this involves a moral lie, such as is wont to beget tyranny. Republicans, such as be worthy of this name, ought to bestow everyone a greater freedom, than did the monarchists. Bereft of the moral right to speak about freedom necessarily are those, who admit of freedom only for themself and for their own.

The self-appointed worker and soldier organisations already for half a year have been committing outrages against the rights of man, they live to deny freedom. It is impossible to deny not only the right, but also the duty of the workers to organise for defending their essential interests and for the increase of their societal standing, but with us the soviets from the very start of the Revolution have entered upon the path towards a class dictatorship, of a peculiar twist to a monarchical dictatorship, and this has turned into a destruction of freedom in Russia. The outrage against the freedom and dignity, the integrity of the word reached its extreme expression, in the playing out of the Kornilov tragedy. All at once darkness has enveloped Russian society and no one has made bold to counter it. The press was terrified and conducted itself unworthily, without any resolve to demand first of all an explanation of the truth, and it swallowed the government's conditional lie about the "mutiny" of General Kornilov[1]. An investigation was begun, and over Russia hung the terrible phantom of a Red Terror, of a self-appointed mob inquiry over those suspected of sympathising with General Kornilov. Fright seized hold upon the woesome Russian society, a fright far greater, than in the most terrible times of the tsardom. Fright always tends to become magnified, but it is characteristic of the spiritual atmosphere of the Russian Revolution. In Russian society started a moral tenseness. Out of fear there were whispers about provocations, causing the Kornilov tragedy. The right even to freely defend General Kornilov, a war hero, a passionate patriot and indisputable democrat, was not given. And only gradually did exposures leak into the press, shedding light upon this dark and grim history. But those nightmarish days have ultimately disclosed for us the absence of the freedom of the word, the manipulation of thought, the stifling of spirit. For us the course of the Revolution has developed into faint-heartedness.

III.

It is necessary loudly to proclaim, that in Revolutionary Russia the freedom of speech, the freedom of thought does not exist, indeed even less so, than in the old and autocratic Russia. The revolutionary democratic societal order tends to read better into the heart of matters and demands a greater conformity of thought, than did the pre-revolutionary reactionary powers, which were too indifferent to every nuance of societal thought and incapable of making sense of it. The censorship by the revolutionary democratic societal setup is more all-encompassing and pervasive, than our old censorship. And it mustneeds be said, that a censorship urged on by the masses of the people is always more terrible, than the censorship by a government power, where much tends to slip by. When the people itself

---

[1] [*trans. note*: General L. G. Kornilov on 28 Aug. (Old Style) /10 Sept. 1917 attempted to restore order during the prevailing chaos under the Provisional Government, and was in turn arrested, denounced and vilified by Kerensky, who relied increasingly upon the support of the leftist socialist soviet elements.]

infringes upon the freedom of thought and speech, this encroachment is more terrible and oppressive, than the encroachment of a government power, -- in this scenario there is nowhere safe. After the revolutionary turnabout the constraints of censorship fell off and there was abolished even the military censorship as is necessary during wartime, but there was not a declaration of the rights of freedom of thought and the freedom of speech, the infringement upon which is a crime against both man and God. A wantonness and dissoluteness of speech is not freedom. This wantonness and dissoluteness has destroyed freedom of speech for us. The freedom and worthiness, the integrity of speech, presupposes a discipline within speech, an inward ascesis. The right of the freedom of speech presupposes a sense of responsibility in the use of words. Every freedom presupposes a disciplining and ascetic effort, and with irresponsibility it always perishes. Those wanton orgies of words, which for all these months have been practiced in the revolutionary socialistic press, have prepared the way for the destruction of all freedom of speech. The wantonness, the dissoluteness and arbitrariness are destroying freedom, for freedom demands the preservation of integrity in man, keeping it clean, a self-restraint. The corrupt manipulation of words destroys the integrity of the word and becomes enslaving. In the revolutionary press occur orgies of verbal corruption. The revolutionary phraseology has degenerated into a quite real perversity. Is it not perverse, all those false cries about "counter-revolution", is it not perverse all these false promises for a speedy start to a social paradise, is it not perverse all these words about the sacredness of the Revolution, about the sacredness of the Internationale, etc.? For the winning of a true freedom of the word it is necessary to fight against this corruption of the word.

  Russian writers, conscious of their calling, their integrity and their responsibility for their native-land, ought to demand a promulgation guaranteeing the freedom of thought and word. But this demand can morally carry weight only in the mouths of those writers, who are observant of the higher integrity of word and thought, who set truth and the right higher than whatever the interests. Over the course of these revolutionary months there has as it were grown dim the integrity and significance of Russian literature and Russian free thought. Too many of the Russian writers have been subjected to stifling street shouts about their "bourgeoisness", about the "bourgeoisness" of all the educated, of all the creators of culture. In them there has not proven a sufficient strength of resistance in the face of the raging elements, they go to pieces and begin themself to pronounce words, inconsistent with the depths of their being. With too many Russian writers there has not appeared their own unique idea, which they are called to introduce into the life of the people, and they instead seek for ideas in that very people, which is itself situated in darkness and in need of light. In Russia there ought to be heard truly free words about that moral savagery and ugliness, to which we have fallen, and these words ought to be raised above the struggle of classes, groups and parties, above the struggle for interests and the struggle for power, they ought to be a reflection of the Divine Word, to which only can be based the sanctity of the free word and free thought, now so abused and trampled upon. This is not a question of politics, this -- is a question of the people's ethics, a question of the religious conscience of the people. The people's conscience and reason ought to possess a centre, a central focus. And such a central focus can only be with the bearers of an higher spiritual culture, free of the slave-like orgies. We inevitably have to renew the spiritual foundations of our life and seek for the inner sources of freedom. A purely external path will drag us down to ruination and slavery. We have no further desire for more slavery, neither the old, nor the new. The revolutionary violence against free thought and words in essence bears within it the seeds of counter-revolution, it is the violence of the old demonic darkness and it cannot be tolerated in a free land.

Democracy and Hierarchy

(1917 - 270)[1]

I.

The moral and aesthetic ugliness of the Russian revolution ought not to hinder us from seeing its enormous significance. In any case its spiritual consequences will be immense. The Russian revolution -- is an enormous experience, which will change the sense of life for the people of the Russian intelligentsia and compel them to think things anew. The traditional history of the Russian intelligentsia has ended, its basic ideas verified in life's experience and its lies exposed. Now forevermore the Russian revolutionary intelligentsia will have no right to say, that a paradise on earth will be established, when they come to power: they have come to power, and on earth is established hell. Truly, the Russian revolution does serve some sort of a great mission, but the mission is non-creative and negative, -- it has to expose the lie and the emptiness of a certain idea, by which the Russian intelligentsia was obsessed and by which it poisoned the Russian people. This idea was borrowed from Western teachings, but it was uniquely adapted in the Eastern Russian element and taken to unprecedented extremes. *The Russian revolution is an exposure of the lie of democracy considered as a supreme principle of life, an experiential evidence of what the tyrannical triumph of the egalitarian passion can lead to. Russians are in the grips of the egalitarian passion, the thirst for a mechanical and materialistic leveling.* This egalitarian passion is being experienced in Russia with a pathos of religious fervour and it bears the character of a demonic obsession, directed at the destruction of everything qualitative in existence, of everything distinct, of everything heightening. In the Russian revolution the hierarchical principle has been violated to such a degree, as in no other revolution in the world. The demand for equality in it will soon be spread not only to the lower

---

[1] DEMOKRATIYA I IERARKHIYA. Article originally published in the weekly "Russkaya svoboda", 15 oct. 1917, № 24-25, p. 5-10.

rungs of the human world, but also to the lower rungs of the natural world, to animals, plants and minerals, right down to the atoms of matter. The whole cosmos will fall apart into atoms and each atom will demand itself an equal position with all the others, and each will acknowledge itself sovereign. The entire producing of man by nature, his elevation over the lower natural order is already an aristocratism, is already an hierarchism, which ought not to suffer the egalitarian passion sweeping everything from its path.

The French Revolution was bloody and terrible, but also in it there was not the complete destruction of that hierarchical principle, upon which rests the whole order of the state and society, of all civilisation. Western Europe even after all its revolutionary turnabouts has remained hierarchical, and in it have been preserved the traditions of all the civilised manner of societal life. Western Europe acknowledges gradations, differences, degrees, it admits of elevation, the selection of the best, a selection of qualities. Russian revolutionaries though have perceived these Western traits as "bourgeois". Truly in the West there is much that is "bourgeois", but a vile "bourgeoisness" is always as the result of destruction of hierarchism, always it is a revolt and appropriation by the unworthy, the ignoble, the worse. And the Russian revolt against every hierarchism is leading to a state of the worse, the unworthy, the ignoble, and the Russian negation of "bourgeoisness" readily gets transformed into a very worst sort and very boorish "bourgeoisness" all its own, a very ugly sort of philistinism. The Russian revolutionary democratism is essentially hostile to the hierarchical foundations of the whole of civilised cultural existence, of all civil and societal existence. This is a barbaric individualism, with the arbitrary will of each individual, who with himself wants to start off the history of the world, revering nothing higher than himself. And this is nowise a question of this or that political aspect, this is a question of one's own revolutionary morals, of one's own sense of life, of one's own direction of religiosity. At the root of the Russian revolution lies not so much a false politics, as rather a false morality. Russians often become nihilists out of moral impulses, and they experience their nihilism as a moral or even religious truth. They deny the Divine values and spiritual realities, God, fatherland, truth, beauty, they reject all the established qualities in the name of the truth and justice of levelling and the levelled well-being of people. Russian revolutionary nihilism rejects the Divine world order, it does not accept the hierarchical structure of the cosmos. This egalitarian nihilistic passion is deeply anti-cosmic, it revolts against hierarchical degrees of being and it thirsts for an equitable non-being, an equality within nothing, in emptiness, in an impoverishment, in a stripping away of all the forms of cultural existence, in an empty freedom from all hierarchical values. Dostoevsky with genius revealed the dialectics of the Russian egalitarian nihilism. Ivan Karamazov also was an advocate of suchlike a repudiation of cosmic hierarchism in the name of equality and an equal happiness of people. The Legend of the Grand Inquisitor provides quite much by way of the metaphysics of Russian nihilism, democratism and socialism, although its action is transferred over to the Catholic West. Very characteristic is this Russian repudiation of God, the world, history, culture, as representing inequality. Down with everything, in the name of equality!

II.

Such a characteristically Russian phenomenon, as Tolstoyanism, is bent on destroying all the richness of existence through egalitarian a passion, in it is active a sort of demonic moralism. And how characteristic Tolstoyanism is of Russian people, by it are poisoned even those, who do not regard themself Tolstoyans and have nothing in common with the Tolstoyan teaching. The war and revolution have shown, how innate to the Russians is the spirit of the Tolstoyan non-resistance. The traditional Russian populism has always been inspired by that same egalitarian passion and always it has been hostile to the hierarchism of culture. The social question for Russian populism has always been exclusively a question of distribution and division, never of creativity or production. The kingdom of God upon earth, for which Russian people so strive, while living under oppression, presents itself first of all as a kingdom of equality, as an overall levelling, as the abolishing of all the historical hierarchies, of all the qualitative heights. The finest Russian people have spoken about the all-humanness and the all-worldness of the Russian spirit. But the misfortune and sickness of the Russian spirit mustneeds be sought in the confused and jumbled mixing up of the all-unity, which includes within it the fullness of all the degrees of being, of all the gradations, of all the hierarchies of individuality from that of individual people up through nations, confusing it with a simplifying and levelling down process, in which all the degrees fade and perish, together with all the individual gradations and hierarchies. And therefore also to Russians the unity of mankind would seem an abolition of nations. With this is connected the deep anti-historicism of the Russian intelligentsia, its moral non-acceptance of those sacrifices for human well-being and human equality, which are gained by history with its creativity of cultures and states. Russian people are tempted by an instantaneous leap across into an absolute unity and absolute equality, without the arduous path of history, without the steps, without the hierarchical distinctions and sorting out of the best. The traditional Russian morals does not ascribe significance to personal responsibility, to personal merit, to a selection through personal qualities. Russian morals do not love strength, all strength it regards as diabolical, and not Divine, and for it the immoral is every exalting and every hierarchically higher a position, based on merit, worthiness and quality. With grief it mustneeds be acknowledged, that this is not an Aryan morals. Many see in such a moral mindset the Christian nature of the Russian people. But I tend to think, that this is an enormous misunderstanding. Christianity -- is hierarchical. True sacrifice -- is a show of strength, and not of weakness.

The entire world-concept and worldview of the Russian intelligentsia was bound to lead to namely suchlike a revolution, as the Russian revolution has proven to be. Within it has been dominant the spirit of non-being, a spirit of levelling, submerged down into nothingness, into desolation, the spirit of a mixed confusion and destruction of all distinctions and matters of worth. For the instincts of the masses of the people, itself still dark but moreover having lost its faith, this new religion of an universal levelling and confusion, the universal obliteration of all hierarchical distinctions and hierarchical qualities has proven very tempting and attainable. The lower elements among the people, lacking in awareness, uncultured and betraying the faith of the fathers, have perceived democracy as the toppling of every hierarchical subordination, of every qualitative process of selection, of the triumph in the revolt by a mechanical quantity. In the moral guise of our revolutionary democratism it is a boorishness that has won out, the casting down of every noble aspect in the respecting of that which is qualitatively higher, more worthy, more valuable, spiritually stronger. Each one albeit most insignificant, at the bottom of his spiritual culture, in his giftedness, in his moral aspect, has sensed himself a tsar and autocrat, and has felt himself the bearer of a sovereign power. A lack of understanding for the propriety of an hierarchical ordering, the propriety of acknowledging and respecting the higher, is characteristic of the boorish. Slaves might see some higher condition in a revolt against everything, that is higher. The soldier might consider it degrading to his dignity to show respect to a general on merit. He would see it worthy to have a levelling confusion, wherein each would be a general unto himself. The prompting of suchlike a sense of worth in soldiers would lead to a shameful flight and treason, i.e. to a total loss of honour.

III.

Upon this basis the nation has arrived at the point of suicide. Upon this basis has collapsed not only the army, which can only exist as an hierarchical organism, but the state also is falling apart, culture is falling apart, every societal accord and structure is going to pieces, the person is in ruin. An evil malice towards neighbour, against whatever was set higher, be it material or spiritual, is set at the foundations of Russian revolutionary democracy. It is a pitiful and shabby foundation, upon which it is impossible to build anything, whether be it the state, culture, economic life, or even spiritual life! The destruction of every hierarchy is a monstrous and ugly bit of confusion, a denial indeed of the cosmic principles of societal life. The structure and accord of the societal is truly but an inexorable part of the structure and accord of the cosmic. Anarchy is a destruction of the cosmos, the rising up of chaos and its getting the better of every hierarchy. The Russian passion for equality in what should otherwise not be is likewise a denial of the personal principle, and this rather -- is a passion for impersonality, the drowning of the person in the chaotic element, in chaotic collectivism, in an overall unqualitative hodgepodge. The personal principle is inseparably bound up with hierarchism, with the universal cosmic structure, and it presupposes distinctions, elevations, qualitative dissimilarities. The person withers and perishes, when it is forced into a compulsory equality with all other persons, when every increase of its abilities, its remarkableness, its qualitative uniqueness is retarded and stunted by a levelling down in equality with its neighbours. This -- is an affront for the finest, and an indulging of the worst. In the realm of a mechanical equality, of all and everything jumbled together within a collective mass, there becomes possible only powerless persons. The Church -- is a model of true hierarchism, -- within it is the personal principle, to which is ascribed absolute significance, co-united with an hierarchical Sobornost'-communality, with a mystical hierarchy, but there is no levelling hodgepodge, there is not the coercion of the person towards equality with every other person. This cosmic hierarchism pervades also the entirety of culture, which is based upon a selection of qualities and the elevation of the more valuable. This cosmic hierarchism pervades also the entirety of the civil aspect, upon it rests every authority, which, in the words of the Apostle Paul, is from God, and this is true also in regard to the democratic states. The destruction of every hierarchism in the state, in society, in culture, in religious life, is a return to the primordial chaotic condition, it destroys man, who is of the highest hierarchical rank in the universe, and it betrays man into the power of the lower chaotic elements, which pretend upon an equality with man. And indeed man himself is an hierarchical organism, in which all the parts have to be subordinate to the supreme centre. Amidst the destruction, however, of this hierarchical subordination man tends to disintegrate, in him perishes the image and likeness of God.

The democratic principle is perceived by us in a terribly distorted form. What is true in democracy, is also a searching out of ways of selection of the best, the averting of a false hierarchism and the establishing of favourable conditions for true hierarchism. The aristocratic principle is lodged within the intents of a representative democracy. And democracy is a seeking of ways of establishing a governance by the best. Democracy does not invariably exclude an higher hierarchy. A free, a self-determining and self-governing people can acknowledge the higher truth of an hierarchical structure, the selection of the finest and the subordination of the lower to the higher. Democracy has need of nurturing in a true hierarchical spirit, and without this it decays and falls apart spiritually. "Bourgeoisness" in the ugly sense of this word is also a destruction of true hierarchism, a mistaking of the worst for the finest, the occupying of a position, not corresponding to qualities and worth. Snobism is the denial of true hierarchism and a slavery to a false hierarchism. A democracy, which regards itself utmost and the sole principle of life, is already subordinate to nothing, and is certainly both a lie and a temptation. And this tempting lie of democracy is most of all manifest in the Russian revolution. But in democracy there is also its own subordinate truth, which aids in the triumph of a true hierarchism over the false hierarchism. Final still and utmost remains the truth, proclaimed by Plato: the ideal form of governance can only be aristocratic, the dominion of the best, the noblest, the most gifted, the spiritually strongest. This is also the true hierarchism, upon which only can be based states and cultures of peoples. There should be wrought out and passed on predominantly a nobler and more gifted race, which would be called upon to determine the fate of the world and the fate of peoples. But the seeking out of representatives of this race and the summoning of them to rule -- is a very complex and tortuous process. The worst very often get to rule. And the question about the relationship of the selection of the best for a consistent historically noble race is more complex, than the representatives of a primitive democratic metaphysics tend to think.

The casting down of a selection of the best is a cosmic act of destruction, an infringement upon the Divine world-order. The very appearance of cosmic being is on the order of a distinction in glory of the sun from the moon, of one star from another star. The same principle ought to pervade the entirety of societal life and ought to reveal in it the paths towards the appearance of a true hierarchy, and it ought to set itself in opposition to the spirit of a levelling non-being. In the Russian revolution has appeared the spirit of an envious and vengeful casting down of every hierarchy, not only earthly, but also heavenly, the coelestial hierarchy. This ignoble spirit is undermining the spiritual health of the Russian people, debilitating it and readying it for a woeful future. Upon this path creativity is impossible, since creativity -- is hierarchical, and not democratic, it presupposes the heights and the prevailing of qualities. One who has no desire to admit the higher, falls then under the grip of the lower. Such is a law of world justice. Having risen up against God and nowise revering the holy, one slithers down like an animal before idols and grovels before serpents. Man cannot free himself of a religious venerating, and when he ceases religiously to revere the higher, he begins religiously to revere the lower: in the human heart the Anti-Christ gets substituted for Christ and creates its own godless hierarchy.

The Objective Groundings of the Societal Aspect

(1917 -282)[1]

I.

The course of the Russian revolution has revealed, that our basic and essential demand is a demand for enlightening, for knowledge, for a more conscious attitude towards societal life. We are beset by darkness, and it directs our unconscious elemental movements. In this darkness are immersed not only the masses of the people, but also wide circles of the Russian intelligentsia. The Russian revolutionary intelligentsia, which pretends to convey light to the people, has never been truly enlightened, nor educated and cultured, it was semi-enlightened, its consciousness was devoted only to a superficial enlightenment. And an half-enlightened, superficial enlightenment is worse than that complete lack of enlightenment, in which the people tended to live, if the people has not as yet lost its immediate organic faith. A superficial enlightenment leads readily to a nihilistic negation of all sanctities and values. Among the half-enlightened Russian intelligentsia also was begotten the nihilism, which many tend to see as an unique offspring of the Russian spirit. When this semi-enlightened nihilism spreads to the masses of the people and replaces in the soul of the people the extinguished faith, it then begins to destroy all of national, state and cultural life. And then we begin to recognise, that most of all we are in need of genuine enlightenment, which has nothing in common with ratio-judgemental and negative enlightenment. A genuine enlightenment would have to begin for us, other than where it begins for the semi-enlightened, -- with a cognition of the objective principles of the societal aspect. And then there would not occur these orgies of a perverted social visionary dream from a subjective human arbitrariness, which now

---

[1] OBЪETKTIVNYE OSNOVY OBSCHECTVENNOSTI. Article originally published in the weekly "Narodopravstvo", 23 oct. 1917, № 13, p. 7-9.

occurs. The ratio-judgemental enlightenment, i.e. half-enlightenment, is powerless to reveal the objective reason in societal life, its objective principles, it always favours human subjectivism, it nourishes a disdain for history and for the ignoring of the natural grounds of societal life. For the semi-enlightened Russian intelligentsia, every lawful measure in natural and societal life represents something sufficiently as such "bourgeois", and thus for the revolutionary and proletarian mentality is non-binding. "Bourgeois" likewise also appear all the norms of the societal aspect, ledged in general within reason and the conscience. Any consciousness of societal life as conditioned by objective cosmic principles seems a product of "bourgeois" thought to those, who think as proletarians,[1] i.e. without any traditions of thought, without any connections with the deep wellsprings of life. Such a "proletarian" mindset does not want to know of fatherland, does not want to know of origins, i.e. it disdains the deep fundamentals of all things, the deep roots. This is also a nihilism hostile to culture, proclaiming in everything a limitless license of sons, having broken off all connections with the fathers. Suchlike a "proletarian" semi-enlightened intelligentsia mindset also does not attempt to uncover nor perceive the quite profoundest grounds of the societal aspect, since this would lead into the mysterious depths of cosmic life and would limit the human arbitrariness.

The proletarian semi-enlightened intelligentsia mindset sees in societal life, on the one hand, the subjective interests of people and groups of people exclusively, their evil will, their violence and exploitation, which also comprises the content of history, and yet on the other hand, it sees the struggle against all this and the limitless possibility to attain a perfect social order by way of an organising and active will, be it proletarian or intelligentsia. Such a sort of superficial mindset unites an extreme pessimism as regards the past (all filled with evil) with an extreme optimism as regards the future (all filled with good). This state of consciousness begets much hatred, malice and disunity. All the energy of soul is directed against those evil-doers, which impede the establishing of an ultimate equality and social paradise on earth. These evil-doers for the Russian revolution have received the name "bourgeoise" and to them are ascribed desperate acts, conspiracies and intrigues. What thus monstrous

---

[1] By "proletarians" I mean a particular type of thought, and not the mindset of the workers, who can also think otherwise.

dimensions of the evil-doer role are assumed by the heap of capitalists, while in contrast to this is the noble role of the proletariat, who have to contend against this heap. History becomes defined exclusively by the evil and good subjective will of people. In this conception, a complete moral irresponsibility is uniquely combined with an eternal moral labelling of people behind the objective societal order. The semi-enlightened, the "proletarian" mindset is totally convinced, that if at present it is impossible to introduce into Russia a socialistic order, then this is exclusively because that the evil will of the bourgeoise neither desires nor permits of it. And if this bourgeois will can be countermanded by way of armed insurrections, by violence and destruction, then socialism will be realised. Mr. Lenin has even reached such a forgetfulness of the abc's of Marxism, of the social elements and economic aspects of knowledge, that he proposed the arrest of 100 capitalists and from this thoughtless act he anticipates the approach of socialism! The revolutionary psychology, as adduced by Marxism, ultimately has to deny objective science. Marxism represents an hodgepodge of semi-enlightenment, i.e. of subjectively proletarian thought, together with authentic enlightenment, i.e. with elements of objective social science. But Russians have predominantly adopted for themself the semi-enlightenment of Marxism, i.e. the class point of view, admitting over them of nothing higher, no higher court of judgement.

II.

There is no sort of possibility to beat into the heads of the Russian socialists the objective truth of Marxism about the developing of the productive forces as an economic basis for socialism, about the dependence of distribution upon production, about the legitimacy of social developement, about the reactionary aspect of all the socialistic experiments, in lessening the productivity of labour, etc. Everything objective bounces off away from the semi-enlightened intelligentsia and proletarian mindset, does not penetrate into it, and this consciousness is incapable of being interested in truth, of devoting itself for however short a time to a disinterested knowledge, it -- remains but elementary and emotional. The semi-enlightened aspect of the class philosophy of history explains everything by the evil will of the exploiters, and it is incapable of perceiving those objective principles of state, societal and cultural existence, which arise with every capricious act of people. And thus, the semi-enlightened in the service of class maliciousness cannot and do not want to perceive, that many an inequality is not in the evil will of some exploiter, but rather has an objective underlying cause and justification for that level, in which human culture finds itself. An equality, not corresponding to the degree of victory of man over the elemental powers of nature, would lead to yet greater impoverishment and need, and culturally it would throw mankind backwards. The social question is first of all a question of production, and not distribution, this -- is a question of mastery of the elemental powers of nature. The remarkable Russian thinker, N. F. Fedorov, was correct, when he said, that the social question is to a greater degree a question of the knowledge of nature, rather than sociology. The demand for levelling into poverty is a reactionary demand, hostile to the creativity of culture. In the sickening and tormentive question about poverty and neediness in the masses of the people, quite of secondary a significance is this, that a comparatively small heap of people has attained wealth and happy a condition. This -- is a moral question. The need expresses itself not so much with the material rise of the rich and exploiters on their side, as rather the objective poverty of mankind, the low level of culture, that of the mastery of the elemental powers of nature. No sort of divisiveness can resolve the problems of poverty and need, and such per se tends to drop lower the level of mankind. The question however concerning the establishing of the inner brotherhood of people is a question religious and moral, and not economic and social.

In truth, the direction of our consciousness and our thinking upon objective, upon disinterested explanations of truth is one of the methods of treating our sickness, is a setting free from social malice and hate, which makes for slaves. The pathos for objectivity leads to a more favourable understanding of socialism, as a regulation of elemental powers, i.e. first of all, as a problem utmost cultural and material, and spiritual. The socialism of envy and revenge should be surmounted. The fury, malice, hatred, the thirst for blood and violence will cease, when the masses of the people is enlightened by socialism on the point, that in Russia at present socialism is impossible and so is an unlimited improvement of condition of the workers and peasants, that a full social equality is impossible not only because, that it is the bourgeoise and the possessing classes not wanting this, but rather first of all because, that it is impossible objectively, because this runs counter to the immutable laws of nature, because the poverty of Russia does not permit of this, with its industrial backwardness, amidst the unculturedness of the people, the spiritual incapacity of Russian society, etc. If socialism is possible (and it is possible only conditionally, since to a remarkable degree it is an abstraction), then it will be possible only as the result of the utmost developing of productive powers, of an intensification of culture, only by the begetting of the riches of the people, by that surfeit of abundance, which gains a creative productiveness in all the spheres of life. Socialism is a luxury, which only the rich can permit themselves, it presupposes immutable objective conditions. Socialistic experiments in a backward and impoverished land are essentially reactionary, they disorganise and throw matters backwards. The Russian revolutionary socialism, the Russian revolutionary populism -- are begotten of the Russian backwardness, of the Russian extensive thrift in economy, material as well as spiritual.

III.

The denial of objective principles of sociability brings with it a fierce chastisement. The objective reason fiercely smites the foolish. And in this is an inherent justice. The Russian revolutionary socialism, sundered off from everything objective, is essentially an unique form of an abstract rationalistic folly. It desires as it were and heedless of results to rationalise societal life, to subject it to its own fanatical idea of egalitarian justice, not reckoning with the mysteried and cosmic fundamentals of society, and for this God deprives it of its senses. Socialism denies everything mysterious, all the mystical powers of history, and its folly -- is a folly of the rational judgement. A total and ultimate socialism is already impossible because it seeks to produce a given societal form upon a limited territory of the earth from out of the world entirety, set apart from cosmic life, and upon this isolated circle it wants to impose its own law. A perfect societal form would be possible only in a perfect cosmos, after evil would have been torn out by the roots from the natural order. The societal form is a phenomenon of cosmic life, it is connected with all the cosmic thousands of mysterious threads, the cosmic energies eternally break forth into every societal form, itself seemingly a shut-in system, and they topple over all the utopias of a social paradise. Cosmic life is a complex hierarchical system, it forms everything by degrees and gradations, in it is set apart at the head the sun from the moon and star from star, and in this is no chance inequality, it has deep bases. The cosmic harmony in societal life presupposes likewise degrees and gradations, and their complete displacement is an uprising against the Divine world-order. The existence of the state (independent of form of government) possesses objective, cosmic, and in the final end a Divine basis. And when one proclaims, the state is but the organisation of a class domain and serves these or some other class interests, in saying this one undermines the objective existence of the state. Upon this path one undermines all culture also. When one talks about "bourgeois" and "proletarian" culture, one spurns the values of culture, of culture per se ascendant over human interests and caprice, and reveals instead the beast in man. A sociability, in which would be completely lost every connection with the world totality and lacking any objective basis -- would be a beastly sociability, even though it be created in the name of humanism. And with the victory of Bolshevism in Russia there would also be created a beastly life.

Insofar as it is both possible and desirable to have a partial socialism, it ought to be subject to objective principles of state, national and cultural existence, it cannot be only the subjective caprice of a class, with the childish fury of the human will -- isolated within itself and setting itself highest of all. The source of the evil, the untruth and suffering of life derives not in that there exist classes of evil-doing exploiters and violent governments, but rather in this, that "all the world doth lie in evil", that every human will is infected by sin, that there exists a mutual responsibility in the face of world evil and sin. The law within nature and the law within society is not the source of evil, but rather the reaction of an objective good against evil, against the chaotic element. The legitimacy of truth and the legitimacy of society is of the realm of just law for a sinful world, in which is impossible the graced Kingdom of God, impossible a blessedness without redemption, without a proceeding through Golgotha. This is also the truth of the Old Testament, the truth of the law, the truth of the Ten Commandments. The chaos has to be subordinated to law. The capricious release of sinful chaos is not liberation, and in it man sinks down and perishes, as does the image and likeness of God within him. And insofar as revolution sets loose a sinful chaos and denies the truth of law, in it then is a godless principle, a principle dark and evil. The path to an higher, free, graced life lies through law, through the subjection of chaos to an objective norm. The ultimate uprising of class against class, of interest against interest, the ultimate revolutionary atomisation of society is a partial return to the primordial sinful chaos, an avoidance of submission to a sense of law and a lack of desire to go through redemption for new life. For a Christian people this is a great temptation and a testing of its spirit. The objectivity of science and scientific knowledge is in essence a submission to a sense of law, and with in this objectivity there is an Old Testament form of astuteness. And there is a point, at which coincides a religious enlightenment with a naturo-realist enlightenment. The Russian people most of all now has need of a liberating objectivity via religious and scientific enlightenment. And this enlightenment has to begin with the recognition of objective truth.

Concerning a True and a False Will of the People

(1917 - 283)[1]

I.

After the fall of the old Russian monarchy, the revolution entrusted the fate of the Russian state to the will of the people. In accomplishing the will of the people, the Constituent assembly was convened on the basis of an overall elective right. This too is a pure democracy, a purely people's sovereignty. For more than half a year the revolutionary element rages, the revolution "developes" and "deepens", many self-appointed organisations make pretense at expressing the will of the people, but over them all becomes ascendant the idea of a Constituent Assembly, as the last resort for which all appeal. All want to hear the voice of the sovereign people, for so long silenced. Certain of the Bolsheviks had the audacity to declare, that for them the will of the Constituent Assembly would not be binding and that they would bring down a Constituent Assembly, such as would be hostile to their aims. The Bolsheviks -- are not democrats, they are not adherents of the principle of "bol'shinstvo", the will of the majority. Nor are they formalists in regard to the will of the people. For them most important is the holding of the people's will, directing it. And they aspire not towards the sovereignty of the people, but to a class dictatorship. They are ready to go the path of a coercive rule by the "men'shinstvo", the minority (the revolutionary proletariat of the capitals) over the majority of the Russian people. The French syndicalists, with whom the Bolsheviks have points in common, likewise are antagonistic to the principles of democracy, and for them the idea of democracy is essentially bourgeois. All except for the Bolsheviks stand upon the point of view of a revolutionary legitimacy, unstable and half-fast as it may be. All haplessly

---

[1] OB ISTINNOI I LOZHNOI NARODNOI VOLE. Article originally published in the weekly "Narodopravstvo", 30 oct. 1917, № 14, p. 4-6.

grasp at the illusory legality of the Provisional Government in the present and at the indisputable legality of the Constituent Assembly in the future. And essentially it is only the Bolsheviks that are the bearers of the revolutionary element in its pure and extreme form. True, this pure form of the revolutionary element has proven very vile and dirty, but such is the very object. The principles of democracy -- involve a revolution-based legitimacism, which sits upon a fine edge and any second can slide off to one or the other side. The revolutionary turnabout has opened before the Russian people all the paths for a free self-determination. Let us consider, whether indeed the people has freely determined itself in the months following the revolution and whether indeed it will freely determine itself in the Constituent Assembly, which is to be convened in the very near future?

      The will of the people -- is more mysterious a matter, than various sorts of rationalists tend to think. And it is not so easy to find the means of its perfect expression. A quantitatively-mechanical expression of the people's will cannot be perfect. The people is not a mechanical complex of quantities. The people -- is a living existent, living across the expanse of all its history. And the defining of the will of the people is not a task of arithmetic, it is rather an organic process. The will of the people, which over a long period will determine the fate of Russia, has to be qualitative, and not quantitative. In the expression of the people's will there ought to be revealed a certain objective truth, and not some middle ground of intersecting and clashing interests. It would be a mistake to be interested exclusively by the formal signs of expression of the people's will while being completely without interest in the content and direction of the people's will. For everyone, who believes in the existence of truth and right, the spiritual condition of the people cannot be a matter of indifference, as regards the state of its inner freedom at the moment of manifesting its will, the truth pervading this will. Only a poverty of spirit, an inner void and emptiness can stand exclusively for a formal people's sovereignty and bestow an unconditional significance to the will of the people, irregardless of its condition. In an abstract democratism and constitutionalism there is a certain falseness, set at the surface aspect of life. What is important is not only this, that the will of the people be expressed and that in accord with it should be determined the fate of Russia, but also this, that the people's will be directed to good, so that it should manifest the truth of God, and not the falsehood of the devil. The people's will, just like every empirical human will, cannot be idolised into a god, cannot be avowed a last resort, for higher than it -- is absolute truth, value, God. The autocracy of the people ought to be repudiated the same, just like the autocracy of the tsar, just like every autocracy. The autocracy of the people ought to be delimited by higher principles, by supreme values. The Christian cannot accord divine honours to Caesar, nor can he accord divine honours to the people. The autocracy of the people is the same as the kingdom of Caesar and it likewise is incommensurate withe the infinite nature of the human spirit. If the will of the people in its quantitative majority were to destroy freedom and wreak havoc with spiritual values, then there would be no sort of grounds to give way before it. I can be forced physically to submit to an evil will, but not submit morally. The principle of formal democracy therefore cannot already be the utmost principle of societal life, and democracy itself can vary, can be higher or lower, it can be inspired by truth or be in the grip of a lie. And this means, that democracy has need of nurturing and a spiritual nobility, of being subject to higher values. Higher than the will of the people stands the will of God, and only in the will of God can there be sought the guarantee, that the truth of man and the freedom of man should not be crushed and violated. Within human arbitrariness there is not this guarantee.

II.

From a philosophic and religious point of view how might be considered the people's will, as expressed in Russia over the span of these revolutionary months? The estimation can only be very pessimistic. There is happening a most shameful falsification of the people's will, a very brazen sleigh of hand and violence. The Russian people even after the revolution is not determining itself freely, from within, from the depths. Its will is being violated, from the top with the revolutionary bureaucratism there is being prescribed for it, what it ought to think, what it ought to want. The revolutionary bureaucratism of the intelligentsia falsifies the will of the people just the same, as when the old bureaucratism falsified it. They lied before, when they said, that the will of the people -- was the Black Hundreds, and now they still lie, when they say, that the will of the people -- is the Red Hundreds. The Soviets of Worker, Soldier and Peasant deputies now play the role, as earlier was played by the Union of the Russian People and other Black Hundred organisations, by force of terror.

Nicholas Berdyaev

The will of the peasantry -- the largest portion of the Russian people -- we do not really know, and in any case it is not expressed in the Soviet of Peasant deputies, in which there are no genuine peasants, and it is primarily but a thrown-together front of an intelligentsia, alien to the Russian people. Demagoguery always falsifies the will of the people, it plays upon the dark instincts and passions of the masses of the people, in order to coerce the people and make it subject to itself. The demagogues find their interest consists in this, that in the people there has not blazed a light, as should be a weapon of knowledge in guarding the people against all the temptations and acts of violence. The demagogues always snare their fish in the murky water. They are afraid of the light. The peasantry wants to possess a larger holding of land, but this does not mean, that the peasantry -- are Socialist Revolutionaries. The soldiers do not want to make war, but this does not mean, that the soldiers -- are Social Democrats. The people need bread, but this does not mean, that the people confesses a revolutionary socialism. Such a foreign intelligentsia contrivance, as socialism, is alien and unintelligible for the Russian people.

Our people in its masses is still dark and itself it still does not know, what it wants, it has still itself not determined its own will. The people lives by elementary instincts and does not know, what state and social arrangement is best. Our people is grievously sick, sick in soul, and it is experiencing a deep crisis, it has lost the light of the old faith and has not discovered any sort of new light. The people is situated in a slavery to its own sinful instincts and passions, it is easily tempted and deceived, easily coerced. This very simple and clueless people, which at present is the master of Russia, makes pogroms and exposes to the greatest dangers the values of our national, state and cultural existence, helpless and defenseless of soul. Each one is able to go and direct his will to whichever side pleases him, to a pogrom against the bourgeoise and cultural society, the same just like a pogrom against the Jews and the revolutionaries themself. Free and with defense is only that one, who has a spiritual centre, in whom ha not been shattered and weakened the moral core. But with the peasants and workers at present the spiritual centre is already lost, the moral core has weakened, they have become situated in the greatest of spiritual slavery and helplessness. When I am at the street meetings, the faces of those speaking have produced a painful impression upon me. It would seem, that they are splitting apart the brains of the clueless people out of their inability to resolve the tasks set before the people. This -- is a cruel aspect of history in regard to a people, kept in forced darkness. And here this people, when particularly it has the darkness condensed in it and around it and itis sick of soul, it is then called on to decide the fate of the Russian state, to determine the life of future generations. The elections to the Constituent Assembly will happen in abnormal conditions both physically and of soul, falsified conditions of the will of the people. It is essential to desire, that a sovereign people should express its will at such a moment of its existence, when within it should be born an inner light, when it is healed in soul and ceases with its convulsive obsessions, when it should become inwardly free, and not so enslaved to the sin of greed and malice, when it subjects its will to an higher truth. In an emotional state, in a fit of irritation, in moments of spite, jealousy and malicious mistrust there cannot be an healthy showing of the will of a man. The same can be said also about a people. The will of the people ought to decide the fate of the whole people, the fate of Russia, and it cannot at this responsible moment be fragmentive, in it there ought to be a sense of wholeness, an illumination with the idea of a single Russia. But the idea of the oneness of the people at present has dimmed in the Russian people, and therefore it is difficult to decide the fate of the whole.

III.

The freedom of the will of the people is not a formal concept, it presupposes the victory of good over evil within the will, the victory of God over the devil. The devil -- is a liar, he falsifies the will of the people, he works a sleigh of hand. He gives the illusion of boundless freedom, a formal freedom, but in essence he enslaves the will within people. Boundless freedom always devours itself, it burns in a void, in emptiness, in trifles. The sinful will is always non-free, it is the captive of the dark powers. The will most free -- is an holy will. The sinful will can become free only through redemption. The redemption from sin makes man free. Here is why true freedom is only in Christianity. It is necessary to guard against transforming the sovereignty of the people into a worship of the people. The people's will cannot be and ought not to be made a god of. It is impermissible to accord divine honours to the human will. What is proper for respect should be what is great within man, the valuable within him, his sanctity and genius, his high stature, and not simply man per se as such, not everything relative to man nor to the mechanical tangle of people. And therefore the entire task consists in this, that there should be manifest the utmost will of the people, inspired by the utmost values, respecting the sanctities.

It seems to me to be secondary a sort question, whether it is necessary to postpone the Constituent Assembly. And this cannot leave morally a good impression, when the struggle for the finishing touches to the Constituent Assembly is bound up with whatever the special interests. It is time already to look at all this with a deeper and inward point of view. We ought first of all and most of all to desire, that there should be created an healthy spiritual atmosphere for expressing the will of the people, that there be found conditions, favourable to the raising of the will in its qualitative aspect, in its value. And for this, it is necessary to awaken the light in the soul of the people and free it from the enslaving sinful instincts and temptations. At all levels, in all the classes of the Russian people there ought to appear a thirst for redemption, the sense of guilt ought to win out over the pretensive sense of making claims. And this sense of guilt ought to be particularly strong among the classes, governing in the past. But from the Christian point of view nowise exempted can be even those, who now make pretension to rule. There is little hope in this, that the spiritual restoration of health of the people will be accomplished by way of a peaceful evolving. It is all too evident, that only catastrophes will restore to health the soul of the people. Only grievous tribulations and tragically experiential re-examinations of false ideas will awaken a better awareness. Rational deductions cannot be persuasive as regards an higher vital truth. And it would be proper first of all to stop bestowing absolute significance to such a conditional and relative matter, as the Constituent Assembly. For many at present the Constituent Assembly is a master, which will come and reason everything out. But it is impossible to rely so totally on a master, which can be either good or bad. The Constituent Assembly itself per se is but an empty form, which can be full of whatever sort of contents, good as well as evil. And all the efforts ought to be directed to the attaining of this good content... It is not the formal will of the people that is dear to us, but rather the will to good. We seek the mighty expression of good, of value, of the higher will of the people.

When a man is psychologically disinclined to leave a spiritual legacy, then this act is morally and juridically for naught. A spiritual legacy demands the attentiveness of the one making it. At the Constituent Assembly, the Russian people will be making a spiritual legacy for the coming generations. For this utmost responsible act, it ought to be healthy and attentive of soul. But there are grounds to fear, that by the people's sickness of soul and its unattentiveness will be devised a counterfeit and falsification of a spiritual legacy. Our generation in the course of the given hour cannot decide the fate of Russia, in usurping the will of generations past and the generations to come. The people in a condition of health and attentiveness ought to decide the fate of Russia not by its arbitrary will, giving in to the force of momentary whims, but in an accordance of its will with an historical existence of a great past and a great future. The people is not a mechanical mass of recent day history, it is an assembled collective person as it were of a thousand years existence. And only such an assembled collective will, conscious of the preeminent bonds of time, will not be falsified, will not substitute the great whole with instead an insignificant part. In Russia is occurring the spiritual struggle of those, who believe in objective, absolute good and truth, and who desire the triumph of such, against those who believe only in the well-being of the person and in the interests of the human masses and who want the triumph of such. And in comparison with this basic religious opposition, all the other remaining oppositions, connected with the struggle of interests, are unimportant and unsubstantial.

Has There Been in Russia a Revolution?

> *We have lived and continue to live only for this, in order to serve as some sort of important lesson for generations distant, who have to make sense of it; we now however, in any case, comprise a blank gap in the moral world-order.*
> **Chaadayev**

(1917 - #284)[1]

I.

The seizure of power by the so-called "Bolsheviks" for many would seem some sort of a terrible catastrophe, something completely unanticipated in the destinies of the Russian Revolution and of Russia. There are to be found even people, who out of naiveté or out of deceit declare, that there has ensued the final stage of the struggle of the workers and peasants against the capitalists and land-owners, the final clash of the people against the possessor clashes. Mr. Lenin has regarded it possible to declare, that at the end of February in Russia in Russia it was a bourgeois revolution, overthrowing tsarism, and at the end of October there occurred the socialistic revolution, overthrowing the bourgeoise, i.e. a process, which amongst the advanced Western peoples takes centuries, but which in

---

[1] BYLA LI V ROSSII REVOLIUTSIYA?. Article originally published in the weekly Journal "Narodopravstvo", nov. 1917, № 15, p. 4-7.
A date of "19 November 1917" for this article is indicated in earlier Paris reprint: Tom 4 of Berdiaev Collected Works by YMCA Press, in the collection of 1917-1918 Berdyaev articles under the title, "Dukhovnye osnovy russkoi revoliutsii (Stat'i 1917-18)" ("Spiritual Grounds of the Russian Revolution (Articles 1917-18)", Paris, 1990, p. 102-112. However, the 1978 Klepinine "Berdiaev Bibliographie" indicates only "nov. 1917".

backwards Russia happened in some several months. Since our life has begun to become reminiscent of a nightmare, everything appears to us in an exaggerated form. We have completely lost the perspective on events. I venture for myself to think, that everything happening in Russia -- is of the sheerest phantasms and hallucinations, in all this there is nothing substantial and genuinely real. That what has occurred most recently, is very tormenting and grievous in the perspective of the personal life of people. Blood has been spilled, there have been and will be many innocent victims, human life has become still more precarious and unbearable. But it mustneeds be realised, that nothing essentially has changed, nothing new has occurred. There has been a shifting about of atoms, yet staying in the same inert condition, and it cannot change anything on any side. Generally within the Russian Revolution nothing new is transpiring, in it is no sort of a genuine movement. And that, what we call revolution, is but the power of inertia, is a dead immobility in facing the judgement of an higher spiritual life. In the cycles of chaos and anarchy never indeed will there be a genuine stirring and creative newness. The chaotic shifting about and revolvings of dead matter moves nowhere and nowise creates new life. In the souls of people and in the soul of the people, in the wellsprings of creative energy nothing has changed, nothing new has been born. All the same old instincts are active, all the same old feelings. The new man is not being born. Nor has any new soul been born within the elements of the Revolution. Everything has remained very old in Rus', all the psychology of individual people and whole groups has remained the old. The whole societal fabric is being pulled and torn apart, like a rotting bit of matter. The souls of people are slaves' souls all the same. The masquerade change of attire ought not to fool anyone. Under the new masks are still too apparent the old faces. Slaves are prone to violence, in which not a single feeling has changed, in which no sort of glimmerings of a new and better consciousness is evidenced, they stroll and drive about in the costumes of the new and free people. But the beastly gruntings are all the time heard under the masks, which fool only people very naive and very ignorant.

It is laughable and absurd, what is being seriously said among us about the "Bolsheviks", about refuting them, while they dispute about the paths of developement of the Russian "Revolution". All this, as children tend to say, is not for real, all this is not the genuine thing. The whole Russian "Revolution" is an onerous nightmare, dreamt up for the Russian people out of its incapacity and sickness, it is a phantasm, created by a disordered imagination of a people weak and having lost its spiritual centre. It is as though the nightmares and phantasms of an insane asylum have been set free and go about howling across the Russian Land. Everything happening is but an illustration for "The Devils" of Dostoevsky, a book truly prophetic. Everything is inescapable, as in a nightmare, everything keeps repeating and returning, the demons circle about, and it is impossible to break free from this devilish circle. The demon-driven power of Messrs. Lenin and Trotsky and the non-populist character of their power is describable the same, as was describable the demon-driven and non-populist character of the power of Messrs. Stuermer and Protopopov. From the former time nothing essentially profound has changed. Everything old is repeated and acts but under new masks. The stormy processes occur but at the surface. These processes are but the rot of old clothes of a Russia unreborn. We are experiencing the consequences of our old sins, we suffer from our inherited ills. In Russia there has been no sort of a revolution. It is time already to tear off the masks and expose the genuine realities. The Russian Revolution is a sheerest phantasm. In it there are no essential signs of a revolution in the Western European sense of this word. The old power, the old monarchy was not overthrown by the Revolution, it rotted, became decayed and ingloriously fell, like a rotten apple falls from the tree. But the poison from the rotting of old Russia has remained within the organism of the people and it continues to undermine the life of the Russian people. Still, here among us, these processes of the rotting of old Russia are considered as "the developing and deepening of revolution". The hideous nihilism, triumphing in these processes of disintegration, is an evidence of the old Russia, and not the creativity of a new Russia. In Russia the ruling power fell, and it was not replaced by any sort of a new ruling power. There has ensued a chaotic sort of interregnum, a fruitless and uncreative troubled period of anarchy. It would be the same incorrect to term as revolution the catastrophe happening with Russia, just as it would be incorrect to term Pugashevism as a revolution. The catastrophe is not a change in the forms of the state, it is not the building up of a new ruling authority with an organising of its powers, it is the breaking up of a state, powerless to organise whatever it might as a state power. In this the Russian Revolution is infinitely distinct from the French Revolution, in which there was active a strong civil national instinct of the people. With us however there is no sort of a new, an organising and constructive power, having arrived to replace the old and disintegrating powers. That which we tend to call "revolution" is but a continuous disorganisation and disintegration, the death of the state, of the nation, of the culture.

II.

The course of the Russian "revolution" is not a drama, moving along developing from one act to the next. In it there is not a true dramatism, there are not true heroes. The course of this "revolution" is more reminiscent of a very chaotic cycle. The inescapable aspect and lack of resolution are especially characteristic of it. And for us rather quickly has ensued a revolutionary wasting-away disease. We are experiencing not so much a revolutionary, as rather a distressed era. Everything has become poisoned in this era, all are joyless, all are unhappy, with everything there is a murkiness in the depths of the soul. The makers themself of the "revolution" sense neither joy nor uplift, in them is no genuine faith. The Russian "revolution" suffers from the hounding of old age, it has not experienced a period of youth, of youthful enthusiasm, of the youthful attraction with liberating ideas. All the revolutionary ideas have long since already become weathered, all the revolutionary words have grown stale. The aesthetic and morally sensitive man can no longer without a tinge of shame recourse to revolutionary terminology. It is impossible to endure this yawning abyss with all the revolutionary concepts! Everything has long since already chilled down and turned to ice under the revolutionary phrases, there is no feel of the heat of the human heart, there is not the heat of human thought. The old words, pronounced by representatives of the old approach, have become weather-beaten over the course of a century. Revolutionary words straight off have come to seem old and weather-beaten over the course of but several months. During the first days of the revolution no energy of sacrifice was spent in struggle against the old ruling powers. The old ruling powers fell without struggle and resistance, and victory came too easily. Much spite had however accumulated in the past, from the old slavery and the old abasement. And they began to search out an object for this unresolved spite. The objectivisation of the spiteful feelings created the counter-revolutionary fiction of the "bourgeoise". They poisoned masses of the people with an inhuman malicious hatred towards the "bourgeoise", understood in a very broad sense, as the whole of cultured society. The "bourgeoise" itself however uncovered a wont for disorganisation, passivity and yielding, unseen in history. From the very beginning of the "revolution" the Russian was obsessed by a craven fear of counter-revolution, and in this shameful fear is sensed a terrible powerlessness, the absence of youthful faith, of youthful enthusiasm. In the inquest over counter-revolution there is something to the utmost degree ignoble. The makers of the "revolution" discovered their spying instincts, traits characteristic of a decrepit and decaying power. All this is conceivable, if there be finally admitted the truth, which for the time being is evident but to few, -- that in Russia there has been no sort of revolution, and what there was is but a continuing disintegration and rotting of the old, only a prolonged chaos and lack of statecraft, only the developing and deepening of an arbitrary power.

For a long time already we are living under the dictatorship of a "revolutionary democracy". And in this regard the "Bolshevik revolution" has brought with it nothing new. But what does this "revolutionary democracy" represent, which they want to pass off as an organising and creative power? This is first of all the lording it up of ignorant and destructive soldier-recruits, the lording it up of bayonettes in the hands of ignorant people, the primitive instincts of which have raged unchecked over the course of eight months. The Russian Social Democrats, students of K. Marx, have recognised the bayonettes of soldiers as the chief defining factour of historical developement. Certain of them, calling themselves "Bolsheviks", are even convinced, that the bayonettes of soldiers can radically alter the correlation of economic factours. Such a militaristic rebirth of Marxism is truly amazing, it was possible only in the murky East, in a completely non-cultural land. In this there is something Turk-like. There are grounds to think, that Western people will look upon the Russian "revolution", as though it were Chinese or Turkish. It is a monstrous falsehood to declare, that the lording about of soldiery, grounded in physical violence, has any whatever relationship to socialism, to "the idea of a fourth estate", as it was understood by Marx, by Lassal and other Western socialists. The illiterate dark mass of soldiers, unaccustomed to all actual work, are those selfsame soldiers, upon whose bayonettes not long ago still rested the old arbitrary rule, and they are not given to any whatever perspective of socialistic thinking or socialistic feelings for the working class. "Bolshevism" rests upon the same sort of soldiers bayonettes, upon the selfsame dark and crude physical force, upon which rested also the old decaying ruling powers. Nothing has changed.

The masses have remained in the same state of darkness. Where is that new psychological insight of the proletariat, to be worked out by collective industrial labour, which the Marxists always have considered as a necessary premise of socialism? Is it the signs of this new psychology in the disorderly mobs of soldiers, pocketing the grain, lighting cigarettes and committing violence against peaceful citizens? It is no accident that in the dark masses that it is so difficult to differentiate the "Bolsheviks" from the Black Hundredists. And the "socialistic revolution" of recent days is very easy to confuse with counter-revolution. This is the same spirit, those same approaches of violence and terror, the same outrage against freedom and right, the same jeering at the worthiness of man. And the hatred towards the "bourgeoise" is an age-old hatred of the dark East towards culture.

III.

The Russian people continues to decay out of a lack of strength, from a tyrannic anarchy, from churlish ignorance and darkness, from a lack of organisation and discipline, from the absence of guiding constructive powers. The "Bolshevik revolution" is one of the moments of the falling apart of old Russia, one of the transformations of the old Russian darkness. In all this there is no similitude to revolution, to democracy, to socialism, to any sort of deep change in society and the people. All this -- is a subtle and vicious masquerade. The principles of arbitrary rule and despotism continue their triumphant march and they incite to orgy. In the old Russian arbitrary rule there was too much of the anarchistic and too few objective legal principles. And at present the anarchy and arbitrary rule are killing every right, every objective and legitimate truth. In old Russia there was not a sufficient respect for man, for the human person. But at present this respect is even less so. In entire classes of society man is denied, the person is not respected, and in regard to the classes of society admitting the revolutionary assertions, there is committed a spiritual homicide, which all too easily passes over into a physical homicide. The oneness of the human race is denied to a larger degree, than during the time of slavery. Even during the time of the slavery of serfdom, even during the time of the serf-owning right privileged Christians all the same still saw in both serfs and serf-owners a man, the image and likeness of God, i.e. at a particular depth they surmounted all the conditional and class oppositions and impediments. The present vicious and malicious division however into a world "bourgeois" and a world "socialistic" is an ultimate betrayal of Christianity and an ultimate denial of man, as one race in God. In this likewise can be seen a requital for old sins, for old discord and falsehood, but it would be madness to see in this something new, creative, transformative of life. The convulsive and monstrous end of the old man is impossible to conceive of as a principle of an new and better life.

"Bolshevism" has prevailed with its principle of "revolution" and in its present triumph there is nothing new. All the "developing and deepening of the revolution" has happened by decree of the "Bolsheviks", has been inspired by their spirit, if this can be called spirit, and gradually it has taken on the principles proclaimed by them. The other revolutionary socialistic parties, the Mensheviks and the Socialist Revolutionaries, went in tow with the "Bolsheviks", though they were less consistent and the same poison in them was less condensed and concentrated. The Mensheviks and the Socialist Revolutionaries will never decisively and radically rise up against the "Bolsheviks", since the "Bolsheviks" for them were people of the same faith, sinners perhaps, but not heretics. True-believers do not burn sinners in the bon-fires, they burn only the heretics. But for every Social Democrat and Socialist revolutionary, not having concurred with the Bolshevik tactics, the heretics however -- are all those not socialists by faith, all those not believing in the socialistic revolution and the socialistic happiness. And in the victory of the "Bolsheviks" over the other socialistic groups there is an immanently inner justice, this -- was a national punishment for their own particular sins. The sickness had to run its course to the end, had to be lived out to its extreme consequences. Why has there occurred such a deluge of "Bolshevism" throughout all the Russian Land, and why did it attain such an easy victory? This is first of all connected with the war. "Bolshevism" is the line of least resistance from the national and elementary instincts of every dark and unenlightened human nature. "Bolsheviks" eventually became all those, who did not want to make war, who did not want to sacrifice anything, but who want as much as possible to receive more. What is termed as the Russian "Revolution" and what at present it has come to, reveals one shameful and sad fact for us: the Russian people did not hold up under the great challenge of the war, in the terrible hour of the world conflict it weakened and began to fall apart. It spiritually was not prepared for the world struggle, it lost every idea of a purpose for this war. And without a great idea or purpose it is impossible to go forth to sacrifice and suffering. The bloody fratricidal struggle on the streets of Moscow is but an episode of the world war. The German poison has done its job.

The moral however, which the Russian "Revolution" teaches, is quite simple and elementary, though also bitter for us. It has become necessary to part company with many of the Russian illusions, with the Slavophils, the Populists, the Tolstoyans, the lofty-minded anarchists, the revolutionary-messianists, etc, etc. It is necessary to repent and be humbled, to sacrificially admit the elementary truth of Westernism, the truth of culture, the harsh truth of law and norms. The Russian people has lost faith, has betrayed the eternally sacred, and civilisation it does not possess, to culture it is foreign. And we have need of the lengthy workings of civilisation, in which there is its own secularised religious truth. It is necessary for Russia to again pull itself together. The great tribulations confirm the truth as of Chaadayev, and not the Slavophils. At present we are experiencing a period of profound moral and spiritual collapse. Even in our cultural segment many have fallen so low, that they have given in to the mass hypnosis and have come to believe the vilely ignorant view, that at present is occurring a final clash of class interests, a final struggle of the people against the bourgeoise. When the Russian people awakens from its hypnosis and spiritually sobers up, they will comprehend, that every great struggle in the world is a spiritual struggle, a clash of varying ideas. It has to be admitted, regretably, that terming it "bourgeoisness" signifies at present but an elementary level of culture. In the lower levels of Russian life -- is a primordial darkness, everything there is elementary, everything still is in the primitive past. At the summits of spiritual life, however, there occurs the clash of differing spirits and ideas, there the devil fights it out with God. In the midst of the struggle it is perceived as the clash of the "bourgeois" world and the "socialistic" world. But both these worlds stand upon the same basis and are inspired by the same earthly spirit. The bitter spiritual struggle is complexly interwoven into this middle range material struggle, and from this middle range admixture it is necessary to distinguish the higher and pure spiritual principles and to set them in opposition to the triumphing darkness and triumphing churlishness: it is but the utmost spiritual struggle that ought also to manifest itself in the middle realm, as a struggle for creativity of culture within the darkness round about us.

The Tasks of a National Democracy

(1917 - 285)[1]

I.

The so-called "revolutionary democracy" pretends to speak on behalf of the Russian people and wants to get Russia involved in peace negotiations. And this is a basic lie and switching about of our revolutionary ideas. In the "revolutionary democracy" are not those authentically from the people. Is it not striking, that in the Provisional Soviet of the Russian Republic in all total has been only one peasant and this peasant sat on the extreme right, as the representative of the union of landed property-owners? In the Soviets of Peasant deputies sit no Russian peasants, but rather assembled from abroad intelligentsia, foreign to the Russian people. Does our "revolutionary democracy" posses an organic connection with Russia? In it there is nothing Russian. It is impossible to say, whether or not the representatives of the "revolutionary democracy" have been patriots and have had a native land. But their native land is not Russia. Our native land is a thousand years in existence. Their apparent native land exists but for all of six months, and their native land -- is revolution. They -- are not Russian patriots, but rather patriots of revolution and of revolutionary a people. Over these months has been born among us not only a revolutionary patriotism, but also a very extreme revolutionary chauvinism. They want to subject all the peoples of the world to the will of the Russian revolution. The revolutionary democracy sees the Russian revolution as a light from the East, which is to enlighten all the peoples of the West. But this light, intending to subjugate all the world, is expressed exclusively in a torrent of words, quite weathered and since become trite, along the line of "without annexations and indemnities", "the self-determination of peoples", etc. all this self-serving hollow talk half a year already has demoralised and undercut the Russian

---

[1] ZADACHI NATSIONAL'NOI DEMOKRATII. Article originally published in the weekly "Narodopravstvo", 13 nov. 1917, № 16, p. 5-7.

people and the Russian army. Internationalism upon Russian soil is an inverted inside-out German nationalism or the nationalism of foreigners having settled in Russia. But as regards the peculiar Russian passivity and the obsessiveness characteristic of Russians, many Russians tend to sense the internationalism, as a Russian revolutionary messianism. This revolutionary messianism has already inflicted grievous wounds to the Russian national soul and national body. The revolutionary self-conceit has degraded Russia and oppressed the Russian people, subjecting it to foreign principles. The revolution has inflicted a painful blow to Russian national feeling and the many ugly aspects have tended to evoke against it the healthy reaction of instincts of a national self-preservation and the instincts for a national creativity.

In Russia there ought finally to form healthy a *national democracy* with a strong instinct for a national self-preservation, of a deep sense of a connection with the past in Russian history, with a broad basis among the masses of the people, with a decisive social reformism in its programme. The national democracy would have an organic connection with the authentic Russian people and would express its spiritual visage. It needs to be stressed, that the issue involves not the national in general, as they now love to express it, but rather concerning a nationally-Russian democratic trend. From the growth and crystalisation of such a trend to remarkable a degree would depend the future of Russia. In our political and social groupings there is a gaping emptiness, which ought finally to get filled in. There, is where has to be born the new trend, there -- is the most important, the most central, the most fiery grounding of Russian life. At that point, wherein is born the national democracy, would awaken the element of the Russian people. It mustneeds finally be admitted, that all our parties to a remarkable degree represent a fiction and behind them lies concealed absolutely nothing, on what they promise in their slogans. None of our parties is ultimately based upon the Russian people. But many of them speculate upon the dark instincts of the people and upon the most loutish interests of the moment. It is striking, that in the existing groupings there are no groupings quite essentially most for real, which would comprise the core of all the future Russia, a non-national and Russian grouping. *Russian* has seemed something forgotten and overlooked in Russia at the moment of the great historical turnabout. The revolutionary aspect is exploited for non-Russian ends, such as are hostile to our national entity.

The Russian state encompasses many a nationality and it exists not only for Russians, but for all the nationalities settled within it. But the Russian and even more precisely the GreatRussian nationality comprises that strong and mighty core, which has created the Russian state and Russian culture, it comprises the subject within Russian history. Around this core has grown and spread all our many-tribed state. The *Russian* people has radiated around itself the energy, which civilly and culturally has united and formed the great totality. It subjugated other nationalities not by force only and by wars, but also by its great language, by its great literature, before which bow even those peoples, who would prefer to separate from the Russian state and heap scorn upon the Russian tribe. Russian culture has proven itself by that higher culture, which has brought together the weaker and less advanced peoples of Russia towards higher a spiritual life, and the mighty and enormous Russian state which has defended many a people and provided the forms of civil an existence. It would be a crying shame to consider the great-powered Russian people as an aggressor and oppressor and identify its role with that of the coercive politics of the old regime.

II.

It is impossible to formally understand the principle of the self-determination of peoples. This self-determination has to be commensurate with a real balance, with the spiritual and material strength of peoples. And to the strength and balance here of the Russian nationality it is impossible to compare with the strength and balance of other nationalities, inhabiting Russia. The Russian nationality indeed is the prevailing and dominant nationality. With the Russian people there is an exuberant power, which it ought not restrain, but rather provide the other peoples of Russia, providing them the defense of their enormous state, the benefit of its enormous economic organism and the values of its spiritual culture. It is improper to allow the vilification of the Russian people on the part of all the foreigners, which is seen during the era of the revolutionary crisis. In the past the Russian people was not only the oppressor, as now they seem to want to paint it, it was also a provider of benefit, it united lesser peoples towards great an historical life. And here in a moment of great historical crisis the very existence of the Russian nationality is subjected to doubt, it has proven disorganised and even its right to organise is denied. The Russian national consciousness has been struck ill and debilitated. Russians have been too accustomed to be under an official guardian and too inclined always to let everything up to the policeman. Some have been very satisfied with this externally privileged position, which granted them power, others however have been ashamed to be Russians from this privileged position. But the Russian energy, the Russian self-initiative was undermined both for these, and for those. And here, when the old guardianship fell, when the policemen were snatched away, then the Russian people was left disorganised and weak, and it feels itself as though a stranger in its own native land, in its own state, upon its own soil. All the other nationalities are readily organised, they display great energy and manifest exorbitant pretensions. The Russian nationality exists only in the quality of citizenship, at the same time when other nationalities exist both as self-promoting nationalities, and as possessing Russian citizenship, i.e. representatives with twofold a power. Yet this cannot lead to a weakening of the Russian nationality. It everywhere is rendered representative not proportionally to its historical significance. The Russian state, which has as its vocation to serve the Russian idea in the world, can become transformed into a bland state comprised of nationalities, and Russian culture can be rendered a bland international culture, in which it is impossible anymore to recognise the Russian spiritual image. Such a position endangers the very existence of a great and unified Russia with its singular and unrepeatable individuality and singular and unrepeatable mission in the world. The Russians are too grievously wont to atone for their sins of the old regime. Many do not want to see in the Russian people an uniter and creator, only a violator.

In the free Russia there arises the Russian national question, which had been obscured by the coercive national politics of the old regime. Now however it is already possible and there ought to be posited this question in essence, without any false moral reflections. Basic and urgent it seems to me is the organisation of the Russian nationality as that core, which has to preserve the unity of Russia and create the possibility of a transition to new life in connection with the legacies of Russian history. I have been especially persuaded as to the importance of these tasks after a few sessions of the Commission on National Questions of the transitional Soviet of the Russian Republic, which could be termed a commission on the dividing up of Russia. The Russian nationality has its own singular spiritual visage, reflected in Russian religiosity, in the Russian great literature, imprinted upon the whole of Russian culture, and this visage cannot vanish from the world, it ought not to dissolve away into a Russian internationalism, it ought also to be valued for all the world. If there be not for us a conscious organisation of the Russian nationality, which will subsume itself to a great idea, then there will be instead an outraged national feeling, unenlightened and guidable by nothing, and it can overflow into a movement of violence and pogrom. Jewish pogroms also at present are already occurring and can assume very ugly forms, to the shame of the Russian people. Healthy nationalism has nothing in common with human hatred.

III.

An organised and enlightened national democracy ought to create the conditions of life, in which would be possible the co-friendship of the Russian people with all the peoples inhabiting Russia. All the peoples of Russia ought to receive a cultural autonomy, but with the preservation of the centralised unity of Great Russia. The Russian people is not merely one of the peoples, inhabiting Russia, it also is Russia, it bestows to Russia its unrepeatable visage. Russia is not an assemblage of a land, is not a mere union of various nationalities. Russia was born in the world for the realisation od some singular a Russian idea. And in this great and extensive idea there is nothing restrictive nor oppressive, it -- is of benefit for all the peoples of the Russian land and for all mankind, within it there is universality. But for this, that the Russian people should realise in the world an idea, it has to be strong, has to possess a mighty state, has to sense itself an unified people and master of its land. A movement, which arises upon the basis of an awakening of the Russian consciousness, cannot be primarily a movement of the governing and possessing classes, it has to go into the depths of the people's Russia. It likewise cannot be primarily an intelligentsia movement, though at the head of it there ought to stand a national intelligentsia -- the bearers of the national mindset and national conscience.

A national party for us does not exist, though there are currents, from which it could be formed. For lack of a national party, the People's Freedom Party could fulfill this role for us. But this party lacks in itself a national essence and is bereft of a basis in the people. For this, it is too academic. This -- is a statist party, and it became national by virtue of the external conditions of the war and revolution as regards its political tactics. The People's Freedom Party is not so much national, as rather national in general. It is national in the Russian, and in the non-Russian sense of this word. And still it must be said, that this party -- is very democratic in its programme, but insufficiently democratic in its psychology, it does not enter into the thicket of the people's life, and it fails to resonate with any sort of the heartstrings in the soul of the people. I admit the merits of this party over these past grievous months, in its staunchness, its lofty intellectual level. But the cause of the weakness of this most organised and most defensive of state-national politics in parties has to be sought in the absence of an extensive and strong national basis of the people. Such expressions, as "more leftward" or "more rightward" to the Cadets seems to me trite and empty, and in these words is nothing essential and real. It is time already for us to get free from the grip of words and pass over from the superficial aspect of every movement "leftwards" and "rightwards", to rather a movement at depth, where "leftness" and "rightness" lose all meaning. But as regards this superficial and conditional terminology, the national democracy, about which I speak, will be "leftwards" to the Cadets as regards its connection with the masses of the people and in its social programme, including elements of the reform socialism, and at the same time "rightwards" to the Cadets as regards its sharp national character, together with an acknowledging of an hierarchical principle, as regards its connection with the historical past of Russia, since it will comprise in itself elements of a conservative connection of the times of and a respect for religious and national ancestral legacies. The formation of a true national democracy in Russia presupposes altogether different a spiritual grounding, altogether different a world-outlook, than that, which prevails in our intelligentsia circles becoming intruded into the masses of the people. A revolutionary worldview cannot but be superficial, it is always bereft of profound a spiritual basis. Revolutionism can only be but for the moment, it cannot be a prolonged condition. And in the very primal basis of a revolutionary democracy lies a false presupposition, that there is possible and desirable a permanent revolutionism and that the revolutionality manifests a creative principle. But a new democracy has to finally surmount the revolutionary aspect and become transformed into a creative national democracy. This will represent a winning out of constructive principles over principles disorganising and destructive. A national democracy has to possess other spiritual foundations, than those, upon which rest all our parties, and these foundations can only be religious.

The Germanisation of Russia

(1917 - #286)[1]

I.

We live from day to day, not knowing, what tomorrow will bring. The dark abyss stretches open beneathe us and at any moment it can swallow up all our blessings and values. It would be difficult to establish some measure of law within the swirlings of these dark chaotic elements and foresee the future. Actually, all is occurring not thus, as we would think. But it would be improper to forget one thing. Russia -- is not an isolated island. It -- is an inseparable part of the world organism, connected by a thousand threads with the life of other peoples. The collapse and ruin of Russia cannot be a matter of indifference for the rest of the world, for all the great powers and for all the cultural peoples. All are interested in the fate of such a gigantus, as is Russia. If the weakening of Russia can cheer many, then its total collapse has to be disquieting. This collapse is disquieting not only for our allies, but also for our enemies. Germany has done all it could for the weakening of Russia and its collapse during the time of war: it has played upon Russian weakness and Russian ills, the Russian darkness and Russian baseness, it has stopped at nothing in deceitful struggle, has not been squeamish about stooping to the vilest, most repugnant methods. And it has succeeded, it has found a favourable soil in the passivity among elements of the Russian people, in the corrosive ideas of the Russian intelligentsia, in the betrayal by bunches of riff-raff. Germany will have defeated Russia in close alliance with the destructive and corrupt forces, acting within Russia itself, through a betrayal by the Russian people of itself, its native land and its idea in the world. But it mustneeds be said, that also for Germany itself the too far gone collapse of Russia is unsafe and undesirable. The Russian anarchy -- holds great a temptation. For the intention of exploiting Russia, there would still be

---

[1] GERMANIZATSIYA ROSSII. Article originally published in the weekly Journal "Narodopravstvo", [...] 1917, № 17, p. 2-4.

needed the preserving of some sort of power, though subverted and bereft of independence. Germany wants to germanise Russia and gradually transform it into its colony. Thus is its projected aim. But even Germany itself acknowledges the unsafe aspect of the experiment of the anarchistic communism in Russia. These efforts ought also to seem unsafe and not a matter of unconcern for the other peoples of Europe, friendly towards us. Too many interests are invested in Russia, it is too indebted, too many natural riches are hidden in Russia. The creditors indeed love us. The total impoverishment of Russia through its delirious anarchistic experiments and its ultimate disappearance from the world civil-legal order represents a danger and harm for all the world.

It is a great matter of shame and humiliation for every Russian, not bereft of a sense of national dignity, to realise, that Russia, the hitherto great Russia, the dreadsome Russia will enter into a period of international and forceful deciding of its fate. The worldwide balance of powers will not allow Russia ultimately to fall apart and perish. The clashing and opposing struggles of interests of the great powers will put limits to the dismemberment of Russia. But this is quite vexing a comfort, it likens Russia to Turkey, which long already has been propped up through a diplomatic balancing act. Prior to this limited humiliation and shaming of Great Russia, a world power encompassing an entire enormous world of East-West, it will be preceeded by those, who in a frenzy of revolutionary chauvinism have shouted, that the Russian revolutionary democracy will instruct all the peoples of the West with the light of internationalism and revolutionary socialism, the brotherhood of peoples, etc, etc. Those, who have demanded a speedy cessation of the war and by this having undercut the army, have terribly further burdened and prolonged the war. Those, who have proclaimed the slogans, "without annexations or indemnities" and "the self-determination of peoples", are getting the world ready to make very grievous annexations and indemnities and without any self-determination of peoples. Those, who have wanted to ply all the world with revolutionary phrases, have surrendered Russia into slavery to the world. Such is a natural punishment for allowing lies and deception. The internationalist Germanophiles love to say, that having Russia threatened upon England and America is nowise better, than being dependent upon Germany. Better it be already dependent upon that, which one loves and serves, i.e. upon Germany. A power debilitated and inwardly dismembered will always be dependent upon others and in slavery. And indeed the idea of a mighty Russia and the unity of Russia is something our internationalists have always regarded as bourgeoisly imperialistic. There has not been a will to might with that revolutionary democracy, which wanted to lead behind it the peoples of Europe, and there has not been a consciousness of the worth of Russia. The poison of an international Bolshevism has been active throughout all the revolutionary democracy, in all these Mensheviks and Social Revolutionaries, and it has afflicted he organism of Russia. All these people have been patriots of revolution, and not patriots of Russia. they have all sought to save the revolution, and not their native land. They have laid waste their native land, and each step towards the "developing and deepening" of the revolution has been transformed into a betrayal and treachery towards their native land, into a victory for Germany.

II.

Russia has been rendered non-mighty and powerless to continue with the international struggle, not only as regards whatever the goals and ideas, but also as regards its fundamental inviolability and worth. The voice of Russia cannot be heard in the affairs of the world. The world will become shut off for us. And Russia can assist no one, liberate no one. Those very people, who in the international conflict have not admitted it necessary to have a strong army and regarded it sufficient to rely upon words, in an internal struggle will rely exclusively upon bayonettes. The disorganised and weakened army will become transformed into a weapon for a fratricidal civil war. The anti-militarists will become transformed into very extreme militarists. The goal, which Germany has pursued, will have been attained: the war will cease at the front and be carried on back at the rear, Russians will stop fighting Germans and start fighting Russians instead. After this, Russia would be ultimately weakened and the Russian people given over to the capricious whims of other peoples, their fate dependent upon some shreds of mercy. Internationalism will not lead Russia forth onto the world stage, but the rather shove it back into Asia. The world role of Russia would be done for. The Slavic world would fall back afront the Germanic world, separating us from Europe.

How to make sense of all that is happening, from more extensive an historical perspective? The catastrophe happening with Russia is merely one of the points along the way of a long historical Germanisation of

Russia, a Germanisation of the Slavic East. This also is an historical aim of the Germanic world, posited by them in former times. Marx was conscious of this "mission" of the German people no less, than were the verymost rightist German imperialists. Germanism has striven by various paths towards the realisation of this goal: paths both spiritual and material. Germanism first of all set itself the task of weakening the Russian national will and the Russian national consciousness. And this has proven very successful over the span of two centuries. The Social Democratic internationalism -- is one of the final steps towards the weakening of the Russian will, of the enslaving of the Russian mind. Germanism has long since poisoned Russian thought and undermined the Russian will. This has occurred both at the summits of the spiritual life and the lower aspect of the material life. Kant and Marx alike have Germanised the Russian soul. The Russian state powers have been Germanised. The Russian Church has been Germanised into a synodal structure, the Russian intelligentsia has been Germanised, Russian economic life has been Germanised. At the moment, when the war began and there occurred the clash of the German world and the Slavic world, already long before had been set in place the process of the Germanisation of Russia and it continued to the extent, that Russian resistance was weakened. We lost our own idea. We were all he time waging the war in a sort of moral ambiguity. This ambiguity was there alike both in the right, and in the left camps, and both prior to the revolution and after the Revolution. The genius of the nation had its revenge in the betrayal of the Russian idea. The Germanophiles have consisted of both the Russian Black Hundredists and Russian Social Democrats. Both the one and the other were ready to betray Russia in the name of the triumph of either reaction or the triumph of revolution, in the name of the old dynasty of the Romanovs or the new dynasty of the "Revolutionary Democracy". We slid down the facets of separate a world. If one of the moral causes of the downfall of the old powers was manifest by its suspected treason and betrayal of Russia, then a thousand times moreso has happened treason and betrayal by the Revolution over the span of is developement -- in the internationalism and Bolshevism.

And the most terrible thing of all is this, that the Russian people itself in its enormous dark masses has remained passive, it has become a weapon for the evil powers acting through it, directed upon the destruction of Russia. It has been taken in by the internationalist Bolshevik propaganda, as a line of least resistance for its unenlightened instincts. It went along with those, who proposed to be more dear to it, and surrendered its soul. It completely swallowed the German poison both unconsciously and passively, in a deep darkness, not knowing what would happen. It betrayed to Germany the Russia, which belongs not to it alone, but also to its fathers and grandfathers, its sons and grandsons, all the entire thousand year Russian people and the God-created Russia. And it, this dark people, is terribly responsible, since not totally without responsibility are average people, created by God. But the greatest responsibility falls upon that revolutionary intelligentsia, semi-enlightened and obsessed, which has accepted and spread throughout all the organism of Russia the German poison under the alluring guise of internationalism.

III.

Russian internationalism is merely the reverse side of German nationalism, only one of the methods of the Germanisation of Russia. The Bolshevik turnabout is merely an aspect in the victorious Germanisation of Russia, an ultimate crash of the Russian will and dimming of the Russian consciousness. It is not by chance that our internationalists so love our enemy Germany and so dislike our allies England and France. They have all the time shouted about English capitalists and French imperialists and have said comparatively little about German capitalistic imperialists. The internationalist orientation in international politics in practice has always seemed a German bias and anti-English orientation. Internationalism is a vile gas, released by German imperialism upon other peoples, weakening them and forming a misty fog around them. Over Russia it is quite terribly criminal a thing, which will be bewailed for many a long generation. Our grandsons and great-grandsons will curse the criminal act of our revolutionary generation, for having consigned them to a miserable and paltry existence. This revolutionary generation in its social carousings and orgies has squandered riches not belonging to it, of the worth of all the Russian people in its past and future generations. Part of the present day generation has betrayed Russia, has doomed it to a miserable slave-like existence. The Russian utopias have ended up poorly, they have gone into serving the enemy of our native land, have been rendered into pliant tools. Russia could have merged from the war glorious, powerful, free and granting freedom. It would have brought to completion a matter of many centuries, would have realised the age-old aspiration of the Russian people

-- it would have received a free access to the Southern seas, so needful for the Russian grain-agriculture, it would have resolved the accursed Eastern question, an age-old source of wars, it would have liberated oppressed nationalities, it would have smashed the grip of German imperialism and kept it restrained. But the Russian people in the dark depths of its free will became callous to its concerns in the world, it succumbed to a diabolical temptation, it permitted evil powers to violate it, it succumbed to deceptive promises, to flattery with the greedy instincts of he present day. And Russia will emerge from the war dismembered, weak, miserable and dependent. After the orgies of the present day will follow a fierce reckoning. The great national totality is the source of life of all the parts. But the great totality has been forgotten and brought to ruin by the self-asserting parts. Russia has fallen apart into atoms and each atom has regarded itself a god.

Every relegation to dependence is humiliating and grievous for Great Russia. But being rendered dependent upon Germany is especially dangerous and intolerable. Germany -- is our mighty neighbour, and long ago already Germany has striven to render Russia into its own colony. Germany has an exceptional capacity to depersonalise those peoples, upon whom it extends its influence, it mangles their soul. The German spirit is terribly dangerous for Russia, it tempts the Russians, and it can enslave them. The German world -- is the age-old enemy of he Slavic world. England is less terrible for us, it is farther away from us, has less pretensions concerning us, its interests are less contrary to ours. Spiritually it cannot enslave Russia, its spirit does not tempt Russians. Germany is spiritually stronger than England and within it lies concealed a dangerous spiritual poison for Russians. Likewise dangerous is also the material poison of Germany, that economic slavery, which it will bring us, if it emerges victorious. It will enmesh us with a thousand threads. The Germans will exploit our riches and transform us into their slaves. Spiritual slavery results from material slavery. It would be a crazy dream, to imagine that Germany would heed the appeals of the Russian revolutionary democracy and produce also for itself a socialist revolution! The German Social Democrats -- are pliable and culturally bourgeois, they are for the large part faithful German imperialists. Marx himself was a German imperialist (vide my article, "The German Influences and Slavism", in issue No. 6 of "Narodopravstvo"). The Russian Revolution repels the peoples of the West by its dark, Eastern Asiatic image.

We have to gather all the powers of our spirit, to gather all, of what has remained in Russia healthy, bright, true, all the remnants of our national ill and national sense of reason, in order to oppose this Satanic onslaught by Germanism both outward and inward. Let Russian people, having preserved fidelity to their idea, their faith, their great legacies, let them withdraw into the catacombs, if evil ultimately triumphs over the surface of the earth, and herein make ready for the resurrection of Russia.

The "Bourgeois" World and the "Socialistic" World

(1917 - 288)[1]

> "There will remain the five unsatiated Senses, and the sixth insatiable Sense (of Vanity); the whole *daemonic* nature of man will remain, -- hurled forth to rage blindly without rule or rein; savage itself...".
> Carlyle, "The French Revolution" [2]

I.

The Russian people has manifest itself, in hitherto unprecedented a way, as having become a world falling apart into a "bourgeois" world and a "socialistic" world. The unity of the human race, as God's race, having a common origin, in Russia now is ultimately being undone. Russian mankind is falling apart into two hostile races. "Bourgeois" man and "socialistic" man have declared each other to be wolves. In Russia the idea of class has killed the idea of man. Russian people have ceased to approach one another, as man to man. The ideologues of the "socialistic" world, its prophets and apostles, want to believe, that in this falling apart of mankind, in this rift of all continuity and all unity there will be born the new man. The old world, the old man has to perish. In the conflagration of the Russian socialistic revolution, which is to be transformed into a worldwide revolution, the old "bourgeois" world will be burnt up, and upon its ashes will be created the new "socialistic" world. The Russian Bolsheviks, insofar as they can seriously speak about it, is also to be that new race,

---

[1] MIR "BURZHUAZNYI" I MIR "SOTSIALISTICHESKII". Article originally published in the weekly "Narodopravstvo", 25 dec. 1917, № 18-19, p. 3-6.

[2] Thomas Carlyle, The French Revolution, 1837, Bk I, Ch II, p.13.

which denies every connection and any continuity between these two worlds, and which wants to destroy utterly all the old, all the legacy of the past. And in this they are akin to the futurists. This race, having spurned everything noble and everything venerable, as prejudices of the old world, has set about an enormous experiment of the creation of a new "socialistic" world, in which there will no longer be anything of the "bourgeois". In Western Europe there is this "bourgeois" type of socialism that predominates. But the Russian revolutionary socialism, having attained its own perfect expression in Bolshevism, scorns and repudiates this "bourgeois" socialism, and it has pretensions to teach the "bourgeois" peoples of the West a true socialism, a true revolutionism. A new race is to be born in Russia and from Russia it will convey to all the world the goods news about a perfectly new world. The pretension is enormous, in truth "messianic". Suchlike was the Russian and Slavic "messianism" as confessed by Bakunin, for whom the red glow of the world conflagration was to have begun from Russia, and who believed in a revolutionary light from the East. Mr. Lenin also has proven to be a peculiar Slavophil, an Eastern "messianist" -- he would betray and destroy Russia in the name of its world-revolutionary mission!

It would be very interesting and instructive to investigate and to learn, what is it new that this Russian "socialistic" world brings with it, and what is it of the old in the "bourgeois" world that it repudiates? Is there a new soul born in the socialistic race, having set about with such worldwide pretensions and attempting to realise them in such bloody acts of violence? In perceiving this, one might have to stand off to the side of the struggle of these two worlds, and he would have to rise above the clash of interests in this struggle, and he might grant, that there was much evil, much that was vile and low in the "bourgeois" world, and that in the "socialistic" world there is its own truth, there are of necessity elements of good. The final times of the existence of the old "bourgeois" world were not noted for their comeliness and beauty. And let us suppose, that this one, who wants to comprehend the nature and meaning of the occurring clash of the two worlds, with all his heart desires a transformation of our ugly old life, and desires also the overcoming of slavery, sin and lawlessness, along with the birth of a new man, of a new human soul. The will towards the new, the better, the transformed life can be not only a "socialistic" will, it can be likewise a religious and Christian will. The one who is authentic, not merely external, but deeply a Christian cannot be satisfied with the old "bourgeois" life, based on violence and hatred, he desires a "new heaven" and a "new earth", and he desires deeper and more radical changes and improvements, than the verymost revolutionary socialist. And the "socialistic" world can seem to him all that same old world, the old world of sinful man, the slave to his passions, to his wicked and greedy instincts, all that selfsame "bourgeois" world, but with a mechanically new rearrangement change of its covering and garb. Has not the "socialistic" world inherited all the "bourgeois" sins and vices, does it not indeed desire a "bourgeoisness" somewhat more equitably distributed, and to attain but a limited developement and perfection? The revolutionary-socialist experiment, performed upon hapless Russia, reveals quite much and teaches much. One discovers, that the "socialistic" world with its malice and hate disdains all the best, the best that was in the "bourgeois" world, all the enduring sanctities and values of the past, of one's fathers and grandfathers. All this while it accepts and increases everything bad that was in the "bourgeois" world, all the sins, the ills and depravity of the past, all the darkness of the fathers and grandfathers. In its sense of wicked vindictiveness this "socialistic" world preserves a continuity with the past, in its feelings of spiteful envy it remains tied to the past, like a slave. And thus it has remained faithful to the most greedy traditions of the past. There has remained still "the five unsatiable senses, and that sixth insatiable sense -- vanity".

II.

The Bolshevik "socialistic" world arising in Russia gives the impression of being the scum of the "bourgeois" world, of the sick and stinking vapours of the past, the effluence of some old darkness. From the Russian people there issues forth an unclean spirit. Where indeed is the new man and the new values in our purely soldierly, bayonette style "socialistic" revolution? The "socialistic" world has not evidenced the slightest signs of creativity. The old world was creatively rich, and from it the "socialistic" world steals all its values. Socialism itself is the product of the creativity of the "bourgeois" world, and its values were created by the children of the "bourgeoise" -- Saint-Simon, R. Owen, Marx, F. Lassalle, and certainly not by the children of the "proletariat". The socialistic ideas, like all ideas, -- are the product of a "qualified" world, qualified in education, talent, culture. In the "socialistic" world arising among us, there is no necessary qualification for creativity, neither a material nor a spiritual qualification. Everything occurring in Russia produces the impression of a destruction of the old world. But this destruction is produced by the negative and decayed powers of the old world, having arrived at a condition of chaos and collapse. The souls of people, remade by the "socialistic" revolution, are old to the point of terror, their instincts are age old, their feelings and thoughts inert, and in all their appearance is to be recognised the old beastly nature of man, acting also within the "bourgeois" world and therein wreaking the most wicked deeds of this world. But with this beastly nature there has finally been snatched off all the fetters, it has emerged from under the restraining law of civilisation, the law of the state. There was much violence in the old "bourgeois" world, many an outrage against man. Has the newly appeared "socialistic" world repudiated and conquered this old evil? No, and it commits a thousand times moreso the violence and greater outrages against man. This "new" world has repudiated neither the violence nor the outrage against man, but rather in its principle and in its idea it has repudiated all the worthiness of man, everything venerable and noble, as mere prejudices. This new world has taken its wont for violence from the old world, but manifests it in nowise limited and in nowise veiled a form. The Russian "socialistic" world has taken the bayonettes from the "bourgeois" world and given them unlimited power over the life of the miserable Russian people. It took from the old world the prisons, borrowed from it the spying and gave these old elements unlimited power. The old "bourgeois" world did not very much love freedom and as regards its spiritual incapacity it did not know how to live in freedom. But the new "socialistic" world hates freedom and extirpates it without a trace. Foreign to this new world is the very idea of freedom and man and the sacred rights of man.

There was much greed in the old "bourgeois" world, much ugly egoism. But has the new "socialistic" world repudiated and conquered this old evil? No, the avarice and egoism in it has moreover intensified and it governs life all the more impudently. The difference is only in this, that on the old world the avarice and egoism was in people, not yet having lost the distinction between good and evil, and these vices were not elevated into the pearl of creation, not reverenced as sacred, but were admitted rather as sin and weakness, whereas in the new "socialistic" world these lower principles are acknowledged as sacred and lofty, since this world admits of nothing higher, than the self-assertion of man, than his well-being, satisfaction and pleasure. The "bourgeois" world was a sinful world, an avaricious world. The "socialistic" world however seeks to sanctify this sinfulness and greed, it kills the sense of sin and wants to make man completely self-sufficing, it wants to render him insolent. To the sins of the "bourgeois" world, the "socialistic" world has moreover added a still devouring and fierce envy, and has acknowledged it as an utmost social virtue. If earlier the people of privileged an existence were the landowner and capitalist, then now those of a privileged existence have become the workers and the peasants. Man is evaluated as regards his outward, his social guise, and not as regards the inner, his spiritual qualities. And there is created no new life, in which ascending the heights would be man, the human image, the human visage.

III.

In the final times of its existence the "bourgeois" world had become little spiritual, and very materialistic. But is the "socialistic" world any more spiritual, is it any less materialistic? Alas, but no, it is more materialistic, it ultimately would extinguish the spirit, it even does not forget about the spirit, but rather would deny and exterminate it. The materialism of the "socialistic" world, loathing all the supreme spiritual realities and spiritual values, is a socialism, borrowed from the "bourgeois" world, but intensified and assuming a character all-encompassing. The "bourgeois" world became doubtful in the spiritual realities and the spiritual values, it lost faith in the other world, it became non-religious. The "socialistic" world creates its kingdom upon this non-belief and this non-religiosity of the "bourgeois" world. But it elevates its atheism into a religion and is proud of it. The "socialistic" world leads the utilitarian "bourgeois" spirit onto the foundations of its own being. The old "bourgeois" world still all the same tended to doubt in the grandeur and propriety of its unbelief, it was divided on this, and in its bright moments it condemned its own godlessness. The "socialistic" world in this regard was more consistent, it smugly experiences its godlessness, it is proud of its unbelief. If the "bourgeois" world be accused of rendering the human person and the human soul into a means and tool of material interests and into a material social means, then still even more does the "socialistic" world sin in this -- it fails to see the human person, it does not know the human soul, it knows of nothing, besides the material social means.

Nicholas Berdyaev

This world is totally cast out upon the surface, in it there is no depth. Everything bad, evil, vicious in the old "bourgeois" world is slavishly borrowed by the smug "socialistic" world, it copies it and developes it even further. The new "socialistic" world is also a strengthening of the forever and everywhere spreading of "bourgeoisness", with dulled a sense towards sin. It repudiates not the sin, but rather the awareness of sin and repentance.

But in the old "bourgeois" world, the world of our fathers and grandfathers, there was not alone the bad and the evil, -- in it there were great sanctities and great values. In the old "bourgeois" world there was holiness and genius, in that world was Pushkin and St. Seraphim. In the "socialistic" world there will be no more saints and geniuses, -- they are denied by all the fundamentals of this new world, they will be forcefully submerged into the dull grey impersonal masses, into the qualityless collective, they will be hated, along with everything lofty. The new world will dissolve away every quality into the collective. There was many a fine and good prejudice in the old world, now repudiated. To such "bourgeois" prejudices belongs the acknowledgement of basic distinctions between good and evil, obligatory for every moral human being. The "socialistic" world of the Bolsheviks has gone beyond that side of good and evil, it has fallen not into immorality, but rather into a moral idiotism. This world has gone beyond that side of the law of civilisation, yet not above the law where already would be a kingdom of grace, but rather below it, wherein is the beastly kingdom. The old "bourgeois" world acknowledged the "prejudice" of what is right, though consequently also insufficiently, though also too often betraying it. The new "socialistic" world ultimately destroys every sense of what is right, it repudiates the very idea of what is right. The old "bourgeois" world created GreatRussia, the great Russian state, it acknowledged the prejudice of patriotism, of national honour, of duty for the fatherland. The new "socialistic" world has abolished the state, has dismembered Russia, has transformed our native land into an heap of rubbish and made a mockery of the patriotic feeling, of national honour and worth, in forms yet unprecedented in history. The "bourgeois" world was nonetheless compelled to reckon not only with material qualification (in the over-estimation of such was its weakness and sin), but also with spiritual qualification, with the qualitative principle in the human person, with education, with talent, with cultural developement. The "socialistic" world has repudiated all the qualitative ascendant distinctions, all the spiritual points of excellence, and it surrenders the human person for devouring by the quantitative mass, it extinguishes every individual light within the impersonal dark mass. It repudiates the "prejudices" concerning the person, about its responsibility, about its worth, about its primordial freedom. This was a Christian "prejudice", a "prejudice" revealed to us by God Himself. The "socialistic" world has repudiated the old "prejudice" about God. Herein is its secret. It has accomplished a betrayal of eternity. It has repudiated everything eternal also in the old "bourgeois" world, all the enduring values, and it has accepted everything corruptible from it, all its greed, all its spiritual slavery.

A spiritual restoration of health will ensue then, when they grasp, that the world is not divided into the "bourgeois" and the "socialistic", and that "bourgeoisness" and "socialisticness" -- are abstractions, which relate to a very complex and multi-faceted actuality, as much spiritual, as material. There remains the eternal division and opposition in the world of good and evil, of beauty and ugliness, of truth and lie, of God and the devil. This opposition is not an opposition of human interests, but rather higher and deeper. Relief will ensue then, when they grasp, that the idea of a "socialistic" paradise on earth also is a transforming of our life on earth into an hell. In this phantasmic paradise "there remains the daemonic nature of man; savage per se, it will hurl forth to rage blindly without rule or rein". It is necessary to think not about an earthly paradise and not about bliss, but rather about the fulfilling of arduous the duty, about the realisation of the truth of God.

Personal Good and Supra-Personal Values

(1917 - 287)[1]

I.

The Russian revolution represents an enormous experiment, it provides rich experiential material for consideration in the area of the philosophy of society and the philosophy of culture. Revolutions usually are viewed as a triumph of the societal effort. In a revolutionary epoch everything personal, intimately inward, recedes to secondary a plane, is crowded out. The person is compelled to become subordinate to society and societal interests. Such is one of the aspects of revolution. But there is possible an altogether different aspect. And then, for example, the Russian revolution in its current form can represent the atomisation of society as a whole, the atomisation of the state, the atomisation of the nation, the atomisation of Russian culture, the disintegration of the whole and of the continuity of Russian history. In a revolution, inspired by the ideals of class socialism, the perspective of personal good always takes precedence over the perspective of supra-personal values. The personal, the partial, the group-greed triumphs over the supra-personal, the in-common, over the entirety, over values, inspired beyond the limits of the immediate and empirical human life. Revolutionary socialism is an indubitable denial of supra-personal values, the indubitable atomisation and disintegration into parts of every objective reality, as might be regarded eminent above human psychologism. The revolutionary class socialism is a triumphing of psychologism over ontologism, the triumph of subjectively capricious conditions of people and human groups over objective principles, over supra-personal Right and Truth. This destructive type of modern socialism possesses little in common with the idealistic and aristocratic socialism of

---

[1] LICHNOE BLAGO I SVERKHLICHNYE TSENNOSTI. Article was originally published in periodical "Russkaya mysl', 1917, bk. XI-XII, p. 33-39.

Plato, for whom first of all there does exist the great totality and the supra-personal values of Right and Truth, not dependent upon the caprice of person and class.[1] Materialistic communism is in essence a pseudo-individualism, an extreme atomism. And this individualistic atomistic perspective of personal good bears within it its own punishment, since it leads to a denial of the value of the person, of the value of individuality. There triumphs instead the fabrication of artificial persons. Materialistic socialism is an extreme nominalism, it denies the reality of the in-common, the reality of nation, the reality of the state, the reality of Right and the reality of God.

Only through inconsistencies and through philosophic naiveté is there acknowledged by this type of socialism the reality of class and the reality of the individual man and his good. In actuality, it is rendered into the realm of abstraction and thus loses touch with anything of the concrete. The process of atomic pulverisation and the crumbling of being ought then to be taken further, it ought then to be extended to each human person, the reality and integrality of which then there are no grounds to admit of, and thus also to each societal group. The reality, such as the international proletariat terms it, is certainly a purest fiction, an abstraction from an abstraction. The proletariat, as something entire and unified, does not exist -- it breaks down into diverse groups of workers, with various outlooks and diverse interests, eternally unsteady and changing. To assert for some particular man, that he is a proletarian, and that this defines his human aspect entirely is, certainly, a feckless abstraction. This abstraction gets in the way of encountering the living human being. The rub consists in this, that the reality of the human person upon the basis of a materialistic socialism cannot be established. The person is rendered merely a combination of atoms, only a bunch of perceptions, it -- is merely a tiny drop within the sea of social and natural mediums. And in this the name of man becomes unjustified, in it there is no real energy. Yet nonetheless the welfare, the happiness, the satisfaction of the man, of the human person is admitted as some higher value, to which everything is subordinated. Every supra-personal value, the value of religion, of morality, art, science, philosophy, the state, law, nationality etc has to thus become subordinated to the good of the person, its satisfaction, its subjective aims. This is

---

[1] Vide R. Pohlmann [Robert, 1852-1914], History of Ancient Communism, p. 75-76.

already the highest, to which the ideologues of socialism are capable of going, beyond which ends discussion of class struggle and the triumph of the proletariat. There thus gets replaced any sort of a significance of supra-personal values and there triumphs instead the welfare and good of the person, but bereft of any ontological basis. The exclusive assertion of personal value is rendered hostile to the value of person, since the value of person presupposes the Divine within it. All this -- is for the human person, for its good, but the human person as such becomes unreal, it disintegrates, just like everything else in the world. Humanism, which promotes human welfare and human value, lacks any sort of authentic groundings in the objective order of being, it rests upon subjective an illusion, it apotheosises and makes a god of man, who is a chance and ephemeral phenomenon of natural and social necessity, which as such possesses no sort of self-existent core. The whole of reality gets displaced in the name of man, but man himself thus becomes unreal, he himself falls away along with the falling away of all the other remaining realities. *The reality of man presupposes the reality of all the degrees of being, the reality of that which, is higher than him. The person is a composite of worldwide hierarchy, and the person is unthinkable outside of hierarchy.*

II.

Two outlooks upon societal and historical life tend to oppose each other and their conflict represents a choosing of different values, a serving of different gods. For the one, the positivist humanistic outlook, the highest purpose -- is in the good of each individual person, higher than which there is nothing. The pathos of this outlook -- is in the equality of all human persons. There is no freedom nor creative uplifts by way of inspiration with these people, who hold to this view on life. The freedom of the person becomes subordinated to the equality of persons. Its chief aim rests not upon this, that there should be attained the higher qualities of the person, it higher freedom, its higher flourishing, so that within it be revealed creative values, but rather instead, that all persons should attain one common level, in order that none be higher nor lower on account of others, in order that heights be made level with hollows, that no person should sacrifice for anything higher than man, that each person be admitted of equal value with every other person, irregardless of his qualities and attainments. In this theory of the person the actual content of the person tends to play no sort of role, its greater or lesser aspect, its qualitative strength, its unrepeatable uniqueness. And to the person then has to be assigned a place in life nowise in measure to its spiritual energy and its qualitative attainments. An equal place for each person is determined mechanically. The pathos of such a personalistic outlook is not creative, but moreso distributive. The idea of the creative person is totally foreign to this mindset. Any creative eminence is considered dangerous for a levelling and distributive sense of justice. The theory of person in Russian populism has not been creative, but rather distributive a theory, directed first of all and most of all against the division of labour and against differentiations within society. Suchlike a theory of the person and the struggle for individuality was brilliantly developed by N. K. Mikhailovsky. He essentially struggled for an impersonal person, for the person everyone and all, for the equality of persons, for individuality, bereft of all individuality. In the name of suchlike a person, society has to be rendered dull, all alike, bland, has to be devalued of all supra-personal values.

Such a sort of the triumph of person would be to the withering of societies, of nations, states, the denial of historical tasks with their great remoteness. In the terminology of Nietzsche, ultimately there would triumph the morals for the love of the here and now over the love for the remote. This personalistic morals would displace the sacrifices, by which are obtained the stirrings of history, the formation of states, the creativity of cultures. The most extreme expression of such a sort of morals is in Tolstoyanism. L. Tolstoy -- was an extreme individualist in regard to everything historical, and his individualism is destructive and atomising in its action. In the name of the part, of the individual human good, Tolstoy sets aside the entirety of world history with its sacrifices, its sufferings, its further goals. The division of labour, the differentiations within society, the historical hierarchism is for L. Tolstoy, just as it is for N. Mikhailovsky -- the chief source of evil. There are two types of individualism -- the individualism of Tolstoy and the individualism of Nietzsche -- and their attitudes to the positing of many a theme is directly the opposite. The teaching of Tolstoy is very concerned with the welfare and good of each person, but to the utmost degree it is unfavourable for a vivid and creative manifestation of the personal principle. Nietzsche is totally unconcerned over the welfare of the person, of every person, but indeed he calls for a vivid and creative manifestation of the personal principle, that the person should strive towards remote and supra-personal goals. In this lies concealed a certain antinomy. *The teaching, which is based upon the welfare of the person and in its name repudiates supra-personal values, proves unfavourable for personal creativity, for personal flourishing. Whereas the teaching, which first of all is oriented towards supra-personal values, to the supra-personal, towards the remote, is very favourable for personal creativity, for personal flourishing.* All the creative persons within history in their paths are closer to Nietzsche, than to Tolstoy. The creative personal principle inevitably presupposes uplift, ascent, inequality. The spirit of levelling is murderous for the person, clips the wings. The individualism of Tolstoy is in essence extremely hostile to the person, knows not the face. Likewise also the personalism of Mikhailovsky -- is vapid and illusory. Neither in Tolstoy nor in Mikhailovsky is there the living creative person nor an actively alive creative history. The creative person cannot but be oriented towards supra-personal values, towards the remote. For the establishing the greatness of states can stand the strong creative person. For the positivist humanistic denial of the state in the name of personal good, in the name of the partial, can prove to be not the person, but merely the dull and impersonal masses. Populism of the Tolstoyan type always is immersed in the collective and therein seeks its criteria of truth.

III.

Socialism essentially is based upon such a sort of a positivist humanistic teaching about the person, although also it insufficiently reveals this teaching. Even in Marxist socialism can be discerned a moralistic teaching, that at the basis of history, at the basis of culture, at the basis of the state lies a sin-fall into inequality, the exalting of some and the lowering of others, sacrificing the good of persons comprising the people. And thus does Marxist socialism hurl an anathema against all prior history, as sinful and transgressive. In this, Marxism unexpectedly aligns with Tolstoyanism. The actual and good history, inwardly justified, begins only with socialism. In the past there was a realm of evil necessity, and in the future mankind awaits a realm of blessed freedom. The connection of time is broken. There is no historical process of succession in the life of peoples, and even the peoples as such do not exist. The people becomes transformed into an agglomerate of individuums and groups, guided by interests. Marxism does not admit of any sort of historical aims, bequeathed by ancestors, received from the past. It is powerless to exit history, it dwells wholly within its necessity, it has no religious power to surmount history, but yet there is the pretending to begin history with itself, as the start. And thus Marxist socialism signs a death sentence on historical nations and states, and converts the human masses into an abstract Internationale, transforms it into an abstract international proletariat, which also it considers as the true mankind. In this new and abstract humankind are to be demanded from the person no sort of sacrifices in the name of the supra-personal, and the good of the person, equal with every other person, will be posited as the keystone. It will lead to a socialising of persons, but exclusively in the name of their good. And thus will perish the state, when there ceases the sacrificial aspect of the person and its subordination to supra-personal sanctities. There will perish the nation, when it falls apart into separate individuums and classes, reinforced only mechanically, not wanting to know anything higher than itself.

A society, grounded upon such a sort of nominalistic individualism, was not without insightful a basis termed by K. Leont'ev as a "simplistic confusion", i.e. a withering and fading of peoples and states, and to this he contrasted the society of a period of "complex flourishing", when they were also more vivid, creative, tending to uplift the person above the average level. With the reactionary-romantic pathos characteristic of him, K. Leont'ev exclaims: ""Martyrs for faith were there under the Turks; under the Belgian Constitution though will be scarcely even any venerable ones". "The aspects of egalitarian progress -- are complex, coarse of aim, simple in thought, in ideal, in influences etc. The goal of everyone -- is that of the average man, bourgeois, docile amidst millions of precisely the same average people, likewise docile". The social ideal, based upon individualism, displacing every supra-personal sanctity, -- is a bourgeois ideal, the ideal of a "paltry earthly all-bliss, of an earthly radical all-triteness". The opposing view upon societal and historical life derives first of all from supra-personal, supra-human aims and sanctities. It acknowledges the value of historical nationalities and historical states, it is inspired by values religious, moral, cognitive and aesthetic, by the values of creative culture, which cannot be made subordinate to the bliss of the individual person. This perspective does not admit of a mechanical equality of persons, it instead transfers the centre of gravity to the qualities of the person, to its achievements, to its uplift and it connects the qualities of the person with a revealing in it of supra-personal values and supra-human sanctities, with its creative energy, directed towards the highest. The teaching about the person in Mikhailovsky and many of the socialists is that of empty a person, not filled with any worldly or Divine content. And this teaching cannot, for example, forgive the great Greek culture for having been based upon slavery, holding this grievance against it, just like with all of history, always in which great qualitative achievements have been bound up with human sacrifices. This moralism eternally harping upon personal welfare does not allow for the coursings of personal creativity. The second perspective finds justification of personal sacrifices in the name of higher values. This justification is connected with faith in that moral and mystical world-order, which transcends the empirical life of the person and in which the person has its own eternal fate. When Ivan or Peter makes an historical sacrifice in the name of some supra-personal purpose, unconsciously, this is done in the name of their own utmost fate, transcending the bits of their own empirical existence. Here is why the fundamentals of nationality, of the state, of culture in essence are profoundly irrational and mystifying. Rationally, reasonably it is impossible to justify the sacrifices of personal life and its subordination to the great entirety with its remote aims. The ultimate collapse of the religious sanction, the triumph of a nominalistic materialism would be to the collapse of peoples, states and cultures, their atomisation and disintegration.[1] Socialism however attempts to create a new religion, which looks to enslave the person.

IV.

A genuine flourishing of the person, of its creativity, of its genius is possible only amidst an acknowledging of supra-personal goals and supra-human sanctities. Without this, the person has nowhere to ascend to, it vanishes into its own emptiness. Mikhailovsky's theory of the person, so dear to our socialistic populists, renders the person bland and one-sided. The vivid clarity of the personal principle, its flourishing, is connected with an uplift and does not endure restraints in the name of levelling, does not endure the glancing at others, as though to not outdistance them.

---

[1] Vide the 1894 book of Benjamin Kidd [1858-1916] entitled "Social Evolution", in which is posited the interesting question about the necessity of a supra-rational religious sanction for social developement.

Spiritual democratism, which is the reverse side of such a sort of personalism, seeks to render the person impersonal, lacking in originality, to extinguish within it the will to genius. The positivist humanistic teaching about personal good, setting it foremost, tends to extinguish man and extinguishes also society and the state, it lowers the qualitative aspect in the name of the quantitative. The second type of world-outlook transfers the centre of gravity from the quantitative to the qualitative, and for it highest of all is not the welfare and satisfaction of the person, but rather values and sanctities, not such which reasonably and rationally are admitted as profitable and needful for the empirical life of people, but rather such, which irrationally and mystically are needful for the higher, the remote, the mysterious purposes of life. The human soul possesses infinite a value, but the empirical and earthly life of people cannot be endowed with such a value. The winning out of the second type of world-outlook and attitude towards life will raise the creative originality of the person and will render society itself more vivid, beautiful, many-sided -- nations and states would flourish, and have style. There is needful an ultimate defeating of that prejudice of the Russian populist sociology, that in order for the person to become differentiated, society has to become levelled, rendered grey and simplified. A qualitative selection is needful in the life of persons and in the life of peoples, of states, in their cultures. When there is a withering and fading of peoples, states and cultures, there is a withering and fading also of the person. Persons cannot lead abstract an existence, they live within great totalities, within their national cultures. We stand at a crossroads, two paths open before us, two spirits oppose each the other. One of the paths, one of the spirits, inspiring its path, a path to non-being, is the spirit of non-being. This mustneeds be revealed and exposed. The exclusive emphasis on a perspective of personal good is very impropitious for the revealing of the person in Russia, for the strengthening of personal initiative, of personal responsibility.

Concerning Creative Historicism

(1917 - 56,1)[1]

I.

Our time merits being termed "historical" quite especially, -- it is compellingly oriented towards history and the historical. Even people profoundly "*private*" in their outlook on life are attracted to historical interests, they admit of historical purposes, they read historical books for establishing instructive analogies. Events lead to a thinking about history. They begin to admit the inapplicability to concrete history and concrete historical tasks by the customary schema, the abstract sociological, the moral and religious doctrines. "History" involves its own totally unique spiritual activity, has its own specific values. But there can be great misunderstandings with the words "historicism" and the "historical" view on life. One mustneeds get beyond a mere schoolish dabbling in words. As paradoxical as it might sound, yet it has to be said, that it is quite most difficult to meet with a sense of history and true historicism among the professional historians. The scientific pursuits of history, on the one hand, provide much, but on the other hand, they also dull and kill the intuitive sense of what is happening in history. The historicism of historians tends to debilitate, to clip the wings, to weaken the creative historical impulse. Man gets too overwhelmed by the historical past, and this becoming overwhelmed tends ever to increase. Historians however seek to render this burden beyond the pale. The massiveness of history can become so great, that it deprives man of all creative historical power. Not merely once have the dangers of historicism been noted. And there can result also the pessimistic thought: man in the past created history, because back then he was not overwhelmed by history, he was not so beset by a backwards

---

[1] O TVORCHESKOM ISTORIZME. Article was originally published as 1st entry in collection of articles entitled, "Vetv'", by the Club of Moscow Writers, 1917, Moscow, publisher "Severnye dni", the book comprising 326 total pages.

oriented historicism. The man of past historical epochs was young and fresh in his impulse towards historical creativity, he was less tied up with historical knowledge, by the massiveness of the historical past, he created an historical tradition, but he was not overwhelmed by it. The memory of modern man is too overwhelmed, he is too much accustomed to think about the historical past, the cross-currents with strata of various historical eras have rendered him a sceptic, reflecting over every elemental impulse towards historical creativity, and he generally gets too much caught up in the "about". Modern man tends too much to think, to write "about something", and his concern is a concern "about something", and so he does dare to think and to write "something", to discover his own creative impulse. This legacy is to be sensed also in its overwhelmed aspect. The memory about the historical past and the knowledge of the historical past as it were hinders the creating of history, undermines the boldness. "Historicism" leads to scepticism and a weakening of the will. But there is possible also a totally different historicism.

In most profound a sense of the word, history is a myth-creating. Myth is a most essential and real content of history, its certain primal occurrence, its first-life. Historians however in what they do generally tend only to kill the myth, and by this they obscure the possibility of getting at the living, the inner mythogenic process of history. The medieval papal theocracy, the Renaissance, the Reformation, the great French Revolution -- all these vivid moments of historical creativity had at their basis the myth, and in this myth they derived their creative energy. And those, who seek ultimately to put a stop to the mythogonic process, -- they seek ultimately to put a stop to historical creativity. Myth is a great dynamic power within history, it is not "about something", but rather "something", not about history, but rather history itself, its inner constructive energy. It would have been impossible to make the great French Revolution without the myth concerning freedom, equality and brotherhood, concerning the rights of man and the citizen, concerning the modern natural condition. And the Renaissance would have been impossible without the humanistic myth. Granted that these myths may be exposed by history, granted their pathos might impair the most remote historical process -- yet they have created history and without them history is incomprehensible. At the basis of the myth lies deeper a reality, than at the basis of all the disclosures of the historians, -- the reality of the creative human spirit. These real myths, are upon what medieval history has been based. But it would not be real to construct our life and seek to create future history upon the basis of medieval myths. Reactionary traditionalism is the ossifying and deadening of the old myths, a cessation of the mythogenic process of history. And it requires all one's powers to fight against an identification of historicism with such a traditionalism. History -- is not that, what was, not these threads, which stretch from the past, and restrain us, history -- is that, what is eternal, as a dynamics of spirit. Historicism ought to be applicable to the very depths of spiritual life, and history itself perceived, as a dynamic aspect of spirit, as spiritual life, within the creative process.

II.

To live exclusively in the past, with the creativity of the past, the thoughts of the past, means to live vampire-like a life. This -- is not a fidelity to the creative past, but rather a betrayal of it. Too great a guarding, with a traditionalistic faithfulness to the medieval period and its great myths is a betrayal of the creative aspect of the medieval period, to its living mythogonic process. A restoration never becomes faithful to the spirit of that, what it restores. Someone who, for example, would merely repeat the old fathers and teachers of the Church and in slave-like a manner follow after them, would not be faithful to their spirit. They were then indeed modernists, innovators, creative figures for their times, and not merely restorers, not traditionalists, not merely derivative. And this is true in regard to every creative stirring within history, both in the sphere of thought, and in the sphere of action. Only a creative dynamics, only a continuation of the living mythogonic process signifies a fidelity to the creative spirit of the past. The traditionalism of the restorers least of all signifies a fidelity to the spirit of those, who created in the past, who were alive with the myth-creating. Each era has need of its own living myths, creating history, it cannot be alive with the old myths. And our era has need of new myths. A creative historicism presupposes a turning to the dynamic powers of history, to living energies, and not to authoritarian traditions; not to ossified myths is creative historicism oriented, but rather to the mystery of historical creativity, to the living myth-creativity of history. The historical man is that one, who has created history, who acutely senses and understands the mystery of history, as a mystery of formation. And thus, Napoleon was to the utmost degree an historical man.

History is not a given, history is foremost a great task. And to understand past history -- means inwardly to perceive this great task. But history is not a tabula rasa, some blank slate, and to create history does not mean to begin it from the beginning, from nothing. The historical succession per se, the historical legacy and tradition can be perceived inwardly, as a continuative dynamic process. There indeed does exist a sacred tradition within history, but it is dangerous for the creativity of history, when it becomes conflicted, like something inwardly stiffly obstructive, when the attitude towards it is rendered as though mineralogical, rather than biological. A revolutionary nihilistic denial of tradition reflects an incapacity inwardly to perceive the mystery of history. The historical attitude towards life is to the highest degree active, and not passive an attitude. History is a continuing creativity, not an end and not the beginning, but rather a mid-point. In this mid-point there is a continuative motion, impulses, bursting forth from the realm of freedom, from the creative arbitrariness of man. Only the combining of successive tradition with the creative caprice of man creates history. Creative historicism presupposes audacious initiative, the imposing upon man of great responsibility, presupposes freedom and the arbitrary aspect of man, all which receive sanction and approval only afterwards. Historical figures and the actions wrought by them only with time are admitted as great and valuable, though to begin with, such may seem mere chance and caprice. The element of risk is involved in historical activity, without it is impossible any sort of historical movement and change, and one, who takes upon himself the responsibility of initiative, becomes open to reproach for arbitrary and capricious activity. But this necessitates a free choice of paths, an audacious resolve, an assent to the risk of being accused of being arbitrary. The giftedness of the historical figure -- is in an intuitive divining of that which can become a creative power of history. But that, what the historical genius or talent intuitively surmises, can seem capriciously arbitrary. One needs only to remember, that the sacred tradition and legacy in its time involved a certain creative capricious aspect and seemed a matter of chance. There exists a special pathos in history, which inclines towards historical activity and historical creativity. And everything, created by this pathos, at first seemed doubtful.

III.

Not so very long ago, yesterday still as it were in Russia, traditionalism had great power and the old myths, weathered and moribund, all still governed life. But a true and creative historicism almost did not exist among us. The Russian soul lived either in the depths, remote from history, or was dreamily fixated upon the end of history, or remained in private a manner of life. Russian revolutionism is totally anti-historical, hostile to the creativity of history. The Russian soul as it were could not decide to accept history, taken aback by the cruelty and amorality of the historical process. Russians desire not so much history, the historical dynamics, the struggles and dramatism, as rather a total condition of the miraculous and catastrophic within the Kingdom of God. At the opposite pole however, Russians love calm and from lethargy are ready to remain in swinish a condition. The Russian idea is of a rightful social order, be it religious or non-religious, and thus usually it tends to bypass historical tasks. Our national aesthetic sense has been til now foreign to any historical gesture. It is not by chance that Tolstoyanism has seemed so characteristic of the Russian soul. And is this not connected, with our still not having entered into a period of world historical existence and not having been called to historical activity? In our civil life the tradition of the past has boundlessly prevailed. In our society, however, there has been very readily a radical break with all tradition, and this breaking off has been irresponsible, since it has not been subjected to the testing of historical activity. This testing has ensued today.

Creative historicism is neither traditionalism, nor is it that of revolutionism, its pathos is not a pathos of contrivance and disclosing, nor a pathos of destruction. This rather -- is a pathos of creativity. Creative historicism is deeply contrary to the "partial" view on life, always fearful and timid, always inclined to a guarding of well-being, always regarding history from the perspective of a given generation, a given Peter and Ivan. *The moral pathos of creative historicism is a pathos of love for the far off, and not love for the here and now.* Love for the here and now is static, love for the far off -- is dynamic. The audacity to create history is like a flash of lightning upon the mountain summits. This pathos in a supreme sense is aristocratic. With creative historicism can be united individualism of the Nietzschean type, but not unitable is the individualism of the Tolstoyan type. In a profoundly conceived progressive imperialism is the spirit of a creative historicism. But inauspicious to this spirit is every sort of populism, oriented towards the here and now and frightened by the far off. When Russia ultimately enters upon the path of historical constructiveness, it will emerge from the period of populist outlooks and ideologies. At the basis of creative historicism lies a mystical principle, but this mystical principle mustneeds be sought out within the creative "I", in the creative historical person, in the new myth about the revelation of man himself, and not in the historically traditional forms, not in the old powers and not in a new elemental wisdom of the people. Within the Russian consciousness there has to occur a turnabout towards such an historicism, and this turnabout will occur, though imperceptibly. First of all it has to be manifest in a free and independent thinking about history and historical tasks, thinking not under the massive crush of the old prejudices and doctrines. In our progressive thinking there has been no little of an inert conservatism, and there has been too little boldness. And the historicism in Russian thinking always has been quicker to avoid the creative historical impulse, than to consolidate it. Traditionalism turns backwards, revolutionism however pulls sideways, to a detour, to a disruption of historical movement and constructiveness. But in the depths for us is beginning a great upheaval, a starting upon the creativity of history, oriented towards a greatly attracting far off. We have to become historical people, have to grasp the mystery of historical constructiveness.

Translator note: This article is somewhat confusing as to its gist, it seems to be speaking in veiled references to some fluidly changing issues or events not readily apparent to us, as they might have been "in context" back then. Adding to our confusion is that this article was written and published *sometime* in the year 1917, a very dramatic year which spanned the collapse of the old regime and the "February" and the "October" Russian revolutions... As it is, the peculiar tone of this article seems an example of the "spoken unsaid"...

Is Social a Revolution Possible?

(1917 - 9)[1]

I.

The question, whether a social revolution is possible, is at present irresponsible and tends to disrupt the consciousness of the Russian people, it is throw out to the broad masses of the workers and peasants and evokes division and dissension. A great revolutionary turnabout has occurred in Russia, it has led all to movement and opening for the toiling masses of the Russian people a broad and free path to a new life. Those, who altogether not so long ago were in almost total enslavement, now are called to the people's rule and to a deciding of the fate of the Russian state. The transition over the space of several days from a despotic monarchy, which even after 17 October 1905 remained autocratic in essence, this transition to a democratic republic is, certainly, very radical a political revolution. This revolution has already occurred and has prepared the way for all the subsequent history of Russia, dependent upon the Constituent Assembly, to be convened upon the basis of common, equal, direct and secret electoral ballot rights, i.e. upon the basis of purely the power of the people, purely a democracy. For the Russian people this opens up all the possibilities, without setting any sort of hindrances upon its path. It was not a social struggling of classes that led us to the political turnabout, but rather the irreconcilable clashing of the old powers conflicting with all the classes of society, with all the Russian people, with all the nation. The old powers betrayed Russia, they had gone rotten and had to fall. But the all-national political turnabout opened up all the social contradictions, it exposed all

---

[1] VOZMOZHNA LI SOTSIAL'NAYA REVOLIUTSIYA? Pamphlet published under the auspices of the Moskovskaya prosvetitel'naya komissiya pri Vremennom komitete Gosudarstvennoi Dumy (Moscow Elucidation Commission on behalf of the Committee of the Provisional State Duma); Moscow, 1917, 24 p.

the festering social ills. With a debilitating lateness there has occurred the political liberation of Russia. We have facing us the experience of the Western European history of the XIX Century, which demonstrated, that a purely political liberation does not liberate quite yet for real the people of toil, that even in political democracies it is possible to have a material oppression, that political revolutions themself per se do not diminish the gap between the rich and the destitute. In Russia, at the present late hour of history, there cannot yet be the increase of purely liberal ideas, such as there was in the West. The so-called "bourgeois liberalism" has never been popular in Russia, and the attitude towards it has always been contemptuous. The word liberalism derives from the word for freedom [i.e. the Latin word "*libertas*"], and liberalism itself per se, liberating the person and assuring its rights, cannot be "bourgeois". In freedom and rights there is nothing "bourgeois" and they always represent a great good. The label "bourgeois" however has been applied to liberalism in the economic sphere, amidst which the whole of economic life is given over to free competition, and the state and organised society do not meddle in it. But there can also be a liberal socialism, i.e. based upon freedom and rights. The Russian revolution did not advance any sort of original new ideas. But in it, undoubtedly, there began to predominate socialistic ideas over liberal ideas, not only in a bad, but also in a good sense of the word, and thus in it right off was sensed an insufficiency of political liberation and the necessity of social liberation.

The working class of the large cities always plays a remarkable role in revolutionary turnabouts, it comes out onto the streets and in the ensuing struggle tips the scales towards revolution. During the days of the revolution and in the first months after it, the working class has played a large political role, more than corresponds to its social significance in that enormous and mysterious organism, named Russia. And still to play a large political role among us is the peasantry, attired in soldier's great-coats, and the role of the peasantry will grow, since it comprises a large portion of the Russian people. But this significance and power of the workers and peasants does not correspond to their level of organisation, their awareness, their societal experience and societal concepts, which are very insignificant. It is difficult over the span of several weeks or even several months to get organised thus, to find such experience, awareness and knowledge, in order to attain a predominant positive significance within the enormous social organism of the Russian state. The significance of people and entire classes for the improvement of life is determined not only by the quantities, but also by qualities. If a destructive role be played by any of the masses, standing at some lower level of enlightenment, then a role constructive, positive and creative can be played only by those masses, which would stand at higher a level of culture. It is impossible to decide social questions, whilst knowing nothing at all about them, not having any sort of preparation or experience. It does not suffice to have determining special interests and certain feelings and mindsets. And it still needs mentioning, that we do not know the voice of all the Russian people, -- of this enormous and mysterious entirety -- concerning the social disposition of Russia, or about the deciding of the agrarian and workers question. The voice of the Soviet of the Workers and Soldiers deputies cannot be admitted as the voice of all the Russian people. This still is but a voice of some of the parts, a partial voice. Only the Constituent Assembly is fully empowered to decide the social questions in Russia. And first of all it mustneeds be admitted, that these questions are very difficult and complex and their resolution demands great preparations. In social life it is impossible to do anything by coercive means in a short space of time. It is possible to destroy much by such a path, but impossible to build up anything. This question is not a mere political matter, which in a single day can be replaced by something else. Every developement in the social order of human societies is a prolonged and slow process. This involves a change in the actual cells, in the primordial fabric of society, in the attitude of man towards nature and of man to man. And herein this change in the fabric of society, in the attitude of man towards nature and of man towards man, a change both economic and psychological, cannot be sudden, cannot become visible in a short instant of time, like unto the overthrow of a political power. And this means also, that there can only be a social evolution, but there cannot be and never will be a social revolution.

II.

Revolutions never happen reasonably. They therefore also occur, because all the preceeding course of events were not only unreasonable, but also involved a reason-bereft resistance to every developement, to every improvement, to all reforms. It would be strangely odd to expect and demand the reasonable from revolutions. Revolution can represent a significant event in the life of the people, in it can be burnt up the old evil and also the revealing of a path to new life. But the times of a revolution never go lightly, in it there does not ensue the happiness of a people, and this time always is a time of tribulation for the people, in it there is much madness. Revolutions never bring about what is expected from them, they always disillusion. The great French Revolution taught us this: from it they expected a paradise upon earth, but what issued from it proved too reminiscent of hell, and it led to results insignificant in comparison to their expectations. After the great French Revolution there resulted not one continuous democratic republic, but rather several, and only after 80 years was a democratic republic re-established. And thus always it has been in history. And in the Russian revolution there is too much repeating itself, not new and original, as would seem to people not knowing history or having forgotten it. It is not the first time in history that they have sought to transform a political revolution into a social one, into a radical change of the social economic ordering of society and correlative classes. Such an aspiration has occurred in almost all large scale revolutions. Amidst all the revolutionary turnabouts, though perchance having been very "bourgeois" as regards the historical moment and the corresponding historical forces, the toiling folk await their ultimate liberation. Always are born dreams and utopias, which then are mercilessly destructive of life. Evil in this world always proves stronger than good, and this evil is evidenced both in those, who strive for a social paradise, and in those, who oppose them. The attempt at transforming a political revolution into a social one was already done in France in 1848 and led to the regency of Napoleon III for a long while. The hour of social revolution had not happened then, nor did it occur even later, in 1871. In 1871, after the catastrophe of the Franco-Prussian War, when France was humiliated and broken, in Paris was introduced the Commune, in which was realised a dictatorship of the minority of Parisian workers over the majority of the other people. This experiment ended very badly. The Commune drowned in blood. The socialist movement was thrown backwards. The republic established after this was glaringly bourgeois. This experiment yielded no sort of real conquests for the workers. Suchlike efforts occurred also in former times; fiery dreams about a social paradise more than once held sway with the popular masses. And always, when this ended, with the forcibly installed social paradise giving the people not more, but less, -- it again threw matters backwards. The attempts at a coercive "social revolution" never have and never will provide bread to a starving people, and these attempts bring disorganisation into economic life among the source providers of food, and they lessen the quantity of bread. These efforts will never lead to the brotherhood of people, they instead introduce division, malice and hate. Bread is provided by social organisation, by the increase of the productivity of labour, by social reforms. The path to brotherhood follows upon the moral and spiritual regeneration of people, a change in the man himself. If the heart of a man be full of malice and hate, if the man be guided by greed alone, then brotherhood cannot be possible. In the era of the Reformation in Germany during the times of the peasants wars there were attempts by forcible revolutionary means to introduce a kingdom of social justice, a kingdom of God's righteousness upon earth. John of Leiden created a coercive brotherhood, the kingdom of Sion. Luther sensed, that this was all a false movement, that it would not lead to good, and he opposed it, though also not by altogether good methods. In place of brotherhood, instead of the kingdom of God upon earth, there ensued terrors, mutual destruction, hatred and blood. The socialist Lassalle [Ferdinand, 1825-1864] even admitted that the peasant wars, with their social demands, did not correspond to the real correlation of forces and historical tasks of that time, in that they were moreso reactionary, than progressive. Brotherhood, the kingdom of God upon earth cannot be attained through a revolutionary turnabout. The Kingdom of God is to come imperceptibly. This remains an eternal truth.

III.

And here yet again in history, in an atmosphere of revolutionary intoxication, when everything has split apart, they want to transform the recent political revolution into a social revolution, into a socialist revolution, all at once they want to do it, instantaneously to overleap the long series of steps, traced ahead by the peoples of Western Europe, and to realise the most extreme social goals, to realise the realm of an ultimate social justice and truth. The Russian revolution wants to be made into a worldwide revolution, to renew all the world, it hopes to attract into following it all the peoples of the West into the fire of a social revolution, in which all the old world will be burnt up and a new world created. And the Russian Social Democrats fall thus into contradictions, which can evade detection. They are all the time saying, that the Russian revolution is bourgeois, and not proletarian, and yet they want, that in this bourgeois revolution the proletariat should play a chief role and realise its social demands. Such a demand is not initially apparent, and yet it is humanly perceptible. Someone, in living burdensome a life, tends naturally to dream about a speedy attaining to a better and more happy life. No one can blame the workers for tending to go too far in their desires, their dreams and expectations. But blameworthy are those socialist intelligentsia, who throw out the extreme social slogans, in the realisation of which they themself do not believe, and yet they do this in order to draw the masses over to their side. These socialists, who hold to the teachings of Marx, tend to forget the fundamentals of Marxism. Marx taught, that to the bourgeoise belongs a progressive and revolutionary role within history, while it enables a productive industrial process, while it is yet in thriving a phase; he taught, that socialism is possible only amidst the heightened developement of the productive industrial powers of a country, and that socialism is justifiable only then, if it increases the productivity of labour, and that socialism can be realised only after a prolonged process of social developement and social organisation. Socialism is impossible in a country industrially backwards, amidst a lack of organisation, amidst an insufficient awareness and insufficient enlightenment of the working class. Our Social Democrats well know this. Neither the condition of Russian industry, nor the condition of the working class in not having experienced any sort of organising history, tends to provide the Marxists any real grounds to anticipate a speedy realisation of socialism. For in miracles, however, and in an instantaneous spiritual regeneration of mankind, they do not believe. As regards our socialist populists, they tend to assume too much of themself, in asserting, that the enormous and manifold masses of the Russian peasantry imperceptibly are for socialism and are for the socialisation of the land. All this will prove more complex, than it seems.

Marxism has undergone a prolonged process of developement. The socialistic teaching of Marx and Engels initially coalesced in the revolutionary atmosphere of Europe after the 1848 revolutions. And in the first period of Marxism, in the days of its youth there was belief in the possibility of an impending social revolution. Marxism comprised in itself two sides: one -- an objectively scientific, which spoke about the laws of social developement, about the inter-dependence of all changes in distribution and about the realisation of social justness of the conditions of industrial productivity, whereas the second side -- was subjectively a matter of class, which posited the realisation of socialism as dependent upon the activity of the working class itself. These two sides of Marxist socialism frequently fall into contradiction. In Russian Marxism there has always been predominant the second side, with the first side relegated to secondary a plane. The Russian Social Democrats have believed and do believe in this, based on their faith in the possibility of a quick social revolution. In the objective and scientific side of Marxism, however, have occurred great changes, which have undermined the fundamentals of the theory of a social revolution. According to Marx, the catastrophe of capitalist society inevitably has to occur by virtue of the developement of the contradictions within it, of the concentration of capital, of overproduction and crises, and of the progressive grinding down of the working class, from which will grow discontent and class discord. These theories were constructed under the influence of the initial period of capitalistic developement in England. But further developement did not follow out the path indicated by Marx, that of a path of developing contraries, of an increase in catastrophes and a worsening condition of the workers. Within capitalistic society itself began a mitigating of evils and the dark sides, with an improvement of the position of the workers by virtue of their organisation and their planned-out struggle for an improvement of their condition, forestalling catastrophes by way of social reforms and a mitigating of the contradictions. Capitalistic industry adapted itself to the new and ever newer conditions of its existence, and proved more stable and vigourous, than Marx imagined. But its nature is changing. Workers organise into unions and prove to be more and more an influence in economic life and in the life of the state. The state is changing in the relationship of workers and capitalists and is defending the interests of labour. There occurs not a worsening, which would tend to lead to social revolution, but rather there occurs an improving, i.e. the reforming of society, via social evolution. The workers become citizens, and they thereby find a fatherland.

IV.

There is occurring a gradual change in the social fabric, a regeneration of society, a process, which in physiology would be termed molecular, i.e. a social evolution, and not revolution. On the one hand, there is a growth in the productivity of labour, making the people as a whole richer, and on another hand, there is a change in the psyche of people, their attitude to one another. Without a spiritual changing of man, without a moral regeneration, winning out over the excluding grip of egoism and selfish interests, and thereby establishing between people the possibility of unity and brotherhood, -- no whatever socialism, no whatever social rebirth, can possibly be or be spoken of. While the masses of workers and peasants are situated in darkness, while deprived of an elementary enlightenment and awareness, while in it there remains unawakened a moral and social consciousness winning out over egoism and personal interests, it is impossible to speak about the realisation of socialism seriously, and with a sense of responsibility. With a rather low level of culture, when there is not yet a spiritual self-discipline and spiritual tempering of the person, the typical masses of the workers and peasants tend to understand the slogans of socialism in a personally selfish sense, taken exclusively and applied in meaning to their own gain. The dark masses tend to conceive of socialism not only unsocially, but even anti-socially. In the idea of socialism there enters the regulation and organisation of the whole, the struggle against anarchy and disorganisation in economic life. Such an understanding of socialism existed in Plato, its founder in antiquity. But on the social and cultural level, in which at present a large portion of the toiling masses of the people is situated, impulsively cleaving to the old order in darkness, there triumphs not the socialistic idea, directed towards the great totality, but rather an hostile greed towards anything social, amidst the private interest, the uprising of parts against the whole. In the name of selfish special interests there is no focusing on the destruction of industrial productivity, nor the ruin of the agricultural economy. What thus is occurring is neither social revolution nor social evolution, but rather the disorganisation of the economic totality, its destruction and throwing everything backwards. And the first social task, facing Russia, is the task of the enlightening of the people, an enlightening both mental and moral, the uplift of its culture, its spiritual regeneration. Without this, there can be no deciding of the question of daily bread. Much of what is happening at present in Rus', and which is termed "social revolution", is a direct path leading to hunger, to deprivation and that scarcity of bread, which there has been til now for the workers. If the workers and the peasants fail to thus become conscientious and morally responsible for having always in view the interests of the whole of Russia, wherein only can be the source of their sustenance, if the part rises up against the whole, then there will not be a bettering, but rather a worsening of their material position.

A society is always reformed and improved upon by a working together of the classes, and not by a divisiveness into two parts each hateful and destructive towards the other, not by a civil war. One class alone, rising up against all the other classes, cannot better the society, cannot bring about social brotherhood. It will never happen, what Marx thought, i.e. the transformation of the greater part of mankind into the proletariat. There will remain all the other classes and sub-classes, which will be impossible to destroy, impossible to force. In the social struggle inevitably will ensue a moral moment. The idea of socialism ought to be not only an economic, but also a moral idea. Without a moral grounding even economics itself falls apart into an heap of trash. An ethical socialism would lead to the elimination of the possibility of a violent social revolution, always as such based upon hatred, upon class interest, upon a wish to know no sort of an higher truth. This has to be understood first of all by the possessing classes, the economically dominating. There has been no lack of threatening forebodings.

Of these classes, much depends upon a changing of the moral atmosphere, in which the modern social struggle occurs. It is impossible, certainly, to demand from the average sort of whatever class to have too lofty a moral level and to make too great sacrifices. But in the possessor classes, the so-called "bourgeoise", there both can and ought to awaken a civil and moral awareness of the truth of socialism, of a truth neither of class nor materialistic, and the inevitability of the socialising tendency within industrial and economic life. A social revolution therefore only gets considered necessary, if there does not occur social improvement, developement, the struggle against social evil, the growth of good and justice. It is based upon the principle: the worse the better. But when there occurs a creative social evolution, when society assumes solid a form, when there is a growing of the moral unity of the people and a consciousness of social duty, then social revolution, the pathos for a social revolution, dissipates. Socialism then ceases to be a religion, it is rendered practical, a real social politics, subsumed to higher aims. The religious feelings would get redirected upon worthier and loftier matters, and upon God.

V.

If one employ words in more profound and conscious a context, then it mustneeds be said, that there never have been and never will be social revolutions. Possible are merely political revolutions. "Social revolution" would involve a prolonged, almost unforeseeable process, it would perchance involve a change of attitude of man towards nature, i.e. a growth of moral power. And this also means, that under the concept "social revolution" can only be understood as social evolution. And indeed, even the increase of the "productive powers of man", of his ability over the natural elements, is not exclusively a material and economic process, for this process possesses spiritual a grounding. It is bound up with the organising and self-discipline of the human will. Dissoluteness in man, moral corruptness in him leads to a downfall in social creativity. And this can occur with an entire people. It is especially important, that Russians understand, that the deciding of the social question first of all depends upon social creativity, and not upon division and destruction. Even if the struggle for power can lead to political revolution, to the overthrowing of the old powers and the installation of the new, then still never can it lead to a social revolution. In the enormous, complex, socio-economic life of peoples nothing can be accomplished by plottings, uprisings and revolts, nothing positive can be begotten of violence and seizures. Blood, spilt in a civil war, in the uprising of class against class, will not cultivate the ground and ready the harvest, will bring no benefits, will not feed nor clothe, will not save from hunger and cold. Hatred and malice of one class towards another will not lead to social brotherhood, will not eliminate divisiveness and discord. And the social question, is a question about bread, about clothing and blood, about brotherhood and the uniting of people, about suchlike an organising of the great entirety, amidst which there will not be the deprived, there will not be the oppressed and the hungry and each as is able will develope his quality as person. It needs moreover to be made clear, that in social life everything is very complex and difficult, and simplistic extreme slogans solve nothing. How complicated the agrarian question is, and how divided is the peasantry in its resolution! By a thousand threads social life ties in with the enormous and mysterious life of nature and with the no less enormous and mysterious life of the human spirit. But in nature itself and in the human spirit itself is lodged a sort of evil, which is not so easily overcome and defeated. Many improvements occur within human life, many for all the people, much of the old evil is falling away not to return, and there will be gained daily bread for all the people, not only material, but also spiritual bread. But a paradise upon earth will not ensue. And ahead of mankind will lie prolonged a path towards higher a life. The attempts however at social revolutions can only lead to disorganisation, to a destroying of the people's economy, to a crash of industrial productivity, from which the workers first of all would suffer. And then would come about not a social paradise, but rather a social hell, with grievous want and hostility, with blood and destruction, with reactions and a turning backwards. Into this hell would tend to thrust the toiling people, those who seek to tempt it with a quick realisation of a social paradise.

VI.

Russia -- is a land industrially backward, as has become sufficiently evident during the time of war, and in it still has to get developed a capitalistic industrial productivity. But this industrial developement cannot simply involve a repetition of that of the Western countries, especially as was with the first period of the history of capitalism in England. Russia will make the transition to higher an industrial culture, enriched by the experience of other peoples, and in different an historical time, when there will no longer be any sort of justification for hypocritical economic individualism, when the moral enthusiasm for the idea of cut-throat competition will have become impossible. With us forthwith will ensue a struggle against the dark and evil sides of capitalism and there will occur a gradual socialisation, a state regulation of economic life. The workers will organise, will form unions, and within the capitalistic society itself will improve their position and increase their significance within industrial life. The factory setup will gradually shift from being autocratic to instead constitutional, not impeding personal initiative. At higher a degree of developement and amidst a greater organisational ability, of awareness and enlightenment, the working class will be in a condition more directly to participate in the industrial arrangement. But this is a very complex matter of social evolution and of social reforms, of the working together of classes, and not some sort of social turnabout, in which one class seeks to exterminate the other. The true point in socialism mustneeds be sought in the idea of a regulating of the whole, the conforming of all and everything withe the interest of the social organism, i.e. the surmounting of anarchy and social hostility, of social egoism within society. The socialisation of society is also to a large degree a matter of its organisational ability, of the extensive mutual pretensions of its parts and its members. The bourgeois capitalistic society has facing it prevailing personal and class interests. Social idealism has to win out over this dominance of personal and class interests and selfishness. The workers accuse the industrialists of greed, but if they themself can oppose against this greed nothing except their own selfish greed, then towards a new better life, towards greater a truth they will not arrive. In their private life, people can be guided by selfish interests through weakness and sinfulness. There is much egoism in everyone. But when social life involves uniting and grouping exclusively in accord with selfish interests, no sort of truth and justice then obtains, no sort of higher life can obtain through this. A socialism exclusively materialistic and of class would itself blow up. Only in the uniting in the name of an unselfish idea, in the name of truth and right, can lead to a new, a better and finer society. A new man has to be born, a new human soul. Without this, all social revolutions will be merely a switching of clothes, only a deceptive changing of the externals. Slaves have to cease being slaves, actively be rendered and not resist becoming free, not merely wearing the costumes of the free, whilst in soul remaining slaves, slaves to their own passions, their own interests, their own proclivities towards violence, received from their old life. Socialism gets transformed into a slavery, if it does not foster freedom within the human soul. The war has evoked towards life an altogether especial form of socialism -- a military socialism, a state socialism primarily. We see manifestations of this socialism each day on the ration-cards for bread and sugar. In Germany this socialism has reached an especially high degree of developement. On this side is also a movement in England, a land with an aversion towards state meddling and oversight. This military socialism is working out the trends of state regulation and the organisation of economic life. And to return to the past, to an exclusively private and individualistic economic arrangement of the people is neither desirable nor possible. But this military socialism does not provide any sort of basis to feel, that a social revolution is nigh at hand. On the contrary, it renders social revolution still more unnecessary and impossible. Within the entirety of the people, into which enter all the classes, there is awakening an healthy state feeling, which promotes a better organising of economic life and the securing of sustenance for all. All these are facts, not foreseen by the teachings of Marx and class socialism. The future social order is impossible to foresee. It never turns out, as the various social teachings would imagine it. It is possible only to say, that within economic life will begin to be discerned tendencies towards socialisation. But this socialisation will transpire by complex paths and manifold means. In this regard, the cooperative movement will have no less a significance, than state socialism. And that which is accepted in various teachings and theories termed as "socialism", will always be too premature, or too late. A "socialistic revolution" is impossible, whilst society is insufficiently prepared economically and morally, insufficiently reformed and developed, and a social revolution is not needed, belatedly, when society has gone far forward upon the path of social reforms, upon the path of a moral regeneration. The English form has to be admitted as the highest form of the socialist movement. English socialism is both more practical, and more idealistic, and this -- is a socialism economic and cultural, not revolutionary political. The revolutionary political form of the socialist movement does not improve the position of the workers, does not provide bread. Moreover, this form of movement distorts the moral awareness of the workers, grips them in a tension of malicious and hateful feelings. And there is no sort of a justification for this, that in the Russian socialist movement there should hold sway the German Social Democrat form. Socialism always tends to become national. With each people is its own form of socialism. The French socialism is unlike the English, and the English -- unlike the German. The Social Democrat form is an exceptionally German form of socialism. And if there be possible a Russian socialism, in accord with the character of the Russian people, then it ought to convey a moral and even religious character. And this means, that a socialist movement ought to be, on the one hand, practical and reform oriented, and on the other hand, idealistic, oriented towards higher aims, an higher truth.

VII.

The revolutionary class socialism ought to be discarded, from both a scientific and from a moral point of view. It not only fails to correspond to actuality and is refuted by the course of history, but likewise it is in contradiction to the moral nature of the human person and to its religious hopes. Socialism of such a sort distorts and maims the soul of the Russian people, violates it with foreign teachings imported from Germany. Revolutionary socialism is a type of pseudo-religion, which wants to be a substitute for true religion in the soul of the people. The soul of the people cannot live without sanctities and here instead of the Divine Christian sanctities, upon which this soul has been nourished and lived by, they want to forcibly attach it to a sanctity, in which God is replaced by the material ordering of earthly life, to make a god of the proletariat itself, of its will and interests. This -- is a religion of flattery to man and the people, a religion of self-apotheosis, a making a god of oneself. The people cannot live by such a religion, since every people, just like every man, can spiritually live only by sanctities, which are loftier than himself. The attracting aspect of a social revolution is in its seeking to be a religious attraction. And it has to be exposed for its religious lie and nothingness, unmasked in its desire to enslave man by a dream, which can lead only to slavery and downfall. A full, total and ultimate socialism -- is impossible, it is merely a false and enslaving dream. But there is possible a socialism which is partial, practical, reforming, and this socialism ought to be in accord with an higher culture, subordinate to higher cultural aims. The Russian revolution will have its own social side, which will impel bold social reforms. But about a social revolution it is impossible for us to speak seriously and responsibly. These discussions have to be viewed, as demagoguery, as the flaming up of class passions, without an inner faith, that this will lead to a socialistic success. By way of flattery and lie they want to win the masses over to their side. With the most sincere among the Social Democrats and the Social Revolutionaries there is an unhealthy dreamy aspect, mixing up theory with practice, material order with a religious sense of sanctity, this world with the other invisible world. But amidst a new lofty moral level with people there also cannot be a perfective societal setup. It is love, and not hatred, that will lead to a perfective society.

The revolution in Russia has happened and has ended. And now there can be either a positive building and construction of new life, or destruction and disintegration. That what they now tend to term as continuing revolution, is merely a disintegration of revolution, which can lead to counter-revolution and new slavery. In this sinful world, there cannot be a leaping over from the realm of necessity into the realm of freedom, a matter about which Marx and Engels have also spoken. The regeneration of mankind, its liberation from the enslavement to nature -- is from external nature, whereas from his own inner nature -- it is a matter spiritual, and not only material, not only social. Without this spiritual aspect, distinct from every social revolution, man never will be free. In the great deed of the liberation of man a partial socialism also does play its own subordinate role. But this is a socialism for every conscientious man, for whom truth stands highest of all, and it ought to be a socialism that is moral, national, of the state and cultural, i.e. it has to subordinate itself to the good and truth, to the utmost good aspects of nationality, the state, of culture, truth and freedom. The Russian socialist movement either will be conscious of itself as connected with the national and state unity of Russia, with the purposes of Russian culture, with the moral composite of the Russian soul, or it will decompose and rot, having given nothing to the toiling folk. Our social question can be decided only in connection with the greatness of Russia itself. The socialist movement will be fruitful and creative, if it frees itself from the phantasm of a social revolution, which in practice, in life, leads only to disintegration.

The People and the Classes in the Russian Revolution

(1917 - 10)[1]

I.

The Russian revolution -- represents the greatest turnabout within the life of all the Russian people, in all its historical fate. Such turnabouts occur once in a span of centuries, and in them are active all the forces of the people, not only of our generation, but also past generations. No one can claim, that what belongs to all the Russian people across the span of its history, belongs merely to only one class, only one group, only one party. The turnabout of a millennium has happened in the life of the Russian state and the Russian people, and in the face of this remarkable fact there tends to fade all the class and party disputes and reckonings. When they say, that the working class has wrought the revolution and that it has an exclusive right to it, then this sounds false not only in regard to those, who participated in it at the present hour of Russian history, but also in regard to all the past Russian history. The right to it could be claimed also by the Decembrists, struggling for political freedom a century still back and the Russian intelligentsia over the span of a century suffering martyrdom for the liberation of the Russian people. Children of the nobility, ignoring their class position, went to the people and sought to be of service to it. It would be unjust and ignoble to forget about all those, who by their martyr's life and death prepared for the Russian revolution, and instead to call to mind only one class, which by its support during the days of revolution helped assure its triumph. The revolution occurred so readily, the old powers fell so unhindered namely, because that the turnabout involved an impulse of

---

[1] NAROD I KLASSY V RUSSKOI REVULIUTII. Pamphlet published under the auspices of the Moskovskaya prosvetitel'naya komissiya pri Vremennom komitete Gosudarstvennoi Dumy (Moscow Elucidation Commission on behalf of the Committee of the Provisional State Duma); Moscow, 1917, 15 p.

all the people, and in which participated from top to bottom all the classes and groups -- the intelligentsia, the nobility, the industrialists, the many-millioned peasantry, garbed in the grey military great-coats, the workers and all the parties -- from the nationalists and Oktyabrists to the Social Revolutionaries and the Social Democrats. All came out onto the streets, all were exposed to danger. Our revolution, the most bloodless and unimpaired of all the great revolutions, -- was engendered by the sense of self-preservation amongst all the people. And in its State Duma, the president Rodzyanko was a revolutionary the same, as were the workers out on the street. And when Rodzyanko decided, that the State Duma would head the organisation of revolutionary powers, he predetermined the fate of the revolution, he averted a civil war, a bloody struggle, which could imperil it. The Russian revolution was national moreover, still in that within it was expressed the characteristic traits of the Russian people -- the absence of revenge and a bloody reprisal, and in its first days the death sentence was abolished.

When a great historical turnabout occurs, then within it always there is a line, which corresponds to the interests and the tasks of the whole, -- of all the Russian people, of all the state. Beyond the life of individual people, of individual social groups and classes there exists moreover the enormous life of the entire people and it is not some simple composite of the lives of these individual people, groups and classes, it possesses its own soul and its own tasks in the world. To search out this all-national line, to follow along it and remain faithful to it -- means also to hold truly to the people's and the state's politics, means to serve one's fatherland, to save it from collapse and ruin, to organise within it a new better life. And in the name of this great task, to which we are called not only by the demands of the people's self-preservation, but also the impulse towards historical creativity, all the classes are called towards restraint of their interests, towards putting them into accord with the interests, the goals, the demands and needs of Russia. Each Russian man is not only a class-man, a worker, an industrialist, landowner, peasant, merchant, but likewise also he is a free citizen of his fatherland and state. And the citizen in him has to win out over the class-man. He needs more to be a citizen of the Russian state, than an industrialist or worker, a landowner or peasant, and he needs to love his fatherland more, than his class. Class is not the native land of a man, with it is connected only the externals of a man, while in his depths however a man is connected with his authentic natal sources, with the whole organism of the people. And all Russian people at some level of depth are closer to one another, despite their belonging to various classes, than they are to the Germans, the English and the French. The people is more extensive a matter, than is democracy, which is a part of the people. All Russian people have to remember, that Russia exists, and it is not only workers and industrialists, peasants and landowners, with their opposing interests. Russia already existed, when there were not these classes, which now oppose each other, and it will exist, when there will no longer be that class ordering of society, which now exists. Yet Russia can be inflicted a grievous wound, from which it will bleed and not quickly be corrected, if everyone thinks only about himself, if they forget about it and allow it to be lacerated in a raging struggle of class interests. Only those class interests are morally justified and deserve support, which are in accord with the interests of Russia as a whole, of the Russian state and all the Russian people, which is not some sort of mere class. The change and improvement of the position of the toiling masses of the Russian people, of the peasantry and workers is not only necessary and just, but also is called for by the demand of restoring to health the whole of Russia, and to avert the decaying of the Russian people. But if all the growing demands for the improvement of the lot of the workers and peasants is accompanied by a wrecking of Russian industrial productivity and the agrarian economy, if it all leads to economic chaos and a lessening of industrial productivity, then such a movement will have become detrimental to the essential interests of Russia and the Russian state and cannot be deserving of sympathy. We face ahead great social reforms, and they will come to benefit the Russian people, if these are organised and directed towards the social totality, rather than destroy it in the name of private interests. It is immoral to think only about one's own class. The truth of a class, rather than the interests of a class, can be its contribution to the history of the people. When the nobility among us came to hinder the liberation of the peasantry, in being concerned about its own interests, it ceased to play a creative role in Russia and thrust itself onto the path of decay and decline. And in 1905, when extremist revolutionary currents set forward maximalist demands, not corresponding to the condition of the Russian people, they brought about the demise of the revolution and for 10 years were bypassed by life.

II.

Russia exists not only for a single moment, not only for that hour, in which we happen to live with our own limited interests, the life of Russia -- is that of a thousand years, and it connects all our dead ancestors with all our coming descendants. And to understand the revolution is possible only for one, who is able to grasp the connections of time, one who in the present does not ignore the past and the future. And such a person lives an historical national life, keeping alive the memory about the great past, bout the old fighters for freedom and who has concern for the far future, not merely casting about greedily for gain during the present day. Not only will we die together with all our limited interests, but there will vanish also from the arena of history the various class goals with their interests of the present day, and Russia will yet be, and all the Russian people, as a great totality, who live within it, and through it also within mankind. A century, perhaps, will pass, and descendants of people of the revolutionary epoch will recollect, whether they loved their Russian ancestry, whether they were concerned about all the passed down to them riches and blessings of Russia, both the spiritual and the material, all the values of culture, whether they thought not only about the partial, but also about the whole, not only about the interests of the present, but also about the greater welfare of the future. And with pitiful pretensions there is the showing off of individual classes and groups to ascribe exclusively to themself the honour of making the revolution and themself achieving its conquests. Then will be rendered the judgement of history over us, disdaining partiality of person and class interests. And this judgement, verily, will acknowledge, that in 1917 in Russia there occurred not a class revolution, that it occurred not from the social conflict of classes and that a great mistake in this was made by those, who sought to bestow on it the character of a fierce social-class struggle, who had no such sufficient grounding and justification in the experiencing of that moment. This undermines the unity of the revolution, pushes part of Russian society onto the path of counter-revolution and endangers the conquests of freedom. The only real winning course can be with that line of movement, which expresses the greatest national unity of all the people, which does not fragment Russia into irreconcilable mutually exclusive parts from each other, which is a line centring round the people, expressing the will of all the people, of all the Russian nation. Democracy, as an expresser of the will of the people and the power of the people, cannot be a matter of class, it has to be national. And the very basics of democracy contradict any attempts at a dictatorship from whatever the class, its attempted violence against all the enormous multi-faceted Russian people.

The old powers, in sowing hatred, discord and division, set the Russian people on the brink of ruin, and the people was able to save itself only in a surge of unity, which led it to freedom. The revolution therefore only succeeded, because there was unity in it. And the dark forces would very much want to sow discord and division and through this to return themself to power. Thus it always was and always will be in history. Division, an inner hostility and anarchy in a free Russia is most of all the desire of our enemies -- the Germans and the underground lurking adherents of the old order, the old powers. But one mustneeds believe, that the old is gone and for it there is no return. Now facing the Russian people stands the task of constructing a new free life, a task of creativity and not destruction. The free citizens, from which henceforth the Russian people is comprised, are called to responsible constructive work, they cannot revolt in the manner of slaves. The free path opens widely before all. And if the first days of free life, when first in all its own history the Russian people is called to a free ordering of its fate, if such be overshadowed by evil discord and hatred by classes, in which perish any thought about Russia and the whole of the people, then this gloomy darkness will haunt all the further history of Russia and the Russian people. The first days in the liberation of a people from age old slavery ought to be joyful days, which will call forth remembrance in the memory of a people, as its early youth of existence as citizens. But such a memory will remain about our revolutionary period, only if all the Russian people, belonging to various classes, avoid assuming a class perspective, and conquer in themself the exclusive grip of class interests, if all sense themself spiritually one people, dwelling at the bosom of their one common mother -- Russia. Thus ought the free citizen of the free Russia to sense himself, responsible for his native land. The exclusive prevailing of the class point of view is destructive of citizenship and can lead to civil war. And those, who do not want to spill the blood even of their enemies -- the Germans, would instead wind up spilling the blood of the brothers -- Russians.

With the industrialists and the workers there exist differing interests, and they can always find grounds for mutual social hostility, just like with the landowners and the peasants. But both these and those -- are

Russian citizens, and neither the one nor the other can tear himself away from Russia as an entirety and yet find sustenance from Russia, both these and those had need of freedom, and they shared in the liberation of Russia. Irregardless of the differing interests of the industrialists and the workers -- both are interested in the growth and flourishing of Russian industrial productivity. To wit, that our industrial productivity should not go into an ultimate disorder and decline, all classes of the population have an interest in this. On the growth of the provisioning powers of Russia is dependent the power and the greatness of the Russian state, and the well-being of all the Russian people. In a land industrially too backward, ravaged and impoverished, there can be no deciding of any sort of social questions and there cannot essentially be improvement in the position of workers and peasants. And according to the teachings of Marx, socialism is possible only amidst a very high developement of productive forces and obtains only in the instance, if it increases the productivity of labour. Social reforms in Russia at present presuppose a working together of classes.

III.

They are incorrect, who say, that in the victory of Russia over its enemy, Germany, are only interested the capitalist industrialists, only the bourgeois, who need markets and enrichment, and that it is for them that the Russian people is shedding its blood. The victory over Germany is needed for all the Russian people, for all the Russian workers and Russian peasants, for all our remote descendants -- it is needful for Russia, and not only for some whatever class. If Germany defeats Russia, then the danger threatening us -- is not only, that it might annex part of our lands. A still greater danger -- is in this, that it might economically enslave the Russian people. Russia would be transformed into a colony for the Germans, and the Russian workers would fall into slavery to the German capitalists. All the Russian people, all the Russian workers and peasants are dependent upon the economic flourishing and prospering of Russia, upon its economic freedom. Industrialism exists not only for the industrialists, it exists for all the land, and its interests -- are interests for all the people. And if Russia should win and receive the straits and free access to the southern seas, then this would be a great good thing for al the people, for our grain merchants, for the peasants and the workers, and not only for the capitalists, not only for some whatever class. The workers have an interest in the power and flourishing of Russia and they cannot be indifferent to the greatness of Russia, they cannot be unfeeling to the shaming and humiliating of Russia. The workers -- are citizens, this is their native land, they -- are not slaves, not outcasts, bereft of feelings of fatherland. A conscientious and free patriotism is the measure of a free citizenry.

    The industrialists can think about their own group interests, and strive towards an increase of profits, coming into conflict with the whole, just as the workers can think too exclusively about their group interests, and strive towards a realisation of extreme social demands, amidst present conditions not fully compatible with the well-being and security of the Russian state. But both the one and the other can play a positive historical role only to the extent of subordinating their own interests to the whole, to the purpose and welfare of Russia, of the Russian state, of all the Russian people, as Russian citizens and patriots of their fatherland in the most genuine sense of this word. Every class, proving egoistical and thinking only about itself, dissociating itself from the entirety and letting Russia get torn apart, cannot but be bypassed in the constructing of a new life in Russia, cannot but be pushed aside by the true and just feelings of the people. About this ought to be mindful also the leaders of the workers, if they want to creatively participate in the building and ordering of the new Russia. The struggle for exclusive power of various classes and groups will tear apart Russia and lead to chaos and anarchy, it is hostile to the very idea of Russia as a totality. The power of rule can only be unified and of all the people by its nature. And powerful can only be that rule of power, which expresses the greatest unity of Russia, which corresponds to a course national and of the state in common. Such a power of rule cannot involve the power of rule of whatever one class, which always would be but a dictator, i.e. a bully over the greater part of the Russian people. Such a power of rule can only be instead a supra-class power of rule. And it has to be with a continuing with that unity, with which the Russian revolution began and which gave it its victory. The power of rule at present in Russia is not a right, but rather an onerous duty, a burden and ascetic like a feat. The raging struggle for the power of rule distracts from the responsible matter of the organising and building up of Russia. The state power of rule has to be a principle, ascendant over human caprice, and it has to conscientiously subsume itself to the service of truth.

IV.

The interests of Russia have to be felt, as the interests of all the classes, of all the Russian citizens. Without a great cohesion into one people, into one state, Russian people of all classes would be transformed into a formless heap of dirt. A positive attitude towards one's native land and one's state, towards one's people and its history provides for the moral and civil sustaining of the person, surmounts the boundless prevailing of egoism and developes the capacity for self-sacrifice. No one class can separate itself from the whole of the people and the state, can set its own interests in opposition to the interests of the state, to the interests of Russia. For otherwise it tends to destroy the sources of its existence and dooms itself to perishing. Class struggle within human societies is inevitable, as long as mankind fails to rise to an higher degree of spiritual perfection. But it can course along in accord with national and state unity, not tending towards its destruction. The supra-class perspective not only reinforces the unity and power of Russia, but also the very existence of the Russian people in the world. An exclusive class perspective however divides and pulverises Russia and subjects to doubt the very existence of the Russian people as a whole. But classes are transitory a thing, which were not and will not be, whereas the Russian people will remain, and the name of Russia will continue to exist in the world. The revolution was made, in order to save Russia, and not in order to divide it up into parts and besmirch its name. A liberated people still more remains a single people, than is a people, situated in slavery. And now finally has to be heard the voice of all the people, and its will has to be manifest in the Constituent Assembly, gathered together upon the basis of the in-common, direct, equal and secret vote. Various classes will participate in the Constituent Assembly, various interests, in it will be present and in it will be inevitable a social struggle, a struggle for these or some other social reforms. But in this, however, the Constituent Assembly has to heed the nation as a whole, and it has to determine the form of governance, the fundamentals of the state and social construct of Russia. And prior to this forming of the collective will of all the nation, no one can arrogate to himself the right on their own to determine the fundamentals of this arrangement, no such prerogatives belong to any one class. Let the consciousness of all the Russian people take form and become crystallised in determining the course for the nation in common, as regards our further history.

The wording, "the people", is impossible of comprehension in a social-class sense. The Russian people is not some sort of social group, is not the peasantry or the working class or all the common folk, all the toiling classes of society merely. The Russian people is a great totality, a thousand years alive, it was there prior to the formation of the present social order of society and it will be there still, after there is no longer this social order with all its classes. And the true voice of the people is the voice of a thousand years spanning its history, with all its past and its future generations. In revolutions tend to fall decayed powers, but in the life of the people remains the historical connection with time, the historical flow of succession does not disappear. A class, living for itself alone and opposing itself to all the other classes, can sense itself as sundered off from Russian history, from its legacies. But an entire people cannot sense itself thus. In the people, as a whole, there has to be found an accurate sense of what is needful for Russia, how to arrange it. And all our hope rests on this, that in the Constituent Assembly will resound this voice of the people, not as some class, but as a great totality.

V.

The Russian revolution was patriotic as regards its fundamentals and as regards its character. It occurred, not because one class roe up against another, the workers against the industrialists or the peasantry against the landowners, and not because of an acuteness of class contradictions and class struggle. Before the revolution itself, there had not occurred any such acute social class struggle, it was not the chief ill within Russian life, the motives for the turnabout mustneeds be sought elsewhere. The final blow was struck the old powers, when its unpatriotic, its non-national character of betrayal in regards to Russia was exposed. The old power fell first of all, because it had neither the will nor the ability to defend Russia from external dangers, because it left the Russian people defenseless and unarmed in facing a threatening enemy. The old power fell, because it assumed hostile an attitude towards all the Russian people, towards all the strata, all the classes. It had become insufferable for all, even for the rightist circles. An acute class struggle did not beget the revolution and it was not begotten by the revolution. It as it were came from the outside, from the sidelines it entered into the national revolution of all the people and attired itself in the garb of outmoded teachings. There began a struggle against the "bourgeoise", although quite unclear for many, what this all-encompassing word means, and was seized upon by wider and ever wider circles, to which are beginning to be numbered even the more moderate representatives of the socialist currents. And the frightening thing is, that as "bourgeoise" are beginning to be labelled the creative powers of the land, which actively desire to build up Russia, to organise in it a new life, to save it from disintegration and ruin. And as "bourgeoise" are beginning to be called the cultural and educated segment, endowed with knowledge and societal experience. Here is to what sort of pitiful results the fomenting of class struggle leads, evoked not by the urgent demands of life, but rather by abstract teachings or unenlightened instincts.

The Russian revolution by its conquests will reinforce freedom and lead to a new and better life only, if it remains patriotic and of all the people, both in facing the outward enemy, and the inner dangers of discord and dissolution. It can proceed only in unity and only in unity can it consolidate its conquests. If however disunity prevails, then the revolution might destroy itself. Merely to work out new social slogans -- means not developing nor consolidating the liberative aspect of the revolution. We know already from the course of the great French Revolution, that a revolution can decompose and lead to a new Caesarism, -- the extremes readily conjoin. The extremities of revolution too often lead to the extremities of reaction. We, as Russians, ought to be mindful of this, enriched by the experience of Western Europe. They tried to transform the revolution of 1848 in France into a socialistic revolution. But this ended pitifully and led to the accession of Napoleon III. Very pitifully ended also the experiment of the Paris Commune. In these instances typically the working class, too excessive in its demands, threw everything backwards and for a certain while stood aside from a direct building up of life. This can occur also in Russia, if the class struggle in the Russian revolution goes too far and tears apart the unity of the revolution. The state has its own life and its own laws, in withstanding the struggle of classes and social groups, and when collapse and ruin threaten it, it will find its own inner strength and save itself. And then the power of the state itself will drive back onto a secondary plane those classes and groups, which have proven hostile to its destiny and have transgressed the fundamental laws of its existence.

Progressive only is that class, which has its interests in accord with the interests of the whole state, with all the nation. And irregardless of how revolutionary in the externals some class might be, if in the struggle for its own interests inflicts wounds upon the whole of the people, the whole state, it does not serve towards the creative progress o the people, and at such a moment cannot be called truly progressive. This is true in regard to all classes. The state and the nation imperatively demand every class, that its struggle with other classes be subordinated to higher interests and aims. In this demand resounds the voice of all the entire people with its long historical fate. And to this voice of all the people, of all of Russia, it is needful to hearken, and not merely to the voices of individual self-asserting classes. This voice sounded forth during the first days of the revolution and only it can consolidate its work and appeal for the building up of new life. The Russian people cannot forget its Christian upbringing and cannot allow, that its soul becomes poisoned by class hatred. And the struggle itself for the improving o the lot of the toiling folk has to be subsumed to an higher truth. But it would be hypocritical to call for self-restraint by the toiling folk, who always have been in an economically oppressed position, and not to appeal for self-restraint on the part of the rich, the industrialist capitalists and landowners, who have the ability to offer the greatest material sacrifices in the name of native land and the state. The holding of property obligates, and the possessing classes ought to demonstrate in deed, that the general interests of the nation and the state for them stand higher than class interests. Only conscientious social sacrifices will guard and strengthen the moral unity of the Russian people, which is so very necessary for the salvation of Russia and Russian freedom.

The Free Church

(1917 - #013)[1]

I.

In the life of the Russian people there has occurred a turnabout, which entails beyond it enormous consequences, not only material, but also spiritual. Such catastrophes do not happen often in the history of a people. Something had to have changed in the soul of the people, in its spiritual composition, in order for it so suddenly to alter the foundations of its historical existence. It is only on the surface level that such changes seem sudden and instantaneous, in actuality they are the result of a prolonged and profound inner process. Religious life always serves as the primal basis of every people, it is the basic wellspring of its nourishment. And the organic complex of the life of a people begins to crumble away then, when in the religious life of a people there has occurred a crippling fracture, when some sort of lie has penetrated into religious life and idolatry has poisoned the soul of the people. Such an idolatrous lie has poisoned the life of the Russian people and swayed it from the true faith. The Kingdom of God and the kingdom of Caesar, separated apart by Christ, have become jumbled together in Rus': "Caesar" became substituted for "God", and to "Caesar" was the requital due "God". But every creation of an idol and graven image of itself enslaves, it deprives of freedom. Only worship of the One, the Living God, makes people free. From the time when the imperial power of the autocracy was transformed into an idol, into something idolatrous not only for worldly life, of the state, but also for life religious and churchly, the Russian Church lost its freedom, and fell into slavery. Dostoevsky from Orthodox a perspective said, that the Russian Church has

---

[1] SVOBODNAYA TSERKOV'. Pamphlet published under the auspices of the Moskovskaya prosvetitel'naya komissiya pri Vremennom komitete Gosudarstvennoi Dumy (Moscow Elucidation Commission on behalf of the Committee of the Provisional State Duma); Moscow, 1917, 31 p.

been in paralysis from the time of Peter the Great. The Slavophils Khomyakov, Yu. Samarin and I. Aksakov, and the prophet of universal a Christianity, Vl. Solov'ev, wrote much about the abnormal position of the Russian Church within the Russian state, about its captivity by the state power. The official Russian Church was transformed into a government department, into a ministry of the Orthodox confession. During the final years of the reign of Nicholas II this abasement and enslavement of the Church reached unprecedented dimensions. The upper Church hierarchy, in worshipping Caesar like God, fell under the sway of the rascal and khlystyite Grigorii Rasputin. By virtue of his exclusive influence upon the tsar and tsarina, almost the whole of those comprising the Holy Synod was rendered into "Grigorians", and not Orthodox, becoming composed of the cronies of Grigorii Rasputin. The Petrograd metropolitan Pitirim and the Moscow metropolitan Makarii were of the "Grigorian" confession. The Church's upper hierarchy, having lost all sense of churchly propriety, became so mixed up with the Rasputinite element, just as did the upper bureaucracy. It has long since lost any spiritual influence upon the people. The finest Orthodox people, believers not out of fear, but out of conscience, have viewed the Holy Synod with contempt. Orthodox missionaries, who were as such the agents of the corrupt state power, just like gendarmes and police detectives, have poisoned the religious life of the people, they have inspired an abhorrence towards the Church, their activity has led to a falling away from the Church and to the growth of sectarianism. There has arisen the expression, the "official Church", and it has served as a blocking screen over the true and eternal Church of Christ, and it has made being within the Church impossible for many. Russia received from Byzantium an onerous legacy, it acquiesced to the Byzantine temptation and bears from it the grievous consequences. The pre-death hours of Russian tsarism are reminiscent of a page out of Byzantine history with its intrigues and deceits, with its falsehood, with secret influences, with conspiracies and betrayals, with the slavery of the Church to all sorts of rascals, with a special role of women and their favourites. The soul of the people was in dismay over all this, such as had occurred in churchly life, from the servile idolatry of the spiritual powers in facing the growing might of the state. This dismay and division in the soul of the people found expression in the dissipation of the religious energy of the Russian people into a multitude of sects as well as a complete falling away from Christianity. The greatest preserving was done by the Old Ritualism, the

Old Believers, since they sought to preserve their faith at a distance away from the "official ecclesiology".

Revolutions are inevitable in the life of peoples, but they are always a matter of sickness, they always bespeak the accumulated evil from the past; the detritus of evil of the Russian state and churchly life have set an unhealthy imprint upon the spiritual aspect of the Russian Revolution, with similarities to that, as happened during the major French Revolution. The Revolution has proven bereft of positive spiritual foundations, it was not the result of an accumulation of creative spiritual energy, it has come about chiefly through the putrid processes of rot from the Old Order. Within the elements of the Revolution there has not been heard the voice of the liberated Church. The Free Church is as it were totally absent from the active powers of the currently happening Russian history. The Church, even after the Revolution, after its liberation from the grip of the old powers, seems to play but a servile role. Within the life of the people, in dealing with the Revolution, there occur stormy spiritual processes. And within the souls of simple and ignorant people, old sanctities and idols fall in an instant and new ones arise. But the Church in all this does not play any sort of active and creative a role. Though indeed the Russian people with its enormous masses always has been a Christian and Orthodox people, and the Church in the past was a great initiating force in Russian history, the significance of which cannot but be acknowledged even by people who are non-believers. But it is only the Free Church that can have spiritually an influence upon national life.

What kind of effect has the Revolution had upon churchly life? Has there occurred for us a turnabout not only political, social and in way of life, but also a religious turnabout? No, the religious turnabout for us is still in the future, it will come about only after this, when the people will have spiritually worked its way through the experience of the Revolution. The experiences of the revolutionary epoch can lead to a religious renewal. Meanwhile, however, the Church has mechanically accepted the Revolution, almost as though it did not sense the catastrophic events taking place. The Church had become so abased in the Old Order, so enslaved to the old powers, the religious hierarchy so morally dissolute, that the outward powers of the Church were unable to play any sort of active role in the historic turnabout. If there was any sort of religious energy that might act, then it was underground, invisible. The Name of Christ had become forgotten amongst the revolutionary element and it was not in His Name that the revolutionary upheaval was made. The revolution took place within the "kingdom of Caesar". But the Church was connected by a thousand threads with the "kingdom of Caesar" and the catastrophic changes within it cannot but have an impact upon its life. The Revolution struck a blow to the old connection of Church and state and inwardly has led to a stirring within the whole churchly organism. The Church had become free, just like everything in Russia. So they say and so it seems from the side-lines. But it would be insulting to the dignity of the Church to think, that it could receive its freedom outwardly from the Revolution, from the changes in the world outside Christianity. The Church can draw forth its freedom only from within its own depths, from Christ its Head, and it itself is the wellspring of freedom for people, living in the slavery of passions and sins. How are we to reconcile this contradiction?

When they say, that after the Revolution the Church was set free from its long slavery to the state, then this inwardly and religiously can be understood only thus, that the temptation of idolatry afront Caesar, to which churchly people and the Russian Church were subjected on its human side, has vanished, it fell away and has given churchly people a moment of free choice of an utmost religious path. From a deeper point of view the old connection of the church with a state, enslaving it and degrading it, was a partial separation from the Universal Church of Christ, which the gates of hell will not prevail against. But for church people, who now face the tasks of a restructuring of the entire churchly order of things, new temptations are possible, there can arise the fashioning of new idols and a new slavery. The autocratic imperial power, having so deformed our church life, has fallen, the Church has been liberated from this idol. But the "kingdom of Caesar" continues to live in new forms. An idol can be created whether from democracy, or from socialism, or from the people itself, and church life can fall into slavery to these new idols. The free Church has to be free not only from the old state, from the autocratic kingdom, but also from the new state, the kingdom of democracy. And in this transitional time, in which we live, the Russian Church has been faced with great trials. The Eastern Orthodox Church is entering into a boundless freedom. And this boundless freedom is a tremendous testing of the spiritual powers of churchly people, of churchly humankind. In this human freedom there can begin divisions in place of church unity, there can be the enslavement to a new idol, as occurred within Protestantism. For the Russian Church's impetus in our troubled and changeable days it is most important to realise, that the Free Church has nothing in common with Protestantism, and this Russian religious renaissance cannot be some sort of a movement towards a Lutheran Reformation. The inevitable restructuring of the Church upon democratic principles ought not to include within itself anything of the "Protestant", and it should be in accord with the precepts and traditions of the OEcumenical, the Universal Church. In the externals, with the historical structure of the Church there is no other sort of principle besides the elective principle, besides democratism and to conceive it otherwise is impossible, unless one acknowledge papism and if the holy tsardom had not fallen. But inwardly in the Church there ought to be preserved an eternal hierarchism. The free Church -- is hierarchical. If it became democratic, then it would fall under the grip of human arbitrariness, it would lose its connection of succession from Christ and the Apostles.

II.

The infamous downfall of the imperial power in Russia cannot be a matter of indifference for eastern Orthodoxy. The Russian Revolution should have a greater significance for the Orthodox Church, than all the Western revolutions had for the Catholic Church. The Catholic Church is not broken up into autocephalous national churches, it always was little dependent upon the state and the nation, it possesses its own independent hierarchical structure, headed by the pope. No sorts of any revolutions within states or nations alter essentially anything within the structure of the Catholic Church, its organisation remains worldwide. This is not so in the Eastern Orthodox Church. The Eastern Orthodox Church, although it defines itself as the Church Universal, in fact was at first primarily the Byzantine Church, and then the Russian Church. The Eastern Orthodox Church does not possess an outward universal unity nor an outward universal organisation, it does not possess a centre, which could be connected with any sort of state or national rule. The Orthodox Church from the time of Constantine was always in fact a matter of nation and state. The autocephaly, the national self-independence of the Church is the source of its slavery, and not its freedom, since the autocephalous national church inevitably falls into dependence upon the state power, and inevitably subjects itself to the national element. The autocephaly of the Russian Church meant its being headed by the tsar. At first in Byzantium, and then in Russia the nationalising of the Orthodox Church was interwoven and held in place by the imperial power, which was accounted as sacred. The Byzantine emperor was of a sacred rank within the Church, and his role was exclusive. This sacred significance of the imperial power passed over from Byzantium to Russia, it was transmitted on to the Russian tsars and emperors. Even if they did not speak of it as such, it was a tendency towards Caesaropapism, i.e. the acknowledging of the tsar as the head of the Church, both in the Byzantine and in the Russian Church. The Byzantine imperium and the Russian tsardom regarded themselves as sacred rulers and the Church gave blessing to this self-awareness of the ruler. Neither the power of the Byzantine emperor, nor the power of the Russian emperor was merely a mundane worldly state power, this was a spiritual power, a theocratic power. The sacred Byzantine imperium long ago disintegrated and fell. The theocratic hopes, connected with the imperial power, passed over to the Russian tsardom. Moscow was acknowledged as the Third Rome. And now there has fallen the sacred Russian tsardom, the last holy kingdom in the world.

There has burst forth a great historical chain of events, striking a blow to the matter of state and Church. The Eastern Orthodox Church imperceptibly has survived a catastrophe: it has lost a limb, which over all the expanse of its history it regarded as sacred and holding in place the outward organic unity of the Church. The sacred imperial power created the outward appearance of the unity of the Orthodox Church, by force it held down and kept all parts of the Church in co-subordination. The Eastern Orthodox Church itself has failed to notice, how it has entered into a domain of boundless freedom, unknown by the Western Catholic Church, nor existing either within Protestantism. There has ended the worldwide historical period of life of the Eastern Church, which began with Constantine. Outwardly the Church has returned to the condition, which existed prior to Constantine. Inwardly, however, churchly mankind on the one hand has become enriched, which on the other hand overwhelmed by the enormous and difficult experience of all its history, and by the demands of modern mankind. There has fallen off the rotting limb, through which infection had come to all the whole churchly organism. And in the organism of the Eastern Church what happened, was but that nothing replaced it. The Church became free, but this freedom was exclusively formal, it was the freedom of a choice of path, a negative freedom. The free Church in the positive sense of the word, in the religious sense, is a spiritual power, it is a religious capacity, of knowing its own direction.

The free Church is the One, Universal Church of Christ, having apostolic succession from Christ its Head, drawing forth all its revelations from its own depths in contrast to all the fickle elements of "this world" and the temptations of "the prince of this world". This Church dwells eternally and the gates of hell cannot prevail, but the outward image of the free Church is twofold or threefold, it is enveloped by the trappings of this world and distorted by the dominion of the failings and sins of the masses of mankind. All the divisions within the Universal Church, all the disputes, all the temptations and distortions come from the human element, without the free activity of which there could not be the Church, as Divine-human an organism. And now the human element within the Church is summoned to an exclusively spiritual direction, towards a concentration of churchly will-power. The catastrophe within the Universal Church must be lived through, it signifies an upsurging of human energy and human activity within the Church.

III.

It is necessary to make a distinction between churchly freedom and religious freedom. Churchly freedom is the freedom of the Church itself, its independence from the state. In this sense, the greatest churchly freedom is within the Catholic Church, which moreso is independent, than the Orthodox Church, or than the Protestant Church, which even cannot be termed a church in the strict sense of the word. Churchly freedom is an utmost churchly worthiness, of which we have too little, a pride not personal, the human is always sinfully so, but rather the churchly pridefulness of the sanctities of the Church, upon which nothing in the world ought to infringe. Churchly freedom is a strengthening of the Church, a defending of it from the surging elements of the world, preventing the disintegration of the Church. Religious freedom however, religious freedom of conscience, is altogether a different principle. Churchly freedom already presupposes a definite and strong faith and is concerned over its fate in the world. Religious freedom is a freedom of the choice of this or some other faith, of this or some other religious path. It is oriented towards the human person and guards not the faith itself, but rather the freedom of faith, the freedom of a love for a confession.

Nicholas Berdyaev

Coercion in matters of faith is impossible. To come to any faith is possible only by the path of freedom. And this most mustneeds be said for the Christian faith, since Christianity itself is a religion of freedom. To confess Christ is possible only by freely having accepted and having come to love Him. Where there is the Spirit of Christ, there also is freedom. Knowing the Truth of Christ, is to be made free. The Spirit of Christ breathes, whithersoever it will. The freedom of conscience for the Christian is not exclusively formal a principle, as it might appear to non-religious people, it is an inner principle of Christianity itself, as a religion of freedom, the religion of the free filiation-sonship of man to God. The Church is preeminently a kingdom of freedom, a kingdom of grace, in distinction to the state, -- a being the kingdom of necessity and force. In the Church everything ought to be accepted freely, everything ought to be the object of love. Compulsion and coercion in matters religious, in matters churchly, signifies but a false and distorted relationship between the Church and the state, between "God" and "Caesar", it always transpires within a sphere civil, and not churchly, it always makes use of the sword of Caesar, since the Church itself possesses no weapons for compulsion and force. Both the Church Catholic and the Church Orthodox, when they resort to coercion and force in matters of faith, always make use of the sword of Caesar, and they debase themself to the kingdom of necessity. Wherefore herein it can be said, that the loss of religious freedom and the coercion over the religious conscience always has led and has to lead to the loss of churchly freedom, to the enslavement of the Church to the state, by the means of the implements it makes use of. The Free Church does not possess the wherewithal to violate religious freedom, it lacks the tools for this. Its sword, by which it cleaves the world, is a sword that is spiritual, and not material. The greatest freedom in the Church was that prior to Constantine, not when it was the one chasing and persecuting, but when they chased and persecuted it. Within Christianity then the churchly freedom and the religious freedom coincided. After the uniting of the Church and the state, the Church lost its freedom when it infringed upon religious freedom, when "God" and "Caesar" became confused.

The Gospel words of Christ to "render unto Caesar the things that are Caesar's, and unto God the things that are God's", is also an eternal Christian resolution of the question concerning the relationship of the Church and the state, a riddle which the Christian world has to resolve. With these words Christ divided the two kingdoms, He affirmed churchly freedom and religious freedom, and religiously He justified the existence of the state, as an independent and necessary principle in this world. The wisdom of these brief words is extraordinary and it resolves the enigma spanning across the whole of Christian history. It was only Christianity that first placed limits to the all-powerful might of the state, such as existed in the ancient world. The Christian revelation also promulgated religious freedom, the freedom of the boundless human spirit, incommensurable with any state, or any kingdom of this world. Paganism was powerless to guard the freedom of the human spirit against the unknown boundaries of infringements by the state, the kingdom of Caesar. The great wise men of the ancient world could not accomplish this liberation of the human spirit. The apotheosis of Caesar, the cult of Caesar also takes to the limit the unbounded power of the state, the religion of the kingdom of this world. The "things of God" were ultimately bestown "unto Caesar". And here then, when the world was in worship of Caesar as God, Christianity came into the world with the good news about God, crucified upon the Cross for the sins of the world, God the Redeemer. Man was filiated in sonship to God and within man was revealed a boundless freedom, an infinite spirit, surpassing all the kingdoms of the world. Christianity revealed the infinite worth of the human soul, the eternity enclosed within it, and its independence from the elements of this world. Man, redeemed by the Blood of Christ, is liberated from the dominion of the lower nature, he ceases to be a slave, he spiritually stands on his own feet. When the first Christians refused to worship Caesar and underwent tortures, they eternally affirmed within the world a religious freedom, the freedom of the human spirit, and they set in place the foundations of the free Church. The Christian Church gave blessing to the state power, acknowledged its positive mission in the world, but it did not permit of its apotheosis, of an absolute obedience to it, and from its side it refused infringement upon the boundless life of the human spirit. The things of God ought entirely to be bestown to God. This truth was sealed by the blood of the martyrs. For every state there is a moral boundary regarding the Church and the transgressing of this boundary is already a demand for bestowing to Caesar the things of God, i.e. it is a betrayal of Christ and of that commanded by Him. Only Christianity promulgated freedom of conscience. Thomas Aquinas indeed promulgated the religious right of rising up against the state power and he went so far, that he even justified regicide, if that ruler transgressed the religiously allowable limits. This limiting of the powers of the state was possible only upon the basis of the Christian consciousness. The denial of freedom of conscience, of the freedom of the human spirit, has always led to the enslavement of the Church by the state, both in the West and in the East. The Christian world has not always remained faithful to the Christian revelation about freedom, it was exposed to temptations and fell.

IV.

The Free Church signifies likewise the affirmation also of freedom within the state, the guarding of the boundless rights of the human soul from the infringements both of state and of society. Freedom of conscience is a right, received not from citizenship in society, nor from the state, nor from democracy, but rather from the spiritual life, from Christ Himself. The fact that democracy of itself does not guarantee freedom of conscience, is something which can be seen from that apostle of democracy, J. J. Rousseau, who denied freedom of conscience, he regarded as obligatory for each citizen his own pitiful and contrived religion, and he did not recognise any sort of inalienable rights for the human person. The sovereign nation and democracy as it were at their pleasure can deprive man of any right, since here the source of every right of man lies not within man, not within his boundless spirit, but in the external, in the will of the people, in the majority of voices. But the majority of voices can at its pleasure take away from man that which it at its pleasure prescribes him. This is a return to the ancient, the pagan power of the state over the human soul. Freedom of conscience was also denied by that apostle of socialism, K. Marx, and by the social-democracy subsequent to him. In the social-democratic teaching there does not exist a boundless nature of the human soul and its inalienable rights. Man is rendered entirely a child of the material societal means, he receives everything from it, he is totally dependent upon it, and he possesses nothing unique to himself. Socialism itself per se guarantees the rights of the freedom of conscience just as little, as does democracy. In the social-democratic programme there is a paragraph, which proclaims, that religion is a private matter. But this is only a formal method of disposing of religion. The social-democratic freedom of a religious conscience does not presuppose the existence of the religious conscience itself, as a principle unique to the human spirit. As regards its own teachings of belief, Marxist socialism is deeply hostile to every religion and is hostile most of all to the Christian Church. To be a genuine Christian within the social-democrats is an impossibility, though the Christian can acknowledge the partial truth of socialism.

The Church has to be free from the elements of this world. And the Church then can be the source of freedom for every human soul, living within society and the state. The Church defends the human soul from the dominion of the elements of this world, from the pretentions of "the kingdom of Caesar" for transgressing every boundary, even though such should assume the form of democracy and socialism. But the Church ruling within the state and through the state is a Church dependent, it loses its freedom and cannot be a source of freedom, nor safeguard freedom. A Church resorting thus to rule cannot be the free Church, its spiritual power is always undermined and diminished. The free Church cannot be an official, ruling Church. We know this only too well regarding the fate of the Russian Orthodox Church. The Western papocaesarism and the Eastern caesaropapism -- are two temptations, enslaving the Church to the elements of this world, to the kingdom of Caesar. In the West the Church was more free in its original foundations, but it transformed itself into a state and utilised the weapons of a state. In the East the Church was subordinated to the state in its primal foundations and likewise was utilised by the state. Now in the East, in Russia, the Church is entering into a new world period, wherein its structure has to be rendered democratic. And the whole purpose of this -- is so that this new democratic structure of the Church does not become a new form of its dependence upon the kingdom of Caesar. Yet always it is proper to remember, that the Church is a kingdom qualitative and not quantitative, within its structure can be an elective principle, but nothing in its spiritual life is decided by majority voice-vote. The hierarchism of the Church is a guarantee of its freedom. Democratism however, passing over into the inner life of the Church, can become a source of slavery, since it places the spiritual values into dependence upon a majority of voices. And insofar as within the Church there has to be manifest human activity and human creativity, it has to be manifest as humanly qualitative, and not quantitative.

V.

It would be very erroneous to think, that the Reformation created the Free Church, that within Lutheranism the Church became more free, than it was in Catholicism. Within the Lutheran Reformation there was a negative truth, and no little there was a just criticism and a just indignation against the moral decline of the Catholic world, against the human sins of papism. But the Lutheran Reformation was a secularisation of the Church, remaking it into a state-Church and subordinating it to the elements of this world. Freedom of conscience was acknowledged within Protestantism only as something relatively so, the faith-toleration of Luther was limited. But most importantly, the promulgation of religious freedom was surrendered away into the domain of being developed by the elements of this world, it lost its own unshakable churchly foundation. If one might speak, with pushing the point about the Protestant Church or Protestant Churches, then it is that they surrendered over into the hands of the princes and became subject to the territorial principle. Ultimately, there was extinguished the idea of the Free Universal Church. Luther did not liberate the church from the state, but rather the state from the church. The church was abased also within Protestantism in the triumph of the state-church. The human defects of Catholicism ought not to prevent us seeing, that at its core there was a greater religious truth, than in Protestantism. In Catholicism in the West, and not in Protestantism, there is preserved the eternal sanctity of the Church and the true churchly freedom. The Catholic world fell into the sin of pride and self-affirmation, considering itself the fullness of the Universal Church and denying the whole of Eastern Christianity. But Catholicism is an inalienable and great part of the Universal Church, inwardly one, and only on the outside, as regards human limitations, in ruin. At present, the consciousness of the Russian Church stands at the crossroads and is subject to the danger of swaying towards Protestantism in this or that form. Our Church has to be reformed and we await the religious rebirth of the Russian people. But in Russia a Protestant Reformation is impossible. This would be a betrayal of the Russian religious spirit and the Russian religious vocation.

Sects of the Protestant type have long since already existed in Russia and in the latter times they all tend towards the Baptists. The position of the official Church within the old order quite assisted in the spread of sectarianism and provided all the sects, including also the Baptists, the aura of being strugglers for religious freedom, the prestige of persecution. In the new, in the free Russia, this abnormal appearance should tend to cease. And then will be manifest all the limitedness and defect of sectarianism, for which always there was seen a portion of religious truth, its one only ray of light, while not allowing for all its fullness. The religious poverty of the Baptists and their profound opposition to the Russian national spirit has to be evidenced in an atmosphere of churchly and religious freedom. From the hands of the sectarians would be removed their chief weapon -- there would no longer be the coerciveness of the ruling official church, and the church hierarchy would no longer be officials of the state power. It mustneeds be remembered, that Protestantism in its fatal developement was a secularisation of religious life, and therefore also a loss of religious freedom through processes, transpiring in this world. Elements of Protestantism have long since already entered into the life of the Russian Church. The synodal churchly structure, established by the will of the autocrat Peter, was a triumph of state absolutism. This was a process completely analogous to that, which led in the West to the system of the state-church. The so-called Jozefism, i.e. the system of the Austrian emperor Jozef II, which subordinated the Catholic Church within the limits of his empire to the state, was the introduction of a Protestant spirit into Catholicism, a Protestant subordination of church to the territorial principle and the princely power. The lack of freedom of the Russian Church came about from the Protestant spirit of our civil realm since the time of Peter. The greatest churchly freedom has been within the Old Ritualism, the Old Believers. The whole synodal period of the Russian Church was already a secularisation, a making mundane of churchly administration. The princes of the church, appointed to the Holy Synod, were agents of the imperial power, and during the final period they were agents of Grigorii Rasputin. And the task of the free Church in the free Russia is the restoration of the spiritual character of churchly power. The forceful actions of the Uber-Prokurator in the new Provisional Government, directed at cleansing the composition of the Holy Synod, are justified, since the old staff of the Holy Synod was imposed upon the Church by the old order; it was not in a true sense churchly, and the revolutionary powers ought to undo and liquidate the old compulsory connections of church and state, so that the Church as already free might recreate its structures. The Uber-Prokuratorship, which is to be transformed into a Ministry of Confessions, ought not in future to play any sort of churchly role, but the first Uber-Prokuratorship after the Revolution has to display an exceptional power, just as ought also in everything to be manifest by the Provisional Government of the transitional epoch. This is but the liquidation of the sinful past. When the lived-through experience of the Revolution provides depth to our religious life, then it will become clear, that the Church cannot be fully free, if it remains nationally-isolated and cut off from universal Christianity.

VI.

The free Church and the free Russia ought with love to turn to the Western Catholic world and to seek with it an inner unification into the Universal Church. The division of the Christian East and the Christian West can be justified only as the expression of two types of Christian spiritual experience, which ought to be preserved within the Universal Church. The division of the Church itself and the taking of a separate part from the whole is but human a sin and human self-assertion. But the unification of the churches is impossible to expect, as resulting from the Unia or a confab of churchly rulers of East and West. This external path will lead to nothing, except political intrigues. And least of all can it be wished, that the Orthodox Church should reunify with the Catholic Church, by renouncing its own spiritual path and its own truth. Reunion can be expected only from an inward turning of the two Christian worlds each to the other with love. Such is one of the worldly tasks, which faces the Free Church in Russia. But the Russian Church has many inward tasks, left unresolved under the old order, under the old relationship of church and state. Such first of all is the task of reunion with the Old Ritualists, the Old Believers, the overcoming of the historical schism within the Russian Church. For the reuniting of the Old Ritualists with the Orthodox Church, which was termed official and which forever has ceased to be official, there can be no sort of religious impediments. The Old Ritualists are Orthodox people entirely and the schism transpired within "the kingdom of Caesar". The people's religious sensitivity was aroused over the bestowing of "the things of God" "unto Caesar". In the persecution of the Old Ritualists there was accumulated a tremendous religious energy and there was formed a powerful religious discipline. This energy ought now to go towards the renewal of the Russian Church. Under the current conditions the disdain for unity can be perceived, as the manifestation of a religious egoism. Much religious energy in Russia has been dissipated upon the sects, and much of it in turn was squandered in the struggle against the Church and against the fullness lodged within it. Sectarianism is always a rising up of the part against the whole, in it there will never become that universal Christian spirit, which only is what gives freedom. Within the sects there is no freedom in the spiritual sense of this word, their freedom is purely negative, and not positive. The sects are doomed to degenerate, in them always there prevails a rationalistic spirit and the religious energy, accumulated in the sects, falls away and loses itself in worldly elements, torn off from the religious churchly centre. In the sects there is an endless and ugly splintering. The sectarians await not the free Church, but rather freedom from the Church. The question about the sects -- is an agonising question of Russian churchly life. But its resolution can be very much mitigated by the turnabout happening. Churchly freedom and religious freedom ought to lessen the quantity of sects, and they would remove a whole series of reasons for falling into the sects. People having accepted Christ in their hearts would return to the Church and would remain in it. Into the sects, however, would go and would stubbornly remain in them only those, who in their spiritual depths have broken off from the Universal Church and in something have betrayed Christ. The free Church of Christ in a free Russia would, actually, be in number less a quantity of members, than with the official church, in which formally, according to passport, all Russians have belonged. Many would fall away from the Church. But the lessened quantity would make up for it with an increase in quality. In the Church would remain only its worthy and faithful sons. The true Church of Christ maintains itself upon the qualitative, and not upon the quantitative. And in the interim would be at least some few righteous, at least some few faithful to Christ, and the Church will exist upon the earth. The freedom of falling away does not terrify the free Church. But the boundless religious freedom, opening forth before the Russian people, is a testing of the strength of its spirit.

VII.

Great danger threatens from a mixing up of religion with politics. The triumph of democracy and socialism can facilitate acceptance of the renewal and growth of Christianity. The Christian Church cannot be against true freedom, equality and brotherhood. Moreover, true freedom, true equality and true brotherhood are possible only within the Church. In the democratic socialistic "kingdom of Caesar" everything is based upon necessity and compulsion, and people can become attracted to one another through common interests, but never are they rendered brothers. Socialism knows of "tovarisch-comrade", but it does not know of "brother". The social class struggle can be acknowledged as a bitter necessity, but never can it be acknowledged by Christian truth and blessing. Christianity sees an utmost truth in this, that one gives off one's riches to neighbour, but sees it not in this, that one takes away what is of the neighbour. Christianity does not believe, that the kingdom of God can be attained by an outward path and material means, nor that it be possible or desirable to want compulsory virtue and compulsory social brotherhood. The kingdom of God comes unnoticed and externally its triumph is impossible within the bounds of this sinful world. Christianity demands a spiritual sobriety in the matters of this world and does not allow for boundless social fantasising. All the chiliast religious movements, awaiting the quick onset of a sensual thousand-year reign of Christ on earth, always were heretical and hostile to the Church. They all rest upon this mistake, which also is Montanism, the denial of mutual responsibility and a responsibleness for the evil of the world, on a denial of the working and burden of history, on a mixing up of the absolute and the relative. And at present in Russia there can arise similar kinds of chiliast movements, in which everything gets jumbled, and revolutionary socialism gets accepted as the onset of a thousand-year reign. Principles, anti-Christian in spirit, can be mistaken for Christian ones, they can tempt with equality, imperceptibly demolish the churchly hierarchism and destroy every quality, everything, that rises up. The Church of Christ can be democratic as regards its outward structure, but inwardly it is aristocratic and hierarchic, just like everything in the Divine order of the cosmos is hierarchic and aristocratic. This has to be clearly recognised within our churchly stirrings, so that the Church should not fall into a new slavery, so that it not be humbled before a new "kingdom of Caesar". It would be a fatal error to mistake the political and social energy as being a religious and churchly energy. The most radical political and social turnabout of itself is insignificant in the face of eternity, it changes nothing in the life of the Church. The churchly impetus is still forward, it has to have its own inner wellspring.

 The new democratic state will not be a Christian state, just as the old autocratic state was not. The new state power ought to receive its blessing from the Church, just like any power, insofar as it fulfills its purpose. The authorities bear not the sword in vain. The state has a mystical basis, although this does not at all mean, that the state is theocratic. Even the secularised state in democratic republics preserves its mystical, trans-rational basis. The free Church cannot from the outside make the new Russian state, as yet unknown and enigmatic in its structure, to be Christian and Orthodox. In the old order the Christian Orthodox character of the state degenerated into an hideous lie, into ugly hypocrisy and coercion. In the new order there ought first of all to be honesty and truthfulness. Inevitably the state will be secularised. Nor does it even exclude the possibility, that the Church will be persecuted. But the Free Church can in the measure of its spiritual power from within influence the life of the state and spiritually direct it upon the path of truth. Insofar as the Russian people remains a Christian people, its Christianity has to be expressed in its state, it has to influence it from within, to define not the body of the state, but rather its soul. The Free Church remains only but an inward spiritual power in the state and its activity will be dependent upon the religious energy of the people itself, on its fidelity to Christ and His Church. The Free Church in the free Russia has to be more active, than was the official Church in the old order.

VIII.

In the question concerning the relationship of church and state, for every Christian more important and more precious is the freedom of the Church, than the freedom of the state. Unbelieving people, hostile to church, want a separation of church from state, in order to free the state from every influence of church, so as ultimately to secularise it. The separation of church and state in France was conducted by the militant atheistic ministry of Emile Combes and assumed the form of a persecution against the church. The French form of the separation of church from state cannot be desired for Russia and in any case such a form of separation the Church itself would be unable to accept. For the Church better to be persecuted, than itself to persecute, and persecution could even lead to a strengthening of religious energy. Persecution of the Catholic Church by the anti-Christian forces of the French Republic led to a renewal of Catholicism. But the Church itself cannot desire, that they should persecute it, and therefore it cannot separate itself from the state in the French method, which is singularly radical. The division of church and state is always conditional and relative a matter, it cannot be absolute within the external plane of life. The Church by a thousand threads is connected with the kingdom of Caesar. Yet there has to be a radical religious division of the two kingdoms -- of God and of Caesar. This means also, that the Church has to be free and that "the things of God" ought never to be bestown "unto Caesar". But in the outward historical plane the state penetrates all the pores of life, even the Church represents for the state a component part. And herein arises the question, whether the Church be an institution publicly-legal or partially-legal? The state of a Christian people comprising it overwhelmingly cannot acknowledge the Church as a partial-legality institution, equating it with some sort of partial society. If also there ought not to be an official and ruling church, then indeed the Orthodox Church cannot occupy an exclusive position in Russia, for the Russian people. This is determined not by the state privileges of the Orthodox Church, but by its churchly and religious prerogatives, its connection with the heart of the Russian people, with the spirit of Russian history, with the vocation of the Russian people within the world. The Church of Christ ought to become a prevailing spirit and inward power of the Russian state. We ought to desire, that the free Russian state in form should be secular, while in spirit Christian, so that within it the cruel beastly principle not win out, though it be with the most progressive and democratic trappings.

The Russian people is experiencing a spiritual and religious crisis. The soul of the people goes about its path in agitation. This crisis began already long ago. Long ago the Christian faith was jostled and shaken. This found expression also in the enslavement of church to state, in its creation of the idolatry of "Caesar", in a falling-away from the Church, in sectarianism, in the growth of unbelief, in the triumph of materialism in life. In the people at present the Revolution has cast down the old idols, but there has begun the creation of new idols, the idols of "Revolution", "Democracy", "Socialism", "Internationalism", and many others. The Living God, Christ, has long ago already become forgotten, and His Name is not to be heard in these storms and catastrophes, which the Russian people experiences. To the new Russia there can be put this selfsame question, which Vl. Solov'ev put to the old Russia: "What sort of East desirest thou to be, the East of Xerxes or of Christ?" The "East of Xerxes" can be not only a beastly cruel autocracy, it can be also a beastly cruel democracy. In democracy can be revealed the human image, reflecting the image of God, but there can be revealed also the image of beastly cruelty. And the Russian people is at the crossroads. In the Revolution there has been burnt away the old lie, the old hypocrisy, the fetters have fallen away, which held tight the Church to the decaying power of the state. But if the religious will of the people takes to the false path, then there will reign a new lie, a new hypocrisy, and new fetters will be set upon the Free Church of Christ. In such a time it is necessary, that the voice of the Free Church ring out, that it ring out not only concerning the question of the external arrangement of the Church, but also concerning the more profound, the inward questions of religious creativity, connected with the fate of man and mankind. Within the Church there ought to blaze the fire of eternal truth, which the surging of the elements of the world cannot extinguish.

IX.

All the hopes for the renewal of the Russian Church have been set upon convening of a Sobor-Council. Since the year 1905 the Russian Orthodox world has been living with the hope, that the local Church Council would resolve all the burning questions of Russian ecclesial order and renew the ailing body of our Church. Under the old order there were made insincere preparatory steps towards the Sobor, but its convening seemed impossible. The old powers were afraid of a Sobor. The conciliar principle in the Church was smothered. After the fetters were removed from the Church, the convening of the Council was rendered a possibility, and it is being convened, without sufficient preparation within the churchly currents and churchly organisation from below. We need the Sobor. Without it the Free Church cannot restructure itself on new principles. But one should not overestimate the significance of the Council and put too great an hope upon it, since then one will not be disappointed. It is impossible to expect from the Russian local Sobor, to be convened in the near future, a religious creativity, and resolution of the religious headaches of modern mankind. It is unlikely that a prophetic spirit should breathe within it. The Sobor will be the same way as the churchly people are. The local Church Sobor of itself cannot create that creative religious energy, if such exist not within the churchly people elected to the Sobor. If the religious energy in the people be weak, then it will not be great either at the Sobor. The Sobor will, in all likelihood, be concerned with what can be called "the churchly prosaic", with questions of the relationship of church and state, and of churchly manner of life. The most important thing, that the Sobor could do, would be to conclusively liquidate the old relationships of church and state and reconstruct churchly life upon elective and democratic principles. There are no special grounds to hope, that at this Sobor the voice of the Free Church of Christ would authoritatively and mightily resound concerning the catastrophes being experienced by Russia and the world. There are grounds to be apprehensive, that as regards churchly creativity they might accept a denial of the old order and the establishing of a new democratic order. But in this there would still be no sort of churchly creativity. And herein there might be a tendency towards Protestantism. Within Protestantism was no religious creativity, no sort of new revelations. Religious creativity does not negate the old revelation and tradition, but rather gives a new revelation and initiates a new tradition. The Russian Revolution, as in every revolution, is not the revelation of new life, of a new spirit, it is rather but the consequences of the old sins, the crisis of the old sickness, God's chastisement for allowing in the past an intolerable lie. A creative religious stirring lies still for the future, after the experience of the Revolution will have been lived out in the soul of the people.

Freedom of conscience cannot be for the churchly Christian consciousness merely a formal principle, it cannot be rendered into a religious indifference. The Christian freedom of conscience presupposes the existence of a religious conscience and a positive religious energy, which is something non-binding for a negative freedom of conscience, such as is proclaimed by unbelievers, unconcerned and indifferent to religion. Christian freedom of conscience possesses and has its source in Christ, the Deliverer, the Bestower of all freedom. Freedom having been received through Christ, this freedom cannot be deprived from a single human soul, it has to be granted to all. We desire churchly freedom and religious freedom, but we wish for it from within our faith, for the triumph of the working of Christ in the world. But this nowise means, that for the Christian it can be a matter of indifference, as other people might confess their faith, in that they are prepared to accept "religion as a private matter", as non-religious liberals and socialists admit for this. For non-religious liberals and socialists religious freedom is a negative freedom from religion. For Christians, however, religious freedom is the positive source of their religion. Religious freedom is the path to the triumph of the working of Christ in the world. Churchly freedom guarantees better the spiritual triumph of the Church in the world, than does the chaining of the Church to the state and the use of the weapons of the state in matters of the Church. Religion however is not a private matter, as an indifferent liberalism hostile to religion would tend to affirm, religion is an universal matter, it makes pretense to be the fullness of everything. Religion as the fullness of all, of being everything in all, is done not by way of external theocratic pretensions, not by way of a compulsory Christian state, but by its own inner spiritual power, directing the world. A chiliastic faith in the triumph of the thousand-year reign of Christ in this sinful world, in a sensual thousand-year reign of Christ upon the earth cannot be acknowledged as a churchly faith, and it cannot be spiritually justified. Such a chiliastic hope always was a slippery slope within religious experience, the mixing-up of various planes, the forgetting of apocalyptic prophecies about the growth within the world of the power of an anti-Christian spirit and of the Anti-Christ. The manifestation of this spirit is too apparent even now already. And all the positive Christian powers ought to unite for counteracting the rising surge of the anti-Christian powers. The state, society and culture are that neutral medium, which is subject to the influence of these contrary spiritual principles, in which transpires the spiritual struggle. It is impossible to render the state and culture externally and forcibly Christian, they ought to remain principles formally free, revealing their own particular powers. But a diverse spirit can inspire the state and culture. There stands ahead an inevitable and great religious struggle of two spirits, of two world principles. And in this worldwide struggle the voice of the Free Church of Christ, One an Universal, ought to resound from within, from the depths, as the voice of spiritual life, free from enslavement to the elements of the world, rising above everything political, above every temporal power, free from all temptations, such as were repudiated by Christ in the wilderness, but through which mankind passes. The churchly stirrings have to become animated by a new spirit, by a new life, and in it ought to be heard new words. Fidelity to the eternal in the old ought not to hinder the creative stirrings in the Church. The Free Church will be faced with new tasks, with new themes, with new torments of the human spirit. But the deciding of these tasks and the relieving of these torments presupposes a spiritual surge, of which as yet there is not. The Free Church has to itself manifest the greatest spiritual energy, wherein nothing in its life can be imputed to the state and its organs.

Class and Man

(1918 - #290)[1]

I.

The struggle of classes fills the whole history of mankind. It is not a discovery of the XIX and XX Centuries, although in these centuries it assumed new acute forms. This struggle occurred way back in the ancient world and there already it had quite varied appearances. Much that is instructive can be gleaned from the book of [Robert von] Pohlmann [1852-1914], "History of Ancient Communism and Socialism". Certain pages bring to mind the chronology of our own days. The social uprising of the masses always and everywhere was alike as regards its psychological atmosphere. Too much gets repeated in social life, and it is difficult to imagine new combinations and settings. There was many a class communistic movement in the past, and they often assumed a religious hue. Suchlike communistic movements were especially characteristic of the era of the Reformation. The elemental communism of the lower classes is one of the oldest principles, periodically arising and making an attempt to topple the individualistic and hierarchical principles. Communism -- is as old as the world, it was there at the cradle of human civilisation. Many a time within history have arisen the lower peoples, and there was the attempt to do away with all the hierarchical and qualitative principles within society and to establish a mechanical equality and mixing. This disruptive leveling and simplification of society always was non-correlative with the progressive historical tasks, with the cultural level. Periodically within history have occurred deluges of chaotic darkness which have striven to topple the societal cosmos and its laws of developement. Such a kind of movement over and over continually could become quite reactionary and throw off a people backwards. The socialist

---

[1] KLASS I CHELOVEK. Article originally published in the weekly Journal "Narodopravstvo", January 1918, № 20, p. 2-4.

Nicholas Berdyaev

Lassal did not regard as progressive the peasant wars of the Reformation era, he regarded them as reactionary, i.e. contrary to the basic historical tasks of that time. And in elements of the Russian Revolution are active likewise the same old, reactionary forces, in it is stirred up the ancient chaos, lying beneathe the thin layers of Russian civilisation.

The class struggle, the original sin of human societies, tended to deepen and change during the XIX Century. In this progressive century human society became very materialised, it lost its spiritual centre, and the beastly greedy man attained an extreme intensity and expression. The moral character of the bourgeois-capitalistic century makes the struggle of classes for their interests all the more brazen, than in former centuries. And this is connected not with the fact of industrial developement, which is a good per se, but with the spiritual condition of European society. The spiritual poison in this society went from the top down, from the dominating classes to the oppressed classes. The materialistic socialism of Marx and others, having concentrated in itself all the poison of the bourgeois godlessness, failed to restrain itself amidst a more acute perception of the fact of class struggle, -- it sanctified this fact and ultimately subjected man to the class. The means of struggle ultimately eclipsed the higher aims of life. Materialistic socialism, enslaved by the economic aspect of capitalistic societies, denies both man and human nature in common, it acknowledges only the class-man, only class collectives. There is begotten an altogether peculiar sense of life, it is only the masses that feel and they altogether cease to sense the individual man. Class represents quantity. Man however represents quality. The class struggle, elevated into an "idea", has obscured the qualitative image of man. In our harsh era, with all the veils torn away, the naively amusing old mode of idealism is already an impossibility, impossible too is a turning away from the ugly fact of class struggles, from the perceiving of class antagonisms and class solidifications, distorting the nature of man. Class antagonisms and class distortions play an enormous though unappreciated role in social life. But upon this fact of nature ought not to depend our moral judgements and our reflections concerning the spiritual image of man. Human nature can be distorted by the class position of a man, the outward aspects of a man can become determined by class greed and class limitation. But the spiritual core of a man, the individual human image never is determined by class, is not dependent upon the social medium. And anyone, who denies this, winds up denying man, and commits a spiritual homicide. It is godless and immoral, in place of man with his good and bad traits, to see only some collective substance of bourgeois or proletariat. Such an idea of class kills the idea of man. This murder theoretically is committed in Marxism. Within elements of the Russian Revolution it gets to be committed practically and for real in dimensions yet unseen within history. The "bourgeois" man and the "socialistic" man cease to be people for each other, brothers by the One Father of the human race. Within this revolutionary element there cannot be a true liberation of man, since man is negated within his primal basis. The liberation of class as it were constrains and enslaves man.

II.

From such time as the world became Christian and accepted baptism, within its religious consciousness it acknowledged, that people -- are brothers, that we have One Heavenly Father. In the Christian world the master and the slave as regards their social trappings cannot look upon each other as wolves, in their sin perhaps they can, but they cannot in their faith. In their moments of clarity, in their spiritual depths they have admitted each other as brothers in Christ. The Christian world has remained a sinful world. It fell, it betrayed its God, it did evil, in it people hated one another, and in place of the law of love they fulfilled a law of hatred. But the sin of hatred, of malice and violence was recognised by all Christians as sin, and not as a virtue, not as a way to an higher life. The faith in man, as the image and likeness of God, has remained a belief of the Christian world. Man may have been bad, but his faith was good, and good was the spiritual foundation itself, lodged within Christ and His Church. Yet within the Christian mankind there occurred a grievous crisis. The soul of peoples and the soul of nations sickened. Faith became impaired, and there ceased to be a belief in man as in the image and likeness of God, since there had ceased to be a true belief in God. The very spiritual foundations of life became altered. Socialism was not to blame for this spiritual downfall, it occurred earlier. Socialism but slavishly adopted this unbelief in man and in God, it merely takes it to the limit and gives it a common expression. The unbelief in man led to the apotheosis of man. The struggle of classes ceased to be a socio-economic fact, it became a spiritual fact, it spread to all the junctures of human nature and human life. There did not remain a single corner of the human soul, within human experiences and human creativity, not intruded upon by the struggle of classes with their interminable pretensions. The theories of economic materialism anticipated and corresponded to the new human actuality -- economism, flooding across all the scope of human life. And upon this basis was lost within human society a singular law of the good. The "bourgeois" good and the "socialistic" good want to have nothing in common between them, and over them stands nothing higher, of a single good. And therefore there is no longer a direct relationship of man to man, there is only the relationship of class to class. Revolutionary socialism, as transpiring at present in Russia, ultimately kills the possibility of the brotherhood of people on principle, in its new faith, in its very idea. And as regards this new faith, there is no longer man, there is only the bearer and declarer of an impersonal class substance.

Not only is it that the "proletariat" and the "bourgeoise" are not brothers to each other, being rather instead wolves, but also the proletarian is not a brother with his fellow proletarian, being rather instead "comrades", comrades in interests, in woe, in togetherness of material desires. Within the socialistic faith, comrade has replaced the brother of the Christian faith. Brothers were united one to another, as children of the One God, through love, through a common spirit. Comrades are united one to another through a commonness of interests, through hatred for the "bourgeoise", through a like material basis to life. Comrades in their comradeship have a respect for class, but not for man. Such a comradeship kills at the root the brotherhood of people, not only the higher unity of Christian mankind, but even the modicum of unity of civilised mankind. The French Revolution made bad use of the slogan, "Freedom, Equality and Brotherhood". But brotherhood it did not realise and did not attempt to realise. The socialistic revolution imagines, that it can and ought to realise brotherhood. But it realises only comradeship, bearing an unprecedented divisiveness into mankind. Equality is not brotherhood. Brotherhood is possible only in Christ, only for a Christian mankind, since this -- is a revelation of a religion of love. The idea of brotherhood is derived from Christianity and outside of it, it is impossible. The pathos of equality is the pathos of jealousy, and not of love. Movements, begotten by the passion of a leveling equality, breathe vengeance, they do not want to be sacrificial, but rather to take away. Brotherhood -- is something organic, equality is however something mechanical. In brotherhood is affirmed every human person, in the equality of "comrades" there however vanishes every person into the quantitative mass. In the brother triumphs man, in the comrade there triumphs class. The comrade becomes a substitute for man. Brother -- is a religious category. The citizen -- is a political category, a state-legal category. The comrade -- is a pseudo-religious category. The "citizen" and the "brother" have justification. But through the idea of the comrade, class kills man. Man to man is not a "comrade", man to man is a citizen or brother, -- a citizen in the state, in worldly society, and a brother -- in church, in the society religious. Citizenship is connected with law; brotherhood is connected with love. The comrade denies law and denies love, he admits only common or contrary interests. In this conjunction or disunion of interests, man perishes. Man needs either a citizenly relationship to himself, laws acknowledging him, or a brotherly relationship to him, a relationship of free love.

III.

The Russian people has to go through the school of citizenship. In this school has to be worked out a respect for man and his rights, there has to be perceived the dignity of man, as a being, living within society and the state. Every man and every people has to go through this stage, it is impossible to overleap it. When slaves in revolt declare, that the citizen condition for them is unnecessary and not to their liking, that they at once can pass directly over to an higher condition, then usually they fall into a beastly condition. The school of brotherhood works out the love of man for man, the consciousness of a spiritual commonness. This -- is a religious plane, which ought not to be confused with the political plane. It would be unseemly and dishonest to transfer a miracle of religious life over to the life political and social, bestowing the relative with an absolute character. A compulsory brotherhood is impossible. Brotherhood -- is the fruition of a free love. Brotherly love -- is a blossoming of spiritual life. With the citizen however everything can be obligatory. Everyone can demand a respect for his rights, the acknowledging in him of man, even if there is no love. The socialistic comradeship is in its idea a forced virtue, a coercion to association, greater than that, which a man voluntarily would wish. "Comrade" is an impermissible muddling of "citizen" and "brother", the mixing together of in society of state and church, the substituting of one plane by another, not that and not this. And these past months the word "comrade" in Russia has assumed a laughable and almost shameful significance. With it is connected for us the destruction of citizenship and an ultimate denial of a brotherhood of love. The class in the guise of the "comrade" has risen up not only against class, but class has risen up against man. In the raging of class hatred they have forgotten about man. Man however is an authentic and enduring reality. It is man that inherits eternity, and not class. Every class is a temporal and transitory phenomenon, it once was not and again will not be. Man is what is concrete. Class however is an abstraction. Within this abstraction are conjoined complex social interests and complex social psyches. But these abstract conjunctions can never form an authentic reality, a real value. The "proletariat" of the socialists is an abstract "idea", and not a reality. In reality there exist only varied groups of workers, often differing in their interests, and in their manner of soul. Yet they want to compel the workers themself to submit to the abstract idea of the proletariat. And to this bloodless abstraction, like to an idol, they offer human sacrifices.

Class is likewise lacking in that reality, which is had by the nation, and the state. Class -- is a very relative mode, it can occupy only a very subordinate position. Everything regarding "class" relates to the outward trappings of life, and not to the core. The attempt to posit at the basis of the fate of society the idea of class and the fact of class is a demonic attempt, it is directed at the extermination of man, of nation, the state, the church, all the genuine realities. Class, that to which they ascribe the supremacy, undermines everything of value and distorts all the vital settings of value. The working class, persuaded, that it is the sole chosen class, leaves no place for living, it steals and cripples everything. In Russia there will be no free citizenry, as long as Russians live under the power of the demonic idea of class. And this dark class idea will extirpate the remnants of brotherhood in the Russian people, as a Christian people. The hypnotic effect of the class idea distorts even socialism itself and bestows it a destructive and suicidal character. If socialism were possible and allowable, then at its foundation ought to be put man, and not class. Against class absolutism it is necessary to preach a crusade. In the darkness of the Russian people, in the grip of a false idea, deceived and abused, there ought to awaken man, the human image and the human dignity. The conceit and impudence of class are not an human worthiness, in them man perishes. In the masses of the workers and the peasants not only does man not awaken, but ultimately he becomes forgotten and sinks into the element of dark instincts. The Bolshevik collectivism also is a final obscuring in

Russia of the human principle, of the human person, of the human image. The proletarian class communism on Russian soil is an experiencing of a primitive human communism. The revolution has set loose this communistic darkness, but it has done nothing in the life of the masses of the people for the developement of a free citizenry. A new and better life will begin in Russia, when the bright spirit of man wins out over the dark demon of class.

Spiritual and Material Work in the Russian Revolution

(1918 - 291)[1]

In Memory of Feodor Feodorovich Kokoshkin

"Each belongs to all, and all to each. All are slaves and in slavery are equal... The first duty is to undertake a levelling of education, science and talents. The high level makes science and talents accessible only for those of higher abilities and the higher abilities are not needed. Slaves ought to be equal: without despotism still there would neither be freedom, nor equality, but in the herd there has to be equality, and herein is the Shigalevism... To level the heights -- is a fine thought... not needed is a rounded education, the sciences suffice... The thirst for a rounded education is already an aristocratic thirst".

Dostoevsky "The Devils" ("The Possessed")

I.

In the social consequences of the Russian revolution there is very much of the paradoxical and unanticipated. It is nowise necessary to seek there for the fundamental conflict, in where usually they would seek it. And it is not that a social group falls victim to it, one which was due to fall according to the popular theory of revolution. The social, and the deeper and spiritual essence of the Russian revolution mustneeds be sought not in the clashes of the working classes with the possessing classes, not in the struggle of the proletariat with the bourgeoise, but first of all in the clash of vital interests and in contrast different feelings on life within the

---

[1] DUKHOVNYI I MATERIAL'NYI TRUD V RUSSKOI REVOLIUTSII. Article originally published in the weekly "Narodopravstvo", 21 jan. 1918, № 21-22, p. 3-6.

representatives of material work from those of spiritual work. There is a very deep conflicting of work that is quantitative in contrast with work that is qualitative, and this for the fate of Russia -- is a tragic clash betwixt the "people" and "culture". The people has risen up against the works of Peter and Pushkin. The causes for such traits in our woesome revolution are lodged very deep in the past. In comparison with this basic opposition, discerned within the elements of the Russian revolution, all the other remaining oppositions tend completely to fade away, those which have so occupied the customary thinking. Certainly, within the Russian revolution occurs the clash and struggle of "socialistic" interests of the toiling masses against the "bourgeois" interests of the possessing classes; certainly, there is discerned in this a struggle of a type of "socialistic" thinking against a type of "bourgeois" thinking. But for our revolution, unique in its social and cultural setting, there is much that is distinct from the European revolutions, these clashes and this struggle are not spiritually indicative and substantial. The peculiar tragedy of the Russian revolution -- is in the opening apart of a yawning abyss, the separating and the setting in opposition the world of spiritual work, mental, creative, the work of the creators of the values of culture and the welfare of the state, apart from the world of material work, lacking the qualitative, a world barbarically hostile to every culture and every state. In Russia has occurred the clash of barbarity and culture, a barbarity enormous in its extent against a culture very small in its extent. The revolution has not awakened in the people the thirst for light, for any movement upwards. On the contrary, the dark element amongst the people is dragging the cultural heights downwards, demanding a lowering to their qualitative level. Material work displays an exclusive pretension to lord it over spiritual work. All the intellectual and spiritual work of many generations, all the accumulated values and benefits of a civilised existence, are declared "bourgeois" and unneeded.

    A genuine workers movement, making constructive efforts to surmount the evil sides of the bourgeois-capitalist order, in Russia does not exist nor can it exist, since Russia is a land industrially backwards, our proletariat are comparatively few in number, insufficiently organised and insufficiently developed. With us there are not yet the economic, nor the moral-psychological premises of a workers socialism, directed to the organisation of work, to the organisation of production, and less so anarchistic, than in the individualist-capitalist economy. The Russian "socialism" is but a Western European euphemism for the Russian backwardness and the Russian wont for revolt. In Russia, a land predominantly peasant, culturally backward and undisciplined, in this historical hour, when for the element of the people have fallen all the external restraints and the fetters have been shaken loose from the inner spiritual bonds and connections, there has transpired the clash of a world intellectual, educated, spiritually qualified against a world of the quantitative masses, not endowed with any kind of qualification. This -- is a clash more profound, than between a qualified world and the world of labour, in the material sense of this word. The conflict of the quantitative principle with the qualitative principle, in which falls victim the qualitative principle, -- here is what has proven fatal in the Russian revolution. The acute aspects of the Russian revolution have proven suicidally directed against culture and its servants. The masses thirst for distribution, they have no desire to lift themself up to an higher life, always based upon creative work. The revolution has proven neither progressive nor creative, but rather instead reactionary, showing a clear preference for the elements of darkness over the elements of light. The uprising of the "socialistic" world against the "bourgeois" world in the Russian revolution nowise signifies the struggle of organised labour against the exclusive domination of capital, against the power of the possessors. This -- is a secondary aspect. The mass of soldiers, making the revolution, are incapable of a positive organising of labour, and instead disorganises the work and creates a realm of lethargy and idleness. A substantial trait in the Russian revolution is the uprising of the uneducated against the educated, of the uncultured against the cultured, of the ignorant against the knowledgeable, of quantitative material work against work that is qualitative and spiritual. And it is characteristic, that the psychology of those rising up is not one of labour, but rather a consumptive psychology. The will of the uprising masses is not directed to the organisation of labour, not to the regulation of the social totality, but upon confiscations and consumption. This -- least of all is a psychology of producers. Production holds no interest for the revolutionary masses. This but at a glance shows, how much authentic work has a spiritual basis and presupposes the moral self-discipline of the toiling. A materialistic attitude towards work leads to a decay in work, and upon this unhealthy basis there can flourish only but lethargy and idleness.

II.

Material work, sundered from every spiritual basis, cannot defend itself. Only an organised productive work can defend itself, always presupposing a moral self-discipline. Suchlike a strength of organised and self-disciplined labour has not been evidenced in the Russian revolution, nor was it prepared for in all our preceeding history. Here is why the toiling masses at present destroy the production, they wreck the industrialism and the agrarian economy, and deny work itself. It is needful always to remember, that the productive initiative belongs to the spiritual toil, that to it belongs the guidance in the economic life of the land. The economic foundations of spiritual-cultural life in Russia are crumbling, since the spiritual foundations of economic life have come apart, and there has decayed the moral and religious discipline of the working person. It is impossible to deny the rights of material labour to an organised improvement of its position and the increase of its societal weight. Labour has its own sacred rights, and it ought not to be situated under the exclusive and unlimited power of capital. The relationship of labour and capital cannot be regulated individually, left to the exclusive power of personal competition, -- they are subject to state and societal regulations. This can be admittedly an inheritance of the modern consciousness. But the rights of labour cannot be conceived of, as the rights of quantity against quality. The principle of quality is represented not by capital, but by qualified work. Capital however makes it possible for qualificatory work to realise its own productive and creative goals. The higher right belongs to qualitative work, and the highest right belongs to creativity. In the world of human labour there is its own hierarchy, its own ascending and descending steps. And labour can be organised only hierarchically, not mechanically. This was excellently understood by such people, as John Ruskin, who stands many an head higher than the socialists, in their proclaiming of an all-equal work lacking in the qualitative. Ruskin was faithful to the noble Platonic tradition. The divisions within labour is a law of cosmic life. The toppling of the hierarchy of work, in which the higher quality receives its corresponding place, is a reactionary revolt, throwing everything backward, lowering the level of culture, exterminating all values. Such a reactionary revolt, destroying the hierarchy of work and the hierarchy of values, is occurring at present in Russia.

The Russian revolutionary-socialistic movement does not organise, but rather disorganises production, and it is essentially hostile to labour. The Russian "revolutionary democracy", in regards to the "bourgeoise" which it wants to exterminate, understands by this not the class of capitalists, not the industrialists and merchants, not those qualified as the "haves", but rather all the educated and cultural world, all those endowed with intellectual quality. The spiteful hostility is stronger against the "educated", than it is against the "haves". This is very characteristic. The socialistic ideology has always limped in this, that it was an ideology of material labour lacking in the qualitative, that it denies in work the hierarchical principle, that it does not provide a corresponding place for quality, ability, education and calling, that it mechanically levels the working and excludes the possibility of a selection of the best and their predominance in societal life. Materialistic socialism, taken in purely an abstract regard, leads in fatal a manner to a selection of the worst and to their predominance, and it tends to end up in mob rule. And if Western socialism, being more cultured, tends to sin by its lack of attention to the significance of qualitative spiritual work, then Russian socialism, revealing its completely barbaric nature, goes farther and is prepared to threaten the representatives of this higher work. To make the mountains level with the valleys -- herein is the pathos of Russian socialism. This is also the "Shigalevism", with genius revealed by Dostoevsky in "The Devils". This is also the "Makhaevism", which fifty years back foresaw the results of the Russian revolution and gave an extreme [anti-intellectual anarchistic] expression to Russian socialism. Within this Russian socialism there stirs the hatred towards everything lofty, towards every spiritual predominance. The slighting of mental work, connected with education and giftedness, as reflective of privilege which has to be cast down, is a spiritual pitfall and morally ugly. One both can and ought to struggle for the uplifting of the mental, the educational and cultural level of the workers and the peasants, the working classes, and it is dreadful, that so little was and is being done for this. But it is impermissible, and in the deepest sense of the word reactionary, in the name of democratisation and levelling to lower the spiritual level of the cultural stratum, to sacrifice quality in the name of quantity. The working people has to be ennobled and aristocratised -- herein is the sole intent and permissible form of democratisation. Insofar as that within the socialistic workers state it presupposes a lowering of the level of education amidst a compulsory cultural and spiritual levelling, it is a completely reactionary and demonically dark idealism, and it will be to the extinguishing and enslaving of the human spirit.

III.

The Russian revolution is gripped with a passion for levelling, it responds with a black envy towards everything uplifting, every qualitative predominance, towards higher a spiritual level. Having lost its faith and become submerged in darkness, the people does not want to receive light from the more enlightened, it wickedly spurns every attempt to enlighten it. With us nothing can go from the top downwards. The "people" has fancied, that it itself is capable of everything, that it knows everything, that from hence everything issues forth from it itself. The "people" in the deluge and triumph of Bolshevism first of all rose up against the intelligentsia, and in this there was a just payback for that nihilistic venom, by which the "intelligentsia" had poisoned the people. But in this is likewise a terrible illusion and self-deception. In actuality, the "people" proves to be a manipulated tool in the hands of a bunch of demagogues, it remains in a state of slavery, since it has not a liberating light. As a victim of the people's spite, fanned further by demagogues for their grip of power over the "people", first of all falls the most cultural stratum of the intelligentsia, the least blameworthy in spreading the nihilistic venom. Everyone "educated" evokes hostile an attitude towards himself on the streets, in the carriages, everywhere, where the quantitative masses gather. We might remember the attitude towards doctors during the time of the cholera epidemics. This dark pogrom-like instinct has now received its sanctioning in the Russian socialistic realm. The people expels as useless all the rural intelligentsia, as the "third element". Certain intelligentsia, essentially, privileged to have come from abroad, and foreign-most to the people, yet the most demagogic in deportment, expel other intelligentsia, more involved and standing closer to the people's life, those not having resorted to a demagoguery devoid of conscience. The people, left remaining in that selfsame darkness, in which it was earlier, but having taken on a totally superficial socialistic tint, spurns the mental work, the work, connected with the qualities of education, giftedness, a specialised calling. To a "socialistic" people quite unneeded have seemed the learned, the writers, the jurists, the teachers, the engineers, the agriculturalists etc. The locksmith or the porter is on the same level with the educated specialist, with the man of experience, knowledge and ability. The whole hierarchy of intellectual work from the highest representatives of spiritual creativity down to the most modest representatives of the toiling intelligentsia, alike teachers of the people, are spurned out of feelings of spite. This ends up with a predominance of former criminals or spies.

The war already has begotten an entire series of economically paradoxical consequences. The pay for material work has very much risen, without any correlation to the growth of productivity of work. The common labourer has begun to earn notably more, than a representative of qualitative intelligentsia work. One who is learned can fall into a worse position, than the unskilled workman. The masses of the toiling intelligentsia amidst an immeasurably expensive live are doomed to an half-starved existence. The favourable situation of the peasants has quite risen, they were more secure with bread and they have stowed away more money in reserve. The peasants strive for a bourgeois manner of gain and their socialism is but an outer veil. The revolution has given sanction to an economic paradox, on the strength of which material work has received such preferential treatment over work that is mental and spiritual. At the height of its developement under the Bolshevik power, the revolution dooms to a death by starvation and to the perishing of almost all the toiling intelligentsia, all our have-not cultural stratum. Here is the social result of the revolution, here is what social group it is that first of all falls victim to our "socialistic" revolution. The genuinely qualified bourgeois, though, also experiences greater shocks, but he however yet has all the possibility to exist and in the final end to preserve his capital. Grievous blows are being struck at Russian industrialism, which is one of the basics of the existence of all the Russian people and of the workers themself first of all, but the representatives of the industrialist class can survive these times, they possess the means for life. The intelligentsia cannot perish in the literal sense of this word. I speak not about those intelligentsia, who unashamedly exploit the revolutionary element to their own benefit and make a living off of this, I speak instead about the intelligentsia, who create and sustain Russian culture. There is occurring a selection of the worst and the expulsion of the best people. It threatens the danger of the perishing of our cultural level. They are abolishing all the material foundations for the functioning and creativity of Russian culture. After an orgy there is a grimly sober accounting to face. A miserable existence threatens all the Russian people. Only an inspiring of the representatives of material labour can restore the significance of spiritual labor. Without a spiritual restoration of health, even the economic developing of the nation becomes an impossibility. Now however the vicious Russian revolution commits reactionary and demonically-dark misdeeds. Against this "Shigalevism" there have to rise up all the spiritual forces of Russia.

The Power and Psychology of the Intelligentsia*

(*this article was written prior to the Bolshevik takeover)

(1918 - #292)[1]

I.

Here already it has been several months, with Russia facing unresolved tasks -- to create a strong state power from an human material, totally unprepared for the holding of power and for determining the fate of the state, unprepared as regards all its past, unprepared as regards its mental frame of mind to not be called to power nor rule in the state. Over the course of the "unfolding" of the Revolution the power gradually passed over to the Russian revolutionary intelligentsia, to the Russian Social Revolutionaries and the Social Democrats, i.e. to people, who in their dreams never imagined, that they might actually come to power, and whose whole world-outlook and psychology denies the very principle of holding power. The tumbling over from the underground into a ministry -- is no easy thing, it can be mentally maddening. The Russian socialistic intelligentsia had no presentiment, had no thoughts, which might have prepared it for holding power. The Russian revolutionary-socialistic intelligentsia had crystalised into a peculiar race, into a peculiar variety of people, which could be recognised even by its physical appearance, and this race was incapable of governance. Its governing and holding of power is anthropologically, psychologically and morally something ridiculous. This variety of people cannot create an aesthetic style of holding power, as might be but repulsive. The shouted about lack of power is not only aesthetically repulsive, -- its aesthetic non-acceptability is likewise an

---

[1] VLAST' I PSIKHOLOGIYA INTELLIGENTSIYA. Article originally published in the Journal, "Russkaya mysl", jan.-feb. 1918, p. 95-100.

indicator of spiritual unpreparedness and untruth. By all its very blood and all its thoughts our revolutionary intelligentsia has always denied the holding of power, and for it the struggle with the autocratic power passed over into a denial of the state, the nation, and history. The revolutionary intelligentsia has lived with utopias and dreams of a perfect social order. And at that blissful point in time, when this social order ensues, it presupposes the absence of every sort of holding of power, since every having of power is from evil. Prior to this desirable moment, however, there has to be an irreconcilable opposition to every sort of power, there being needful permanent revolution. The absolutisation of the revolutionary psychology makes impossible any participation in the holding of power. The Russian revolutionary does not imagine it possible for him to participate in power prior to the realisation of socialism, and yet he would tend to imagine for himself the realisation of socialism as the final blessed surmounting of every holding of power, of everything to do with the state. For him the holding of power would either be something too premature, or too belated. He is accustomed to experience a religious absoluteness in societal life, where everything is relative. And this distorted religious feeling has not been to a strengthening morally, instead it has led to a moral distortion and decay. The soul of the Russian intelligentsia has fallen under the grip of false gods and idols.

    No sort of positive habits of constructive a societal and state outlook have preceeded the sudden and catastrophic appearance in power of the Russian intelligentsia. The intelligentsia has been accustomed to sense itself alienated from its native land, from its history, from the legacy of ancestors, from the whole of the state and the people. Never has there opened before it the perspective of the span of history and never has it directed its will to creative tasks. Its psychology was caught up in its own narrow circle, stuffy and stifling. This world of the intelligentsia has been completely self-enclosed world, dwelling within its deeply provincial interests, its own party considerations, speaking in its hideous jargon, setting itself in opposition to the breadth of the universal and historical. This was a sectarian like little world with all the peculiarities of the sectarian psychology. Foreign to it was a language national and a language all-human. The sectarian is not capable of thinking about the great entirety nor is he able to direct his will to this entirety, and in this he is distinct from the churchly man, who senses himself within the universal whole. The sectarian psychology of the revolutionary intelligentsia has led to an extreme simplification of the thinking process. All the complexity of life has eluded his sight, visible only is a direct straight line, God's whole manifold world is rendered either on the "right" or the "left". The sectarian psychology of the intelligentsia never was creative nor productive, it was totally in the grip of a thirst for division and redistribution. The intelligentsia sectarians never wanted to recognise any sort of objective principles of societal life, and to them this seemed "bourgeois". The fate of the state and society was relegated by them to the domain of human subjectivity, everything was explained by the evil or good will of people and classes. The cosmic and natural grounds of human society always remained unconceivable and unacceptable for the intelligentsia sectarianism. Limited by nothing, the subjective moralism has led to an immoral violence against the objective nature of society and state, to the immoral denial of principles, set higher than the subjective arbitrary will of people and their subjective well-being. This has been a moralism of the underground and the renegade, for which there does not exist any great mystery of the whole nation and world, there does not exist any mutual responsibility. And here now the elemental historical surging wave lifts to the summits of power these sectarians, accustomed to live in the underground, as renegades from the national entirety, and to deny the state, the fatherland, and the pre-eminence of history.

II.

The whole revolutionary history of the Russian intelligentsia has accustomed it to irresponsibility. It never was summoned to responsible deeds within Russian history. The responsibility for the woeful state of Russia, for all the evil of Russian life, the intelligentsia tended to lay on "them", the ruling power, in opposition to the people, but never upon itself. The banishings, the prisons and the executions morally strengthened the sense of irresponsibility. The hapless Russian intelligentsia was accustomed to a persecuted position and in everything it regards as blameworthy its persecutors. One who lacks the vocation for a constructive life, who as it were is thrown overboard, is one who is deprived the possibility to develop and strengthen in himself a sense of responsibility. The intelligentsia was accustomed to confess the most irresponsible theories and utopias, which never were credible in actual experience. In its self-contained little world, the intelligentsia came up with the most extreme teachings, but never did it seriously prepare itself for the vital testing of these teachings. For several days prior to the turnover, the representatives of the revolutionary intelligentsia did not even realise, that it had befallen their lot to take upon themselves the responsibility for the fate of a great state. Even after the turnover occurred, when all the obstacles on the paths to democracy had fallen, the revolutionary democracy relegated to the Provisional Government almost the same structure, as it had applied to the old government, it transferred over its old habits onto the new Russia. It is incapable of putting aside its underground and mutinously negative revolutionary psychology. The professional revolutionaries have continued on with making revolution even then, when there is no one and nothing to make it against. The irresponsible sense of revolutionary opposition has been totally carried over also into the liberated Russia. And it mustneeds straight out be said, that the Russian revolutionary intelligentsia is, perhaps, a very inert and very reactionary inheritance, received by the new Russia from the old Russia -- it lives in the old, it breathes with the old and negative feelings, it is incapable of being pervaded with a creative psychology. This -- is the product of people, organically incapable of the constructive view for a new life.

These people started with this, with committing an immense crime -- in the dark masses of the people they spread the seeds of class malice and hatred and brought about the act of the rising up of class against class in monstrous proportions, auguring the death of the state and the nation and transforming Russian life into a living hell. Then these very people became alarmed at the deed wrought of their hands, they tasted the bitter fruits of their destructive work and hastily they began to do the elemental schooling of state and national learning, and certain of them by rote began to pronounce the word fatherland. Having received the rule of power, they began without success to set right certain of their mistakes, for example, they tried to revive the army, but alongside this they made ever newer and newer mistakes. The Russian socialistic intelligentsia faces the danger of being swept away by the very element in the people that it has set loose. The revolutionary intelligentsia itself began to destroy the liberated new Russia, and having come to power, it is powerless to try to set right the consequences of its destruction. It has not been the creative, but rather the destructive deeds that brought the Russian socialists to power, and this path has begotten a tragically impotent holding of power. The weave of soul of these people is such, that they are incapable of rule. The holding of power

-- is not an intelligentsia trait. When the revolutionary intelligentsia ceased to be persecuted and changed into persecutors, they displayed features of a frightful moral ugliness. They were incapable of worthily bearing the burden of power, since first of all they understand power as a right, and not as an obligation. *For one to worthily hold power, it is necessary to be done with the revolutionary psychology, to get into communion with the mystery of the whole and the mystery of succession.* "Revolutionary ruling power", just like "revolutionary order", -- is an absurd word combination. The attempts to create a "revolutionary ruling power", relying upon the revolutionary psychology, over the course of several months have made for an atmosphere in which the governing power is creating bedlam and has begotten appearances morally ugly. After the revolutionary turnover occurred, it became necessary to organise in Russia a new order of life, to enter upon construction and creativity. Instead of this healthy path -- a path of national renewal, -- with us they produced a revolution on to infinity, they set upon a path of destruction and lacked the ability to give up on the old revolutionary psychology, begotten of oppression and slavery. The revolutionary democracy cannot rule, this -- is an old, and not a new democracy. As a builder of life, as the builder of a new Russia there can be only the democracy of a new type of outlook, with a developing sense of responsibility, with a developing instinct for productivity, with a strong awareness of the national and state totality and having a bond with the historical past, i.e. a creative national democracy. The democracy ought also to create an aristocracy, i.e. the selection of the finest. The revolutionary democracy, however, which is but the revolutionary intelligentsia, is putting the finish to its history with the Russian Revolution.

III.

Our socialists simultaneously fight for power, while in every way which they can they discredit the "bourgeois" holding of power, and they are likewise afraid of the holding of power, they do not want to take upon themselves the fullness of responsibility. Having lost neither their shyness nor scruples, the Russian socialists are ill at ease over what in the Revolution they tended to call "bourgeois", yet the socialists are now at the top, and the bourgeoise squeezed into the background. This -- is a paradox of the Russian Revolution, which disquiets the Russian socialists, such as are not ultimately bereft of a sense of responsibility. The socialistic structure at present cannot be introduced into Russia, a land industrially backward, wretched and uncultured, with its working class unenlightened and unorganised, and amidst an indisputable social antagonism of the peasants and workers. And indeed the socialistic order is an abstraction, while manifold social reforms are what is concrete. The radical socialistic experiments at present are throwing Russia backwards, splintering it. And forthwith the socialists demand participation in the organisation of power, without them cannot be made the "bourgeois" revolution, but they have need of them only as a smoke-screen, in order to shift from their own shoulders the immense sense of responsibility. As soon as s coalition is formed, the socialist elements demand, that the bourgeois elements completely fulfill their programme. Such indeed was the attitude of the old powers towards the liberal elements of Russian society: in dangerous moments they were prepared to call on them, but with them it was a matter of preserving intact the old regime. The socialist influence has caused much woe and has led Russia to great disgrace, but the socialists do not want to assume completely upon themself the answerability for these misfortunes and this disgraceful state of affairs. The revolutionary democracy is fighting for total power, yet it does not want to deal with that power, which unexpectedly has fallen to its lot.

It is with fear that the representatives of the socialist intelligentsia have scampered up to the summits of power. Their own shouts against the bourgeoise have placed them in a tragic position. They have morally fallen out on top. These people could morally undergo persecution, but they cannot morally undergo being in power. The ruling ability does not flow in their blood, they do not belong to the sort that are rulers. The Russian socialist intelligentsia having power is a phenomenon of tragic impotence. It cannot create an aesthetically viable style of holding power and it is doomed to a moral unseemliness and collapse. A man, having fallen into a situation too unsuited and impossible for him, becomes impotently paralysed, he aesthetically becomes lacking in ability and it is only with difficulty that he remains upon the moral heights. History has set a trap for the Russian socialist intelligentsia, and beyond the ecstatic moments of its power and glory it faces a grievous payback. To me it is quite clear, that with the Russian revolutionary intelligentsia being in power and with its experiments, which it makes upon hapless Russia, represents its finish, its graveyard, the proving out of the falseness of its basic ideas and principles.

With us the ruling Russian socialism is now taken too seriously, we are too frightened and beset by it. This however -- is a false perspective. All this prevailing "revolutionary democracy" is but an expression of Russian chaos and Russian darkness. This is a matter of illusions and mirages within Russian life. Within the Russian Revolution there has been too much of the unreal, many a declaration which can be snatched away at any moment, and theatrical forms, nowise active of real personages. The authentic realities lie hidden, and the real interplay of powers is not at all such, as it would seem on the surface. With us there was created a myth about the Bolsheviks, and this myth has assumed the appearance of reality, but the Bolsheviks also shake with terror at the prospect of counter-revolution and the return of the old masters, and they belong to a sort, not for long called to rule. Momentarily their rule will be a spectre, one of the nightmares of the great soul of the Russian people, nothing more. Sooner or later in Russia there has to be a real, a strong national state power. This power might be varied in whatever its shading, but it cannot be a power of the revolutionary intelligentsia, -- a breed, doomed to extinction. There will be a new power, stronger and more integrated, not consumed from within by the old sicknesses, not debilitated by moral reflections, and capable of fulfilling severe duties. There cannot be in power those, who still on the eve did not know, whether war is permissible and justified in defense of the fatherland, who were doubtful whether to maintain order in the land by forceful measures and thereby avert anarchy, and who reflected Hamlet-like over the repulsive severity of every manner of state. The coming Russian democracy, if it is to be, will have nothing in common with what at present is called "revolutionary democracy". And if we are to have an healthy socialist movement, then it will have nothing in common with the Russian revolutionary socialism, now having its orgy. Russia has to find itself a manner of people, truly capable of rule, a new aristocracy.

The Ruin of Russian Illusions

(1917 - #280)[1]

I.

The catastrophe, termed the Russian Revolution, through all the degradations, tribulations and disappointments, has to lead to a new and better awareness. Such an experience in the life of a people cannot but enrich and sharpen our perceptiveness. But a crisis of soul will have to precede this perceptiveness with a readiness for repentance and humility. The light will be begotten after an inward cleansing and ascesis. This -- is a law of spiritual life. And it is needful to be aware, that all the whole thinking portion of Russian society, that which has esteemed itself as the bearer knowingly of ideas, has within it something to repent and be cleansed of. Beliefs and ideas -- are answerable matters, from them come emanations of liberating truth or enslaving ideas. The greatest responsibility for the evil triumphing in life is borne by those, who conceived of it initially in idea, those first few who in their distorted spiritual experience gave in to deceitful and false illusions. The Russian intellectual Intelligentsia, belonging to various camps, having lived by illusions, was inspired by a false faith and phantasmic ideas. And here has begun the hour of pay-back. It has become time, when this must be recognised under the compelling weight of vital experience. Only but few

---

[1] GIBEL' RUSSKIKH ILLIUZII. Article originally published in Journal "Russkaya mysl'", sept.-oct. 1917, p. 101-107.

N.B. possible erratum: YMCA Press Berdiaev Tom 4 text provides on this "Gibel'" article at conclusion the bibliographic citation of: "Russkaya Mysl' *jan.-feb. 1918*", with no page number indication, which differs from the *sept.-oct. 1917* citation (#280) within the Klepinina "Berdiaev Bibliographie". To preserve proper continuity with the Klepinina enumeration of Berdyaev's works as indicated in the "Bibliographie", the "*sept.-oct. 1917*" rather than the "jan.-feb. 1918" issue date is tentatively is here used.

have realised this under the free pull of creative thought. We remember the irritated and indignant attitude towards "Vekhi" ("Signposts"), even in those circles, which now through bitter experience perceive the truth of "Vekhi". But justice in regard to the authors of "Vekhi" is difficult to expect.

The Russian Revolution in its fateful and fatal course of developement signifies the ruin of Russian illusions, -- be it of the Slavophils, the Populists, the Tolstoyans, the anarchists, the revolutionary-utopianists or the revolutionary-messianists. This -- is the end of Russian socialism. The quite most opposite Russian ideologies have tended to assert, that the Russian people stands higher than European civilisation, that the law of civilisation for it has no force of decree, that the European civilisation is too "bourgeois" for the Russians, that the Russians are called to realise the Kingdom of God on earth, the kingdom of an higher truth and justice. This has been asserted on the right by the Slavophils, adherents of the Russian religious and national uniqueness, just as it was asserted on the left by the revolutionaries, socialists and anarchists, who were nowise less than the Slavophils as adherents of an Eastern uniqueness, and to the bourgeois West they opposed the revolutionary light from the East. Bakunin confessed a Russian revolutionary messianism. And he continues to be confessed also by those, who all these terrible months keep shouting, that the Russian revolutionary democracy will instruct all the peoples of the West in socialism and the brotherhood of peoples. This Russian light, which is intended to enlighten all the peoples of the world, has also led Russia to an ultimate abasement and shame.

All the ideologies of this type, gripping the Russian Intelligentsia both by mind and by heart, were based on a faith in the people, in the wisdom of the people and the truth of the people. Among the Populists on the right, standing upon a religious basis, the faith in the people was better grounded and justified, than with the populists of the left, standing upon a materialistic basis. Slavophilism was the sole serious Russian ideology, for which one can have deep esteem. The religious populism is an illusion and self-deceit, from which we are being cured at dear a price, but this idea is not bereft of depth. This idea was so deeply embedded in the consciousness of the people, that it religiously sanctified the Russian autocracy and rendered impossible any sort of evolution of the monarchy. And thus the religious populism gave Russia a shove, seeing in the autocracy an utmost truth, and pushing it onto the path of catastrophe. The revolutionary populism is lacking in depth, it is based upon darkness and muddled consciousness, and to a remarkable degree it is the product of backwardness and churlish ignorance, the fruit of the extensive Russian economic system. Revolutionary chauvinism is a very ugly and vile form of chauvinism. Russia at present is torn apart by orgies of this revolutionary chauvinism, shouting "we shall toss up our hats in victory" over all the world, subjugating all the world by revolutionary chatter. It is time already to recognise, that all the forms of Russian Populism -- are illusions, begotten of the Russian cultural backwardness; they signify a servile dependence of the Russian cultural segment upon the darkness of the people, the loss of all the qualitative aspect of Russian life into rather the quantitative. Faith in the "people" always was a pitfall and weakness of Russian thinking people, afraid to take responsibility upon oneself and decide for oneself, where is truth and right. The mean-spirited and craven tend to think, that the source of truth and right lies outside them, within the element of the people, in the mass of the people, in the people's faith or the people's toil. From the very summits of thought and spiritual life very remarkable Russian people in their aspirations have fallen downwards and in their contact with the lower aspects of the people's life they have sought for an higher wisdom. For some this was a religious wisdom. I. Kireevsky suggested reverencing the sanctity of the icon, because the people prayed before the icon and had sanctified it with their poklon-bowings and kisses. For others this was a social wisdom, a truth of the workman's life, a truth of life, close nigh to nature. But all were afraid of their own higher cultural life as something not right, as a falling-away from the natural and blissful world-order. L. Tolstoy was the most extreme expression of this Russian Populism. And in him was combined the religious populism with the social populism.

II.

The Russian faith in the "people" was a form of idolatry, of worshipping man and mankind, of fashioning for oneself an idol from the external masses. The faith in the people, as the common-people, as peasants and workers, was a faith in an empirical quantity. The object of this faith is not conditioned by its qualities, its inner value, as something close and understandable for the believer. A member of the Intelligentsia, while believing in the people, will have tended not to know the soul of the people, not grasp it within himself, kindred to him in his depths, but instead will have worshipped the people, as something unknown and foreign to him, beckoning by its remoteness. The true soul of the people, the soul of the nation, as a mystical organism, is undefinable by any sort of sociological signs, it was rather a soul, graspable first of all in the proper depth of each son of the people, but it was obscured by the populist ideology and by the populist illusions. The Russian consciousness itself was muddled and contaminated by the social-class point of view regarding the people, by its dependence upon the empirically given, the hypnotic effect of the quantitative category. For the populist consciousness the people was a substitute in place of God, and service to the people, its well-being and happiness substituted for service to truth and right. In the name of the people, as an idol, they were ready to sacrifice all the greatest values and sanctities, to destroy all culture as being the basis for inequality, every lifestyle, as being a legacy of their fathers and grandfathers. The religion of the "people" is truly a religion of non-being, of darkness, of the all-swallowing and all-consuming abyss. The idea of the people, as defined under social-class aspects, is a falsification of the idea of the nation, indefinable by any sort of social-class aspects, and it encompasses all the classes, all the groups and all the generations, past and future.[1] The populist ideology -- is purely an Intelligentsia ideology, the expression of having been torn asunder from the "people" and in opposition to the "people". For the "people" itself populism is an impossibility. The best people from amongst the "people", from the lower working class, have striven towards the light, towards knowledge, towards culture, towards an escape from the people's darkness, and they have never idealised the "people" nor worshipped it.

The "people" for a long time has been silent. Various ones self-appointed have attempted to speak for it. But the impotent and people-worshipping Intelligentsia expected, that people will finally speak and have its own say, which will be a light for all the world, and that this light will enlighten the peoples of the West. The Revolution has gotten mired down, the old ruling powers have fallen and demolished all hindrances to the expression of the will of the people. The "people" has received its possibility to speak. The Russian revolutionary Intelligentsia, all gnawed at

---

[1] Vide my article, "The Populist and the National Consciousness", in Russkaya Mysl' for July-August 1917.

within from the chronic ills, and having poisoned the people with vicious nihilistic feelings and thoughts, have begun shouting, that in "the revolutionary democracy" will be revealed a sort of truth never before heard nor seen in the West, the light will dawn from the East. But this truth and this light has been expressed in nothing, besides mere meaningless abstract formulas on the order of "without annexations and indemnities", "all the land to the working people", etc. The Intelligentsia shout about all this, having borrowed its formulas from half-baked and maladapted Western teachings. But what did it reveal of itself and what was discovered by this "people", in which the Russian Slavophils and the Russian Revolutionary-Populists believed, and in which believed Kireevsky and Hertsen, Dostoevsky and the "going to the people" generation of the 70's, in which believed also the Russian religious seekers and the Russian Social Democrats, reborn into being Eastern populists? This "people" has discovered a primitive savagery, darkness, hooliganism, greed, the instincts for making pogroms, with the psychology of slaves in revolt, it has shown forth with the beastly snout. With its own say the "people" remains inarticulate, its own true say has yet to be born in the people. Behind all this terror, behind all this darkness of the people, the responsibility rests first of all upon the classes in command and upon the Intelligentsia. Some had no desire to enlighten the people, and instead held it down in compelling darkness and slavery; others bowed before the people as an idol and brought it a new darkness in place of light, a darkness semi-enlightened with an Intelligentsia nihilism. And in this most terrible and responsible hour of Russian history there stands among us for the elementary good of state and culture, for national worthiness, only a thin and nowise numerous cultural segment. this segment is easily to be torn through, and beneathe it is discerned a yawning abyss of darkness. The immense and dark realm of peasants swallows up and consumes all the good and values, within it drowns every human face. Many an excellent lover of the people has felt revulsion, at what they have seen and have heard. Not so altogether long ago the "people" was of the Black Hundreds and with soldier bayonettes they upheld the arbitrary rule and dark reaction. Now Bolshevism has won out with the people, and with the same soldier bayonettes it upholds Messrs. Lenin and Trotsky. Nothing has changed. The light has not enlightened the soul of the people. There reigns that same darkness, that same frightful element under but new trappings, under new masks. The realm of Lenin is nowise different from the realm of Rasputin.

III.

All those obsessed with populist illusions both from the right and from the left have to perceive, finally, that it is impossible to worship the "people" and it is impossible to expect from it some truth, unknowable for a more cultural stratum, -- the "people" is in need of enlightening, an uplifting, the communing with civilisation. The acclaimed Russian humility has been in essence a terrible pride and self-conceit. And it has become time, when there is necessary for us, finally, a more genuine, a more simple and elementary humility, humility not in the face of the wisdom of the Russian people, but rather in the face of the law of civilisation, afront culture, afront the light of knowledge. The enormous dark peasant realm has to proceed down the long path to civilisation, of enlightening and illumination. This -- is a worldwide path of developement and only through it can there be evidenced the national essence and the national calling. The Dionysian orgies of the dark peasant realm threaten to transform Russia, with all its values and good, into mere nothingness. The raging dark element has to be brought into a norm, made subject to law. Without this it is impossible to dream about any sort of higher vocation for Russia, since even Russia itself will have ceased to exist. The Russian people is not above the law, , this -- is an illusion; it is not some sort of a state of grace, it -- is beneathe the law, and in its notable masses it is in a state of beastliness. Such an admission represents also genuine religious humility, more humble, than the totally arrogant and self-conceited words about Holy Rus' or about an Internationale-Socialist Rus'. Russians have muddled up freedom with chaos, they have made an hodge-podge of the very low with the very high, of uppermost infinity -- with uttermost low infinity. And our generation is paying dearly for this confusion. The Russian people still is in need of elementary truth, it has not yet passed through the elementary sciences, but it regards itself as having overleaped all the sciences by some higher wisdom. The tragic experience of the Russian Revolution confirms the elementary truth of Westernism. This -- is not the ultimate truth, this -- is a pre-ultimate truth. But even a pre-ultimate truth has become needful to the extreme. It is time already to repudiate the Russian illusion, that for Russians exclusively needful is only the most final and ultimate. It is time already to be healed from the utopianism, from the pernicious social visionary dreaming, it is time already to religiously humble oneself in facing realism, with laws dealing with the relative and the intermediate.

Among Russian thinkers, the most correct was Chaadayev. Vl. Solov'ev in much also was correct, he was free of the populist illusions. Gogol saw in Russia the beastly snouts and then he repented of this. Now the Gogolian snouts are triumphant. Slavophilism however is dead in all its views and forms. The faith in Holy Rus' now sounds unendurably false and a lie. There is need to get concerned over this, that Rus' should preserve something of an human semblance, so that in Russian man there should not perish ultimately the image and likeness of God. Many ideas of the Russian great writers have suffered a terrible collapse. Dostoevsky prophetically foresaw the demonic aspect of the Russian Revolution in "The Devils" ("Besy"), he hinted at the demonic metaphysics of revolution in "The Brothers Karamazov". With genius he caught sight of much in the nature of Russian man, in the peculiarity of the nature of the Russian revolutionary Intelligentsia. But all the positive ideas of Dostoevsky have proven to be illusions, and now they sound like a lie. L. Tolstoy has to be acknowledged the greatest Russian nihilist, a destroyer of all values and sanctities, a destroyer of culture. Tolstoy has triumphed, there has triumphed his anarchism, his non-resistance, his denial of the state and culture, his moralistic demand for equality in poverty and non-being and submission to the peasant kingdom and physical toil. But this triumph of Tolstoyanism has proven less gentle and delightful, than it appeared to Tolstoy. He himself would hardly be happy in suchlike a triumph. There has been exposed the godless nihilism of Tolstoyanism, its terrible poison, devastating the Russian soul. For the salvation of Russia and Russian culture, and with red-hot iron, there needs to be burnt out from the Russian soul the Tolstoyan morals, so debasing and destructive. Tolstoy himself was infinitely higher than this morality, but he carried still the terrible poison of a false morality, in which was concentrated the broad average flow of Russian feelings, of Russian moral illusions and Russian defects of moral service. One of the greatest Russian geniuses has proven himself a progromchik out of moral zeal. He intensified among Russian people the all-leveling egalitarian passion.

The end has come for all the basic lines of Intelligentsia thought and currents, be it the lines leading from Kireevsky, and so likewise the lines, leading from Hertsen. Slavophilism, Populism, Tolstoyanism, Russian religious self-conceits and Russian revolutionary self-conceits -- are at an end, tragically lived out. There is no movement further along those paths, further along opens up the abyss of non-being. Russian illusions have ended in an ugly orgy. But its hypnotic effect soon will pass. After a cleansing from sins, from the old lies, it is necessary to begin a new life upon new paths. Worn down with sufferings, the Russian people has to reorient itself onto the long path of civilisation. In their souls will be born other thoughts, with a different and better consciousness. The soul of the Russian people will be tempered within a more austhere morality. Russia has its own mission, distinct from the mission of Germany, France and England. But the fulfilling of this mission lies through culture, through a duty of obedience to the burdens of civilisation. We have mistaken our backwardness for a point of excellence, as a sign of our higher calling and our greatness. But the terrible fact is that the human person for us is drowning in a primitive collectivism, and this is nowise a point of excellence, nor a sign of our greatness. It makes totally no difference, whether this all-engulfing collectivism be that of the "Black Hundreds" or of the "Bolsheviks". The Russian land lives under the power of a pagan khlysty-like element. In this element gets submerged every face, it is incompatible with personal worthiness and personal responsibility. This demonic element can pull forth from its bosom no true face, save only the likes of Rasputin and Lenin. The Russian "Bolshevik Revolution" is a dreadful worldwide *reactionary* phenomenon, just as reactionary in its spirit, as the "Rasputinism", as the Black Hundred khlystyism. The Russian people, just like every people, has to pass through a religious and cultural discipline of the person. And for this, it is needful to repudiate Russian illusions. The perishing of these illusions is not at all a perishing of the world. For us it is not given to know the times and seasons of the end of the world. And is not the eschatological and apocalyptic investigation of the religious populists of all the Russian woes and the Russian sins -- is this not one of the Russian illusions and temptations, begotten of the Russian self-conceit?

The Spiritual Foundations of the Russian People

(1918 - 293)[1]

I. The People and Culture

I.

Cast onto the sidelines of life in the days of the triumph of its old ideas and hopes, the Russian intelligentsia social stratum has facing it much to re-evaluate after the catastrophes experienced recently. Too many of the traditional ideas and values have not held up under the tribulations of life. And first of all there has to be reviewed and re-evaluated the traditional intelligentsia attitude towards the people and culture. For such Russians as are people of a radical intelligentsia mindset and likewise semi-intelligent, always characteristic on the one hand has been a faith in the people and a worship of the people, and on the other hand a sceptical attitude towards culture and a dislike for culture. In Russia there was never anything in the way of the spirit of the Renaissance, and with Russians there was never a surfeit of the joy of creativity. The most creative Russian people created not from a joyful exuberance, not through carefree impulse, but through suffering and torment, with overstrained nerves, with sickly reflection, with a lack of confidence of creating their own truth. Russian people of various trends have believed, that wisdom is innate by nature in the people, a wisdom otherwise unattainable, and so they have awaited the liberation of the people, which would lead to a revealing of this wisdom. On the other hand, they little believed that there is wisdom in culture and that only a cultural people, a people, having risen to its loftiest level of developement, could reveal all the possibilities hidden within it. Upon this groundwork there transpired an idealisation of the people's innate darkness, and this led to a bowing in worship to the quantitative masses. The idealisation of the people's darkness and the worship of the toiling masses

---

[1] DUKHOVYE OSNOVY RUSSKOGO NARODA. Article originally published in "Narodopravstvo", 1 feb. 1918, № 23-24, p. 3-7.

is alike characteristic both for the Russian Populists, and for the Russian Social Democrats, and both the one and the other regard the cultural segment as "bourgeois" and therefore situated in falsehood and non-truth. Such a sort of viewpoint is morally very close to Tolstoyanism -- wherein only those physically toiling know truth. And thus already for the representatives of mental and spiritual work truth is something hidden, because they -- are the privileged. The moral condemnation implicit in this division of labour conveys a condemnation of culture, a non-acceptance of those sacrifices, by which it is gained. It mustneeds be said, that Marxism initially began in Russia as a teaching moreso cultural, than the old populism, it demanded an higher intellectual level, and it rose up against the idealisation of the Russian backwardness. But further on, the Marxism among us became subject to a populist degeneration, and the Russian Marxists likewise began to idealise the darkness, if it be connected with the working world, and also to disdain culture, as the product of a privileged world. The Social Democrat ideology of non-qualified work in everything gives a preponderance to the quantitative, it denies the significance of ability, education, experience, vocation, and therefore inevitably it assumes an hostile attitude towards culture. There becomes established a completely mechanical equality, independent of the qualities of person, of cultural level. The mechanical, materialistic socialism looks upon man as an arithmetic unit, as the bearer of a certain quantity of work, -- of no significance for it is the qualitative distinctions between people, there does not exist for it individuals with various effect and various significance within the social organism.

    Physical labour has factual a preponderance, by its quantitative strength. And socialism establishes a new aristocracy based on quantity, an aristocracy of physical toil. According to this teaching, truth and right are better revealed under the conditions of physical toil, than under the conditions of spiritual toil and creativity. For the socialist-materialists, the "people" has preeminently a material basis. For a religious populism, such as Tolstoyanism for example, this basis rather instead is religious. But the "people", which is thought of as close by nature to truth and right, is however not then the great entirety, encompassing all classes and all generations, rising above all the social categories and walls of partition, -- the "people" becomes instead only the common people, and for some it is primarily the peasants, for others it is the workers, the toiling classes, set in opposition to the possessing classes, and to the cultural segment.

The Russian people all expect, that in the hour of its liberation from oppression this "people" will have its new say about a new life, that it will disclose some particular truth of its own. Our cultural stratum never conceived of its own worth per se and of its own true calling, it was almost ashamed of its culturedness, did not see in it a true light, the criteria of truth and right, and it always sought for these criteria on the outside, in a darkness, not infected by the sin of culture for the "people". A large number of Russian writers are of suchlike a psychology. Among them, it is difficult to find the awareness of an high worthiness and vocation of the writer, they almost all have something of Tolstoy in them. Sickly reflections always have eaten away at the Russian intelligentsia, in it there was never a sense of manly strength, a shedding of light from an inner source. In Russia, there was never essentially a spiritual aristocracy, sensing its vocation to be a guiding power in the life of the people, and within the Russian intelligentsia segment there was always a sickly reflective attitude towards culture, which was conceived of as deriving from non-truth and abuse. Tolstoyanism -- is a characteristic phenomenon of the Russian spirit. Almost all Russians somewhere in the depths of their souls tend to yield before the Tolstoyan moral views as something unattainably lofty. Yet from this selfsame moral source issues forth also this, that the man of the Russian intelligentsia is dogmatically convinced of the truth and justice of socialism, and socialism for him is not problematic in its moral basis.

II.

European man reveres creative cultural values, he finds inspiration in them, whereas Russian man reveres however the people, finds inspiration in service to the people. This traditional Russian worship of the people is not at all connected with the culture of the people, with an heightened qualitative level of the people, and it is quick instead to set in opposition the people and culture, as a sort of truth to non-truth. Russian intelligentsia people are essentially always inclined to think, that culture is something "bourgeois", and that it is proper for Russians to stand higher than this. And thus thought both the conservative Slavophils, and the revolutionary Westernisers. The current, which derives from Hertsen, always regarded culture with suspicion as begotten of "bourgeoisness", and it idealised the peasant kingdom, and worshipped the "people".

Nicholas Berdyaev

The extreme right camp and the extreme left camp coincide in their suspiciousness and hostility towards culture, and alike they have both tended to idealise the unenlightened element in the people. Bolshevism is totally akin to the Black Hundreds in this. In political life, this affinity is expressed in a likewise hostile attitude towards truth. The cultural stratum in the Russian intelligentsia is very thin and vulnerable in the darkness surrounding it, and in essence it has capitulated before the vast peasant realm and powerlessly yields before its alluring dark abyss. Its idolatry of the "people" reflects an insufficiency of manliness and a betrayal of its cultural mission. Such an impotent and reflexive psychology has quite hindered the cultural raising of the people, has impeded the matter of its enlightenment. One cannot bring light into the darkness, if one be not convinced in the particular source of the light, if one does not have in himself a firm spiritual support and faith, independent of the human masses surrounding him. The intelligentsia has been impotent to provide the people with enlightenment, but it instead poisoned the people with its semi-enlightenment, destroying what was sacred for the people and flattering the darkest instincts within the people.

Our radical revolutionary intelligentsia in its masses always has been semi-enlightened and little cultured. It was doubtful of higher culture, neither having attained it, nor experienced it. The Russian method of surmounting culture and its instead assertion of the Russian people, as standing higher than culture, is not particularly impressive. In Russia, it is with too great an ease that culture is surmounted by those, who have never tasted of it, who have never perceived its values and its efforts. The Russian schoolboy all straightly assembled in line regards himself of higher standing than culture, though he has read but a couple of brochures, he basically knows nothing and has experienced nothing. It is altogether a different spiritual matter of gravity, when European man thirsts to surmount culture, and be freed of its burden and pass on to an higher life, and for him each cell is pervaded by a sacred devotion to culture. This -- is a tragic process. And this -- is very serious. The Russian wont for standing above culture too often becomes but a barbarism and nihilism. The Russian attitude towards culture is also that of an age old nihilism, by which are too easily overcome, and by all too easily denied. This nihilism is deeply ingrained in the Russian people and assumes dreadful forms, when amongst the people there is a falling away from faith and the old sanctities grow dim under the pressure of the semi-enlightenment flooding over it.

And the "people" fiercely takes revenge upon the "intelligentsia" for the destruction of the old sanctities by its negative semi-enlightenment. The revolutionary intelligentsia has not had an authentic culture nor has it conveyed such to the people. But neither did it have a religious faith, it lost its pearl of Christianity and fantastically came to believe in its own non-belief, in a whole series of negative dogmas, which seemed immutable to the semi-enlightened consciousness. What could it give to the people? During an historical transition, during a most responsible hour of Russian history, it awakened in the people greedy and wicked instincts, it blessed those instincts and then it itself became frightened of its own nihilistic deed. Here is the bitter fruit of worshipping the people and of hostility towards culture. These days wide circles of the radical socialistic intelligentsia are fearful, that a triumphant Bolshevism will consign Russian culture to pogroms and plunderings, that it will deny literature, that it will deny spiritual toil and cast on the sidelines all the intelligentsia, all the cultural segment. But this is not an accidental act of malice by the Bolsheviks. This -- is the payback down a long path. Everything happening during these dark days has its reason in the people worship and nihilistic attitude towards cultural values, of which guilty are even those, who are now fuming about it. A betrayal of the spiritual grounds of life cannot go unpunished, its consequences have to follow, in order that there be a rebirth to new life.

III.

It is tragic for the fate of Russia and the Russian people, that the Orthodox religious upbringing, received by the people, insufficiently forestalls the nihilism and the raging storminess of the dark chaotic elements. Russian Orthodoxy has created forms of dazzling sanctity, it has nurtured in the people the worship of sanctity and the sacred, it has provided the much-suffering Russian people the possibility humbly to bear its grievous lot, and it has opened up to each human soul the path to salvation. But Russian Orthodoxy has not provided that tempering of the personal and the people's character for historical life and for the creation of culture, which in the West was given by Catholicism, and variously by Protestantism also. The religious upbringing of the people has not been favourable for culture. Our clergy has not provided the people the necessary enlightenment. In the people has been religiously nourished a spirit of humility in regard to the ruling powers, but therein quite entirely has not been nourished the spirit of activeness and self-discipline. In all its past, there has been no preparation of the people for self-government. In the Russian Orthodox mindset there is lodged a peculiar populism, a mistrust towards culture and the cultural stratum. This mistrust extends not only to the atheistic intelligentsia, which also does not merit different an attitude towards itself, but also to the hierarchy with higher a culture. In the West, Catholicism contended against a godless culture, against an anti-Christian enlightenment, but it itself created a great culture, the Latin culture of the West, and as such it sustained not only a sacred devotion to the church, but also a sacred devotion to culture, it nurtured the person for a life within history and for work within civilisation. The results of this nurture in a secularised form have remained in people, having lost the Catholic faith. Completely foreign to Catholicism was a people-worship, hostile to culture. Never on Catholic soil was there begotten an idolatry of the people and of the national wisdom of the people. They tended to see wisdom in the universal Church, in the Church's mentality, but not in the element of the people. With us, however, there has been almost no sacred devotion to a culture, created and sanctified by our Church.

We taste at present the bitter and poisoned fruits of the false Russian attitude towards the people and towards culture. By bitter experience we are learning, that it signifies an uprising of people, not yet having accepted culture and threatening culture, bearing with it an uprising of the quantitative masses, not admitting of any sort of qualities, and casting aside every norm and law. This is a setting loose of the primitive chaotic darkness. The laws of state, the laws of civilisation for awhile are holding in check the dark and beastly chaos, threatening the annihilation of all the cosmic harmonic order, similar to how the natural order of laws holds it in check within the world entirety. Bowing in worship to the people, as a fact, as an unenlightened quantity, is a godless idolatry. The people, as a fact, as an empirical given, cannot be held sacred, it is itself first of all in need of the sanctity, which it can set as higher than itself, and in need of light, which should enlighten its natural darkness, bound up as it is with the original sin of mankind and with the fall of man into a beast-like condition. It is not the people that merits a religious attitude to itself, but rather man, as in the image and likeness of God. Culture itself per se ought likewise not to be made a god of, but in culture there are values, which bear in them a reflection of the Divine light and which merit respect and an attentive attitude. The people, as an empirical fact, does not merit veneration and worship, in it is impossible to seek out the criteria of truth. But in the depths of the people's soul are hidden the possibilities of an higher life and these possibilities ought to be brought into an active condition through culture. The people, revealing in itself higher qualities, the people as enlightened and in a noble sense of the word cultured, is a task, and not a given. The higher creative spiritual life is attainable but for few, it is not subject to democratisation. But many can and ought to be qualitatively uplifted, so as to overcome the power of darkness. Only in the measure of their overcoming of this darkness is it that a people is summoned to active historical life, to the determining of the fate of its state. The enlightening of the darkness presupposes hierarchical steps. Here is why, to the tasks of culture belongs a spiritual primacy over the political tasks, and why the principles of an evolutionary process of developement ought to morally be set higher than the revolutionary principle. Overcoming the people's darkness now bursting forth upon us is not attainable alone by measures political, be they revolutionary or counter-revolutionary, it presupposes rather the awakening of a religious light in the soul of the people. And foremost of all, there has to happen a radical turnabout in all the value perspectives at the spiritual summits of Russian society, a turning away from the idolatry and idealisation of the people's elementalness and a respect for values and for the creativity of spiritual and material culture. Our people, bereft of any sense of humility before culture and without a creative attitude towards culture, is destined for disintegration and ruin.

Nicholas Berdyaev

II. The People and the Church

I.

During these dark and terrible days for Russia it is not infrequent to happen to hear complaints against the Church. Why is the Church silent, why has the Sobor not said its powerful say about the terrors, being experienced in Russia, and about the spiritual collapse of the Russian people? Granted, the Church ought not to be occupied with politics, granted that it ought to stand infinitely higher than the political struggle. But indeed, it is not about politics that is being discussed. Russia is perishing. The soul of the people has become depraved and fallen so low, as never before, and greed and malice, envy and vengefulness entirely rule Russian life. The complaints against the Church, it would seem, and in part against the Sobor, do have some basis. Thus, prior to the revolution many were perplexed, why the Church was not raising its voice against the evil of autocracy, against the depravity of the ruling powers, against the realm of Rasputinism. It is of little help, that those speaking thus and making various demands on the Church too often tend to speak this from the sidelines, from afar, while they themself are not in the Church and long since already have fallen away from the Church, but in difficult moments are prepared to recourse to the Church out of utilitarian political considerations. Those very intelligentsia, who did everything they could for the destruction of the Church, and who over the course of half a year undermined faith within the people, now have grown frightened of the fruits of their activity and are prepared to cling outwardly to the Church, as to an anchor of salvation. They grumble, that the Church as it were has forsaken the people, is insufficiently concerned about it, insufficiently provides it guidance during the difficult moments of its historical life. Granted this is true. But indeed there is also anther side to the matter, about which people tend to forget, and for whom the question about the Church -- is an external question. The people itself has forsaken the Church, itself has fallen away from the Church, itself has deprived itself of the Church's help, its graced gifts. Set before man and the people is the freedom to either be in the Church or to fall away from it. Salvation can only be a free matter. The Church holds no one by force in its house. Force can only be the doing of the state. The revolution has made much apparent, an in this perhaps is its singular significance, it has made separate the spheres of churchly freedom from that of state force. The Russian revolution has discovered this old truth, which for many was insufficiently clear, -- it is not only the Russian intelligentsia that betrayed the Church and fell away from it, as one might tend to think and speak, but also the Russian people has betrayed the Church and has fallen away from it. And this weakening of the religious energy of the Russian people occurred already long ago. Whereof -- is the weakness and infirmity of the visible Russian Church, which so distressed and tormented the finest, the most religious Russian people. Whereof also is the possibility of the terrible words about the paralysis of the Russian Church. It is needful to ponder over this strange Russian contradiction: the Russian people has declared itself the most religious, indeed a singularly religious people in the world, but the Russian Church has been in degradation, in infirmity, in paralysis.

If in the old Russia, prior to the revolution, the Church for long a time was situated in a condition of enslavement to the autocratic state and was governed despotically -- at one point by Pobedonostsev, and at another point by Grigorii Rasputin, if after the revolutionary turnabout the Church remains powerless to set right the godless element in the people and is unable to exert definitive an influence on the fate of Russia, then this signifies not an infirmity of that Church of Christ, against which the gates of hell will not prevail, but rather an infirmity of the people of the Church, a spiritual fallenness among the people, a weakness of faith, the loss of a religious assuredness. The people of the Church, the churchly mankind, comprises an indispensable part of the historical life of the Church upon earth. But there is impossible the mighty manifestation and thriving of the Church in historical life, if the people to a notable degree has betrayed the faith and fallen away from the Church. The Church will prevail, even if there remain all but only three righteous ones. The Church is grounded upon the qualitative, and not upon the quantitative. But when there falls away from the Church and betrays it the human quantity, the mass of mankind, the Church as it were withdraws into the depths, is rendered moreso a catacomb Church, and it is impossible to expect from it a mightiness in historical happenings. A man having betrayed the Church just like a people having betrayed the Church cannot rightly lay any sort of demands upon the Church. If in the Russian Orthodox Church there has been almost totally no sort of parish life, no real sort of Sobornost'-communality, then the blame lays not upon the Church of Christ with its inviolable sanctities, but upon the churchly people, upon the human sins of the hierarchy, upon the human religious infirmity. Too weak in our Church has been the expression of human activeness. And those, who by their religious outlook sanctioned and blessed this weakness of human activeness, are guilty of the weakening and fallen condition of churchly life. The infirmity of the Church is but only our own religious condition of infirmity, is only the projection outward of our religious impotence and lack of faith, the absence in us of boldness before the Lord. The activeness of the Church within historical life presupposes a positive religious strength on the human side of the churchly organism. The weakness and fallen condition of the Church, the abomination and desolation in place of the holy reflects the weakness and fallen condition of the churchly people, the faithlessness of man.

II.

The course of the Russian revolution has already made apparent, for us as Russians, one bitter truth, which it is necessary bravely to recognise. In light of the churchly consciousness of God-manhood there ought to be a reconsideration of the old position on the exclusive religiosity of the Russian people, a position supported both by the Slavophils, and by most Russian writers. To continue to assert this would be a terrible falsehood and lie. The prolonged weakness, the lack of independence, the paralysis of the Russian Church cannot but evoke a suspicious attitude towards the people of the Russian Church, and towards Russian religiosity. For a God-bearing people, in which the religious faith and religious conviction were strong, would not have allowed it, that its Church would have fallen into a condition so lacking in independence, it would rather have made its Church a determining power in its history. Formerly, during the time of St. Sergei of Radonezh, the Church indeed was a determining force in Russian history. But this was very long ago. Back then the people were otherwise. Back then the spirit of the times throughout all the world was different. From the time of the [Old-Ritualist or "Old Believer"] schism within the Russian Church the churchly people grew weak. The especial religiosity of the Russian people long ago already became subject to doubt. In the masses of the people this religiosity always was half-Christian and half-pagan. But even this age old semi-paganism of the Russian people is religiously nonetheless infinitely higher and more noble than the non-belief and nihilism, which all more and more is now engulfing the people. Better it is to worship some fetish, than merely oneself, one's own greed, one's own whims. The semi-enlightened intelligentsia subsequently has killed off the remnants of faith in the masses of the Russian people. And regardless how bitter it be, it needs to be admitted, that the Russian people now is less religious, than many of the peoples of the West, and that the religious culture in its soul is weaker. A total nihilism quite readily has taken hold upon Russian man. And it is time to stop seeing in this nihilism the reverse side of an exceptional Russian religiosity, which always had to be all or nothing. This nihilism is a terrible sickness of the Russian spirit, which it is necessary to stop idealising.

    We tend to grumble, that God has forsaken us and that His Church does not provide us graced aid, as might become a source of strength for us, might help us deal with the terrors of our time and save Russia from ruin. But we too much tend to forget, that we ourself have forsaken God, have done nothing for Him and for His Church, and that our culpability before Christ cannot but have an inner chastisement. There is the direction of movement from God to man; it always occurs within the Church and in it graced gifts come down from above. But there is also a reverse direction of movement, of a response, from man to God. The supreme religious life is always a meeting of the love of God with the responsive love of man. But here it mustneeds be admitted, that this responsive movement of human love is too weak and infirm in each of us and in all the Russian people. From whence issues such gloom and such terror in our life? In the very difficult moments of life we are ready to have recourse to God, we remember about Him and express pretensive demands on the Church, but we ourself do nothing for God nor do we want even in the Church to manifest any sort of sacrificial human activeness. In our luminous moments we believe, that Christ -- is our Redeemer and Saviour, and we are prepared to seek help in the love of Christ for us. But our own love for Christ, our response is weak and insignificant. Christ suffered for us, His blood eternally has been shed for the redemption of our sins, and eternally His Golgotha sacrifice is made for our salvation unto life eternal. But we do not want to ease the burden of Christ's sacrifice by our own sacrifice, our own love. We become almost indignant, that the Church should be silent and inactive, when we are perishing, when the people is perishing, we express vexation and we then demand the forceful intervention of Divine Providence, which still not so long ago seemed to us so unnecessary. But the people is perishing through its own betrayal, through its own spiritual fallenness, from its own baseness. God cannot and does not want to force evil a freedom upon people. Christ expects the free love of man. Many of us now, as Russian Christians, are powerfully afraid in the face of the approaching darkness, powerfully we loathe the sowers of darkness, but weak is our free love for Christ, and amidst us there is no brotherhood in Christ. Such a spiritual atmosphere cannot be favourable for the receiving of the graced help of Christ. And from the sidelines, from afar, it is impossible to assimilate anything in the Church and it is impossible to put forth any sort of demands for the Church. Each ought to be in the Church and make apparent by his own renewal the powers of the Church over our sinful world.

III.

Many an expectation has been bound up with the Sobor. But the Sobor can only be such, as the churchly people comprising it. If the religious energy in the people of the Church is weak, then it cannot be powerful even at a Sobor, for a Sobor unites and consolidates the religious energy, but it cannot create it ex nihilo, from human a vacuum. That especial grace, which is operative in a sobor, presupposes also an especial recoursing of man to God. The Sobor is convened at a difficult time of religious fallenness and religious betrayal by the Russian people, after a too long period of enslavement and paralysis of the Russian Church. It was not preceeded by any sort of churchly stirrings from below, in the life of the people, in the primary cells of the Church. The hierarchy of the Russian clergy have not been at the height of their calling, and within it for ages there has been nurtured passivity, the obedience to every authority, and there has not been worked out the proper consciousness of the dignity of the Church. The hierarchy of the Russian Church are not accustomed to speak powerful words, and they have not been true spiritual guides of the people. And this weakness of the Russian clergy has a sort of basis in the weakness of the churchly people themself. The people has both a secular power and the spiritual power such as corresponds to it. And so no one should be surprised and outraged, that the Sobor is not speaking sufficiently strong words about the fate of Russia. Strong words in the Church religiously presupposes tender hearts in a receptive people. Those having stony hearts tend to hear nothing and to learn nothing. Here is why in the missives and literary celebrations of the Sobor there is much of the conditional and the rhetorical, and in it there is too much a sense of the sham under the old churchly style. A new churchly style there is not, since there is not the religious energy, in strength akin to the religious energy of former times. And there is not the sense of a sufficiently deep connection between the Sobor and the people. And the Sobor remains insulated from the stormy ocean of the people's life. There is not the breath of a creative spirit at the Sobor, since there is not this vital breath within churchly mankind, in the churchly people. The Church wound up in a condition of complete disorder, and the Sobor has had to concern itself over arranging the existence of the Church, with a determining of its relation to the state, with the re-establishing of the Patriarchate, etc. But the Sobor has proven not atop those religious themes, which have tormented a minority of the Russian religiously hungering people. The Sobor can be an organ of churchly renewal, but it cannot itself create the churchly renewal.

A people can live a strong and healthy historical life only in the instance, where it possesses the strong and healthy spiritual foundations of life. Without these fundamentals the entire material life of a people gets shaken to pieces. The spiritual foundations in the life of a people can only be upon religious grounds, such only as provide for the discipline of soul. These grounds of disciplining the life of a people cannot be provided by abstract philosophy or an abstract morality. These spiritual grounds have to have their own symbolics. Symbolic signs have a magic-like effect over the soul of a people, and their abolition results in ruination. An army thus collapses, when its symbolic standards are destroyed. The religious life of the masses of the people is all bound up with cultic symbolism, and it is possible only in the Church, within the concrete historical Church, it can only be in churchly life. When the mass of the people falls away from the Church, it falls away also from all religious life, it loses the spiritual foundations of its life. The stirrings of sectarianism in the people, which to many might seem a transition to an higher type of religiosity, ends up in total rationalism and unbelief. The fateful process of the falling away of the mass of the people from the Church occurs also in the West. But the nurturing of the human soul there was such, that even after the loss of faith and falling away from Christianity, there has remained a strong residue in the form of norms of civilisation and culture, reflecting a secularisation of religious virtues. The Christian consciousness of the distinction between good and evil has remained with the peoples of the West and keeps them from complete collapse. In the Russian people, lacking in civilisation, and with a loathing for the common realm of culture, the falling away from Christianity instead results in the collapse of all the spiritual foundations of life, i.e. a purest nihilism. Russian man regards everything permissible, if there is no God, if there is no immortality. Dostoevsky revealed this. This was confirmed also by the Russian revolution. The so-called cultural values live but for few. We need to own up and admit, that the Western peoples up to the present remain religiously stronger, than the Russian people. Russians -- are religiously brittle and unstable. To certain select souls among the Russian people there is revealed a vastness and unboundedness, unknown to the peoples of the West, but in its masses, the Russian people is falling into nihilism. A spiritual renewal, the upsurge of spiritual energy can begin only after a process of repentance. In the "people", as bearers of the true faith, it is impossible to believe anymore. We have to turn inwards into ourself and from our own depths initiate churchly unity and creativity. A churchly populism is a lie and a pitfall. The select among the intelligentsia have to restore the faith of Christ among the people. But henceforth the churchly people will comprise a minority. To the old ways of religiosity there is no return. There is beginning instead a period of deliberative religiosity. The world is entering into a new period of growth.

Russia and GreatRussia

(1918 - #296)[1]

I.

The nucleus of Russia -- has been subjected to a maximum of disintegration in the process of revolution, it has become the hearth of Bolshevism. Many see in Bolshevism even a characteristically GreatRussian phenomenon. In the GreatRussian tribe there is a metaphysical sense of hysteria and tendency towards an impaired obsessiveness. And this has always been sensed in the GreatRussian sects, in the self-immolators [samosozhigiateli], in the khlysty, with genius it was reflected in the creativity of Dostoevsky, this belongs to the inability to admit of a relative right, in an exceptional tendency towards the extreme limits. LittleRussians [i.e. Ukrainians] are more reasonably inclined, in them is a strong instinct for self-preservation. In LittleRussia was not that spiritual tension, evoked by the Mongol Yoke, and always there too have been stronger Western influences. There is no GreatRussian nationality, just as there is no LittleRussian nationality, there is only a Russian nationality. But there exist tribal peculiarities, which to deny is impossible. And the GreatRussian peculiarities have proven fatal during the course of the Revolution. The powers, having assembled GreatRussia, has now abolished its own thousand-year work of building. The Russian Revolution is essentially distinct from all the former revolutions in the world, and most of all from the French Revolution -- it has broken up Russia, one and great, and it has grievously wounded the Russian national sense. Russia -- the greatest state in the world -- has crumbled apart in a few short months, having been transformed into an heap of rubbish. The work of the whole of Russian history, the work of assembling together Russia from the time of Ivan Kalita, the work of Peter the Great, the work of the whole of Russian culture -- of Pushkin and Dostoevsky -- is abolished, is destroyed, is

---

[1] ROSSIYA I VELIKOROSSIYA. Article originally published in the weekly Journal "Nakanune", № 3, apr. 1918, p. 4-5.

declared an unneeded, evil work. In the Russian Revolution has become apparent a dark reactionary element, hostile to historical progress, hostile to every culture of a grand style. Such a renunciation of one's own history, such a betrayal of a great historical legacy has never and nowhere ever been. This -- is a suicide of the people, a refusal of its great past and great future in the name of the greedy impulse of a given moment, from the nihilism, gripping the soul of the people. The presently living generation of the Russian people has not held up under the historical tribulation, it has failed to want to bear the sacrifices, which the great tasks demand, it has recoiled from the legacy received from its forefathers, belonging not to it alone, but to all the descendants. Russia great and united, the great and united Russian state, the great and united Russian culture, was created not by our generation, for behind it stand the exploits, the sacrifices and efforts of many generations, of all the whole Russian people over the expanses of its thousand-year existence.

The Russian people has its own singular and indivisible destiny, its own allotted portion in the world, its own idea, which it is called to realise, but which it can betray, which it can betray by the power of the human freedom inherent in it. The falling apart of the temporal connections, a complete rift between the past and the future, the desecration of the great graveyards and memorials of the past, the thirst for a destruction of everything former and departed, and not its resurrection for eternity, is a betrayal of the idea of the people, as a great whole, is a betrayal of the values, those non-transitory as regards its significance. The Russian people in a most responsible hour of its history has renounced the great in name of the small, the far-off in the name of the near, values in the name of a well-being illusory and transitory. Elevated to the place of Peter it is Lenin and Trotsky, to the place of Pushkin and Dostoevsky -- Gorky and some no-name people. Pushkin foresaw this possibility and with genius revealed it in "The Bronze Horseman" ("Mednyi Vsadnik"). There occurred the revolt of Evgenii, the hero of the "Bronze Horseman", against Peter, the revolt of childish people with their childish and partial interests against the great destiny of the people, against the state and against culture. And transgressed was the legacy of Pushkin:

> Beautiful art thou become, city of Peter,
> And unshakable stand, like Russia.
> Let the conquered element
> With thee become reconciled:

> Their enmity and captivity of old
> May the Finnish waves forget,
> And by vain spite not disturb
> The eternal dream of Peter!

The appearance of Pushkin himself only because Peter "had stretched Russia upon the rack", he brought it into communion with world culture and prepared for Russia the allotment of a great people. But the childish Evgenii did not want to accept the great destiny of the people, he recoiled with fear in the face of the sacrifices, which this destiny demands.

> Well tis, O wondrous builder!
> Whispered he, spitefully shuddering,
> Bye and bye concerning thee.

He could not reconcile himself with the ruin of his own personal and particular hopes, he could not take the clash of the great deed of Peter against his own childish deeds, against his own childish fate. A large part too of the Russian Intelligentsia have not reconciled themself with this, and now too the Russian people in revolt support it not. In the Russian Revolution and in the limiting Bolshevism expressing it there has occurred a revolt against Peter and Pushkin, the destroying of their creative work. The prolonged path of ideas of the Russian Intelligentsia from Belinsky on led to this revolt and destruction. The traditional Russian Populism always was hostile to having a great state and a great culture, it always demanded a casting down of values in the name of the people's well-being and the people's interests, the destruction of qualities in the name of quantity.

II.

Many naive and inconsistent people think, that it is possible to repudiate Peter and preserve Pushkin, that it is possible to make a split within the single whole destiny of the people and its culture. But Pushkin is inseparably bound up with Peter, and he recognised this organic bond. He was an imperial poet, that of a great-powered Russia. Dostoevsky too is bound up with the deed of Peter and with all the Peterburg period of Russian history. The peculiar Slavophilism of Dostoevsky did not prevent him from appreciating Peter differently, than the old Slavophils regarded him. Every hero of Dostoevsky -- is a Peterburg hero, of the imperial period of Russian history. Within their soul was reflected all the complexity of GreatRussia. The Russian great literature is bound up with the Russian great state. Russian literature told all the world about the existence of a single inseparable Russia, spiritually united by its one prevailing Russian language. The emanations of the GreatRussian language subjugated all the peoples, inhabiting Russia, by its spiritual strength they had to recognise the Russian literature as their own literature, and it evoked the awareness of belonging to a singular great literature of Pushkin and Gogol, of Dostoevsky and Tolstoy. But now this prevailing significance of the Russian tongue has been infringed upon. The first to infringe have been the Ukrainians, who are committing an apostacy from the people of Pushkin and Dostoevsky, casting aside the dominant Russian language in the name of a LittleRussian dialect, to divide up Russia. There are proving thus victorious the spirits of particularism, of provincialism, of separatism. These spirits, these little devils are destroying Russia and Russian culture the same, as is the big devil of internationalism. There is being denied from various ends the existence of Russia, of the Russian people, of the Russian idea. The Russian aspect is being replaced by partial and particularistic definitions, among which is to be also the GreatRussian. The GreatRussian people as it were does not want to exist any longer, it gives way to some new, some partial small formations, it is crushed from above by the abstract monstrosity of the Internationale, and from below by the egoistically-shallow national self-assertions.

Here is why it is necessary straight out and decisively to declare -- there is no sort of uniquely GreatRussian culture, just as there is no uniquely LittleRussian culture, there is only a single Russian culture, united by the Russian great language, which is not a mere GreatRussian language. There is no GreatRussian history, there is only a Russian history. The formation of a northern GreatRussian state and GreatRussian culture would be a completion of the falling-apart of Russia, brought on by the sickness being experienced by Russia, as to its idea of itself. That there are provincial-district peculiarities of GreatRussia and the GreatRussian tribe, just like with LittleRussia and the LittleRussian tribe, no one denies. But the nationality is Russian only, and not GreatRussian nor LittleRussian, the culture is Russian, the state is Russian, encompassing many provincial peculiarities. GreatRussia is but one central core of Russia, around which formed the Russian state and Russian culture, but the whole significance of this core is in this, that it has been the bearer of Russian might and the Russian cultural idea.

III.

Russia is not only a geographical concept, it is not only to be measured by its material expanses. Russia is first of all a spiritual concept, it possesses an inward scope, not attached to any sort of gubernias nor districts... Russia exists spiritually, as does the Russian people and Russian culture. It was conceived of within the thoughts of God, and its existence transcends our limited empirical existence. To destroy the intent of God is not within the powers of evil human caprice. No sort of material catastrophes can kill the spiritual existence of Russia. If from Russia there were to remain only one of the GreatRussian gubernias and within it only a small pile of people were to remain true to the spiritual existence of Russia and the idea of Russia, then even upon this small expanse, in this small pile Russia would continue to exist, and to pass over into the eternal. And banished even to the catacombs, we would continue to sense ourselves sons of Russia and would maintain fidelity to the Russian great culture of Pushkin and Dostoevsky, similarly like as, we would continue to sense ourselves Christians and sons of the Church, even after persecutions against the Church would drive us into the catacombs and there it behoove us to make our prayers. No sort of any external and material fate can compel us to betray the Russian idea. Fidelity to the end is possible even then, when there remains still no earthly hopes. And we would the sooner still lose all earthly hopes. Russia can still resurrect. Perhaps, it has to die, in order to resurrect to new life. In this is a great mystery of Christian redemption, existing not only for individual people, but also for entire peoples. Suffering is included in the Russian idea, as a necessary inner moment. Better there exist a suffering, sick and disorderly Russia, than such well-ordered and self-satisfied states of GreatRussia, LittleRussia, WhiteRussia and other areas, conceitedly regarding themselves independent totalities.

The falling-apart of Russia, the separation of its borderlands has placed the GreatRussian centre in a tragic position. And it is necessary to restore to health and reorganise the GreatRussian centre of Russia. This is fully justified and healthy a movement. But it ought not be made subject to the infectious sickness of going to pieces and provincial particularism. The colonisation of the borderlands, which transpired across the whole expanse of Russian history, was not some evil oversight, this was an inwardly justifiable and necessary process for the realisation of the Russian idea in the world. The so-called GreatRussia itself per se could not have and cannot exist, it would be consigned to a miserable and wretched existence. It is impossible to think of GreatRussia without the south, without its riches. And it is impossible not to see a terrible betrayal and a terrible transgression in the destruction of all the whole work of Russian history, in its realisation of the idea of Russia.

The Russian people has had to pass through an unprecedented humiliation and downfall, so that in it might be awakened a conscious national feeling and a conscious national activity. The persecutions starting up against the Church can have a tremendous significance in the restoring to health of the Russian people and its liberation from evil obsessions. The Revolution has infringed upon the holy and the saintly within the people's soul, it has disclosed its anti-Christian nature, as earlier it disclosed its anti-national nature. And if the Russian people be still alive, if it has not ultimately perished spiritually, then in it there has to awaken an acute religio-national feeling. A great people can worthily exist, if it remains in its depths faithful to the eternal spiritual basics of its existence. France even after all its downfalls and changes remains at its basis a France medieval, Catholic, chivalrous, in it has not died off finally that spirit, which stirred the ancestors of the present-day French in their crusades. This has been sensed during the time of the war. The Orthodox Church is something holy not only for every believer, but also for the great entirety, the great spiritual repository of Russian culture, the spiritual basis for life of the Russian people. With the Church also is bound up the Russian idea, the vocation of the Russian people in the world. If the Russian people were ultimately to cease being a Christian people, then it would lose its significance in the world. There has to be perceived the Russian idea, national and religious, leading us out onto the world stage, and surmounting every sort of isolating national provincialism. History moves towards unification, and not towards disunification, i.e. Christianity has to conquer the pagan particularism within it. The Russian idea, inspired by an universal Christianity, will conquer also the terrible devil of internationalism, -- that horrid distortion of the idea of the universal oneness and brotherhood of mankind.

The Recuperation of Russia

(1918 - #297)[1]

I.

Russia is grievously sick. This sickness has as its material symptoms the disintegration of our state and social organism. But at its core -- this is a spiritual, and not physical sickness. The visibly material roots of the societal life of the people lie are hidden in the invisible depths. These depths always involve the spiritual life. Russia cannot be healed by material means alone. Not only the body, but also the soul is sick. Russia's restoration to health presupposes first of all the healing of the spiritual foundations of life for the Russian people and the guiding circles of the Russian Intelligentsia. The false ideas of the Intelligentsia have yielded their poisoned fruit. The Intelligentsia now is bound to realise its sins and mistakes and convey to the people healthier ideas, in which there will be a rebirth of energy. We know, those which are the ideas that have devastated Russia, and we know, that the rebirth of Russia can only be with ideas the opposite to these. To the spirit causing the decay there needs to be opposed a spirit life-creating. At the groundworks of the material life of peoples therein lies the spiritual principles of their life, and this is a truth deeper, than that superficial truth, which is preached by economic materialism. Now even in the newspapers, which always have a disdain for religion, they have tended to state, that without religious foundations the state cannot exist. This truth is penetrating even the most positivist-minded parties. The economic life of the people, its economic productivity depends upon the discipline of the person, upon the spiritual aggregate of the people, upon its religious type. A series of scientific investigations has uncovered a connection between the economic developement of England and the religious upbringing of the English people. This connection has extended also to other lands. Catholicism in its own way, and Protestantism

---

[1] OZDOROVLENIE POSSII. Article originally published in weekly "Nakanune" № 6, (May) 1918, p. 1-2.

in another have nurtured the peoples of the West for an historical life, they have worked out the forging of character, necessary for the creation of culture. Catholicism is pervaded by the spirit of universalism. But it also developes and provides the discipline of person. In Catholicism there was always a dynamic energy, which has played a guiding role in world history. The Orthodox religious upbringing has been unfavourable for the historical life of peoples; it teaches little for a societal and cultural sense of building, it little disciplines the person. Orthodoxy [eternally wavers][1] between a maximalism of sanctity and the minimalism of a quite base manner of life. Russian Orthodoxy has created dazzling forms of sanctity and nurtured in the people the cult of sanctity and the saints. But very little was done for the developement in Russian man by way of integrity and responsibility, for the religious strengthening of energy in him, such as is needful for the creativity of history and culture. In the Russian religiosity there has always predominated features of the Eastern passivity. In this type of religiosity the personal principle has always been weakly expressed. The person is dissolved always and drowned in the natural collectivism, which is mistaken as being a spiritual Sobornost'-Communality. Many psychological features of the Russian Orthodox religiosity in a secularised form have passed over into the atheistic Russian Intelligentsia. The Orthodox upbringing has not left in the soul of Russian man solidly firm deposits in the form of the cultural virtues of the norms of civilisation, such as the religious upbringing of the West has left. Russian man all too easily passes over from the religious condition into a condition totally nihilistic. If there is no God and immortality of the soul, then for Russian man everything appears permissible. He can go about stark naked. The Russian Revolution has uncovered the deficiency of the religious upbringing of the Russian people. The spiritual foundation of the Russian state, of the Russian economy, of Russian culture is shaken apart with an extraordinary ease. The person within Russian man has been subjected to fragmentation, in it has been lost the spiritual centre. Faith has weakened within the Russian people, and civilisation within it has not been apparent. The Intelligentsia long since already has fallen away from the Christian faith and has been inspired by another faith, a socialistic faith in an earthly paradise to come. This faith has not provided any sort of discipline for the person. The

---

[1] Here a torn section in the newspaper -- with an approximate rendering.

unhealthy social dreaminess has led to a wantonness of the person. The socialistic faith has paralysed the sense of responsibility and begotten an immeasurable pretensiveness. Russian man jumps across from the primitive collectivism over into the socialistic collectivism. The schools of personal discipline and personal responsibility have been skipped by him. If the Orthodox faith of Russian man has not been fully favourable for personal creativity and historical activity, then a socialistic faith is anew likewise unfavourable for this. The Eastern aggregate of religiosity has tended to abase man, and when the religious faith has weakened, man is set free into a completely chaotic, undisciplined and sick condition. When I criticise the Orthodox religious upbringing, it is the Church least of all that I want to condemn, and the gates of Hell will not prevail against it, but I have in view the Russian type of religiosity as regards its human aspect. This type is weak in its defensive ability against passing over into a condition completely chaotic and nihilistic. But only the Church has taught the Russian people truth, and without the Church the Russian people cannot be saved from spiritual death.

II.

Russia's recovery of health first of all presupposes the transition of its guiding Intelligentsia circles away from its materialistic and atheistic mindset, which has led to moral decay and spiritual impairment, to pass over instead to a religious consciousness, i.e. to a renewal of the spiritual foundations of life. In the Russian religiosity itself there ought however to be revealed more active and more responsible an human principle. Worst of all would this mean, certainly, that I should want for Russia something on the order of a Lutheran Reformation. The Lutheran Reformation ran out its course in the West, and it corresponds neither to the character of the Russian people, nor to the historical task of Russia. But in Russia there is occurring a vast and sickly turn of events, and it cannot but be accomplished by religious reform, by a religious renewal. With quite some basis it can be said, that for Russian religious life it is necessary to seek further the unification of the Churches and the awakening of human activity within the Church. The fact, that at the Sobor there was not brought up the question about the reunification of the Churches, nor about the possibility of creative developement within the Church, indicates merely, that it gathered moreso to address the problems of a period of religious impairment for the people of the Church, rather than for a period of religious upsurge. But the upheavals from the Revolution cannot but lead to a religious deepening and awakening of religious energy within the people, worn down and disenchanted in the social promised lands. The religious recovery of health and the rebirth of the Russian Intelligentsia and the Russian people has to convey for itself something completely other, a more creative and more responsible attitude towards life.

At the societal foundation there has to be set other principles and other values, than those, which up til now have obtained for us. The Populist idea of reallocation and division, completely having taken hold amongst the Russian Intelligentsia and readily accepted by the Russian people, moving along the course of least resistance, has brought Russia to ruin. In the name of this idea Russia has been torn and broken up into shreds. This idea in practice, seemingly so exalted for a whole series of generations, has led to an all-Russia pillaging, to the plundering of the state and to famine. The egalitarian passion is leading us towards non-being. Russia and the Russian people need to be healed of its obsessive idea of division and leveling. This is a pernicious and basically anti-religious idea, since it has nothing in common with Christian love, and it has to be opposed by ideas of creativity and instincts of productivity. Upon this path more quickly would be fed the starving, than upon the paths of division and compulsory leveling. After the rapacious orgies of divisions and leveling in Russia there will arise a new differentiation, and the creative person will be of note. And after the terrible tribulations, inequality will be acknowledged as something good and of value, with its necessity for the spiritual and material advancement of the very masses of the people. Russia has been brought to ruin by the false idea of class and "the people", taken in the social-class sense of the word. This idea, which evokes emotion, is nigh close to being an obsession, and it is killing man in Russia, it has filled Russia with hatred and malice. In the name of service to a suffering "people" there was shredded the moral grounds of the relationship of man to man, there was rendered impossible the respecting within man of the image and likeness of God. The idolatrous approach towards the "people" has hindered the revealing and developing within it of the human person. Russia's recovery of health has to come from ideas completely the opposite: from the idea of the person, perceiving itself as a free, responsible and creative power, from the idea of the nation, as a reality, transcending all social classes, from the idea of the state and the idea of the

Church, as preeminent realities. Russia is in need of serious social reform, to create a new forging of the moral character of the Russian person. Russia is perishing because of its long idealisation of weakness. But it will be restored to health and be reborn from an idealisation of strength, for the acknowledging in strength of a moral and spiritual significance. Russia is perishing from an irresponsible social visionary-dreaminess. It will be restored to health by a social realism. Russia is perishing from its anarchistic instincts and anarchistic ideologies. It will be strengthened by instincts and ideas for statecraft. Russia is perishing from the Russian inclination towards collectivism, in which drowns the person, a collectivism variously religious and mystical, and otherwise materialistic and economic. For the recovery of health and rebirth of Russia, a certain dose of healthy moral individualism is necessary for Russian man. Russia needs the selectivity of qualitatively uplifted persons. In Russia there is need to push to the highest intensity for personal initiative and personal responsibility. Russia is perishing from the irresponsibility of Russian man, who leaves everything to the social medium, or to fate, or to an omnipotent autocratic government, or to an all-powerful proletariat. Russia will be restored to health by a lifting to the highest degree the responsibility of each person. Each has to accept upon himself as much as possible a greater responsibility and a lessening of pretensions, of demands. Russia is perishing from the irresponsible pretensions of everyone and from the weak sense of duty in everyone. It will be restored to health, when the awareness of duty in the Russian people wins out over the pretentiousness. With Russians the sense of duty has almost atrophied, and therefore their sense of right has become shaky. For the restoration of Russia to health there is necessary the strengthening in Russian people of a sense of duty.

III.

It is necessary to get free from the old Russian sentimentality, from a false feeling of sympathy and sentiment, from the excessive grip of the feelings and emotions, in which tend to drown the will and reason. It is necessary to cultivate in oneself more austhere virtues: with them only can history be made. Russia is perishing from an extensiveness of the Russian soul and Russian culture, and from a weak intensiveness of work. Russia will be restored to health and reborn by a greater intensiveness of the Russian soul and Russian culture, and by a lifting of the intensiveness of work. The spiritual discipline of the person has to bear with it also a discipline for work, the denial of which is shaking to pieces the economic life of Russia. Russia is perishing by bowing to the quantitative and by the denial of the independent significance of qualities and qualitative selection. It has to be restored to health and renewed by a respecting of qualities and qualitative selection and with a limiting of the power of the quantitative by qualitative principles. With this is connected the revision of our traditional attitude towards democracy, which includes in it great dangers, if it is not subject to any sort of higher qualitative principles. The Revolution has revealed, that the people itself does not with us desire a pure sovereignty of the people and too that it is incapable at the given level of developement. The people in the depths of its soul awaits such qualitatively select ones, who forcefully will lead it forward to more human a life. In the recovery of Russia to health it is necessary to surmount those Tolstoyan moral views, which are widespread in Russian society. These moral views have paralysed the creative energy of the Russian person, they have rendered powerless the Russian people in the hour of the world struggle and as it were snatched away the weapons from their hands, when the enemy has set foot upon our land. The Russian non-resistance, the Russian passiveness, the Russian pacifism -- are unhealthy phenomena. These are virtues not so much Christian, as rather Buddhist.

For the recovery of Russia to health it is necessary to surmount all the forms of Russian populism and its worship of the people, in whatsoever the form they be manifest, -- whether religious or materialistic, whether Slavophil or revolutionary. The Russian Revolution represents a finish to our Populism, both its triumph and its ruination, its bitter fruit and its end. This populist mindset always has been a great impediment for the transition of Russia over to an higher culture, and for the growth of Russian might. The populist mindset is incompatible with the setting of creative historical tasks. And in it there is a rebellious irresponsibility. The sentimental populist preachings have finished very badly, they have ended up with cruelty and brought misfortune to the Russian people. Those, who made the people's welfare their ideal, have wound up destroying the civil and economic foundations of the existence of the Russian people, all which can only be the sources of every manner of well-being. Those, who have created for themself a moral aura around the sorrows and sufferings of the people, have destroyed the moral foundations of the existence of the Russian people, without which man is rendered a wolf to his fellow man.

And thus always it happens with a false and irresponsible sentimentality, with a moralism, ripped off away from the deep spiritual and religious truths. We have tasks facing us of renurturing the character of the Russian people and the Russian person. In the life of the individual man there occur grievous crises, when he is nigh close to perishing. And after such a crisis the man tends to collect his spiritual powers, he pulls himself together and gets disciplined. Such a condition an entire people can also experience. If the Russian people even after such terrible tribulations and crises does not collect its spiritual powers and discipline itself, then it may perish, and fade from the historical scene. For the political and state rebirth of Russia there is necessary the spiritual rebirth of the Russian person, a re-invigoration of the Russian soul. This also would be a principle oriented towards a national renaissance. Russian man is perishing from lack of will. He lives primarily by feelings. And his thought process is too emotional and bound up with interests, he dislikes the objective, he is bereft of the pathos of objectivity. And the recovery of health for Russian man must be by way of the strengthening of the will in him; the recovery of health will be for him a strengthening of the powers of reason, in seeking objective truth. Through bitter and painful experience we know, what spiritual principles have led Russia to ruin. And we have to recognise, that to save it can only be by the opposite principles, only by a different spirit. This different spirit and these different spiritual principles have to be preached by the wide circles of the Russian Intelligentsia, who have to convey to the people antidotes to those poisons, with which they for a long time have poisoned it. Russia can be reborn and has to be reborn, it will still be great and powerful. But for this we need to be inspired with the idea of the greatness and strength of Russia.

The End of the Renaissance

(Regarding the Contemporary Crisis of Culture)

(1922 - #17 | 60,1)[1]

The school delineations of history into the ancient, the medieval and the modern, are becoming quickly outmoded and will be discarded from textbooks. "Modern history" is ending and there is beginning something unknowable, an historical epoch not yet named with a name. We depart from all the customary historical shores. This was acutely felt, with the onset of the world war. Then already to people the more far-sighted it became clear, that a return to that peaceful "bourgeois" life, which existed prior to the exploding of the catastrophes, would nowise occur. The tempo of historical changes: it is rendered catastrophic. And thus it always happens amidst the transitions to new historical eras. People, attuned to what is to come, long since already have sensed the onset of catastrophes and have seen their spiritual symptoms beneathe the external trappings of well-ordered and tranquil life. Events in the spiritual actuality tend to play out earlier, than in the external historical activity. In the soul of modern man something got shaken loose and into flux earlier, than the historical bodies were shaken loose and into flux. And thus, now that all the world is passing over into a state of flux, ought not to surprise those, who have been attentive to the stirrings of the spirit. In our days outwardly it would seem, that the old, the forever foundations of the European world have shaken loose. Everything in the European world is in an upheaval of

---

[1] KONETS RENESSANSA. Written 1919 in Moscow; first published as booklet in Peterburg, publisher Epoch, 1922 (Kl. № 17).
  Subsequently included in the Berdyaev-edited anthology, "SOPHIA: Problemy dukhovnoi kul'tury i religioznoi philosophii" ("SOPHIA: Problems of Spiritual Culture and Religious Philosophy") -- Berlin, Obelisk, 1923 (Kl. № 60,1); The "End of the Renaissance" comprised the 1st of 3 articles by Berdyaev within this Sophia anthology, p. 21-46.

displacement from its customary and ordered place. Nowhere and in nothing is there a sense of a firm footing of ground -- the ground is become volcanic with eruptions possible everywhere both in a material, and in a spiritual sense of the word. The Old Light, central Europe, is being supplanted by a New Light, by the far West, by America, and by the far East, enigmatic for us, the almost spectral Japan and China. And inwardly, in the old Europe, arise elemental principles, unsettling the foundations, upon which rests its ancient culture, connected still with antiquity. It would be myopically near-sighted to deny, that Europe has facing it the undergoing of a crisis of culture, of world historical a significance, and the consequences of which will extend into the remote and unknowable future. It would be naive and shallow to imagine, that it is possible simply to get a firm restraining grip by external means on that destructive whirlwind process, to which our old sinful world has been subjected, and to return, with but smallish changes, to that old life, which we lived prior to the world catastrophes of the war and revolution. We enter upon a realm unknowable and unavoidable, we enter joylessly, without bright hopes. The future is dark. We can already no longer believe in the theories of "progress", which so absorbed the XIX Century and on the strength of which would have to be begotten a future always better, more beautiful and more comfortable than the departing past. We are more inclined to believe, that the better, the beautiful and the consoling are to be found in the eternal, and not in the future, and that it was there also in the past, insofar as the past partook of the eternal and created of the eternal.

How does one make sense of this crisis of European culture, which long since already had started at various ends and which now is reaching its limit of outward expression? Modern history, having its conception during the era of the Renaissance, is ending. *We are experiencing the end of the Renaissance.* At the summits of culture, in creativity, in the realm of art and in the realm of thought long since already has been sensed the draining away of the Renaissance, the ending of an entire world era. The search for new paths of creativity has been also an expression of the end of the Renaissance. But that which occurs on the summits of life has also its own expression down lower. At the lowest levels of social life is being readied the end of the Renaissance. For the Renaissance signified an entire type of world perception and culture, and not merely one area of higher culture. Human life, and the life of peoples represents an entire hierarchical organism, in which are irreparably connected the higher and lower functions. There is a correlation between them, of what happens at the heights of spiritual life and in the lower levels of the material life of society. The end of the Renaissance is the end of an entire historical era, of the whole of modern history, and not merely of certain forms of creativity. The end of the Renaissance is an ending of that humanism, which served as its spiritual basis. The humanism was however not only a revival of antiquity, not only a new morality and the stirrings of science and art, but likewise a new sense of life and a new attitude towards the world, giving birth to the dawning of modern history and defining this history. Here though this modern new sense of life and the new attitude towards the world is coming to an end, exhausting all its possibilities. The paths of humanism and the paths of the Renaissance course towards their endpoint, there being nowhere further to go along these paths. The whole of modern history has been an inner dialectic of self-revealing and self-negating of those humanistic principles, which were lodged at its basis during its birth. The humanistic sense of life long since already has lost its freshness, it has gone old and can no longer be experienced with such a pathos of feeling, as during the days of the young turbulence of humanism. Within humanism have been discerned destructive contradictions, and a sickly scepticism has further sapped the humanistic energy. The faith in man and in his autonomous powers has become shaken. It was an impetus to modern history, but modern history has shaken this faith. The free rovings of man, knowing no sort of higher power, not only have not reinforced his faith in himself, but ultimately have weakened this faith and have shaken the awareness of the human image. Humanism has not reinforced, but has the rather debilitated man -- such is the paradoxical result of modern history. In his self-assertion man has lost, and has not found himself. If European man had tended to enter into modern history, full of self-hoping faith in himself and his creative powers, if everything had seemed to him at the dawning of this history a matter of his artifice, to which he would set no bounds nor limits, then he is emerging out of this modern history and entering into an uncertain era in a great dismay, with a tattered faith in his own power and the might of his artifice, exposing the danger of ultimately losing the core of his own being as a person. Man is emerging from modern history in not pretty a shape, and there is a tragic lack of correlation between its beginning and its end. Too many an hope have proven broken. The very image of man has gone murky. And spiritually sensitive people are wont to turn back to the Middle Ages, to find there the true foundations for human life and anew to rediscover man. we live in an era of spiritual decline, and not of spiritual ascent. We cannot repeat anew the words of Ulrich von Hutton [1488-1523], spoken by him at the dawn of modern history: "spirits have awakened, joyous to be alive". The aim of modern history has not succeeded, it has not glorified man, as it sought to glorify him. The promises of humanism have not been fulfilled. Man has grown infinitely weary and is ready to consider every sort of collective, in which ultimately disappears already the human individuality. Man cannot endure his desolateness, his aloneness.

* * *

In the Renaissance human powers were set free and their sparkling play created a new culture, formed modern history. The whole culture of that world era, which in the textbooks is termed modern history, was a testing of human freedom. The new man himself wanted to create and to order life without any higher help, without Divine sanction. Man got torn away from the religious centre, to which he had been subordinated during all his life in the Middle Ages; he wanted to go his own self-set, willful way. At the beginning of this path it seemed to the new European man, that for the first time was being discovered man and purely human activity, suppressed in the medieval world. And til now there are still many, blind in their humanistic faith, who are wont to think, that humanism at the onset of modern times has revealed man. but in our era, stressed out over all the contradictions of life and having delved into all its principles, some begin to understand, that in the self-conceit of humanism was a fatal error and self-deception, and that in the very primal basis of humanistic faith lay concealed the possibility of a self-negation of man and his downfall. When man tore himself away from the spiritual centre of life, he tore himself away from the depths and passed over onto the periphery. His removal from the spiritual centre has made man all more and more superficial. Having become bereft of the spiritual centre of being, man has lost also his own spiritual centre. Such a decentralisation of the human being was destructive of his organic order. Man ceased to be spiritual an organism. And then, at the very periphery of life, there arose pseudo-centres. The subordinate organs of human life and their subordinate functions, having freed themself from the organic connection with the true centre, then arrogated to themself being the centre of life. And from this, man has been rendered all more and more superficial. During the XX Century, at the height of the humanistic era, European man emerges already terribly empty and exhausted. He does not know, where is the centre of his life, and he has no sense of depth beneath him. He consigns himself to trivial an existence, he lives as though in two dimensions, as an inhabitant of the surface of the earth, not knowing, what is over him and what is under him. And there is an enormous difference and an enormous lack of correlation between the beginning of the humanistic era and its end. At the very beginning of the free erupting of the powers of the new European man, it marked a splendid and unprecedented flourishing of human creativity. Never yet, it would seem, had man attempted such a creative ascent, as during the Renaissance era. Back then had begun the free creativity of man, his free artistry. But he was still nigh close to the spiritual wellsprings of his life, he had not yet withdrawn so remotely from them onto the surface level of life. The man of the Renaissance was twofold a man, belonging to two worlds. And this tended to determine the complexity and the richness of his creative life. It is impossible still now to posit the beginning of the Renaissance exclusively as a rebirth of antiquity and as a return to antiquity. In the Renaissance were quite many Christian elements and medieval principles. Even such a typical man of the XVI Century, as Benvenuto Cellini [1500-1571], a man of the latter portion of the Renaissance, was not only a pagan, but also a Christian. And therefore the Renaissance was not and could be totally pagan. People in the Renaissance found nurture in the spirit of antiquity, they sought in it the wellsprings of free human creativity and images of perfective form, but they were not people of the spirit of antiquity. These were people, in the souls of which raged storms from the clashing of pagan and Christian principles, those from antiquity and those from the medieval. In their souls could not be the classical sereneness and wholeness, forever lost, and their artistry could not create fully finished, complete, classically perfective forms. The soul of Christian man had become infected with a sense of sin, a thirst for redemption and the striving for another world. This was a finish to the ancient, pagan world. And with an inner inevitability was the transition to Christianity. Within history is possible a revival, a reorientation towards past creative eras. But no sort of a revival can become a going back, the restoration of an old, already bygone creative era. The principles of bygone creative eras, to which the revivals resort, act in very complex a new medium, in very complex an interaction with new principles and tend to create types of culture dissimilar to the old types. And thus the Romantic movement at the beginning of the XIX Century was not a return to the medieval, and in it the medieval principles, towards which the Romantic turned, became refracted within the soul of man, in the experiencing of a complex new history, and produced results very dissimilar to the medieval. However much Friedrich Schlegel [1772-1829] may have recoursed to the medieval, he was very dissimilar to medieval man. Thus too, people of the Renaissance were not similar to people of the ancient world, to the Greeks and the Romans. They had the experiencing of the Middle Ages, they were baptised, and the water of Baptism could not be wiped away by any sort of recoursing to antiquity, by any sort of their superficial paganism. The paganism within the European Christian world could never become deep, it was always superficial. It could render complex the soul of European man, but could never create wholeness. And so complex was the soul of the people of the Renaissance, that they could not be rendered into good pagans. This duality and complexity of people of the Renaissance can be studied in the creativity and in the fate of a central figure of the Quattrocento -- Botticelli [1445-1510].

The Renaissance began back in the deep Middle Ages and its first foundations were fully Christian. The soul of medieval man, a Christian soul, awakened to creativity. This creative awakening occurs already during the XII and XIII Centuries. It is marked by a fragrant blossoming of sanctity, an high ascent of the spiritual creativity of man. It is accompanied by a flourishing of mysticism and the Scholastic philosophy. The medieval rebirth created the Gothic and the painting of primitives. The early Italian Renaissance was a Christian revival. St. Dominic and St. Francis, Joachim of Flora and Thomas Aquinas, Dante and Giotto [di Bondone, 1267-1337] -- this is already the genuine Renaissance, the rebirth of the human spirit, of human creativity, not having lost the connection with antiquity. In the era of the Renaissance, medieval and Christian, there was already a creative attitude towards nature, towards human thought, towards art -- towards the whole of life. The early Renaissance in Italy -- the Trecento [1300-1399] -- was the greatest era of European history, the highest point of ascent. The arisen creative powers of man were as though an answering revelation by man to the revelation of God. This was a Christian humanism, conceived from the spirit of St. Francis and Dante. But the great hopes and prophecies of the early Christian Renaissance were not realised. Much in it was before its time. Man still faced a passing through a great dividedness and falling away. He had to put to the test not only his own powers, but also his own weakness.

The Quattrocento was predominantly an era of twofold a separation. And then occurred the stormy clashing of Christian and pagan principles, leaving its imprint upon all the creativity. In the creativity of the Quattrocento there was not a perfect conclusion, in it were searchings of stronger attainments. But there is a special fascinating aspect to this incompleteness and unconcludedness. The twofold separation of the Quattrocento speaks to the impossibility of purely a pagan revival within the Christian world. And the very unsuccess of the Quattrocento -- is a great unsuccess. The formal attainments of the creativity of the Cinquecento [1500-1599], of the high Roman Renaissance, produce the impressions of greater completeness and larger successes. But this formal perfection and success -- are illusorily classical. Nothing truly classical, fully complete upon the earth, is possible in a Christian world. And it is only by chance that all the creativity of the Cinquecento rapidly led to a moribund academism and decline. The twofold separation spiritually within the Cinquecento passed over into a falling away, into a deadening of the Christian soul. The humanists of the eras of the Renaissance did not break ultimately with Christianity, they did not come out against church, but they were religiously cool and indifferent people. Their hopes were on a revealing of man, ultimately oriented towards this world and turning away from the other world. And they lost the depth. Man as revealed by them, the man of modern history, had no depth and was compelled to wander life on the surface. On the surface, free from the connections with the deep, he would test out his creative powers. He does much, but comes to exhaustion and a loss of faith in himself. Not by chance did human individuality in the XVI Century instigate and approve of terrible transgressions. Humanism liberated human energy, but it did not spiritually elevate man, it left him spiritually empty. This was already foreordained in the very fundamentals of humanism. At the primal basis of modern history lay a rift of man from the spiritual depths, an estrangement of life from its meaning. There was a fatal lack of correlation between the doings of St. Francis and Dante and the doings of the XVI and XVII Centuries. The Renaissance created much that is great, it introduced many values into human culture. And yet however it did not totally succeed, its very task has proven impractical. The early Christian Renaissance did not succeed, and the late pagan Renaissance did not succeed. From the Renaissance has proceeded the impetus of modern history. Within history there always occurs a tragic lack of correlation between the creative task and the factual realisation. In modern history has been realised something altogether different, than what the first humanists and the creative people of the Renaissance dreamt of. Did they think, that the consequence of their new sense of life, their severing from the spiritual depths and the spiritual centre of the Middle Ages, their creative beginnings -- would lead to the XIX Century with its machines, with its materialism and positivism, with its socialism and anarchism, with the exhaustion of spiritual creative energy? Leonardo, perhaps, the greatest artist of the world -- is a culprit in the machinisation and materialisation of our life, its loss of soul, its loss of higher meaning. He himself did not know, what he was preparing. The Renaissance, on the strength of its spiritual foundations, in its consequences had to undermine itself. The Renaissance set free the creative powers of man and expressed the creative upsurge of man. In this was its truth. Still however it disconnected man from the spiritual wellsprings of life, it denied the spiritual man, who alone can be a creator, and it asserted exclusively the natural man -- the slave to necessity. The triumph of the natural man over the spiritual man in modern history had to lead to the desiccation of creative powers, to the end of the Renaissance, to the self-destruction of humanism.

The Renaissance was a great commencing of the search for the free playing out of human powers. Man fancied, that perhaps the whole of life should become a matter of his artifice. Man had recourse to that nature, which in the Middle Ages he sensed as set in evil. He sought in nature the wellsprings of life and of creativity. And at the beginning of his turning towards nature he had a sense of nature as alive and inspiring. From nature was snatched away its curse. They ceased to fear its demons, which had so frightened medieval man. Modern man imperceptibly entered into the cycle of natural life. But he did not become united with nature inwardly. He spiritually subjected himself to its materiality, but remained disconnected from its soul. The Renaissance held concealed within it the seed of death, since at its basis lay the destructive contradiction of humanism, which exalted man, it ascribed to him immeasurable powers and at the same time it saw in him merely a limited and dependent being, not knowing spiritual a freedom. In having exalted man, humanism deprived him of God-likeness and enslaved him to natural necessity. The Renaissance, based upon humanism, revealed the creative powers of man as a being natural, and not spiritual. But natural man, sundered off from the spiritual man, does not possess an infinite wellspring of creative powers, he becomes drained and winds up on the surface aspect of life. This also finds expression in the final fruits of modern history, which have led to the end of the Renaissance, to the self-negation of humanism, to the emptiness of the superficial and to having lost the centre of life, to the desiccation of creativity. The free play of human powers could not continue endlessly. And in the XIX Century this creative playing out already was ending, and there is no longer to be sensed a surfeit, there is felt instead a sparseness, with the difficulty and burden of life on the increase. The basic contradiction of humanism deepens and reveals itself across all the expanse of modern history. It leads to humanism passing into its opposite. The humanism of L. Feuerbach and Auguste Comte -- preachers of the religion of mankind -- possesses already little in common with the humanism of the era of the Renaissance. It goes farther, it deepens the basic contradiction of humanism, but in it there is no longer still a creative abundance of powers, and in it is felt the approach of inner catastrophe. The Middle Ages preserved the creative powers of man and prepared for their splendid flourishing in the Renaissance. Man entered into the Renaissance with the medieval experience, with the medieval preparation. And everything authentically great in the Renaissance had a connection with the Christian Middle Ages. But now man is entering into an unknowable future with the experience of modern history, with its preparation. And he enters into this era not full of creative powers, as during the era of the Renaissance, but exhausted, debilitated, dispirited, empty. And upon this it is proper to ponder deeply.

* * *

Humanism had its first, its most creative and splendid manifestation in the Renaissance. And the whole creative and humanistic era of history comes from the spirit of the Renaissance, can be termed Renaissance. In this, its first manifestation, humanism recoursed to the eternal sources of human creativity -- to antiquity. But currently it is impossible still to think, that the creative disclosing of humanism within the Renaissance occurred from a return to paganism, from a pagan relapse within the Christian world. This -- is a superficial and erroneous view. Humanism took nourishment from antiquity, but it was a new phenomenon, a modern phenomenon, and not of ancient history. The creative activity of man was already lodged within Catholicism. And all the great European culture, the Latin foremost of all, was at its basis a Christian and Catholic culture. It was rooted in the Christian cultus. Catholicism itself was already saturated in antiquity and having transformed it, it assimilated into itself the ancient culture. The ancient culture lived throughout all the Middle Ages within Catholicism and was carried over by Catholicism into modern times. Hence only did the Renaissance prove possible into modern times. And the Renaissance was not directed, as was the Reformation, against Catholicism. There was in Catholicism an immense human activity, it was manifest in papism itself, in the world power status of the Catholic Church, and in the creation of a great medieval culture. And in this, Catholicism was always distinct from Eastern Orthodoxy. Catholicism not only led man to heaven, it created beauty and glory also upon the earth. In this was the great secret of Catholicism: the striving for heaven and life eternal creates beauty and fashions might within the temporal earthly life. The asceticism of the medieval Catholic world was a fine preparation for creativity, it preserved and concentrated the creative powers of man. The medieval asceticism was a great school for man, it provided a great forging of spirit. And the European man of modern history lived, by what he had acquired in this school, and he owed it all to Christianity. No sort of new a spiritual school, forging and disciplining of spirit, would European man been able to have. He grew his powers, he applied himself and he exhausted himself. And if spiritually he remained alive, then it was thanks exclusively to the Christian foundations of his soul. Christianity continued to live on in him in a secularised form and did not permit him reaching the point of dissolution.

    Humanism, at the onset of its appearance, was still nigh close to Christianity, and it drew upon two sources: from antiquity and from Christianity. And it was creative and beautiful as regards its results in the measure of its proximity to Christianity. When humanism became sundered from the spiritual depths and made its transition over to the superficial surface level, it began to degenerate. Humanism did not immediately begin to assert man without God and against God. Not such was the humanism of Pico della Mirandola and many of the theosophists of the Renaissance era. But in humanism was concealed already the seed of the falling away and apostacy from God, and from it sprouted that humanism of modern history, which now gives forth its final fruits -- the negation of man. Only that humanism, which was lodged within Christianity and draws upon it whilst not disclosing to the end its revelation, -- such affirms man and creates beauty. It only is connected with antiquity. Humanism, having broken away from Christianity, in the final end breaks away also from antiquity and is destructive to man twice over, severing both his ancient and his Christian groundings. This will become apparent as regards the final fruits of humanism. The sacred tradition of culture by a thousand threads is connected with the sacred tradition of the Christian Church, and a total break with this tradition leads to a downfall of culture, to a lowering of its quality. The exhaustion of the Renaissance in modern history, the weakening of its creative energy was through its estrangement both from Christianity, and from antiquity. And those partial revivals, which modern history knows of, were from a return both to Christianity and to antiquity. Modern European man lives by ancient and medieval principles, or he becomes exhausted, becomes empty and collapses. The twofold splitting of the Renaissance, an inner fracture, experienced by the man of the Renaissance, constitutes the theme of modern history. *In it unfolds the self-destructive dialectic of humanism -- the affirmation of man without God, and against God, the denial of the image and likeness of God in man which leads to the denial and destruction of man, and the assertion of paganism against Christianity which leads to the denial and destruction of antiquity.* The image of man, the image of his soul and body, was formed by antiquity and by Christianity. The humanism of modern history, having broken with Christianity, departs from the ancient foundations of the human image and shatters the human image. The Reformation was another manifestation of that process of modern history, which formed the Renaissance; it likewise was begotten by the humanistic movement, by the uprising of man in modern history. But the Reformation was formed by a different racial temperament, than was the Renaissance, formed by the temperament of the Germanic race, northern, remote from the sun, bereft of plasticity in artistic giftedness, but endowed with its own unique spiritual depth. The breath of modern spirituality was conveyed into European culture by the Germanic race. The Renaissance however was not an uprising and protest, it was creativity. In this -- was the beauty of the Renaissance, in this its eternal significance. The Reformation however was moreso an uprising and protest, than religious creativity, it was directed against the primacy of religious tradition. The creative aspect was in the German mystic -- a great manifestation of spirit, and not the Reformation, which proved religiously fruitless. There was in the Reformation initially much that was Catholic, it was a phenomenon within Catholicism. Luther was a rebellious Catholic monk, in him boiled Catholic a blood. And everything profound and genuinely religious in the Reformation was connected with the eternal truth of Christianity, was a thirst for the cleansing, the renewal and rebirth of Catholicism itself. There was with Luther a moment, one only moment of great truth. Rightful was his thirst for spiritual freedom. But in his denial he strayed from the path. The rebellion and protestation of the Reformation engendered that process of modern history, which led to "enlightenment", to rationalism, to revolution, to the contemporary positivism, socialism and anarchism. The "Enlightenment" of the XVIII Century was a far-removed offshoot of the Renaissance, a manifestation of the spirit of humanistic self-assertion. But in the "enlightenment" dries up the creative spirit, in it the Renaissance becomes desiccated. The rationalism of the XVIII Century -- is a phenomenon deeply distinct from the creative era of the Renaissance, but genetically is connected with it. The Enlightenment is an inward punishment of the Renaissance, a retribution for the sins of humanistic self-affirmation, the sins of betrayal of the Divine wellsprings of man. Thus, the Bologna school was an inner punishment of Michelangelo and Raphael, a deadening of spirit, lasting into the XVI Century. Upon these paths the creative spirit becomes desiccated. Savonarola also was concerned about the false paths of the Renaissance. The Renaissance creatively became exhausted, lost contact with the sources of its sustenance, but it engendered a stormy historical movement, in which there would no longer be so great a creativity. The French Revolution, the positivism and socialism of the XIX Century -- all these also are consequences of the humanism of the Renaissance era, and the drying up of the creative spirit of the Renaissance. All this -- was a transformation of humanism.

* * *

By the time of the Renaissance there had accumulated a profusion of the creative powers of man. It produced a splendid blossoming and then was supplanted by the whole of modern history. Man was indebted to the medieval asceticism for this creative abundance. The powers of man had been preserved. But the man of modern history proved ungrateful to that spirit, which had guarded his powers. In modern history the creative abundance was expended and the powers of man became spent. It was fated for the European man of modern history to live out all the humanistic illusions to the end, in order to arrive at the height of the historical era at self-destruction, at a shaking to the very foundations of the human image. Everything compels one to think, that the earthly historical path of mankind is but a testing of the human spirit, merely the preparation for some other sort of life. All the accomplishments of history themself represent great unsuccesses. The Renaissance did not succeed, the Reformation did not succeed, the Enlightenment did not succeed, and there did not succeed revolution and the growth of its illusions based upon the Enlightenment, nor will there succeed the socialism emerging in the world. In the historical life of mankind there is never realised the goals that man has set himself. But there are created great values, which man has not consciously set himself. The Renaissance did not succeed, it did not achieve perfection and completeness in earthly beauty and earthly joy through a rebirth of antiquity. But it did create great values amidst its quite unsuccessful impressions of immortal beauty. Suchlike were the unsuccesses of the Quattrocento. From the Renaissance has derived modern history. But also the Reformation, and the Enlightenment, and the French Revolution, and the positivism of the XIX Century, and socialism, and anarchism -- all this was already a disintegrating of the Renaissance, a disclosing of the inner contradictions of humanism and a gradual impoverishment of the creative powers of man. The farther removed from the Renaissance that European man has gotten, the more his creative powers have dried up. His greatest upsurges have been connected with a return to the medieval, to the Christian sources, as for example, at the beginning of the XIX Century in the Neo-Romantic and Symbolist movements. There are strong grounds to think, that the creative powers of man can be revived and that the image of man can be restored only through religiously ascetic an era. Only such an era, returning to the spiritual wellsprings of man, can concentrate the powers of man and avert the dissolution of his image. For this, man has to arrive at the heights of his modern history, assaulted anew from all sides by the danger of being done in by demons. It is impossible to arrive at any sort of new Renaissance after the exhaustion and squandering of the spiritual powers of man, after the prodigal wandering the wilderness of being, after the shaking of the very image of man. If one offer an analogy, we then are approaching not to a Renaissance, but rather to the dark aspect of the Middle Ages and we shall have to pass through a new civilised barbarism, and a new religio-ascetic discipline, before there dawns a new era, of a yet unknowable Renaissance. But has it all thus already passed away into historical life, that there will not anew awaken the creative powers of man directed at the other world? The powers of natural man are finite. The self-conceit of natural man leads to his downfall, since he abjures the wellsprings of life. Natural man, estranged from the spiritual man, creates an illusory life, he becomes captivated by illusory well-being. There mustneeds be admitted a law of life, that man in this finite and relative earthly life creates beauty and value only then, when he believes in another life -- infinite, absolute, immortal life. An exclusive orientation of man to this finite and death-bearing life, in the final end saps the creative energy of man, leads to smugness and self-gratification, renders man empty and superficial. The true creator can only be the spiritual man, having his roots in the infinite and immortal life. But humanism has repudiated the spiritual man, has betrayed eternity for time and affirmed the natural man upon the finite surface of the earth. And the net result is this, that in having too high an opinion of himself, the natural man is defenseless against the natural elements and the spirits of the earth besetting him from all sides. The human visage cannot be guarded by the powers of the natural man alone. It presupposes the spiritual man. Without moments religiously ascetic, limiting and setting distance, subordinating the lower to the higher, the existence of the person is unthinkable. But modern history has been posited upon the illusion, that there is possible a flourishing of the person without these religio-ascetic moments. Modern history, in deriving from the Renaissance, has reflected the growth of individualism. But individualism has proven ruinous for the human individuality, destructive of the person. And we are experiencing a tortuous end of individualism, such as is bereft of all spiritual groundings. Individualism has desolated the human individuality, has made the person bereft of form and content, has disintegrated it. Suchlike are the laws of life: the human individuality is reinforced, flourishing and with content, when it admits of supra-personal and supra-human realities and values and subordinates itself to them; the human individuality is weakened, desolated and in decline, when it denies them. Individualism renders aimless all the directions of the will of the human individuality, as having no direction, no purpose. And to this void of content man has been brought by a false humanism; it has transformed the human soul into a desolation. But within humanism has been posited a great task, the great theme concerning man.

This theme reveals itself throughout the tragic dialects of modern history. And the appearance itself of humanism cannot be considered purely a loss, purely evil. This would be static a view. The humanistic effort has also a positive significance. Man within his destiny had to undergo the experience of it. Man has had to proceed through freedom and in freedom to acknowledge God. In this -- is the meaning of humanism.

* * *

Those transformations of humanism, which occur in the second half of the XIX Century and early XX Century, represent an ultimate extinguishing of the Renaissance, the ultimate exhaustion of its creative powers. the free and dazzling interplay of abundant human powers comes to its end. The spirit of the Renaissance has followers no longer. Everything spiritually significant and creative at the end XIX and XX Century was oriented upon the religiously Christian wellsprings of man. The pagan currents of this period are superficial and in them it would be vain to seek the spirit of antiquity. Trans-cultural man is experiencing not a Renaissance, but rather a decadence. Decadence is one of the forms of a finishing off of the Renaissance. At the summits of the culture of modern history man has grown exhausted and broken, grown wasted under too complex a burden, stripped away from the religious centre of history. Man cannot endure the abject loneliness, into which the humanistic historical era has plunged him, -- he becomes disoriented from this aloneness, he invents substitutes and surrogates for spiritual community and spiritual connections, creates for himself pseudo-churches. The extreme sociologism of world feeling and world awareness is also the reverse side of a profound lack of community, the profound aloneness of man. The inwardly disunited atoms attempt externally to unite with one another. The extreme sociologism, in its philosophic sense, is merely the reverse side of extreme individualism, the atomisation of human society. The human individuality arising in the era of the Renaissance lived still within organic spiritual entities and was nourished by them, it did not itself represent a broken away atom. It played freely and created, having still beneathe it a spiritual grounding. It did not cleave so tightly to socialness for the saving of itself from aloneness, from spiritual and material starvation. The socialness, transformed into a religion, represents an indisputable end of the Renaissance, the exhaustion of the human individuality, such as arose during the era of the Renaissance. Extreme individualism and extreme socialism -- are two forms of the ending of the Renaissance. And in both one and the other becomes shaken the human individuality, grows dim the human image. Abstract humanism, severed off from the Divine groundings of life, from spiritual concreteness, has to lead to a destruction of man, of the human image. The human image, as in every authentic reality, obtains in but a spiritual concreteness, a conjunctedness, in which the Divine unity embraces within it all the human multiplicity, and it instead disappears when in abstraction, is torn away. The humanistic process in modern history reflects a transition of man from spiritual concreteness, in which everything is organically conjuncted, towards instead an abstracted rupturedness, in which man is transformed into an isolated atom. In this departure from concreteness towards abstractedness the man of modern history has hoped to receive his emancipation, to affirm his individuality, to discover creative an energy. Man desired to become free, to draw away from that grace of God, which restored the image of man and spiritually nourished it. Humanism is a denial of grace, a separation from grace. But only life manifest as concrete is in grace, life external to grace -- is abstracted a life. Upon this basis arise all the illusions of humanism. That which has seemed to man as a liberation, as a finding of his individuality and creative energy, turns out rather to be an enslavement of his spiritual being to the natural cycle, and is a downfall of the person. This is ultimately to be sensed at the heights of the humanistic process in modern history. Humanism has dealt with man not concretely, not in his spiritual connections and conjunctive aspects, but abstractly rather, as a self-sufficing atom of nature. This path did not immediately obtain during the era of the Renaissance. But it has become all more and more evident across the span of modern history. This path inevitably has had to lead to an extreme individualism and an extreme socialism, as the two forms of atomisation, of the abstraction-derived disintegration of society and the person.

    The two dominant figures of the thought of the modern era -- Fr. Nietzsche and K. Marx, with acute a genius have been manifest as the dual forms within the self-negation and self-destruction by humanism. With Nietzsche humanism negates and destroys itself in individualistic a form, with Marx -- in collective a form. An individualism that shoves all aside and also an abstracted collectivism are begotten of one and the same principle -- the drawing away by man from the Divine basics of life, a falling away from concreteness. Nietzsche -- was the child of the humanism of modern history and also its victim; he is a retribution for its sins. In the life's fate of Nietzsche, humanism passes over into its opposite. Nietzsche senses man, as a shame and lowliness, he thirsts for the surmounting of mere man, his will is directed towards the superman. The morals of Nietzsche do not acknowledge the value of the human person, it breaks off with humanism, it preaches fierceness towards man in the name of the superman goals, in the name of the remote and distant, in the name of the heights. The superman substitutes in Nietzsche for the loss of God. He cannot and does not want to hold on with, as he entitles it, the human all too human. In the superman individualism of Nietzsche the image of man perishes. The image of man likewise perishes in the supra-human collectivism of Marx. Marx spiritually derived from the humanistic religion of Feuerbach. But in it, though in otherwise a manner, humanism passes over into its opposite, degenerates into anti-humanism. Marx sense the human individualness, as something deriving from the old bourgeois world, and he demands the surmounting of it within collectivism. The morals of Marx do not admit of the value of the human person -- he makes a break with humanness, and he preaches fierceness towards man in the name of the collective, in the name of the coming socialistic Zukunftstaat, the coming future state of things. The collective substitutes in Marx for the loss of God. He likewise already cannot and does not want to hold on to man, to the human; in the collectivism of Marx, truly, there is something inhuman and contra-human, in it vanishes the human person, grows dim the human image. The collectivism of Marx does not admit of the human individualness with its infinite inner life, which the humanism of Herder and Goethe not so long still before had acknowledged and acclaimed. Marx -- is a legitimate child of modern history the same, as is Nietzsche. And in both the one and the other transpires the end of the Renaissance, but differently. Nietzsche was oriented towards the Renaissance, he wanted to live the creative upsurge of the Renaissance, but he had passed already into a new dimension, in which there was already no returning to the basics of the historical Renaissance. Marx was ultimately repelled by the Renaissance, as being something from the "bourgeois" world, and he thirsted for a new realm, in which would be impossible such creative exuberance. Neither the matters of Nietzsche, nor the matters of Marx, have reflected a triumph of man, they were merely an exposure of humanistic illusions. After them has become impossible already the sentimentally pretty humanism, has become impossible already the emotional rapture with humanistic ideas, impossible the naive faith in humanness. Man likewise gets denied by Max Stirner, who inflicts strong blows on humanism. The average human realm, the realm of self-contented humanness will decompose and be overcome; there will emerge the end-points, the limits, the bounds of man will be transgressed. Upon anything human it will be impossible to hold on. Together with this, there ends also the Renaissance, which was a creative playing out of the powers of the average human realm, with the pretense to create a perfective, happy and beautiful life within humanistic a realm. This humanistic realm has been shattered by modern history. The broadening and spreading of the humanistic realm, its democratisation -- is a fact fatal for its existence. Creative humanism can exist only in a small and select portion of human society. Thus it was also during the era of the Renaissance. The Enlightenment and Revolution have produced a levelling process within the humanistic realm and have prepared its inward disintegration. The Renaissance was based upon inequality and was made possible, by virtue of inequality. The thirst for equality, gripping modern mankind, reflects an ending of the Renaissance. This -- is a matter of entropy, a turnabout, within social life.

* * *

The end of the Renaissance is historically accompanied by the disintegration of the entire organism, of everything organic. In the Renaissance was still preserved an organic mode of life. Life still was hierarchical, as also is all organic life. Back then there had only still begun the process of secularisation which, in the final end, had to lead to the mechanisation of life, to a falling away from the whole organic order. At the beginning, during its first stages, this secularisation was adopted as a liberation of the creative powers of man, as joy at their free playing out. *But the human powers, issuing forth from organic a condition, inevitably are made subject to mechanical a condition.* This was not immediately apparent. For a certain while man lives in the illusions, that he is free from organic bounds and from being mechanically chained down. This interim period, when the modernly new European man senses himself free from the organism and not subject as yet to mechanism, holds sway during the historical Renaissance and its close during the XVII and XVIII Centuries.

At the summits of European society play out human powers, torn off from the depths, but not yet with a sense of their subjection to a levelling mechanical aspect. But in Europe during the XIX Century occurred one of the most terrible revolutions, the likes of which have been most trying for mankind throughout all its history. Into human life victoriously entered the machine and disrupted all its entire organic rhythm. The machine disrupted all the age-old order of human life, the organic connection with the life of nature. The machinisation of life destroys the joyfulness of the Renaissance and renders impossible the creative exuberance of life. The machine murders the Renaissance. It readies the modern historical era, an era of civilisation. Culture, full of sacred symbolics, withers. People of the Renaissance did not know and did not understand, that they were readying in the world a triumph of the machine, that the ultimate egress from the Middle Ages had to lead to a realm of the machine, to a replacement of the organic order -- by the mechanical one. The organic order of life is hierarchical, i.e. cosmic. In the cosmic organism the parts are subordinated to the whole, maintaining connection with the centre. In the organism the centre projects the goal of life to the parts. Every organism is an hierarchy. When parts separate themself from the whole and cease to serve the goals, situated in the organic centre, they imperceptibly subjoin themself to a lower nature. The era of the Renaissance took pride, in what it discovered not only in man, but also in nature. People of the Renaissance were oriented towards nature with favourable an attitude, they studied nature and copied its external forms; they ceased struggling against the sinfulness of nature, which people of the Middle Ages had waged. And the Renaissance orientation towards nature in its first period was accompanied by a rapture over natural forms and joyousness over natural life. But the soul of nature in its depths was not discerned by the people of the Renaissance, since in the Renaissance had not arisen the spiritual man, to whom only can be revealed the inner essence of nature, there had arisen rather the natural man, oriented towards the surface aspect of natural life. Only the few mystics and theosophists of the era of the Renaissance penetrated deeply into nature. In the Renaissance was begotten not only an artistic, but also the scientific-cognitive attitude towards nature. In this was an enormous significance of the era. And from which has come the historical triumph of science as regards nature, which prepared the way for the great technical discoveries of the XIX Century and led to a dominance of the machine over human life. The historical end of the Renaissance thus has proven incongruent with its beginning. The initial joyous attitude towards nature became reborn into an awareness of the inevitability of a grievous struggle with it by way of the machinisation of life. Our era already no longer imitates the forms of nature, nor seeks in them the forms of perfection, as did the era of the Renaissance, it instead leads a struggle against nature, it is inwardly alienated from it, nature is regarded by it as a dead mechanism, and it places the machine in between man and nature. The attitude towards nature by modern civilised man is also an ending of the Renaissance. The inner dialectic of the Renaissance towards nature leads to a self-negation of this attitude. The end of the Renaissance is murderous to nature, just as it is murderous to man. This -- is an immanent tragedy of modern history, which has to be overcome. The machine was prepared for by the Renaissance, and the machine kills the Renaissance, destroys the beauty of life, such as is given birth by the creative exuberance of human powers.

The consequences of the incursion of the machine into human life have proven incalculable. They have extended also into the spiritual life of man, upon all his creativity. Science and art have proven fascinated by the process of machinisation, upon them also is the imprint of that splintering of the organic wholeness, which the machine produces in all the spheres of life. Modern art in its most recent trends breaks with the Renaissance, since it ultimately also breaks with antiquity. In modern art, oriented exclusively towards the future and worshipping the future, they tend to be given over to a laceration of the human body and its eternal forms. In it ultimately perishes the human image. Futurism, which represents rather more serious a symptom, than might seem, destroys both the image of nature and the image of man, i.e. wants ultimately to abolish the effect of the Renaissance, which was all oriented to the eternal forms of nature and of man. Futurism represents an ending of the Renaissance. It is destructive of the accomplishment of Leonardo and Michelangelo. Futurism marks an ultimate breaking away from antiquity, from the principles of the eternal forms in art. The eternal perfective forms, sought by the Renaissance, have two sources: nature and antiquity. Futurism repudiates both the one and the other source. It seeks out its images of perfectness not in nature and not in man, but in the machine. Futurism is situated in the grip of a process of the machine-like calculation of every natural and human entity. The futurists are consumed with process, a concept of which they themself do not understand, since the level of their awareness and knowledge is too low.

It remains indisputable, howsoever futurism be appraised, that the image of man, the soul of man and the body of man perish within futurist art, lacerated and torn by inhuman whirlwinds, from which remain mere scraps. The Cubism however of such a great artist, as Picasso, takes into account the human body and dissembles the artistic image of man. The futurist art, in which the trendy currents of tomorrow replace those of the present day, goes still further in the laceration of the human image. The solidly firm boundaries of all the natural forms are transgressed, everything passes over into everything, man passes over into inanimate objects; newspaper declarations, pieces of glass and footwear flash into every natural form and shatter it. The forms of the human body -- are ancient forms, and their destruction is also an ultimate breaking with antiquity. Futurist poetry likewise decomposes the human soul, it inserts into the human soul those selfsame newspaper declarations, bits of glass and footwear, it enslaves the soul to the noise of automobiles and aeroplanes. The dissolution of the human soul had begun already in Impressionism. The soul of man has broken down into mere moments. Ultimately is lost the centre of soul. The self-affirmation of man leads to a perishing of the human image. Man becomes estranged from his eternal spiritual sources, he becomes subject to the pulverising grip of time. Futurism is begotten of man's self-affirmation. But futurism represents an ending of humanism, its self-negation. In futurism man becomes lost to himself, ceases to realise his own uniqueness. Man dissipates off into the inhuman whatever masses. In futurism man becomes enslaved to inhuman collectives. And not by chance, futurism has proven akin to the most extreme forms of social collectivism. The process of being done with and dissolution of the Renaissance, the tearing apart and destruction of the human image can be observed in the creativity of A. Bely, one of the most remarkable artists of our era. A. Bely has an affinity with futurism, but in much he stands heads above all the futurists. In the creativity of A. Bely transgressed are all the natural boundaries, all the creative forms; in it man and the whole cosmos are blown apart by maelstrom whirlwinds. It is impossible to find the human images within this creativity. The human image becomes indistinguishable already from that of a lampshade, from that of the avenue of a large city; it sinks away into the cosmic infinitude. Characteristic of our era, the creativity of A. Blok is a transgressing and demolishing of all the ancient and Renaissance forms, it signifies a departing from nature, from man and from God. This -- is an ending of the Renaissance, the end of the humanistic era. Contemporary art is all and all more caught up in this ending of the Renaissance, with the perishing of human and natural forms. Into it intrude barbaric principles, it rends and claws with barbaric sounds, barbaric gestures. The dynamism of this art tears at the cosmic rhythm. The positivism of the XIX Century was already an indisputable principle contributing to the end of the Renaissance. Positivism was begotten by the spirit of the Renaissance, but in it this spirit became exhausted. In positivism there is no longer the creative exuberance of knowledge, no joyful rapture in knowledge unwravelling the secrets of nature. Positivism is already a recognition of the limitedness of human powers, is a staleness regarding knowledge. For positivism the secrets of nature become shut. Positivism clips the wings of man. In the era of the Renaissance the knowledge of nature was the result of a joyful approach to knowledge. A typical man of the Renaissance was Pico della Mirandola -- the direct opposite to all positivism. And the pathos of Leonardo was the opposite to positivism, but in it already was lodge the seed, from which positivism would grow. In all the areas of the Renaissance was borne the seed of its own perishing, its own end, dissimilar to its beginning, in the area of knowledge, just like it is everywhere. The positivism of A. Comte has two opposite sources, which from various sides are destructive to the spirit of the Renaissance: the rationalism of the Enlightenment and the spiritual reaction within the French Revolution. A. Comte was a distorted Catholic, a Catholic in reverse. In him are many medieval elements, in him occurs a return to medieval hierarchicalism, to organisation and authority; he wants anew to subordinate both knowledge and life to the human spiritual centre and to halt the intellectual anarchy of modern history. It is not by chance that A. Comte so highly esteemed J. de Maistre [1753-1821] and learned much from him. These medieval and religious, though in distorted a form, principles of the Comtean positivism did not become prevalent in the further developement of positivism and even were vexing for the positivists. But in the most "positivistic" of the elements of positivism they represent a reaction against the spirit of the Renaissance. Positivism quickly began to go into decline and evidenced the exhaustion of the creative principles of cognition. At present already it is impossible to seriously speak about positivism within philosophy. In European philosophy long since already holds sway not positivism, but rather critical philosophy, acknowledging Kant as its spiritual father. Critical philosophy can be investigated, as one of the latest phases of the Reformation.

In contemporary German gnosseology the Reformation issues forth with its final, intellectually most refined fruits. If at the start of modern history, in the sources of the Reformation that there occurred an uprising of man, wherein man proclaimed his right to self-determination, then at the ending of modern history in the intellectual consequences of the Reformation man wants as though to be freed of himself in the process of cognition, to overcome himself, to rise above every anthropomorphism. Contemporary German philosophy in the figures of Cohen, Husserl and many others leads first of all to a struggle against anthropomorphism; it is contemptuous towards man, it sees in man the source of relativity and instability in cognition, it aspires to a non-human cognitive act. In critical gnosseology there is something reminiscent of Cubism, it likewise decomposes the organism of human cognition into categories, just like Picasso and others dissolve the human body into cubes. This is a process of analytic splitting apart and dismembering organic wholeness. The image of man perishes within critical gnosseology. It likewise itself signifies an ending of the Renaissance, in it likewise become exhausted and expires the Renaissance spirit of creative exuberance. And within cognitive knowledge, upon the paths of its autonomous self-determination and self-affirmation, man arrives at self-negation and self-destruction. Having lost the spiritual centre and the spiritual wellspring of his being, man loses also himself, his eternal image, he betrays himself into the grip of something non-human. In the medieval Scholastics it is far easier possible to find man, than in the gnosseological Neo-Scholastics. Contemporary gnosseologism -- is the product of an era of spiritual decline. One and the same process of the self-destruction of man upon the groundings of humanistic self-assertion occurs everywhere. Within theosophy is dissolved, is dismembered and flattened down the integral image of man; it is betrayed away to rending by astral whirlwinds. Contemporary theosophy is hostile to man and his creative exuberance, in it there is nothing of the Renaissance. It likewise is destructive of the personal principle, just like positivism is destructive of it, just like the gnosseological criticism is destructive of it. Theosophy no more believes in the reality of the human person, than does the very typical materialistic naturalism. It is likewise a materialistic naturalism destructive of man, transferred over to the spiritual realms. Such theosophic figures of the era of the Renaissance, as Paracelsus, loftily exalted man and set before him creative tasks. But such theosophic figures of our era, as Steiner, though he also calls himself an anthroposophist, ultimately enslave man to a cosmic evolution, the meaning of which is incomprehensible, and the path revealable by it for the self-accomplishment of man is not a creative path. The theosophy is a denial of God, the anthroposophy is a denial of man. Man -- is merely a passing transitory moment of cosmic evolution, he has to be surmounted. The theosophic trends of our era reflect the exhaustion and dying down of the creative exuberance of man. In them the human individuality is quenched and the free play of its powers ceases. Man loses his inward spiritual centre and instead seeks it in complex and disintegrative cosmic forces. The theosophic knowledge contemplates the corpse of nature and the corpse of man. All the prevailing intellectual life of our era stands under the standard of the ending of the Renaissance. The naturo-scientific character of education reflects a break with the Renaissance. Even the solidity of the Renaissance physico-mathematical world-concept of Newton has been shaken by modern physics. The teachings about entropy, about radioactivity and the falling-apart of the atoms of matter, about the law of relativity, represent a genuine physical apocalypsis.

* * *

Characteristic to our era are socialistic tendencies. They pervade not only economic and political life, but also the whole of modern culture, all contemporary morality; they exemplify a particular feeling in life. Socialism is merely the reverse side of individualism, merely the result of the collapse and dissolution of individualism. Upon the paths of the atomisation of society lies in wait socialism, as an inner dialectical inevitability: a certain sort of principle has to lead to socialism. Both socialism, and individualism are alike hostile to an organic world-sense and world-perception. Socialism is merely a vivid symptom of the end of the Renaissance, within it ends the free play of the exuberant human powers of modern history. The human powers are connected and needfully subsumed to a centre, but the centre is no longer religious, but instead social. The pathos of the creative individuality is replaced by the pathos of a compulsory organised collective effort. The human individuality becomes subject to collectives, to the masses. The image of man is overshadowed by the image of the impersonal collective. In regard to every creative exuberance there is established suspicious regulation. The centre of gravity in life is transferred over to economics, whereas for the sciences and the arts, the higher creative culture, the spiritual values, everything gives way to "superstructures". Man is transformed into an economic category. Socialism possesses humanistic a basis and humanistic a source; it is begotten of the humanism of modern history, it would have been impossible without the self-affirmation of man and without the transferring of the centre of gravity of life to human welfare. But within socialism the humanism comes nigh to self-negation. Man with his individual soul and his individual fate is subordinated to non-human collectives. The proletarian class consciousness is no longer humanistic, but rather an anti-humanistic consciousness. Man is replaced by the class. The value of man himself, of his individual soul and his individual fate is denied. Man is transformed into a means for the societal collective and its growth. Humanism gives birth to humaneness, as a special moral outlook. This humaneness was a moderateness within the human realm. It becomes dislodged within proletarian class socialism. Socialism reflects an end to humaneness, the exposure of its illusions. Socialism is an exposure of everything lofty, connected with humanism -- the humanistic sciences and arts, the humanistic morals, the whole humanistic culture. Crumbled into ruins is the whole humanistic "superstructure" and laid bare is its basis, its foundations. This basis and foundation proves to be economics, class economic interests. And man, indeed, torn away from the spiritual centre and the spiritual wellsprings of life, has then a material basis of life, and all his exaltedness -- is a false exaltedness. Man dissolves into interests, the singular human nature -- the humanness -- vanishes, becomes stratified into class natures. Marx was right for the bourgeois European society of the XIX Century -- in him the humanness, which Herder regarded as the goal of history, was subjected to dissolution, and in him the economic basis plays too great a role, and the whole of higher culture too reminiscent of a "superstructure". Economic materialism too passively reflects the condition of human society, its spiritual apostasy, its enslavement to the material side of life. This -- is a self-dissolution of humanism, an ending of the Renaissance, the ruin of illusions, the illusions of a realm of "humanness", the exposing of the impossibility for man to be a creator after he has torn himself away from God, has rebelled against God. As regards its cultural consequences, socialism represents an indisputable ending of the Renaissance. The spirit of socialism is a death of the spirit of the Renaissance. For socialism, human life is no longer still a matter of the creative human art, the free play of exuberant human powers.

Nicholas Berdyaev

The Renaissance -- was aristocratic, it created themes, which were free from the oppressive necessity of life. For socialism, proclaiming a death sentence to all aristocratism, human life is a matter of grievous necessity and collective toil. In the socialistic order there does not remain any sort of a free creative exuberance, unregulated and not subordinate to the material centre. The Renaissance was a proclamation of the rights of man, of human individualness, first of all in the sciences and the arts, in the intellectual life, and then also in political life. Socialism opposes to the rights of man the rights of the collective, which is not humanness, and in which are delineated inhuman features. In the collectivism, to which humanism has arrived in its historical dialectics, there are abolished all the rights of man, there is abolished freedom of thought itself, from which began the Renaissance. All thinking is rendered compulsory and subject to the social faith-confessing centre, i.e. what occurs is a return to the Middle Ages, but already not on religious, but rather material a basis, on the basis of materialistic an anti-religion. The end of the Renaissance signifies the exhaustion and destruction of the personal principle within human societies, the principle of personal creative initiative, personal responsibility, with instead a triumph of the collective principle. The end of the Renaissance is to be noted not only within socialism, but also within anarchism, no less characteristic of our era. Modern history, born of the Renaissance, is characterised by a rich flourishing of the state aspect; from this it is distinct from the Middle Ages, when the state awareness was weak. The medieval period was international, universal. The modern period -- is a period of national states. At the basis of modern states rests an humanistic self-assertion of man, initially in the monarchies, then in the democracies. But the humanistic national states of modern history bear within them the seeds of self-negation. A purely humanistic rule by the people undermines the religious grounding of the state and creates the basis for its anarchistic collapse. Anarchism is an ending of the Renaissance era state. In anarchism occurs not only a self-negation of the humanistic state, but also the self-negation and self-destruction of the personal principle, the ultimate crash of individualism within its apparent extreme triumph. The personal principle has been very closely and inseparably connected with the state civil principle. In anarchism, however, there win out all the same collective mass elements, hostile both to the person, and to the state. The spirit of anarchism -- is not creative a spirit, in it is a malicious and suspicious hostility towards all creative exuberance. Anarchism wants as though to destroy everything, such as was created by the Renaissance. In it is a retribution for the falsity of humanism. When the thirst for equality takes hold in human societies, -- there is an ending of everything of the Renaissance, of all creative super-abundance. The pathos for equality is a pathos of envy towards foreign a being, towards different a being, is the impossibility to affirm a being in itself. The passion for equality is a passion for non-being. Modern societies are in the grip of a passion, which transfers the centre of gravity of life from a creative assertion of a being in itself into a jealous denial of being in an other. Suchlike only can be infirm a society.

* * *

The Renaissance began with an affirmation of creative human individualness. It has ended with a denial of creative human individualness. Man without God ceases to be man -- in this is the religious meaning of the inner dialectics of modern history, the history of the flourishing and ruin of humanistic illusions. Left alone to himself and inwardly empty, man is rendered a slave not to higher and supra-human, but rather to lower and non-human elements. The human spirit becomes quenched and in the grip of whatever non-human spirits. The formation of the religion of humanism, of the ultimate making a god of man and the human is also a beginning of the end of humanism, its self-negation, the drying up of its creative powers. The flourishing of humanness has been possible only as long, as man has sensed and conceived as set beneathe him and in his depths are principles loftier, than he himself, whilst he has not torn himself away ultimately from the Divine groundings. In the era of the Renaissance there was still with man this feeling and this awareness, there was not yet an ultimate rift. And European man across the whole span of modern history has not ultimately broken away from his religious groundings. Therefore also only has been possible humanness, has been possible a flourishing of human individualness and human creativity. The humanism of Goethe had religious a basis, it was bound up with faith in God. Man, bereft of God, is plunged into the impersonal and inhuman element, he is rendered a slave to an inhuman necessity. In our era there are no longer the free, the Renaissance-like playing out of human powers, which created Italian art, and Shakespeare, and Goethe. In our era at play are non-human powers, elemental spirits, oppressing man and darkening his image. Man now has not gotten free, but is rather fettered by inhuman elements and by their designs they entangle man. Man has received his form, his image through the actings of religious principles and energies. The chaos, in which the human image has gotten lost, cannot be overcome by human powers alone. The formation of the human cosmos has been likewise a matter of Divine powers. The man of modern history, towards its end having fallen away from the Divine powers and refusing their assist, falls anew into chaos, renders unstable his image, shakes its form. The creative energy of man does not become concentrated, but instead dissipated. The formation of a reservoir of creative energy presupposes a preservation of the forms of the human image, presupposes boundaries, distinguishing man from the formless lower stages. This reservoir becomes ruptured, and the creative energy from it gets poured away. Man becomes bereft of his forms, his boundaries, he becomes defenseless against the poor infinity of the chaotic world.

If we are experiencing the end of the Renaissance in the modern currents of art, in futurism, in the modern currents of philosophy, in critical gnosseology, in theosophic and occult currents, and finally, in socialism and anarchism, which occupy so dominant a place in the societal life of our era, then likewise we are experiencing it also in the religious and mystical trends. In certain currents the humanism inwardly decays and in this process of decay is also pulled in the image of man, the forms of man. In other currents the humanism gets surmounted by higher principles, and man seeks the salvation of his own image, of his forms, in the Divine groundings of life. But in both the one and the other instance the historical Renaissance ends and there occurs a return to medieval principles, at one point the dark principles of the Middle Ages, at another its luminous principles. In humanism there has been a betrayal of sanctity, and in this betrayal man is being paid back in his history, suffering one disappointment after another. There is now beginning a process of the barbarisation of European culture. After the refined decadence at the summits of European culture there had to occur an incursion of barbarity. And in this regard the world war will have had a fatal significance for the fate of Europe. Cultural and humanistic Europe has exposed and rendered itself defenseless against the inward and outward incursion of barbarity. The dull grumblings of a subterranean barbarity have long already been heard. But the declining European bourgeois society has done nothing for the saving of the old and eternal sanctities of Europe -- it has lived unconcerned, reckoning upon an endless prosperity. The twilight of Europe is beginning. (Vide my article, "The End of Europe", written in the year 1915 and appearing in my anthology of articles entitled, "The Fate of Russia".) European societies are entering upon a period of senility and dotage. There can ensue a new chaos among peoples. There is possible a new feudalisation of Europe. In the history of mankind one cannot have progress exist along straight an upward line, a progress in which the people of the XIX Century so believed, to the extent that they could make of this faith a religion itself. In the history of societies and cultures are to be noted organic processes, in which there is a period of youth, followed by maturity and old age, there is a flourishing and then decline. We are experiencing not so much the beginning of the new, as rather the end of the old. Our era is reminiscent of the end of the ancient world, the fall of the Roman Empire, the exhaustion and desiccation of Graeco-Roman culture -- the eternal wellspring of every human culture. The modern trends in art are reminiscent of the loss of perfective ancient forms and the barbarisation of that era. The social and political processes of our time are reminiscent of those processes, which occurred during the era of the emperor Diocletian, the processes leading to the feudal enslavement of man. The religio-philosophic and mystical searchings of our time are reminiscent of the end of Greek philosophy, and thence the mystical searchings -- the thirst for an incarnated god, for the appearance of a god-man. Our era approaches spiritually nigh to that of the universalism and syncretism of the Hellenistic era. A great angst envelopes the better part of mankind. this -- is a sign of the onset of a new religious era.

* * *

Humanism has to be lived out to its end. Its paths are now passing, and it has to be surmounted. The inner, the self-destructive dialectics of humanism has provided enormous an experience to mankind. And a return to that rather more simple a condition, in which European man prior to the humanistic era of modern history was situated -- is impossible. Modern history has rendered twofold, has aggravated and exposed everything in man. In this is its chief meaning, and not in the positive conquests and achievements. The searchings of modern history provide great a significance. In humanism something was opened, a great theme posited. Yet now is ending the life of man sundered off from the religious centre and inevitably there is a searching for a new religious centralisation of life, i.e. a spiritual immersion at depth. Man in all the spheres of his creativity cannot further remain on the surface level, on the periphery of being. He has to either begin movement into the depth, or ultimately become winded and empty. From the great upheavals and tribulations of our time has to occur a deepening. European man is being faced with an ultimate freeing from the illusions of humanism. It becomes already impossible to go the middle way. There is occurring a split into two opposing sides: upwards and downwards. By many indications we are approaching a new historical era. To an era, similar to the yet dark Middle Ages, to the VII, the VIII and IX Centuries, prior to the medieval rebirth. And many of us tend to feel ourself akin to the last Romans. This -- is a noble self-feeling. Something of this feeling awakened also in the new Christian soul of Bl. Augustine, when danger threatened Rome, when the barbaric world burst forth. So also at present: many of us can sense ourself the final last and faithful representatives of the old, the Christian, European culture, threatened by great dangers both inward and outward. Through such a danger there is possible a new, though rather too barely civilised, barbarisation necessary to carry forth with the unfading light, as once it was carried by the Christian Church. Only in Christianity is ultimately revealed and preserved the image of man, the visage of man. Christianity has freed man from the demons of nature in the pagan world tearing at him, freed him from demonlatreia. Only the Christian redemption has provided man the possibility to lift himself up and stand on his feet; it severed man from the entrails of the elements of nature, into which man had fallen, to which he had become enslaved. the ancient world readied the form of man; in it awakened the creative energy of man, but the human person was still not freed from the grip of the natural elements, the spiritual man was not yet born. The second, the not of nature, but rather of spirit, birth of man has occurred in Christianity. And humanism received its true humanness from Christianity, it cannot find it only in antiquity. But humanism in its developement tore away the humanness from its Divine roots. And here, when humanism has ultimately torn man away from the Divinity, it has turned also against man, and has begun to destroy the human image, because man -- is in the image and likeness of God. When man desired merely to be in the image and likeness of nature, only the natural man -- he made himself subject to the lower elements and lost his true image. Man is anew torn at by demons, and he is powerless to withstand and resist them.

The spiritual centre of the human person has been lost. *In this turning of humanism against man -- is the tragedy of modern history.* In this -- is the cause of the fatal failure of the Renaissance and of the inevitability of its end. People in our time are wont to say, that Christianity also has been a failure, has not realised its expectations, and upon this they base the futility and meaninglessness of a return to it. But the fact, that European mankind has not made a realisation of Christianity, has distorted and betrayed it, cannot be valid an objection against its truth and veracity. Christ also did not promise the realisation of His Kingdom upon earth, He said, that His Kingdom is not of this world, He predicted prior to the end a paucity of faith and of love. The untruth of Christian mankind is human an untruth, human a betrayal and failure, human a weakness and sinfulness, and not Christian an untruth, not an untruth of God. All the righteous indignation against Catholicism can be directed against Catholic mankind, but not against the genuine sanctity of the Catholic Church. Man first distorted Christianity, he besmirched it with his own failings, and then ultimately he revolted against it and betrayed it, blaming the Christian truth itself as responsible for his own sins and failings. The creative spiritual life is not a matter of God only, but also of man. To man has been granted great freedom, and it involves a great testing of the power of his spirit. God Himself as it were expects from man creative activity and creative results. But rather than this, than directing his creative image towards God and devoting to God of the free abundance of his powers, man instead has squandered and wasted his creative powers in self-affirmation, in a return to going in circles upon the periphery. In this there is much to be sad over. It seems, that the beautiful is fading and dying, that it is impossible still to have the free playing out of human powers, that the free human individualness is come to an end. But it would be shallow and cynical to surrender to grief. The capacity for a renewal of human nature -- is infinite. But to believe in a spiritual rebirth of man and human creativity is possible now only through a deepening of Christianity, through an ultimate revelation of the image of Christ in man, through a fidelity to the Christian revelation concerning the human person. Within Christianity there has not yet been fully revealed its anthropology, its revelation concerning man is not yet concluded. In this is the meaning of the positing by modern humanistic history of the theme concerning man. But modern Europe has gone off afar in its betrayal of the Christian revelation concerning the human person and has surrendered itself to the lacerations of elemental

tempests. And thus it has allowed within its culture a chaotic principle, which can plunge Europe into a period of barbarity. But no sort of tempests, no sort of chaotic elements can extinguish the light of the Christian revelation concerning God, concerning man and concerning the God-Man.
The gates of hell will not prevail over it. And therefore the source of the light will abide, irregardless how great the manifest darkness. And we ought to sense ourself not only like the last of the Romans, faithful to the old and eternal truth and beauty, but also oriented towards the unseeable and coming day, when will rise forth the sun of a new Christian Renaissance. Perhaps, it will be in the catacombs and happen merely for few, perhaps, it will be only at the end of the times. To us it is not given to know. But assuredly we do know, that the eternal light and the eternal beauty are invincible against any sort of darkness and chaos. The victory of quantity over quality in this finite world over the other infinite world is always illusory. And therefore without fear and despondency we have to enter from the waning day of modern history into a medieval night. May there fade away the false and deceiving light!

* * *

My theme is European, and not Russian. Russia has remained on the sidelines of the great humanistic movement of modern history. Within it has not occurred the Renaissance, the spirit of the Renaissance is foreign to Russian people. Russia, to a significant degree, has remained the East and remains the East even in our day. Within it has always been insufficiently revealed the personal principle. In it has not been the resplendid blossoming forth of the creative human individuality. But the Russian people have adopted for themself the final fruits of European humanism in the period of its self-dissolution and self-destruction, when it ultimately has become directed against the human image. And no other people has gone to such extremes and destructions of the human visage, of human rights, of human freedom. No other people has displayed such hostility towards creative exuberance, such malicious jealousy towards every flourishing of human individualness. In this is something terrible for us, as Russians. We are living through in very extreme a form the end of the Renaissance, not having experienced the Renaissance itself, not having the great remembrance of past creative profusion. The whole entirety of

Astride the Abyss of War and Revolutions

Russian great literature has not been Renaissance-like in its spirit; in it is not sensed a profuseness of powers, but rather the strain of sick a spirit, a tortuous search for salvation from ruin. In Pushkin alone has been something Renaissance-like, but his spirit has not prevailed within Russian literature. We now experience a futurism hostile to the Renaissance, not having experienced the creativity of the Renaissance; we experience socialism and anarchism hostile to the Renaissance, not having experienced the free flourishing of a national state; we experience philosophic and theosophic currents hostile to the Renaissance, without having experienced a Renaissance rapture of knowledge. To us has not been given to experience the joyousness of a free humanity. In this -- is a peculiarity of the bitter Russian fate. But with us there has to be an anguishing over a spiritual deepening and the seeking of the Divine grounding of man and of human creativity. Is there possible for us a religious sanctioning of creativity, which in Russian religiosity never obtained? With this is connected the possibility of a spiritual rebirth of Russia. Can we, as Russians, be capable of at least sharing in a Christian Renaissance? But for this we would have to undergo a great repentance and cleansing, and by fire we would have to burn away the superstitions and idolatry of a false and rotting humanism in the name of the Christian idea of man.

The "Living Church" and the Religious Rebirth of Russia

(1923 - # 60,2)[1]

I.

Two sorts of people are doomed to a lack of understanding concerning the essence and the meaning of the Revolution -- the externalistic revolutionaries and the externalistic counter-revolutionaries. Both the one and the other are bereft of freedom of spirit, cast about upon the surface aspect of the revolutionary process and in the grip of evil passions; and both the one and the other believe, that the Revolution will destroy the old life and build a new life. The external revolutionaries think, that the Revolution will destroy the old, the ugly and evil life, and make for a new, beautiful and good life. The external counter-revolutionaries think, that the Revolution will destroy the old, beautiful and good life, and make for a new, an ugly and evil life. Some sense themself as builders of a new life, others -- the restorers of the old life. This -- is eternal a self-deception, an illusion, arising from concentrating our gaze upon the surface superficiality of life. The inner meaning of the revolutionary process is altogether otherwise, and it remains hidden for those, who let their grasp of the meaning become subject to negative emotional reactions. The Revolution, every revolution (and not only the hapless Russian Revolution) does not represent a breaking off from the old life and a making for a new life. Revolution as regards its metaphysical essence is an effect of the rot and disintegration of the decay and mustiness of the old life, the cast-off garbage of the old order. In it continues to act the old, but in a condition

---

[1] "ZHIVAYA TSERKOV'" I RELIGIOZNOE VOZROZHDENIE ROSSII. Article was originally published in the Berdyaev-edited anthology, "SOPHIA, Problemy dukhovnoi kul'tury i religioznoi philosophii" ("SOPHIA: Problems of Spiritual Culture and Religious Philosophy") -- Berlin, Obelisk, 1923; comprising the 2nd Berdyaev article therein, p. 125-134 (Kl. № 60,2).

downward and dissolute. Old souls, chained like slaves to the past, are what act in revolutions. The inner impulsive principles in revolutions are such, that they cannot create a new life. When the souls of people, social groups and entire peoples permit themself to have unlimited an hold over them the negative feelings of malice, hatred, envy and vengefulness, they become slaves of an harsh and putrid past, they cannot get separate from it. People in a revolution become incapable of seeing the eternal in the past, in them is no resuscitative spirit, they remain attached to their malicious and vengeful feelings towards the rot in the past and they lack the ability to turn their view towards what is to come, to get free from this past. Revolution only externally seems to be oriented forwards, inwardly it always is oriented backwards. This obsession with the past, degenerating into an hatred towards it, into malicious destruction and reprisals, is also the predominant impression of the revolutionary aspect. When a revolution, in recovering from its vengeful and malicious feelings, attempts to turn itself forwards, it creates very unrevolutionary, very banal and trite things, it evidences its own emptiness. When the Russian Revolution committed acts of revenge, when it was under the evil obsession against the old "bourgeois" world, it produced very revolutionary an impression, it had revolutionary a pathos and alarmed all the world by its maximalism.

When the Revolution turned towards the future, it started at construction, it formed NEP, it opened a market with kielbasa-sausages, it instituted trusts and started to produce impressions altogether unrevolutionary, very "bourgeois", bereft of idea and pathos. Revolution is in a condition where it either hates the past and destroys it, or else partially restores it. But there are in it no creative powers. Revolution in its metaphysical essence is a diminishing, a degradation of being, it is not ontological, not existentially durable. It is merely a reflective mirroring of inward failings, spiritual sicknesses. revolutions therefore always become unsuccessful, successful revolutions there are not and cannot be. They always beget not that, towards what they have striven, they always pass over into their opposite. Revolutions possess metaphysically reactionary a nature and this mustneeds be revealed and exposed. Revolutions become the allotted fate of peoples, the tragic fate of peoples, and it is necessary to recognise them, as the expiation of guilt. But there is nothing more pathetic, than idealising them and worshipping them.

In this selfsame fallacy are situated also the external counter-revolutionaries. They no less than the revolutionaries define themself negatively, and not positively. They think, that they can restore the old life. But in actuality they are immersed in the revolutionary destructive torrent and often become one of the powers of failure. They likewise are unable to pass over to a positive creativity, just like with the revolutionaries. The spirit of the times conveys destruction, and yet there wins out the spirit of eternity, conveying the resuscitation of all life. One and the same evil often appears in history under various guises. The ominous shades of the past overshadow the revolutionary process. And the destructive and despicable element of the past tends to avenge itself, as manifest in revolutions in the most repulsive forms. The genuinely eternal in the past, however, withdraws into the hidden depths of life. Revolutionaries and counter-revolutionaries, each waging a struggle for their interests, cannot free themself from the burden of the past and make the transition to a better life, since they do not want to begin with the essential thing, that would free the spirit for creative work, -- with repentance. The revolutionaries will always be slaves of an evil past and powerless to create, since at the basis of their world-view they deny repentance, they remain unrepentant sinners, i.e. burdened by the evil past. The same with those, who fight against the Revolution and upon whom the Revolution has struck a grievous blow, often in principle they admit of repentance, but do not want to repent of the sins, which have led Russia into revolution, not wanting to cleanse themself of the spirits of malice. Thus the revolutionary and counter-revolutionary processes represent various sides of one and the same failing, they remain locked within an inescapable vicious circle. The demons of malice tear at the soul and body of the Russian people, and unrepentant souls render impotent the attempts to create life.

II.

Revolution is a process involving all sides of life. And in Russia is occurring a geological upheaval, rattling and shaking all the substrate of life. And it cannot be imagined, that it would not affect the life of the Church. In the religious life of the Russian people long since already has been something impropitious. Within the Orthodox Church has lived the Russian people in its enormous masses. Without the Orthodox faith it could not have held up under its grievous history. And with the Church is connected the highest upsurges of Russian history. But the entirety of the XIX Century was filled with an awareness of the sins and ills of our spiritual life, of the unfortunate aspect of our churchly arrangement. It evidences a rift between the people and the intelligentsia, between society and the ruling authority. A weakening of faith, a disintegration of spiritual wholeness precedes revolutions. The better sort of Orthodox people over the course of the XIX Century denounced the ulcers of our churchly life and sought paths towards churchly renewal. Even before the revolutionary darkness itself had thickened to the point of cutting its way across the Russian Church and the Russian state had been sensed, that the chastisement from God had to break loose. It suffices to call to mind the fateful image of Grigorii Rasputin. The intelligentsia had long since fallen away from the faith and had poisoned the people with their nihilism; into the people imperceptibly filtered down a negative "enlightenment"; the upper classes of society, the nobility, the bureaucracy, the bourgeoise had an external attitude towards the faith and in utilitarian a manner were prepared to make use of it for their own interests; while at the summit of the ruling authority was an affliction with a mystical infirmity. The New Testament command of Christ: Bestow unto God what is of God, and unto Caesar what is of Caesar, was not fulfilled, "God's" and "Caesar's" got all jumbled together. Christian social truth, Christian brotherhood in the Russian Orthodox kingdom was not realised. And therefore they would attempt to realise social truth not through the freedom of Christ, but through the coercion of the Anti-Christ. The Church had become passive, since the times and the seasons had not yet ensued. The state, the realm of Caesar, was the active element. It was active prior to the Revolution in a certain direction and it became active after the Revolution in a direction of the polar opposite. The dysfunctions and ills of our churchly life are evidenced not by the fact, that the state lorded it over the Church, that the uber-prokurators oppressed the Church. This -- is external a view, a non-religious view upon the historical fates of our Church and state. On the contrary, the inner weaknesses and infirmities of our churchly life on its human side made it subordinate to the state and gave an especial role to the uber-prokurator. Pobedonostsev, a sincerely believing man, was not to blame for the fact, that our Church was insufficiently free. The inward lack of freedom in churchly life evoked the state civil authority of Pobedonostsev within the Church. That which transpires within the depths of spiritual life, determines the outward order of life. The enslavement of the Church to the state of Caesar is merely a reflection of the condition of the Church itself, in its human aspect a lack of revealedness of Christian community, and not an offspring begotten of the evil will of the state. The holy Russian monarchy fell, because it had lost its religio-mystical point of support in the Church, it felt too great a dependence of the Church upon itself, at a time, when it itself was in need of spiritual a support. The Russian empire assumed a form of humanistic self-affirmation, in it began to govern a ruling power deriving from man, and not from God.

And then ensued the fateful hour, when there fell apart the great bond, uniting the Orthodox Church with an Orthodox kingdom from the time of Constantine the Great. The Church as it were returned to its condition prior to Constantine, it felt a sense of great and frightening freedom. And it came up face to face with the raging elements of this world. The kingdom sacred for the Church itself ceased to hamper the Church with its protection, but a clashing with a godless realm stood before it. The Church began hastily to reorganise itself. And in this urgent deed there were not yet signs of a religious creativity. The restructuring of the Church was determined by a change of relations with the state, with the secular elements and the processes occurring in them. At the height of the historical catastrophe, there were no religious stirrings evident within the Church during the first period of the Revolution. The Revolution had not yet affected the Church inwardly. The Church assumed but a defensive posture, and guarded its sacred matters against the obtrusion of the secular world upon it. Within the elements of the Revolution the Church evidenced a great stability in comparison with other historical entities, which quickly became subject to disintegration. It was the sole spiritual refuge. Russian priests proved far loftier, than might be expected of them from the historical past of the Russian clergy, unaccustomed to struggle and resistance. But the Revolution, like an infective illness, has its own inevitable course to run out to the end, it is impossible to stop it. There had to ensue a moment, when the Revolution would directly and grievously impact the Church, when it not only would begin persecution against the Church, but also would affect inwardly churchly life itself. And then arises the monstrous phantom of a "Red Church". Will this be a religious stirring, will there be creative life in it, be a breathing of the Spirit? What signifies the appearance of "the Living Church"? Is this the beginning of a Russian Reformation? Are there signs of regeneration in the "reformed Church", the church of bishop Antonin [Granovsky]?

Nicholas Berdyaev

III.

The revolutionary process has entered into churchly life and there once again has evidenced its non-creative character. But revolution in the Church possesses rather moreso a paltry and reflective, not independent character, than in the state and social life, -- it tails along after the Revolution. The revolution in the Church is not a churchly and religious revolution, it is merely the mirroring of the social and political revolution, an adaptation to it, an infecting of it with toxins. In any case, Lenin and Trotsky are more primal, more independent a phenomenon, than the priest Kalinovsky and bishop Antonin. Bishop Antonin goes in tow with Lenin and conforms to him, and not the reverse. This quasi-churchly effort follows in tow with the political movement, fulfills the dictates of the social and political revolution. Within churchly life has begun a class struggle between the white and the black clergy. The sacristans, the cantors and the most democratic part of the white clergy have come to sense themself a "proletariat" and have become pervaded with a revolutionary class consciousness. The struggle against the episcopacy and monasticism has become a struggle against a churchly aristocracy and bourgeoise. The "Living Church", the "Church of Reform", and all the other labels, from a churchly-inward, religiously-inward point of view do not signify anything regarding "life" in the Church, nothing of a "renewal" of the Church, no sort of a churchly reformation or religious revolution. On the contrary, from religious a point of view, all these appearances are quite "reactionary". The Revolution has radically effected a separation of the Church from the state, and the Church has entered into an era of putting to the test a great freedom. I am speaking, indeed, concerning the human element in the Church. The Divine element within the Church can neither be enslaved nor liberated. The Church has come to face not only an irreligious and secular state, but a state openly godless and anti-Christian. It has to determine its attitude towards the new kingdom of Caesar (Caesar in the Gospel is the appellation not only of monarchy, but also every secular domain, albeit a socialistic republic). The Church has stood above the political struggle, its attitude towards the Revolution has been spiritual, and not political. This has to be admitted to the enormous merit of Patriarch Tikhon. The Orthodox Church has remained aloof, in it has not been a great creative stirring, but also neither a servile "reaction", i.e. an adaptive fawning towards the new kingdom of Caesar. And here the apparent reform and renovative moments in the Church, as manifest in the so-called "Living Church", are the foremost to bestow that which is of God "unto Caesar", the kingdom of this world. The "Living Church" has prostrated itself before the godless Caesar, it surrenders the Church to the grip of the state, renders the Church a tool of the most godless of states, it shows forth a slave's low-bowing craven spirit, it has loved foremost of all "the world" and that, which is of "the world". It writes hypocritically upon its banners the word freedom and it tramples the freedom of the Church, the freedom of religious conscience. The "Living Church" gives itself over into the power not only of an anti-Christian state, but also of an anti-Christian "enlightenment", of an anti-Christian rationalism. It begins its activity with denunciations against those, for whom execution threatens. It does not promulgate any sort of creative religious ideas, it speaks only about a subordinating of the Church to the new state, about the accepting of Communism by a new church. Among the activists of the "Living Church" is also that part of the churchly hierarchy afflicted with rationalism, which firstly did not hold up under the testing of freedom sent down from on high, renouncing freedom and giving in to the temptation of the Grand Inquisitor in the name of the millions upon millions of happy "infants". It is difficult for one to imagine a movement, which to such a degree is bereft of all independence and all creative power. I shall not mention about the wont for bribery among certain of its activists, about their possible connection with the organs of the political police, for this is not the principal question, nor does it interest me. We shall grant, that the initiators of the "Living Church" are sincere and unselfish. But in that case how shallow the figures! Not a single religious thought, no sort of a creative upsurge, no sort of signs of an awareness, advancing beyond that, by which the Russian religious thought of the XIX and XX Centuries has lived! This yet again makes evident, that the revolutionary element reflects a force of qualitative lowering, and not uplifting, in it, always there come out on top the elementary and simplifying principles. When bishop Antonin gave talks at the Peterburg religio-philosophic gatherings [occurring 1901-1903], the minutes of which were published in "Novyi Put'", he stood at greater an height of religious consciousness, there were put to him themes more complex and deep, than when he undersigned the proclamation of the "Living Church" and founded a "Church of Renovation". A decline occurred, a "democratisation" of the qualities of religious themes.

Nicholas Berdyaev

The repeating of trite phrases, that Christianity is communistic and that the first Christians were communists, does not evidence any sort of signs of a creative religious thought. This communism is a borrowing from the outside, from a worldly revolution, it was received from the hands of Lenin and Trotsky, and it does not signify the arising among us of any sort of a religious Christian socialism, in which would be its own truth. The "Living Church" is merely the spectre of a vile and putrid past, only the stench of the old rot, a reproducing in new setting of the old relationships between the Church and the state, of the old enslavement of the Church, the evidence long since already of happenings that have killed the Spirit in churchly life, of the triumph of rationalism within our churchly hierarchy. The "Living Church" is a Rasputinism, a debauchery of the revolutionary era, a profligate turgidness and pollution of spirit. In it the bishops and priests are appointed through the organ of the state political administration. This is also the production of profound religious "reaction" within churchly life, a quenching of the Spirit, the loss of spiritual freedom, the freedom of the children of God, a filial sonship with God through Christ the Saviour. This -- is not a religious movement, in it are no signs of a religious energy. This is nowise a reformation. Luther was of religiously fiery a nature, in him there was religious an idea, albeit false, but there was religious a fire. The "Living Church" is merely the uniting of the revolutionary ruination and disintegration of a rationalistically minded circle of Orthodox hierarchs, their being drawn in to this elemental process of atomisation. This -- is a phenomenon politically and from life, non-religious, signifying a loss of spiritual wholeness, a loss of spiritual freedom and spiritual resiliency in regard to the elements of the revolution, hostile to everything of spirit. It signifies a weakening of the mystical effort within churchly life, in which long already have been indications of the signs of a falling away from a churchly ontologism. The Russian Revolution, certainly, is a manifestation of spiritual, and not only political an order. But in this its aspect it signifies merely a militant assault of natural spirits against a spirit, rooted in God. In this quasi-religious church movement is evidenced the total absence of the unique ideal of Christian society. It consents to serve a foreign master, it is ready to accept an ordering of society, based upon malice and hatred, envy and revenge. Within the Orthodox Church even earlier there was not revealed a Christian societal awareness. The old society likewise was not Christian, in it was lie and untruth, which also led to the Revolution. But greed and envy, malice and vengefulness were not raised into the pearl of creation, were not made into a religion. Everything for the old society was accountable to an awareness of sin and repentance. The new society ceases to be conscious of sin and wants nothing of repentance. And therefore the old lie and untruth within it is intensified. Only a liar or a lunatic is able to assert, that in revolutionary Russia there is moreso Christian brotherhood, than in pre-revolutionary Russia. Of Christian brotherhood there was too little even earlier, but now it has become even less so, all the societal relationships have become saturated with malice and hate. Christianity has never been inclined to teach, that the brotherhood of people can appear as the result of a class struggle involving material interests, that a Christian community can be begotten from evil violence. But those active in the "Living Church" evidently have believed in this. They have come out on behalf of the oppressed -- a matter genuinely Christian, but as though not having noticed, that the oppressed already succeeded in being transformed into oppressors. Christianity ought however to actively defend the oppressed and spiritually censure the persecutors. This is something at odds with those, who threaten prison, execution and exile. The tempting allure of communism among churchly activists is begotten in part upon the basis of greedy class interests of a churchly "democracy", in part also upon the basis of an horrid confusion of brotherhood in Christ with a compulsory uniting of people in the Anti-Christ. The "Living Church" is not a disclosing of authentic life within the Church, it is merely the stench of the rot and corruption in the past, the arising of images of the old sin and the old untruth, the manifestation of a lowly cowering and groveling afront a triumphant power, of a passive surrendering of oneself to the disposition of the non-spiritual powers of this world. This is merely another side of the image of that selfsame sickness and untruth within our churchly life, as expressed also in the Karlovtsy Synod, in the attempts to render the Orthodox Church into an obediently pliant tool of externally manipulative and greedy restorationist intents. Metropolitan Antonii Khrapovitsky, himself a foe to the Imyaslavtsi Name-Praisers, is a rationalist and political the same, as are the activists of the "Living Church". Too many tend to take advantage of church for political ends. The creative process in our churchly life is still outwardly not in evidence. The strong element within it has been merely a fidelity to churchly sanctities. The creative process can only be by an evidencing of the spirit of the love of Christ, which would possess also its own social expression.

IV.

All the attempts at the reformation and renewal of the Church within the revolutionary element tend to have nothing in common with the genuinely creative themes of the Russian religious thought of the XIX and XX Centuries. Evidently, in the conflagration of the revolutionary element the Church can either guard itself, can defend its sanctity from the destructive processes, or it can adapt itself to a revolutionary aspect foreign to it, abjuring its own sanctity, it can either be conservative in the profound and best sense of this word or it can enter upon the path of apostacy. A creative churchly rebirth within the revolutionary process cannot be discerned. And thus it was also in the French Revolution. Catholicism before the Revolution was in decline, and at the time of the Revolution a significant portion of the Catholic clergy apostacised from the faith. After the Revolution, at the beginning of the XIX Century there began a Catholic renewal and it continues on to our day. I have no doubt, that after the Russian Revolution, after the inward spiritual reaction against it, after pondering the enormous effect experienced in it, that in Russia there will be a religious and churchly rebirth. This renewal will be creative, and not simply a matter of restoration. Only by it can there also be the salvation of Russia. For the Church, the Revolution will have positive a significance. All these years in the depths of Russia, in the souls of Russian people occur molecular processes, which also will lead to this renewal. The Russian intelligentsia, traditionally hostile to religion, will turn to religion. But for awhile still this inner movement cannot be manifest. On the surface we shall see either the "Living Church" or the Karlovtsy Synod, two offspring of the revolutionary process of disintegration, and not of the process of creativity. Creativity will ensue after the externals of the Revolution, as a manifestation of an inward revolution of spirit. This inward revolution of spirit might seem to externalist revolutionaries as something counter-revolutionary, but it never will be simply a restoration of the old, of the old life, of the old spirit of decay. In the eternal within the past will combine with the creativity of the new religious life, and in the eternal will be attained an unity of the past and the future. Across the span of the XIX and XX Centuries there was in Russia an original and creative stirring of religious thought, there was passionate a religious searching. Chaadaev, the Slavophils -- Khomyakov and I. Kireevsky, Yu. Samarin and

Astride the Abyss of War and Revolutions

I. Aksakov, Dostoevsky, K. Leont'ev, Vl. Solov'ev, Bukharev, N. Fedorov, V. Rozanov and the modernmost religio-philosophic currents -- what an amazing wealth of Russian thought, what a depth in the setting of religious themes, how intense a spiritual thirsting! The dominant currents in the Russian intelligentsia tended to bypass this spiritual current, not having taken advantage of this wealth. And the official Russian theology, the official churchly currents almost failed to have contact with this enormous spiritual life. Characteristic to Russian religious thought was a prophetic spirit, it had presentiment of much, it foresaw and predicted much. Dostoevsky, K. Leont'ev, Vl. Solov'ev knew about the revolution, transpiring within spirit earlier, than it transpired within the surface aspect of history. And here now the terrible moment has ensued. All the Russian religious and philosophic thought, all the Russian great literature was toppled down into the dark abyss, proved unneeded for the revolutionary process. The Revolution had other teachers, those, who enjoyed greater a popularity, but in whom was no breath of creative Russian genius, of religious a genius. The Revolution was not the work of Chaadaev and Khomyakov, of Dostoevsky and Vl. Solov'ev, it was the work of Belinsky and Dobroliubov, of Chernyshevsky and Plekhanov. In the Revolution was embodied not a single genuinely great and original Russian idea, but within it acted a large and sickly Russian element, amidst the genuine foreboding of great and original people. The ideas however were very banal and shallow Western ideas. And when reform and renewal attempts began in the Church, there began also processes of adaption to the Revolution, and then all these "Living Church" and "Church Revivals" began to enrich the churchly consciousness and churchly life not with Chaadaev and Khomyakov, not with Dostoevsky and Vl. Solov'ev, but the rather with Belinsky and Chernyshevsky, Plekhanov and Lenin. This -- is the remarkable fact. The Russian priests of the "Living Church" have shouldered the shallow booklets of Russian socialism, of the Russian nihilistic enlightenment, but nowise have they shouldered the books of Russian great creative figures, those inspired by a prophetic religious spirit. They tended to pass on from the seminary lesson books over to the five-kopeck brochures of Russian Marxism. Khomyakov and Dostoevsky could moreso teach these priests, striving for renewal, about the freedom of the Church and freedom of spirit, than can Chernyshevsky or Lenin! Chernyshevsky and Lenin can represent but captivity and enslavement for the Church.

Nicholas Berdyaev

The Slavophils were nowise religious conservatives, though they were faithful to the ancestral sanctities and traditions. If one peruse the philosophico-theological articles of Khomyakov concerning the Church and the articles of I. Aksakov on the churchly question, then in their teachings about Christian freedom and love -- for them Christianity was first of all the religion of freedom and love -- it is possible to find the grounding for a religious reforming (not in the sense of a Reformation) and renewal of the Church. They exposed the sins and ills of our historical churchly order with an extraordinary radicalism. And with Dostoevsky, with Vl. Solov'ev, with Bukharev, with Fedorov and suchlike, it is possible to find prophetic presentiments of a new spiritual epoch in Christianity. But the official Russian churchliness and the official Russian revolutionness have remained stuck in the impasse between the Orthodoxy of metropolitan Philaret, the uber-prokurators and rationalist bishops, alien to authentic spiritual experience, and the socialism and materialism of Chernyshevsky and Plekhanov. Rather moreso spiritual, hidden, mystical currents within Orthodoxy have been bound up with the aspect of the startsi-elders, with the pilgrim wanderers, and they at present still find for themself an expression in the Imyaslavtsi Name-Praising, which the rationalistically minded bishops have little love for, in the humble priest-elders, in which also one mustneeds seek out the authentic religious life of contemporary Russia. The activists of the "Living Church" -- are the inheritors of the official, bureaucratic, synodal uber-prokurator style rationalistic Orthodoxy, and not of the mystical Orthodoxy, the Orthodoxy of saints, startsi-elders, wanderers, the Orthodoxy of the mystical piety of the people, seeking the Unseen City, the New Jerusalem. All the present day churchly reformers and renewers -- are rationalistic alike down to the marrow of their bones, as are a significant portion of our churchly princes. Their type is the opposite to the spiritually experiential type in religious life. They are making for a churchly revolution, when they ultimately repudiate all the revelations and mysteries of Christianity, when they transform the Church into a community, wholly devoted to materialism and socialism, when in the Church they cease to perform the sacraments, and the priests then renounce the faith in Christ the Saviour and snatch off their cassock. This -- is the limit for the churchly revolution. But in the churchly persecution, rather than adaption to the revolutionary dissolution, there has to begin a process of spiritual deepening. From the bosom of the churchly will begin a creative religious rebirth, which will be the continuation of a genuinely spiritual, mystical Russian Orthodoxy and provide a churchly reply to the religious questionings and religious agitation of Russian religious life. In the Church there cannot be revolution, there cannot be even reformation, ought not to be even restoration. The Church lives by the revelation of the Holy Spirit. And the creative religious process of the Church is a revelation of the Spirit within Christian mankind. The religious rebirth in Russia, without which Russia cannot be saved, will be a mystical, and not rationalistic, fulfilling of the great hopes and expectations of Christianity, and not by a borrowing and adaption to that revolutionary socialistic world, which lives and breathes in an apostacy from God and in a struggle against the truth of Christ. It will overcome the falsity and lie of the old world, but it will overcome by the power and the truth of Christ.

frsj Publications

1.) **N. A. BERDYAEV** "*The Philosophy of Inequality*"
   1st English Translation of Berdyaev's 1918/1923 book,
   "*Filosofia neravenstva*" (Kl. № 20).
   (ISBN-13: 9780996399203 / ISBN-10: 0996399208)
   406 pages (6/4/15)

2.) **N. A. BERDYAEV** "*The Spiritual Crisis of the Intelligentsia*"
   1st English Translation of Berdyaev's 1910 book,
   "*Dukhovnyi krizis intelligentsii*" (Kl. № 4).
   (ISBN-13: 9780996399210 / ISBN-10: 0996399216)
   346 pages (6/19/15)

3.) **FR. ALEKSANDR MEN'** "*Russian Religious Philosophy:
   1989-1990 Lectures*" -- 1st English Translation
   Published in 25th Year Commemoration of Fr Men' Memory
   (ISBN-13: 9780996399227 / ISBN-10: 0996399224)
   (ISBN-13: 9780996399265 / ISBN-10: 0996399267) *Paperback*
   214 pages (7/14/15)

4.) **E. SKOBTSOVA (MOTHER MARIA)**
   "*The Crucible of Doubts: Khomyakov, Dostoevsky, Solov'ev,
   In Search of Synthesis -- Four 1929 Works*".
   (ISBN-13: 9780996399234 / ISBN-10: 0996399232)
   166 pages (5/20/16) 1st English Translation

5.) **N. A. BERDYAEV** "*The Fate of Russia*"
   1st English Translation of Berdyaev's 1918 book,
   "*Sud'ba Rossii*". (Kl. № 15).
   (ISBN-13: 9780996399241 / ISBN-10: 0996399240)
   250 pages (10/1/16)

6.) **N. A. BERDYAEV** "*Aleksei Stepanovich Khomyakov*"
 1st English Translation of Berdyaev's 1912 book,
 "*Алексей Степанович Хомяков*" (Кl. № 6).
 (ISBN-13: 9780996399258 / ISBN-10: 0996399259)
 224 Pages (5/8/17)

7.) **N. A. BERDYAEV** "*Astride the Abyss of War and Revolutions:
 Articles 1914-1922*" -- 1st English Translation of a collection
 of 98 articles penned by Berdyaev covering the period of
 WWI & Russian 1917 Revolutions
 (ISBN-13: 9780996399272 / ISBN-10: 0996399275)
 (ISBN-13: 9780996399289 / ISBN-10: 0996399283) *Paperback*
 742 pages (7/24/17)

*   *   *

Forthcoming Works in Preparation:

N. A. BERDYAEV "*Sub Specie Aeternitatis:
 Essays Philosophic, Social and Literary (1900-1906)*".
 1st English Translation of Berdyaev's 1907 book,
 "*Sub specie aeternitatis. Опыты философские, социальные
 и литературные (1900-1906 гг.)*". (Кl. № 3).

N. A. BERDYAEV "*The Philosophy of Freedom*"
 1st English Translation of Berdyaev's 1911 book,
 "*Filosofiia svobody*" (Кl. № 5).

www.ingramcontent.com/pod-product-compliance
Lightning Source LLC
Chambersburg PA
CBHW050522300426
44113CB00012B/1920